Microsoft®
Expression Blend™
Bible

Microsoft® Expression Blend™ Bible

Gurdy Leete and Mary Leete

Wiley Publishing, Inc.

Expression Blend™ Bible

Published by
Wiley Publishing, Inc.
10475 Crosspoint Boulevard
Indianapolis, IN 46256
www.wiley.com

Copyright © 2007 by Wiley Publishing, Inc., Indianapolis, Indiana

Published simultaneously in Canada

ISBN: 978-0-470-05503-8

Manufactured in the United States of America

10 9 8 7 6 5 4 3 2 1

For general information on our other products and services or to obtain technical support, please contact our Customer Care Department within the U.S. at (800) 762-2974, outside the U.S. at (317) 572-3993 or fax (317) 572-4002.

Library of Congress Control Number: 2007926001

Trademarks: Wiley, the Wiley logo, and related trade dress are trademarks or registered trademarks of John Wiley & Sons, Inc. and/or its affiliates, in the United States and other countries, and may not be used without written permission. Microsoft and Expression Blend are trademarks or registered trademarks of Microsoft Corporation in the United States and/or other countries. All other trademarks are the property of their respective owners. Wiley Publishing, Inc., is not associated with any product or vendor mentioned in this book.

Wiley also publishes its books in a variety of electronic formats. Some content that appears in print may not be available in electronic books.

About the Authors

Gurdy Leete is the coauthor of *Macromedia Flash 8 For Dummies* and four other popular books on Flash. He has also published 19 essays about the frontiers of computing, and his books on Flash have been translated into Arabic, Chinese, Dutch, French, German, Italian, Norwegian, Russian and Spanish.

Gurdy teaches digital imaging, graphic design, Web design, video, and animation at Maharishi University of Management in Fairfield, Iowa, where he has been a pioneer in using digital media applications in undergraduate art and design classes for 15 years. Prior to joining faculty, he worked as a 3-D animator under the direction of magician Doug Henning. Gurdy is also an award-winning graphics software engineer and user interface designer, and has worked for clients such The Learning Company, Sierra, Scott Foresman, and numerous others. He holds a B.F.A. and M.F.A. in Film-making from the San Francisco Art Institute.

Gurdy is the owner of Flying Haystacks Design, a digital media studio specializing in innovative Web design. You can view his work on the Web at www.flyinghaystacks.com, and you can reach him by email at gurdy@flyinghaystacks.com.

Mary Leete was a contributing author for *Fifty Fast Macromedia Flash MX Techniques*, and co-wrote *OpenOffice.org For Dummies*. Her book *Free Software For Dummies* received highly favorable reviews in the *Chicago Tribune*, the *Los Angeles Times* and elsewhere. She has a B.S. in Computer Science and a Masters in Professional Writing, and lives to write code as well as write about it. Mary has extensive experience as a systems analyst and programmer with a multitude of software on way too many platforms.

Mary is also a freelance Web designer and video producer, and an award-winning screenwriter, and she has written under contract for the producer of *The Buddy Holly Story*, among others. She's the editor of the Web site www.interactivedesignertips.com, where you may download many of the files for the tutorials in this book, read the latest news on Interactive Designer, and more. You can contact her at mary@interactivedesignertips.com.

Credits

Acquisitions Editor
Tom Heine

Project Editor
Katherine Dvorak

Technical Editor
Zach Szulaka

Copy Editor
Kim Heusel

Editorial Manager
Robyn Siesky

Business Manager
Amy Knies

Vice President and Executive Group Publisher
Richard Swadley

Vice President and Executive Publisher
Bob Ipsen

Vice President and Publisher
Barry Pruett

Project Coordinator
Kristie Rees

Graphics and Production Specialists
Denny Hager
Jennifer Mayberry

Quality Control Technicians
John Greenough
Christine Pingleton

Proofreading and Indexing
Aptara

Acknowledgments

We'd like to thank the many people who supported our vision for this book and helped us every step of the way. We'd especially like to thank our wonderful acquisitions editor, Tom Heine, who's moving on to exciting new ventures, and hope very much that we'll have the chance to work with him again.

We also must thank our fantastic project editor, Katherine Dvorak, who always stayed on top of everything, and made it so much easier for us to write this book. Her superb competence and her constant helpfulness are an inspiration.

And we thank our technical editor, Zach Szukala, for his outstanding work in reviewing so many details of our book so reliably and quickly, and for all his thoughtful and constructive advice.

Finally, we'd like to thank our fabulous literary agent, Laura Lewin at Studio B, for all her work on our behalf.

Contents at a Glance

Contents

Contents

Contents

Part III: Designing with Type 227

Contents

Contents

Contents

Introduction

A study published in 1995 by Masaaki Kurosu and Kaori Kashimura showed that when people used one of two functionally-identical ATM machines — one with an aesthetically pleasing user interface and another with a less beautiful user interface — the users were more adept at using the more pleasant-looking interface. (If you'd like to check it out, the study was titled "Apparent Usability vs. Inherent Usability: Experimental Analysis on the Determinants of the Apparent Usability," published in the *CHI '95 Conference Companion.*) This study was performed in Japan in the mid-1990s and later replicated by Noam Tractinsky in Israel with even more dramatic results.

Why two almost identical ATM displays would produce dramatic differences in usability was startling to some in the computer industry. But additional studies have continued to show that more beautiful designs are easier to use and are more likely to be used.

This phenomenon has important implications for the future of computing, particularly as computers are increasingly capable of presenting high-resolution, highly interactive audio-visual content.

Microsoft Expression Blend makes it possible for you to take advantage of the implications of this research finding, and this historic change in computing capabilities, by providing you with easy-to-use, cutting-edge tools to bring Windows and Web applications to a whole new level of beauty and effectiveness using Microsoft's powerful Windows Presentation Foundation (WPF).

Blend makes it easy for you to create beautiful and compelling user interfaces without getting bogged down in writing code. Microsoft has created a simple new mark-up language, called XAML, that can specify all the details of high performance user interfaces for the next generation of Windows and Web applications, without the need for any complicated procedural computer code. Blend, in a sense, is your WYSIWYG user interface for the creation of XAML code. Blend, provides you with numerous ready-made, highly functional WPF controls and panels that you can use to quickly assemble sophisticated user interfaces — often without any programming. And Blend works seamlessly with Visual Studio to make it easy for you or developers to add procedural code to the user interfaces that you create, in a seamless back and forth work flow.

Blend makes it easy for you to design a new generation of applications that are built to look great and take pervasive advantage of digital media. Blend provides you with intensive support for deeply integrating multiple layers of animation, 3D, audio, video, vector graphics, sophisticated typography, custom controls, and automatic data binding into your user interface, and provides you with advanced styling tools that make it easy for you to make extensive use of transparencies, opacity masks, lighting effects, and more, to make your user interfaces visually stunning.

About This Book

We've strived to make *Microsoft Expression Blend Bible* an information-packed, friendly guide to designing compelling, highly usable, and richly interactive user interfaces for the next generation of Windows and Web applications. You may use the book as a complete guide to Blend, by proceeding step-by-step from the basics to advanced developer topics via the sequence of tutorials that you'll find distributed throughout the book. We think you'll also find that the book functions as a comprehensive reference to Blend, by thoroughly explaining how to use every important tool and component of the software. We've designed each chapter of the book to serve as a mini reference manual for each of the most important aspects of Blend.

We've tried to design *Microsoft Expression Blend Bible* for anyone who is interested in creating spectacular and effective interfaces for Windows or Web-based applications using next-generation technology. Blend contains ground-breaking features that are useful to every Windows and Web application user interface designer, so we think the book can be useful to anyone creating Windows or Web applications, from novice to professional. Our goal has been to get you up and running and creating terrific user interfaces for Windows and Web applications with maximum speed and minimum effort, while also providing you with a complete set of background and reference information that is easily accessible whenever you need it.

Throughout the book, we think you'll see that we also explore deep principles of design and usability that you can put to work to successfully deploy all this cool technology, in order to create highly satisfying user experiences. We explain and showcase these deeper principles by presenting and illustrating throughout the book:

- Principles of interactive design
- Strategies for conceptualizing the user experience
- Principles of graphic design, typography, and 3-D design
- Examples of new user interface techniques, and
- Principles of animation that you can use to create cinematic user interfaces

So this is not only a book about using new technology. It's also a book about ways to create interactive experiences of a much higher quality than ever possible before. We see this as a book that's as much about design as it is about technology, and we hope you find that helpful.

How To Use This Book

You can read this book sequentially from cover to cover like a really big novel, if you'd like to study every important facet of Blend and next-generation interface design. But we've also tried to write the book in such a way that you can start anywhere. For instance, if animation is your passion, then go ahead and start with Chapter 14. Or if you just want to delve into controls and panels, head for chapters 16 and 18. If you want an in-depth overview of Blend, you may want to check out Chapter 3. Don't worry about missing stuff. If there's something we think you need to know when you read a section, we add a Cross-Ref icon, to refer to related sections in other chapters.

This book contains numerous practical examples that you can work with and modify to create useful features for your user interfaces. You can download the computer files for these examples from our Web site, `www.blendtips.com`. You can also view there many of the book's figures in full color.

If you have something specific you are looking for, then the Table of Contents contains a detailed view of the contents of the book. You can browse through it to find out where to go. Or check out the index — it's big, and we don't leave much out.

Also, we use a convention when referring to selecting items from a menu. We use ⇨ to replace the words "and then choose." This saves time, because instead of saying, for instance, "Choose Tools from the menu and then choose Make Tile Brush and then choose Make Visual Brush", we just write "Choose Tools ⇨ Make Tile Brush ⇨ Make Visual Brush."

Icons Used in This Book

Here and there, you'll find icons in the margins of this book, pointing out the following:

 With this icon we alert you to potential perils or pitfalls, and how you can avoid them.

 Here you'll find a cross-reference to other portions of the book where you can find additional information on the current subject.

 The Note icon provides you with additional background information on the current topic, or information about miscellaneous additional options.

 Here we offer advice or point out handy techniques that you can use to solve problems or make faster progress.

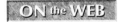 This icon points you to additional information, software, or examples that are available on the Web and related to the current topic.

How This Book Is Organized

This book is divided into six parts, focused on these six main topics as they relate to Blend:

- Next-Generation User Interface Design
- Vector Graphics

- Typography and Flow Documents
- Cinematic User Interfaces
- Controls and Layouts
- Code, Data Binding, and Integration

For added excitement, at the end there's a glossary.

Let's take a quick tour now of each part of the book.

Part I: Designing Next-Generation User Experiences

This part presents you with an overview of how to use Blend from start to finish, and gives you a comprehensive reference guide to the functions of the tools and palettes of the Blend interface. Explore in Chapter 1 the new tools for the next generation of user interface experiences — video, audio, animation, animated transparencies, opacity masks, real 3D, data-binding, ready-made controls, and customized controls — and how to put them all together in innovative and highly effective new ways. Learn to use the Blend interface, and find a step-by-step guide to each palette of the Blend workspace in Chapter 2. See how to choose panels, insert controls, and add data binding, and how to proceed through the entire process of interface design from conception to fulfillment, in Chapter 3. Then learn how to deploy your application for the Web or Windows in Chapter 4.

Part II: Creating and Transforming Vector Graphics

This part is your guide to Blend's powerful tools for creating and modifying the look of vector graphics in your user interface. Investigate the inner workings of the Pen, Line, Rectangle, Ellipse, Pencil and Selection tools and Blend's tools for aligning, stacking, rotating, scaling, and skewing your vector graphics in Chapter 5. Find out how to transform your vector art with color, gradient fills, glows, spotlights, opacity masks, transparency, and more in Chapter 6. Learn to create and edit styles for shapes, paths, panels and controls, apply them as resources within your project, use the powerful tools of Microsoft Expression Design, and import artwork into Blend in various ways in Chapter 7. Then explore principles of graphic design that you can use to enhance your user interface in Chapter 8.

Part III: Designing with Type

Unless your user interface is entirely driven by audio or video, text is probably a key link between you and your user. How that text appears can play an important role in the success of your user interface. In this part you can learn both the practicalities and the subtle nuances of adding type to your application. See how to create text controls and flow documents (with automatic resizing and user-adjustable text sizes) and how to use them in your application design in Chapter 9. Explore Microsoft's new world of enhanced typography, which allows you to add swashes and other flourishes to your text, in Chapter 10. Then in Chapter 11 find guidelines on how to choose the right font, font size and font color, where to find fonts, and how to apply principles of typographic design to your interface design to make it more usable, appealing, and meaningful.

Part IV: Creating Cinematic User Interfaces

This part plunges you into the world of 3D, animation, video, and audio. Learn how to add 3D to your application in Chapter 12, as well as how to create 3D objects and animations in Zam3D and import them into Blend. Discover principles of 3D design that you can use to make your user interface more immersive, more intriguing, and more effective in Chapter 13. Find out how to add video and audio to your interface, create a video player, animate 3D models, use visual brushes, and assign triggers to control timelines in Chapter 14. Then in Chapter 15 see how you can use animation principles of staging, anticipation, timing and storytelling to create cinematic user interfaces that will charm and inspire your users.

Part V: Constructing Controls and Layouts

Controls and panels are the fundamental building blocks of your user interface design. Blend supplies you with many ready-made Windows Presentation Foundation controls and panels that you can use to quickly construct highly functional user interfaces, or you can completely customize your own controls, without writing any code. Blend's ability to create custom controls is nothing short of awesome. You can delve into the template of the control and change its look however you want — even rebuild it completely from scratch while maintaining its functionality, so that your progress bar remains a progress bar whether you make it slide, spin, or do triple somersaults. Find out about all the ready-made controls available to you, and the various techniques to create custom controls, in Chapter 16. Then grab principles of usability design (such as Fitts' Law, Hick's Law, and others) that you can use to create next-generation user interfaces in Chapter 17. Find out all about canvas panels, dock panels, grid panels, stack panels, wrap panels, and others, and how you can use them to build a high performance user interface, in Chapter 18. Then discover how you can take advantage of usability principles to enhance your panel layouts in Chapter 19.

Part VI: Coding, Data Binding, and XAML

This part shows you how to work with computer code (or programmers who write computer code) to enhance your user interface, how to connect your application to data sources such as databases and news feeds, how to integrate your applications with existing Windows Forms applications, and how to put everything together for optimal performance. Get an introduction to how you can add even more functionality to your user interface (such as draggable and resizable objects, Open File and Save File dialog boxes, navigation systems, and objects animated in code) by using Blend's code-behind file, event handlers, the .NET Framework, and C# code in Chapter 20. Find out how to use the deeply powerful technology of data binding to connect your controls to XML data sources such as databases and RSS feeds — without programming — in Chapter 21. Understand more about XAML code and how you can edit it to further customize your user interface in

Chapter 22. And, in Chapter 23, see how to integrate your application with Windows Forms applications, and what you can do in Blend to maximize the performance of your Windows or Web application.

Glossary

New words and phrases for a new generation of user interface design — we try to explain them all here. Just browsing through the glossary may help you get up-to-date on this revolution in Windows and Web application design.

Where to Go From Here

If you haven't done so already, you probably want to get Blend and install it on your computer right away, so that you can start using any of the information here that interests you.

You can find the computer files for all the examples in this book, news about Blend, and more at our Web site www.blendtips.com.

You can contact Gurdy at gurdy@infinityeverywhere.net and Mary at mary@blendtips.com. We can't provide you with technical support for Blend, but we'd love to hear your comments about the book.

Best of luck creating the most fabulous Windows and Web applications ever!

Part I

Designing Next-Generation User Experiences

Chapter 1

Exploring New User Interface Techniques

Expression Blend is part of a suite of new products from Microsoft that aim at making it radically easier for designers and developers to collaborate in designing extraordinary user interfaces for Windows Vista, Windows XP and the Web.

Blend supports a new paradigm for user interface design for both Windows applications and Web applications, primarily by taking unprecedented advantage of two advanced computer hardware and software technologies:

- the hardware-accelerated 3D graphics that are common on today's computers and
- the automatic generation of *XAML* code, Microsoft's new XML-based language for rapid construction of sophisticated user interfaces.

Blend exploits these technologies to make it quick and easy for you to create user interfaces that deeply utilize rich media content, that are highly interactive, that can be driven by customized controls, and that attain new levels of usability and aesthetics for end-users to enjoy — often without requiring you to write code.

Building Rich Interactivity with Vector Graphics, Animation, 3D, Video, and Audio

At the basis of Blend is the Windows Presentation Foundation (WPF), the new graphical subsystem of Microsoft's .NET Framework 3.0 that is deeply integrated into Windows Vista. WPF was designed from the outset to provide advanced support for video, audio, 3D graphics, vector graphics, animation, bitmap graphics, advanced typography, and data binding. WPF, for example, supports *flow documents*, which automatically optimize the readability of documents for different window sizes and screen resolutions, and WPF supports a wide range of pre-built controls that designers can quickly plug into a user interface — and that they can quickly customize to a remarkable degree, even by adding animation, video, and 3D content right into the controls themselves.

Blend is also designed so that you can merge the steps of creating your prototype of the user interface design with the creation of the real user interface. You can design your user interfaces with controls that work even during the prototyping stage. Blend's numerous ready-made, functioning controls are easy to customize in both appearance and functionality, and can resize automatically to any screen resolution or according to the user's preference. You can activate many of the controls, including menus, buttons, sliders, and list boxes, without needing to do any programming. And within Blend you can link these functioning controls to live external data sources such as databases, RSS feeds, and more — again without writing any code. All this enables you to bring the user interface design to a level of functionality that can actually be the basis of the full-blown application, rather than just a graphic mockup of a user interface that needs to be re-implemented by a programmer.

When designing smaller applications that don't require much back-end programming, you can use Blend as a stand-alone tool that can help you create Windows or Web applications from beginning to end. Or you can use Blend in conjunction with other graphic design tools such as Microsoft Expression Design, and with programming tools such as Visual Basic .NET and C# in Microsoft Visual Studio. You can, for example, import artwork from tools such as Expression Design into Blend, and you can integrate with Visual Basic .NET or C# code as a back end to the user interface that you create in Blend. If you do this, you can continue to modify your design in Blend even after the Visual Basic .NET or C# code is connected to it. This gives you tremendous flexibility and the freedom to be creative at every step in designing and implementing your user interface.

Blend makes it easy for you to use a combination of video, audio, animation, 3D content, bitmap images, vector graphics, and sophisticated typography as interactive elements of the design of your user interface. You can use these separately to make up the different components of your interface, or you can use them in conjunction with one another, as shown in Figure 1.1. For example, you can import videos and play them on their own small, animated 3D planes that can resize to full screen when clicked. And you can do it without programming. You may or may not want to get so fancy. But the capability exists in this program to create user interfaces using a wide range of media in a wide range of combinations and to do so with greater ease than has ever been possible before.

CROSS-REF Chapter 3 includes instructions for playing movies on animated 3D screens and creating triggers to resize each of them to fill the window when the user clicks.

FIGURE 1.1

These buttons, consisting of video on animated 3D planes, are examples of Blend's capacity for merging video, animation, 3D, and interactivity.

Designing your application with vector graphics

Microsoft Expression Blend provides you with a wide range of tools that you can use to build your own vector graphics or to import vector graphics already built in Microsoft Expression Design or other applications. Figure 1.2 displays just a few vector graphic objects that you can create from scratch in Blend.

CROSS-REF See Part II for detailed information on how to create and manipulate vector graphics within Blend.

Vector graphics allow you to zoom in on objects without any apparent loss in detail. In user interfaces, this is a distinct advantage for vector graphic images compared to bitmap images, which can become fuzzy and start showing individual pixels when scaled too large. Because monitors are increasing in size and resolution, it's becoming increasingly important to use vector graphics as much as possible to avoid those chunky pixels.

FIGURE 1.2

Vector graphic objects created in Expression Blend.

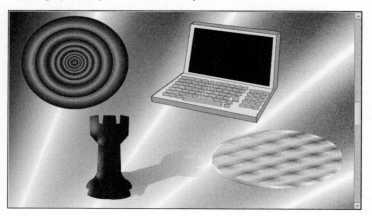

The vector graphic-based user interfaces that Blend produces can be completely scaled to any size automatically by the application in order to fit the monitor resolution of the user. With the addition of a few resizing controls, you can also enable users to scale any component of the interface you designate. Without doing any programming, you can divide an application window into sections, called a *grid*, and add a few controls so the user can resize any of the sections of the grid. Or you can allow the user to resize text in text boxes by adding sliders. This easy scalability of elements provided by Blend makes better user experiences possible for both you — the designer — and for the user of your designs.

Designing with type

WPF flow documents allow for greater readability of text across all window sizes and monitor resolutions. They offer automatic resizing, as shown in Figure 1.3. The FlowDocumentReader is the most fully featured type of flow document viewers and has three modes: Page mode, Two Page mode and Scroll mode, and includes a slider to allow the user to resize text — plus it offers a search option.

You can also add images, controls, animations, and video into flow documents.

CROSS-REF   For more about creating and using flow documents, see Chapter 9.

FIGURE 1.3

Flow documents resize optimally for their window size and screen resolution, and can contain user interface elements such as, the slider and buttons shown here.

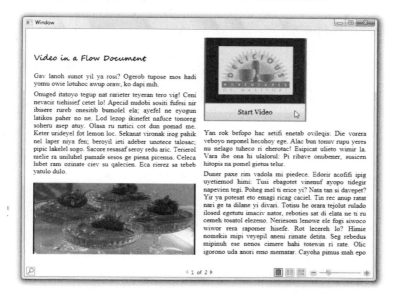

Blend offers a wide range of text controls. Labels are available to provide access key support, so that users can access controls easily from the keyboard. Blend's enhanced typographic support allows you to add different styles of type while using the same font — you can add swashes and ligatures and more to your user interface. You can also use Expression Design to create sophisticated typographic designs and import them for use in Blend.

 **CROSS-REF** For more about enhanced typography, see Chapter 10.

Incorporating animation into your design

Blend provides you with multiple timelines in which you can animate your vector objects, controls, 3D objects, video, or bitmap images on 3D planes — practically anything you could want to animate. You can define two points on a timeline as keyframes, and Blend fills in the changes in the objects on the timeline between the two keyframes. On a keyframe you can change something about an object, such as color, rotation, position, size, and any combination of those or more, and Blend creates the animation between the two keyframes for you. For example, you can animate buttons to move or rotate when you move your mouse over them. Or you can animate colors of controls to change when you use them. You can also connect an object to a motion path that defines the path on which the object moves between the keyframes.

You can also let the user take control of an animation by creating buttons that animate objects in various ways. Maybe you want the user to control a 3D model of a product, such as a new car, so he can see it from all sides — even underneath. Or how about a submarine, as shown in Figure 1.4? Pressing any button causes the submarine to rotate in 3D space to its new position. It's interesting to note that the animation can kick in from whatever the current position of the object is. This is called handoff animation and is one of the many new features of WPF that Blend supports.

The timelines that Blend uses, shown in Figure 1.4, not only support extensive animation capabilities, but also sophisticated control of video and audio playback as well.

CROSS-REF   For more about animation in Blend, see Chapters 14 and 15.

FIGURE 1.4

Creating an animation in the Blend interface to control the position of the 3D submarine.

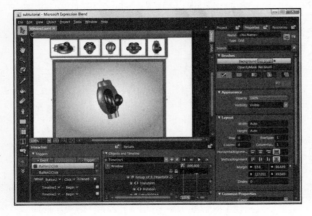

Including 3D models and animation

In Blend, you can make any image into a 3D plane that you can then animate. And you can change that image to a video, creating an animated video on a 3D plane, as shown in Figure 1.1. Or, you can import 3D objects from other programs. And with Zam 3D from Electric Rain (www.erain.com) you can import both the 3D object and its animation into Blend, because Zam 3D exports in XAML, the user-interface markup language the Expression family of programs understands.

NOTE XAML is the Extensible Application Markup Language, an XML-based standard developed by Microsoft to define media-rich user interfaces for Windows XP or Vista applications and Web applications. User interfaces designed with XAML can take full advantage of Windows Vista's rich media presentation capabilities, while remaining completely separate from the rest of the application code. This simultaneous separation and integration makes it easy for designers to work on their own with XAML-generating tools such as Blend to develop highly functional graphical user interfaces. Programmers can then quickly integrate these interfaces with Web application code or Windows application code that they create by using, for example, Visual Studio development tools (including Visual Basic, Visual C#, and so on).

XML is the Extensible Markup Language, which is increasingly used for creating common information formats that can be used to share data between computers on the World Wide Web and elsewhere. XML is similar to Hypertext Markup Language (HTML), the standard language used by Web pages, but unlike HTML it can be easily extended to create new information formats. Like HTML, XML is a standard developed by the World Wide Web Consortium, which is led by Sir Tim Berners-Lee, the inventor of the World Wide Web.

You can also import 3D objects from any program that exports an OBJ file, which is a commonly used 3D file format. For example, in Figure 1.5, the text on the right is wrapped onto a sphere imported from an OBJ file created in Blender 3D (www.blender.org). The 3D animation on the left in Figure 1.5 was created in Zam 3D and imported into Blend.

Blend also lets you position 3D lights, move 3D objects in 3D space, add materials to 3D objects, and more. It can even animate already existing 3D animations—for example, you can import a rotating 3D object from Zam 3D and then create a fly-by animation of it in Blend.

CROSS-REF For more about using 3D models and animating in Blend, see Chapters 12 and 14.

FIGURE 1.5

A rotating 3D object created in Zam 3D on the left and a 3D sphere with text mapped on it on the right.

Playing video

It's becoming more apparent every day that video is going to be a major component of the new age of user interfaces. Video is compelling, and computers now are sufficiently powerful to use this medium extensively. Blend supports many video formats including: ASF, AVI, DVR-MS, IFO, M1V, MPEG, MPG, VOB, WM, and WMV. Basically, all the file formats that Windows Media Player 10 supports are available. Blend also allows you to play video at various resolutions, including High Definition (HD). You can play the video on any part of the interface that you specify for video, and you can allow the user to resize the video image interactively. You can provide the user with video playback controls as well as volume controls, or you can make your application control when the video is played, paused, or restarted. You can also play video on a 3D object, have it conform to the 3D surface, and even make it possible (and easy) for the user to animate the position, scaling, and rotation of the video on the 3D surface.

Video and audio can be added to the same timeline that is used for animation. You can define triggers, such as a mouse-over or mouse-click on a button, to start or stop the audio or video from any point in the timeline that you specify without using any programming. Figure 1.6 shows an example of a video player created in Blend.

 For more information about using video in Blend, see Chapter 14.

For more information about controls and layouts in Blend, see Part V.

FIGURE 1.6

A video player created in Blend that automatically resizes for all window sizes.

Using audio

With Blend you can create presentations containing recorded audio, or you can attach audio to buttons so that when the user moves the mouse over the button, the audio plays. Why have silent user interfaces? Speech and music are integral parts of the world. They can now be integral parts of user interface design. With Blend, you can also allow users to control their own volume and playback, or you can even provide them with an MP3 player to select and skip through multiple tracks of audio, as shown in Figure 1.7.

Blend supports all the audio file types that Windows Media Player 10 supports, such as AIF, AIFC, AIFF, ASF, AU, MID, MIDI, MP2, MP3, MPA, MPE, RMI, SND, WAV, WMA, and WMD.

FIGURE 1.7

You can add your own custom-designed MP3 player to your application's user interface.

CROSS-REF For more information about using audio in Blend, see Chapter 14.

For more information about controls and layouts in Blend, see Part V.

Adding images

Bitmap images can be added into a Blend document and resized and positioned precisely. Bitmap images can be added into controls, such as buttons. You can give images glows using opacity masks or bitmap effects. For example, the collage in Figure 1.8 has opacity masks assigned to each bitmap. You can change them to 3D to animate them like photos flying in space. You can add them to flow documents and wrap text around them. Images can resize along with the container that holds them, or you can specify that they do not resize. Unlike vector graphics, images may become jagged when magnified, but you can specify a maximum size that they can be enlarged to, as well as the minimum size that they can shrink to. You can also specify precisely what part of the image is focused in on if the image gets clipped in a smaller window. (The Viewbox control allows you to do this.)

CROSS-REF   For more information about using images in Blend, see Chapter 6 and Chapter 9.

FIGURE 1.8

Opacity masks have been added and text overlaid onto this collage of images to create art for a button.

Creating Innovative and Elegant User Interfaces

Blend provides you with an array of standard layout panels and pre-built controls such as list boxes, menus and buttons to assist you in creating user interfaces. These layouts and controls can be so easily deployed and activated that the designer no longer needs to design first and then implement. The implementation can be part of the design process. This saves time and allows you to more precisely craft your user interface design — and to immediately see how it actually works. Many other features of Blend also save you time, including:

- The ability to nest objects, to create hierarchical designs that are easy to manage (as described in the section "Nesting layout panels and controls for a hierarchical design" later in this chapter)

- The ease with which you may integrate interactive video, audio, 3D, and animation into your designs

- The Objects and Timeline palette, which contains a list of objects that makes it easy for you to navigate through complex hierarchies in your design

All this makes it possible for you to spend more time on finding creative and elegant new approaches to user interface design.

Choosing and customizing controls

Blend provides you with WPF system controls that are standard for Vista and Windows XP applications and that you can use to quickly design your user interface, or you can customize controls and create your own look. The controls available in Blend include the following:

- Menus
- Tabs
- Toolbars
- List boxes
- Combo boxes
- Group boxes
- List views
- Tree views
- Scroll viewers
- Buttons
- Radio buttons
- Check boxes
- Progress bars
- Sliders
- Grid splitters
- Resize grips

Blend allows you to customize your controls by adding borders and backgrounds of different colors, gradients, images, transparency values, opacity masks and bitmap effects. And you can add text of any size and color in any font you choose.

You can also customize controls by editing styles, as well as editing control parts (also known as templates), to give your control an entirely new look, and to change the way your controls react during different stages of interactivity. For example, Figure 1.9 shows a stack panel with buttons that have their styles modified so that the buttons animate to a larger size during a mouse-over.

FIGURE 1.9

In Blend it's easy to create customized controls such as these buttons that enlarge during a mouse-over.

Figure 1.10 shows an example of a progress bar that has been radically changed from the WPF ProgressBar below the slider into the dial that appears as a speedometer above the slider. The progress bar and the dial are both the same kind of control, yet they appear entirely different. The slider is used to test the action of both progress bars.

Blend also allows you to create a custom control, using a UserControl document, and Blend adds a tool button in the Asset Library to allow you to instantiate your user control in Blend, just like you add a button or list box or any control. You don't need to write any code to create a customized control in this way, although you can add code to enhance its functionality, if you want.

CROSS-REF   Creating custom controls and editing the styles of controls are discussed in detail in Chapter 16. Modifying the template of a list box is discussed in Chapter 3.

FIGURE 1.10

A standard WPF progress bar on the bottom is transformed into a speedometer on the top.

Choosing layout panels

One of the things that you will probably do in the early phases of designing an interface is to choose the layout panels that you'll employ in the user interface. (You can see examples of the different types of layout panels in Figure 1.11.) Then in these panels, you'll place child elements. *Child elements* are objects placed inside another object. These objects can be more panels, or vector art, text controls, buttons, other controls, and more. The layout panels include:

- **Canvas:** You can place all elements in this panel wherever you want them. Objects in canvas panels generally don't resize when the canvas panel itself resizes.

- **Grid:** A grid panel can be sectioned off, and nested elements placed into those sections. You can add grid splitter controls so users can resize each section independently. Objects in grid panels can resize both horizontally and vertically when the window is resized.

- **Stack:** An element placed into a stack panel is automatically positioned next to the previous element in the stack, horizontally or vertically depending on the direction of the stacking desired.

- **Dock:** Elements in this panel are docked around the edges of the application window.

- **Wrap:** An element placed into a wrap panel is automatically positioned to the left of the previous element unless there is no room, in which case a new line is started, just as with text wrap in a text box.

- **Border:** This adds a border around any panel, control or other object.

CROSS-REF   For more information about adding child elements into layout panels, see Chapter 3. For more information about laying out objects in the grid panel and other panels, see Chapter 18.

FIGURE 1.11

The canvas, grid, dock, stack, and wrap panels

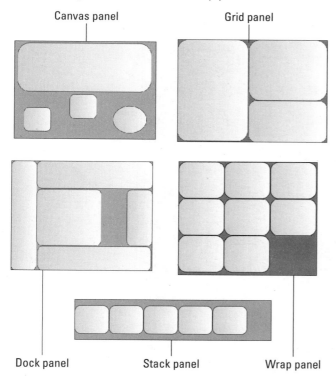

Canvas panel   Grid panel

Dock panel   Stack panel   Wrap panel

Nesting panels and controls for a hierarchical design

With Blend, you often place the controls for your user interface into a layout panel, but you can also place panels within other panels or controls within other controls. Nested objects, which are called child elements, inherit properties from their parents—for example, they move with the parent when the parent is moved, or they become invisible if the opacity of the parent is set to 0. Some panels or controls can take a single child element, such as a border panel or scroll viewer. Other panels or controls can take many child elements, such as all the panels, except Border, listed in the previous section of this chapter, as well as menus, list boxes, combo boxes, tree views and more. And some controls, such as sliders, progress bars, and grid splitters, accept no child elements.

The Objects list in the Objects and Timeline palette contains all the information about what is nested in what, as shown in Figure 1.12. You can open or close the expanders to explore deeper levels of nesting.

FIGURE 1.12

The image is nested inside a button which is nested in a wrap panel which is nested in a border panel.

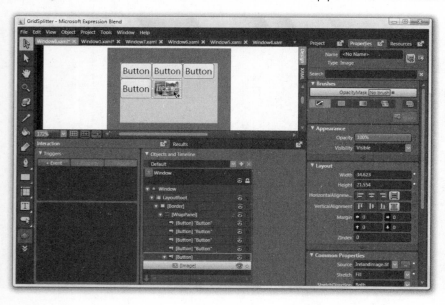

When objects are nested, they are still readily available. You can select any particular nested element of your program—to modify it or move it, for example, by double-clicking it several times until the actual element is selected, So if your image is inside a button inside a wrap panel inside a grid panel, as shown in Figure 1.12, you may need to double-click on the image three times and then single-click it to select the image rather than the panels or the button. Fortunately, this is easier than it sounds, because a large yellow border appears around what is selected to make it obvious what is selected, and double-clicking is fast. When a yellow border appears around an object, then the object is *active*. To make an object inactive, just double-click somewhere else.

 **TIP** You can also click on the name of the object in the Objects list to select it.

Nesting makes things much simpler for the designer. You can stack objects, wrap them, place them in sections of a grid, and then move the objects around in their layout panels as a single unit. It makes the task of creating many parts of a user interface simpler by allowing you to compartmentalize objects and controls.

Adding bitmap effects

Blend offers five bitmap effects that you can apply to your controls and other vector objects. They are Bevel, Blur, Drop Shadow, Outer Glow and Emboss. These bitmap effects are a powerful way to add sophisticated imagery to your user interface. For instance, you can give any image the look and feel of a button by giving it a bevel, as shown in the upper left in Figure 1.13. Then you can use Blend's Make Button tool to transform your image into a button. Or you can use the Outer Glow bitmap effect to make your buttons glow when they are pressed or moused over. You can also give your objects drop shadows to add a 3D look to your user interface, and you can add depth to the drop shadow when a tool, for instance, is dragged. You can also use the blur bitmap effect to add a glow to text, as shown in Figure 1.13. The blurred text is behind a text box that contains the same text with a transparent background.

FIGURE 1.13

Bitmap effects applied to images and text.

Using styles and templates

Maintaining consistency in your application is an essential part of making your user interface design highly usable. To aid your efforts in balancing the consistency and interactivity that you need in your interface, you can create and use styles and templates in Blend. You can add animations to styles or you can add property triggers to trigger the change in appearance of a style due to a property change for its object type, such as when the mouse is over the control, or when it is pressed. Blend also offers templates to define the control parts of a control, and how the control parts respond interactively to property changes and events. Using a template, you can define a control that appears radically different from its default WPF control, yet consistently maintains that new look.

You can make styles and templates available as resources within a single window, or within the entire application, or save them in resource dictionaries and make them available to other applications as well. Styles, templates, and resource dictionaries provide you with a way to extend the flexibility of your design, because changing a style or template can result in immediately changing every instance of that style or template.

Linking to data

Using Blend, you can link your controls to different sources of data. For example, you can link your controls to data from RSS feeds, and you can also link to data in databases. Blend allows you to link to two kinds of data formats: Common Language Runtime (CLR) Objects and Extensible Markup Language (XML).

- *CLR Objects* are data items that are usually stored in an ObservableCollection object in the code-behind files. You can read in data from a database into a data table in the code-behind file, and then convert it into an ObservableCollection. Then it can be added as a CLR Object data source in the Data palette of Blend and linked to controls.

- XML, as noted earlier in this chapter, is similar to HTML except that it is extensible. Because it is extensible, the user can create custom tags for data according to certain rules so that the data can be more easily understood by other computer software. These tags can be, for example, the names of fields in your database. You can link to a database and bind controls, such as a list box or combo box, to any field or fields of the database. In Figure 1.14, for example, an XML data source supplies information from Wikipedia.

CROSS-REF   For more information on linking controls to data sources, see Chapter 21.

ON the WEB   For a great example of how powerful flow documents can be, especially when linked to data sources, go to `http://firstlook.nytimes.com/` and check out the New York Times Reader.

FIGURE 1.14

The Wikipedia Explorer, developed by Dot Net Solutions, here displays Wikipedia's listing for Windows Presentation Foundation.

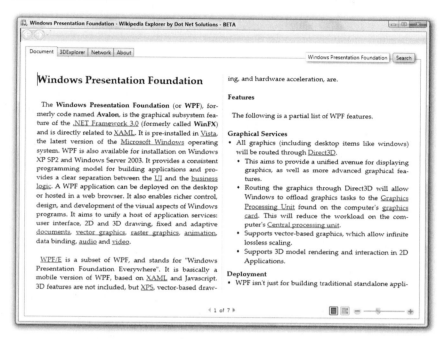

Increasing Productivity by Increasing Collaboration

In your application, you may want to import sophisticated art that is externally created, and you may also want to connect your user interface design to a back end of complex programming to run the various tools and features that you design into your interface. For this you may want to rely on the work of others. Blend is designed for collaboration both with other designers and with programmers. In large applications, Blend provides the link between the graphics and the back-end programming environment.

Microsoft Expression Design can export (among other things) XAML code, the same format in which Blend stores its data (as described in the section "Including 3D models and animation" earlier in this chapter). So, vector objects created in Design can be imported into Blend easily.

You can also import 3D objects and animation from Zam 3D, which also exports into XAML code. You simply add the xaml file into your project and open it in a document window. Then you can cut and paste its objects into any other window, page or user control in your project. And you can import any 3D object in the popular OBJ format, along with its accompanying MTL (material) file.

The XAML code output by Blend is designed to integrate with projects created with Visual Basic .NET and C#, the popular programming languages from Microsoft. When you create a project in Blend, you can choose between Visual Basic .NET or C# code for your *code-behind files*.

Each document in Blend, such as a window or page, has an accompanying code-behind file which you can use to connect your user interface elements to advanced functionality provided by Visual Basic .NET or C# code. For example, when you want to create code for an object (such as a button, for example) in Blend to make it respond to some event (such as a mouse click, for example), then you type in a name that you want to give to the event handler, and Blend generates the code to create the event handler and opens Visual Studio which pastes the code into the code-behind file and opens to the correct place for you to enter your code into the event handler. If you don't have Visual Studio, you can still open the code-behind file and Blend automatically generates code and places it into the clipboard, which makes it easy for you to paste it into the code-behind file. Then you can type more code into the method that Blend created. (Using Notepad is good for this, although it doesn't offer nearly the functionality of Visual Studio, which provides you with IntelliSense auto-completion, debugging aids, and lots more. But Notepad can be handy for a few lines of code here and there.)

Developers working in Visual Studio and designers working in Blend can work on the same project at the same time. When the project is modified and built in either application, a message appears in the other application, asking whether the project should be updated in that application.

CROSS-REF For information on importing graphics from Expression Design, see Chapter 7 and Chapter 10.

For information about using Visual Studio to publish applications and create XAML browser applications for the Web, see Chapter 4.

For more information on modifying and adding code in Blend, see Chapter 20.

For more information on importing 3D art and animation from Zam 3D, see Chapter 12.

Exploring Examples of Innovative User Interfaces

Blend makes it easy to integrate video, audio, animation, 3D, and vector graphics into your user interfaces and thus to take advantage of the extra graphics power of the Windows Presentation Foundation. You may find it useful to merge this use of rich media in interface design with other innovative ideas, such as, for example, user interface ideas taken from the trailblazing work of designer Kai Krause in the 1990s, which we describe next. These ideas may not be useful in every situation, but they have all been put to work in innovative applications to which Krause contributed, such as Kai's Power Tools, Kai's Power GOO, Kai's Photo Soap, Kai's Power SHOW, LivePicture, Poser, and Bryce.

ON the WEB You can find Kai's Power Tools at www.corel.com, Poser at www.e-frontier.com, and Bryce at www.daz3d.com.

Big windows

The idea of using big windows is to immerse the user in the application. For example, if you play a video, you may want to use the entire monitor space while hiding or minimizing the controls. Or if you are in an application, you may want to hide whatever you can to make the window that the user needs as big as possible, as shown in Figure 1.15. Monitors are only so big, and ideally, the user should be able to see only what he or she needs to see for the task at hand. Making use of the entire monitor space without any pixels consumed by a virtual desktop may be advantageous, but you may be able to do more than that by having menus or toolbars disappear when they're not needed. Making use of all the space available can help users keep their attention on what's most important to them.

FIGURE 1.15

The default for the 3D modeling, rendering, and animation program Bryce is to basically take over your whole computer screen as one big window, which works well.

Rooms

Allowing users to work in an environment that focuses just on the single task that they are performing without the distraction of other environments is a big asset. Rooms are big windows laid out for the different features of the application. Rooms can give the feeling of spaciousness in the design, just as many big rooms in a house can make a house feel spacious and opulent. So you may want to give the user lots of rooms.

The design of each room should display its functionality. For example, whatever tools you offer specifically for a room should probably be large and prominently displayed so that when the user chooses a room, the functionality of the room is obvious. Perhaps only the tools or objects needed for the user's current task are visible, so that everything in the room is geared to the task at hand.

Minimized interfaces

Offering users the tools they need when they need them may simplify a user interface and increase user productivity and satisfaction. Tools, controls, and menus can pop up when the user needs them (as shown in Figure 1.16) and disappear when the user doesn't need them.

FIGURE 1.16

Pop-up menus like the ones shown here in the 3D modeling program Poser can help minimize the user interface until it's needed.

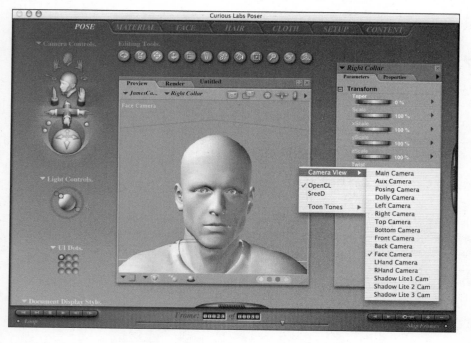

Drag-and-drop desktop tools

Tools that actually look like the tools you may use in real life such as paintbrushes or magnifying glasses, as shown in Figure 1.17, may be useful whenever they can be incorporated into your user interface design, because this adds a natural and familiar element to your application. The tools can be resized to appear large and cast shadows when used. For example, paintbrushes can contain the paints on their tips, which might resize according to the user's preference, and the tips of the paintbrushes might bend as the color is applied. This provides an obvious benefit because users can see the size and color of the brush precisely where they plan to apply it. Users don't need to look over to a distant tool palette to see what they're doing.

Or you might provide your users with drag-and-drop tools that allow them to, for example, drag items that they'd like to buy into a shopping cart, or to drag videos into their "favorites" lists.

FIGURE 1.17

A Zoom tool may become a more appealing and familiar tool when it looks like a magnifying glass and even creates a shadow as it enlarges an area of the screen.

Visibility on demand

In many applications, the number of tools may be more than the user cares to see all at once. Some applications, such as Blend, assign tools to toolbars that can be made visible by choosing them from a menu. Another method might be to have the names of tools grayed out (as shown in Figure 1.18), but appear when you press a key or move the mouse over them. This could let the user see what's available and know where the tools will be when they are needed. Depending on your application, whole groups of toolbars or other controls might appear when a single button is clicked or key is pressed.

FIGURE 1.18

Interface items may be grayed out until they are needed, as menu items are grayed out here in Bryce until the mouse moves over them.

Mouse-overs

Tools can become invisible or small when not used, but when the mouse rolls over the small or invisible tool area, they can pop up and become large and visible and functional once again, as shown in Figure 1.19.

FIGURE 1.19

It may be helpful for tools to become more visible when the mouse passes over them. Here in Bryce, a light glows when the mouse passes over the light.

Memory dots

Offering the user a quick means of switching from one window to another can definitely be a useful addition to the application. For example, the Windows Task Bar shows the applications that are open and allows the user to click on any one of them to quickly go back and forth. This feature, however, does not need to take a large portion of your application. It can be implemented via small buttons or even small dots. For example, buttons could switch you from one window to another within an application.

You may provide several memory dots in your interface design, which when pressed by default take the user to the main screen of your application. From there, whenever the user wants to go to another part of the program, while remembering where he was, he can click another memory dot and start from the main application page again. The original memory dot remembers where the user left off.

Transparencies and shadows

You can give your user interface a 3D look by adding shadows. The magnifying glass in Figure 1.17 casts a shadow, which gives it a floating appearance. Shadows create two effects on the user. First, they may subconsciously give the user the clue that the objects are draggable so that the user quickly understands how to use them. Second, the shadows may give the application more visual interest.

You may also want to include bitmap effects and opacity masks to create glows and lighting effects in your application design. Glows around objects highlight them, and make them more visible without increasing their size. And you might want to use partial transparency to make tools less visible when they're not being used or not needed.

CROSS-REF   See Chapter 7 for more information about transparency, opacity maps, and glows.

Metawindows, drawers, and scrapbooks

A metawindow is a window into the entire world of your application where you can see the entire functionality of your application at a glance, somewhat like the example shown in Figure 1.20. The user may choose the tools he wants to use or what room he wants to enter, or how he wants to proceed in the application from the metawindow.

FIGURE 1.20

A metawindow may show you the entire functionality of an application at a glance. In this Poser metawindow, many tools are accessible at once.

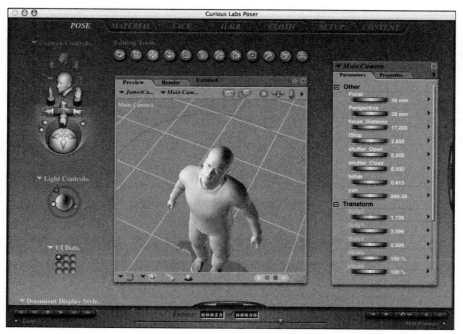

Drawers are collections of tools or features that can pop out when clicked, as shown in Figure 1.21. Drawers can actually look like drawers or stacked trays, or they can have expanders that indicate that they exist (although that doesn't seem like as much fun).

FIGURE 1.21

You can store all kinds of handy things in drawers. In Poser, the drawers on the right store actors, props, clothing, and more.

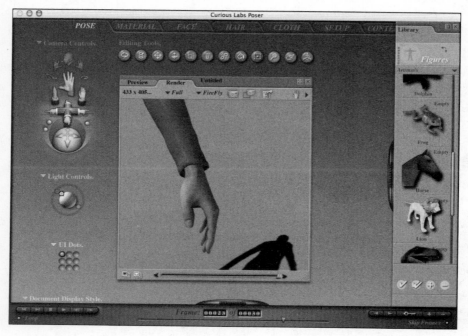

Scrapbooks can be a more inviting version of a file folder. A file cabinet full of folders may seem cold and impersonal, but a scrapbook may seem warm and comfortable. In which container would you rather place your images, artwork, or whatever the output of your application is? Of course, if your application creates spreadsheets, maybe they do belong in a file folder.

Even more ideas

The previous user interface ideas are just a few that you may wish to try when using Blend. But don't stop there — Blend makes it easy to push the art of user interface design ahead to an entirely new level, deep into the next generation of advanced user interfaces. You may, for example, want to use Blend to explore:

- *ZUIs* (Zooming User Interfaces) — described by Jef Raskin in his book, *The Humane Interface: New Directions for Designing Interactive Systems* (Addison-Wesley, 2000)

- User interfaces based on layers of movable filters, such as the Magic Lenses proposed at Xerox Parc in the 1990s

- Collaborative, online 3D user interfaces, similar to the Croquet Project, being developed by Alan Kay (one of the designers of the SmallTalk programming language) and others

 **For more information about the Magic Lenses project at Xerox Parc, point your Web browser to www2.parc.com/istl/projects/MagicLenses/.**

To learn about the Croquet Project, see www.opencroquete.org.

For online demo movies of next generation Web interface and interaction designs, visit Max Kiesler's DesignDemo blog at www.maxkiesler.com/index.php/designdemo/.

For late-breaking news on innovative user interfaces of the future, check out the Nooface blog at www.nooface.com.

Summary

- You can use Blend to quickly and deeply integrate high quality and highly interactive digital media into your user interfaces — within Blend you can add video, animation, and audio, use 3D tools, import bitmap images, create vector graphics, bind to live data sources, and manipulate text in sophisticated ways to create next-generation Windows applications and Web applications.

- Blend provides you with ready-made WPF controls, and also allows you to radically customize the look of a control while retaining its functions. For example, with Blend you can embed animation, video, and 3D graphics inside your controls.

- The grid, canvas, stack panel, wrap panel, dock panel, and border are the most important panels provided by Blend. Within these panels you can nest objects, controls and other panels, to create a hierarchy of objects that can help you to organize the complex structure of a user interface.

- You can use Blend's styles and templates to maintain consistency in your design as well as to make global changes easily. You can also create and use resource dictionaries to make your styles and templates available to other projects, and to import styles and templates.

- Blend is designed to facilitate collaboration between the artist and the developer — for example, Blend imports a variety of digital media formats, including XAML from Expression Design, Zam 3D and other WPF design applications, and it seamlessly communicates with Visual Studio.

- Blend's extensive support for automatic generation of XAML user interface code and for the advanced capabilities of accelerated 3D graphics and audio-video playback in contemporary computer hardware makes its easy and practical for you to make new breakthroughs in the user experiences provided by applications that you design for Windows and for the Web.

Chapter 2

Working with the Workspace

I n this chapter, you learn about the major features of the Blend application. You explore all of its panels and palettes and their uses, as well as how to customize the workspace and get started using Blend.

This chapter is designed to get you up and running in Blend as well as give you a vision of its possibilities. You can use this chapter both as a guide and as a quick reference. If you're new to Blend, you may appreciate the overview that this chapter provides. If you already know the basics of how to use Blend, then feel free to skip this chapter and use it as a reference when you need the information here.

IN THIS CHAPTER

Getting started

Customizing your workspace environment

Adding controls, layout panels, text, vector objects and 3D to the artboard

Understanding Blend's panels and palettes

Creating and Testing a Project

The first thing to do when getting started with Blend is to create a project. When you create a new project, Blend creates a project folder and all the files you need to get started with a blank project. As you build up your project, your project folder grows to include the XAML code files that Blend generates, your project's image files and media files, the code-behind files for each window and page in your project, your project's resource dictionaries, the .exe files that Blend creates when the project is built, and more.

To create a project, open Blend, and in the welcome screen that appears, click the New Project button, as shown in Figure 2.1.

FIGURE 2.1

Creating a new project in the Blend welcome screen.

In the Create New Project dialog box that appears, you can either choose a Standard Application or a Control Library. (If your intention is to create a user control, then choose Control Library, otherwise you probably want to choose Standard Application.)

Type a name that has no spaces in it, choose a location for your project file, and choose a programming language — Visual C# or Visual Basic, whichever you prefer for the language for your code-behind files. Then click OK.

CAUTION Blend project names can't contain spaces.

A new project appears, as shown in Figure 2.2, with a window as its default document type. The large white area is the artboard, and the Toolbox is to the left. The Interaction panel is below the artboard. You access the Projects, Properties, and Resources panels by clicking the tabs of the panel on the far right.

FIGURE 2.2

A new project open in Blend, with the expanders open in the Project panel.

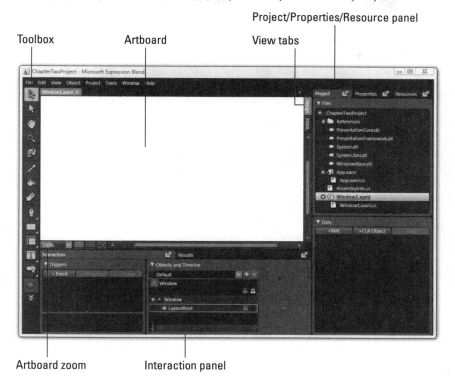

Project/Properties/Resource panel

Toolbox   Artboard   View tabs

Artboard zoom   Interaction panel

To view the XAML code for the window, press the XAML tab in the artboard, as shown in Figure 2.3.

Viewing the code files

Blend makes use of two types of code: markup code and procedural code. The markup code is the XAML code, which can control the following:

- The appearance of your application, including some built-in functionality of controls
- Data binding
- Creating animations, adding media files, and assigning event triggers
- The appearance of controls during property triggers (such as when a mouse moves over a button)
- Calling of event handlers

The procedural code is either C# or Visual Basic, which you can use to implement interactivity beyond the interactivity that the markup code can control. For example, you can use procedural code to:

- Enable the user to drag or resize an object.
- Make it possible to navigate through multiple pages in your application
- Create pop-up windows
- Bring up the Open File dialog box and other common dialog boxes
- Write data to files
- And lots more

To view the XAML file for a window or other currently open document in your project, click the XAML button at the top right-hand corner of the artboard. The XAML appears, as shown in Figure 2.3. While you are creating your user interface, you undoubtedly will need to work with the XAML code itself at times, although it may be only for very easy tasks, such as adding a frame that allows you to host Web pages or XAML pages in your window, or re-arranging the order of paragraphs in a flow document. Or you may want to go deeply into the structure of the XAML code and find new ways of using XAML to perform tasks that may not be implemented yet in a WYSIWYG manner in Blend.

CROSS-REF   **For instructions on adding frames, see Chapter 3. For more about flow documents, see Chapter 9.**

FIGURE 2.3

The XAML code file in the artboard.

To view the code-behind files or the XAML code files for your application, you can open Notepad and choose File ➪ Open. (Be sure to change Text Files to All Files in the Open dialog box.) Then navigate to the project folder and open any of the files, as shown in Figure 2.4. The document in the background is the App.xaml file. The files shown in the Open File dialog box with .xaml.cs extensions are C# code, and the other files are XAML. Both kinds of code files are combined by the Windows Presentation Foundation to create a single .exe file when you build the project.

TIP You can also right-click on the code-behind file or XAML file in the Files palette of the Project panel and choose Edit Externally. This brings up XAML files in Notepad and code-behind files in Visual Studio or Notepad, depending on your settings. Normally, you'll access the XAML code files in Blend, and the Visual C# or Visual Basic code files in Visual Studio, although you may also want to use Notepad or any other editor of your choice from time to time to access the code files.

CROSS-REF For more about using the code-behind file, see Chapter 3 and Chapter 20.

FIGURE 2.4

Using Notepad to view the code files.

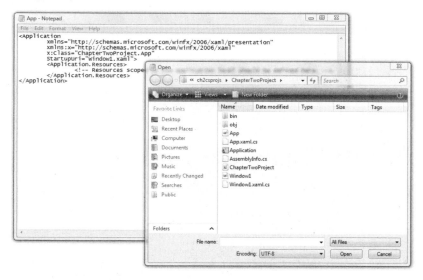

Resizing your window or page

You can resize your window by clicking Window in the Objects list in the Interaction panel. Then object handles appear around the window, allowing you to resize it. (If the window is larger than the artboard, see "Zooming the Artboard" later in this chapter.) Choose the Selection tool from the

Toolbox and drag the object handles to resize your window. You can also resize your window by changing the Height and Width properties in the XAML code or in the Layout palette in the Properties panel.

Building and testing your application

To build your application, choose Project ⇨ Build Project. This creates the .exe file in the bin/Debug folder of the Projects folder. To test your project, press F5, or choose Project ⇨ Test Project. Figure 2.5 shows an example of a blank application being tested.

> **TIP** When you have more than one document (for example, more than one window or more than one page) in your application, be sure that you assign the startup document by choosing Project ⇨ Set As Startup ⇨ (your window name or other document name here).

FIGURE 2.5

Creating a blank application.

Customizing the Blend Workspace

Blend allows you to customize your workspace in many ways. For example:

- You can change from the default dark theme to the light theme. The light theme is shown in Figure 2.6. To set the theme to Light Theme, choose Tools ⇨ Options, click Workspace, and choose Expression Light for the Theme.

- You can resize the palettes to make them larger, which is also shown in Figure 2.6. This can be handy when, for example, you're creating a gradient with multiple gradient stops, and you want to precisely position them.

- You can dock and undock panels as well as resize them. To dock or undock a panel, click on the button in the upper right-hand corner of the panel. To resize a panel, click and drag the resize grip at the bottom right of the panel. Blend's panels are: Properties, Project, Resources, Interaction, and Results. Figure 2.7 shows panels that are undocked and resized.

FIGURE 2.6

Blend's light theme.

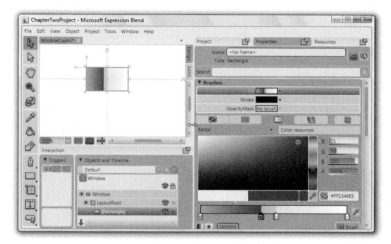

FIGURE 2.7

You can undock and resize Blend's panels.

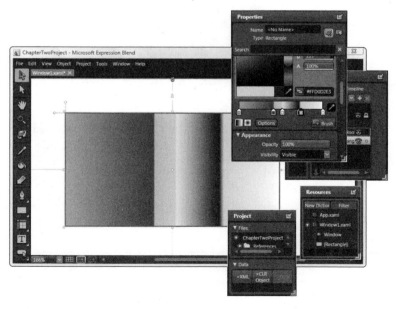

- You can add color to your Blend background surrounding the window or page in the artboard. To change the background color, choose Tools ⇨ Options and select Artboard. Then click the Color radio button and click the color swatch. A color picker appears. Choose the color that you want. We chose yellow for Figure 2.8, although for most of this book, we chose white.

- You can close panels selectively to expand the size of the working area for the artboard by choosing the panels to close or open in the Window menu. For instance, in Figure 2.8, the Interaction panel and Results panel are closed, freeing up space for the artboard.

FIGURE 2.8

Choosing to close a panel in the Window menu.

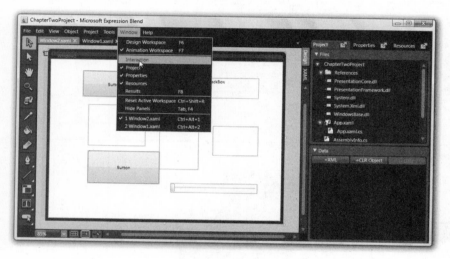

- You can close or show all panels by pressing F4 or the Tab key. This affords you maximum space for working in the artboard.

 To get your workspace looking like it was when you created your project, choose Window ⇨ Reset Active Workspace.

Using the Artboard

The artboard is where you create your user interface. You can add objects to the artboard and manipulate them in the artboard. The artboard contains two views: the design view, which is the default, and the XAML code view, which contains the markup language that defines the look of your application. The design view is actually a WYSIWIG representation of your XAML code.

When you make changes to the contents of the artboard in the design view, Blend automatically modifies the XAML code of your project to describe those changes.

You can position, rotate, and scale both 2D and 3D objects in the artboard using the Selection tool in the Toolbox. The 2D objects may be controls, layout panels, text boxes, or 2D vector objects. The 3D objects can be images that you convert into 3D, or 3D objects imported into Blend.

Creating a sophisticated user interface is not difficult using Blend, but you must know a few basics in order to begin. For example, you need to know how to add objects to the artboard, how to be able to move, resize, or rotate your objects, and how to select and deselect objects.

Adding vector objects

To add objects to the artboard, you can click the button for the object in the pop-up toolbar in the Toolbox. These toolbars are arranged by type. For instance, all text boxes are in one pop-up toolbar, vector objects in another, controls in another, and layout panels in another. You can add an object to the artboard in two ways:

- Double-click the button for the object in the pop-up toolbar in the Toolbox. This places an instance of that object in the upper left-hand corner of the artboard. You can click the Selection tool to drag it wherever you want it.

- Single-click the button for the object, and then click and drag in the artboard to specify its size and location in the artboard.

The object appears with object handles surrounding it. We describe how to manipulate these object handles in the section "Using object handles" later in this chapter.

Drawing simple paths

You can use the Pencil tool, Pen tool and Line tool to draw simple paths, as shown in Figure 2.9, in the following ways:

- To draw a path using the Pencil tool, click the Pencil tool in the Toolbox, or if that is not showing, click the Pen tool and continue to hold the mouse down, so that the Pencil tool appears in the pop-up toolbar, and then click the Pencil tool. Then click and drag in the artboard.

- To draw a path using the Pen tool, you can do the following:
  - To draw straight lines, click the Pen tool, and then click wherever you want in the artboard to create nodes. Straight lines appear between the points you clicked to create. Double-click to stop creating nodes.
  - To draw curves, click the Pen tool, then click and drag in the artboard. The line that you drag is the control handle that defines the curve that you plan to create. Click again in the artboard to create your end node and a curve appears.

■ To draw lines using the line tool, click the line tool, click where you want the beginning node of the line to be in the artboard, and drag to where you want the end node of the line to be.

TIP Here's an easier way to create curves using the Pen tool or Line tool: create straight lines first, and then click the Direct Selection tool and hold the Alt key while dragging a straight line into a curve.

CROSS-REF For more information about drawing vector objects, see Chapter 5.

FIGURE 2.9

Blend's five drawing tools.

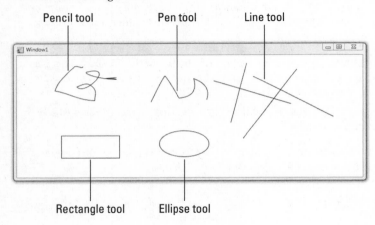

Adding controls

You add controls in the artboard in the same way that you add rectangles and other vector objects. For example, to add a button, you can click the button tool in the Toolbox and then click and drag in the artboard to specify its location there, or you can double-click the button tool and the button appears in its WPF default size in the upper left-hand corner of the artboard.

CROSS-REF For more information on controls, see Chapter 16.

Adding layout panels to the artboard

To add a layout panel (such as a grid, canvas, stack panel, wrap panel or dock panel) to the artboard, find its button in the layout panel pop-up toolbar in the Toolbox and double-click it, or single-click it and click and drag in a section of the artboard to make it appear there. To make the layout panel active so that you can add children into it, click the Selection tool in the Tools palette and double-click on the layout panel. A yellow border appears around it. Now you can double-click on controls, other layout panels, shapes, and more in the toolbox, and instead of the object appearing in the upper right-hand corner of the artboard, they appear in the upper right-hand corner of the active layout panel. To make the layout panel inactive, you can double-click outside the layout panel.

 You can also add objects into a layout panel by dragging an object while pressing Alt.

CROSS-REF Layout panels are discussed in many chapters of this book, although they are discussed in detail in Chapter 18. Feel free to skip ahead to explore them more thoroughly.

Using object handles

When you create a shape, path, control, or layout panel, it's enclosed with eight object handles, as shown in Figure 2.10. You can use these object handles in the ways described in the following list. When you create a path, the object handles do not show — only the nodes show. To make the object handles visible, select the path by clicking the Selection tool in the Toolbox.

Using object handles, you can do the following:

- **Resize the object.** Move the mouse over any object handle. When the cursor becomes a straight double-arrow, as shown in Figure 2.10, click and drag to resize the shape.

- **Rotate the object.** Move the mouse over any corner object handle. When the cursor becomes a curved double-arrow, as shown in Figure 2.10, click and drag to rotate the shape.

- **Relocate the center of rotation.** Move the mouse over the small round point in the center of the object. This is called the center of rotation. When the cursor becomes four arrows pointing up, down, right, and left, click and drag the center of rotation to a new location.

- **Adjust the corner handles of a rectangle.** Click and drag a corner handle to curve the corners of a rectangle.

- **Skew the shape or path.** Move the mouse near a middle object handle. When the cursor becomes a double-arrow with a slanted line through it, you can click and drag to skew the shape or path.

FIGURE 2.10

Skewing, resizing, rotating, and adjusting corner handles on a rectangle.

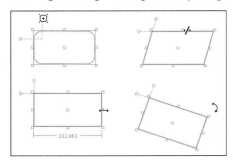

TIP In the Transform palette in the Properties panel, you can also perform all of the above transformations, except adjusting corner handles. You can use the Appearance palette for that.

Selecting objects with the Selection tool

In Blend you can select a single object, such as a shape, path, layout panel, or control, or you can select many objects at once, or you can select everything in the artboard.

- To select a single object, click on the object, or click on the name of the object in the Objects list. (If an object is nested within a layout panel or control, then you can double-click the object so that the layout panel or control becomes active and then select the object. If the object is deeply nested, you may need to double-click several times before being able to select the object. This is known as *drilling down*.)

- To select several objects at the same time, click and drag over several objects at once, or press and hold the Shift key while clicking objects individually in the artboard or while clicking their names in the Objects list.

- To select everything on the artboard, either press Ctrl+A, or choose Edit ➪ Select All.

- To deselect an object, click the object (or its name in the Objects view) while pressing and holding the Control key. Or click on another object to select that instead.

- To deselect all objects, choose Edit ➪ Select None, or press Ctrl+D.

TIP Instead of drilling down to select a nested object, you may find that often you may select a nested object more easily in the Objects list of the Objects and Timeline palette in the Interaction panel.

Selecting objects with the Direct Selection tool

When you select part of a path using the Direct Selection tool, the individual nodes of the path appear. You can edit the nodes of a path by moving the nodes, or selecting and deleting nodes, or pressing the Alt-key and changing lines into curves and reshaping existing curves, as shown in Figure 2.11.

TIP Shapes in Blend have no nodes, so it only makes sense to Direct Select a path and not a shape. If you want to transform a shape into a path so that you can manipulate its nodes, you can convert it to a path by choosing Object ➪ Path ➪ Convert To Path.

FIGURE 2.11

Pulling curves using the Direct Selection tool.

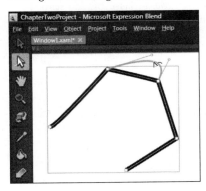

Positioning your object in the artboard

You can move your selected shape, path, control, or layout panel around in the artboard in the following ways:

- Use the arrow keys to nudge your selected object. To move it faster, press and hold Shift while using the arrow keys.

- Set values in the Layout palette for the position of the object.

- Set values in the Transform palette for the relative position of the object.

- Move the object by using the Selection tool to select it and then clicking and dragging it to a new location.

CROSS-REF The Transform palette is described in Chapter 5.

The Layout palette is described in detail in Chapter 18.

Adding text

When you want to add text to the artboard, first you must determine what text control to use to contain it. In Blend you can display text in a TextBox, RichTextBox, TextBlock, PasswordBox, Label, or FlowDocumentScrollViewer. For a more in-depth look at all of these text controls, see Chapter 9. But here are some basic instructions:

- **TextBox** and **Label** don't accept paragraph formatting. You can format the entire TextBox or Label in a single stroke, for example, by giving it a font or font size, but you can't format different paragraphs with different fonts or font sizes. A TextBox can be editable by the user, and a Label is not editable by the user.

- **TextBlock** can format selected text using the Font tab and List tab of the Text palette, but not the Paragraph tab or Line Indent tab. It's also not editable by the user.

- **RichTextBox and FlowDocumentScrollViewer** can be edited fully using the Text palette. These are flow documents. RichTextBox can be editable by the user, but FlowDocumentScrollViewer is read-only.

 You can also use FlowDocumentReader and FlowDocumentPageViewer to display text in your application by adding a simple tag in XAML. See Chapter 9 for the details.

- To add a text control to the artboard, click the text control button of your choice in the Toolbox, and click and drag in a section of the artboard to make it appear there. Or simply double-click the text control button in the Toolbox.

- To add text, you can either select the text control in the artboard and right-click on it and from the pop-up menu that appears choose Edit Text, or you can select the text control using the Selection tool, then click again so that a cursor appears. (Be careful not to double-click, because this will make your text box the active container, and you can't edit text while it's in this state. If you double-click accidentally, then double-click outside of the textbox to make something else such as the LayoutRoot the active container, and try again.)

 Sometimes in this book, we use "text box" to refer to any text control, because that is a more commonly used term than "text control."

Formatting text using the Text palette

You can use Blend's Text palette to:

- Specify fonts, font sizes, margins, and line heights
- Apply bold, italics, or underlining to text
- Align text
- Create lists with bullets and assign indentation for outlines

All the above formatting can be applied to a RichTextBox or FlowDocumentScrollViewer. Other text controls can make use of the above formatting in more limited ways. For example, in a TextBox text formatting is applied to all the text in the TextBox, and you can't format selected text separately.

Selecting text

To apply text attributes to text in rich text boxes, you can either select the text or select the entire text control. However if you apply text formatting to the entire text control, this does not change attributes applied to individual text that was already assigned different attributes.

You can select text in Blend in several ways. First, click the Selection tool and then click the text control twice slowly (not with a regular double-click) so that a cursor appears in the text, or right-click on the text control and in the pop-up menu that appears choose Edit Text. Then do one of the following:

- Select a single letter or a block of text by clicking and dragging over the text to select it.
- Select a word by double-clicking on the word.
- Select a paragraph by triple-clicking in a paragraph. Or when assigning margins, alignment, and line height, you can simply click anywhere in the paragraph once, and the formatting that you assign is applied to the entire paragraph.
- Select all the text by clicking in the text box and pressing Ctrl+A or choosing Edit ➪ Select All.

Selecting fonts, font sizes, and font styles

Choosing your font and font size carefully is important in conveying your message to your viewers, so that you use letterform shapes that are consistent with your message and that don't detract from it. To specify a font, font size or font style for some text, select the text, click the Font tab in the Text palette (shown in Figure 2.12), and choose a font from the pop-up Font list box, or choose a font size from the pop-up Font Size list box, or click the B (Bold), I (Italic), or U (Underlined) buttons.

FIGURE 2.12

Blend's text palette.

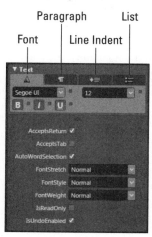

CROSS-REF For more about using principles of typographic design in the process of choosing your font, font size, and font style or for information on how to add more fonts to the list of fonts that you choose from, see Chapter 11.

Customizing line heights

The space between lines is called *leading* in the world of print media, because in the early days of printing, printers set type made of lead, and they used strips of lead to create space between the lines. Blend calls this attribute of text the *line height*. The optimal line height is typically the type size plus 1 to 4 points (1 point = 1/72 of an inch) if you are using type in the 9- to 12-point type range.

Blend sets a default line height that may put more or less space between the lines than you want. You can accept the default line height, or you can define your own. To define your own line height, select the paragraph or paragraphs that you want to format, click the Paragraph tab in the Text palette, and choose the Line Height that you want from the drop-down menu.

To adjust the line height between paragraphs, you can select a paragraph, choose the Paragraph tab of the Text palette, and choose a number from either the Paragraph Spacing After or Paragraph Spacing Before drop-down list. This number represents the number of points added to the amount of space Blend would normally place between paragraphs. You can also choose a numerical Line Height from the Line Height pop-up list, but you may want to leave it at Auto or NaN (which stands for Not A Number and is the same as Auto.)

Flow documents automatically resize their line heights to optimal sizes, so it's recommended that you leave them with line height set to Auto.

Aligning text

You can use the alignment of text to guide the viewer's eyes on the screen. The text's alignment makes it clear how text is to be read and brings a sense of relatedness to whatever objects are aligned with that text. Objects having the same alignment are viewed as a cohesive whole — whether the objects are aligned to the right, left, or center.

You may want to align your text to the right, center, or left — or to both the right and the left, which is known as *justified text*. To do this, you can select the paragraph or paragraphs that you want to align. Then click the Paragraph tab of the Text palette, and choose Left, Right, Center or Justify from the Horizontal Alignment drop-down menu.

Setting margins

You can set margins for an entire rich text box or flow document scroll viewer, or for individual or groups of paragraphs within a rich text box or flow document scroll viewer. You can also specify the amount of indentation for the first line of your paragraphs. To set your margins, select the text or select the rich text box, and click the Line Indent tab in the Text palette. Then choose a value from the Left Indent box, Right Indent box, or First Line Indent box to adjust the left margin, right margin, or the amount of indentation for the first line of your paragraphs, respectively.

You can also set margins for your entire text block, text box, label, rich text box or flow document by selecting the Text control, opening the expander at the bottom of the layout panel, and assigning Padding values to the text control, as shown in Figure 2.13.

FIGURE 2.13

You can set Padding values in the Layout palette to set margins, as an alternative to using the Line Indent tab of the Text palette.

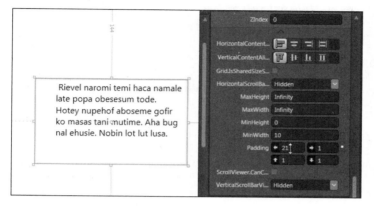

Creating Lists

You may find that you want to create lists and use bullets for text in your user interface. Blend provides you with many characters that you can use as bullets for your lists:

- Numbers for a numbered list
- Letters (uppercase and lowercase)
- Roman numerals (uppercase and lowercase)
- Various squares and circles

STEPS: Creating a Numbered, Lettered, or Bulleted List

1. Position your cursor in the first line of your list.
2. Click the List tab of the Text palette.
3. Choose a number from the Indent box to specify the indentation for your list.
4. Do one of the following:
   - For numbers, choose Decimal.
   - For uppercase or lowercase letters, choose UpperLatin or LowerLatin.
   - For Roman numerals (uppercase or lowercase), choose UpperRoman or LowerRoman.
   - For bullet shapes, choose Box, Circle, Square, or Disc.

   A bullet appears in the line with your cursor.
5. Continue typing. Every time you press Enter, your text is indented and a new bullet character appears.
6. To stop typing bullets, press Enter after your last bullet, and choose None from the Bullet Character list.

If you want to assign an indentation other than what is available from the list, you can click the XAML Code button near the top-right corner of the artboard and find the code that reads:

```
<FlowDocument>
                <List MarkerStyle="Box" MarkerOffset="10"
                      <ListItem>
```

(MarkerStyle could also equal Circle, Square, or whatever you chose from the Bullet Character list.) Then change the 10 to whatever number you desire.

 **CROSS-REF** For more information about XAML Code, see Chapter 3.

Zooming the artboard

Blend's zoom feature for the artboard is powerful. You can zoom in to increase your images' size up to 6400 percent and you can zoom out to view the artboard at 3.13 percent of its normal size. Zooming in lets you deal with the fine details of your images. Zooming out lets you increase the size of the artboard and what can be contained in the artboard greatly, and allows you to view the entire artboard and its contents in a single screen. To zoom in and out of the artboard, move your cursor over the Zoom control at the lower left-hand corner of the artboard (shown in Figure 2.2), and when the cursor changes to arrows facing in four directions, click and drag upward or to the right to increase the zoom, and downward or to the left to decrease it. You can also press the drop-down arrow and choose from some standard zoom sizes, including Fit To Screen. Or you can click in the percentage field and type in a number representing the percentage of zoom you want to view.

TIP Use the Pan tool in the Toolbox to center your zoomed image on the artboard. This is quicker than using the scroll bars.

Snapping objects to snap lines and grid lines

In Blend you can make your objects snap to a grid of any size that you specify. You can also snap to other objects and assign a margin to maintain space between the objects. And you can snap objects to the edges of the layout panel that the objects reside in and assign a padding distance between the edge and the objects.

Figure 2.14 shows the three buttons to the right of the Zoom control at the bottom of the artboard. The left button shows and hides the snap grid. The middle button toggles on and off snapping to the grid. The right button toggles on and off snapping to snap lines, which automatically align objects to the edges of other objects or the edges of the layout panel that the objects reside in.

FIGURE 2.14

A button snaps to snap lines.

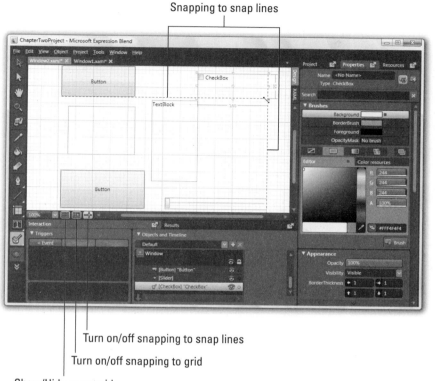

Snapping to snap lines

Turn on/off snapping to snap lines

Turn on/off snapping to grid

Show/Hide snap grid

To adjust the size of the grid, as well as the snapping margins and padding, choose Tools ➪ Options, and click the Artboard button in the dialog box. Options appear as shown in Figure 2.15.

- To adjust the spacing of the grid lines, type a number of pixels into the Gridline Spacing text box.

- To specify the margin when snapping to objects, type a number of pixels into the Default Margin text box.

- To specify the padding between the edge of a layout panel and an object snapping to it, type a number of pixels into the Default Padding text box.

FIGURE 2.15

Setting options for snapping and gridlines.

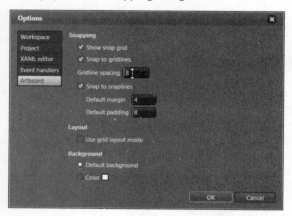

Using layers

In Blend you can organize your objects in layers that you create. You can lock or unlock all objects in a layer, or hide or show all objects in a layer, by clicking the buttons beside the layer name in the Objects palette. To create a layer, choose Tools ➪ Create New Layer, and a layer name appears in the Objects palette. Use the buttons on the Objects list to lock or unlock or hide or show layers. You use these buttons to lock, unlock, hide and show individual objects, too.

Adding 3D objects

To add a 3D object to the artboard, choose Project ➪ Add Existing Item and browse to select the 3D object in the form of an OBJ or XAML file and click OK. If you add an OBJ file, then be sure to also add the .MTL file. (Choosing Add Existing Item copies the files to the project folder and adds them to the Files palette.) If your file is an OBJ file, then right-click on its name in the Files palette of the Project panel, and choose Insert. Or, if your file is a XAML file, then double-click it in the Files palette, select the 3D object in the artboard, choose Edit ➪ Copy, click the tab for your window (above the artboard), click in the artboard, and choose Edit ➪ Paste. The 3D object then appears on the artboard.

Or you can add an image to the artboard and convert it to a 3D object. To convert an image to 3D, first add it into the project by choosing Project ➪ Add Existing Item. (You could also choose Link To Existing Item, although adding it into the project folder is probably much more common and easier.) Then right-click on that item in the Files palette, and in the pop-up menu that appears choose Insert. Then choose Tools ➪ Make Image 3D.

The 3D object resides in a Viewport3D control in the artboard. You can position and manipulate the control, to resize, re-position, or rotate the object. You can also manipulate the actual 3D object within the Viewport3D, whether it's a 3D image or an imported 3D object, by doing one of the following:

■ Click the Camera Orbit tool in the Tools palette, and then click and drag in the object to manipulate the camera view of the object. Click and drag while pressing Ctrl to pan the camera view, and click and drag while pressing Alt to zoom in or out.

■ You can display the transformation handles, shown in Figure 2.16, by clicking the Selection tool in the Tools palette and double-clicking on the 3D object.

   ▪ You can use the arrows on the ends to move the object along an axis, as shown in Figure 2.16 in the image on the bottom.

   ▪ You can use the boxes to scale the object, as shown in Figure 2.16 in the image in the upper right.

   ▪ You can use the curved bars to rotate the object, as shown in Figure 2.16 in the image in the upper left.

CROSS-REF See Chapter 12 for more information on 3D objects, including information on manipulating 3D lights, adding other 3D objects into a Viewport3D, adding animation, adding materials, and lots more.

FIGURE 2.16

Using the 3D transformation handles to move, rotate, and scale a 3D image.

Rotate along Z-axis   Resize along Z-axis

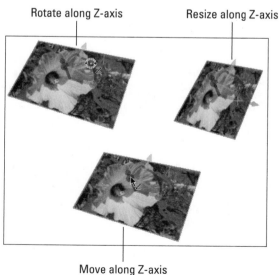

Move along Z-axis

Auto sizing

In Blend you can specify whether or not your vector objects automatically resize in height, width, or both as your window resizes. For instance, the user may be able to click and drag the edges of the application window to resize it, or to click an expand button to resize the application window. This feature, which allows a vector object to resize according to the size of an application window, is known in Blend as Auto Size. This feature is often crucial to enabling your application to be aesthetically appealing regardless of whether the application window is viewed small or large — low resolution or high resolution. For example, the video player on the right in Figure 2.17 appears with the proper proportions of the screen and the controls as the video player on the left, even though it's in a larger window.

FIGURE 2.17

We specified the controls to become smaller in proportion to the size of the screen, in the video player on the right, than the video player on the left which required larger controls because of its smaller window size. (*Video image courtesy of* www.deliciousadventures.com.)

Sizing considerations are different for different controls and objects and are discussed throughout this book. For instance, objects in the grid panel usually can resize both horizontally and vertically. Objects in stack panels can resize in one direction. And objects in canvas panels usually don't resize at all.

CROSS-REF Chapter 18 describes how layout panels resize objects.

If the Height and Width of an object are set to Auto in the Layout palette, then a vector object will usually resize automatically if it is nested inside a grid. The default LayoutRoot for a window is a grid. (LayoutRoot is the layout panel that fills the window that you're creating for your application.) To allow objects to resize, you can type Auto into the Width and Height properties in the Layout palette, and sometimes that successfully changes the sizing to Auto, but the methods in the following section may be more successful more often.

Fortunately it is easy to change one kind of layout panel into another just by selecting the layout panel, right-clicking, choosing Change Layout Type from the context menu that appears, and choosing the layout panel that you want.

Setting the Width and Height properties to Auto

To set the Width and Height properties of an object to Auto, first be sure that the object is nested in a grid panel. (The LayoutRoot is usually a grid.) Then:

- Select the object and choose Object ➪ Auto Size ➪ Width, Height, Both, or Fill (if you want to fill the parent layout panel).

- Switch to Grid Layout mode. To do that, choose Options ➪ Tools and choose Artboard. Then select the Use Grid Layout Mode check box. Then you can view the margin adorners which are the icons at the edges of the grid that appear each time you select a child element of the grid. When the margin adorners are all closed, then the object will resize. When one or more margin adorners are open, then the object does not resize. Figure 2.18 shows an example of clicking an open margin adorner in Grid Layout mode in order to close it.

FIGURE 2.18

Auto sizing only the width property of a custom button by opening a margin adorner in the Grid Layout mode.

NOTE Grid Layout mode in a visual way lets you assign how an object within a grid is to be autosized — which is a pretty cool feature.

Not all controls and objects can have their width and height set to Auto and still function normally — for example, a list box can't.

CAUTION Sometimes when you close one margin adorner, the margin adorner opposite to it opens. When this happens, then give up, and try the following tip.

 When your object refuses to resize, but you still want it to do so, try nesting it into a Viewbox. For more information about Viewboxes, see Chapter 16.

Using Make Same for Size Uniformity

Make Same is a simple feature that allows you to set the size of two or more objects to the same size. To use Make Same, select more than one object, and choose Object ➪ Make Same ➪ Width, Height or Size. Blend automatically sets the width, height, or both of the uppermost object to the same width, height, or both as the bottommost object.

Your Panels and Palettes at a Glance

The Blend interface includes five panels and over a dozen palettes. Palettes are contained in panels. Blend's five panels are Properties, Project, Interaction, Results, and Resources. This section gives an overview of the function of each panel and highlights the features of its major palettes.

Using the Properties panel

Every object in the .NET Framework has properties that are associated with it. These properties define the appearance and functionality of an object. The WPF assigns default properties to its controls and layout panels, allowing you to use the controls and layout panels with their default properties, or allowing you to change the properties. You can change Properties in many ways by using the Properties panel. And they can also be changed in other ways as well.

The Properties palette displays the properties of the currently selected item. Using the Properties palette you can do the following:

- Assign values to a property using any of the palettes. For example, you can assign a Brush to a Background of a Text box.
- Bind a property of one object to a property in another object, or to a data field in a data source. Do this by clicking the Advanced Properties Options button that is beside many properties in the panel. For example, in Figure 2.19, the Value property of the progress bar is data bound to the Value property of the slider. Properties that have data binding have a border around them in the Properties palette, signifying this state.

CROSS-REF   For more information about data binding, see Chapter 3 and Chapter 21.

For more information about assigning values to properties in the code-behind file, see Chapter 20.

FIGURE 2.19

Properties with data binding have bright borders around them.

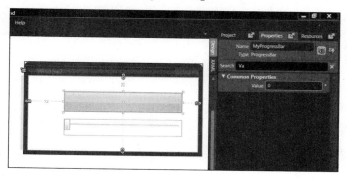

Because the Properties panel is quite large and consists of many palettes, it includes a search feature that allows you to search for the property that you want to find. In Figure 2.19 we searched for the Value property, although we could have found it easily in the Common Properties palette. The search results show only the properties that correspond to the phrase that you searched for.

The Properties panel contains the Brushes palette, Appearance palette, Layout palette, Transform palette, Events palette, Common Properties palette and Miscellaneous palette, all of which we describe next. It also contains the Text palette for specifying fonts, font sizes, and text-related options, described earlier in this chapter.

The Brushes palette

The Brushes palette, shown in Figure 2.20, allows you to assign colors, gradients, opacity masks, image brushes, drawing brushes, visual brushes, and transparency, as appropriate, to the following (and more) in selected objects:

- **Background:** Layout panels and controls have backgrounds rather than fills.
- **BorderBrush:** You can change the appearance of a border for objects that have borders.
- **Fill:** This is the area between strokes in vector objects.
- **Foreground:** This generally applies to text.
- **OpacityMask:** Almost every object in Blend has an opacity mask that causes the object to be visible when the alpha value of the opacity mask is equal to 1 and invisible when its alpha value is equal to 0. Assigning a linear gradient, for example, to an opacity mask where the opacity mask fades from an alpha value of 1 to 0 creates the effect of the object fading to invisibility in a linear manner.
- **Stroke:** These are the lines and curves of a vector object.
- **TextBackground:** This is the background color of each line of text.

FIGURE 2.20

The Brushes palette.

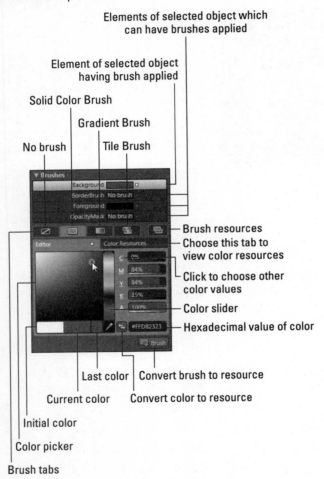

Elements of selected object which
can have brushes applied

Element of selected object
having brush applied

Solid Color Brush

Gradient Brush

No brush   Tile Brush

Brush resources

Choose this tab to
view color resources

Click to choose other
color values

Color slider

Hexadecimal value of color

Last color | Convert brush to resource

Current color   Convert color to resource

Initial color

Color picker

Brush tabs

In the Brushes palette, you can choose an element of the selected object that you want to change in the preceding list, and then click on one of the following brushes to open a new pane in the palette:

- **Gradient:** A color space, color picker, and a gradient bar appear, which you may use to assign a linear gradient or a radial.

- **No Brush:** No new pane is required. The fill, stroke, or whatever you select from the list becomes invisible.

- **Solid Color Brush:** A color space appears in which you may choose a color.

- **Tile Brush:** Use this to tile an image or pattern.
- **Brush Resources:** Apply resources in this tab, including the following:
  - **Drawing brush:** This applies vector art as an image that you can use as a brush to fill other vector objects.
  - **Image brush:** This applies an image as a brush to fill other vector objects.
  - **Visual brush:** This is like a camera view of a layout panel, animation or video, which can be applied like a brush on an object.

CROSS-REF The Drawing brush, Image brush, and Visual brush are defined in the Tools menu and described in Chapter 6.

The Brushes palette also includes a color eyedropper tool, a color picker, and sliders to assign color and opacity, using any of four color spaces: HLS, HSB, RGB and CMYK. To choose a different color space, click on one of the letters of the existing color space and choose another color space from the pop-up list.

You can assign gradients in the Gradient tab, adding as many gradient stops as you like by clicking in the gradient bar, and deleting gradient stops by dragging them away from the gradient bar. Select a gradient stop to assign it color.

From the Options button you can choose gradient modes. These modes can apply when the Brush Transform tool makes the gradient smaller than the object, and you have a choice of what to do with the extra space. The gradient modes are:

- **Pad:** Fills the extra space in the object with the color of the last gradient stop.
- **Reflect:** Fills the empty space with a mirror image of the gradient.
- **Repeat:** Repeats the gradient in the empty space. This mode is shown in Figure 2.21.

FIGURE 2.21

A gradient with Repeat mode assigned in the Brushes palette.

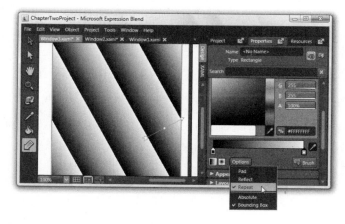

The Appearance palette

The Appearance palette lets you specify the visibility and opacity of an object, and specify the width of a stroke. It also allows you to choose the look of how lines join at their nodes. The bigger the stroke size, the more apparent the difference in the three kinds of joins:

- **Bevel Join:** Appears more rounded but has some point in it
- **Miter Join:** Appears sharp and pointed
- **Round Join:** Appears completely rounded

The Stroke palette also lets you set caps, which are the shapes at the ends of lines.

You can also use this palette to assign bitmap effects.

CROSS-REF For more information about assigning bitmap effects, see Chapter 6.

The Layout palette

This palette shows you the properties set for a selected object in terms of how it relates to the layout of the panel that it resides in. If the selected object is in a grid panel for example, then in the Layout palette you can specify a row and column in the grid for the selected object. You can set margins to determine the position of an object within a layout panel, and you can set the size of the object. For more information about Auto as a size, see the section "Auto Sizing" earlier in this chapter. The Layout palette is invaluable for enabling you to set properties that result in a fully resizable user interface.

CROSS-REF For lots of information about the Layout palette, see Chapter 18. Feel free to skip ahead, if you want.

The Transform palette

The Transform palette lets you assign any of the following to a selected object, either relative to its current position or relative to its original position. You may want to use the Transform palette when you need to precisely specify scaling, rotation, or position.

- **Center Point:** To move the center point in an X, Y, or Z direction by typing the number of pixels.
- **Flip:** To flip horizontally, vertically, or on the Z-axis.
- **Position:** To assign values for X, Y, and Z offsets in pixels.
- **Rotation:** To assign a specified number of degrees of rotation to an object for the X-, Y-, and Z-axes. In Figure 2.22, for example, the Blender monkey is rotated by clicking and dragging upward in the Y Angle property in the Rotation tab.
- **Scale:** To assign a percentage of scale to an object in the X and Y directions (and in the Z direction for 3-D objects).

■ **Skew:** To skew a selected object by assigning a value (in pixels) for an X skew or a Y skew.

CROSS-REF For more information about the Transform palette, see Chapter 5.

FIGURE 2.22

Rotating a 3D object using the Transform palette.

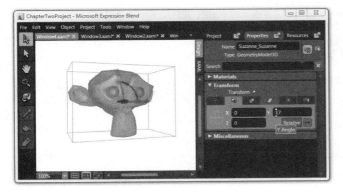

The Events palette

Use this palette to create event handlers. You can access this palette by clicking the button at the top of the Properties panel. Events might be a button click, or the selection of an item in a list box. Figure 2.23 shows an example of an event handler being added to a button in the Events palette. In the bottom part of the figure is the code-behind file with the event handler (named HideTheEllipse) that was placed into a clipboard by Blend and added using Ctrl+V. In addition we added a line of code to make the ellipse disappear when the button is pressed. If you're running Visual Studio at the same time as Blend, then the event handler is added automatically and you just need to type in the lines of code.

For more information on finding and opening the code-behind file, see the section, "Viewing the code files" earlier in this chapter.

TIP Be sure to build the project in Blend before assigning an event. And build the project in Visual Studio before testing it in Blend, or save the Notepad file if you are using Notepad to add code to the code-behind file.

CROSS-REF For more information about creating event handlers and writing code, see Chapter 3 and Chapter 20.

FIGURE 2.23

Assigning an event handler to a button, on the top. On the bottom is the code-behind file with the code generated by Blend, plus the single line of code manually inserted by us.

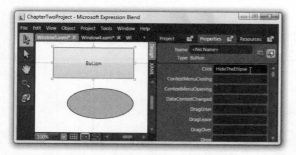

Common Properties palette

This palette contains the properties commonly modified for a control. For instance, the properties you may want to change often in a slider include its Maximum, Minimum, SmallChange, and Orientation. These properties are all found in the Common Properties palette. This palette allows you to explore the functions of a control more easily without needing to sift through dozens of properties to explore the purpose and scope of the control. This palette also provides you with a way to easily set and data bind common properties.

The Results panel

The Results panel reports errors in your XAML code when you click the Design tab after being in the XAML Code view. This happens because XAML code is compiled for errors whenever it is modified. So, if you make changes in the XAML code and some problem occurred, you will see that problem immediately when you click the Design button. Figure 2.24 shows an example of an error that a missing closing tag in a XAML document created. The Results panel displays the line number of the code at fault. (Or sometimes it refers to the line after the problem has occurred.) Checking the Results panel to correct a problem can save you oodles of time.

When you test your project, the Results panel also gives an in-depth explanation of any errors in the C# or Visual Basic code in the code-behind files.

FIGURE 2.24

Error messages from improperly written XAML code, or errors in procedural code in the code-behind file are all listed in the Results panel.

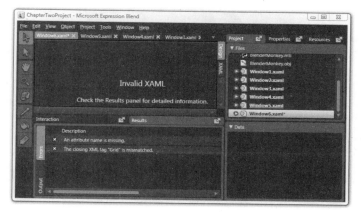

 The Results panel can also give you information about the 3D objects in a selected Viewport3D, such as how many vertices they contain.

 For information about adding C# or Visual Basic code to your project, see Chapter 3 and Chapter 20.

For information about writing and editing XAML code, see Chapter 3 and Chapter 22. XAML code is also discussed in many other chapters, as well.

The Interaction panel

You can use the Interaction panel to create animations in Blend, as well as assign property and event triggers, which allow you to control timelines or change the appearance of objects based on a property change or an event. Using the Interaction panel, shown in Figure 2.25, you can also add audio, or video to your project. You can have multiple timelines, and the timelines can contain animation, audio, video, or any combination thereof, on multiple tracks.

In Blend, you can animate the properties of objects. For example, you can animate the size, position, or orientation of an object, plus you can animate any of its other properties, such as its gradient fill or its opacity or its opacity mask to add light effects to the animation. You can animate 3D objects, controls, layout panels, and more.

CROSS-REF For more information about using the Timeline palette, see Chapter 14.

Animating the lighting of a 3D object using the Interaction panel.

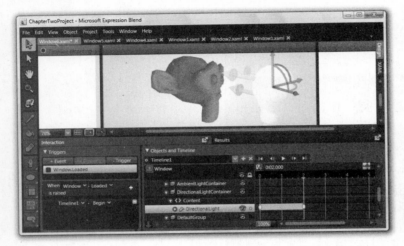

Objects and Timeline palette

Use this palette to add animation, audio, and video to your project. You can add tracks, keyframes, and multiple timelines. This palette also provides playback controls so that you can view your animations in the artboard without needing to build the project.

The Objects and Timeline palette also contains the Objects list, which allows you to select objects in the artboard.

Triggers palette

This palette, shown in Figure 2.25, lets you specify events and property changes that trigger the playing of a timeline or the change in appearance of an object. Events that trigger the playing of a timeline might be a window being loaded, or a button being clicked. And you might want to use a property trigger, for example, to give a control a different look when a mouse is over the control, to let the user know that it is ready to respond.

The Project panel

The Project panel contains two palettes: the Data palette and the Files palette.

The Files palette

In the Files palette, you can access the following items:

- **Code-behind files:** These files have an additional file extension .cs or .vb depending on whether you choose C# or Visual Basic as your procedural language when you create the project. To open this file, click the drop-down arrow beside the name of the window or page and double-click the code-behind file.

- **Image and media files:** Image files, audio files, and video files that you add to your project reside in the Project folder, and they're listed in the Project panel. You can choose to copy the file to your project folder or simply link it to your project. To add an item, choose Project ➪ Add Existing Item or Project ➪ Link To Existing Item. To add one of these files to the artboard, right-click on it in the Project panel and choose Insert.

- **References folder:** This contains dynamic link libraries, which are necessary for the processing of the code in your projects.

- **3D imported objects**

- **XML files:** XML data sources are discussed in detail in Chapter 21.

- **Pages, Windows, UserControls, resource dictionaries, and other XAML documents:** These are windows and pages that exist within your projects. Or they may be Zam 3D animations or other imported XAML documents. They all have .xaml as their file extension.

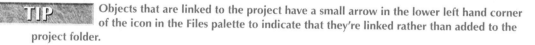 **TIP** Objects that are linked to the project have a small arrow in the lower left hand corner of the icon in the Files palette to indicate that they're linked rather than added to the project folder.

Here are some of the ways you can use the Files palette:

- You can make an item appear in the artboard by right-clicking on it in the Project panel and from the pop-up menu that appears choosing Insert.

- You can set a page or window as your start-up (which is the first that plays when you test a project) by right-clicking on it in the Files palette and choosing Startup from the context menu, as shown in Figure 2.26.

FIGURE 2.26

Assigning the start-up by using the Project panel.

CROSS-REF   For more information on adding images to your project, see Chapter 6.

CROSS-REF   For more information on using resource dictionaries, see Chapter 7.

The Data palette

In the Data palette, shown in Figure 2.27, you add or delete data sources. Data sources can be of two types:

- CLR (Common Language Runtime) object data sources.
- XML data sources. These data sources are often RSS feeds.

CROSS-REF   For more information on data binding, see Chapter 3.

Click the plus sign to add data sources and click the minus sign to delete a data source. Once you add a data source you can drag a field into the artboard, and create controls to bind the data. For example in Figure 2.27, the BBC's RSS feed from `http://newsrss.bbc.co.uk/rss/new-sonline_uk_edition/front_page/rss.xml` is added as a data source and placed into a list box in the artboard. Once in the artboard, you can edit its template and improve its look and functionality greatly.

FIGURE 2.27

The BBC RSS feed is added as a data source to the project and placed into a list box in the artboard. From there you can adjust the look and its functionality.

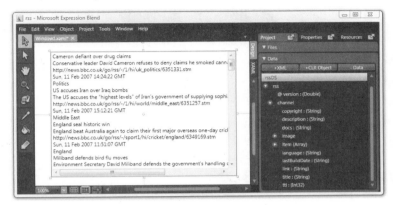

The Resources panel

The Resources panel allows you to add, edit, rename, and delete resources from your project, and to link resource dictionaries to your project. In Blend, *resources* are items saved for repeated use — they can be colors, brushes, styles, templates, and complex objects. Resources can be defined on three levels: document, application, and resource dictionary. The Resources panel allows you to change resources from one level to another, as well as edit resources. Figure 2.28 shows an example Resources panel.

FIGURE 2.28

The Resource panel allows you to organize your resources in three categories: application, document, and resource dictionaries.

Color and Brushes resources are created in the Brushes palette and can be applied from there. Other resources can be created by editing a style or a template. Templates are contained in controls and define the look of the control for different states of a control. One way to create a resource is to select an item that has a style or template that you want to modify, and choose Object ➪ Edit Control Parts (Template) ➪ Edit A Copy, or Object ➪ Edit Style ➪ Edit A Copy. Give your style or template a name or accept the default name. If you want to add your resource to a resource dictionary, click the Other Document button in the Create New Style dialog box and choose the name of the resource dictionary.

To apply a resource, select an object, and choose Object ➪ Edit Control Parts (Template) ➪ Apply Resource ➪ (name of template), or choose Object ➪ Edit Style ➪ Apply Resource ➪ (name of style).

CROSS-REF For more information about resources, see Chapter 7 and Chapter 16.

Working with the Toolbox

The Toolbox is at the left side of the Blend window (as shown in Figure 2.2). It includes the following tools, starting from the top of the Toolbox:

- **Selection:** Use this to select objects, move objects, resize objects, rotate objects, and more. Also, you can use this in conjunction with double-clicking to make layout panels and controls active, which means they are ready to accept child elements.

- **Direct Selection:** This tool shows the nodes of a vector object as well as its control handles for curves and allows you to move the nodes and reshape the curves. When used while pressing the Alt key, you can create and reshape curves without the need of using the control handles.

- **Pan:** Use this tool instead of the scroll handles to view parts of the artboard that are not visible.

- **Zoom:** Zooms in on the artboard.

- **Camera Orbit:** Use this to orient 3D objects in 3D space.

- **Eyedropper:** Assigns attributes, such as a brush, to a selected object by clicking on the Eyedropper and clicking on another object.

- **Paint Bucket:** Assigns attributes of a selected object, such as its brush, to another object by clicking the Paint Bucket tool and then clicking on another object.

- **Brush Transform:** Allows you to control the size and angle of gradient fills, as shown in Figure 2.21.

- **Pen, Pencil**

- **Ellipse, Rectangle, Line**

- **Panels: Grid, Canvas, StackPanel, WrapPanel, DockPanel, ScrollViewer, Border, UniformGrid, Viewbox**

- Text: TextBox, RichTextBox, TextBlock, PasswordBox, Label, and FlowDocumentScrollViewer

- Controls: Button, CheckBox, ComboBox, ListBox, RadioButton,ScrollBar, Slider, TabControl, GridSplitter

- Asset Library: This is described in the next section.

CROSS-REF For more information on using the Selection, Direct Selection, Pen, Pencil, Line, Rectangle, and Ellipse tools, see Chapter 5. And, for more information on using the Brush Transform tool, see Chapter 6.

Using the Asset Library

The Asset Library, shown in Figure 2.29, contains many different kinds of controls, including user controls that you create in the UserControl XAML document. It also includes simple controls, which are offered to allow designers to more easily customize the control, in certain cases. And the Asset Library lists the project's media files.

FIGURE 2.29

Blend's Asset Library.

Many of the system controls available in the Asset Library are also available from the pop-up toolbars in the Toolbox. The system controls that are only found in the Asset Library are:

- **BulletDecorator:** This is an element of the CheckBox and RadioButton.
- **ContentPresenter:** A container used to add content to a control in order to keep the content separate from the template of the control. This is an element of a button and can contain media files, as well as a Viewport3D. It accepts one child element.
- **Expander:** A drop-down arrow for opening a panel of information.
- **GroupBox:** A control that accepts two child elements. It has a simple border and allows you to add a title.
- **ListView:** A list in which each column can have a resizable heading, allowing the user to resize columns. This is not completely implemented in Blend at this writing, but you can add XAML code to make it functional.
- **PopUp:** Elements of menus and combo boxes.
- **ProgressBar:** A control to which you can data bind the Value property, to create progress bars.
- **ResizeGrip:** A control, usually placed in a corner of a layout panel or other control, that makes it possible for the user to resize a layout panel or control. This requires code in the code-behind file.
- **ToolBar:** A panel with an overflow tray that you can add items to. The user can open the overflow tray to see any overflow.
- **TreeView:** A hierarchical structure in which parts that are opened or closed are indicated by small boxes with a plus sign or a minus sign beside the header.

CROSS-REF For more information about adding controls to your project and creating custom controls, see Chapter 16. Most of the system and simple controls found in the Asset Library are described in Chapter 16, although some are described elsewhere. The Bullet Decorator is discussed in Chapter 18. The ListView is described in Chapter 21.

Summary

- Blend offers a flexible workspace in which you can create your own optimal layout for greater productivity.
- You can add, select, and manipulate layout panels, controls, vector objects, 3D objects, and more in the artboard.

- The panels that Blend provides are

  - The Properties panel: For assigning and organizing properties of objects.

  - The Interaction panel: For creating animations, adding media files, and assigning triggers.

  - The Resources panel: To organize resources and link resource dictionaries to your project.

  - The Project panel: To organize the files of your project as well as data sources.

  - The Results panel: Provides detailed error messages for the XAML code and code-behind files, when necessary.

- The major palettes that Blend provides are:

  - Brushes palette: To add colors, gradients, opacity masks, and drawing brushes, image brushes, visual brushes, brush resources, and tiling to your objects.

  - Common Properties palette: This includes properties commonly set for controls and other objects.

  - Data palette: To add data sources and to data bind controls to them.

  - Events palette: To assign event handlers to events and create event handler methods in the code-behind file that you can customize by adding code.

  - Files palette: Contains items in your projects such as windows, image files, other projects, media files, reference folders with dynamic link libraries, resource dictionaries, and more.

  - Layout palette: To aid you in laying out your user interface, so that it looks good at all screen resolutions and window sizes.

  - Appearance palette: To apply bitmap effects and assign stroke widths and stroke-related features.

  - Text palette: To assign fonts and font sizes and to format text.

  - Objects and Timeline palette: To create animations and add media files.

  - Triggers palette: Makes it possible for you to assign triggers to control timelines.

  - Transform palette: Scales, positions, rotates, skews, and flips 2D and 3D objects.

Chapter 3

Designing a Next-Generation Interface

Blend makes it possible to create rich, immersive user interfaces quickly. In this chapter, we examine the kind of workflow that can make this easy. Rather than concentrating on technology, we suggest that you focus first on the needs of end users, then thinking out of the box to create innovative, compelling interface designs, assembling richly interactive interface components, connecting the components to live data, and testing your functioning designs on users. Then repeat the whole process a few times to improve your design until you have a charming and highly functional user interface that's everything you hoped for.

In this chapter we investigate the process of developing an application, including the principles involved in conceptualizing it, as well as practicalities of creating it. We explain how to use grid-splitters to allow the user to resize sections of the user interface. We also show how to data bind element properties, such as data binding a slider to control a progress bar. We create an RSS news feed reader. We also discuss the fundamentals of coding in XAML and creating event handlers in the code-behind files. And we discuss what document types are available for use in Blend, and how to navigate between the document types and the Web.

Conceptualizing the User Experience

Computer applications are used to accomplish specific tasks. The way in which a task is accomplished — the steps a user must take within the application to complete his goal — creates what is called a *user experience*. The nature of that experience is important to the user's overall perception of the application. If the user interface creates a positive experience for the user, then the user is going to be able to make much greater use of the application and will want to use it.

If users are going to use your application for any amount of time, which is probably what you hope is the case, the experience that you create for them with your user interface may almost be as important to them as the outputs of the program. Your program may be competing with other software applications that can produce similar results — or you may even be competing with activities that are unrelated to your application but may be more enjoyable than using it.

Creating a compelling and useful user experience may have a tremendous influence on the level of success of your software.

One way to look at an application is that it often takes input from the user and transforms that input into some sort of output that is useful to the user. To begin to design your software, it is useful to create a diagram of inputs on the left and outputs on the right. Between the inputs and the outputs is the user interface that captures the user inputs and hands it over to the code, which transforms the input and usually gives it back to the user through the user interface again.

Once you are fairly clear about what your user wants the inputs and outputs of your software to be, you have a lot of flexibility about what happens in between. Computers now are capable of supporting a rich user interface with compelling digital media elements such as video, audio, 3.D, animation, and beautiful graphics that are all highly interactive, immersing the user in a world of possibilities and solutions. The WIMP (Windows, Icons, Menus and Pointing device) interface of Windows and the Macintosh (shown in Figure 3.1) has served the world well in thousands of applications, but it takes almost no advantage of the tremendous increases in the computing power of personal computers since the introduction of the Macintosh in 1984.

When beginning to design your application, instead of thinking, "How can I implement a user interface for my application using a standard WIMP interface?" you might instead start out by thinking, "Is there a highly efficient, effective, and even inspiring way for the user's inputs to be transformed into desired outputs if the user is immersed in a highly interactive virtual digital world with powerful computing resources?" Then work backward from that to see what's practical with today's technology.

FIGURE 3.1

The standard user interface of the typical personal computer has not changed much in more than 20 years, in spite of enormous increases in computing power. The user interface of Mac OS X isn't much different from that of the original Macintosh of 1984.

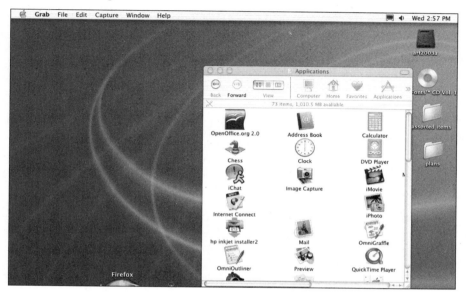

Using Metaphors

The standard WIMP user interface, as exemplified in the Windows and Macintosh interfaces, uses a metaphor of a desktop in which you can place your documents, store them in folders, and put them into a trash can, as shown in Figure 3.1. It's been a useful way to think about information that we store on a computer. Using this metaphor has some drawbacks in areas where it may cause some confusion and ambiguity, and that's probably a common feature in using metaphors in user interfaces. But metaphors are nonetheless useful because they are a quick way for the computer user to mentally map the functionality of an application to something familiar.

Using metaphor is a great way also to come up with creative solutions. The Synectics creative-problem-solving method, developed by a group of consultants in New England starting in the late 1950s, demonstrates that you can use metaphors to make familiar problems seem strange in order to arrive quickly at unique ideas that can be mapped back to practical solutions. It's fascinating how easily these strange ideas can be mapped back to the familiar world of the problem for an innovative solution. Metaphors provide you with a quick way to think out of the box by connecting a familiar problem with something strange and then linking back from the strange to the familiar.

Very powerful kinds of metaphors that you might want to use are archetypal themes, archetypal imagery, and storytelling. Incorporating elements of any of these in an enjoyable and natural way into your user interface design may make the user experience more appealing and meaningful and even help to uniquely brand your software. Archetypal themes can be rebirth, victory in the face of extreme adversity, and the power of ethical action. Much of the imagery in the world around us has archetypal qualities that we may perceive — for example, when we see images of eyes or flowers or the ocean, or of forests, the moon, or a cowboy hat.

If you can make your application use the elements of storytelling, then you really have a chance to more fully engage your users. You might consider creating for your application a setting, characters, plot, and mood with a beginning, middle, and end, so each user session creates a narrative experience into which the user is drawn to supply certain inputs — that's Act I, the beginning of a story. Those inputs are transformed perhaps via human and computer interactions, and that's Act II, the middle of the story. Then the users' inputs are transformed into a useful form that is passed back to the users as outputs, and that experience is Act III, the conclusion. In this way, you can provide a richer context for your application and for the users' experience of it. Of course, this may be ridiculously annoying if it isn't all relevant to the users' needs, so you'll want to tailor your use of storytelling in a way that is constantly relevant to what your user is really looking for.

For example, say your assignment is to create a new kind of software package to create art. Instead of the metaphor of a canvas used by so many paint and draw programs, you could choose other metaphors. Perhaps you could choose the metaphor of a gold mine, and in your software you have tools to dig into and reveal permutations of patterns, as if by cutting off slices of variously colored wax pellets that are melted together. Or maybe you might use the metaphor of a lab with a chemistry set, where you have different art objects or art styles or patterns in assorted test tubes. Then you dump varying quantities of each art content item into a beaker, mix them up, heat them up or cool them down, and then somehow magically take snapshots of slices of what's inside the beaker from different angles and depths. Or maybe this is an art program to generate images of people, so you use a Mr. Potato Head metaphor to assemble different facial features and clothing.

None of these approaches uses the paint-on-canvas metaphor, and perhaps if you came up with a few more ideas like these and combine them, you might end up with something that's pretty interesting and useful.

Moving from Thumbnail Sketches to Mockups

After you have conceptualized the big picture of what you want to accomplish in your user interface and the kind of experience you want the user to have, you can start to think about what kind of user interface you want. Here again it's important to start with the big picture. We suggest that you don't just sit down in front of Blend and start putting buttons on the screen. Instead do what graphics designers in other media do. Make a dozen or a hundred or a few hundred thumbnail sketches that are the size of a thumbnail or of a postage stamp — or of a large postage stamp if you think that's really necessary. You may find it easier to make these sketches with pencil and paper rather than with a mouse and a computer screen. Or maybe use a drawing tablet with your computer.

You can and should do this even if you can't draw. There isn't much room to draw in a sketch the size of a postage stamp anyway. So, if you need to put people in the user interface, draw stick figures. If you have a big block of text, represent it by drawing a few horizontal lines. Outside the postage stamp area, put arrows with callouts, to note what each part of the sketch is. This is intense work, but it's much faster than mocking up a whole interface that is not really optimal. If you make your sketches, in a few minutes or an afternoon, you'll have tried dozens of interface ideas in a surprisingly short period of time, and that makes it much easier to quickly latch onto a really good one. Then when you sit down in front of Blend, everything is much easier, because you already know where you want your interface elements to go.

> **TIP**   Spending a little time on thumbnail sketches puts you way ahead of the game. Then take advantage of the speedy way in which you can create a functioning interface in Blend to quickly put together mockups of your application that you can try out on members of your target audience.

Your final design is probably going to be far better if you go through this cycle early and often: thumbnail sketches, mockups, testing with members of your target audience, repeat. Videotape your testers using your mockups in a comfortable environment but without any help from you, and while your videotape is rolling, have them talk aloud about what they see and what they're thinking. You'll be amazed at how much you learn and how fast you can make progress at creating a really great user interface.

Drawing all those little pictures, trying multiple designs instead of using the first one that occurs to you, having people try your mockups and telling you what they think of them, and then repeating the process may seem like a huge hassle. However, it's much more fun to do that and end up with a great user interface that creates a terrific user experience and produces output that's truly helpful to the user.

Starting with thumbnail sketches

When I worked on debugging my programs in my first programming job, my boss told me that sometimes the only way to locate the bug was to take a walk. It sounded strange, but whenever I had a perplexing problem that I couldn't figure out, I'd go for a walk and somehow the answer would pop into my mind. The point of this story: you probably don't want to start designing your user interface directly on the computer. Do it by creating thumbnail sketches with a pencil and paper.

Find a quiet, light-filled space. Get out a piece of paper, and start either with your main screen, or your metawindow — the one window that lets the user see everything about the program — or start with the different rooms in your interface and work your way up to the metawindow. You can start at the bottom and work your way up, or start from the top and work your way down.

Start with the objectives of your application. Then, for example, you might create one virtual room in your interface for each objective.

Creating the user interface

Once you have your sketches, you can start the actual layout of your windows. Until now, designers have often accomplished this by using a graphics program such as Photoshop or Illustrator to create prototypes of window layouts. But now, by using Blend, you can accomplish this by creating functioning layout panels and controls.

Choosing your document types

When you open a new project, it generally opens to a Window, although you can change this. If you choose File ⇨ New Item, you have the choice of choosing Window, UserControl, Page, and ResourceDictionary. They do the following:

- **Window:** Offers a resizable window that when used with a grid as the LayoutRoot can shrink and expand the contents when the window resizes. However, it doesn't have the same navigation abilities as a Page. See the section "Planning your navigation system" later in this chapter for more information.

- **Page:** Like a Window, except that it doesn't resize its LayoutRoot when resized, and it has more sophisticated navigation abilities. See the section "Planning your navigation system" later in this chapter for more information.

- **UserControl:** Allows you to create a control that you can access from the Asset Library and add into the artboard, just as you add any control. The user control has an associated code-behind file that developers can use to add procedural code to the control. The user control also has another wonderful use. Because it's very similar to a Page, but is assigned a specific tag that can be accessed in the XAML code, the user control is ideal for containing content that can be navigated to within ContentControls in windows or pages. This is discussed in the section "Planning your navigation system" later in this chapter.

CROSS-REF   For more information on customizing controls, see Chapter 16.

- **ResourceDictionary:** Contains resources, which are reusable items such as brushes, styles, and templates that can be shared with other projects.

CROSS-REF   These are discussed in detail in Chapter 7.

Choosing and adding the layout panels

Often the layout panel you use as the main panel of your application is the grid. This layout panel gives you the flexibility to allow its contents to resize in both directions if the grid panel resizes. It also allows you to break up your window into many sections. In fact, the default LayoutRoot panels of all windows and pages are grid panels. (However you can change the LayoutRoot to a different layout panel by right-clicking on its name in the Objects list, choosing Change Layout Type from the pop-up menu that appears, and then choosing the layout panel that you want to change to.) Other layout panels are the dock panel, stack panel, canvas and more. These layout panels are described throughout the book, but they are discussed in depth in Chapter 18.

If you use a Grid panel — or if you just use the artboard (which is a grid panel by default) — you can place grid splitters into your application to enable the user to resize any section of the grid.

Creating a user-resizable grid

The LayoutRoot of your window is a grid panel by default, but if you have more than a couple of sections that you want to resize, you may want to nest more grid panels into the artboard for greater flexibility. In the following example, the user interface is divided into five sections that can be resized. As you resize one section, the other resizes to take up the available space. Figure 3.2 shows the five resizable sections. It takes two grids plus the LayoutRoot and four GridSplitters to achieve the effect. Here are the steps to add resizing capabilities to your user interface:

FIGURE 3.2

GridSplitter controls allow you to resize your grid sections. This window has five resizeable grid sections.

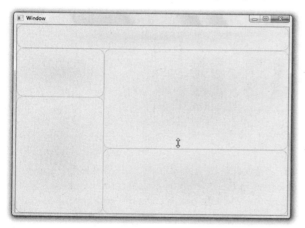

> **NOTE** When performing these steps, if you ever double-click an object and a yellow border appears around the object by mistake, you can double-click outside the borders of the artboard to remove the yellow border. (First be sure the Selection tool is highlighted in the Toolbox; if not, then click it.)

STEPS: Creating a Resizable User Interface

1. To do this, choose Tools ➪ Options and select Artboard, then select Use Grid Layout Mode. You can also change the background color, if you want — we changed ours to white.

2. In a new window, zoom out the artboard so you can see the edges of the LayoutRoot, choose the Selection tool and double-click in the LayoutRoot to make it active. Then move the mouse over the light blue line on the top and left edges of the LayoutRoot to create a grid line across the artboard, as shown in the upper left in Figure 3.3. When the grid line is positioned where you want to divide the artboard, click. The grid line becomes a blue line. (To move the line, click and drag the triangle at its top or side. To delete the line, click the end of the line to select it and press Backspace.) Create a vertical grid line as well, as shown in Figure 3.3 on the upper left.

FIGURE 3.3

You can section the artboard to create columns and rows.

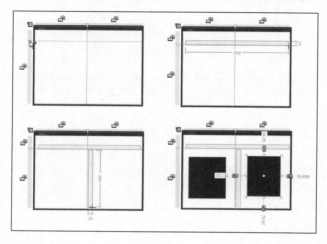

3. Add a grid splitter above the top of the horizontal grid splitter, as shown in the upper right in Figure 3.3. To do this, click the GridSplitter button in the Toolbox, and click and drag in the grid to draw in the grid splitter. Be sure not to cross the grid line when you draw it. Also add a grid splitter next to the vertical grid line, but not crossing the other grid splitter, and not crossing any grid line, as shown in Figure 3.3 on the lower left.

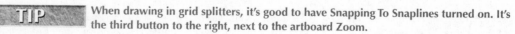

TIP   When drawing in grid splitters, it's good to have Snapping To Snaplines turned on. It's the third button to the right, next to the artboard Zoom.

4. Add grids into the lower sections of the LayoutRoot. To add a grid, click the Grid button in the Toolbox, and click and drag to position it into a section. Select each grid and give it a background color in the Brushes palette, as shown in the lower right in Figure 3.3, so that when you test the grid splitters, you'll see the effects better. Different colors may be a good idea. Then select the grids one at a time and choose Object ➪ Auto Size ➪ Fill. This fills them to the size of the section of the LayoutRoot. Select the grid in the same section as the grid splitter and choose Object ➪ Order ➪ Send To Back.

5. Test your grid splitters by choosing Project ➪ Test Project, or pressing F5. (If you need to set your window as the Startup window, then choose Project ➪ Set As Startup ➪ your window name.) They should look something like ours, shown in Figure 3.4. If the grid splitters don't function, then in the artboard be sure they don't cross any grid line.

FIGURE 3.4

Testing the grid splitters.

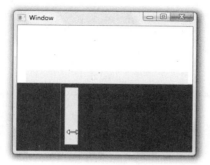

6. Choose the Selection tool and double-click one of the grids to make it active. A yellow border should appear around it, and the bar that allows you to create grid lines appears, as shown in the upper left in Figure 3.5. Click to create a horizontal grid line. Then draw another grid splitter above or below that grid line, as shown in Figure 3.5 on the upper right. (Make sure the grid is still active when you do this.)

FIGURE 3.5

Adding more grid splitters.

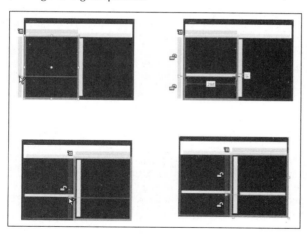

7. Choose the Selection tool and double-click the other grid to make it active. Then add a horizontal grid line to that grid, as shown on the bottom left in Figure 3.5. Then draw a grid splitter into it either above or below the grid line, as shown in Figure 3.5 on the bottom right.

8. Test your grid splitter again to see how it functions, by choosing Project ⇨ Test Project or pressing F5. It should appear similar to Figure 3.6.

FIGURE 3.6

Testing all the grid splitters.

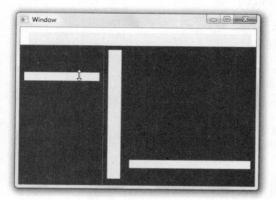

> **TIP**   Grid splitters don't have to be visible in the application window, although you can't set their Visibility to Hidden or give them No Brush in the Brushes palette. What you can do, however, is set the Alpha value of their brush to 0 in the color space, or you can set their Opacity to 0 in the Appearance palette.

9. Select each grid splitter individually and set its Alpha value to 0 in the Brushes palette. Set the background of the two grids to No Brush.

10. To add rectangles with nicely rounded corners as a background to your resizable grid sections, add the rectangle to the top upper section in the LayoutRoot, and give the rectangle rounded corners by clicking the Selection tool and adjusting the corner radius handles. In the Brushes palette, give your rectangle a color or gradient for its fill.

> **TIP**   Grid splitters can't function when they are beneath other objects. Be sure your grid splitters are the topmost objects in your application window.

11. Select the rectangle and choose Object ⇨ Order ⇨ Send To Back.

12. Be sure the Selection tool is highlighted in the Toolbox, and double-click a grid to make it active. Then draw in two rectangles, one in each section of the grid. Select each one at a time and choose Object ⇨ Auto Size ⇨ Fill, so they fill their sections. Select the rectangle in the same section as the grid splitter and choose Object ⇨ Order ⇨ Send To Back.

13. Repeat Step 12 for the other grid. You can also choose the LayoutRoot and give it a nice color, since it is visible near the rounded corners of the rectangles.

14. To be sure that all your rectangles will resize correctly in any window size, select them all individually and be sure that all the margin adorners are closed. If any are not closed, then click on them using the Selection tool to close them.

> **NOTE** Grid splitters have Auto set for either their width or height, depending on their orientation. This is automatic for this control, So if you select a grid splitter, be sure that one of the margin adorners in one direction is open, and don't try to close them all.

Inserting controls

Blend offers many ready-made controls that you can build into your design and make functional in many ways without programming. To insert a control into your user interface, first determine into which layout panel or control you want to nest the control. You can nest controls into other controls as well as into layout panels. For instance, you may want to add a check box into a menu item, or you may want to add radio buttons into a rich text box, and so on. In Blend, a layout panel or control in which you nest another object is called a *container*.

An object that you put inside a container is called a *child element* or *nested element*. For example, each of the two grids placed in Figure 3.5 have two rectangles as their children. Containers may accept one child element, or several child elements. For instance, the Border panel accepts one child element, so any object you place into it replaces any other object that was in it. (However, the one child element could be a layout panel, such as a grid panel that contains many child elements.)

Any object that is added into the artboard is added into the *active* container. Blend allows one active container at a time in the artboard, and one layout panel or control must be the active container. By default, the active container is often the LayoutRoot. But you can assign any control or layout panel that accepts child elements to be the active container. You can spot the active container easily because it has a yellow border around it, and a yellow border around its name.

To make a layout panel or control the active container, which means it's ready to receive a child element, you can do any of the following:

- Double-click the name of the object in the Objects list. A yellow border appears around its name.

- Choose the Selection tool and double-click on the object in the artboard. You may need to double-click several times to work your way down to the object that you want to designate as your container. A yellow border surrounds the container, as shown earlier in Figure 3.5.

To change the active container to another container or to the LayoutRoot, double-click on the other layout panel or control, or double-click on the LayoutRoot. Double-clicking outside the artboard automatically makes the LayoutRoot the active container. Make sure the Selection tool in the Toolbox is selected before you double-click, unless you're double-clicking in the Objects list.

To nest a child element inside a container, you can do any of the following:

- Drag the object into the active container (or any layout panel) while pressing Alt. For example, in Figure 3.7, the image of a flower is dragged into the rich text box while pressing and holding Alt.

FIGURE 3.7

Inserting an image into a rich text box by dragging it while holding Alt.

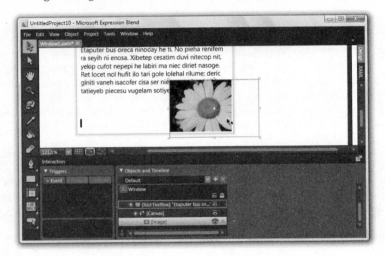

 Sometimes when trying to drag an object into an active container, you need to first click the object in the Objects list to select it. Then you can drag it in while pressing Alt.

- Double-click the button of an object in the Toolbox, and it appears within the yellow border of the active container.
- Click on the name of an image file or media file in the Project panel; then right-click and choose Insert. It appears in the active container.
- In the Objects list, drag the name of the object into the name of the active container while pressing Alt, as shown in Figure 3.8.
- Click on the button of an object such as a control in the Toolbox, and click and drag anywhere in the artboard. The object generally remains where it is, even if it is outside the active container, but it is actually nested within the container—it just has large margins set that make it appear outside the container.

FIGURE 3.8

FIGURE 3.8

Dragging the name of an object into the name of the active container while pressing Alt.

Adding Animation and Video

In Chapter 1, we described how Blend can allow you to map video onto 3D planes and animate the 3D planes, as well as allowing the user to click on any 3D plane, causing that video to resize to the size of the window. The animated 3D planes with video are shown in Figure 1.1. In this section, we'll investigate how to create them. First, we'll look at how to map a video onto a 3D plane using a visual brush and how to animate it. Then we'll describe how to create the animation that increases the size of the video to fill the window, and how to assign the trigger so that the animation plays when the video is clicked. And all this can be done without code!

Mapping a video onto a 3D plane and animating it

Blend allows you to create a visual brush using a video. You can map the visual brush onto an image that was converted to a 3D image. The visual brush replaces the image on the 3D plane. Then you can animate the 3D plane. Here's how to do it.

Steps: Creating a visual brush and mapping it onto a 3D plane and animating it.

1. To create a 3D image, first add an image into your project — choose Project ⇨ Add Existing Item, select your image, and click Open. Also add the video files that you want to appear, using the same process.

2. Right-click on the image in the Project panel, and choose Insert. Choose the Selection tool and resize your image to a size about 30 percent larger than you want your 3D video to be. Select the image if it's not already selected, and choose Tools ⇨ Make Image 3D.

3. Click the Camera Orbit tool, and click and drag downward in the 3D image while holding the Alt key. Your image resizes to a smaller size. Keep resizing it until it reaches the size you want. (Doing this resizes the image smaller than the Viewport3D, so that when you rotate the image, the image doesn't get clipped by the sides of the Viewport3D.)

4. Right-click on a video in the Project panel and choose Insert. You can size it very small, choose Tools ⇨ Make Brush Resource ⇨ Make Visual Brush Resource, and click OK. (If you want to hide the video, you can cover it with a rectangle that is the same color as the window background, but deleting it also deletes the visual brush.)

5. To apply the visual brush to the 3D plane, click the Selection tool and select Model in the Objects list. It's nested in Content, which is nested in ModelContainer, which is nested in Viewport3D. In the Materials palette in the Properties panel, click in the Material swatch, click the Brush Resources button, and choose the visual brush that you created in step 4.

6. You can test it by pressing F5, then choose Default as the Timeline and repeat steps 2-6 to add as many videos on 3D planes as your application requires.

7. To animate a 3D plane, click the Create New Timeline button, select a Viewport3D, and click the Record Keyframe button. Then move the playhead forward in time, and move the Viewport3D to a new location. You can also click the Camera Orbit tool, and click and drag on the 3D plane to rotate the plane in 3D space. You can continue to move the playhead forward and change the location and 3D angle, creating as many keyframes for your animation as you like. To loop forever, right-click on the gray time span bar on a track, choose Edit Repeat Count, click the Loop Forever button, and click OK. Click the Turn Off Record Mode button when you are finished. (If Edit Repeat Count does not appear, then click the expander to view more levels of the tracks and try again.)

8. Press F5 to test your 3D animated video.

CROSS-REF   For more information about animating 3D objects, see Chapter 14.

Setting an event trigger for the 3D plane to resize the video

Suppose you have multiple videos, like in Figure 1.1 and you want the user to choose the one he wants to view by clicking on it. When he clicks on a video, it resizes to full-screen. You can do that by animating the resizing in a timeline and setting an event trigger to trigger the timeline to start.

To create the timeline to resize the video, select the Viewport3D, and click Create New Timeline. Then move the playhead to about one second and, using the Selection tool, size the Viewport3D to take up the entire window. (You can resize it larger than the window, if you like). Then click the red Record Mode button to turn recording mode to off.

To create the event trigger to trigger the timeline to play, select the Viewport3D, and in the Triggers palette, click Window.Loaded. In the pane below, choose Viewport3D instead of Window and MouseUp instead of Loaded, choose the name of the timeline that you just created, and accept the default, which is Begin. You also need to stop the other timeline that animates your video. To do that, click the plus sign beside MouseUp in the Triggers palette, and then, from the new timeline list that appears, choose the name of the timeline created in the previous section, and choose Stop.

Now you can test your project by pressing F5.

CROSS-REF   For more information about animating objects, see Chapter 14.

Data binding controls

Data binding is a powerful tool that you can use to add a great deal of functionality to your application, often without any programming. Blend allows you to bind data to controls in two major ways:

- **Element Properties.** You can bind the value of a property of one object to a value of a property of another object. This is known as data binding element properties. For instance, you can bind the value of a slider to the size of some text, or the value of the slider to the rotation of a 3D object. In this section, we discuss how to bind the value of a slider to the value of a progress bar.

- **Data Sources:** You can bind data from a database or RSS feed to a list box, combo box, or other control. Any data from an XML or CLR object data source can be used in Blend. All RSS feeds and files with .xml extensions can be used as XML data sources. In the example in this section, we data bind an RSS feed to a list box to create an RSS feed reader.

 See Chapter 21 for more information about data binding.

Binding Element Properties

To bind an element property of one control to an element property of another control, you first need to be sure that the type of property is the same. For instance, you cannot bind Visibility to the Value property of a slider, because you can specify the Visibility property as Hidden, Visible, or Collapsed, but you can't specify it as a number unless you convert it. However, you can bind the value of a slider to the Opacity of an object, because they are both numbers, and they're the same type of number.

The following is an example of how to data bind the Value property of a slider to the Value property of a progress bar.

STEPS: Binding Element Properties

1. Create a slider in the LayoutRoot of your window by clicking Slider in the Toolbox and then clicking and dragging in the artboard. In the Common Properties in the Properties panel, change Maximum to 100.

2. Open the Asset Library in the Toolbox and choose ProgressBar from the Controls ⇨ System Controls tabs. Then create a progress bar in the artboard by clicking and dragging in the artboard.

3. Select the progress bar in the artboard, and click the Advanced Properties button beside the Value property in the Common Properties palette. From the context menu choose Data Binding.

   The Create Data Binding dialog box appears, as shown in Figure 3.9.

FIGURE 3.9

The Create Data Binding dialog box.

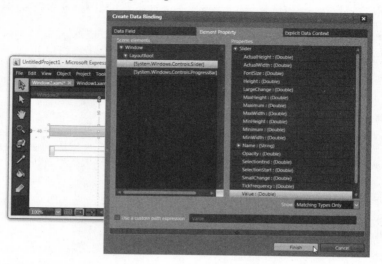

4. Click the Element Property tab, choose the slider in the list on the left, choose Value in the list on the right, and then click Finish. The Create Data Binding dialog box disappears.

5. To make the controls fit gracefully in their window, you can resize the window by selecting Window in the Objects list and assigning it new Width and Height values in the Layout palette.

6. Test your project by choosing Project ➪ Test Project, or pressing F5. Be sure the window is the startup window. If it is not, then choose Project ➪ Set Startup ➪ (your window name), and then test the project. Your window appears, and when you drag the slider, the progress bar moves accordingly, as shown in Figure 3.10.

FIGURE 3.10

The Value property of the slider is bound to the Value property of the progress bar.

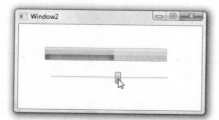

You can use ready-made value converters, or create them yourself, to bind data between properties with values of different types.

For more information about value converters, see Chapter 21.

Binding to Data Sources

In this example, we'll bind data to an RSS news feed. RSS news feeds generally offer descriptions of articles and then links to Web pages where the articles reside. In Blend you can create an RSS news feed reader which displays the descriptions and creates hyperlinks to navigate to the links. The first step in doing this is adding the XML data source (the RSS news feed) to your application. Then you want to data bind the information to an items control such as a list box, and edit the template of the list box to make the data look more appealing. The following are the steps for creating the RSS news feed reader.

STEPS: Binding an RSS Feed to a List Box

1. Create a new page by choosing File ⇨ New Item and click Page. Then click OK. In the Data palette in the Project panel, click the +XML button.

2. In the Add XML Data Source dialog box, shown in Figure 3.11, type or paste the URL of the RSS feed that you want to link to. For instance, we chose `http://newsrss.bbc.co.uk/rss/newsonline_uk_edition/front_page/rss.xml`, which is an RSS feed from BBC News. Then click OK.

FIGURE 3.11

Type or paste the URL of the RSS feed in the Add XML Data Source dialog box.

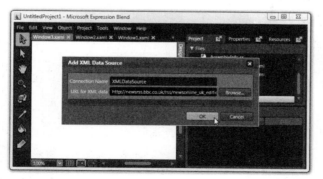

3. In the Data palette, open the expander for RSS, and then open the expander for Channel, as shown in Figure 3.12.

4. Find item (Array) in the Channel section of the Data palette, and drag it into the artboard. When you release the mouse a menu appears, as shown in Figure 3.12. We selected ListBox.

FIGURE 3.12

When dragging the item (Array) into the artboard, a pop-up menu appears.

5. In the Create Data Binding dialog box, shown in Figure 3.13, click OK.

FIGURE 3.13

The Create Data Binding dialog box.

6. In the Create Data Template dialog box, deselect the items that you do not want to see in the list box. For example, in Figure 3.14, we're deselecting Guide and Link. You can see a preview of the data in the Preview pane on the right.

FIGURE 3.14

Deselect the items that you do not want to view in the Create Data Template dialog box.

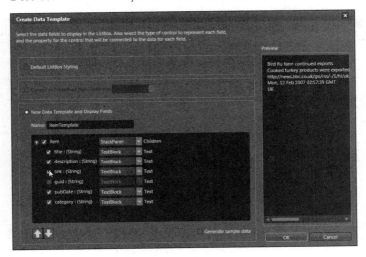

7. Click OK. A list box appears with the RSS feed data, as shown in Figure 3.15.

FIGURE 3.15

A default look for data from an RSS feed.

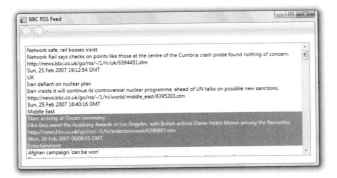

8. To edit how the data looks, you may want to first resize the list box. Then you may want to change its template by selecting it and choosing Object ⇨ Edit Other Templates ⇨ Edit Generated Items (Item Template) ⇨ Edit Template. The containers that make up a single item in the list box appear, as shown in Figure 3.16. It shows the StackPanel as the layout panel for the information to be contained. We want to change that to a grid. To do that, right-click on the name in the Objects list and choose Change Layout Type ⇨ Grid.

FIGURE 3.16

Changing the container of an RSS feed to a grid.

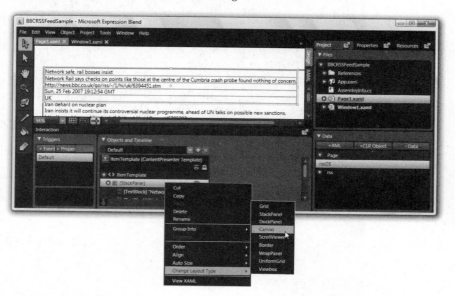

   If Change Layout Type ⇨ Grid doesn't work, try Group Into ⇨ Border, and then change the StackPanel to a grid using Change Layout Type ⇨ Grid.

9. Expand the grid by pulling down on the object handles to make some room for laying out the item template. You can add grid lines to the grid to section it off, and then assign the different text elements into the different sections of the grid. Here are some other changes that you might make, the results of which are shown in Figure 3.17:

   ■ Adjust the text wrapping of the text elements to Wrap in the Text palette. (Click the Expander).

   ■ Change the background of the grid.

   ■ Change the font and font size for the different elements.

FIGURE 3.17

Modifying the look of the data from the RSS feed.

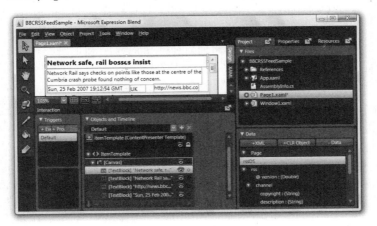

10. Click the Scope Up button beside ItemTemplate in the Objects list to exit the template, and test your project by choosing Project ➪ Test Project. Our RSS feed is shown in Figure 3.18.

FIGURE 3.18

A new look for the RSS feed.

CROSS-REF For information on activating the links to bring up the Web page, see Chapter 21.

Planning your navigation system

The Windows Presentation Foundation offers many ways to navigate among your documents or on the Internet during run time. Pages are ideally suited for navigation, but we include some ways to navigate using windows, as well. Here are the major ways to navigate:

- You can use hyperlinks to navigate between pages, as well as to HTML pages. Hyperlinks are probably the easiest of all the ways to navigate. They are discussed later in this section.

- You can use event handlers to navigate between pages. (You can also navigate to html pages, too, using event handlers.) Use this method when you want to use a control, such as a button, instead of a hyperlink. The code for this is described in detail in Chapter 20.

- You can bring up XAML page documents or HTML pages inside frames in XAML pages or windows. This is described later in this section.

- You can create content in a UserControl and navigate using event handlers that set the content property of a ContentControl to a UserControl. This is a powerful way to navigate, and its code is simple. This is described in detail in Chapter 20.

- You can create pop-up windows. This is also described in Chapter 20.

- You can use layers or the ZIndex order to bring up new content. This is described in Chapter 20.

- You can create or use existing XML data sources and navigate among the data records. This is described in Chapter 21.

- You can create flow documents, which offer several ways to organize the navigation of a single large text document. This is described in Chapter 9.

CROSS-REF   Feel free to check out Chapter 20 to get the scoop on navigation. Or check out Chapter 9 for how to create flow documents. Also Chapter 21 goes more deeply into hyperlinks and data binding to data sources. It's certainly not required to read this book in order, so feel free to skip around.

Assigning Hyperlinks

Using Hyperlinks, you can navigate from XAML pages to XAML pages or from XAML pages to HTML pages. Hyperlinks are simple to assign. First create a page by choosing File ⇨ Add New Item, choose Page, call it Page1.xaml, and click OK. Then create a text block to contain your hyperlink. You can create a hyperlink in either a TextBlock or in a flow document viewer, such as FlowDocumentScrollViewer, FlowDocumentPageViewer or FlowDocumentReader.

To create a TextBlock, for example, click the TextBlock button in the Toolbox, and click and drag in the artboard to create the TextBlock. Then type in your text and select the text that you want to use as a hyperlink. Click the Hyperlink button in the Text palette and type a URL or XAML page name in the Hyperlink URI input box. For example, if you want to bring up Page2.xaml, then type Page2.xaml into the input box. (Don't forget to create a Page2.xaml and add some content into it, so you can test your hyperlink.) Or if you want to bring up a URL, then type the URL, such as http://www.google.com.

To test your hyperlink, choose Project ⇨ Set As Startup ⇨ Page1.xaml. Then choose Project ⇨ Test Project. When you click the hyperlink in the application window, Page2 replaces Page1 in the application window.

Adding frames into windows to navigate between pages

To view HTML pages or XAML pages inside a window or a XAML page, you need to add a Frame control to host the pages within them. Frames can be any size you want, from a small part of the window or page to the entire window or page. Figure 3.19 shows an example of a frame that is set to the same size as the LayoutRoot within a window. Frames can be useful for navigating among pages, when you either want to size the frame smaller than the window or page that contains it, or you want to use a window and not a page to navigate.

FIGURE 3.19

Hosting Internet Explorer in a Blend application window.

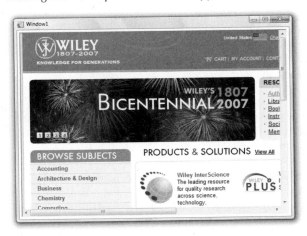

To create a frame to host a XAML page or Web page, perform the following steps:

STEPS: Creating a Frame to Host a Page

1. In a new window, click the Rectangle tool in the Toolbox, and click and drag in the artboard to create a rectangle (or anything—it just simplifies adding XAML code when the artboard contains something already. You delete it in step 3.)

2. Click the XAML tab in the artboard and type the following in the line above the Rectangle tag

   ```
   <Frame Source="http://www.wiley.com/"/>
   ```
   or whatever URL you want.

3. Click the Design tab, select the Rectangle, and delete it. Test your project by choosing Project ➪ Test Project.

By the time you read this, you can probably also set the Source property in the Common Properties palette, although that doesn't work at this writing.

CROSS-REF   For instructions on adding buttons to bring up new content into a frame, see Chapter 20. And see Chapter 21 for instructions on data binding an XML file to a list box and clicking on the list box items to bring up links into a frame.

Converting to Full Functionality

Using Blend you can create major parts of a functioning user interface design without writing any programming code. When converting to a full application, however, some programming, or maybe a great of deal programming, may be necessary.

You can add code to your application in two places: you can add code in the XAML code editor, which you can view by clicking the XAML tab in the upper right corner of the artboard, or you can add code to the code-behind files.

Most documents that you create in Blend have a code-behind file, in which you can easily create code for event handlers that you name using the Event palette. For example, you can assign an event handler to run when the user moves the mouse over an object. The Event palette includes over 70 events to which you can assign an event handler, including DragOver, MouseRightButtonDown, MouseLeftButtonDown, MouseEnter, MouseLeave, KeyDown, and KeyUp. Some of these events may be related to objects, such as MouseEnter, and others may not be, such as KeyDown and KeyUp. For more about using the code-behind file, see the section later in this chapter, "Adding code to the code-behind files."

When you add controls, layout panels or other objects to the artboard, Blend automatically generates the XAML code for those objects and instantly adds it into the XAML code file. Blend also adds the XAML code for animations, media files, and data binding. Normally there may be no need to delve into the XAML code, although it's important to understand the basics. And some results can't be achieved in your application without modifying the XAML code files or the code-behind files.

The code-behind files can do almost anything in your application, because C# and Visual Basic offer so many more capabilities than XAML. But for anything that deals with the visual design of the application, you want to use XAML whenever possible. By using XAML code rather than C# or Visual Basic, you can view your application in Blend's Design mode, without having to build your project and run it outside of Blend to view your design after you make each change in your code. And XAML code is easier to work with than C# or Visual Basic code, because it's not procedural code.

When designing your user interface, probably the most XAML coding is required in creating and editing flow documents. It's all simple coding, but the following section defines some basics.

Adding and Editing XAML Code

Extensible Application Markup Language (XAML) is a declarative language that can be used to create user interfaces, just as HyperText Markup Language (HTML) can be used to create Web pages. XAML is based on Extensible Markup Language (XML) and follows the same rules as XML, although XAML contains specialized tags that can be processed by Windows Presentation Foundation, a primary component of .NET Framework 3.0, the new application programming interface that is an integrated part of Windows Vista.

CROSS-REF This section is meant to get you started with editing XAML code. For more information on editing XAML code, see Chapter 22. And for more information about using XAML code to modify flow documents, see Chapter 9.

Working with opening tags and closing tags

XAML code is written with angle brackets around names of objects, and properties, also known as attributes, within the angle brackets. For instance, you can write:

```
<Button/>
```

If you put this into the right place in your XAML code, Blend places a WPF default button in your artboard.

The angle brackets and the information within the angle brackets are commonly called a tag. Properties in a tag can specify the name, location, size, color, transparency, and many other qualities of the element created by the tag. To add properties to a button, you can add them into the tag, as follows:

```
<Button Margin="100,100,100,200"/>
```

To nest objects in a button, you need to create opening and closing tags, as follows:

```
<Button></Button>
```

Then you can, for example, place a rectangle within the button:

```
<Button Margin="100,100,100,200">
<Rectangle Width="10" Height="10" Fill="#FFFFFFFF"/>
</Button>
```

This nests a white rectangle that is 10 pixels wide and 10 pixels tall into the Button.

Adding opening and closing tags to the LayoutRoot

When the LayoutRoot is new and devoid of any objects, the XAML code that creates it is as follows:

```
<Grid x:Name="LayoutRoot"/>
```

If you add a button to the artboard, Blend changes the code to:

```
<Grid x:Name="LayoutRoot">
  <Button HorizontalAlignment="Left" VerticalAlignment="Top"
Content="Button"/>     </Grid>
```

Because nothing is nested in the button, its code is in the form

```
<Button/>
```

Because a button is nested in the grid, its code is in the form

```
<Grid></Grid>
```

If you add anything to the artboard in the XAML code, you have to change

```
<Grid x:Name="LayoutRoot"/>
```

to

```
<Grid x:Name="LayoutRoot"></Grid>
```

and nest whatever you want to add between the opening and closing tags.

Some code formatting rules

Obviously you don't want to see all the XAML code for you application on a single line, and there are also a few requirements for writing correct XAML code. So here are a few rules for writing and formatting your XAML code:

- Insert one or more spaces between properties.
- You can press Enter for a new line between properties, but be sure you insert one or more spaces between properties as well.
- Include no spaces before and after an equal sign.
- Put property values in quotes.
- Use precisely correct spelling and capitalization for each property name.
- Don't omit the end bracket of a tag, or the ending tag for a starting tag — be sure every element and object is written in the form

  ```
  <Tag/> or <Tag></Tag>
  ```

Specifying properties

You can add to or change the properties of any objects in your XAML code, just as you can add or change any property in the Properties panel. Every property of every object has a name and allowable values that can be set for it. Some objects have specific rules about their properties. For example, you can't add a Content property to a button that has a nested object in it. This is because the button's ContentPresenter control takes only one child, which can be either text in the Content property or a nested object.

You always specify properties in the opening tag of the object, and never the closing tag.

To define an object, you can add as many properties as you need.

Color coding

Blend provides color coding in its XAML view:

- Red: Properties
- Blue: Values for properties
- Brown: Tag keywords, such as Button, Grid, Canvas, and many more

Understanding namespaces

For XAML to understand the meaning of a tag, it needs to have a namespace defined for the tag. (XML tags may have different meanings in different contexts. A *namespace* is a place where information about a set of names is stored, so that the context of each name is clear.) At the top of the XAML code file are the following properties for the window

```
xmlns="http://schemas.microsoft.com/winfx/2006/xaml/presentation"
xmlns:x="http://schemas.microsoft.com/winfx/2006/xaml"
xml:lang="en-US"
```

These define what tags are valid to use in your document.

NOTE XAML follows all the rules of XML. It is only the namespaces that are added that change it from XML into XAML.

By default, two namespaces are added. The first provides Blend with information about the WPF controls and objects, such as Button, Grid, and so on. The second is referenced when you need to name an object. This allows the names of objects to be understood by the code-behind files. Both these namespaces are vital to the XAML code, but you can also add more namespaces — for example if you want to use Windows Forms controls instead of WPF controls in your WPF application.

CROSS-REF For more information about adding namespaces, see Chapter 22.

Adding controls

Some controls are available only in the XAML code and have not been implemented in the Blend interface. The Frame control, for example, offers you navigation capabilities and (at this writing) is only available by manually adding it into the code in the code-behind file or the XAML file. An example of adding a frame using XAML code is

```
<Grid x:Name="LayoutRoot">
  <Frame Source="Page2.xaml"/>
</Grid>
```

Adding code to the code-behind files

In Blend, the C# code or Visual Basic code for each document of your user interface resides in a file that is known as the code-behind file and that is listed in the Project panel. Usually each Blend document (including each window and page) in your user interface, can have its own code-behind file, and the entire application that you're designing in Blend also has its own separate code-behind file. You can access all these code-behind files in the Files palette of the Project panel. Usually you need to click the expander by the document name in the Files palette to see the name of its code-behind file.

Blend does not provide an editor to edit the code-behind files, but you can edit them in Visual Studio, as well as in Visual C# 2005 Express Edition or Visual Basic 2005 Express Edition. The Express Editions are available via a free download from Microsoft. Or you can edit the code-behind files in many word processing applications, including Notepad. (In Notepad's Open dialog box, be sure to change Text Files to All Files.)

The code-behind files are located in the project folder, and their file names (for example, Window1.xaml.cs) include the name of the document to which they relate. They have a .cs at the end of their file extensions if they're C# code-behind files or .vb if they're Visual Basic code-behind files.

You can set options in Blend to specify how you want to deal with the code-behind file, as shown in Figure 3.20. Choose Tools ➪ Options and then click the Event Handlers button to choose between using Visual Studio to automatically open and place your event handler into the code-behind file when you add an event, or to manually paste it in using the clipboard and a code editor or word processor such as Notepad.

Using Visual Studio to edit your code-behind files has advantages, because, for example, it provides you with IntelliSense auto-completion, which can make it easier for you to find the keywords that you may want to type into your code. And when testing your application, Visual Studio provides you with more debugging capabilities than Blend does. Nonetheless, if you are using only the bare minimum of code and prefer a simpler approach, you may find that Notepad works well for you. Just be sure to save your file before testing.

FIGURE 3.20

Setting the options for the code-behind files for C# and Visual Basic.

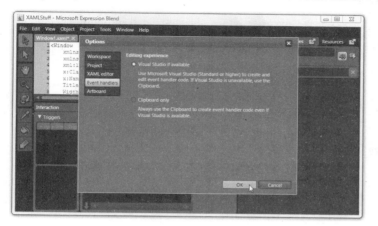

> **CAUTION** If you are planning to run Visual Studio in Vista, and you're not running it in the Administrator account, then you should right-click Visual Studio in the Start menu to start it, and then choose Run As Administrator from the context menu that appears. When a dialog box appears warning you that you are running as Administrator, check the checkbox that allows you not to see the message again. Otherwise, this dialog box (at this writing at least) does not allow Visual Studio to open the code-behind file, and then Blend can't write event handler code into the code-behind file.

You can also open the code-behind files in Visual C# 2005 Express Edition or Visual Basic 2005 Express Edition, but (at this writing) Blend doesn't do this for you automatically.

To edit a code-behind file to assign an event handler, perform these steps:

STEPS: Assigning Event Handlers

1. Before assigning an event handler, you need to give unique names to any objects that will be referenced in the event handler. The button that raises the event in this example can be automatically named by Blend, but other objects that are referenced in the code-behind file, such as the ellipse that we make invisible in this example, need to be named. If an object has brackets around its name in the Objects list, that means it has no unique name. To name an object, such as an ellipse, select it and type in a unique name, such as MyEllipse, at the top of the Properties panel. The name must include no spaces. The name can include numbers or underscores, but it can't start with a number or underscore.

2. Select the object (such as a button for example) that you want to define an event for.

3. If you're using Visual Studio, choose Project ⇨ Build Project from the menu in Blend. This makes Visual Studio aware of your objects and their names. You can skip this step if you're using Notepad.

CAUTION   When using Visual Studio as your editor for a code-behind file, be sure to choose Project ➪ Build Project in Blend before you add any event in the Events palette. You don't need to do this when using Notepad.

4. Select the object that you want to add an event to, and click the Events button beside the name of your object in the Properties panel. The Properties palette shows all the possible events, as shown in Figure 3.21.

5. Type a name to be used as an event handler in the text box beside the event that you want to handle. In Figure 3.21, for example, EllipseDisappear is added as the name of the method for the event handler.

FIGURE 3.21

Typing the name EllipseDisappear beside the Click event for a button, to add this event handler into the code-behind file.

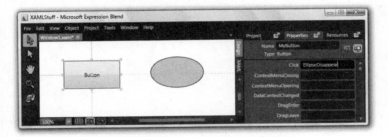

6. Press Enter, and one of two things happens (described in step 7 and step 8, depending on the settings you set in the Tools ➪ Options ➪ Event Handlers settings.)

7. If you are using Visual Studio, it opens to the code-behind file, as shown in Figure 3.22, with the code-behind file already containing the event handler with the method name that you specified in Step 5, along with beginning and ending brackets, ready for you to type your code into. It even locates the cursor near the top of the new method. (Blend is smart enough to start up Visual Studio, if Visual Studio isn't running.)

   If you are using Notepad or another code editor other than Visual Studio, a dialog box appears informing you that Blend has placed the code to create the event handler in the clipboard, as shown in Figure 3.23.

   If you are using Visual Studio, then type the code that you want to add into the event handler. You can make use of IntelliSense to guide you. Visual Studio also automatically adds spaces that you may have forgotten to add, since C# wants spaces around the equals sign, and XAML does not want spaces. (Yikes!) Figure 3.24 shows an example of IntelliSense in Visual Studio. When you are finished adding code, press Shift + F6 to build your project, and click Save in the dialog box that appears the first time you build your project in Visual Studio, and then skip to Step 9.

FIGURE 3.22

Visual Studio opens to the code-behind file with the event handler added by Blend.

FIGURE 3.23

The notice that Blend placed the event handler code in a clipboard for you to add to the code-behind file.

The code that we added is as follows:

```
MyEllipse.Opacity = 0;
```

FIGURE 3.24

Visual Studio's IntelliSense auto-completion feature helps you choose your keywords.

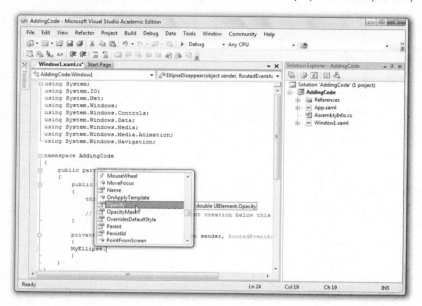

8. If you are using Notepad or another code editor other than Visual Studio, click OK in the dialog box that appears, as shown in Figure 3.23, and then open the code-behind file using Notepad or other editor. (If you use Notepad, be sure to change Text Files to All Files in its Open dialog box.) The code-behind file is in the project folder and has the name of the window with .xaml.cs extensions. Paste your event handler as shown in Figure 3.22, and add your code. You are responsible for making sure your syntax is correct, because you have no automatic IntelliSense helping you out. Choose File ➪ Save.

9. Test your project by pressing F5 in Blend, or choosing Project ➪ Test Project. In our example, when you press the button shown in Figure 3.21, the ellipse disappears.

CAUTION If you are in Blend and you want to edit your code in the code-behind file, you can right-click on the code-behind file in the Files palette and choose Edit Externally. This brings up either Notepad or Visual Studio, depending on your settings. However, Visual Studio is different when you choose Edit Externally, because it does not allow you the option of building the project. In this case, be sure to save your code-behind file by pressing Ctrl+S instead of building your project in Visual Studio before returning to Blend.

CROSS-REF For more about writing code, see Chapter 20.

TIP If you use Notepad to add simple code into the code-behind file, then you don't have to remember to build your project before adding any event in the Events palette in Blend. Also, you can leave Notepad open and quickly move back and forth from Blend to Notepad using Alt+Tab. But for complicated coding, Visual Studio can't be beat.

Summary

- When designing a user interface, don't think about limitations and start from there. Think about what would create the best experience for the user while trying to accomplish his task, even if that includes technology not yet invented, and try to design to that level as much as you can, while still remaining within the constraints of current technology.

- Use visual metaphors in your user interface when they make sense, because they can map the real world to the world of your application, making it easier for the user to make connections.

- You can add grid splitters to a user interface to make it more flexible, allowing the user to resize any sections of a window.

- In Blend you can nest objects into other objects that accept child elements. Any newly created objects are nested into the current active container. One of the layout panels or controls is always the active container in the Blend window, and the current active container is displayed with a yellow border around it.

- You can bind data in two ways: you can bind properties of one element to properties of another, and you can bind data sources to controls.

- In Blend you can bind any RSS feed to a list box, and you can customize the look of the list box.

- The WPF offers a wide variety of ways to navigate in your windows application or Web application that you create. It also allows you to add Web surfing capabilities to your user interface.

- XAML is based on XML, and your XAML code in Blend specifies an XML namespace that provides the links to the WPF controls and properties, and the tags and keywords to instantiate them, in your user interface.

- The code-behind file can be automatically connected to Visual Studio, so that it appears whenever you create an event handler. You can modify and test your project in both Blend and Visual Studio. Just be sure to build your project often, to keep the lines of communication open between Blend and Visual Studio.

Chapter 4

Deploying Your Application Securely

When you're ready to deploy the application that you've created with Blend, you can do so in several ways. You can save it as an .exe file. Or you may want to use Visual Studio to deploy your application using ClickOnce, so that with one click (or maybe two clicks) users can download it, save it on their computer, add it to their Start menu, and run it as a standalone application. Or you can specify that the application only runs when the browser window is connected to the URL of the application. ClickOnce isn't designed for applications requiring involved installation processes such as creating a database, or installing drivers. For those applications, you may want to create a custom installer using Windows Installer technologies in Visual Studio.

You can also use Visual Studio to create a XAML Browser Application (also known as an XBAP) and then design an application in that new project using Blend. Or you can publish *loose XAML code* — XAML code that hasn't been compiled. (Loose XAML code is also known as *markup-only XAML*.)

In this chapter we discuss the steps that you take in Blend or Visual Studio to create and deploy standalone applications, ClickOnce applications, and XAML Browser Applications, and we show how to create and use loose XAML files.

IN THIS CHAPTER

Considering deployment options

Publishing standalone applications

Deploying with ClickOnce

Creating XAML Browser Applications (XBAPs)

Publishing loose XAML files

> **NOTE** In the world of Blend, to *deploy* your application and to *publish* your application mean the same thing: to make your application available to end users.

Considering Deployment Options

Table 14-1 shows the major options for deployment of your Blend project, along with some considerations.

Deployment Options for WPF applications

	Download .exe file from Web	XBAP in browser	Loose XAML in browser	CDROM	ClickOnce (Web)	ClickOnce (Installed)	Windows Installer
Requires IE 6.0 or higher to run	Yes	Yes	Yes	Yes	Yes	Yes	Yes
Requires Windows XP (with .NET Framework 3.0) or Vista to run	Yes	Yes	Yes	Yes	Yes	Yes	Yes
Standalone application	Yes	No	No	Yes	No	Yes	Yes
Requires Full Trust	Yes	No	No	Yes	Yes	Yes	Yes
Offers user easy installation	Sometimes	Yes	Yes	No	Yes	Yes	Often more complicated
Offers installation wizard and custom install	No	No	No	No	No	No	Yes
Allows updates	No	N/A	N/A	No	Yes	Yes	Yes
Project must be originally created in Visual Studio	No	Yes	No	No	No	No	No
Allows the use of code-behind files	Yes	Yes	No	Yes	Yes	Yes	Yes

	Download .exe file from Web	XBAP in browser	Loose XAML in browser	CDROM	ClickOnce (Web)	ClickOnce (Installed)	Windows Installer
Commonly used applications	For non-commercial applications	Yes	No	For large applications	No	Yes	For large applications
Adds name to Start menu and creates Add/Remove program	No	No	No	Yes	No	Yes	Yes

Quick and Easy Deployment of Your Standalone Applications

Every time that you build your project in Blend (by choosing Project ⇨ Build Project or Project ⇨ Test Project), Blend saves your application as an .exe file in the Debug folder inside the bin folder in your project folder. If you find the .exe file in your Debug folder and double-click on it, your application will run. The .exe file may or may not be a standalone application, because it may depend on other items in your Debug folder to run properly. For example, if your project has video files or audio files, they are found with the .exe file in the Debug folder. However, if your project does not require video or audio files, then it may be able to run simply as an .exe file alone. (Bitmap images and XML data sources that are added to the file, using Project ⇨ Add Existing Item, are embedded within the .exe file. Other bitmap images or data sources can be addressed using URLs as absolute addresses.) In any case, the .exe file can often act as a standalone project, and even if it can't, it doesn't depend on files outside your Debug folder, so in that sense your Debug folder is a standalone application.

So, you can deploy your Blend projects as standalone applications simply by making your exe file (or the folder containing audio and video files along with your .exe file) available to others. Making your .exe file available is easy — just publish it to your web site and allow users to download it. They need to save it to their hard drive and run it from there. If your application requires video or audio files, then you can add them into the same folder as the .exe file and compress the folder into one file in ZIP format.

This is a charmingly simple way to deploy your applications, but if your file or folder is zipped, it's more work for your application's users to extract it, and whether it's zipped or not, the users will see a warning to beware of your application when they try to run it. However, this may not bother you or the user — depending on the nature of your application. If you want to avoid the warning, you can deploy your application as an XBAP. This allows your application to run in a secure sandbox in a browser and the user receives no warning. Or deploying it as ClickOnce may also be able to take care of the warning issue, as well as give you the ability to update the application easily, and provide a few other benefits as described in the next section.

Deploying with ClickOnce

Applications created with Blend are WPF applications. ClickOnce is a technology that can deploy and run standalone Windows applications created with WPF or Windows Forms, so ClickOnce works well with the applications that you design in Blend. It's called ClickOnce because ideally when the user clicks on an Install button on a website, the application immediately installs on the user's computer with no further input from the user. ClickOnce doesn't require that the user be logged in as administrator, and it also doesn't require that the user close all programs for the installation to occur.

ClickOnce can deploy your application in one of two ways:

- ClickOnce can download and run the application on the user's computer in cache. The application disappears completely from cache when the connection is terminated.

- ClickOnce can download and run the application on the user's computer and install the application, saving it on the user's computer, adding its name to the Start menu (as shown in Figure 4.1), and creating an Add/Remove program so that the user can easily later remove the application. This is the most common way to deploy using ClickOnce.

FIGURE 4.1

An application deployed on the user's computer using ClickOnce can add your application to the user's Start menu and create an Add/Remove program for the application.

NOTE An online-only ClickOnce application is different from an XBAP because an online-only ClickOnce application must be downloaded to the user's computer, and then runs independently of the Web browser. An XBAP runs in Internet Explorer.

You can also use ClickOnce to easily do the following:

- Provide for automatic updates to your application. You simply upload your updates to a Web address that you specify. You can make updates optional for the user, or you can make them required, as shown in Figure 4.2.

- Specify the frequency of automatic updates.

- Allow the user to revert to the previous version of your application, but only if the latest version is optional.

Also, using ClickOnce ensures that no one can take your application and make it available from any other Web site, because the application doesn't run if it's not downloaded from the proper source. For instructions for installing ClickOnce, see the section "Using ClickOnce" later in this chapter.

FIGURE 4.2

A ClickOnce installed application requesting an update.

NOTE Because ClickOnce downloads the application to the user's machine and runs on it, the user's machine needs to have .NET Framework 3.0 installed. This is built in to Windows Vista, but Windows XP requires a free update to install it. Versions of Windows operating systems before XP can't run any ClickOnce applications, nor can Mac OS X or GNU/Linux — at least not at this writing.

> **TIP** For ClickOnce to work, Microsoft Front Page extensions must be installed on the server from which users download your application. Be sure your server has these installed, or find another server to use for your ClickOnce applications.

Deploying with XBAPs or Other Methods

You may decide to deploy your application in other ways, including the following:

- Publishing your application as an XBAP, to be viewed inside a browser window. Figure 4.3 shows an example of an XBAP application with a FlowDocumentPageViewer. XBAPs run in a secure sandbox within the browser window. See the section "Creating an XBAP" later in this chapter for instructions on creating XBAPs. XBAPs are a good way to publish if your application doesn't require elevated permissions.

- Publishing loose XAML files. Loose XAML files are pages created in Blend that are not compiled and not combined with any code-behind file. Figure 4.21 shows an example of loose XAML code in a browser. For more information about loose XAML, see the section "Creating and deploying loose XAML files" later in this chapter. Loose XAML is considered to be experimental still and not highly recommended, at present.

FIGURE 4.3

An XBAP with a flow document that was designed in Blend. (*Images courtesy of* www.delicious adventures.com.)

CAUTION Loose XAML and XBAPs can only be viewed in Internet Explorer and on computers running Vista or Windows XP with .NET Framework 3.0 installed. However, you can supply a link to alternative content for those unable to view your XAML-based content.

Microsoft also offers customized deployment options using the Windows Installer. If your application requires the installation of drivers or other complex installations, it may be better to use the traditional Windows Installer approach to installing your application rather than ClickOnce. Windows Installer allows you to do the following:

- Run a bootstrapper, which can install a series of required applications, including drivers, along with your application.

- Mark files as optional, and permit users to install them or not at their discretion.

- Run a setup application that initializes the components required by your application.

- Add a shortcut to the Windows desktop.

- Create a file association so that double-clicking files with a particular extension opens your application.

- Provide an installation wizard to supply information about the program as well as a license agreement.

TIP You can deploy your application as a ClickOnce application and still provide the user with a license agreement, if you offer the license agreement in a Web page that links to your ClickOnce link. You can also run your application initially to set things up, by programming your application to run specific code when it runs for the first time on a user's machine.

ON the WEB For more information about Windows Installer, see "Walkthrough: Deploying a Windows-Based Application" at http://msdn2.microsoft.com/en-us/library/k3bb4tfd.aspx.

NOTE Microsoft disallows custom installations using ClickOnce, because they can be complex and introduce errors that can corrupt the user's computer. ClickOnce is designed for simpler installations that don't require much configuration of the user's computer.

Using ClickOnce

ClickOnce is often called ClickTwice, simply because few applications can get by the security warnings that Microsoft imposes on ClickOnce applications. For example, when downloading the Wikipedia Explorer by Dot Net Solutions, the dialog box in Figure 4.4 appears.

Designing your application to avoid that dialog box in Figure 4.4 can be difficult and costly and, often, not even necessary. For example, the Wikipedia Explorer comes from a reliable source and is not an e-commerce application dealing with your credit card information, so users who want it will simply click Install.

FIGURE 4.4

The ClickTwice dialog box.

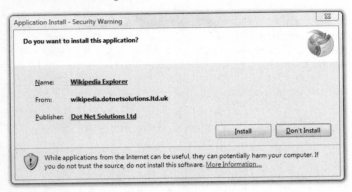

The icon in the message box in Figure 4.4 displays the exclamation point. A stronger warning would be a red X.

Striving for a true ClickOnce experience

Standalone WPF applications were designed to be able to run as partial trust applications with restricted permissions on the user's desktop, but this has not been implemented yet. Currently, all standalone WPF applications require full trust. This may mean that a true "click once" experience may be difficult, since whether or not the user sees a warning depends on the following factors:

- Is your application a full trust application, which is given carte blanche to do whatever it wants on your computer, or a partial trust application which runs in a secure sandbox and does not configure your computer in any way, or requires few permissions, such as WebBrowserPermission or PrintingPermission. However, because all ClickOnce applications are required to be full trust, then permissions are a moot point, although this may change in the near future.

- What URL does the ClickOnce application come from?

- Is the ClickOnce application signed by a trusted publisher? See the next section in this chapter for more information about this.

If the permissions requested by the application are greater than the allowable permissions granted to the trusted publisher and URL, then Windows' Code Access Security (CAS) system displays a warning to the user asking if he wants to elevate the permissions so that the application can run. CAS also determines which warning to show the user.

> **CAUTION** It is possible for IT administrators to configure a user's computer to disallow any ClickOnce application from installing unless it comes from a trusted publisher. They can even specify who the publisher must be.

Trusted publishers

Certificate authorities offer trusted publisher certificates that you can use when you deploy your application using ClickOnce. These certificates include a *public key* that a user's computer can use to verify (via public key cryptography techniques) that it is transferring data from a computer that is controlled by the entity that bought the certificate and not by an imposter.

Using a trusted publisher certificate may mean the difference between a true "click once" experience for the user or viewing a message box with a warning that the publisher is unknown. And even if a warning does appear, it may be a lesser warning.

Trusted publisher certificates can be purchased from several sources, including:

- VeriSign: Prices start at about $400 for a 1-year certificate, but they also insure it. For more information check out www.verisign.com.
- InstantSSL: Certificates from InstantSSL start at about $100 for a year. Check out www.instantssl.com.
- Entrust: They sell certificates starting at about $160 per year. Their homepage is www.entrust.com.

VeriSign and InstantSSL also issue free certificates that are good for 90 days and that you can use for testing purposes.

TIP While it's nice to give the user greater confidence in your application by using a trusted publisher, many users will give your application permission to install anyway, as long as it comes from a website that they trust.

ON the WEB For a list of more certificate authorities, visit http://dmoz.org/Computers/ Security/Public_Key_Infrastructure/PKIX/Tools_and_Services/ Third_Party_Certificate_Authorities/.

Publishing your project using ClickOnce

To publish your project using ClickOnce, you need to do the following, all of which are discussed later in this chapter:

- Sign your application manifest and deployment manifest, so that no one can tamper with your application on the Web.
- Choose your options for how you want ClickOnce to check for updates.
- Inform ClickOnce whether you want your application to be online only, or an online/offline application.
- Specify the URL from which you want to publish your application.

Visual Studio then publishes your application as a ClickOnce application and deploys it on the Web server that you specify. Then any time that you make changes, you can re-publish your application, and Visual Studio updates the version number and re-deploys your application, so that users can automatically receive the updates.

Opening your project in Visual Studio

To publish your application using ClickOnce, you need to use Visual Studio. Blend doesn't publish applications using ClickOnce directly. To open your project in Visual Studio, open Visual Studio and choose Open ➪ Project Solution. Then in the Open Project dialog box, navigate to your project and double-click on the Visual C# or Visual Basic Project file, as shown in Figure 4.5.

FIGURE 4.5

Opening a project in Visual Studio.

To view the Publishing Security settings in Visual Studio, right-click on the name of your file in the Solution Explorer and choose Properties. Then click the Security tab and choose the checkbox labeled Enable ClickOnce Security Settings, as shown in Figure 4.6.

Using the Security tab

Because all WPF standalone applications, including ClickOnce applications, currently require full trust, you can click the Security tab to open the Security features, then click Enable ClickOnce Security Settings and choose This Is A Full Trust Application, as shown in Figure 4.6.

Signing your application manifest and deployment manifest

The signature for your application informs the user's computer whether your application is signed by a trusted publisher, and it's also used to maintain the security of the application on the server.

FIGURE 4.6

The Security tab of the application properties.

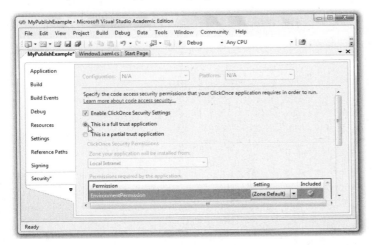

To sign your application, click the Signing tab and select the Sign The ClickOnce Manifests check box, as shown in Figure 4.7. Click the Select From Store button to select a certificate. (This will be called ProjectNameHere_TemporaryKey.pfx, unless you pay for one, as described in the preceding section of this chapter about trusted publishers.) You can see that the certificate is issued to gurdy, which is the name of the administrator account on this computer, as well as the name of the user account. Click Create Test Certificate to password protect the certificate.

Type a password in the Create Test Certificate password boxes and click OK. This adds a key with the file extension .pfx in the project, as shown in the Solution Explorer in Figure 4.8.

Visual Studio then generates the ClickOnce manifests, which are the application manifest and deployment manifest. Their file names both end with .deploy extensions.

To run your ClickOnce application, the user visits your website and clicks on a link to the deployment manifest. The user's computer then downloads the project files, which include the application manifest, and then the user's computer runs the application manifest.

FIGURE 4.7

Adding a password to a temporary key for testing the publishing of the application.

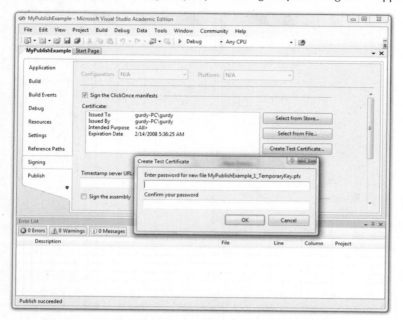

FIGURE 4.8

The file with the .pfx extension contains the key that is the signature for your application.

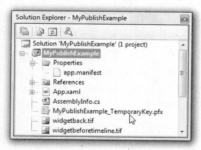

Choosing the options for updates

Once you've added the signature and specified whether your application is a full trust or partial trust application, you can click the Publish tab to publish your application.

Click the Updates button and choose what options you want for updates, as shown in Figure 4.9. Whenever you re-publish an application, Visual Studio automatically increments the version numbers of your application so that users are alerted to the updates. The user then can choose whether to get the new updates or not, as well as which version they want to run, unless you specify a minimum version number allowable.

FIGURE 4.9

Choosing your update options.

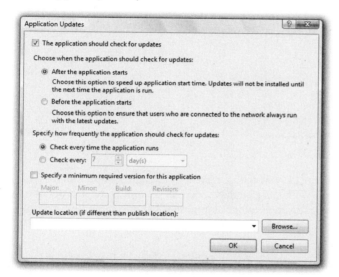

CAUTION When publishing to your local computer as a test, selecting The Application Should Check For Updates may cause an error, and Visual Studio may not allow you to publish the application.

Using the Publish Wizard

Click the Publish Wizard button in Visual Studio to publish your application. The first in a series of dialog boxes appears, as shown in Figure 4.10. It requests a location to publish your application to. Type in a URL or a path specifying the location on the Web or on your computer where you want the Publishing Wizard to put your application. Be sure to add the name of your application to the end of the URL or path.

FIGURE 4.10

Adding your Web address or testing address.

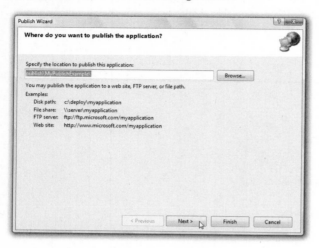

In the next dialog box, shown in Figure 4.11, you choose whether you want the application to be available online only or both online and offline. As we mentioned earlier in this chapter, online mode runs the application in cache, and the application disappears when the connection is terminated. Offline mode saves the application, places the application's name in the Start menu, and adds an Add/Remove program for it.

FIGURE 4.11

Choosing if you want your application to be available online only or both online and offline.

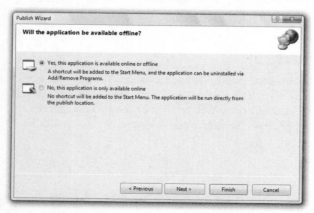

The last dialog box appears. It's a summary page. Look it over, and click Finish.

Your application either gets published, or errors appear in the Error List, as shown in Figure 4.12. Be sure that the server to which you publish your application has Front Page extensions installed.

FIGURE 4.12

Any errors appear in the Error List.

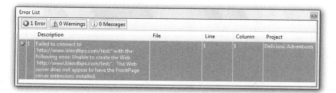

If you are testing ClickOnce by publishing to your own computer, then a window should appear like the one shown in Figure 4.13. Then you can click on Setup to run your application for the first time. This adds your application to the Start menu (as shown way back in Figure 4.1), and adds the Add/Remove program for your application.

FIGURE 4.13

Click Setup to create the link in the Start Menu and run your application.

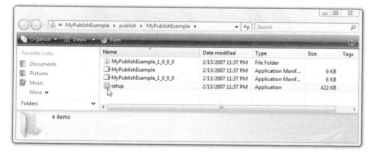

Now you can click the name of your application in the Start menu to launch it. Figure 4.14 shows the project MyPublishExample — the example of handoff animation we build in Chapter 14.

FIGURE 4.14

Enjoying your installed application.

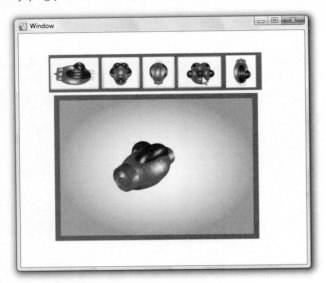

> **NOTE** When making changes to your published project in preparation for publishing a new version, when you open the project in Blend, a window appears with a message that it was modified in another program and asks you if you want to update it. It is certainly important to update it. You also need to build your application in Blend before moving back over to Visual Studio. Choose Project ⇨ Build Project to build it.

Creating an XBAP

If you want to create and run a XAML Browser Application, aka XBAP, you can create the XBAP in Visual Studio and use the tools in Blend to create its look. XBAPs can't perform any operations that require any permissions elevated above the standard permissions allowable for partial trust applications, but that leaves a lot of things they can do.

Creating the XBAP in Visual Studio

The creation of XBAPs is a feature slated to be included in later versions of Blend, but for Blend version 1 they must be created in Visual Studio, and then opened in Blend. Here's how to create an XBAP in Visual Studio:

STEPS: Creating a XAML Browser Application in Visual Studio

1. Open Visual Studio and choose File ➪ New ➪ Project.

In the New Project dialog box that appears, on the left choose NET Framework 3.0, and on the right choose XAML Browser Application (WPF), as shown in Figure 4.15.

FIGURE 4.15

Creating the XBAP project in Visual Studio.

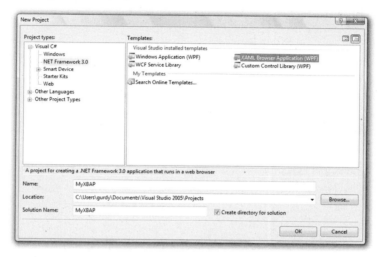

> **TIP** If you don't see .NET Framework 3.0 on the left of the window, then you probably need the Visual Studio extensions for .Net Framework 3.0, and you can find out where to download that by googling "visual studio wpf extension download".

2. Give your application a name (in this example, we call our project myXBAP). Accept the default location or choose the Browse button and select a location for your project. Click OK. The project appears in the Solution Explorer.

3. In the Solution Explorer, right-click on the name of the solution, as shown in Figure 4.16, and choose Properties from the pop-up list.

4. In the Solution 'name of your project' Property Pages dialog box that appears, choose Configuration on the left, click the drop-down arrow in the configuration column on the right, and choose Release (instead of Debug), as shown in Figure 4.17. Then click OK. (You want to do this because you'll probably need to build your application many times before you are finished with it, and this makes it go much quicker.)

FIGURE 4.16

Right-clicking for the Properties.

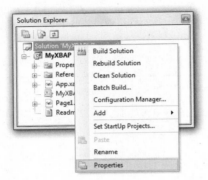

FIGURE 4.17

Changing Debug to Release.

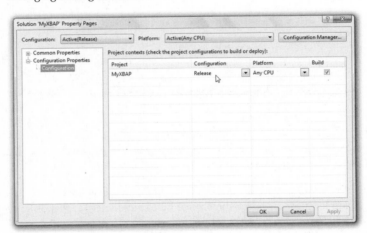

5. Click the drop-down arrow next to Debug on the Visual Studio toolbar and choose Release, as shown in Figure 4.18.

6. Choose Build ➪ Build Solution. (The status bar should read, "Build Succeeded" after a moment or two.)

FIGURE 4.18

Changing Debug to Release again.

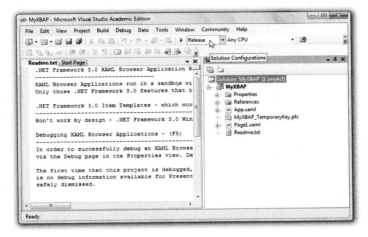

Working with an XBAP in Blend

Now that the XBAP project is created, you can open the .csproj file in Blend and work with it like a normal Blend application. Here's how:

STEPS: Designing in the XBAP file in Blend

1. Open Blend if it's not open. Then in Blend choose File ➪ Open Project, navigate to the .csproj file in the Project folder, select it, and choose Open.

2. A blank project opens in Blend, although it looks different. Don't worry — you'll fix that in the next steps.

3. Click [Page] in the Object list (not the top one, but the next one down) and in the Properties pane, specify a size in the Layout palette, and specify a brush for the Background in the Brushes palette.

   Now you are ready to add content to your XBAP project.

4. If you want, in the artboard you can add rectangles and other vector objects (which you can delete afterwards), test your application by choosing Project ➪ Build Project, open the Results panel next to the Interaction panel, and watch the messages appear as the build takes place. Then choose Project ➪ Test Project to view your XBAP in Internet Explorer, as shown in Figure 4.19.

FIGURE 4.19

Testing your application in an Internet Explorer window.

> **NOTE** XBAPs are a refreshing way to publish your Blend applications and see them instantly on the Internet, without needing to install them. But keep in mind that they are partial trust applications only.

> **TIP** You may want to be sure that Internet Explorer is your default Web browser. Otherwise your XBAP may try to open in a browser that is not compatible.

Transforming a Standalone Application into an XBAP

The 3D submarine animation in the XBAP in Figure 4.19 is the same application as the standalone application in Figure 4.14. To convert a Blend project that was created as a standalone project into an XBAP, first you need to create an empty XBAP in Visual Studio. Then you can transfer the XAML code from the original Blend application to the new XBAP that's open in Blend.

But, before you paste the code, do the following:

- Choose Project ➪ Add Existing Item to add any images and media files or other items that you want into the XBAP.

- Check to be sure that the previous Blend project did not have any references added into the Reference folder. Compare Reference folders in the two projects and add any references into the XBAP that may be missing. Do this in Visual Studio. Choose Project ⇨ Add Reference and find the name from the alphabetical list.

To transfer the code, copy the XAML file from the original Blend application and paste it into the end of the XBAP XAML file. It's much easier if this is a blank page in the XBAP. Then do the following:

- Change </Window> to </Page> in the last line.
- Delete <Grid x:Name=LayoutRoot/> and the next line </Page> above the new code.
- Then delete any duplicate xmlns=...
- Change any Window.Resources to Page.Resources, and any Window.Triggers to Page.Triggers.
- Then all you need to do is get the top few lines looking right, with the opening and closing tags matching and getting rid of any duplicates, and you're done. You can create a blank page and use the XAML code as a guide, to make sure you get the angle brackets and slashes in the correct places.

When you click the Design tab, any errors will show up in a list in the Results palette.

 **For more information about XAML code, see Chapter 3, Chapter 9, and Chapter 22.**

Adding an XBAP or Loose XAML to Your Web Site

You can add your XAML Browser Application (XBAP) or loose XAML page to a Web site in two ways:

- By linking to the XBAP or XAML page from an HTML page
- By adding the content of the XBAP or loose XAML page into an iframe in an HTML page.

XBAPs can harness the full power of the WPF, and be viewed in Internet Explorer 6.0 or higher, as long as the XBAP does not require elevated permissions. However, uncompiled XAML (loose XAML) is much more limited than an XBAP, because loose XAML can't be combined with any code-behind files.

Calling a XAML Browser Application from a Web page

If you have a button or a hyperlink in a Web page, and you want it to open an XBAP, you can do so. Here's some sample HTML for creating a Web page with a link that brings up an XBAP. Be sure your XBAP is in the same directory as the HTML file. Also, if your XBAP uses any audio or video files, add them into the same directory, as well.

```
<!DOCTYPE html PUBLIC "-//W3C//DTD XHTML 1.0 Transitional//EN"
"http://www.w3.org/TR/xhtml1/DTD/xhtml1-transitional.dtd">
<html xmlns="http://www.w3.org/1999/xhtml">
<head>
<meta http-equiv="Content-Type" content="text/html; charset=utf-
8" />
<title>Hi</title>
</head>
<body>
Hi World!
<a href="MyXBAP.xbap"> Click here to see MyXBAP </a>
Bye World!
</body>
</html>
```

Using Iframes

To include your XBAP in your Web page, you can use an HTML iframe to contain it, alongside the other objects in the Web page. First, to keep things simple for now, move your XBAP file into the same folder as the HTML file in the project folder of the Web page. Also move any video or audio files that your XBAP requires into the same folder as the HTML file. In your Web page's HTML code, create an iframe tag where you want the XBAP to appear. Then set the src property of the iframe to the location of the XBAP file. Here's sample code for doing this.

```
<!DOCTYPE html PUBLIC "-//W3C//DTD XHTML 1.0 Transitional//EN"
"http://www.w3.org/TR/xhtml1/DTD/xhtml1-transitional.dtd">
<html xmlns="http://www.w3.org/1999/xhtml">
<head>
<meta http-equiv="Content-Type" content="text/html; charset=utf-
8" />
<title>Hi</title>
</head>
<body>
Hi World!
<iframe height="650"
width="650"
src=" MyXBAP.xbap"> </iframe>
Bye World!
</body>
</html>
```

This code simply puts an XBAP along with "Hi World" and "Bye World" in an otherwise blank Web page.

Creating and deploying loose XAML files

Another way to use Blend to get rich content onto the Internet is to add loose XAML files to your Web pages. Loose XAML is considered by many as somewhat experimental, but you may find it appealing, at least to explore its possibilities.

Blend adds code into its XAML files to support their use with code-behind files. This code, however, does not allow loose XAML to run in the Browser. To eliminate this code in a new file, in Blend choose File ⇨ New Item and select Page, and de-select the Include Code File check box, as shown in Figure 4.20.

FIGURE 4.20

Preparing your page for use as a loose XAML file.

In Blend, you can add any objects to your page that don't require any use of the code-behind file. (Some restrictions may apply, as this currently is not a fully functional method of deploying your content.)

If you have already created a page in Blend and want to use it as a loose XAML page, you can delete the following line of code in the XAML file:

```
x:Class="YourProjectNameHere.YourPageNameHere"
```

You also need to be sure that no event handlers have been assigned to any events. If they have, then delete the events in the XAML code.

Using nearly the same HTML code as in the previous section of this chapter, we can add the loose XAML file. You can bring it up either in its own browser window, or in an iframe. An example of HTML code that can bring up a loose XAML page is as follows:

```
<a href="Page1.xaml"> Click here to see Page1.xaml </a>
```

You can also view the loose XAML page in an iframe, as shown in Figure 4.21. Here's the HTML code for the example; it assumes that Page1.xaml is in the same folder as the HTML file:

FIGURE 4.21

Loose XAML file appearing in a Browser window.

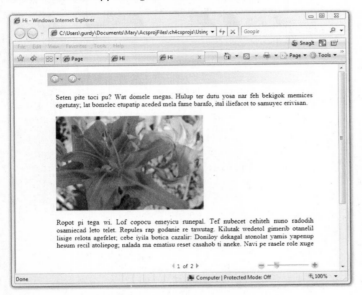

```
<!DOCTYPE html PUBLIC "-//W3C//DTD XHTML 1.0 Transitional//EN"
"http://www.w3.org/TR/xhtml1/DTD/xhtml1-transitional.dtd">
<html xmlns="http://www.w3.org/1999/xhtml">
<head>
<meta http-equiv="Content-Type" content="text/html; charset=utf-
8" />
<title>Hi</title>
</head>
<body>
Hi World!
<iframe height="650"
width="650"
src=" Page1.xaml"> </iframe>Bye World!
</body>
</html>
```

 In our experience, the scroll bars of IE currently do not function well with loose XAML.

Summary

- You can use Blend to create rich content for:
    - Standalone applications that run in Windows XP and Vista, or
    - XAML Browser applications that run in Internet Explorer, on computers running Windows XP with .NET Framework 3.0 or Windows Vista

- You can deploy your standalone application using ClickOnce, which can enable your application to check for and install updates, add your standalone application to the list of currently installed programs in the user's Add/Remove Programs Control Panel, and place your application in the Start menu.

- ClickOnce also lets you run an application without adding it to the Start menu or creating an Add/Remove program. In this case, the application disappears from the user's computer when it's disconnected from the Web page that offers the ClickOnce download.

- XBAP's run as partial trust applications and standalone applications require full trust. Full trust normally prompts the user to affirm that he fully trusts your application. Partial trust requires that the application does not need any elevated permissions to run effectively, and does not require a user prompt to view the application in Internet Explorer.

- If your application requires custom installation, you may want to deploy your application using Windows Installer in Visual Studio.

- To add your XBAP or loose XAML into your Web page, you can host it in an iframe, or you can run it in its own browser window.

Part II
Creating and Transforming Vector Graphics

Chapter 5

Drawing Shapes and Manipulating Paths

In this chapter we explore how to make sophisticated vector graphic line drawings that are infinitely scalable and easily modified. Once you have the line drawings, you can fill them in with colors or gradients, as described in Chapter 6. Blend offers five drawing tools to create shapes and paths. *Paths* in Blend are lines — straight, zigzag, curvy, and so on — that consist of two or more points called *nodes*. Curves or straight lines connect the nodes. Shapes in Blend are two predefined geometric elements: rectangles and ellipses. With these two you can create any shape you can imagine, or you can draw your own custom shapes with the pen tool.

Blend's five drawing tools are as follows:

- **Ellipse:** Use this tool to draw elliptical shapes and circles.
- **Rectangle:** Use this tool to create rectangular shapes, including rectangular shapes with rounded corners.
- **Pen:** You can use this tool to create paths containing straight lines, curves, and closed paths that appear like shapes.
- **Line:** Use this tool to create straight lines. (You can change these straight lines to curves, if you want.)
- **Pencil:** Use this tool to create free-form paths.

> **NOTE** Paths in Blend are not to be confused with motion paths, which are used to specify the trajectory of an animated object. Motion paths are not generally visible, whereas normal paths are generally visible.

In this chapter, we discuss the techniques you may use in Blend for creating vector art using shapes and paths. You can create vector objects as decorative items for your application, or you may want to use these tools to define interesting and unique controls.

Also, we explore the difference between the Render Transform tools and the Layout Transform tools. The Render Transform tools in the Properties panel affect the object they are applied to, without any regard for the layout of the application. For example, an object scaled using the Render Transform tools will have no effect on other objects, if it's in a stack panel. In contrast, an object scaled using the Layout Transform tools will move other objects in the stack panel so it can precisely fit within its new dimensions.

Drawing and Combining Shapes

You can draw Blend's basic shapes by using the Rectangle tool or Ellipse tool. These shapes can be resized, moved, and combined with other shapes and paths to create complex drawings. Except for their size, position, and rotation, shapes are not as easily modified as paths. However, you can convert them into paths and then modify the paths.

Drawing circles, squares, and rounding corners of rectangles

You can use the Rectangle and Ellipse tools to draw perfect squares or circles. Blend also allows you to round the corners of your rectangles, either symmetrically or asymmetrically.

- **To draw a rectangle, ellipse, or line**, click the Rectangle, Ellipse, or Line tool in the Toolbox, and then click and drag in the artboard. You may need to click and hold one of these tools in the Toolbox to see the pop-up toolbar that contains the other tools.

- **To create perfect circles or squares**, click the Ellipse or Rectangle tool in the Toolbox and then press Shift while you click and drag in the artboard.

- **To round the corners of a rectangle**, do one of the following:

  - Select the rectangle and drag either a corner radius handle, as shown in Figure 5.1 on the right. To round them asymmetrically, drag one corner radius handle while holding the Shift key, as shown on the left in Figure 5.1.

  - Select the rectangle, and assign values to RadiusX and RadiusY in the Appearance palette of the Properties panel.

CROSS-REF For information on selecting objects, grouping, snapping to the grid, and more, see Chapter 2.

FIGURE 5.1

You can move the corner radius handles separately if you press and hold the Shift key.

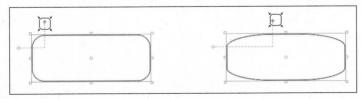

Combining shapes with other shapes or paths

Blend allows you to combine shapes with other shapes, or paths with other paths, or shapes and paths together in five different ways, as shown in Figure 5.2. To combine them, choose the Selection tool, select all the shapes and paths that you want, and then choose Objects ➪ Combine and one of the following:

- **Unite**: Preserves the outer stroke of all the selected objects while eliminating the interior strokes, and uses the fill of the topmost shape or path as the fill for the entire new object, as shown in Figure 5.2.

- **Divide**: Preserves all strokes, and uses the fill of the topmost shape or path as the fill of all selected shapes and paths.

- **Intersect**: Preserves only the segment of the shapes or paths that overlap all the selected shapes or paths. If no such segment exists, then the intersect pertains to the segment of shapes or paths which overlap and contain the topmost shape or path.

- **Subtract**: Leaves only the segment or segments of the topmost shape or path that are not overlapping another shape or path.

- **Exclude Overlap**: Excludes areas overlapped by two shapes or paths or both. Areas overlapped by three shapes, paths, or both are not excluded.

All shapes that are combined with other shapes or paths become paths and can be edited using the Direct Selection tool, as described later in this chapter.

FIGURE 5.2

Combining shapes in various ways.

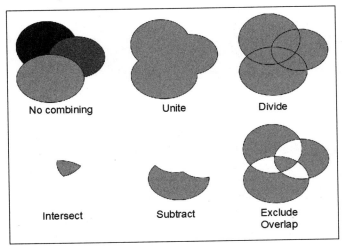

Drawing Paths

Paths are made up of two or more nodes connected by curves or straight lines. Nodes can contain one or two control handles that can define curves. Paths are usually created using the following:

- **Line tool**: This tool is most useful when you want to create a single line or curve containing just two nodes. To create a line, simply click the Line tool and click and drag in the artboard. You can constrain the angle of the line to the nearest 45 degrees by pressing Shift while you click and drag in the artboard. To change the line to a curve, see the instructions in the next section of this chapter.

- **Pencil tool:** Use this tool when you want to create a path as if you're drawing with a pencil. (This works well if you're drawing with a stylus.) To create a path using the Pencil tool, click the Pencil tool in the Toolbox, and click and drag in the artboard. Your lines may appear jagged at first, but after you finish creating your path, Blend smoothes your lines and curves.

- **Pen tool:** This is the most sophisticated tool. To use the pen tool, click on it and click in the artboard for each node that you want to create in your path. Straight lines appear between the nodes. To stop creating nodes, either click on the first node you created and close the path, or click on any tool, such as the Selection tool. As described in the next section of this chapter, you can change the lines to curves, or you can create them as curves.

Paths are flexible and editable because their individual nodes are available for modifying. For example, you can easily change a straight line to a curve, or change the shape of any curve between two nodes. You can also pull the nodes to different locations to make subtle (or drastic) changes in your art. Shapes, on the other hand, do not have nodes available for editing, although you can transform a shape into a path whenever needed by selecting the shape and choosing Object ➪ Path ➪ Convert To Path.

> **TIP** To constrain the angle of the lines created by the Pen tool to the nearest 15 degrees, hold the shift key while clicking in the artboard.

Creating and adjusting curves using the Alt key

Once you create lines or curves, you can easily edit them with either the Pen tool or the Direct Selection tool (the second arrow from the top). The Pen tool and the Direct Selection tool offer the same features and work exactly the same when used in conjunction with holding down the Alt key.

- **To make the line or path segment into a curve, or edit a curve**, select the line or path, click the Direct Selection or Pen tool, and move your mouse over the line or path segment while holding the Alt key. The cursor turns into an angle symbol. When a curve symbol appears beside it, as shown in Figure 5.3, then click and drag to shape the line into a curve or to reshape a segment of a path.

- **To change a curve segment into a straight line**, select the path and click the Direct Selection or Pen tool. Then move your mouse over a node of the path while holding the Alt key. The cursor turns into an angle symbol. When a square symbol appears beside it, as shown in Figure 5.3, then click. The curve defined in the node collapses to a straight line. (You may need to do the same to the other node of a path segment to get a completely straight segment.)

FIGURE 5.3

Reshaping a curve (right) and straightening a curve (left).

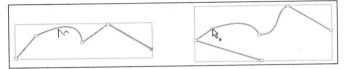

Creating and adjusting curves using control handles

Another way to add curvature to a path is to use a node's control handles. Every node can contain two, one, or zero control handles. Control handles define the tangent and size of a curve and can be adjusted using the Pen tool or Direct Selection tool. Path segments connect the nodes and are shaped according to the angle and length of the control handles. Control handles function as follows:

- **Double control handles** define the curves on both sides of your node, as shown on the left in Figure 5.4.
- **Single control handles** define the curve on one side of the node.
- **No control handle** does not define any curve. Use this for straight lines.

Every path segment between two nodes can be controlled by two, one, or no control handles, resulting in the following:

- An **S-shaped curve, or curve defined by two tangent lines**, which is a segment between two nodes controlled by a control handle on each node, as shown on the right in Figure 5.4.
- A **simple curve**, which is a segment between two nodes controlled by a control handle on one node.
- A **straight line**, which is a segment between two nodes that don't have control handles controlling it.

You can see the control handles when you use the Direct Selection tool to select a node that contains control handles. Selecting a path segment shows the control handles that define the segment. Selecting a node shows the control handles residing in the node. You can pull the control handles and modify their angles or length by using the Direct Selection tool or the Pen tool.

FIGURE 5.4

A node with two control handles (left) and a curve defined by two control handles (right).

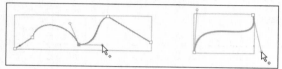

The following steps describe how to create control handles with double, single, or no handles at all, using the Pen tool.

STEPS: Drawing Curves with the Pen Tool Using Control Handles

1. Click the Pen tool in the Toolbox.

2. Click in the artboard where you want one end of your curve to be, and drag. As you drag, a control handle emerges from your node.

3. While still dragging, position the control handle so it represents the tangent line of the curve that you want to create. Release the mouse.

4. Click another point in the artboard, without releasing the mouse until the end of step 5. A curve appears between the two nodes with its tangent being the control handle on the first node.

5. Choose one of the following:

   - **To not define any control handle** for the node, release the mouse.

   - **To define one control handle** for the node, release the mouse without moving it and then click and drag the mouse to define a single control handle that controls the next section of the path.

   - **To define two control handles** for the node, drag the mouse.

6. Repeat steps 4 and 5 for as many nodes as you want to include in your path.

> **TIP** Some artists like to pull each curve as they create it, by alternating the Pen tool and the Pen tool with the Alt key as they create each node. Others like to create a bunch of straight lines and then pull them. And others like to create curves using the Pen tool as described in the steps above. You can do whatever works for you.

Adding nodes, deleting nodes, or closing a path using the Pen tool

Using the Pen tool, you can create new nodes on an existing path or delete nodes. You can continue to extend an existing path that you may have started days ago, or you can close a path into a continuous loop.

STEPS: Adding a Node, Deleting a Node, Extending a Path, or Closing a Path

1. If the nodes of a path are not visible, choose the Direct Selection tool in the Toolbox and click and drag over any part of a path to make the nodes appear in the entire path.

2. Click the Pen tool in the Toolbox, if it's not already selected.

3. Choose one of the following:

   ▪ **Add a node.** Move the cursor over the existing path where you want to add a node, and when a symbol next to the cursor appears as a plus sign (as shown in Figure 5.5), click and drag to create a node in the location you drag to.

   ▪ **Delete a node.** Move the cursor over a node that you want to delete; click when the symbol changes to a minus sign, as shown in Figure 5.5.

   ▪ **Extend an existing path.** Move the cursor over one of the endpoints of the path, and click when the symbol changes to a slanted line or angle, as shown in Figure 5.5. Then move the cursor where you want the next node of the path to be and click.

   ▪ **Close a path.** Click on a node on one end of the path, then move the cursor over the other end node of the path and click when the symbol beside the Pen icon of the cursor changes to a circle, as shown in Figure 5.5.

FIGURE 5.5

Adding and deleting nodes, appending a path and closing a path.

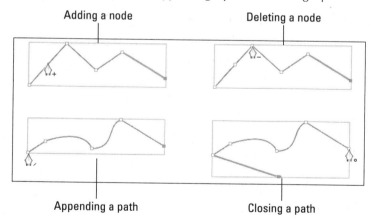

Adding a node   Deleting a node

Appending a path   Closing a path

Converting shapes into paths

Shapes created by the Ellipse tool and the Rectangle tool do not show any nodes when selected using the Direct Selection tool. If you want to give them nodes so that you can modify and refine the way they look, you can convert them to paths.

To change a shape into a path, select the shape and choose Object ⇨ Path ⇨ Convert To Path. Once you convert them, four nodes appear on your rectangle or ellipse.

Editing Nodes with the Direct Selection Tool

The Direct Selection tool is a powerful editing tool with lots of uses for editing paths. Probably its major claim to fame is making the nodes of an entire path appear when you click and drag over a path. But it can also do the following:

- **Move a node** to a new location by clicking and dragging a node, as shown in the upper left in Figure 5.6.

- **Delete a node** by clicking a node to select it and pressing Backspace. You can delete several nodes at a time by clicking nodes while holding the Shift key and then pressing Backspace, as shown in Figure 5.6 on the bottom.

- **Select and move a segment or segments of a curve**. Select a segment by clicking on the segment and drag to move it, as shown in Figure 5.6 on the right. (Use Shift + Click to select more than one segment.) If the segment is thin, zoom in to select it easier.

- **Reshape curves** by pressing and holding the Alt key while clicking and dragging a path segment into a new curve, as described earlier in the chapter.

- **Change curves into straight lines** using the Alt key as described earlier in the chapter.

- **View control handles that define a curve** by selecting a path segment.

- **View control handles residing in a node** by selecting a node.

- **Change the shape of a curve** by dragging a control handle of a selected node. (You can drag one control handle of a node independently of the other control handle on a single node by pressing Alt and clicking and dragging a control handle.)

Some capabilities of the Direct Selection tool overlap the capabilities of the Pen tool and are performed in exactly the same way as the Pen tool — for example, reshaping curves using the Alt key, and changing curves into straight lines using the Alt key.

FIGURE 5.6

Moving nodes (upper left), moving segments (upper right), and deleting nodes (bottom).

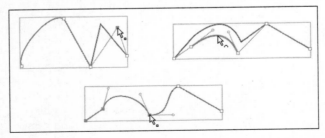

Transforming Objects Using Render Transform and Layout Transform

The ability to scale and transform your artwork gives you access to a whole world of expressive possibilities. The Transform pane of the Properties panel displays the Render Transform tools, which include six features for transforming objects. They are:

- **Scaling:** You can use scaling to create replicas of your shapes and paths in different sizes, which can create the effect of repeating the visual theme of your work in an appealing way.

- **Flipping:** You can use flipping to add symmetry to your vector art. For example, you can copy a path and flip it, then group it to create a symmetric object.

- **Skewing:** Skewing may make your object look more dynamic, just as italic type makes text look more dynamic.

- **Rotating:** Can be used to create sophisticated imagery.

- **Positioning the center point:** The center point is the point around which the object rotates.

- **Positioning the object:** Precise positioning is often the difference between a professional-looking design and an amateurish one.

CROSS-REF These tools not only flip, skew, rotate, and move objects in 2D space, but also allow you to do the same on a Z-axis in 3D space. For more about creating and manipulating objects in 3D space, see Chapter 12.

If you click the arrow at the bottom of the Transform palette, it opens to reveal the Layout Transform tools, which are similar to the Render Transform tools.

Use the Layout Transform tools when you want the transformation to affect the layout of the grid, stack panel, wrap panel, or whatever layout panel the object is located in. Figure 5.7 shows an example of scaling applied to the third rectangle in two stack panels. The rectangle in the middle stack panel is scaled using the Render Transform tool and the rectangle on the left is scaled using the Layout Transform tool. Notice how the Layout Transform scaling affects not just the rectangle, but moves the other rectangle up in the stack panel.

To use any of these tools, click on the appropriate tab in either the RenderTransform or LayoutTransform pane of the Transform palette, and add values into the input boxes. For example, in the Scaling tab you can enter a value between 0 and 1 to scale the object down, and add a value above 1 to scale the object larger. You can also use the mouse, and drag up or right, or down or left when the mouse is directly over the input box (and the cursor changes to a four-directional arrow), although this is not nearly as precise, and may be difficult when dealing with numbers with decimal points. The transformation occurs as you drag, or when you type and the input box loses focus, or when you press Enter. (Instead of pressing Enter, you can also click the arrow beside the Relative button.)

FIGURE 5.7

Scaling a rectangle in a stack panel using the Render Transform tools (middle) and Layout Transform tools (right).

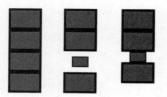

Once you transform an object for the first time, if you want to transform again, you have the choice of viewing the values of the transformation either as relative values or as absolute values. For instance, if you scale an object's width by .5, and you want to double it, you can do one of two things:

- Click the arrow beside the Relative button and the object scales again.
- Click the Relative button and the value changes to 1, and then type .5 again to scale the object more.

The above two actions work in both the RenderTransform pane and the LayoutTransform pane.

Toggling the Relative button allows you to see the values for the transformation of the object from its original size (or position, rotation, skew or center position).

Auto Sizing

When you create your vector art, you may want to take into account how it resizes when the window that it resides in resizes — if it is in a window. You can use the Auto Size feature to choose whether you want its width or height or both to resize automatically when the application is resized. To apply the Auto Size feature, select the object and choose Object ➪ Auto Size ➪ Width, Height, Both, or Fill. (Choosing Fill automatically sizes it to fill its layout panel.) If your object collapses, use the Selection tool to enlarge it to the desired size.

CROSS-REF The Layout pane of the Properties panel also allows you to choose Auto for the width and height values of an object. Using the Layout pane is described in detail for each specific layout panel, such as the grid, the stack panel, and more, in Chapter 18.

Embellishing Strokes

Blend allows you to miter, bevel, or round corners of objects with thick strokes, as well as add end caps to your strokes. To make use of corner joins or end caps, first you need to set your stroke size to a sufficient thickness. To assign the stroke width, select the object; then click and drag in the Stroke Thickness box in the Appearance palette of the Properties panel.

CROSS-REF Expression Design offers many types of strokes that you can use to create interesting line drawings and text and then use them in Blend. For more information about this, see Chapter 7.

Assigning Stroke End Caps

When creating lines or paths, you can cap either of their ends in the following ways:

- **Round cap:** This creates a half circle at the end of the line or path.
- **Triangle cap:** This creates a pointed end.
- **Square cap:** This adds a square to the end of the line or path, so it doesn't really change its appearance, only its length.
- **Flat:** This is no cap. It's the default.

You can use caps to easily add some style to your work. For example, triangle caps are used in Figure 5.8 for the tops of the slanted lines, and round caps are used for the bottoms of the lines. You can use the shapes of the end caps to echo the theme of your work. For example, triangles are pointed and may suggest a more aggressive energy, while rounded shapes may evoke a softer feeling. Of course, the lines or paths need to be fairly fat for the shapes of their end caps to be discernible.

To create end caps, select your line or lines, and click the Expander in the Appearance palette to view more options. Then choose either Flat, Square, Round, or Triangle from the StrokeEndLineCap drop-down menu, and do the same for the StrokeStartLineCap.

FIGURE 5.8

Assign end caps (left) and beveled line joins (middle) in the Appearance palette.

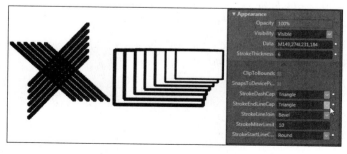

Assigning Stroke Line Joins

While end caps are only available for the ends of lines and paths, you can specify the following corner joins to all vertices of shapes and paths:

- **Bevel:** Slants the outer corners of a shape or path that has a fat stroke.
- **Round:** Rounds the outer corners of a shape or path that has a fat stroke.
- **Miter:** This is the default.

To specify a stroke line join, select your shape or path, and be sure the stroke is wide enough for the stroke line join to appear. Then click the Expander in the Appearance palette to view more options. Choose either Miter, Bevel, or Round from the StrokeLineJoin drop-down menu. If you choose Miter, you can enter a value in the StrokeMiterLimit box. A small miter value creates more of a bevel. A large miter value creates a square join. Figure 5.8 shows rectangles with beveled corners.

CROSS-REF Expression Design offers a wide variety of stroke types. These are described in detail for text in Chapter 10, but can be used for any vector object. You can find instructions for importing vector graphics from Expression Design in Chapter 7.

Creating Complex Line Drawings

If you plan to create your own line drawings, you may want to do it in one of the following ways:

- **Trace your art from a photo or a line drawing.** Tracing photos or drawings takes time, but is fairly easy using the technique described in the next section. Be sure that you own the copyright to any art or photo that you trace, so that you can legally use it.
- **Draw your art from scratch.** This may be more time consuming than tracing your art.

Creating vector art by tracing your photos and line drawings

In an ideal world, photos would come with paths, nodes, and strokes already integrated into them, so that you could animate them, attach events to each, and be able to modify every part of them easily. This feature, of course, has not been figured out by the camera industry. So, in order to transform a photo image or any image that is not already vector art, you may want to trace it.

CAUTION You can't legally publish a tracing of a photo or line drawing unless you have the rights to do so, such as if you created the photo or drawing or if it is in the public domain.

Tracing can be accomplished quickly and easily using the method described in the following steps. For example, it took less than five minutes to create the tracing of the bird in Figure 5.9. And you can add as much detail to your tracings as you want.

STEPS: Tracing a Photo or Drawing

1. Import the image file into the Project panel by choosing Project ➪ Add Existing Item. Select your file and choose Open. The name of your file appears in the Project panel.

2. Double-click on the name of your file in the Project panel, or right-click on the name and choose Insert. Your picture appears in the artboard, and the name of your picture file appears in the Objects and Timeline palette in the Interaction panel.

3. Resize your image with the Selection tool to the size you want. Then either lock the picture in place by clicking on the Lock/Unlock button on the same line as the name of your picture file in the Objects palette, or choose Tools ➪ Create New Layer.

4. Create the main outline of your drawing by selecting the Pen tool and clicking at each vertex in the outline of the object that you are drawing in the photo — wherever any angle exists or where curves change their curvature. Straight lines appear between points. You turn them into curves in Step 6.

NOTE If a white or colored fill obliterates your view of your photo, delete the fill by choosing Fill in the Brushes palette and clicking the No Brush button.

5. When you've added all the points, close the path by clicking the original point, or stop adding points by clicking any tool in the Toolbox.

6. Click the Pen tool again and pull your straight lines into curves by holding down the Alt key, and clicking and dragging the segments of the path according to the outline of the photo.

7. When your outline is complete, deselect your outline by clicking the Selection tool, and lock it by clicking the lock button beside its name in the Objects palette in the Interaction panel.

8. Do the details by choosing another path that you can trace within the photo. Repeat steps 4 to 7 for as many paths as you need to create your tracing. (You can also add some shapes, such as an ellipse shape for an eye, as shown in Figure 5.9.)

9. Make the photo that you are tracing invisible by clicking the Hide/Show button beside the name of your photo in the Objects palette. You can do this anytime while you are tracing. And if you want to delete it from your window or page, click on the image in the Objects palette and press Backspace — you may need to click the Lock/Unlock button to be able to select it.

FIGURE 5.9

You can quickly create vector art by hand-tracing a digital photo.

Drawing vector art from real life

You can also create vector art by drawing from real life. This may not always be as difficult as you think. First, pick a subject that's going to stick around while you draw it. Otherwise, take a picture and use the method described earlier. Look at the shapes that you see in your subject. Use the Pencil tool or the Pen tool to draw the edges of each important form, looking for changes in direction, position, and proportion. As you progress, imagine vertical or horizontal lines being drawn across the forms to see if the parts of each shape are lining up properly. If you've never drawn from real life before, you may suddenly realize how talented you are.

Summary

- Blend allows you to create rectangles and circles which you can combine in many ways to create complex vector objects. Or you can create paths using the Line tool, Pencil tool and Pen tool.

- You can combine shapes in five ways:

  - Unite: Creates one shape from all selected shapes and assigns the fill of the topmost shape as its fill. All strokes except the outermost strokes are deleted.

  - Divide: Creates one shape from all selected shapes and assigns the fill of the topmost shape as its fill. However, unlike Unite, it does not delete the interior strokes.

  - Intersect: Preserves only intersected shapes.

  - Subtract: Preserve only the segment or segments of the topmost shape or path that are not overlapping another shape or path.

  - Exclude Overlap: Excludes any parts of the shapes that are overlapped with one another.

- You can edit paths using the Pen tool and Direct Selection tool in various ways, including:

  - Modifying curves

  - Moving nodes

  - Moving segments

  - Adding nodes

  - Deleting nodes

- Blend lets you modify the curvature of curves in two ways. You can:

  - Hold the Alt key while you click and drag a curve using the Pen tool or Direct Selection tool. This allows you to reshape curves as you drag.

  - Adjust the control handles of a curve using either the Pen tool or Direct Selection tool.

- Blend provides you with a variety of end caps (flat, square, round and triangle) and line joins (bevel, round and miter) that you can add to your strokes.

- You can create complex drawings by tracing line art or photos, or drawing from real life.

Chapter 6

Manipulating Color, Fills, Gradients, and Transparency

Blend provides many versatile brushes that you can use to fill your vector objects, including the solid color brush, gradient brush, drawing brush, image brush, video brush, and tile brush. You can apply these brushes to many elements, including the following:

- Fills or strokes of shapes and paths
- Backgrounds or borders of layout panels or controls
- Text

You can also add bitmap images to your user interfaces and use them in a variety of ways. And you can specify any amount of transparency for each brush or image, by specifying an Alpha value for the brush or the Opacity value for the image. Opacity masks can also generate transparency, and can create gradual changes in transparency for any image or vector object when used in conjunction with gradient brushes.

Blend also offers five bitmap effects that you can apply to your vector objects: bevel, blur, drop shadow, outer glow, and emboss.

You can add compelling imagery to your user interface in powerful ways by using these sophisticated brushes, adding bitmap art, and creating bitmap effects. In this chapter, we explore all these topics.

CROSS-REF In later chapters we explore how to use these brushes interactively, using events and the code-behind file in Chapter 20, and animating them in Chapter 14.

TIP Applying brushes is more than an aesthetic act. Elements of objects that have brushes can respond interactively to mouse events, whereas the elements of objects that have been assigned No Brush do not respond to a mouse event. For example, if an empty layout panel has a MouseEnter event assigned to it and you move the mouse onto the layout panel while the application is running, then the mouse event will only register if the background of the layout panel has a brush applied to it, and not if No Brush is applied.

Using Color Spaces

The Editor tab of the Brushes palette in the Properties panel allows you to choose from four different color spaces. To choose the space that you want click any label, such as R, G, or B from the default RGB color space, and choose a color space from the dropdown list. Figure 6.1 shows the CMYK color space. The color spaces are:

- **HLS:** Hue, Lightness, Saturation
- **HSB:** Hue, Saturation, Brightness
- **CMYK:** Cyan, Magenta, Yellow, Black, as shown in Figure 6.1
- **RGB:** Red, Green, Blue

Hue is the actual wavelength of light on the color spectrum.

Saturation is the purity of hue. If a hue is not mixed with white, black, or a shade of gray, then it is fully saturated. For example, on an overcast day, colors outside are typically highly saturated, because there is no direct sunshine to cast shadows on everything and thus mix blacks or grays into the colors of everything.

Brightness or Lightness is the amount of white mixed in with the hue. More white mixed with the hue results in a brighter color. Maximum brightness is completely white.

Each color space contains an Alpha value that you can use to set the percentage of transparency for a color. Setting Alpha values differ from setting Opacity because Alpha can be set for a single color, which allows you to create gradients that fade to invisibility.

Which color space you use for specifying your colors is up to you. Each color space uses the standard color picker which represents millions of colors. You may not even care what color space you choose, because you can choose colors using just the color picker itself.

To use the color picker, click on the slider to choose the hue, and then click in the color area next to the slider to choose the lightness and saturation of the hue. The upper right-hand corner of the color picker is the fully saturated color and the upper left-hand corner is the color with full brightness or lightness applied to it. Black is added to the colors as you move down the color picker, so that the entire bottom row is completely black.

The rectangles below the color picker represent the initial color, current color, and last color. If only two rectangles appear, then they represent the current and last colors.

The Color editor also provides a color eyedropper, which you can use to choose any color in the artboard or the Blend interface. To use the color eyedropper, click on it and as you move it around the Blend interface, notice that whatever is selected in the artboard changes its fill, stroke, or whatever you defined, to that color.

Every color is also represented by an eight-digit hexadecimal value located in the lower right-hand corner of the Color editor. This code represents 16 million possible colors 256 levels of transparency. The first two digits represent transparency where 00 is transparent and FF is opaque. The last six digits represent all colors from 000000, which is black, to FFFFFF, which is white. If you know the hexadecimal value for the color you want, you can type it in here, and your color appears in your selected object.

NOTE The *CMYK* (Cyan Magenta Yellow Black) color space is normally used for print media, but Blend includes it along with the other color spaces, just in case you want to match the colors on the screen to something in print, and you have the CMYK information for it.

FIGURE 6.1

The Brushes palette with the CMYK color space.

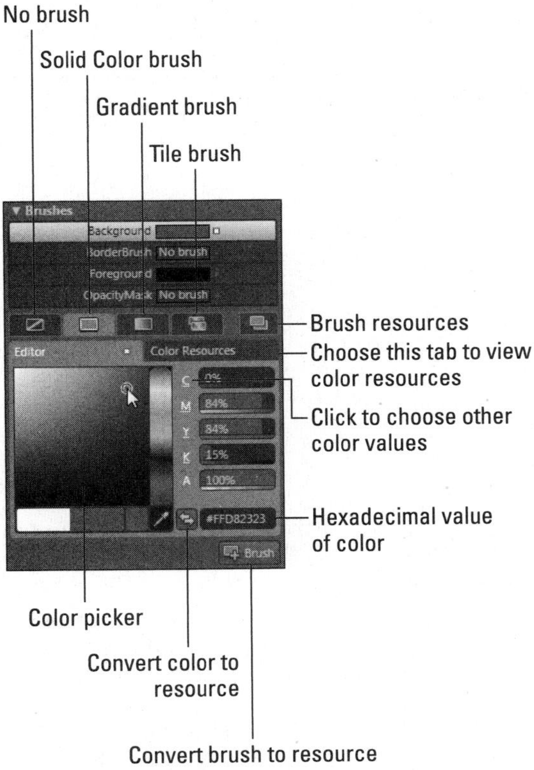

No brush

Solid Color brush

Gradient brush

Tile brush

Brush resources

Choose this tab to view color resources

Click to choose other color values

Hexadecimal value of color

Color picker

Convert color to resource

Convert brush to resource

Creating and Using Color Resources and Brush Resources

Color and brush resources are colors and brushes that you give a name and add to the color resources list or the brush resources list so you can assign them from that list whenever you want to. Every brush that you choose — whether it's a solid color brush, gradient brush, image brush, drawing brush, visual brush or tile brush — can be made into a brush resource. And any color that you specify (whether by using the color eyedropper, hexadecimal values, color spaces or color picker) can be made into a color resource.

You can use color resources when you create new gradients or when you specify the color of solid color brushes, and you can assign brush resources to any object anytime.

Color resources and brush resources are powerful, because if you change the color of a color resource or change the color, gradient, or tiling of a brush (which you can do even during run-time), then all the objects with that resource change accordingly. For example, in Figure 6.2, the gradients in the borders can be changed all at once by editing their brush resource. The same is true for all the image brushes in the centers of the objects.

FIGURE 6.2

If you assign a brush resource to all the borders of the images in the wrap panel, you can easily change them all simply by changing the resource.

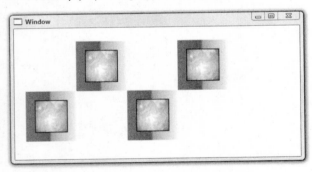

Brush resources and color resources come in two types: system and local. Local resources are the ones that you create. System brush resources and system color resources are created by Microsoft. Using a system color resource or a system brush resource is recommended if you want to conform to the windows themes, so that your application automatically takes on the appearance of the Aero theme for Vista or Luna theme for Windows XP, depending on which operating system the user has.

TIP   Accessibility features of your application may require the use of system brush resources or system color resources to work properly. If you're not using system color resources or system brush resources, you may want to test the accessibility features, and perhaps offer alternatives if necessary.

CROSS-REF For more information on accessibility features, see Chapter 17.

Applying system color resources

To use a system color resource, select an object, choose the Solid Color Brush or the Gradient Brush button, click the Color Resources tab, and choose from the list of system resources.

System color resources are the colors that Microsoft has chosen for standard uses, such as controls, menus, windows, and more. Because Microsoft offers two different looks or themes for WindowsXP and Vista, some of these colors may be different for the different themes. When you assign system color resources, the color may change according to the operating system that the user is working with.

Creating and using local color resources

To create a local color resource, choose a color from the color picker, eyedropper, or specify its values, and click the Convert Color To Resource button that is beside the Hex Value box in the Brushes palette. A dialog box appears asking you to name your color and choose a location to save it, as shown in Figure 6.3. You can choose to save it in the following ways:

■ You can define it for your current document.

■ You can define it to be available for all the documents in your application.

■ You can save it into a new or existing resource dictionary so that it's available to more than a single application. (Clicking the New button allows you to create a new resource dictionary.)

CROSS-REF For information on how to load a resource dictionary and how to organize your resources, see Chapter 7.

FIGURE 6.3

Creating a color resource.

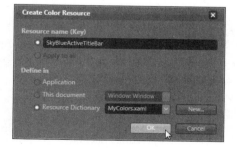

If you create a resource dictionary for your colors and save your color into it, then the resource dictionary gets automatically added to the Projects folder, and the color is added as a local resource in the Color Resources list, as shown in Figure 6.4.

FIGURE 6.4

Applying your color resource.

Applying a system brush resource

To apply a system brush resource, click the Brush Resources tab in the Brushes palette, as shown in Figure 6.1, and choose a brush from the System Resource list, as shown in Figure 6.5.

FIGURE 6.5

Applying a system brush resource.

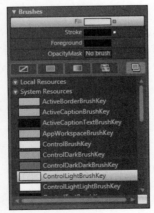

Creating and applying a local brush resource

To create a local brush resource, first assign your element a brush (a solid color brush, gradient brush or tile brush), and then click the Brush button at the bottom of the Brushes palette. A dialog box appears, as shown in Figure 6.6, asking you to name your brush resource and whether you want to define it in the window, the application, or a resource dictionary (which you can create in the dialog box, if you want to). Just as with color resources, you can make your brush resource available in three ways:

■ Define it in the document in which you create it

■ Define it in the application

■ Define it in a new or existing resource dictionary so it's available to more than a single application

FIGURE 6.6

Creating a brush resource.

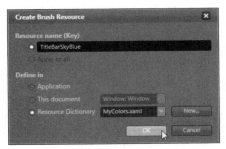

Editing color or brush resources

You can edit your color resources or brush resources in one of two ways, depending on whether the resource is defined in a resource dictionary, in the application or in a window.

Editing color resources or brush resources defined in the application or window

Editing a color resource or brush resource that is defined in your window or application can be performed simply by choosing the resource and clicking on it so that a pop-up mini-Brushes palette appears, as shown in Figure 6.7. You can use the pop-up Brushes palette to change the color or gradient. Changing the color or brush resource automatically updates all the objects assigned that color or brush resource. If your color or brush resource is defined in the application, then all the objects in the application with that color resource or brush resource will change.

FIGURE 6.7

Editing a brush resource in the Properties panel.

Editing color resources or brush resources defined in resource dictionaries

To change color resources or brush resources that are defined in resource dictionaries, right-click on the color in the Resources panel and select a new color from the pop-up Brushes palette that appears, as shown in Figure 6.8. Changing the color or brush resource automatically updates all the objects assigned that color or brush resource. The resource dictionary is also updated, and whatever application uses that resource dictionary in the future will also be affected.

 **TIP**   If you assigned a color resource or brush resource to an object, and no longer want that color or brush resource to apply, simply select it and assign it a new color or brush.

FIGURE 6.8

Editing a color resource in the Resources panel.

Creating and Applying Gradients

Using gradients, you can play with light and shadow. Even simple gradients, such as a single gradient from black to white, can create unusual effects. In Figure 6.9, a skewed chessboard becomes a woven metallic form by assigning a simple gradient of white fading to black to each of the diamonds.

FIGURE 6.9

Assigning a black-to-white gradient to each diamond creates a complex metallic image.

Blend allows you to create your own complex gradients with multiple colors and varying widths of color change in a single gradient. For example, in Figure 6.10, a radial gradient would appear as a rainbow when positioned below another object so that half of the circle is hidden from view.

FIGURE 6.10

Assigning all the hues of the color spectrum to create a rainbow.

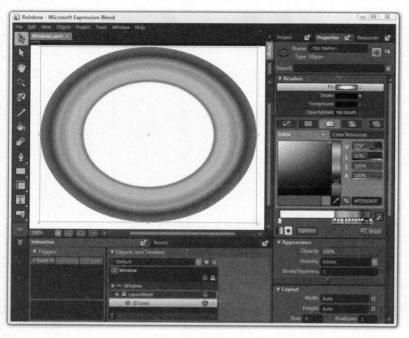

To create a gradient, select an object, and in the Brushes palette, choose the element of the object to which you want to apply the gradient. For example, you might choose Stroke or Fill. Then click the Gradient Brush tab and choose which kind of gradient you want to apply: Radial or Linear. Then click on a gradient stop on the gradient bar and assign it a color, from the color picker or color spaces or the eyedropper, or type in a hexadecimal value in the Brushes palette.

- To add another gradient stop to create more variation in your gradient, click in the gradient bar. (A new gradient stop appears.)

- To delete a gradient stop, click and drag the gradient stop off the gradient bar. (The gradient stop vanishes.)

- To move a gradient stop, click and drag the gradient stop.

CAUTION Some objects do not fill. For example, a triangle won't fill if it consists of a group of three separate lines or paths created either by the Line tool or Pen tool. Your only recourse may be to use the Pen tool to redraw it as a single path. As you create your line drawing, you may want to test each path to make sure it fills as you expect it will.

TIP You may want to select an object by clicking its name in the Objects list of the Objects and Timeline palette, rather than clicking on the object in the artboard. Alternatively, you can double-click objects to drill down to the actual object that you want to apply a gradient brush (or other brush) to.

Adjusting gradients with the Brush Transform tool

Once you assign a gradient to an object, you can fine-tune the gradient by clicking on the Brush Transform tool, which you can then use to adjust the gradient in a multitude of ways. For example, in Figure 6.11 the gradient assigned to the background of the window gives it the appearance of a room, because of the gradient stops applied, and because we used the Brush Transform tool to move the angle of the linear gradient 90 degrees.

FIGURE 6.11

Creating a horizon by assigning a linear gradient and using the Brush Transform tool to adjust it.

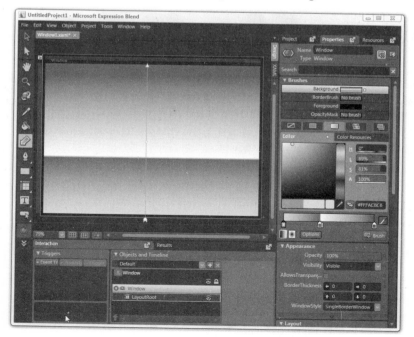

- **To change the angle of a linear gradient,** click and drag either the arrowhead or the feather portion of the arrow, and move the arrow to the desired angle to rotate the gradient.

- **To resize a linear gradient,** shorten or lengthen the arrow by clicking and dragging the arrowhead or the feather portion of the arrow.

- **To resize a radial gradient,** shorten or lengthen the arrow by clicking and dragging the arrowhead, or pull the object handles. (Radial gradients have object handles, whereas linear gradients do not.)

- **To resize a radial gradient giving it a cone-shaped 3D look,** shorten or lengthen the arrow by clicking and dragging the feather portion of the arrow.

- **To move the center of either a linear or radial gradient,** click anywhere in the gradient and drag.

- **To skew a radial gradient,** move the mouse near an object handle in the center of a border line. When the cursor becomes a double arrow with a slanted line through it, click and drag to skew the gradient.

- **To rotate a radial gradient,** move the mouse near a corner object handle. When the cursor becomes a curved double arrow, click and drag to rotate the gradient.

- **To stop using the Brush Transform tool,** click the Selection tool or any tool in the Toolbox.

Repeating and reflecting the gradient

When using the Brush Transform tool, you may notice that when the gradient is smaller than the object, the empty space around the gradient is padded with the last color of the gradient. This is the default, but you can control the color in that extra space by setting the Gradient mode to the following:

- **Pad gradient mode:** This fills the extra space with a single color, as shown on the left in Figure 6.12. The color of the padding is the color of the last gradient stop. This is the default mode.

- **Repeat gradient mode:** This repeats the gradient in the extra space, as shown on the right in Figure 6.12. Use this to create a striped look.

- **Reflect gradient mode:** This creates symmetric stripes, as if each gradient had a mirror image attached to it, as shown in Figure 6.12 in the center.

FIGURE 6.12

The gradient modes from left to right: Pad, Reflect, and Repeat.

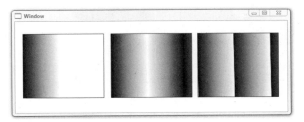

Setting the gradient mode

Use the gradient mode to pad, repeat, or reflect your gradients when your gradient does not fill the object. To set the gradient mode for a gradient, click the Options button in the Gradient Brush tab of the Brushes palette and choose Pad, Repeat or Reflect from the drop-down list. Before or after doing so, be sure to resize your gradient smaller than its container. Remember, Pad is the default, so you probably will see a difference only if you choose Repeat or Reflect.

You also have the option of making the gradient a fixed size, if you choose Absolute in the Options drop-down list, but normally, you want vector art to shrink or expand, so the default is Bounding Box.

Creating and applying stripes using the Repeat gradient mode

You can create stripes by setting the Gradient mode to Repeat as described previously. The smaller you resize your gradient in step 3, the more stripes you achieve. If you want white space between your gradients to achieve an even more striped look, then add two consecutive white gradient stops on the gradient bar with colored gradient stops on each side of the white ones. You can create rainbow stripes by repeating the rainbow gradient, as shown in Figure 6.13.

Once you create stripes, you can apply them wherever you can apply any gradient — for example, as a fill or in a stroke or a background.

FIGURE 6.13

Radial stripes are created using the Repeat gradient mode.

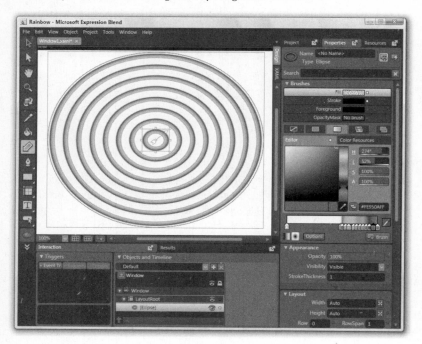

Transferring Colors, Gradients and More

Blend provides an easy way of transferring brushes and other attributes to other objects, using the Eyedropper and Paint Bucket tool. They not only transfer the brush, they can transfer stroke size, text attributes, and Opacity as well.

Using the Eyedropper

The Eyedropper tool copies attributes to a selected object. To use the Eyedropper, select an object that you want to transfer attributes to, and then click the Eyedropper tool in the Toolbox and click on the object that you want to transfer attributes from. The selected object changes its brushes and other attributes to the attributes of the object you clicked on using the Eyedropper tool.

The attributes that are copied are: brushes for the different fills, strokes, background, foreground, border brush, opacity mask, opacity, and stroke attributes, such as thickness and end caps.

Using the Paint Bucket

To transfer different attributes from one object to another (for example, brushes assigned to the stroke and fill, and stroke size), you can select the object that possesses the attributes that you want to transfer, and then click the Paint Bucket tool in the Toolbox, and click an object that you want to transfer these attributes to. In Figure 6.14, an image brush assigned to a selected ellipse is copied to other ellipses using the Paint Bucket tool. (Image brushes are discussed in detail later in this Chapter.)

As with the Eyedropper tool, the attributes that are copied are: brushes, opacity, stroke attributes, and text attributes.

FIGURE 6.14

Assigning an image brush to ellipses using the Paint Bucket tool.

Using Images

Blend allows you to add bitmap images of many types into your project, including TIF, PNG, JPG, GIF, BMP, and more. You can insert images into the artboard and manipulate them just like other objects. For example, you can do the following (and more) with them:

- Move your image, by choosing the Selection tool and clicking and dragging anywhere in the artboard
- Resize your image, by clicking and dragging its object handles
- Use the Transform palette to position, scale, rotate, skew, and flip your image
- Assign your image an opacity mask, which is described later in this chapter
- Animate your entire image, which is discussed in Chapter 14

- Add a bitmap effect to your image, which is discussed later in this chapter
- Transform your image into an image brush

For example, the collage of San Francisco photos in Figure 6.15 was created by adding and positioning the photos.

FIGURE 6.15

Photos of San Francisco are positioned into a collage.

Adding and linking images

Blend offers you three choices for addressing images. You can give your image a relative address, either by choosing Project ➪ Add Existing Item or Project ➪ Link To Existing Item, and then referring to its name in the Files palette. Or you can use an absolute address for your image, such as a file path or URL. Images that are saved as GIF, PNG or JPG file types can be published to a URL and accessed using absolute addresses. Using an absolute address of a URL certainly allows you great flexibility to change the image whenever you want, although it won't appear if the user is not connected to the Internet.

To add your images to the Files palette, you can choose either Project ➪ Add Existing Item or Project ➪ Link To Existing Item. Images that are added to a project are physically copied into the project folder, and they are also physically added into the .exe file when you build the project. This is probably the easiest and most common way of making images available to your application. However it is also possible to link images. Images that are linked are not copied into the project folder and are not in the .exe file, but a link is created by Blend. Once your images are added or linked to the project, their names appear in the Files palette of the Project panel. You can right-click on an image's name in the Files palette and choose Insert to add an image into the artboard.

To insert an image with an absolute address into the artboard, first as a temporary measure in the artboard insert any image that you've added into your project. (You need to do this to get access to an image control.) Then select the temporary image and type or paste the URL of the image you want to use into the Source property in the Common Properties palette. Or you can click the Choose An Image button and browse or type in a file path or a URL. The image with the absolute address replaces the temporary image in the artboard.

NOTE In subsequent examples involving adding images or other items, throughout this book, we often mention only Project ➪ Add Existing Item and not Project ➪ Link To Existing Item. However, you certainly can use the latter instead, or absolute addressing. These are always options, even though we may leave them out for the sake of brevity and clarity.

If you want to change an image from one image to another image, then you can select the image in the artboard, click the down arrow beside the Source property in the Common Properties palette, and choose another image from the list, as shown in Figure 6.16.

TIP To view the contents of your project folder, choose Project ➪ Explore Project. If you do this, you'll see that the images that you add to the project exist there, and the images that you link to the project or used an absolute address are not in the project folder. Images added to the project are included in the .exe file that Blend creates when the project is built.

FIGURE 6.16

Changing an image in the artboard.

Assigning the Stretch Property

When resizing an image in the artboard by dragging a corner handle, the proportions of the width and height of the image remain the same. However, you can resize it so that the proportions of the width and height differ. You can do this by pressing Shift while resizing the image. The object boundaries appear different from the image itself. This is because the object boundaries are displaying an image control whose Source property is the image.

When the image control is a different proportion from the image, then you may want to adjust the Stretch property, which you can find in the Common Properties palette. For example, in Figure 6.17, the image control is taller than the photo of our son, Porter. Blend gives you four choices for handling this. To apply these choices, click the Stretch drop-down arrow and choose one of the following:

- **None:** The image appears in the same size as its original size and is cropped if the shape or path is too small to contain it, or padded with white space if the shape or path is too large. The image on the left in Figure 6.17 has None applied to it and shows only the upper corner of the image in its actual size.

- **Fill:** Your image shrinks or stretches to fit in the boundaries of its image control. For example, the second image from the left in Figure 6.17 uses this type of stretch and is distorted to fit the shape.

- **Uniform:** Your image fills its image control but leaves white space where the image control does not conform to the original size of the image. The image is not distorted. For example, the third image from the left in Figure 6.17 uses this type of stretch.

- **UniformToFill:** Your image fills the image control, and crops itself as necessary so that no white space appears. Except for cropping, the image is not distorted. The rightmost image in Figure 6.17 uses this type of stretch.

CROSS-REF   You can use a Viewbox to define how images are clipped when they are resized, so that when the images resize smaller, they focus in on the area of interest in the image. For more information on how to use a Viewbox to define how an image clips when it does not resize with the window, see chapter 16.

FIGURE 6.17

Four Stretch modes from left to right are: None, Fill, Uniform and UniformToFill.

Adjusting the initial size and resizing using the Layout palette

The Layout palette gives you the power to precisely control the size of an image and how much an image will resize larger or smaller when the window is resized. The default is Auto Size both height and width, but you can also type in values into the Width and Height input boxes, so that it doesn't resize at all, or so that it only resizes the Width, or the Height. And you can specify MaxHeight, MaxWidth, MinHeight, and MinWidth by clicking the Expander button at the bottom of the palette and specifying values for those properties. Then when the application is resized larger the image resizes up to a maximum size and when it resizes smaller it shrinks to a minimum size. You may want to use this feature to prevent the image from enlarging to such a large size that it loses sharpness or shrinking to such a small size that it is no longer discernible.

 For information on adding scroll bars, see "Using the ScrollViewer" in Chapter 16.

TIP Adding your images into sections of a grid panel using the Layout palette is a good way to keep things from shifting around during resizing.

Deleting or removing images from your project

Images sometimes take up a lot of space, so you may want to be selective about what images you want, and get rid of those you don't want. Blend gives you the choice of deleting an image or removing it. Either way, the object is removed from the Files palette.

- Deleting an image removes it completely from the project and the project folder.
- Removing an image removes it from the Files palette, but not the project folder.

To delete or remove images, right-click on the name of the image in the Project panel and choose Delete or Remove From Project.

Using Image, Drawing, and Visual Brushes

In Blend you can create the following brushes to apply images or vector art or the contents of a layout panel as a brush to other vector objects:

- An image brush, to map an image onto a vector object or 3D object. Figure 6.18 shows a photo of our daughter, Jacqueline, in different types of frames using an image brush.
- A drawing brush, to map an image of vector objects onto another vector object or 3D object or layout panel.
- A visual brush, to map an image of a layout panel onto another vector object or 3D object or layout panel. This is great for showing a reflection of a user interface that is constantly changing, for example. Figure 6.19 shows an example of a visual brush as a reflection of a button. You can also use a visual brush to map animations and video onto a vector object or 3D object or layout panel.

You can also use image and drawing brushes to apply a tile brush and tile your images or drawings. For more information about tiling your images, see "Using the Tile Brush" later in this chapter.

CROSS-REF For more information about using a visual brush to apply animations and video, see Chapter 14.

For instructions for applying a drawing brush, image brush, or visual brush on a 3D object, see Chapter 12.

FIGURE 6.18

Using an image brush to frame your images with unusual shapes.

FIGURE 6.19

Using a visual brush to create a button's reflection that changes as the states of the button change.

Creating and using an image brush

To create an image brush, right-click on the image in the Project panel and choose Insert to insert it into the artboard. Then choose Tools ➪ Make Brush Resource ➪ Make Image Brush Resource. Give it a unique name or accept the default, and choose where to define it. (For details on defining a resource, see "Creating and applying a local brush resource" earlier in this chapter.) Then delete your image from the artboard by selecting the image, and pressing Backspace.

You can now apply the image brush by selecting an object, clicking the Brush Resource tab in the Brushes palette, and choosing the name of the image brush from the list. The image brush is also shown in a handy thumbnail to help you identify it in the list.

TIP The last brush you use becomes the default brush. This is true for image, drawing and visual brushes as well. To turn off the image brush (or drawing or visual brush) as the default brush, simply select an object and choose another brush.

Creating and using a drawing brush

To create a drawing brush, select a vector object (which can be either a single vector object, or a layout panel containing vector objects), and choose Tools ⇨ Make Brush Resource ⇨ Make Drawing Brush Resource. Then give the drawing brush a unique name or accept the default, and choose where to define it. (For details on defining a resource, see "Creating and applying a local brush resource" earlier in this chapter.)

Once you create a drawing brush resource, you can apply it by selecting an object, clicking the Brush Resource tab in the Brushes palette, and choosing the name of the drawing brush from the list. The drawing brush is also shown in a handy thumbnail to help you identify it in the list.

Creating and using a visual brush

To create a visual brush, select a control or a layout panel, preferably one that changes in appearance over time, such as a button, or a layout panel that contain buttons, or a video. (You can choose a control or layout panel that doesn't change over time, but then why bother with a visual brush? Use an image brush or drawing brush instead.) Then choose Tools ⇨ Make Brush Resource ⇨ Make Visual Brush Resource. Then give the visual brush a unique name or accept the default and choose where to define it.

To apply a visual brush, select an object, such as a rectangle, a 3D object, or a layout panel, for example. Then select the background or fill or other element of the object that you want to apply the brush to, click the Brush Resource tab in the Brushes palette, and choose the name of the visual brush. To see the visual brush in action, you need to choose Project ⇨ Test Project and change the state of a button or other control. The visual brush changes as well.

Figure 6.19 shows an example of a button with a reflection created using a visual brush. The visual brush is applied to a rectangle and then flipped, skewed and made slightly invisible using the opacity mask. (For more information about how to use an opacity mask, see the section on opacity masks later in this chapter.) When the mouse is over the button, and the button changes color, the reflection also changes color. Figure 6.19 shows the reflection effect for a single button, but it is just as easy to create it for an entire layout panel that contains buttons and other controls.

Editing your Drawing, Image or Visual brush resource

Blend allows you to edit your drawing, image or visual brush resource, just as you edit any brush resource. You can choose any object and click the Brush Resource tab in the Brushes palette to bring up the list of brush resources. Then select the resource and right-click on its thumbnail. This brings up a palette in which you can change the brush resource to a solid color brush, gradient brush, or tile brush, as shown in Figure 6.20.

FIGURE 6.20

Editing an image brush.

Using the Tile Brush

The tile brush works in conjunction with the image brush or drawing brush, as well as the Brush Transform tool in a similar way as Pad, Reflect, and Repeat. If the original object or image that you assigned as an image or drawing brush is smaller than the object it fills, then you can create any of the following effects by choosing them from the Tile Mode menu in the Appearance:

- **FlipX:** Tiles by flipping the object horizontally to create a symmetric copy beside each tile
- **FlipY:** Tiles by flipping the object vertically to create a symmetric copy beneath each tile
- **FlipXY:** Tiles by flipping the object horizontally and vertically to create a symmetric copy beside and beneath each tile
- **Tile:** Does not flip the image as it tiles

To use the tile brush, first assign an image brush or drawing brush to an object. Then use the Brush Transform tool to resize the image brush or drawing brush smaller than the object, in order to leave room for the tiling. Then choose the tile brush tab in the Brushes palette and select the type of tiling you want. Whatever you select fills the object. Figure 6.21 show an example of an image brush tiled inside a rectangle.

FIGURE 6.21

Tiling an image brush in a rectangle.

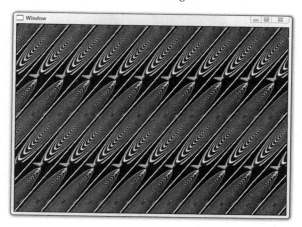

Working with Bitmap Effects

Blend offers six basic bitmap effects which you can use individually or combine. They are shown in Figure 6.22. From left to right and top to bottom, they are Bevel, Blur, DropShadow, Emboss, OuterGlow, and a combination of Bevel, DropShadow, and OuterGlow.

Blend allows you to add bitmap effects to almost any vector object. Each bitmap effect offers several properties that you can change to adjust the effect. The properties for each effect are listed later in this section of the chapter.

 Using bitmap effects requires that your application be granted full trust. If you're creating an XBAP, then you probably do not want to assign bitmap effects to objects.

Creating bitmap effects

To create a bitmap effect, select the object that you want to apply the bitmap effect to, and expand the Appearance palette to view all the options. Then click the down arrow beside the New Bitmap Effect button, and choose the bitmap effect that you want to apply. The effect appears in the selected object, and the default properties appear with their values in the Appearance palette, as shown in Figure 6.23. You can modify the default properties to adjust the bitmap effect.

To remove a bitmap effect, select the object, click the small square beside the New button beside BitmapEffect so that a drop-down menu appears, and choose Reset.

FIGURE 6.22

Bitmap effects: Bevel, Blur, DropShadow, Emboss, OuterGlow, and a combination.

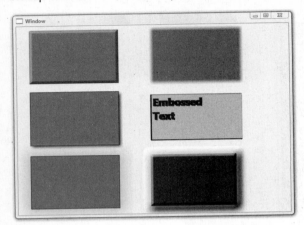

FIGURE 6.23

Adjusting the Bevel bitmap effect.

CROSS-REF To create bitmap effects or change their properties in the code-behind file, see Chapter 20.

Using BevelBitmapEffect

Properties of the BevelBitmapEffect are

- BevelWidth, which you can set from zero (no bevel) all the way to a width that makes the bevel look like a hip roof on a house
- EdgeProfile, which can be Linear, CurvedIn, CurvedOut, and BulgedUp
- LightAngle which you can set from 0 to 360 degrees
- Relief, which adds height
- Smoothness, which gives it an appearance that can vary from crystal clear to somewhat blurred

Figure 6.24 shows an example of three rectangles with the Bevel bitmap effect applied with different values for their properties.

 You can easily turn a beveled rectangle or image into a button by selecting it and choosing Tools ⇨ MakeButton.

 For information about using the Make Button feature, see Chapter 16.

FIGURE 6.24

Three different bevels are created by adjusting the values of the BevelBitmapEffect properties.

Using BlurBitmapEffect

The BlurBitmapEffect offers two properties that you can adjust: the KernalType (which you can set to Gaussian or Box), and the Radius (which allows you to adjust the amount of blur). Figure 6.25 illustrates three blurs using the BlurBitmapEffect.

FIGURE 6.25

Three different blurs are created by adjusting the values of the BlurBitmapEffect properties.

Using DropShadowBitmapEffect

A drop shadow makes an object appear to be hovering over a background and gives the user the impression that it may be moveable, like a tool. Drop shadows can add realism to an application and enhance its aesthetic appeal. The DropShadowBitmapEffect has six properties: Color, Direction, Noise, Opacity, ShadowDepth, and Softness. Figure 6.26 shows an example of three drop shadows. The rectangle in the center has a very high value for Noise. The text on the right is text which is converted into a vector object. To apply a drop shadow to text, you need to type the text into a TextBlock and choose Object ➪ Path ➪ Convert To Path, which converts the text to a vector object. Then you can apply a drop shadow to it.

FIGURE 6.26

Three drop shadow effects.

Using EmbossBitmapEffect

Embossing makes an object appear as a 3D impression. In Figure 6.27, the image on the left is a digital photo, and the images in the middle and on the right are the same image with the EmbossBitmapEffect applied to it, using different values for the effect's properties. The properties for this bitmap effect are LightAngle and Relief. The Relief differed by only a slight amount in the two images, yet created a big difference in the effect.

> **TIP** Embossing can take a lot of computing power. If you have something that you want to emboss, you may want to consider doing it in Expression Design and saving it as a normal bitmap image. Then you can bring it into Blend and use it like any image. In fact, this can work for all the bitmap effects, if you don't want your application to require full trust, or if your bitmap effects are slowing down your application's performance.

The image in the middle and on the right are embossed versions of the original image on the left.

Using OuterGlowBitmapEffect

The OuterGlowBitmapEffect has four properties that you can adjust: GlowColor, GlowSize, Noise, and Opacity. Figure 6.28 illustrates some examples of the glows you can create using Blend. The glow on the right has a high noise value. The glowing text is text which is converted to a path by selecting text in a TextBlock and choosing Object ⇨ Path ⇨ Convert To Path.

Three glows using OuterGlowBitmapEffect.

Combining Bitmap Effects

Suppose you want an object to glow at the same time that it has a drop shadow and a bevel? The bottom right object in Figure 6.22 is an example of this. Blend allows you to combine bitmap effects. To assign more than one bitmap effect to a single object, follow these steps:

STEPS: Combining more than one bitmap effect for an object

1. Select the object, and in the Appearance palette of the Properties panel, click the down arrow beside the New BitmapEffect button, and then choose BitmapEffectGroup from the drop-down list.

2. Click the Button beside Children (Collection) that appears below BitmapEffect in the Miscellaneous palette.

3. In the BitmapEffectCollection Editor: Children dialog box that appears, click the Add Another Item button, and choose a bitmap effect from the drop-down list next to the button.

4. Specify values for the bitmap properties to customize the bitmap effect. You may want to re-position the dialog box so that you can see its effect in your selected object in the artboard.

5. To assign another bitmap effect, click the Add Another Item button again and choose another bitmap effect from the drop-down list.

6. Continue adjusting properties and adding bitmap effects until you are finished. Then click OK.

Changing Transparency

Blend allows you to specify any percentage of transparency for an object or image, accurate to three decimal points (which may be overdoing it a little, but we're not complaining). In the Brushes palette, you can specify any percentage of transparency for any of the following:

- Any element of an object to which you can assign color, such as fill and stroke. Do this by setting the Alpha value in the Solid Color Brush tab of the Brushes palette.

- Any gradient stops of a gradient fill, which can change the transparency gradually in a linear or radial gradient. Set the Alpha value, which is the last box of the color space and has an A beside it. Zero percent is completely transparent. 100% is completely opaque.

- An *opacity mask*, which is a component of every image or object. An opacity mask makes the object transparent where the opacity mask is transparent. You can assign a Gradient Brush to an opacity mask. Wherever the gradient contains an Alpha value less than 100%, the object containing the opacity mask becomes less opaque and more transparent by that much.

Also, in the Appearance palette, you can specify any percentage of transparency for an entire object. You can also set the object to Hidden or Collapsed. A hidden object still takes up space in the user interface whereas a collapsed object contains no space.

Adding transparency to gradient stops of a gradient fill, or doing the same to an opacity mask, can produce many lighting effects that can add interest and realism to your vector art. Lighting effects of this sort, which are discussed in detail later in this section, include:

- Light beams
- Spotlights
- Lighting, as shown, for example, in Figure 6.29

FIGURE 6.29

Using radial and linear gradients with some gradient stops set to an Alpha value of 0 to create dramatic lighting effects in Expression Blend.

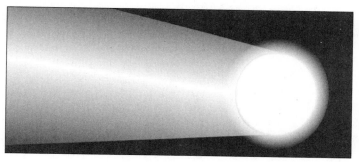

You can also create glows and shadows with the help of gradients that fade to transparency, although these can also be created using bitmap effects.

CROSS-REF   These lighting effects work well with animation. For information about how to animate them, see Chapter 14.

Working with opacity masks

You can assign radial or linear gradients to opacity masks to create interesting changes in the Opacity of an object. Opacity masks that use radial gradients, with at least one gradient stop that has an Alpha value of less than 100 percent, change the transparency in a circular manner either outward from a central point or inward toward a central point. Opacity masks that use linear gradients with at least one gradient stop with an Alpha value of less than 100 percent change transparency in a straight line. You can use the Brush Transform tool to modify the look of the gradient on the object by changing the gradient's size, position, and center.

Figure 6.30 shows an example of an opacity mask in use. The image is an image brush applied to a circle and its opacity mask in the Brushes palette is assigned an Alpha value of zero for the outermost gradient stop. This creates a glow around the inner edges of the circle that the image brush is applied to. This type of glow differs from the OuterGlowBitmapEffect, because the glow is contained within the object it is applied to and not outside the object.

TIP   When assigning an opacity mask to a layout panel, the opacity mask affects all children of the layout panel, as well as the layout panel itself.

FIGURE 6.30

An opacity mask creates a glowing effect around the image brush when one gradient stop is set to an Alpha value of zero.

Setting the Opacity of an object

Opacity differs from an opacity mask of an object because the opacity mask is normally used to change transparency using radial and linear gradients that have gradient stops with Alpha values less than 100 percent. In contrast, setting the Opacity of an object sets it equally for the entire object.

To change the Opacity of an object, set the Opacity slider in the Appearance palette. For example, in Figure 6.31, a rectangle has an Opacity of 50% so that the line art beneath it is visible. (If you want to change the Opacity of an element of an object, such as a stroke or fill, then set the Alpha value of the element using the Alpha value in the Solid Color Brush.)

FIGURE 6.31

The Opacity is set to 50 percent in this rectangle, so that the line art can be seen beneath it.

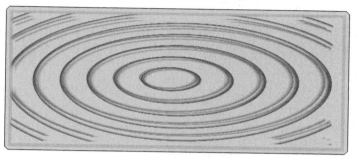

Creating beams of light

By combining gradients with transparency you can generate spotlight effects, as shown in Figure 6.32. Figure 6.33 shows the Blend application window that created the beam of light effect. Beams of light can be any width and any intensity. You can use beams of light in your user interface artwork as static art, or you can animate them as a light show. To create a light beam, create a long thin rectangle filled with whatever color you want your light to be, and modify its opacity mask to have a gradient that is opaque in the middle and invisible on each side. It's good to place the beams of light on a dark background.

FIGURE 6.32

Beams of light created in Blend

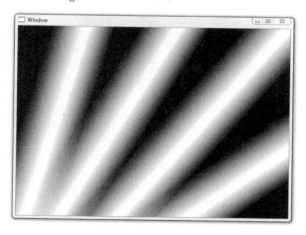

FIGURE 6.33

The opacity mask is set to a linear gradient brush to create the beam of light effect.

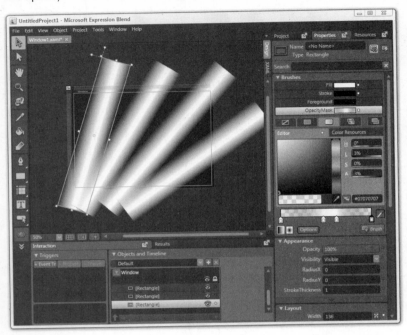

Creating spotlights

You can create several kinds of spotlights. The beams of light in the preceding section might be considered spotlights. A radial opacity mask could represent the end of a spotlight. This could be an opacity mask with a radial gradient that fades to full transparency and made smaller using the Brush Transform tool. Figure 6.34 shows an example of this kind of a spotlight on a digital photo.

FIGURE 6.34

An opacity mask makes a small area of the photo visible while hiding the rest of it.

Making your vector art glow

You can use glows to add interest to your art. You can create some glows by using opacity masks, but these glows don't extend beyond the edges of the object, and the shape of the glow does not always conform to the shape of the object. If you want a glow to extend beyond the object, you can either use the OuterGlowBitmapEffect described earlier in this chapter, or you can use a radial gradient within an ellipse or rectangle placed behind the object.

You can surround whatever you want with a radial glow. Figure 6.35 shows an example of a glow behind a chess rook.

FIGURE 6.35

A radial gradient that fades to transparency is placed behind the chess piece to create a glow.

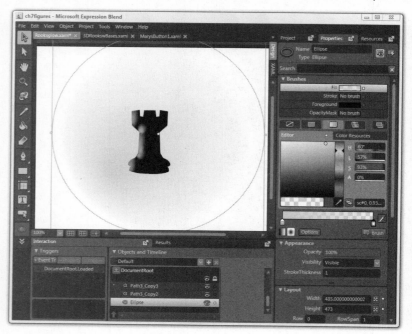

Making shadows

You can create shadows using the drop shadow bitmap effect, or you can create them by copying your object and filling it with gray, and then placing the gray copy where you want a shadow to appear, as shown on the left in Figure 6.36. You need to skew it or resize it, depending on where you want your light source to be coming from. To the opacity mask of your shadow, you can assign a gradient that fades to transparency, as shown in Figure 6.36 on the right.

FIGURE 6.36

The shadow on the left is a solid color. The shadow on the right has an opacity mask with a gradient that fades to transparency.

Summary

- In Blend, you can add colors that you choose to a list of color resources and brushes that you create to a list of brush resources. You can then quickly apply these resources to elements of your interface. If you want to change a resource, then the change automatically appears in all elements to which the resource was applied. You can apply system brush resources and system color resources to user interface elements to be consistent with the Aero and Luna system themes.

- Blend provides you with six kinds of brushes:

  - The solid color brush, to apply solid colors and transparencies.

  - The gradient brush, to create linear or radial gradients

  - The image brush, to map images onto 2D or 3D vector objects

  - The drawing brush, to map vector art onto 2D or 3D vector objects

  - The visual brush, to map videos, animations, and layout panels or controls displaying interactivity onto 2D or 3D vector objects

  - The tile brush, to tile image brushes or drawing brushes.

- In Blend, you can apply color in these ways:
  - Use the color picker
  - Apply a color or brush resource
  - Type in the hexadecimal code for a color
  - Specify values in one of the four color spaces: RGB, HLS, HSB, or CMYK
  - Use the Eyedropper or Paint Bucket tool

- You can adjust your gradients using the Brush Transform tool. This tool allows you to change the direction, size and shape of a gradient, and to move the center of the gradient or skew the gradient.

- When a gradient is resized smaller than the object containing it, you can pad, repeat, or reflect the gradient.

- Blend allows you to add images to your project, and then use those images in the artboard. Blend provides four stretch modes for images: None, Fill, Uniform, and UniformToFill.

- Blend offers five bitmap effects (which you can combine if desired):
  - BevelBitmapEffect
  - BlurBitmapEffect
  - DropShadowBitmapEffect
  - EmbossBitmapEffect
  - OuterGlowBitmapEffect

- You can add transparency to objects in Blend in the following ways:
  - Apply an Alpha value to a solid color brush or to a gradient stop of a gradient brush.
  - Apply an Alpha value to a solid color brush or gradient brush, and then apply the brush to the opacity mask of an image or object
  - Specify a percentage of Opacity in the Appearance palette
  - Choose Hidden or Collapsed in the Appearance palette to hide or collapse an object

Chapter 7

Creating Styles and Using Resources

Blend allows you to create styles and templates for shapes, paths, layout panels and controls, then apply them as resources within the project or import them into other projects. Styles consist of attributes which you can apply to the default look of your shapes, paths, layout panels, and controls, such as scaling, rotation, skew, and bitmap effects. You can animate any of these properties as part of the style, as well.

Templates describe control parts and how the control changes in appearance with events, such as a MouseEnter or MouseDown, and are described in detail in Chapter 16. All controls can have both styles and templates; however, shapes, paths, and layout panels can have only styles.

Both styles and templates can be assigned as resources. Resources are powerful tools for re-using objects. Using resources, you can make changes to a style or template and globally change all the objects with that same style or template applied. For example, after you create a style, you can do two main things with it:

- Apply the style to any object of the same type by applying the resource
- Modify the style after applying it to an object, and in doing so, all objects with that style modify instantly

Modifying styles and templates can aid you in perfecting your user interface during the design of it. Or it can occur during runtime, using events and the code-behind file and can result in sweeping changes to the look of your user interface. A big example of the use of styles in the Blend interface is the ability to choose between its light theme and dark theme.

Because Expression Design and other applications, such as ZAM 3D, generate XAML code, you can seamlessly import resources from them and use them in your project.

This chapter covers how to create and edit styles, organize resources, and create and import resources from Expression Design.

 For information on creating brush resources or using bitmap effects, see Chapter 6. For information on creating new control templates, see Chapter 16.

Creating, Applying, and Editing a Style

Blend allows you to create styles for any object type, including controls, layout panels, vector objects, and text boxes.. Once you create a style, you can apply it as a resource. For more information on resources, see the following section.

You can define styles as resources in any of three places:

- A single window
- Your application
- A resource dictionary

Choosing to define your styles in resource dictionaries has several advantages:

- You can add your resource dictionaries to other projects, and your styles become available to that project.
- Resource dictionaries can act as folders to help you organize your styles in the Resources panel.

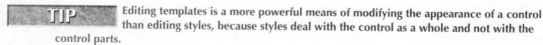 Editing templates is a more powerful means of modifying the appearance of a control than editing styles, because styles deal with the control as a whole and not with the control parts.

 Editing templates of controls is discussed in Chapter 16. An example of adding animation to the style of a control is also discussed there.

Creating a new style

To create a new style, follow these steps:

STEPS: Creating a New Style

1. Draw a shape, path, layout panel, or control, and choose Object ➪ Edit Style ➪ Create Empty.

   The Create Style Resource dialog box appears, as shown in Figure 7.1.

2. Give your resource a name, if you want to change the default name, and choose where you want to define it: your window, your application, or a resource dictionary. Feel free to create a new resource dictionary by clicking New, or you can choose an existing one from a drop-down menu that lists resource dictionaries in your project.

3. If you want your new style to be the default style for every existing object and new object of the same type that you create wherever the style is defined, select Apply to All.

4. Click OK.

You may notice that if you select Apply to All you may not be able to view the object—but the values that you enter take effect for the selected object, as well as all objects of the same type (as well as all future objects of the same type).

5. Make any changes you want to the object using the Properties panel. You can also add animations and triggers using the Interaction panel.

CROSS-REF Details for creating animations are discussed in Chapter 14.

6. When you finish creating your new style, click the ScopeUp button beside Style on the Objects and Timeline palette.

CAUTION You may want to think twice about selecting the Apply to All radio button in Step 3, because it changes all existing and future objects of the same type for the window or application (whichever you selected in Step 2). However, you can always delete a style, as described in the following section.

CROSS-REF If you use the Transform pane to create your style, be sure to choose correctly between Render Transform and Layout Transform. See Chapter 5 for more information.

FIGURE 7.1

The Create Style Resource dialog box

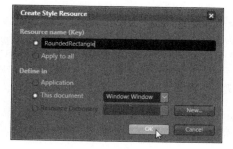

Applying a style as a resource

If you select the Apply to All radio button in the previous steps, your new style is already applied to all objects of the same type, as well as all future objects of that same type that you create.

Otherwise, if you want to apply your style to any object of the same type, first create the object, such as a rectangle to apply a style created using a rectangle, then choose Object ⇨ Edit Style ⇨ Apply Resource and choose the resource from the list of available resources. For example, the rectangle in Figure 7.2 has a style applied to it that is a bitmap effect. It also needs to be applied the Brush resource to make it appear like the others. If your object is a control, then choose Object ⇨ Edit Control Parts (Template) ⇨ Apply Resource and choose the resource from the list of available resources.

FIGURE 7.2

Applying a style to a rectangle

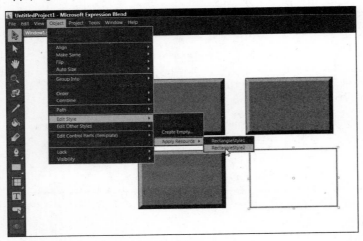

Editing a style

To edit a style, select any object that has the style applied to it, and choose Object ⇨ Edit Style ⇨ Edit Style. You can then use the Properties panel and Interaction panel to make any changes to the style. All changes that you make instantly apply to all objects with the same style applied to them. When you finish editing the style, click the ScopeUp button in the Objects list.

Deleting a style

To delete a style, open the Resources panel, then click the drop-down arrow beside `app.xaml` or the name of the window file to find the name of the style that you want to delete. If it is defined in a window, you also need to open the drop-down arrow beside Window. Then right-click on the name of the style and choose Delete.

Using Resources

Resources are XAML code files that define information for a particular object type or element. Resources may be as follows:

- **Brush resource:** Defines Gradient Brushes, Solid Color Brushes, and Tile Brushes, Drawing Brushes, Image Brushes, and Visual Brushes

- **Color resource:** Defines specific colors

- **Style resource:** Defines a specific style for your objects, layout panels, and controls, as described in the previous section

- **Control Template resource:** Defines the components of your controls and states of the control, such as the appearance of the control during a MouseEnter or MouseDown event

CROSS-REF For more about creating your own controls, see Chapter 16.

When you create resources in your project, you may want to organize them in different ways. For example, you may want to move some into resource dictionaries, or copy and paste some for use in multiple windows. Blend offers the Resources panel, as shown in Figure 7.3, to aid you in organizing resources.

CROSS-REF For more information about creating brush resources and color resources, see Chapter 6. For more information about the basics of XAML code, see Chapter 3 and Chapter 22.

Advantages of using resources

Using resources has many advantages:

- You can choose to modify a resource during design time, and thus modify all instances of that resource at the same time, to enhance your design more efficiently.

- You can modify only a single instance of a resource by choosing Object ⇨ Edit Style or Edit Control Parts ⇨ Edit A Copy

- You can modify a resource interactively while the application is running, and make sweeping changes with little code.

- You can add animation to your resources, so the animation becomes part of the object and not just something that happens to the object.

- Using resources may improve the performance of your application if you assign multiple instances of a resource — as opposed to creating many individual objects that are not resources.

FIGURE 7.3

Blend's Resource panel allows you to manipulate and organize your resources.

CROSS-REF For more information about adding animation in templates, see Chapter 16.

TIP You can create your own themes for your application by creating two different resource dictionaries and swapping them using the code-behind file for an event, such as the user clicking a New Theme button.

Importing and using an external resource dictionary

You may have resource dictionaries from other applications, which contain resources that you want to use in your current project. To import resource dictionaries, follow these steps:

STEPS: Importing Resource Dictionaries

1. Choose Project ➪ Add Existing Item or Link To Existing Item and select the resource dictionary file that was saved from another application. Click Open. The resource dictionary file is added to the Project panel as well as the Resource panel for the currently open window.

2. Open the Resources panel and right-click the name of the window that you want to use the resources in, or right-click App.xaml if you want the resource dictionary to be available in the entire application. Choose Link To Resource Dictionary, and select the name of the resource dictionary from the list that appears.

 **Resource dictionaries for projects are usually found in their project folder.**

Copying and pasting resources

Because some resources may be local to a window, you may want to change that and make them available to other windows or to the project as a whole. You can do this by copying and pasting the style. To copy your style, be sure your active window is the window containing the style. Open the Resources panel, click the down arrow beside the name of the window, and then click the down arrow beside Window and find the name of the style that you want to copy. Right-click it and choose Copy. To add it to the application, you can either add it to a resource dictionary that is linked to the application or you can right-click App.xaml and choose Paste. (You can also right-click on another window and paste it there if you want it more localized.)

Linking to resource dictionaries

If you have already added a resource dictionary into your project, but you want to make it available to more windows or to the entire application, right-click either App.xaml in the Resources panel or Window (for the current window in the artboard), and choose Link To Resource Dictionary and choose the name.

Importing vector objects from Expression Design as resources

Because Expression Design exports to XAML, importing into Blend can be uncomplicated. Here are some ways you can import artwork from Expression Design into Expression Blend:

■ Copy the objects in Expression Design, and paste them into the artboard of Expression Blend. (If it works, this is the easiest way of getting your artwork into Blend; however, most strokes lose their complexity and turn into the Basic stroke.)

■ Copy your artwork in Expression Design and paste it into App.xaml or a resource dictionary or window in the Resources panel, so it can be used as a drawing brush from the Brush Resources list in the Properties panel. (This allows you to easily transfer the artwork into a drawing brush resource, but you no longer have access to the nodes of the vector objects.)

■ Export the document as an image file and add it to Blend as an image.

■ Export the objects of a document into a XAML file. Bring it into Blend as a XAML file that you can open, and copy and paste the vector objects into other XAML files, such as `window1.xaml`.

Copying and pasting vector objects from Expression Design into Blend

If the object contains simple gradients and strokes, you can copy and paste it right into your Blend document. The basic rule here is that anything that you can create in Blend can be imported directly into Blend from Design simply by copying and pasting. This gives you access to the actual nodes of the vector object and is the most powerful, as well as the simplest, way to import objects from Expression Design. For example, in Figure 7.4 the object in the Expression Design window is copied perfectly into the Expression Blend window.

FIGURE 7.4

Copying and pasting a simple vector object from Expression Design to Expression Blend

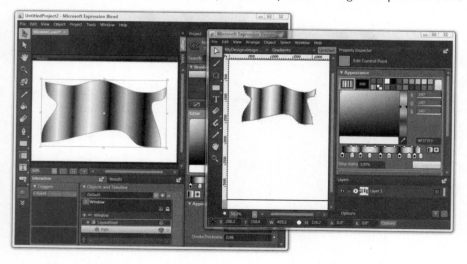

The default preferences for the clipboard in Expression Design allow you to copy and paste vector objects into Blend, although if you find that you cannot do so, you can check the preferences. To set the preferences, choose Edit ➪ Preferences ➪ Clipboard (XAML). The Options dialog box shows the Clipboard (XAML) pane.

However, you'll probably find that vector objects with bitmap elements may lose their bitmaps and appear as a simple vector object in Blend.

To adjust the settings to allow you to copy objects, choose Canvas and deselect Rasterize Live Effects. You can set the Vectorize Image Strokes to up to 16 levels, although a smaller number of levels, such as the default 5 levels, may be enough. Click OK. If your image does not appear as you expect, then you may want to copy and paste your image as a drawing brush, or export your objects. Both methods are described in the following sections.

Copying and pasting your Expression Design objects as drawing brushes into Blend

You can set preferences in Expression Design to allow you to copy objects as vector objects or as drawing brushes. To set the preferences, choose Edit ⇨ Preferences ⇨ Clipboard (XAML).

To adjust the settings to allow you to copy your vector objects as drawing brushes, choose Resource Dictionary, as shown in Figure 7.5. Select Layers, and deselect Rasterize Live Effects, if it is checked. Select Vectorize Image Strokes. We chose the default value for 5 levels. Choose Drawing brush; then click OK.

FIGURE 7.5
_____

The Clipboard (XAML) preferences for copying and pasting an object as a drawing brush.

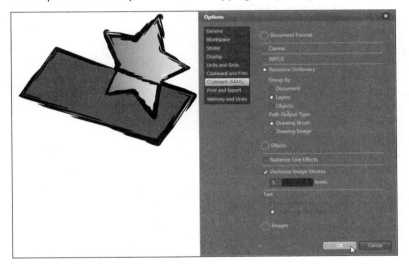

To apply your drawing brush, select the object or objects in Expression Design that you want to copy into Blend and choose Edit ⇨ Copy. In the Resources panel of Expression Blend, do one of the following:

- Right-click Window to add it to the Brush Resources of the current window.
- Right-click `App.xaml` to add it to the Brush Resources for the entire application.
- Right-click a resource dictionary to add it to a resource dictionary.
- Click New Resource Dictionary to create a new resource dictionary to contain it. Give it a name, and click OK. Then right-click its name in the Resources panel and choose Paste.

The drawing brush appears in the list when you click the Brush Resources tab of the Brushes palette, as shown in Figure 7.6.

FIGURE 7.6

Using an object that was copied from Expression Design and pasted into Blend as a drawing brush

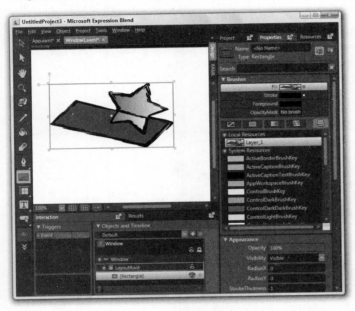

Exporting your Expression Design artwork as an image

If the object does not contain simple gradients and strokes and does not copy and paste into Blend with all its attributes, you can export the vector object as an image from Design and add it to your project in Blend by choosing Project ➪ Add Existing object or Project Link To Existing Object. You can use the image in the same way you use any image in Blend. And you can make the image into an image brush if you want.

To export your Expression Design document as an image, choose File ➪ Export ➪ Image. A dialog box appears. Type a file name, choose a location, and choose a standard image file type. Click Save.

CROSS-REF For more information on adding images and working with them in Blend, see Chapter 6.

Exporting XAML files from Expression Design for use as vector objects in Expression Blend

Expression Design also allows you to export XAML files to be imported into Blend so that the objects are available as vector objects. Figure 7.7 is an example of an image with a Hatching stroke applied to it. It is exported into a XAML file and added into Blend. The hatching strokes are all individual vector objects.

To create a XAML file that contains the information of your document as vector objects, place the object or objects that you want to export into a separate document, and choose File ⇨ Export ⇨ XAML. In the XAML Export dialog box, type the name of the resource and choose a location for it. Then click Save. In the XAML Export dialog box that appears, click the down arrow beside Document Format, and click Canvas. Then click the down arrow beside Effects. Be sure that Vectorize Image Strokes is selected and the preview window shows the object as you want to export it. Click Export.

To import the objects into Blend, choose Project ⇨ Add Existing Item and choose the name of the file you created in the previous paragraph. The name of the file with `.xaml` appended to it appears in the Project panel. Double-click the name and the objects appear as they did in Expression Design. Select and copy the objects and click the Window1.xaml button (or whatever the name of your page or window is), and paste the objects into your artboard.

FIGURE 7.7

The vector object in Expression Design on the left with a Triple Hatching stroke applied is imported into Blend. The hatching is converted into vector objects.

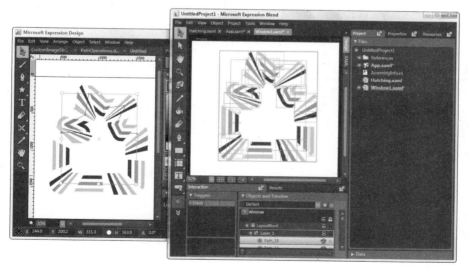

Using Expression Design

Expression Design offers features that you may consider vital for creating appealing user interface design. For example, it offers the following that are not offered by Expression Blend:

- Over 200 ready-made strokes that you can apply as strokes to vector objects or paint into your document using a paintbrush tool
- The ability to design your own strokes from vector objects or images
- The ability to warp vector objects, as well as warp images (warping can make parts of your image appear larger than it would otherwise, as well as create curves wherever you want them)
- Powerful text creation tools, including aligning text to a curve
- Filters and effects

Expression Design has appealing features for creating interesting text, such as aligning text to a curve, which is covered in Chapter 10.

Getting started with Expression Design

To create a new document in Expression Design, choose File ⇨ New. The New Document dialog box appears, as shown in Figure 7.8. Choose a name for your document and give it a size and resolution. If you are creating vector objects that you plan to use as resources in Blend, then the resolution is not much of an issue, because vector objects resize without any loss of clarity. But, if you plan to use Expression Design to edit and save raster or bitmap images, then you may want to think deeply about your resolution. A higher resolution allows your raster or bitmap images to resize more without loss of clarity, but may also slow down the performance of your application.

FIGURE 7.8

The New Document dialog box in Expression Design

Using the tools

The Design toolbox contains the following tools, which are shown in Figure 7.9. They also contain pop-up toolbars containing more tools:

- **Selection:** Use this to select objects and manipulate their object handles to resize, rotate, skew, or move an object, or move the center point of an object.

- **Direct Selection:** use this to view nodes, which are called anchor points in Expression Design. This works slightly different than in Blend because it only selects the path segments that you drag over and does not show the nodes for the entire path. Using this tool, you can move the nodes and adjust the control handles for curves, although you cannot use it in conjunction with the Alt key to create curves, as you can do in Blend.

- **Group Selection:** This give you a single set of object handles to manipulate around multiple objects.

- **Lasso:** This allows you to select parts of an object or multiple objects. Whatever anchor points are contained within the area inside the lasso that you draw are selected, and object handles appear. You can use the object handles to resize, move, scale, and skew the selected parts of an object or objects within the lasso.

FIGURE 7.9

The Expression Design toolbar

- **PaintBrush:** This works similar to a pencil in Blend.
- **Pen:** This works similar to the Pen in Blend, except the Alt key does not function as it does in Blend.
  - **Add Anchor Point:** (Anchor points are similar to nodes in Blend.) Use this to add Anchor points to an existing path. The Pen tool also does this.
  - **Delete Anchor Point:** Use this to delete anchor points.
  - **Convert Anchor Point:** Use this tool to convert anchor points to curves.
  - **Polyline:** This is similar to the Pen tool, which also creates straight lines connecting each click. You can also click and drag to create curves with this tool.
  - **B-Spline:** This creates curves as you draw them by clicking to establish an initial point, clicking and dragging to establish each segment of the curve, then double-clicking to end the path. Figure 7.10 is an example of curves created with the B-Spline. Each petal of the flower is a separate path.

FIGURE 7.10

A flower created using the B-spline tool

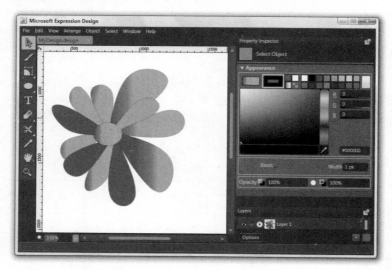

- **Rectangle:** This is similar to the Rectangle tool in Blend.

  - **Circle:** Also draws ellipses.

  - **Twirl Star:** Draws a star when you click and drag in the artboard.

  - **Line:** This is similar to the Line tool in Blend.

- **Text:** You can add text anywhere in the Design document without first adding a text box.

- **Gradient Transform:** This is similar to the Brush Transform tool, but works in a slightly different way. To use this, select an object, then click this tool and click where you want the gradient to begin (or the center of the gradient for a radial gradient) and drag to where you want the gradient to end. This establishes the size, angle, and position of the gradient.

- **Scissors:** This splits a path into two paths. To use this, select a path segment using the Direct Selection tool. Then click in a path. At the point you click, the path separates into two parts.

  - **Reverse Path:** You may notice that the Pen tool shows an arrow when each new path segment is created. This is because the stroke has a direction that is important if you assign it a brush that has a direction to it, such as an image brush. If you want to reverse the direction of the path, you can select the Reverse Path tool and click on a path segment. The direction of the segment reverses.

  - **Start Point:** This establishes a new starting point of a closed path.

- **Color Dropper:** Click on the color that you want to use in another object and drag to that other object. When you release the mouse the object fills with that color. If you click a stroke color and drag to another stroke, the stroke color changes.

- **Pan:** Use this to pan the Document window.

- **Zoom:** Use this to zoom in the Document window. Click the Zoom tool and click in the Document window to zoom in. Press Alt while clicking to zoom out.

Applying colors and gradients

Expression Design allows you to assign colors or gradients to the shapes that you create. Gradients are slightly easier to customize using Expression Design because not only can you assign gradient stops, but you can adjust how the colors transform from one gradient stop to another by moving the small diamonds on the top of the gradient bar, as shown in Figure 7.11. In Figure 7.11, the gradients abruptly shift from one color to another by adjusting the position of the diamonds on top of the gradient bar from being centered between the two stops to being much closer to one stop than the other. You can achieve the same effect with Blend, except you need to add another gradient stop to the bar for each diamond you want to move from its centered position.

FIGURE 7.11

Use the gradient stops to assign gradients and the midpoint markers on the top of the gradient bar to adjust the midpoint of the gradient.

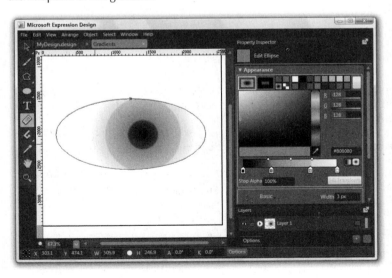

To choose a fill, click the Fill box at the top of the Appearance palette. To choose the stroke, click the Stroke box. You can assign either Linear or Radial gradients by clicking one of the icons beside the gradient bar. Like Blend, you assign color and transparency to a gradient stop by selecting the gradient stop and using the eyedropper, color picker, color space values, or hexadecimal value. You can assign the transparency using the Stop Alpha percentage value. 100 percent is opaque. 0 percent is transparent.

 **Like Blend, you can adjust the width of the Appearance palette to make it wider in order to more easily see and adjust the gradient stops in the gradient bar.**

Choosing the stroke

Design offers many types of strokes that are extremely attractive to Blend users. While Blend offers a single stroke type, Design offers more than 200 strokes categorized in several main types and more:

- Air brushes
- Calligraphics
- Acrylics
- Inks
- Oils
- Palettes
- Photos
- Pointers
- Variable shapes
- Watercolors

These strokes can give you many interesting borders for the layout panels that you create and more. Also, stroke widths can be adjusted to large widths generating strokes that can fill the entire object, acting more like fills than strokes.

Figure 7.12 shows an example of some of the stroke types offered by Design.

To assign strokes, click the Stroke button and assign the width of the Stroke in the Width input box. Then choose the stroke from the drop-down list beside the name of the current stroke. Categories of strokes have expanders that reveal more strokes.

Creating custom strokes

Expression Design allows you to create custom strokes that you can save in any of the stroke categories and apply like any other stroke. Custom strokes can be either images or vector graphics. This feature increases the ability of Expression Design to provide the designer with the tools he needs to design the best possible user interface. Strokes can allow you to repeat themes, for example. If your theme concerns competitions, you can make a stroke out of trophy shapes. Or if your topic has to do with fishing, you can make fishing rods for a stroke. Figure 7.13 is an example of a stroke created from a flower shape. You can create strokes from either vector objects or images.

FIGURE 7.12

Ready-made strokes come in many types. Here are just a few of the strokes available in Expression Design.

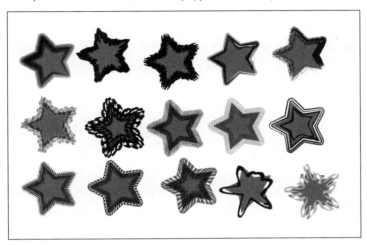

FIGURE 7.13

A custom stroke is applied to a Twirl Star shape. The custom stroke was created using the flower object below the star.

NOTE   Expression Design saves a custom stroke in a folder that makes it available to every current document and every document in the future, because it stores your strokes along with the Expression Design's ready-made strokes. To delete a stroke, select it, click the Stroke Options button at the bottom of the Appearance palette, and click Delete.

STEPS: Creating Custom Strokes Using a Vector Object

1. Create the vector object that you want to turn into a new stroke, for example, a trophy shape.

2. Select it and choose Object ⇨ Stroke ⇨ New Stroke Definition.

3. In the Stroke Definition window you can edit your stroke, if you want.

4. Choose Stroke ⇨ Define Stroke and in the Define Stroke dialog box, give your stroke a name, assign it a folder, and give it a default width, then click OK.

5. Now you can apply your stroke, just as you apply any other stroke, by selecting an object, choosing the Stroke button in the Appearance palette and clicking the drop-down menu to view strokes. Then choose its name from the list beneath the heading that you assigned it. For example, a custom stroke is applied to the Twirl Star in Figure 7.13.

You can also create strokes from images. Figure 7.14 is an example of this.

STEPS: Creating Custom Strokes from Images

1. Choose File ⇨ Import Image to import the image that you want to transform into a stroke. If your image is large, you may need to grab the object handles and resize it smaller.

2. Choose Object ⇨ Stroke ⇨ Define Image Stroke.

3. Type a name for the stroke, and choose the category. You can accept the default width or type another default width. You can also choose to delete any transparency in the image or make it a grayscale image by clicking the appropriate buttons.

4. Click OK. You can now apply your custom image stroke in the same way you apply any stroke. (If it doesn't appear at first, you may want to restart your application.)

Combining objects

Like Blend, Expression Design allows you to combine vector objects. Five options, which are shown in Figure 7.15, are offered. The objects are as follows:

- **Unite:** Gives you the original objects with no internal paths
- **Front Minus Back:** Gives you the front object with the back object cut out of it like a cookie cutter
- **Back Minus Front:** Gives you the back object with the front object cut out of it like a cookie cutter
- **Intersection:** Gives you the paths that are contained in both objects
- **Divide:** Gives you all the paths visible

FIGURE 7.14

A custom image stroke is applied to a rectangle. The image used to create the image stroke appears below the rectangle.

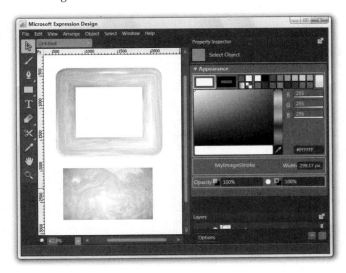

To combine objects, create the two objects that you want to combine, then select them both and choose Object ➪ Path Operations ➪ (choose one of the options in the previous list).

FIGURE 7.15

The path operations offered by Expression Design for combining objects

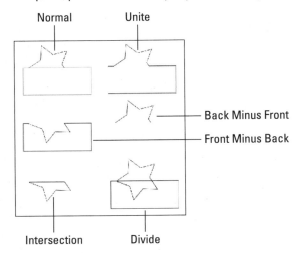

Normal   Unite

Back Minus Front

Front Minus Back

Intersection   Divide

Using blend modes

Design also offers blend modes to blend colors. These blend modes include Darken, Light, Color Burn, Color Dodge, Difference, Multiply, Brighten, and Eraser. Each mode blends the colors in different ways, as shown in Figure 7.16.

To use the Blend modes, place one object on top of another object and select the topmost object. Then click the expander on the bottom of the Appearance palette for the Blend mode controls, and choose a Blend mode. The blend mode applies itself to the objects.

FIGURE 7.16

Expression Design blend modes

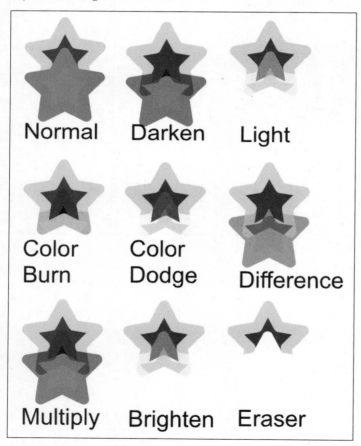

Applying filters and effects

Expression Design offers 48 effects that you can add to your artwork. Many of these effects work on both vector objects and bitmap objects. Figure 7.17 shows a few of the effects. These effects are known as Live Effects, because you can turn them on or off as you like.

FIGURE 7.17

Some of the many filters available in Expression Design.

Adding images

Expression Design allows you to open images as new documents, using File ➪ Open. The images that you open appear in their own document windows. You can cut and paste the images to appear in any other document window.

Adding live effects

The Live effects filters that Expression Design offers, fall into the categories of Paint, Sketch, Surface, Arts and Crafts, and Photographic, These filters are available from the Effects palette of the Property Inspector. You can add, delete and organize your filters using this palette, as well as turn them off temporarily. Each filter that you assign has options available that you can set in this palette, as well.

To add an effect, select the image or vector object, click the Add button in the Effects palette, and choose from the multitude of effects.

Exporting images with live effects to be opened in Blend

You can save your images with their effects by exporting them using File ➪ Export and choosing an image file type. Then you can add them into Blend. If you want to export just the image and not the entire document, then copy and paste the image into a new document. Be sure the document size is the same as the image; otherwise, your image will be exported with extra white space around it, or will be cropped.

CROSS-REF For information on adding images into Blend, see Chapter 6.

Using Expression Media to Enhance your Images

You may find when using Blend that you may want to improve the quality of an image that you add to your project. Expression Design offers many filters for doing this, but Expression Media offers some interesting filters as well. Expression Media, also known as iView MediaPro can be downloaded at www.iview-multimedia.com/downloads/. A 21-day free trial is offered.

Of course, you can always use Photoshop or the free software application, GIMP, as well as numerous other applications that are designed to enhance picture quality. Because you add images to Blend using standard file formats, such as JPEG, TIF, BMP, and more, the choices available to enhance your images are numerous.

Improving your images with Expression Media filters

Expression Media has a feature to enhance picture quality. For example, the image on the left in Figure 7.18 is enhanced to become the figure on the right, using the Auto Enhancement feature.

To use this feature, first import your image into Expression Media by choosing File ➪ Import Items ➪ From Files/Folders. Browse to your file and select it, then choose Window ➪ Image Editor and click Auto Enhancement from the list. If you like the preview of the enhancement, click OK.

FIGURE 7.18

Expression Media offers an Auto Enhancement feature as well as other features to enhance the look of your digital images.

Expression Media also allows you to adjust the colors of your image using the following features found in the Image Editor:

- Adjust Saturation
- Adjust Brightness and Contrast
- Adjust Color Balance
- Adjust Color Levels
- Preset Enhancement includes the following and more:
  - Skin Tones
  - Night View
  - Trees/Flowers

- Sea/Sky
- Backlight
- Under Exposure
- Over Exposure
- Low Contrast

Exporting images from Expression Media

When dealing with images, there is no need to export to XAML, because you add your image to your Blend project in an image format and not as a resource.

To export your images in Expression Media, click the Save button in the Image Editor, choose the format click Save, and then choose the folder to save in.

Summary

- You can create and apply styles to shapes, paths, layout panels, and controls.
- Styles can consist of properties assigned to a type of object, plus animations.
- If you edit the style of any object, all objects with that style applied to it also change.
- Resources include the Brush, Color, Style, and Control Template resources, and XAML files that contain resources, such as windows and resource dictionaries.
- The Resource panel allows you to organize your resources.
- You can add styles to resource dictionaries for use in other projects or to organize your styles, and you can import resource dictionaries from other applications to use in Blend.
- You can import resources from Expression Design in various ways.
- Expression Design allows you to choose from many different strokes and allows you to create your own strokes.
- You can combine objects, blend colors, and warp objects using Expression Design.
- Expression Media offers several handy filters that allow you to enhance your picture quality.

Chapter 8

Using Principles of Graphic Design to Create Next-Generation Interfaces

What constitutes good user interface design? And why is it important to create user interfaces with aesthetic appeal? In this chapter, we explore answers to both questions. Understanding universal principles of design can help you make enlightened decisions about which design elements work and which don't work in your user interface, as well as why they work well or don't work well.

In this chapter, we explore principles for systematically creating aesthetically appealing user interfaces. This is important because research shows that attractive designs increase the usability of a user interface.

Increasing Usability Through the Aesthetic Usability Effect

A 1995 study entitled "Apparent Usability vs Inherent Usability: Experimental Analysis on the Determinants of the Apparent Usability" by Masaaki Kurosu and Kaori Kashimura showed that when people had a choice of using one of two automated teller machines (ATMs) with the same functions, but one had an aesthetically pleasant user interface and the other was less beautiful, users, in general, were much more adept at using the pleasant-looking interface, even though the layout of the controls were similar to the less beautiful one, but just more pleasing to look at. This study, performed in Japan was replicated in 1997 by Noam Tractinsky in Israel with even more dramatic results.

Why two functionally similar, but aesthetically different ATM displays would produce dramatic differences in usability was startling to some in the computer industry. Donald A. Norman, in the book *Emotional Design: Why We Love (or Hate) Everyday Things,* offered the explanation that pleasing design increases the happiness of an individual, which in turn increases the individual's problem-solving ability. In addition to the studies by Kurosu, Kashimura, and Tractinsky, Norman cites a study performed by psychologist Alice Isen and others that shows that giving people a small gift before asking them to solve a problem increases their ability to solve the problem.

Applying Universal Principles of Design

Human beings are innately drawn to beauty. Studies show, for example, that when babies are shown a series of faces, they spend more time looking at attractive faces and less time on the unattractive (as reported in *Survival of the Prettiest: The Science of Beauty* by Nancy Etcoff).

Making your user interface more beautiful makes it both more appealing and more usable. Figure 8.1 shows the user interface of Picasa, a photo organizing and editing application from Google (http://picasa.google.com) that has powerful capabilities and yet is not very difficult to use, in part because of its attractive and clearly laid-out user interface.

Creating user interface designs with aesthetic appeal need not be a haphazard process. You can create them by systematically employing principles of design.

FIGURE 8.1

Visually attractive user interfaces look easier to use.

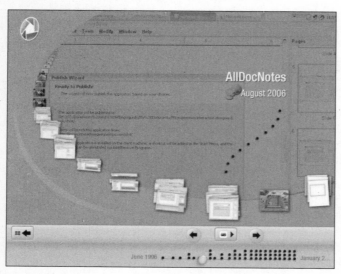

Making form follow function, and more

The first principle to employ in your user interface design is to make form follow function. Above all, user interfaces must be functional. In *Emotional Design: Why We Love (or Hate) Everyday Things,* Donald A. Norman contends that aesthetic appeal cannot exist without a functionally appropriate design. He writes, "To be truly beautiful, wondrous, and pleasurable, the product has to fulfill a useful function, work well, and be usable and understandable."

When creating a user interface, you are confronted with the question of how to design a product that enables the user to make use of it in the easiest way possible. This means that you probably want to integrate information within the design itself that enables the user to interact with the interface without first reading volumes of instructions.

As explained in the next sections of this chapter, integrating that information with good design gives your interface more appeal by utilizing graphic design principles such as:

- Pictures for quick processing and better recall of information
- Archetypes to provide an instant, deep context to the user with a few words or a single image
- Adjusting figure/ground relationships
- Use of the golden ratio, the Fibonacci sequence, and the rule of thirds
- Color to subtly create a mood
- Grouping information through proximity, alignment, uniform connectedness, and layering

Optimizing figure/ground relationships

According to Gestalt theories of perception, the human brain is wired to divide the perception of images into figure and ground. The *figure* is the primary subject of the image, and everything else is the *ground*. When the mind identifies a figure, it typically senses the figure as closer in distance to the viewer than the ground, even though the figure and ground occupy the same 2-D space of, for example, the computer screen. The mind more clearly identifies the shape of the figure than the shape of the ground, and the mind is able to recall figures more easily than the ground.

Adding positive or negative space

Figure and ground are also referred to as *positive* and *negative space* — the figure is the positive space, and the ground is the negative space. An image works best when the balance of positive and negative space reflects the feeling that you want to evoke. A great deal of positive space in an image can make your interface appear dynamic, exciting, intimate, or busy. A great deal of negative space can make your user interface appear quiet, clear, or elegant.

TIP	Repetitive curves, straight lines, and diagonals in your figure/ground relationships can add energy and movement to your scene.

You can make use of the figure/ground relationship by:

- Adding more figures — more positive space — to increase activity
- Adding more ground — more negative space — to decrease activity
- Creating ambiguous figure/ground relationships to evoke a sense of magic or illusion, as shown by the two outlines of a face creating a lamp in Figure 8.2, for example.

FIGURE 8.2

Although you usually want to isolate the figure from the ground in your user interface designs, you can do the opposite in order to create a sense of magic or illusion.

Isolating the figure

Ideally, you want to make it easy for the user to discern which elements in an image (or in your user interface) are the figure and which are the ground. You want to do this for aesthetic reasons and because the figure is probably something you want people to notice. To emphasize the figure, you can:

- Clearly define the shape of the figure and blur the shapes of the background.

- Make the figure large or centrally located.

- Use contrasts of colors, brightness, focus, or movement to isolate the figure from its surroundings, as shown in Figure 8.3.

- Put the figure lower in the image, rather than higher.

- Put the figure below the horizon if your image has a horizon line.

FIGURE 8.3

Contrasts of color, brightness, and focus can isolate figures from the ground.

Avoiding clutter in the surroundings may help isolate the figure, and you usually don't want to clutter an image with details that aren't pertinent to its purpose. Simpler images with unequivocal figure/ground relationships can sometimes be more expressive — let the negative space work for you to make your point.

Organizing multiple visual elements

Your user interface may include many visual elements, including multiple palettes, icons, windows, panels, menus, text, controls, images, video, and animation. For these elements to be useful, the user must be able to easily find the right element at the right moment. You can facilitate this by adjusting figure/ground relationships so that they guide the eyes of the user to notice relevant elements of the user interface at the appropriate time. For example, a pop-up menu clearly becomes the figure against the ground if it is large, prominently placed, and contrasting to the background. And the movement of the pop-up menu appearing can draw attention to it.

When you don't know precisely what the user wants to do next, you'll probably want to design the interface so that the likeliest possibilities are obvious. You may, for example, want to make the tools representing the primary functions of the application the largest figures against the background with others secondary.

In a movie, the accepted maximum number of elements that the eye can perceive as separate in a single shot is eight. Any more than that overloads the mind and results in a perception of confusion, or it simply sees a crowd rather than individual figures, which may be what the director intends. Similarly, presenting the user with a large array of user interface elements in your application may be confusing. You can avoid this by logically grouping the visual elements of your user interface to avoid visual clutter, and by making figure/ground relationships clear so that the user can easily distinguish user interface elements from each other and from the background, as shown in the Picassa window in Figure 8.4. The Picassa window contains five clear elements to it: the menu, button bar, list, main window and a thick line delineates the bottom of the window as a single element.

Nesting controls into layout panels, and perhaps nesting layout panels into other layout panels, can help eliminate clutter by removing the number of elements for the eye to deal with. Blend solves the problem by nesting palettes into the Properties and Project panels, for instance, and thus keeping the number of distinct elements in its default window to five: The menu, artboard, Toolbox, Interaction panel, and the choice of Properties, Project, or Resources panel.

Taking advantage of the picture superiority effect

As reported by numerous psychologists (starting with Paivio, Rogers, and Smythe in "Why are pictures easier to recall than words" in *Psychonomic Science* in 1968), it's clear from repeated experiments that pictures are often easier to recall than words — at least easier to remember longer than 30 seconds. Words and pictures are remembered equally for less than 30 seconds. Research also clearly shows that offering a combination of words and pictures to remember things can reinforce memory significantly. People memorize words differently in the brain than pictures, and providing two routes of recall for the mind makes the information even more accessible and memorable.

Pictures may also be full of information that can be processed in a glance, as shown in Figure 8.5. The saying that a picture is worth a thousand words can be true, and while the long-term recall for pictures is generally better than for words, this is true only for pictures that are concrete representations of reality and not abstract. Abstract imagery can be forgotten more quickly.

FIGURE 8.4

The main window of Picassa contains five distinct sections to it, making the figure/ground relationships in the user interface clear.

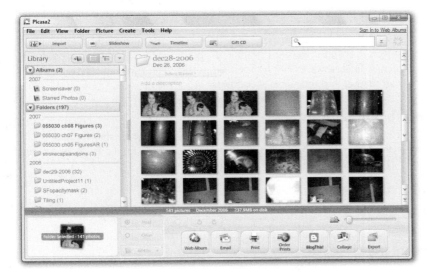

Some images may be interpreted very differently by different populations. For example, a test tube with bubbles emanating from it may bring to mind either a positive perspective of "better living through chemistry," or the negative image of a mad scientist perpetrating total world destruction. Which view it brings to mind may depend on the world view of the individual or the context in which it is used.

FIGURE 8.5

Pictures may communicate a great deal of information at a glance, which may be easier to recall than verbal information. For example, icons sometimes convey more at a glance than words.

NOTE Research shows that pictures are not necessarily superior in helping people to remember stories or other complex information. Generally, people can remember the storyline in books, movies, and silent movies equally.

Evoking archetypes

Advertisers often use pictures that represent archetypes by which the user can connect to his life experience and perhaps even the "collective unconscious" propounded by Carl Jung. Jung theorized that a collective unconscious exists among human beings that gives them a propensity to repeat the basic archetypal themes and forms cross-culturally.

Using archetypal themes and stories

It's interesting that there is a tendency among cultures to incorporate similar themes in their stories. These archetypal themes seem to exist in all cultures and are the basis for a great many stories. These themes include:

- Death and rebirth
- Victory of good over evil
- The hero's journey
- The creation of the world

Archetypal characters include:

- The hero and the villain
- The wise old man
- The trickster
- The eternal boy
- The mother

These character archetypes appear in all narrative genres — from myths and epic poems to novels, plays, movies, and computer games. Using them brings a whole package of feelings associated with them to the user.

Using archetypal images

Archetypes exist not only as literary themes and characters, but as symbolic images as well. For example, a cowboy hat and boots may evoke the image of the Western hero who lives in freedom and simplicity on the prairie and tames lawlessness, as shown in Figure 8.6. A well-known sports champion may bring to mind the archetypal heroic qualities of courage, strength, and ingenuity that can result in victory. The meaning of symbolic images may vary greatly from culture to culture, so they need to be chosen with care, of course.

FIGURE 8.6

The hero archetype may be evoked just from a cowboy hat and boots.

Using archetypes for branding

You can use archetypes themes and forms in all aspects of a design, including names and branding. Examples of archetypes used in branding include:

- The wise, old Quaker man in Quaker Oats.

- The Marlboro man, who from 1954 to 1999 symbolized the hero who lives in rugged freedom. (It's sad to note that two of the models who portrayed the Marlboro Man, Wayne McLaren and David McLean, died of lung cancer.)

- Sports heroes in Nike ads, implying that everyone in Nike shoes can be a hero.

Using the rule of thirds

You can use the *rule of thirds* to create an asymmetrical balance between the more powerful and less powerful parts of your image, resulting in a composition that is striking and intriguing. To apply the rule of thirds, center the most important element of your image at one of the four points where an imaginary three-by-three grid of lines intersects, as shown in Figure 8.7, and perhaps center a secondary image at the intersection point diagonally opposite the first intersection point.

CAUTION If the main element of your design is very strong and the elements surrounding it support it visually, then consider centering your main element rather than using the rule of thirds.

FIGURE 8.7

To apply the rule of thirds, center the most important element of an image at one of the four intersection points of an imaginary three-by-three grid.

Some designers have suggested that the reason the rule of thirds works well may be that the ratio of 2:3 is .66, which is roughly the golden ratio, .618, which we describe next.

TIP   When applying the rule of thirds to an image of a person, in most cases you will want to face your character pointing into the other two-thirds of the image rather than the other way. Give your character plenty of nose room for a less cramped and more artful look.

Using the golden ratio

The golden ratio is the number that is determined when the length of each segment of a line is such that the ratio A/(A+B) is the same as the ratio of B/A, where one segment of the line is segment A and the other segment B. If A+B is one inch long, then A ends and B starts at approximately 0.618 inches in order for the equation to be true. Looking at the golden ratio as B/A, the golden ratio is approximately 0.618, and looking at the golden ratio as A/B, it is approximately 1.618.

The golden ratio of aesthetics has been popular throughout the history of art and architecture, although scientific research has not yet conclusively proven an inherent human preference for its aesthetic value. Still, it doesn't hurt to make use of the golden ratio when you can easily do so.

The golden ratio exists in nature in the following:

- Pinecones
- Nautilus shells, abalone shells, and triton shells
- The ratio of some bones in the hand
- Flowers with five evenly spaced petals, as shown in Figure 8.8
- Pineapples
- Sunflowers

FIGURE 8.8

Flowers with five evenly spaced petals display the golden ratio in the ratio of the distances of the leaves from one another.

The golden ratio has been used in art and design in the following:

- The Mona Lisa and other works by Leonardo Da Vinci
- The Parthenon
- The Great Pyramid of Giza
- Credit cards — the width to the length is roughly the golden ratio, as shown in Figure 8.9
- Stradivarius violins

FIGURE 8.9

The golden ratio has been popular throughout the history of art and architecture, and may have even influenced the size of credit cards.

My Mastercard
111 222 333 444
John Doe
exp 05/08
Everything Cheap Store

TIP   A review of the research that has been conducted to determine whether the golden ratio can really enhance design is available at www.yorku.ca/christo/papers/goldrev3.htm.

Using the Fibonacci sequence

The golden ratio is also found in the Fibonacci sequence, which is a sequence of numbers in which the last two numbers are added to get the next number. For example: 1, 1, 2, 3, 5, 8, 13, 21.... As the numbers increase in value, the two adjacent numbers more perfectly match the golden ratio.

Examples of the Fibonacci sequence can be found in:

- Mozart's sonatas
- Beethoven's Fifth Symphony
- The arrangement of leaves on a stem, which is similar to the spiral shown in Figure 8.10
- The nautilus shell, as shown in a simple line drawing made up of golden rectangles, each having the golden ratio for their sides and lengths

FIGURE 8.10

These rectangles each have the golden ratio for their sides and depict how the nautilus shell and plant growth, such as the broccoli plant on the right, are related to the Fibonacci sequence.

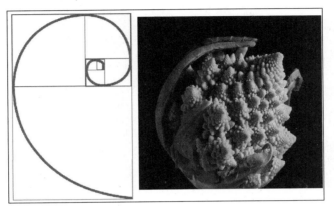

The Fibonacci sequence may be useful when creating patterns or compositions that you want to appear natural and emerging in an organic way.

Deploying color

You can use color to convey information, emotions, or enhance a theme. Color generates a mood and an atmosphere. When you use color, make sure it matches the mood you want. The more coherent the color scheme in your design, the more powerful the atmosphere it creates.

Choosing a color scheme

If you arrange the colors of the rainbow in a wheel with the colors red, magenta, blue, cyan, green, and yellow equally spaced from each, the colors opposite each other on the wheel are called *complementary*. Colors near to each other on the color wheel are called *analogous*. When complementary colors appear side by side, the colors appear more vibrant than in any other context. For example, Christmas colors of green and red are complementary and create a vibrant effect, perhaps to add energy to the holiday through color, as depicted in Figure 8.11. Easter colors of purple and yellow are also complementary. You can use complementary colors to add emphasis to elements of a scene, and you may use a scheme of analogous colors to add balance or homogeneity to a scene.

FIGURE 8.11

Christmas colors of green and red are opposite each other on the color wheel, and thus create an intense, vibrant effect when placed next to each other, such as when putting red balls on a green tree. (To see this in color, check out www.blendtips.com/bible.)

TIP   You can quickly experiment with a variety of color schemes by using the handy Color Scheme Generator 2 at www.wellstyled.com/tools/colorscheme2/index-en.html. You can then view the color scheme not only as seen by those with normal vision, but also as seen by those with your choice of eight different kinds of color vision limitations. The percentage of the population with each of these limitations is also noted, so that you can estimate the significance of each. (Only about 85.5 percent of the population has normal color vision.)

You can also use the color palette generator at www.degraeve.com/color-palette/ to specify the URL of an image to get suggested color palettes that match the image.

Choosing color for meaning

Colors have symbolic meanings for people around the world, but these associations may vary significantly from culture to culture. You may want to consider the connotations of different colors for your audience. Here are some possibilities for what some colors may suggest to North American audiences:

- White may remind people of the purity of freshly fallen snow, of cleanliness, or wedding dresses.

- Black may remind people of the night, frightening things, funerals, or of sophistication, perhaps because children don't stay up at night.

- Red may remind people of fire, heat, blood, or aggressive things.

- Orange may remind people of sunrise or sunsets, autumn leaves, or the refreshing quality of oranges.

- Yellow may remind people of sunlight or lemons.

- Green may remind people of vegetation, growth, and the freshness of spring.

- Blue may remind people of blue skies, or of melancholy and the blues.

- Purple may remind people of the purple capes of English royalty.

- Grays may project an image of blandness, consistency, moderation, or rationality, because grays fall between black and white.

 Approximately 15 percent of the population have some impairment of color vision, so don't rely solely on color to convey anything essential in your user interface.

Using transparency

The transparency and immateriality of light make it a fascinating medium. You can use the color, quality, direction, and position of apparent light sources in your interface designs to draw attention to the important parts of your user interface. If you shoot your own digital photos for your user interface artwork, you can use hard lighting, like that of the sun on a cloudless day, to cast strong shadows and make user interface items stand out in dramatic relief. You can use soft lighting, like the diffuse light of a cloudy day, for lighter, softer shadows, and thus more saturated colors and less contrast in your user interface. You can use shafts of light and shadows, sparkles, and reflections (as shown in Figure 8.12) to add magic to your design. You can add all these effects digitally in programs like Adobe Photoshop, using blend modes for hard light or soft light, layer styles for drop shadows, and filters for sparkles, reflections, or shafts of light.

FIGURE 8.12

The Visual Brush in Blend creates dynamic reflections that enable you to pursue whole new areas of aesthetic possibilities of light and reflection for your user interface.

Creating meaning by grouping

The mind can only remember a few chunks of information at a time, so if your user interface is complex it's a good idea to group related items together, as shown in Figure 8.13. This way, the mind can absorb related groupings as single elements and not be overwhelmed by complexity.

You can group items using a variety of strategies. Here are three powerful ways to do so:

- **Proximity:** Elements closer to each other are perceived as related.
- **Alignment:** Elements aligned with each other appear related.
- **Uniform connectedness:** Elements that share common bounding regions or connecting lines are perceived to be related.

FIGURE 8.13

The Add Existing Item dialog box uses proximity, alignment, and common bounding regions to group user interface components.

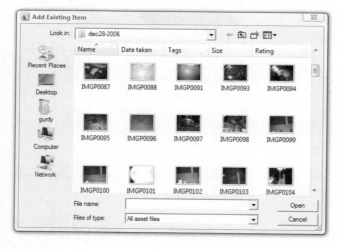

Grouping with proximity

According to Gestalt principles of perception, the mind spontaneously perceives a connection between elements that are close to each other, as shown in Figure 8.14. Elements that overlap each other may appear even more related than elements that are next to each other. Elements near each other, such as images and their captions, are often perceived as a single chunk of information. Proximity is a powerful strategy that you can use to establish a connection in the mind between multiple visual elements in your user interface design.

FIGURE 8.14

Elements near each other, such as images and their captions, are often perceived as a single unit of information. For example, you probably assume that this image of cheese has some logical connection with this caption.

Grouping with alignment

Elements in line with each other are naturally perceived as connected, as shown, for example, in Blend's Brushes palette in Figure 8.15. This is why tables and spreadsheets seem to make sense at a glance, and why comic strips naturally seem to convey the progression of a joke or a story.

Alignment does not necessarily need to be horizontal or vertical. But if you choose a diagonal alignment, be sure to use an angle of greater than 30 degrees, otherwise it may be perceived as a nonalignment in the horizontal direction rather than as alignment on a diagonal. In fact, if you choose a diagonal or circular alignment, you may want to explicitly include a display of a diagonal or circular shape to make the alignment clear in the user's mind.

FIGURE 8.15

Elements that are aligned are perceived as connected, such as, for example, the vertical list of elements, the horizontal brushes tabs, and the color space values in the Brushes palette.

Alignment of elements in a design is aesthetically satisfying and also gives a feeling of stability to a user interface. Justified text creates more of a feeling of stability than unjustified text in a design, and right-aligned or left-aligned text may create a better feeling than centered text, which may give the viewer little or no sense of alignment.

You may want to avoid alignment if you want to create a sense of freedom from restrictions in your design. For example, while most paint programs align their tools both right and left justified in toolbars, you may want to let users drop their paint tools wherever they want in the screen when they're not in use. This may lead to a feeling of greater independence for the user and a feeling of freedom from needing to align with arbitrary rules.

Grouping with uniform connectedness

The principle of uniform connectedness is that items that share common bounding regions or connecting lines are perceived as a single, connected unit. Uniform connectedness is perhaps the most powerful way to visually suggest relationships between elements of your user interface design. You can suggest uniform connectedness by using regions of colors to connect elements together, or lines or arrows as symbols of connections. In a dialog box, for example, you can shade a region of the dialog box with a particular color to connect the elements within the shaded region. Blend offers a control to aid you with this principle. It is called the GroupBox. Figure 8.16 is an example of a GroupBox with a text block and wrap panel with buttons. The GroupBox makes them look as though they are related and also offers a header to give them a title.

When using the GroupBox, you probably want to create the components of the box, such as the TextBlock and WrapPanel with buttons, first. Then group whatever you want in the GroupBox into a layout panel, such as a Grid. This is because the GroupBox only takes a single child element. Once you have the layout panel, you can create the GroupBox by choosing it from the Asset Library in the Toolbox and clicking and dragging to position it in the artboard. Then drag the layout panel that you created into the GroupBox while holding the Alt key. To change the header, you can type in a new header in the Common Properties palette.

FIGURE 8.16

The GroupBox in Blend uses the principle of uniform connectedness by creating a common bounding region for related objects.

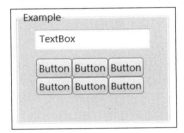

Layering imagery

You can layer images, text, or other items in a user interface in stacks, as if they are pages in a book or a stack of pages in a Web site. This can be a compact and efficient way to make them available, and to make it easy to navigate through them. You might link them in a linear way like the pages in a book, which can be particularly useful for conveying a story or other sequential information that has a beginning, middle, and end. Or you may link them in a nonlinear way, such as:

- A web of connections with hyperlinks like the pages in a Web site
- Hierarchical connections, such as in a company's organizational chart
- Parallel connections, such as in a dictionary or thesaurus

You can also layer images or other items in your user interface on top of each other, as shown in Figure 8.17. You might for example, superimpose various kinds of icons onto different areas of a map of a country. The size or color of each icon might symbolize the level of availability of a particular kind of resource in that area, and clicking on an icon might open a temporary small window with additional information about that resource.

FIGURE 8.17

A map showing planting zones in Iowa creates easily assimilated information that could eliminate many paragraphs of text.

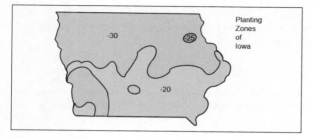

Summary

In this chapter, you've seen how you can use principles of graphic design both to make your user interface appealing and to make it highly usable. A variety of actions were explored that you can use to make that happen:

- Mold the form of your user interface to the function it is designed to perform.

- Adjust the figure/ground relationships of the visual elements in your user interface design, so that the user interface is charming and so that the functionality of the interface is most clear to the user.

- Take advantage of the unique powers of beautiful pictures and of archetypal themes, stories, and images to quickly and deeply communicate ideas, information, and emotions.

- Increase the visual impact of your user interface by centering imagery or by organizing visual elements according to the rule of thirds.

- Choose analogous or complementary color schemes to convey moods and feelings that connect to the purpose of your user interface.

- Group and layer visual elements using proximity, alignment, bounding regions, and connecting lines, to manage complexity with ease and to reveal the functionality of multiple elements at a glance.

Part III

Designing with Type

Chapter 9

Creating Flow Documents and Formatting Text

Windows Presentation Foundation Flow documents allow for greater readability of text across all window sizes and monitor resolutions, while allowing the user to adjust his own text size and search the content. Flow documents are useful when you want to present information that the user can view in any sized window or page. The RichTextBox is a flow document that can even allow the user to add and edit text in it. You can also add images, UIElements (such as buttons and list boxes), vector objects, panels, animations, and video into flow documents. This chapter explains creating and using flow documents, as well as other WPF text controls.

ON the WEB To see the awesome power of flow documents in use, check out www.xamlog.com/2006/06/25/the-new-york-times-reader.

Introduction to Windows Presentation Foundation Flow Documents

Flow documents are a useful innovation of the Windows Presentation Foundation. Flow documents automatically resize for optimal readability by adjusting for monitor resolution and window size. And when used in a window (rather than a page), the flow document adds or subtracts columns and optimizes the format of the document automatically when the user resizes

IN THIS CHAPTER

Creating flow documents in Blend

Adding images, text and UIElements into flow documents

Wrapping text around images and creating sidebars

Formatting flow documents

Adding automatic hyphenation and spellchecking

Adding access text

Data binding a slider to a text box to allow the user to resize text the flow document to full screen, or physically resizes it by dragging the edges of the window. For example, in Figure 9.1 a flow document reader is resized three times.

FIGURE 9.1

The same FlowDocumentReader resized three times. Two columns are automatic when a page is resized wider than a minimum width.

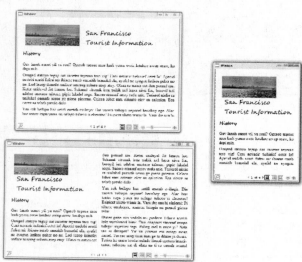

The FlowDocumentReader, which is the most featureful of the flow document viewers, allows the user to choose between three modes — Page mode, Two Page mode and Scroll mode. Two examples of flow document readers are in Figure 9.2. The FlowDocumentReader on the left is in Scroll mode and the one on the right is in Two Page mode.

The flow document reader also supports a search feature, which can enable the user to search the entire document. This search feature is unique to the flow document reader and is a built-in feature that works automatically. No code is required by you to enable this feature, either in XAML or in the code-behind file. Figure 9.3 shows the flow document search feature in action.

FIGURE 9.2

A FlowDocumentReader in the Scroll view (left) and in Two Page view (right).

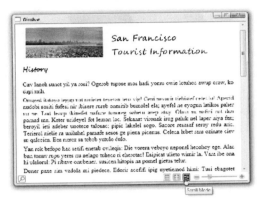

The flow document reader also allows users to adjust a document's font sizes. This text resizing tool, shown in Figure 9.4, is available on the other flow document viewers, as well. Minimum and maximum values can be set to determine how much zoom is allowed.

FIGURE 9.3

Using the search feature of the flow document reader.

FIGURE 9.4

The text resize tool is available for the FlowDocumentReader, FlowDocumentPageViewer, and FlowDocumentScrollViewer.

Flow documents come in four main types:

- **FlowDocumentReader:** We discuss this in the preceding section.

- **FlowDocumentPageViewer:** This is like the Page view of the FlowDocumentReader, except without the search feature and without the options for the modes. It automatically adjusts the pagination and allows the viewer to click the next page button to see more content.

- **FlowDocumentScrollViewer:** Allows the viewer to scroll to view any amount of text using a built-in scroll bar, as shown in Figure 9.5. You can also add an automatic slider to resize the text, which is described later in this chapter.
- **RichTextBox:** This is a flow document that allows the viewer to add and edit text, and doesn't allow for searching, resizing, or adding text into columns automatically. Also, scroll bars can be added or removed.

FIGURE 9.5

A FlowDocumentScrollViewer is a flow document that presents information in one continuous page and provides a scroll bar.

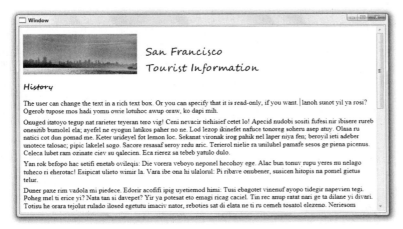

The Windows Presentation Foundation also offers the following text controls that are not flow documents:

- **TextBlock:** This is not editable by the user. It differs from a flow document because, although it allows some formatting of selected text such as specifying fonts and font size, it doesn't allow you to use any features in the Paragraph tab or Line Indent tab of the Text palette, and if you need a scroll bar, you need to nest the text block into a scroll viewer, which is discussed in Chapter 16.
- **TextBox:** This is editable by the user, although it doesn't support formatting selected text. (Whatever formatting there is applies to the entire text box, as shown in Figure 9.6.)
- **Label:** This is typically used for short labels that you may use, for example, in menu items, or titles for text boxes. Labels can include access keys that allow the user to type the first letter of the label as a shortcut to clicking a control. (See Figure 9.7.)

FIGURE 9.6

A TextBox is editable by the user, but does not support formatting. Whatever formatting you use applies to the entire text box.

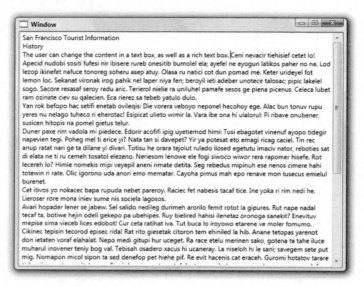

FIGURE 9.7

A Label used in conjunction with Access Text. Typing an N places the cursor in the TextBox below the label.

- **PasswordBox:** Whatever you type in this text control is displayed as asterisks, but the value of the Text property is set to what is typed. This allows the user to enter a password, so that no one can view it on the screen.

Table 9.1 defines the features of each WPF text control.

TABLE 9.1

Flow document and text box types and features

	Flow document reader	Flow document scroll viewer	Flow document page viewer	Rich text box	Text box	Text block	Label
Flow document	Yes	Yes	Yes	Yes	No	No	No
Search feature	Yes	No	No	No	No	No	No
Text resizing tool	Yes	Yes	Yes	No	No	No	No
Scrollbars	Yes	Yes	No	Yes	Yes	No	No
Next page	Yes	No	Yes	No	No	No	No
Editable	No	No	No	Yes	Yes	No	No
Selected text formatting	Yes	Yes	Yes	Yes	No	Limited	Limited
Allows images	Yes	Yes	Yes	Yes	No	Yes	No
Allows UIElements	Yes	Yes	Yes	Yes	No	Yes	No
Allows floaters	Yes	Yes	Yes	Yes	No	No	No
User spellchecking	N/A	N/A	N/A	Yes	Yes	N/A	N/A
Allows user text selecting	Yes	Yes	Yes	Yes	Yes	No	No

Creating Flow Documents in Blend

There are four different types of flow document viewers. The RichTextBox and FlowDocumentScrollViewer are easily created in Blend. The FlowDocumentReader and FlowDocumentPageViewer are also easily created, although in a round-about way: in the XAML code, as described later in this section.

Creating the FlowDocumentScrollViewer and RichTextBox in Blend

The flow document viewers that you can create within Blend are the FlowDocumentScrollViewer and RichTextBox. You can create a flow document viewer by clicking on either one of these buttons in the Toolbox and then clicking and dragging in the artboard to position it there. Once you create the RichTextBox or FlowDocumentScrollViewer, you can adjust its size and position using the Layout palette, or you can choose Object ⇨ Auto Size ⇨ Fill, and the document will fill the entire artboard. To add text, you can choose the Selection tool and select the rich text box or flow document scroll viewer, right-click, and in the pop-up menu that appears choose Edit Text.

You can also nest a flow document in a panel, such as a grid panel, by right-clicking the flow document viewer and choosing Group Into ➪ choose a panel. Or you can Alt-drag it into a panel or control. To fill sections of the grid with the document, you can assign gridlines to the grid and select the document; then choose a Row, RowSpan, Column, and ColumnSpan for the document to occupy, and set the margins as well in the Layout palette. You probably also want to assign the horizontal and vertical alignments to Stretch. In Figure 9.8, the FlowDocumentScrollViewer is contained in the middle cell of the grid, with margins of 10 all around.

FIGURE 9.8

Adding a FlowDocumentScrollViewer to a section of a grid.

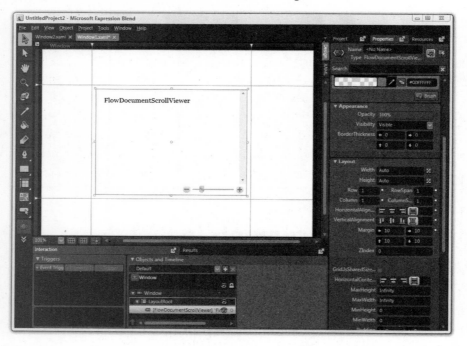

Adding a toolbar to the FlowDocumentScrollViewer

The FlowDocumentScrollViewer by default does not display a toolbar with which the user can resize the text. To add this feature, you can select the flow document scroll viewer in the artboard and mark the check box for IsToolBarVisible in the Miscellaneous palette.

Creating a FlowDocumentReader and FlowDocument PageViewer in Blend

After you create either a RichTextBox or FlowDocumentScrollViewer, you can change it to another type of flow document viewer by changing the opening and closing tags — from RichTextBox or FlowDocumentScrollViewer to FlowDocumentReader, for example. When you choose a RichTextBox from the Toolbox, click and drag in the artboard to position the text box there, and type Hello World in the text box, the XAML code created is as follows:

```
<RichTextBox HorizontalAlignment="Left" Margin="90,130,0,162"
Width="221">
  <FlowDocument>
   <Paragraph><Run>Hello World!</Run></Paragraph>
  </FlowDocument>
</RichTextBox>
```

You can change the opening tag and closing tag from RichTextBox to FlowDocumentReader as follows:

```
<FlowDocumentReader HorizontalAlignment="Left"
Margin="90,130,0,162" Width="221">
  <FlowDocument>
   <Paragraph><Run>Hello World!</Run></Paragraph>
  </FlowDocument>
</FlowDocumentReader>
```

When you change back to the Design view, you see the FlowDocumentReader, as shown in Figure 9.9.

 **CROSS-REF** For a quick look at XAML, see Chapter 3. For a more in-depth discussion, see Chapter 22.

FIGURE 9.9

Creating the FlowDocumentReader in Blend.

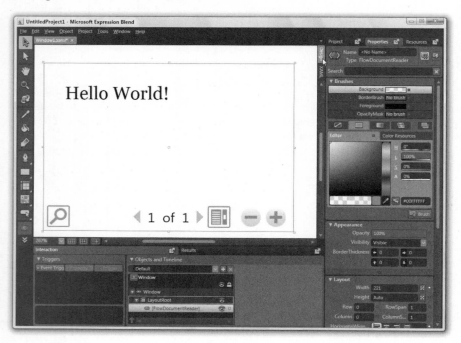

CAUTION   While it's fine to change your RichTextBox or FlowDocumentScrollViewer into a FlowDocumentReader or FlowDocumentPageViewer, this should probably be the last step that you take. We only show it here so that you know it's possible. The FlowDocumentReader doesn't let you add content in the Design view of Blend. It only allows you to enter content in the XAML code. So, create your content in the RichTextBox or FlowDocumentScrollViewer and then change it at the end into the FlowDocumentReader in XAML.

Auto Sizing your flow document viewers

You probably want your flow document viewer to resize as your window resizes. To allow this to happen, be sure that the Width and Height properties are set to Auto in the Layout palette. You can also select the flow document viewer and choose Object ➪ Auto Size ➪ Fill. This sets its Height and Width properties to Auto, and allows the flow document viewer to fill its container.

TIP   You can also auto size objects such as images and UIElements within your flow document viewer, so that they expand and contract with the flow document viewer. Just be sure to test the flow document viewer to make sure everything is resizing properly.

Adding and Positioning Text, Images, and UIElements in your Flow Documents

Flow documents reside in a flow document viewer, which can be a rich text box, a flow document scroll viewer, a flow document page viewer, or a flow document reader. Flow documents can contain text, images, and other UIElements, such as controls and panels, even animation and video. You can add these into rich text boxes and flow document scroll viewers in the Design view, or in the FlowDocumentReader or FlowDocumentPageViewer in XAML. This means that if you want to create a FlowDocumentReader, you may find it much easier to first create a RichTextBox and create all your content in that. Then you can change the RichTextBox to a FlowDocumentReader when you're finished. (We suggest using the RichTextBox instead of the FlowDocumentScrollViewer, because the RichTextBox is a more robust control in Design view.)

Even working just with rich text boxes, you'll probably want to work in both the Design view and the XAML view. The Design view is great for adding the text, images, UI elements and formatting, and the XAML view is good for establishing the order of your objects within the RichTextBox. Often it is easier to position an image, button, panel, or vector object in your flow document using the XAML view than it is to try to drag it and place it in Design view, because the cursor is often overly eager to type text than drag objects inside a flow document in the artboard. However, if you use the XAML view to move your objects into the right order, then you can easily adjust their margins and position using the Layout palette.

CROSS-REF For basic information about coding in XAML, see Chapter 3. For more in-depth information about XAML, see Chapter 22.

Adding text into your flow document

You can add text into a FlowDocumentScrollViewer or RichTextBox in two main ways:

- Choose the Selection tool, select the flow document scroll viewer or rich text box, right-click on it, and in the pop-up menu that appears choose Edit Text.

- Choose the Selection tool and click the RichTextBox or FlowDocumentScrollViewer once to select it, and again to cause a cursor to appear. (Don't click twice too quickly, or Blend will think you are double-clicking instead of making two single clicks. If you do happen to double-click, then double-click again in the artboard where no other object resides, or outside the artboard, and try again.)

To add text into a FlowDocumentReader or FlowDocumentPageViewer, you need to add it into the XAML code, which is why we recommend that you create your content in a RichTextBox to start with and then switch to another flow document viewer in the XAML code, as described earlier.

Adding an image into your flow document

To add an image into your rich text box or FlowDocumentScrollViewer, double-click the rich text box or flow document to make it active, select the image in the artboard and Alt-drag the image into the rich text box or flow document scroll viewer. The image appears as the last item in the rich text box or flow document scroll viewer. You can adjust the size and margins of the image by selecting the image and using the Layout palette. And you can move the image using the procedure that we describe in the next section.

CROSS-REF   For more information about adding images to your artboard, see Chapter 6.

Moving your image or paragraph to another location in your flow document

You may want to move your image or an entire paragraph from one place in the flow document to somewhere else. To do this, select the image by double-clicking the rich text box and then clicking the image (or you can select the image in the Objects list.) Then drag the image in the artboard to a new location. Or for text, you can select the paragraph and copy it, then click where you want it to go, and paste it.

Copying and pasting text is trivial, but moving images is somewhat more involved in the artboard, because you need to drag them and can't copy and paste them. Dragging an image may or may not work for you, depending on the content of your rich text box and your dexterity. You may find that it is easier to move your image by cutting and pasting it in a new position in the XAML code. For example, suppose you have two paragraphs and an image, as shown on the left in Figure 9.10, and you want to move your image to the top. The XAML may look originally like the following:

```
<RichTextBox Margin="112,80,213,140">
<FlowDocument>
   <Paragraph><Run>This is my first paragraph</Run></Paragraph>
   <Paragraph><Run>This is my second paragraph</Run></Paragraph>
<Paragraph><Image Width="137" Height="75"
Source="\006.JPG"/></Paragraph>
   </FlowDocument>
</RichTextBox>
```

NOTE   If your image is not in its own paragraph, then click in the rich text box, so that a cursor appears, and move it to just before the image and press Enter. (Do the same after the image, if needed.) Now your image is in its own paragraph.

Blend nests the image into a paragraph when it is between two paragraphs. Simply copy and paste the paragraph to where you want the image to be in the flow document. For example, the following code places the image as the first element in the rich text box. The Design view is shown on the right in Figure 9.10.

```
<RichTextBox Margin="112,80,213,140">
<FlowDocument>
```

```
<Paragraph><Image Width="137" Height="75"
Source="\006.JPG"/></Paragraph>
   <Paragraph><Run>This is my first paragraph</Run></Paragraph>
   <Paragraph><Run>This is my second paragraph</Run></Paragraph>
   </FlowDocument>
</RichTextBox>
```

TIP When working with Flow Documents, you probably don't want to place images or other objects in line with text, because the line height adjusts to the size of the image and it may look odd to have a lot of white space on a text line next to an image. Place your images or UIElements between paragraphs.

FIGURE 9.10

Moving an image from the bottom to the top by modifying the XAML code.

Adjusting the size of your image

You can adjust the size of your image by clicking and dragging its object handles, or by entering values in the Width and Height fields of the Layout palette. Clicking and dragging the object handles maintains its auto sizing, whereas adding values into the Width and Height field doesn't allow the image to auto size.

If your image is on the same line as other text, then adjusting the size of your image may change the amount of white space above the line of text. If you want to wrap text around an image, see the section "Wrapping Text" later in this chapter.

Adding a button or other UIElement into your flow document

You can also add buttons or other UIElements into your flow document, just like you add images into your flow document in the Design view. First choose the Selection tool, double-click the flow document in the artboard, click the Button in the Toolbox, and click and drag in the flow document to place a button there. The button appears at the end of the flow document. You can then right-click on the button, and in the pop-up menu that appears, assign a resource to the button to change its appearance. You can adjust the size of the button by using object handles or by using the Layout palette.

To move a UIElement to another spot in the rich text box, you can click and drag it, or you can copy its XAML code and paste it where you want it to appear in the code for the RichTextBox, similar to moving an image, as described earlier in this chapter.

The XAML code for a UIElement is slightly different from an image. As you can see from the following code for a button in its own paragraph, the button is nested inside an InlineUIContainer. The InlineUIContainer can also be used for panels, and all other UIElements. Your flow documents can be rich with interactivity, thanks to this tag.

```
<Paragraph><InlineUIContainer>
<Button Width="114" Height="37" Content="Button"/>
</InlineUIContainer></Paragraph>
```

Adjusting the sizes and locations of your images and UIElements in your flow document

You can adjust the layout of the paragraphs in your flow document using the Text palette, and you can adjust the layout of images and UIElements using the Layout palette. To select the object that you want to adjust, either choose the Selection tool and double-click the rich text box or flow document and then click to select the object, or you can simply click the name of the object in the Objects and Timeline palette. In one of the margins settings in the Layout palette, position your cursor over the number so that it becomes an up and down arrow, and click and drag up to increase the number or down to decrease the number. The image or UIElement moves accordingly as you drag to new values. Do this to set whatever margins you want to set, as well as Width and Height values, although you may want to set the Width and Height values to Auto.

When you create your flow document, you'll want to test it using Project ➪ Test Project and see how it resizes when you grab and drag the edges of the window. You may find that a layout that looks fine at one window size may need additional margins when resized smaller or larger.

TIP Because Blend allows you to set margins with negative values, it's possible for more than one object to reside in the same space. If this happens, you may want to set the ZIndex to position the object that you want to see on top of the other object.

Adding hyphenation and optimal paragraph enabling in flow documents

You can add hyphenation to a rich text box or any other flow document. The hyphenation feature can automatically hyphenate text that the user enters, as well as existing text in any flow document, or text generated in a code-behind file.

You can add the WPF hyphenation feature with a simple addition to your XAML code file. To do so, in the FlowDocument opening tag add IsHyphenationEnabled="True". If you add the ability to hyphenate, you probably also want to add IsOptimalParagraphEnabled="True". The OptimalParagraphEnabled statement allows the WPF to add hyphenation in such a way that the text looks natural and not stretched out in any one line. Figure 9.11 shows an example of hyphenation using IsOptimalParagraphEnabled on the left but not on the right.

The XAML code for the rich text box in Figure 9.11, on the left, is as follows:

```
<RichTextBox x:Name="MyRichTextBox_Copy" Height="66"
   Margin="145,84,302,0" VerticalAlignment="Top">
 <FlowDocument IsHyphenationEnabled="True"
   IsOptimalParagraphEnabled="True">
      <Paragraph><Run>Which rich text box is without the
            IsOptimalParagraphEnabled tag?</Run></Paragraph>
 </FlowDocument>
</RichTextBox>
```

FIGURE 9.11

The IsOptimalParagraphEnabled property is set to true in the rich text box on the left and false (which is the default) for the rich text box on the right.

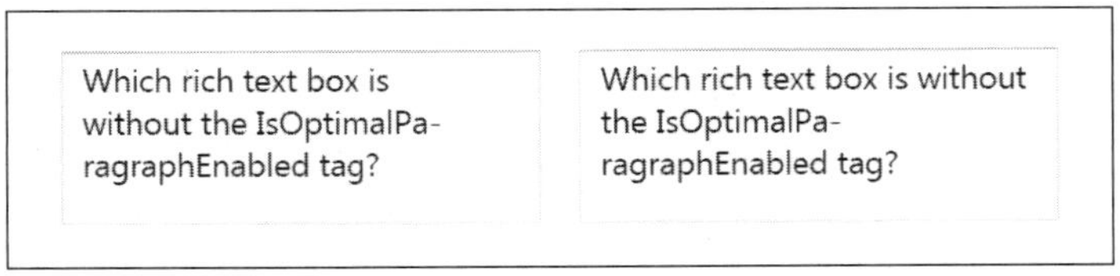

Which rich text box is without the IsOptimalParagraphEnabled tag?

Which rich text box is without the IsOptimalParagraphEnabled tag?

Wrapping text

Wrapping text around objects is a feature of flow documents, but in this first version of Expression Blend this feature can only be added in the XAML code. To do this, you can use a Figure or a Floater. An example of using a Figure to wrap text around an image is shown in Figure 9.12. When the window is resized, the text still wraps. Instructions for using figures and floaters are described in the next sections of this chapter.

Simple text wrapping occurs automatically in all text controls, so that the text wraps from one line to the next and doesn't go off infinitely in a single line. The only controls that do not support simple text wrapping using Blend are Label and PasswordBox. The TextBox control has optional text wrapping that you can turn on or off in the expanded Text palette. To do so, select the TextBox and choose Wrap from the drop-down list labeled TextWrapping in the Text palette. You could also choose WrapWithOverflow.

FIGURE 9.12

Wrapping text around an image using a Figure. Even when resized, the text still wraps well.

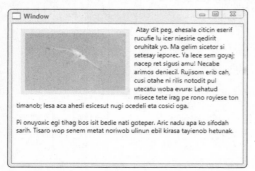

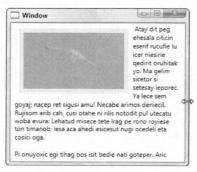

Wrap and WrapWithOverflow

When you have a single word that is longer than the line of your TextBox, then Wrap breaks that word into two so that you can view the entire word in the TextBox. However, Wrap doesn't automatically hyphenate; Wrap just truncates the word at whatever letter you happen to be at when you get to the end of the text box, and continues on the next line.

If you use WrapWithOverflow, then the word doesn't get automatically split and wrapped to the next line. Instead it goes out of sight in the TextBox and does not go to the next line until the user types a space. The entire word is only visible if the user places a cursor in the line and uses the right arrow key to view it.

Using a Figure or Floater to create a sidebar

Figures and Floaters are blocks of text that are not part of the main text, but the main text can wrap around them. You can specify their horizontal anchor, either Left, Right, or Center, and the text flows around them either on the right, left or both sides. Floaters are always anchored to the paragraph that they are nested in. Figures, however, can be either anchored to the paragraph, or anchored to the page or content. When a figure is anchored to a page, then the figure may appear anywhere on the page, as long as it is above the paragraph that it is nested in, and the paragraph is on the same page. Anchoring the Figure to Content, is similar to anchoring it to Page, but more appropriate for a FlowDocumentScrollViewer, which does not have pages. Using Figure instead of Floater gives the WPF more power to find an ideal place for the Figure in the flow document.

An example of using the Figure tag is shown in Figure 9.13. The XAML code that generated the figure is listed below, although some of the text shown in Figure 9.13 is eliminated from the following code, for the sake of brevity:

```
<RichTextBox>
<FlowDocument>
    <Paragraph FontFamily="Segoe Script" FontSize="20"
        FontWeight="Bold">Wrapping Text</Paragraph>
    <Paragraph>Add text here.</Paragraph>
    <Paragraph><Figure Background="#FFF5F5DC" Height="100"
        HorizontalAnchor="PageRight" Width="200">
    <Paragraph Background="#FFFFFFFF" FontStyle="Italic"
        Foreground="#FF0000FF">Text wraps around this text. You can
use text here, or add an image, or any UIElement.</Paragraph>
</Figure>Add text here.</Paragraph>
</FlowDocument>
</RichTextBox>
```

TIP   If you are entering the above code into a new window, then use <Grid x:Name="LayoutRoot"> as the start tag for the LayoutRoot, and use </Grid> as the end tag before </Window>.

FIGURE 9.13

Wrapping text around other text.

Figures versus Floaters

Floaters would look similar to the Figures in Figures 9.12 and 9.13, but the XAML tags would be <Floater> </Floater> instead of <Figure></Figure>, and the HorizontalAnchor would be either "Right", "Center", or "Left" and not "PageRight", since all floaters by default anchor to the paragraph that they are associated with.

Figures also have a HorizontalAnchor property, which you can associate with Content, Page or Paragraph. This equals nine different HorizontalAnchor values that you can set: ContentRight, ContentCenter, ContentLeft, PageRight, PageCenter and so on. Figures also have a VerticalAnchor property, which you can set just like the HorizontalAnchor values, except that you can substitute Top. Center, and Bottom for Left, Center, and Right. And if that's not enough, you can also specify a VerticalOffset or HorizontalOffset as the number of pixels that you want to move from the Right, Center or Left, or Top, Center, or Bottom. So, using Figure, you can anchor your block virtually anywhere you want while allowing the text to resize around it, and the WPF keeps the paragraph that the Figure is nested in nearby, although not rigidly nearby like a Floater.

Wrapping text around an image or UIElement

To wrap text around an image using a Figure, you can change the XAML code for the flow document as follows:

```
<RichTextBox >
  <FlowDocument >
    <Paragraph> <Figure Width="200" Height="100"
Background="Beige" HorizontalAnchor="PageLeft" >
    <Paragraph><Image Source="\006.JPG"
Stretch="UniformToFill"/></Paragraph>
       </Figure> Add dummy text, also known as Lorem Ipsum
here. </Paragraph>
    <Paragraph>Add more gibberish here.</Paragraph>
  </FlowDocument>
</RichTextBox>
```

ON the WEB Not everyone needs a gibberish generator, but if you are looking for one, try www.weirdhat.com/gibberish.php. Another commonly used gibberish generator is found at www.lipsum.com.

Formatting your Flow Documents

You can adjust the spacing in your flow documents by using styles that you add in the XAML code. Using styles can save you from a lot of work by assigning margins to each paragraph in your flow document in one swoop.

You can also specify how wide your columns are, so that when your flow document resizes, it can show multiple columns. You can also specify how much gap you want, and more.

CROSS-REF An in-depth look into the XAML code for creating flow documents is found in Chapter 22, as well as how to add tables into a flow document.

Adjusting the spacing between paragraphs in your flow document

When you create a flow document, you'll probably notice that white space exists between the paragraphs. The amount of white space is a default margin that the WPF assigns to your paragraphs unless you tell it otherwise. Assigning a different value for the margins can be done individually for each paragraph, by setting the Margin property in the Paragraph tag. For example the code Margin="0" creates no space between the paragraphs.

When setting a margin, you probably want to apply it to all paragraphs. But this can be tedious to do one at a time. Instead, you can set a style for the paragraph and apply it to all paragraphs at once. The XAML code to do this is as follows:

```
<FlowDocument.Resources> <Style TargetType="{x:Type Paragraph}">
<Setter Property="Margin" Value="0"/> </Style>
</FlowDocument.Resources>
```

You can place this code beneath the <FlowDocument> tag at the top of your XAML code for your flow document.

Figure 9.14 shows an example of a flow document with the preceding XAML code applied to it.

FIGURE 9.14

A flow document with no margins between paragraphs.

CAUTION Adding margins to paragraphs is slightly different from adding margins to elements in Blend. Margins from two paragraphs do not actually add together to create the size of the space between them. Instead, the larger margin of two adjacent paragraphs becomes the size of the space between them. Keep this in mind when things may be slightly off and you may be wondering why.

Specifying the column width in your flow documents

You can specify how wide you want your columns to be in your flow documents so that when they resize larger, the text fills multiple columns, instead of limiting text to two columns as in the WPF default. To do this, you can set properties in the FlowDocument tag in the XAML. These properties are as follows:

- ColumnWidth: This sets the width of each column. As the flow document resizes larger and this width is exceeded, new columns appear.

- ColumnGap: This specifies the width of the space separating two columns.

- ColumnRuleWidth: If this is set to a value then a line appears between the columns. This is the width of that line.

- ColumnRuleBrush: This specifies the color of the line that separates the columns.

An example of a flow document using columns is shown in Figure 9.15. The XAML to create the columns is as follows:

```
<FlowDocument ColumnWidth="170" ColumnGap="30"
ColumnRuleWidth="2" ColumnRuleBrush="Blue">
```

FIGURE 9.15

Showing multiple columns in a flow document by setting a column width.

Setting Options for Flow Documents and other Text Controls

RichTextBox and TextBox by default allow the user to enter data, but this can be changed. Individual rich text boxes or text boxes can be optionally set to Read-only. They can also be set to accept Returns or accept tabs. These options are available in the Common Properties palette in the Properties panel, as shown in Figure 9.16. Select the control first to view them. Other options in the Common Properties panel are making your text control focusable, hit-test visible, and enabled. Setting tool tips and assigning a cursor are also available in the Common Properties palette.

FIGURE 9.16

The Common Properties palette for a RichTextBox allows you to accept Returns and tabs, and to make the RichTextBox read-only.

Making your text box focusable, assigning a cursor, and adding a tool tip

Allowing your editable text control to be focusable is a prerequisite to allowing a user to type in text or copy text by clicking and dragging in a flow document. But being focusable is not a prerequisite to using the controls of the FlowDocumentReader or the scrollbar of the FlowDocumentScrollViewer, or changing the cursor type or viewing tool tips.

You can set your text control as focusable by selecting Focusable in the Common Properties palette, as shown in Figure 9.17. You can also assign a tool tip for your text control, or change the cursor to a different type when it hovers over the text control.

FIGURE 9.17

The FlowDocumentScrollViewer on the right is focusable and allows you to copy text. The TextBlock on the left is not focusable and does not allow the user to copy text.

Assigning IsHitTestVisible and IsEnabled

If you want the cursor, tool tip, scrollbars and the controls of the FlowDocumentReader to be inactive, and you don't want to allow your user to select text, you can either deselect IsHitTestVisible, or make the control inactive by deselecting IsEnabled in the Common Properties palette. In Figure 9.18, the FlowDocumentScrollViewer on the right has IsHitTestVisible set to false, and the tool tip, scroll bar, and change of cursor are all inactive. This is the same result as if you checked IsEnabled. The FlowDocumentScrollViewer on the left has IsHitTestVisible.

FIGURE 9.18

The FlowDocumentScrollViewer on the left has IsHitTestVisible set to true, and the FlowDocumentScrollViewer on the right has it set to false.

Spell-checking

Blend allows you to see immediately if you have misspelled a word in your text control by underlining misspelled words in red. As you type in a text box, Blend underlines all misspelled words with a red squiggle. When you right-click on the underlined word, Blend offers you its best ideas for corrected versions of the word. You can choose a word from the list, or you can eliminate the red underline by choosing Ignore All and retain the spelling. (Blend doesn't offer the option to ignore just one instance of the word. If you choose Ignore All, then you ignore all the words spelled exactly the same.) Or, of course, you can individually fix the word however you want, so that the red underline disappears.

Blend also allows you to offer this handy spell-checking capability to your users, as shown in Figure 9.19. But spell-checking is not the default in rich text boxes and regular text boxes, as it is in the artboard. You can change that by checking the SpellCheck.IsEnabled box in the Miscellaneous palette. Or you can add SpellCheck.IsEnabled="True" into the XAML code for the text box or rich text box. For example, in the opening tag of the RichTextBox, you can type the following:

```
<RichTextBox SpellCheck.IsEnabled="True">
```

FIGURE 9.19

Automatic spellchecking in a WPF application.

Adding Labels and Access Text

Labels are WPF controls to which you can assign access text, which allows you to enter a letter using the keyboard and automatically create focus in a UIElement, such as a button or a text box or flow document. Figure 9.7 shows an example of a label with the letter N as the access text to bring focus to the text box below it.

Labels can also be used without access text, just by clicking the Label button in the Toolbox and clicking and dragging in the artboard to position a label there. If you want to add access text, here is the procedure: First create the label and give it a name in the Properties panel. Also, create the WPF control that you want to bring focus to using the label, and name the control. Then select the label, right-click, and in the pop-up menu that appears choose View XAML. In the Label tag, we added the following for the label in Figure 9.7:

```
<Label Width="52" HorizontalAlignment="Left"
        Target="{Binding ElementName=NameTextBox}"
Margin="10,3,0,0" VerticalAlignment="Top" Height="25">
    <AccessText Text="_Name"/>
</Label>
```

The NameTextBox is the name of the control that you want to bring focus to. The Width, Horizontal Alignment, Margin, and VerticalAlignment are all generated by Blend according to the size and location of your label.

Data binding a slider to enable text scaling in a RichTextBox, TextBox, and TextBlock

Flow documents automatically supply a control that allows the user to optimize their text size for their visual acuity. This is a good thing, because everyone's eyesight is different, and, for example, older people may need larger type than younger people. Rich text boxes, regular text boxes, text blocks, and labels have no such control, but creating one using data binding is useful and relatively easy.

To use a slider and a text box to allow the user to adjust text size, follow these steps:

STEPS: Adding a Slider and Textbox to Adjust Text Size

1. Create a text box by clicking the TextBox button (or RichTextBox, TextBlock, or Label) in the Toolbox and clicking and dragging in the artboard to position it there. Give it a name in the Properties panel.

2. Assign a text size to the text by choosing a text size from the drop-down list in the Text palette.

3. Choose the Selection tool and click in the text box so that a cursor appears. (You may need to click a couple of times or more.) Type whatever text you want into the text box.

4. Click the Asset Library button on the Toolbox to open the Asset Library palette. Click a slider, and click and drag in the artboard to position the slider where you want it to reside. (Feel free to create gridlines and use the Layout palette to precisely position it in a cell in the grid.)

5. Select the text box and click on the little button beside the FontSize drop-down list in the Text palette. The button has a tool tip "Advanced Property Options". From the drop-down menu that appears, choose Data Binding.

6. In the Create Data Binding dialog box, as shown in Figure 9.20, click the Element Property button at the top, choose Slider from the Scene Elements column on the left, and choose Value from the Properties column on the right. Then click Finish.

FIGURE 9.20

Databinding the text size of the text box to the slider.

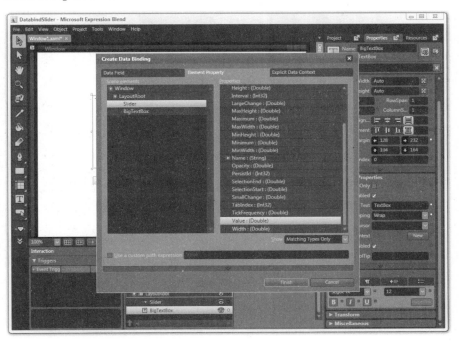

7. Select the slider, and in the Common Properties dialog box, set Value to the size of the default size of the text. When you increase the value of Value (huh?), the text size increases, as shown in Figure 9.21. Set Maximum to the largest text size that you want to allow in the text box, and set the Minimum to the smallest text size. You can also set the SmallChange to 1, so that when the slider is focused, the right arrow or left arrow keys move the slider right or left by 1.

FIGURE 9.21

The text size increases as the value increases in the Common Properties palette.

8. Now you can choose Project ➪ Test Project and see it in an application window, as shown in Figure 9.22.

 **TIP** Naming your slider and text box can help you identify them in the Create Data Binding dialog box.

The text box with its text resizing slider.

Summary

- Flow documents allow for optimal readability, taking into account window size and monitor resolution, and they allow the user to adjust his own text size using buttons or a slider. The FlowDocumentReader offers a search feature, as well.

- Blend provides several text controls that you can use to display text in your applications:

    - Flow documents, which include RichTextBox, FlowDocumentReader, FlowDocumentScrollViewer, and FlowDocumentPageViewer.

    - TextBox: editable by the user, but only allows simple formatting.

    - TextBlock: Not editable. Allows some formatting.

    - Label: Good for short text. Allows only simple formatting.

    - PasswordBox: Types asterisks for whatever the user types.

    - To create a text control, click the Text tool in the Tools palette. and click and drag in the artboard. A cursor appears, and you are ready to type your text. You can create two types of flow documents in this way: a RichTextBox and FlowDocumentScrollViewer. However a FlowDocumentReader and FlowDocumentPageViewer need to be created using XAML.

- You can wrap text around objects in flow documents using Figures or Floaters.
- Flow documents are customizable. You can adjust the size of the columns so they add multiple columns. And you can adjust the margin between paragraphs.
- You can add a slider to allow the user to adjust his own text size by using data binding for rich text boxes, text boxes, text blocks and labels.

Chapter 10

Styling Text and Using WPF Typographical Features

Blend has advanced, flexible typographic manipulation capabilities that allow you to create appealing headings and logos, and add visual interest to your text. In this chapter we discuss how to assign colors, gradients, opacity masks, drawing brushes, image brushes and visual brushes to text, as well as how to convert your text to vector objects and apply bitmap effects to them.

We also investigate the new typographical features of the Windows Presentation Foundation, including support for fonts that contain alternate glyphs such as swashes, ligatures and more. These typographical features are now available to font designers, and we expect to see more and more fonts using these alternatives in the future.

Lastly, we discuss how to use Expression Design to improve the look of your text. Expression Design provides an even wider range of text features than Blend. Design allows you to assign both fills and strokes to your text, and it offers a variety of fills and strokes to choose from. Plus you can create your own fills and strokes. Expression Design also allows you to align text to a path, warp text, and more.

Advanced Typographical Features Available with Windows Presentation Foundation

The Windows Presentation Foundation offers many typographical features that were previously unavailable in Windows. These features are supported by OpenType fonts and are available for font-makers to incorporate into their fonts, and available for you to use in fonts that support them. Fonts can now include optional glyphs, as well as other options such as baseline adjustments. (A *glyph* is a letterform representing a character.) Optional glyphs may include letterforms with the following:

- **Swashes:** These include StandardSwashes, as shown in Figure 10.1, and ContextualSwashes. Swashes can add elegance and bring attention to headings. Contextual swashes are glyphs with swashes that are slightly modified, so that swashes below the baseline don't accidentally criss-cross with the next letter's *descender* — the part of the glyph that extends below the baseline.

FIGURE 10.1

Swashes are an example of new typographical features available with Windows Presentation Foundation. You can specify whether you want the glyph with swashes or without swashes.

- **Capitals:** The optional glyphs for capital letters include SmallCaps, AllSmallCaps, PetiteCaps, AllPetiteCaps, TitlingCaps and Normal. SmallCaps and PetiteCaps give you capital letters that are smaller than your normal-sized capitals. AllSmallCaps and AllPetiteCaps change the text to all capitals, even if you type a non-capital. And TitlingCaps puts more space between the letters of your normal sized capital letters.

- **Ligatures:** These are combinations of two letters in a single glyph. They can provide a handwritten, easy-to-read, or sophisticated appearance to your text. StandardLigatures include the commonly seen ligatures, such as fi, fl, and more. DiscretionaryLigatures are used to allow the font designer to offer interesting letter combinations, some of which are shown in Figure 10.4. ContextualLigatures provide a more appealing glyph in some cases than the standard ligature. HistoricalLigatures are for displaying old typefaces with historical accuracy.

- **Alternates:** These are alternate glyphs that you can use. They include StylisticAlternates, which can serve a wide variety of purposes. StylisticAlternates simply offers an alternative style for your text without needing to switch from one font to another. RandomContextualAlternates use a combination of glyphs to resemble text that is handwritten. HistoricalForms allow designers to present type from times long ago.

Other typographical features that are available are:

- **Variants:** These include Superscript, Subscript, and Ordinal. They shrink the font and adjust the baseline, higher for superscripts and lower for subscripts. They are used for mathematics, footnotes, chemical abbreviations, scientific abbreviations, and more. The Ordinal variant supports the numerical representation of 1st, 2nd, and so on.

- Numerical styles which include the following:

  - **NumeralStyle:** This can include OldStyle, which supports "old style" types of numbers

  - **Fractions:** Can be one of two types, Slashed or Stacked

  - **NumeralAlignment:** This can be proportional or tabular

  - **SlashedZero:** For showing a zero with a slash in it

> **CAUTION** Swashes, as well as other typographic features, may disappear if you assign your text Bold.

Adding Swashes

Swashes come in two types: StandardSwash and ContextualSwash. In the following examples, we assign the swashes to rich text boxes, but you can use any text control. These typographical features are not restricted to flow documents alone.

> **TIP** In the following examples of the XAML code, you don't need to type in all the XAML, just create the text box as you normally do in Blend and add the code that appears in bold to the Run or to the Paragraph. You can even add it to the RichTextBox properties if you want it to apply to the entire rich text box.

Assigning StandardSwashes

Some fonts, such as Pescadero, offer swashes. Swashes can add elegance and appeal to letters, as if they are hand-made calligraphy. Figure 10.1 shows an example of swashes in the Pescadero font. (Pescadero is one of the fonts in the pack of sample OpenType fonts that is distributed with the Windows SDK.) The XAML which specified the swashes is as follows:

```
<RichTextBox Margin="61,38,61,0" VerticalAlignment="Top"
Height="60">
  <FlowDocument>
  <Paragraph>
<Run FontFamily="Pescadero" FontSize="36"
Typography.StandardSwashes="1">Adding Lovely
Swashes</Run></Paragraph>
  </FlowDocument>
</RichTextBox>
```

> **NOTE** The preceding XAML code is formatted for readability in this book. Your XAML code formats differently in the XAML view of Blend.

Assigning the ContextualSwash

Because swashes often intrude onto the space before or after the letter with the swash, sometimes swashes may overlap each other. Assigning ContextualSwash avoids this mishap.

In Figure 10.2, the swashes from Ryan overlap, so we added the ContextualSwashes property to fix it. The XAML code for Figure 10.2 is as follows:

```
<RichTextBox HorizontalAlignment="Left" Margin="33,13,0,0"
VerticalAlignment="Top" Width="115" Height="115">
  <FlowDocument>
        <Paragraph><Run FontFamily="Pescadero" FontSize="36"
 Typography.StandardSwashes="1">Ryan</Run></Paragraph>
        <Paragraph><Run FontFamily="Pescadero" FontSize="36"
 Typography.ContextualSwashes="1">Ryan</Run></Paragraph>
   </FlowDocument>
</RichTextBox>
```

FIGURE 10.2

Contextual swashes remove the offending swashes, as seen in the bottom line.

NOTE Contextual swashes in Pescadero at this time simply revert to no swash at all, so this example is a little misleading. But in a perfect world, or in the final release of Pescadero, you'd probably see a swash at the top of the R but no swash at the bottom to conflict with the L.

Choosing from a variety of capital letters

The WPF gives the font designer the ability to offer several kinds of capital letters. These include SmallCaps, AllSmallCaps, PetiteCaps, AllPetiteCaps, and Titling Capitals. Each has its own appeal. PetiteCaps and AllPetiteCaps are assigned in the same way as SmallCaps and AllSmallCaps — although they need to be included in the font originally to show up any different from the normal caps.

Assigning SmallCaps and AllSmallCaps

Figure 10.3 shows an example of using AllSmallCaps in Blend. The difference between AllSmallCaps and SmallCaps is that AllSmallCaps converts all the letters to small caps, whereas SmallCaps converts only the capital letters to small caps.

FIGURE 10.3
_____

Using AllSmallCaps to create smaller sized capital letters.

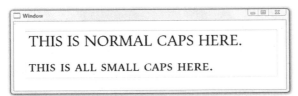

The XAML to create the above figure is as follows:

```
<RichTextBox Margin="26,22,20,0" VerticalAlignment="Top"
Height="112">
  <FlowDocument>
    <Paragraph><Run FontFamily="Pescadero" FontSize="36">THIS IS
NORMAL CAPS HERE.</Run></Paragraph>
    <Paragraph><Run FontFamily="Pescadero" FontSize="36"
Typography.Capitals="AllSmallCaps">This is all small caps
Here.</Run></Paragraph>
  </FlowDocument>
</RichTextBox>
```

> **NOTE** If you assign small caps to the first paragraph, then all preceding paragraphs automatically have small caps assigned to them. To change this, just go into the XAML code and delete Typography.Capitals="AllSmallCaps", and the paragraph reverts to Normal caps.

Adding Titling Capitals

Titling Capitals change all small letters to capital letters, and may add more space into the title by adding more space between letters. The following XAML text is used to assign Titling Capitals.

```
<RichTextBox Margin="40,22,44,0" VerticalAlignment="Top"
Height="57" FontFamily="Pescadero" >
  <FlowDocument>
    <Paragraph><Run Typography.Capitals="Titling">my heading is in
all capitals</Run></Paragraph>
  </FlowDocument>
</RichTextBox>
```

Working with ligatures

Ligatures are a single glyph consisting of at least two letters. Adding ligatures to a font may make it look more natural, or give it more style, or help give it a handwritten look. An example of ligatures in the Pericles font is shown in Figure 10.4 below.

Ligatures available in the Pericles font.

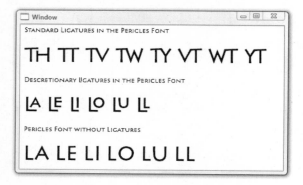

```
<RichTextBox>
  <FlowDocument>
<Paragraph><Run FontFamily="Pericles">Standard Ligatures in
 the Pericles Font</Run></Paragraph>
<Paragraph><Run FontFamily="Pericles" FontSize="36"
 Typography.StandardLigatures="True">TH TT TV TW TY VT WT
 YT</Run></Paragraph>
  <Paragraph Typography.DiscretionaryLigatures="True"><Run
  FontFamily="Pericles">Discretionary Ligatures in the
  Pericles Font</Run></Paragraph>
  <Paragraph><Run FontFamily="Pericles" FontSize="36"
 Typography.DiscretionaryLigatures="True">LA LE LI LO LU
 LL </Run></Paragraph>
  <Paragraph><Run FontFamily="Pericles">Pericles Font without
 Ligatures</Run></Paragraph>
  <Paragraph><Run FontFamily="Pericles" FontSize="36" >LA LE
 LI LO LU LL </Run></Paragraph>
  <Paragraph><Run FontFamily="Pericles" FontSize="36"
 Typography.StandardLigatures="False">TH TT TV TW VT WT
 YT</Run></Paragraph>
  <Paragraph><Run FontFamily="Pericles"></Run></Paragraph>
  </FlowDocument>
  </RichTextBox>
```

The default value for Typography.StandardLigatures is True in Pericles, so to turn off the ligatures, you can't just omit the property. You have to type Typography.StandardLigatures="False".

Assigning Alternates

Alternates include StylisticAlternates, Contextual Alternates and Historical Forms. Remember, that these alternates are only available in fonts in which the font designer explicitly creates the alternates.

Using StylisticAlternates

Pericles is a font that offers three StylisticAlternates. Figure 10.5 shows an example of them. These stylistic alternates show up in the capital letters of the font, so all the text in Figure 10.5 is capitalized. The XAML code for Figure 10.5 is listed below.

FIGURE 10.5

Stylistic Alternates in the Pericles font.

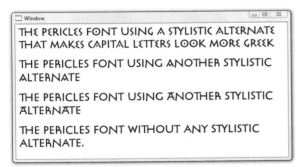

```
<RichTextBox >
<FlowDocument>
 <Paragraph FontFamily="Pericles"
Typography.StylisticAlternates="1">
 <Run FontSize="24">THE PERICLES FONT USING A STYLISTIC ALTERNATE
    THAT MAKES CAPITAL LETTERS LOOK MORE GREEK</Run></Paragraph>
 <Paragraph FontFamily="Pericles">
   <Run FontSize="24" Typography.StylisticAlternates="2">
      THE PERICLES FONT USING ANOTHER STYLISTIC
      ALTERNATE</Run></Paragraph>
 <Paragraph FontFamily="Pericles">
 <Run FontSize="24" Typography.StylisticAlternates="3">THE
PERICLES
    FONT USING ANOTHER STYLISTIC ALTERNATE</Run></Paragraph>
 <Paragraph FontFamily="Pericles">
```

```
    <Run FontSize="24"></Run><Run FontSize="24">THE PERICLES FONT
    WITHOUT ANY STYLISTIC ALTERNATE.</Run></Paragraph>
</FlowDocument>
</RichTextBox>
```

Assigning Contextual Alternates

Contextual Alternates can provide random placements of alternates, giving the text more of a handwritten appearance. The Lindsey font gives you this kind of look by default, as shown in Figure 10.6.

If you are using a font that does not make letters appear differently by default, and that allows you to assign contextual alternates, then you can assign it like you assign the stylistic alternates. The code to assign it is as follows:

```
Typography.ContextualAlternates="True"
```

FIGURE 10.6

The Lindsey font assigns contextual alternates to its text by default, to give a more handwritten look to the font.

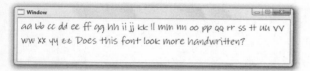

Adding Historical Forms

Historical Forms are available to create a historical look for a font, as shown with the Palatino Linotype font in Figure 10.7.

FIGURE 10.7

Adding a historical look with the Palatino Linotype font.

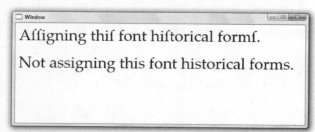

The XAML to create the historical look like that in Figure 10-7 is:

```
<RichTextBox>
  <FlowDocument>
  <Paragraph><Run FontFamily="Palatino Linotype" FontSize="36"
    Typography.HistoricalForms="True">Assigning this font
historical
  forms.</Run></Paragraph>
  <Paragraph><Run FontFamily="Palatino Linotype" FontSize="36"
    Typography.HistoricalForms="False">Not assigning this font
  historical forms.</Run></Paragraph>
  </FlowDocument>
</RichTextBox>
```

Assigning Variants

Variants include superscript and subscript. Superscript and subscript can also be assigned in Expression Design, and the text can be copied into Blend, but if that's too tedious, here's another way to assign them, as long as the font that you're using supports this. To assign superscripts and subscripts in Expression Design and bring them over to Blend, see "Creating Superscripts and Subscripts in Design and using them in Blend" later in this chapter.

Palatino Linotype is a font that supports subscripts and superscripts. To add them, use the following XAML code as a property of the Run tag:

```
Typography.Variants="Superscript"
```

or

```
Typography.Variants="Subscript"
```

Working with Numerical Styles

Figure 10.8 shows numbers transformed into fractions, as well as numbers lined up for easy addition, and the OldStyle numeral style in the Palatino Linotype font.

To create stacked fractions we set the following property of the Run tag:

```
Typography.Fraction="Stacked"
```

For slashed fractions, we used the following:

```
Typography.Fraction="Slashed"
```

For tabulation we used:

```
Typography.NumeralAlignment="Tabular"
```

The default is:

```
Typography.NumeralAlignment="Proportional"
```

FIGURE 10.8

Fractions, numbers lined up for tabulation, and Palatino Linotype's "OldStyle" numeral style.

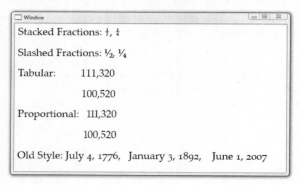

To use Palatino Linotype's OldStyle numerals, we set the following as a property of the Run tag.

```
Typography.NumeralStyle="OldStyle"
```

The preceding code can also be used in the opening tag of a RichTextBox tag or other text box tag, or a Paragraph tag, or other tags, including the Span tag.

The Miramonte font supports slashed zeros. To use them, set the following property:

```
Typography.SlashedZero="True"
```

Customizing Text Controls

Text controls (which include the FlowDocumentReader, FlowDocumentScrollViewer, RichTextBox, TextBox, TextBlock, PasswordBox, and Label) are highly customizable. In this section we use *text box* to stand for all text controls. Here are some basic rules about creating and customizing text boxes:

To change the appearance, size, or position of the text box, click the Selection tool, and then click to select the text box. You can then do any of the following:

- Use the Brushes palette to assign a color, gradient, or transparency to the Background, font, or Border of the text box.

- Use the Transform palette to scale, rotate, and skew the entire text box, just as if it were a vector graphic object.

- Click and drag on the text box's object handles to resize, rotate, or skew the text box.

In Figure 10.9, text is converted into a path and copied, and the two copies are placed slightly off-set on top of a collage of images in a grid panel. The same effect could be achieved by making the background and border of the textbox invisible, and copying the text box.

FIGURE 10.9

You can use text in a wide range of ways in Blend.

Some text boxes may exist only to have text typed into them by the user, and these can also be visually refined in many ways. For example, in Figure 10.10 each side of the border is resized by a different amount, and a gradient and opacity mask is applied to the border. You can specify the border thickness of each side of the textbox in the Appearance palette and assign a gradient and opacity mask in the Brushes palette.

FIGURE 10.10

Borders of text boxes are highly customizable.

Enter your answer here

Scaling and stretching your text

You can scale text in the artboard by doing the following:

- To scale the text box without scaling the font, select the text box, and click and drag the object handles.

- To scale the text box and font at the same time, select the text box, and use the Scale tab of the Transform palette.

When using the Transform palette you can change the X value or the Y value independently, which means that you can scale one of them and stretch your text. This may come in handy if you are trying to create a feeling of being squished together or squashed underfoot. Figure 10.11 shows simple examples of squashed text.

FIGURE 10.11

The same font is stretched horizontally and vertically using the Transform palette.

> **NOTE**   If your text is in a window, and you want the text to scale when the window resizes, you can either change the text into a vector object or nest your text box into a Viewbox. For more information on Viewboxes, see Chapter 16.

Rotating, skewing, and flipping text

You can rotate, skew, and flip text to create special graphic effects that add dynamism to the layout of your user interface. You can also animate text by rotating, skewing, and flipping text. Rotating text may be useful if you create an interface that has controls in concentric circles. Or you may want to rotate text for captions that read vertically instead of horizontally. Skewing can give an interesting effect of dynamism, such as the placards waving in Figure 10.12. And flipping text can give the impression of looking (the wrong way) through a transparent window with text etched on it, or looking in the mirror. Figure 10.13 shows flipped text, although it may be more practical to flip a letter or two for an effect, and not whole paragraphs, but it's fun to see.

FIGURE 10.12

Skewing text boxes.

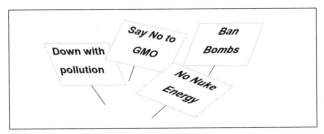

FIGURE 10.13

Flipping text.

To rotate your text box, you can do one of the following:

- Select the text box, move your mouse near a corner handle, and when the curved icon with two arrows appears, click and drag your text box to rotate it. Figure 10.14 shows an example of many letters, each in their own text boxes, with invisible borders and backgrounds that we created and rotated.

- Rotate your text box using the Rotate tab of the Transform palette, just as you rotate any shape or path.

FIGURE 10.14

A rotated and jumbled alphabet.

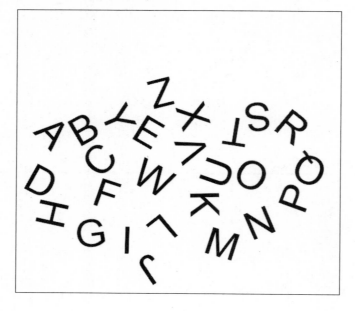

To skew your text box, you can do one of the following:

- Select the text box, and move your mouse near a center handle. When the skew icon appears (it's the straight double arrow with a slanted line through it), click and drag your text box to skew it.

- Use the Skew tab of the Transform palette, just as you skew any shape or path.

To flip your text box, you can do one of the following:

- Select the text box, and choose Object ➪ Flip ➪ Horizontal (or Vertical).

- Select the text box, and drag a center handle over the entire text box, so that your text box shrinks to nothing and then expands out in a flipped version.

- Click the Flip tab in the Transform palette, and click one of the flipping buttons.

Auto sizing your text box

When your application resizes to fit a new window size, your textbox will also resize if its width and/or height are set to Auto in the Layout palette. To do this you can select the textbox and choose Object ➪ Auto Size ➪ Width (or Height, or Both, or Fill). Choosing Fill causes the text box to fill the container, which would be the LayoutRoot or any panel that you nest the text box in. Choosing Auto Size allows your text box to expand and contract according to the size of the window.

Setting maximum and minimum scaling values for your auto sizing

You may want to set maximum or minimum values for your text boxes. You may want to do this because you don't want to require the user to use scroll bars if the text box shrinks, or you don't want lots of white space in your text box if the text box expands. You can test your program out on different monitor sizes to check the effect of shrinking and expanding.

If you want to set maximum or minimum scaling values, you can do so by using the Layout palette, as shown in Figure 10.15. Select the text box, and type values in the Height Minimum, Height Maximum, Width Minimum, or Width Maximum input boxes. In the example shown in Figure 10.15, the MaxHeight and MaxWidth are set to 1200 and the MinHeight and MinWidth are set to 100.

FIGURE 10.15

You can use the Layout palette to precisely position your text box.

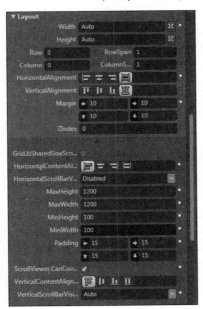

CROSS-REF For more information about using the Layout Palette with text, see Chapter 2.

Converting Text into Vector Graphic Objects

Converting text into vector graphic objects has advantages and disadvantages. Here are some of the advantages:

- You may want your text to enlarge in size when the user resizes the panels. This may be important if you get things to look just the way you want them. However, you can also do this by inserting your text box into a Viewbox.

- You can change the shapes of the letters any way that you want by editing nodes with the Subselection tool and Pen tool. An example is shown in Figure 10.16. Once text is in a vector graphic, you can tweak it to make it unique or merge the letters in a pictorial way. For example, if you are building a Web application for Nike, you can merge letters and words into the Nike swoosh, although using Expression Design may be more full of features for this kind of work.

FIGURE 10.16

Shapes of letters can be manipulated when you turn them into a vector graphic.

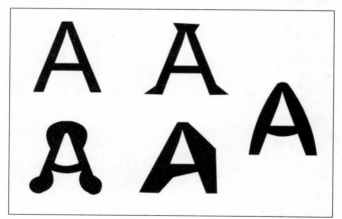

- It gives you more freedom in transforming text when you animate it.
- You may want to get some free clip art from the Wingdings and Webdings fonts, the nodes of which you can edit, as shown in Figure 10.17, if you need to modify them.

FIGURE 10.17

Editing nodes of a Wingding.

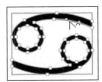

- You can change your text into extruded 3D shapes, which can be useful in animation, or with the right lighting and textures can produce unique artwork that you can use in your user interface.

CROSS-REF For more information on extruding letters to 3D shapes, see Chapter 12. For more information on editing nodes, see Chapter 5. For more information about animation, see Chapter 14.

The main reason you may not want to convert your text into a vector graphic object is that assistive technology for users with impaired vision can't read it. Also, you can no longer use any of the functions of the text box, which include:

- Allowing the user to type text
- Allowing the program to enter text
- Allowing you to modify the text in the text box without having to rewrite everything

To convert your text to a vector graphic, click either the RichTextBox or TextBlock button in the Toolbox .and click and drag in the artboard to position the text box there. Then click the Selection tool, and click once in the text box so that a cursor appears. (Click again, if it doesn't, just be careful not to double-click, or you can right-click on the text box and choose Edit Text.) Type your text and assign your font and font size and bold, italic or underline. Then click outside the textbox and select it again and choose Object ➪ Path ➪ Convert To Path.

Applying Colors and Other Visual Effects to Text

Choose carefully the colors and other effects that you assign to your text, just as you choose fonts carefully, unless you want a carnival look. You can assign the following to text:

- Solid colors
- Gradients
- Drawing or image brushes

- Visual brushes
- Opacity masks
- Bitmap effects (which include bevel, blur, drop shadow, emboss, outer glow, or a combination of bitmaps effects)

Assigning solid colors and gradients to text

To assign a text color, select the text if you are using a TextBlock, RichTextBox, or flow document, or select the textbox if you want the gradient to apply to all the text in the textbox, and choose Foreground in the Brushes palette. Click the Solid Color Brush tab, or Gradient Brush tab, and assign a color or gradient. Two examples of gradients applied to text are shown in Figure 10.18.

> **TIP**   When applying a gradient to text you can utilize the Brush Transform tool, just as if you were applying a gradient to a vector object, as long as you apply the gradient to the entire text box, and not just to selected text.

> **CROSS-REF**   For instructions on creating and manipulating gradients, see Chapter 6. For considerations of what colors you may want to choose for your text and why, see Chapter 11.

FIGURE 10.18

Examples of gradients applied to text in Blend.

> **TIP**   To see the examples shown in Figure 10.18 in color, go to www.blendtips.com/bible.

Assigning drawing and image brushes to text

You can assign a drawing or image brush to text in the same way that you can assign a drawing or image brush to any object. First create the vector art and group it into a canvas or other panel. (For an image brush, add the image to the project and insert it into the artboard.) Then select the vector art or image, choose Tools ➪ Make Brush Resource ➪ Make Drawing Brush Resource (or Make Image Brush Resource), give the resource a name, select where you want to define it, and then click OK.

Once you've created your image or drawing brush, then select the text if you are using a TextBlock, RichTextBox or flow document, or select the text box. Choose Foreground in the Brushes palette, click the Brush Resources tab and assign it to the Brush Resource that you created.

For the drawing or image brush to fill the entire text, you may need to select the Tile Brush tab and choose a Stretch value of Fill or UniformToFill. Figure 10.19 shows an example of text with an image brush (top) and text with a drawing brush (middle). The image and drawing used to create the image and drawing brushes are below.

CROSS-REF For more information about assigning drawing or image brushes, see Chapter 6.

FIGURE 10.19

Examples of an image brush and a drawing brush applied to text.

TIP To see the examples shown in Figure 10.19 in color, go to www.blendtips.com/ bible.

Using a visual brush to play animations inside text

You can assign a visual brush that plays an animation to your text, using the steps described next. In Figure 10.20, an animation plays inside the text, giving the appearance that lights are shining on the text.

CROSS-REF For more information on creating and using visual brushes, see Chapter 6.

STEPS: Playing Animations Inside Text

1. Create your animation to appear inside the text. For our example, in Figure 10.20, we created a canvas, then added two ellipses. Then we created a new timeline, moved the playhead, repositioned and resized the ellipses to create the animation, and then specified that it play forever.

CROSS-REF For more information about creating animations, see Chapter 14.

2. Select the panel containing the animation, and Choose Tools ➪ Make Brush Resource ➪ Make Visual Brush Resource. Then give it a name in the dialog box, choose where to define it, and click OK.

3. Create and select the text that you want the animation to play inside. Choose Foreground in the Brushes palette, click the Brush Resources tab, and select the visual brush from the list of resources.

FIGURE 10.20

Playing an animation inside text using the visual brush.

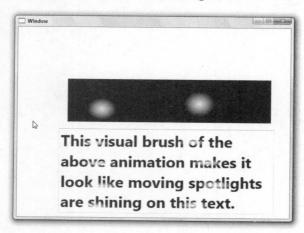

 To see the example shown in Figure 10.20 in action, visit `www.blendtips.com/bible`.

Using an opacity mask with text

In Blend, you can assign a level of transparency to your text using the text's opacity mask. This opacity mask works in the same way as opacity masks for other objects. You can select the textbox and choose Opacity Mask in the Brushes palette, then assign a gradient that fades to an alpha value of 0, or whatever other alpha value you want to set. In Figure 10.21, the text has a linear gradient faded to an alpha value of 0 on each end gradient stop, and an alpha value of 100% in the middle.

CROSS-REF For more information on using Opacity masks, see Chapter 6.

FIGURE 10.21

An opacity mask causes the text to gradually fade out on each side of the text.

Adding bitmap effects to your text

You may want to add bitmap effects to text. For example, you may want to add a bevel to your text to make it look as if it's a statue carved out of wood or stone. Or you might want to add an outer glow to light up your text. Bitmap effects can add a nice flair to a user interface, as shown in Figure 10.22. Drop shadows, for example, can add a 3D effect of floating and movement in an airy, light-filled space to the application. However, bitmap effects can only be added to text that has been converted to a vector object.

If you are deciding whether or not to add any bitmap effects to your text, here are some questions you may want to ask yourself:

- Will bitmap effects enhance the theme of your user application without cluttering the look of the user interface?

- Is the text large and clear enough that bitmap effects are visible while still allowing the text to be legible?

CAUTION Bitmap effects require full trust, so you probably don't want to include them in XBAPs or any other application that requires partial trust.

FIGURE 10.22

Text with bitmap effects applied to them.

To convert your text to a vector graphic, add your text into either a RichTextBox or TextBlock, and then select the rich text box or text block. Then Choose Object ➪ Path ➪ Convert To Path. Then select the converted text and expand the Appearance palette to view all the options. Then click the down arrow beside the New Bitmap Effect button and choose the bitmap effect that you want to apply.

CROSS-REF Instructions to apply more than one bitmap to an object are included in Chapter 6.

Using the Powerful Text Tools of Expression Design

Expression Design has powerful text tools that you can use to create the text that you want, and then you bring that text into Blend to use. Expression Design, as we described in Chapter 7, offers over 200 different types of ready-made strokes, and also gives you the ability to define your own strokes. In Expression Design, text consists of not only the stroke, but a fill inside the stroke as well. So creating letters with borders is simple. You can assign different brushes to both the stroke and the fill, resulting in text that can contain lots of detail that can only be created in Blend with much more effort.

Expression Design also allows you to precisely define the size and position of letters in relationship to each other using its Text palette, and it offers a Warp Mesh feature that you can use to distort and refine your text in various ways. It also allows you to map text onto a path. We describe these features in more detail next.

Creating text in Expression Design

Here are some basics for getting started creating text in Expression Design:

- To create a document in Expression Design, choose File ➪ New, give it a name and a size, and click OK.

- To create text in Expression Design, click the Text tool in the Toolbox, and type in the document window. In Expression Design you do not need to create a text box to contain text — just click the Text tool and type. The text appears wherever you click and type in the document.

- To select your text, click the Selection tool, and click the text in the document window. Handles appear around the text, allowing you to rotate, resize, and skew the text.

- To modify your text, choose the Selection tool, double-click on the text, and a cursor appears. Then change your text.

Using the Text palette

The Expression Design Text palette is shown on the right, below the Appearance palette, in Figure 10.23. The Text palette allows you to select fonts and font sizes and precisely position your text, using the following features:

- Font
- Font Decoration (may include Bold, plus whatever else the font provides)
- Point Size
- Alignment:
  - Left
  - Right

- ▫ Center
- ▫ Right Justify (leaves the last line not justified)
- ▫ Justify All (justifies even the last line)
- ■ Leading (which is the line height)
- ■ Tracking (increases or decreases the space between the letters)
- ■ Horizontal scaling (scales the selected text in a horizontal direction)
- ■ Base Line Offset (moves the text up or down).
- ■ Superscript or Subscript or Normal

You can adjust the settings before you type in the document window, or you can select the text and adjust the settings to modify the selected text. To select text, be sure the Text tool is selected in the Tools palette, and click and drag over the text to select it.

FIGURE 10.23

Creating text with Expression Design.

Applying strokes and fills with the Appearance palette

The Appearance palette, as shown on the right in Figure 10.23, is a great tool for creating visually interesting text. It allows you to specify both the fill and stroke of your text. You can assign how much stroke and how much fill you want, or you can assign no stroke or no fill. You can also assign textures to both fills and strokes.

We describe how to use Expression Design's Appearance palette in detail in Chapter 7. It works the same way for text as it does for any vector object. In short, you assign a brush to your stroke, and assign a brush to your fill, and choose your stroke size. It's very easy to create text with any number of interesting borders using Expression Design. Figure 10.24 shows an example of some text that you can create using various strokes.

FIGURE 10.24

Applying different kinds of strokes using Expression Design.

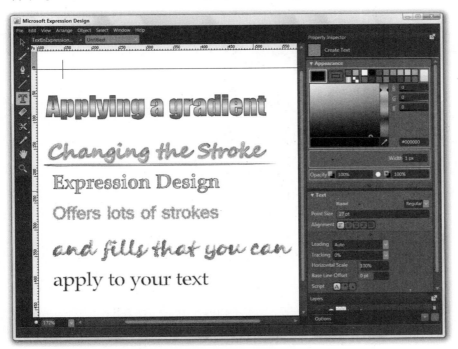

Rotating text in 3D space

Expression Design also allows you to resize, rotate, and manipulate your text in 2D and 3D-like space.

- To resize your text, select it, and click and drag the corner handles horizontally or vertically.
- To rotate your text in 2D, click and drag the side handles.
- To rotate your text giving it a look as if it were in 3D space, click and drag the corner handles, as shown in Figure 10.25.

FIGURE 10.25

Clicking and dragging the side handles rotates text in 2D space. Clicking and dragging the corner handles rotates your text as if in 3D space.

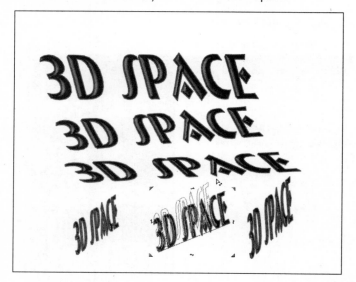

Warping text

Expression Design has a feature known as Envelope Distort, which allows you to warp the geometry of selected text. Basically, Envelope Distort involves placing a warp grid with nodes over the text, and then you can click and drag any node using the Direct Selection tool to distort the grid and thus distort your text. Figure 10.26 shows an example of warping text. Expression Design allows you to increase or decrease the number of nodes in the grid to allow for finer adjustments.

To warp your text, select it, and choose Object ➪ Envelope Distort ➪ Make Warp Group. Click the Direct Selection tool in the Toolbox, and click and drag any node in the grid to change the shapes of your letters.

To increase or decrease the number of nodes in the grid, choose Object ⇨ Envelope Distort ⇨ Increase Resolution to create more nodes, Object ⇨ Envelope Distort ⇨ Decrease Resolution to reduce the number of nodes, or Object ⇨ Envelope Distort ⇨ Reset Grid to reset the grid to its original size and shape.

FIGURE 10.26

Warping text in Expression Design.

Aligning text to a path

Expression Design also allows you to align text to a path, as shown in Figure 10.27. You can easily do this. First create the path and create the text. Then before you perform the alignment, you might want to set the alpha value of the path to 0. Then select both the path and the text, and choose Object ⇨ Text On Path ⇨ Attach Text. The text aligns to the path.

FIGURE 10.27

Aligning text to a path.

Creating Superscripts and Subscripts in Design and using them in Blend

You may want your text to contain superscripts or subscripts. This is easier to create in Expression Design than in Blend, so you may want to create superscripts and subscripts in Expression Design, and copy and paste them to move them over to Blend.

To assign superscripts and subscripts in Expression Design, click the Text tool and type in your text. Then select the text that you want to use as a superscript or subscript, and click the Superscript or Subscript button in the Text palette. The text should visibly change in the document. To bring the text over to Blend, select it so that object handles appear around it, and choose Edit ➪ Copy. Then in Blend, click in the artboard and choose Edit ➪ Paste. The text block that appears may have a height of 0, so you may need to pull the center handle down for the text to be visible.

Considerations for importing text into Expression Blend

You can copy text in Expression Design and paste it into Blend, but you'll lose the fill of your text, and your stroke becomes the Basic stroke, so there's usually not much point in copying and pasting. Instead, you probably want to export your text from Expression Design as one of the following:

- Drawing brush: Does not lose resolution when resized bigger, but can slow the performance of your application. Exporting from Design as a drawing brush is described in detail in Chapter 7.

- Image file: Can lose resolution when resized larger, but may be more efficient in terms of performance. Exporting from Design as an image file is described in the next paragraph.

- XAML file, which preserves your text as a vector object. Figure 10.28 shows an example of text that has been imported into Blend as a XAML file. It is the same text as shown in Figure 10.24 and preserved as vector objects. Like a drawing brush, however, this can be very slow in terms of performance. Exporting from Design as a XAML file is described in detail in Chapter 7.

FIGURE 10.28

Text imported as vector objects from Expression Design into Blend.

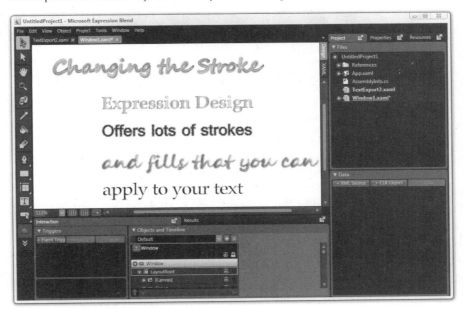

To export your text as an image file, place the text that you want to export as an image in a separate document from any other text on the page. Then choose File ➪ Export ➪ Image. Type in a name, choose a type and a folder, and click Save.

In Blend, you can choose Project ➪ Add Existing Item and then add the text to your project as an image, and use it as an image.

 Before exporting your image from Expression Design, you may want to increase its size to the largest that you want it to appear in your application without losing detail.

 For information about adding images, see Chapter 6.

Instructions for exporting objects as a drawing brush or a XAML file are found in Chapter 7.

Summary

- In Blend you can take advantage of new typographical features supported by WPF in fonts that contain any of the following alternative glyphs:

  - Stylistic Alternates

  - Swashes

  - Small capital letters and petite capital letters

  - Ligatures

  - Fractions that are stacked or slashed

  - Subscripts, superscripts, and more

- You can customize the look of your text and text boxes using the Brushes palette, the Transform palette and Appearance palette. Use the Appearance palette to increase the borders of the textbox. Use the Transform palette to rotate, scale and skew the text or text box. Use the Brushes palette to apply a wide range of brushes to the border, foreground, and background of the text and text box.

- Auto sizing your text box allows it to expand and contract when the window is resized, although the text inside does not change size. You can add maximum and minimum sizes for expansion and contraction.

- Using Blend's Brushes palette you can apply colors, gradients, opacity masks, and add image brushes, drawing brushes, or visual brushes to text.

- You can view animation, video, or the reflection of a panel inside text by creating a visual brush and applying it to text.

- Blend also allows you to apply bitmap effects to your text, so that you can give your text bevels, blurs, drop shadows, glows, and embossing — as long as you convert your text to a vector object.

- Using Expression Design, you can give your text different kinds of stroke styles, give your text borders, assign gradients to the borders and fills, assign patterns or images to your text, rotate text in 3D space, align text to a path, and warp text.

- You can import text from Expression Design either as an image, drawing brush or vector object.

- You can change your text into vector graphics and treat it as a vector graphic object. This gives you tremendous flexibility to make your text look however you want. Of course, the text box is no longer capable of linking to data if you do this, and it also scales as a vector graphic and not as text.

Chapter 11

Using Principles of Typographic Design to Enhance the User Experience

In this chapter, we offer some universal principles for creating compelling and appealing typographic design. The color, size, position, and shapes of your letterforms express a message to the viewer, regardless of their verbal meaning. Text is an art form in itself. It is the job of the designer to make sure the visual presentation of the letters corresponds to the message the words convey.

The way the words are presented on the page is another important area of design consideration. The Gutenberg diagram, for example, describes how the eyes of readers naturally move on a page.

In this chapter we discuss what to consider when choosing fonts in either a Web application or a Windows application. We also analyze how to choose the right text color, size, and styling, and discuss issues such as how the size of your font is influenced by the resizing of your program and how you can deal with that.

Creating Meaning by Thoughtful Selection of the Shape, Scale, Position, and Color of Letterforms

Letterforms have tremendous expressive power. For example, the same word displayed in different fonts can evoke quite different feelings, as shown in Figure 11.1. But the font that you use to display your text is only part of the story. Size, color, and position of the font can also make a huge impression on the viewer. All of these factors can mean the difference between success and failure in your design.

FIGURE 11.1

Same words but different fonts and thus different messages

Choosing and applying the right font

Fonts are plentiful and varied, so you have many choices. Your computer comes with a variety of fonts installed by default, including, perhaps, those shown in Figure 11.2. Thousands more are available on the Web. Choosing the ones you want to use in your application may not always be an easy decision. Let's look at strategies for finding and choosing the best fonts for your particular design.

FIGURE 11.2

Windows typically includes a default installation of a variety of fonts such as these.

Alba	COPPRPLGOTH BD BT	Georgia
Allegro	Courier New	Global Monospace
Arial	Crookie	Global Sans Serif
Baby Kruffy	English 111 Vivace BT	Global User Interface
BANKGOTHIC	Estrangelo Edessa	Gloucn
BernhardFashion	Fab	GoudyHandtooled BT
BernhardMod	Franklin Gothic	Humanst521
Bitstream Vera Sans	Freshbot	Impact
Book Antiqua	Frosty	Jenkins v. 0
Bookman Old Style	Futura	JOKERWOOD
Century Gothic	FuturaXBlk	Kartika
chick	Garamond	Latha
Comic Sans	Gautami	Lucida Console

Echoing the theme of your design

Letterforms are shapes, and the look of those shapes conveys a mood. Shapes that are soft and smooth may create a softer feeling. Shapes that are jagged may create a more aggressive feeling.

Think of the theme of your user interface. Do you want to convey a friendly feeling? Do you want to include some elegant swashes which can draw attention to your headings? Do you want your look to be retro, high speed, relaxed, dazzling, serious, or funny? Do you want to have a font that includes alternate glyphs and slightly shifting baselines to give the reader a sense that it was hand-written? What feeling meshes with your theme? For example, the three fonts shown in Figure 11.3 project completely different feelings. The Bank Gothic MD BT font on the left is wide and thick and looks like it should be chiseled into stone on the façade of a bank. The Bernhard Fashion BT font in the center looks dainty and sophisticated, like a thin, long-legged fashion model. The English111 font on the right looks like script and is not easy to read, but if weddings are part of your theme, then this definitely evokes the script on a wedding invitation.

FIGURE 11.3

Three fonts for three themes

Some fonts reflect their theme by using artwork within their font. This may be like hitting the reader over the head with the theme by projecting the theme to the conscious mind instead of the subconscious. But if you want to project a light feeling or cause a stir in the reader's mind, then you may want to use a font like Frosty, GlueGun, or Jokewood, as shown in Figure 11.4. If you have a theme that you think can be projected in a font, then chances are it already has been done. You can look for such a font among thousands of fonts available on the Internet, as discussed later in this chapter.

FIGURE 11.4

The theme of some fonts is obvious in their artwork — perhaps too obvious.

TIP Some fonts, such as WP Iconic symbols, Webdings, and Wingdings, can be a source of fast and free clip art.

Understanding categories of fonts

When thinking about which fonts to use, it's helpful to think of them grouped in a few broad categories according to basic visual characteristics. One way to group them is to think of English-language fonts as falling into one of four categories: serif, sans serif, script, and decorative.

Serif fonts

Serif fonts have short counterstrokes at the ends of the main strokes of each letter, as shown in Figure 11.5. They resemble letterforms chiseled in stone in ancient Rome, and, in fact, are often called *Roman* fonts. These are the fonts we are most accustomed to seeing in the body of text in books, newspapers, and magazines. When used as body text, they tend to project an air of legibility and normalcy; when used as headlines they may have a dignified, classic look. In print media, which typically has a resolution of 300 dots per inches or greater, and in other fairly high-resolution media, serif fonts may be easier to read than other fonts because the serifs give the eye hints on the structures of the letters.

Serif font families, as shown in Figure 11.5, include:

- *Old Style* or *Renaissance* fonts, such as Garamond, designed by Parisian publisher Claude Garamond in 1617.

- *Transitional* fonts, such as Baskerville, designed by British printer John Baskerville in 1757, in which the contrast between thick and thin strokes increases, with serifs becoming finer.

- *Modern* fonts, such as Bodoni, designed by Italian engraver and printer Giambattista Bodoni in 1788, in which the contrast between thick and thin strokes is even greater, with very thin serifs that are perpendicular to the main stem, rather than gently sloping as with older fonts.

- *Egyptian* or *slab serif* fonts, such as Century Expanded designed in 1895, with heavier serifs than seen before, and a return to less contrast between thick and thin strokes. The serifs are more slab-like — perhaps evoking the square shoulders of Egyptians depicted in hieroglyphics?

FIGURE 11.5

Examples of the letter A in serif fonts from four eras, from left to right: Garamond, an old-style font; Baskerville, a transitional font; Bodoni, a modern font; and Century Expanded, a slab serif font.

Sans serif fonts

Sans serif fonts are fonts without serifs (the fine counterstrokes finishing off the main strokes of a letter), as shown in Figure 11.6. They look clean, rational, efficient, and even austere. The viewer may tend to subtly associate them with modernity. This is not so surprising because almost all sans serif fonts have been designed in the last century, which is more recently than many serif fonts. The uniformity of sans serif letterforms makes them harder to read in long passages in print media. But sans serif fonts are usually easier to read than serif fonts on lower-resolution media such as computer screens, which due to the limitations of current technology often have resolutions as low as 72 dots per inch. On contemporary computer screens, details such as serifs disappear or look fuzzy.

Decorative fonts

Decorative fonts have letterforms that are more elaborate and fanciful, and they may imitate natural objects such as cake frosting, fire, stars, or vegetation.

Script fonts

Script fonts have the fluid strokes of cursive handwriting with letters that are usually connected. They may project an air of informality, elegance, or extravagance, depending on the quality and quantity of curvature and curlicues.

FIGURE 11.6

Examples of (from top to bottom) sans serif, decorative, and script fonts

Font technologies

Blend uses a system called ClearType to position fonts within a fraction of a pixel, so that when the fonts are resized, they can resize without any distortion in the text box. ClearType supports OpenType fonts with either TrueType or Postscript CFF outlines.

> **NOTE** The OpenType fonts were developed by Microsoft and Adobe. They are similar to the scalable TrueType fonts created earlier by Apple. The Postscript CFF (compact font format), also known as CFF font format or Type 2 font format, was developed by Adobe for the WPF to increase the efficiency for rendering times and storage space.

These fonts are created using vector graphics that expand or shrink in size without distortion. For example, if you want to see a font with a size of 72 or a size of 6, it would look the same, although you may need to zoom in or zoom out to see that there is no difference.

CROSS-REF For more information about OpenType fonts and their new features in the WPF, see Chapter 10.

CAUTION Be sure you have the rights to distribute the fonts in an application if you plan to use them in your applications. If the fonts are free fonts that you've downloaded from the Web, you may not need any special permission, depending on the terms under which the fonts were released by their creators. Otherwise, you most likely need to come to an agreement with the publisher of the fonts before you can bundle them with your application.

As we understand it at this writing, letterforms can't be copyrighted under current U.S. law, but the names of fonts can be trademarked, and each computer font file usually includes rasterizing software that is copyrighted. So typically you can't freely share computer fonts unless their creators have expressly dedicated them to the public domain or have released them under the terms of a license that freely permits their redistribution.

Choosing fonts for the computer screen

Computer screens are low resolution compared to print media, which may be printed at 2400 dots per inch. It's a rare computer screen that has 2400 dots across the whole width of the screen, let alone 2400 dots per inch. You may want to have an idea of the range of sizes of computer monitors that your users will have before choosing your font. Many contemporary computer monitors still have only 800 pixels across, although most have at least 1024. With these low-resolution screens, sans serif fonts are more legible for body text. Some fonts, such Bitstream Vera, are even designed for legibility on computer screens and will definitely be good for low-resolution screens. For headlines where the letterforms are bigger, other fonts can be used. But for smaller type, consider sans serif fonts, as shown in Figure 11.7.

If you want to see how a font will look on a low-resolution screen, test it out. Switch your screen resolution to the lowest resolution that you think your user will possibly use and see how it looks. It may look fine, or you may be surprised.

FIGURE 11.7

For body text, sans serif fonts are more easily readable than serif fonts on computer screens.

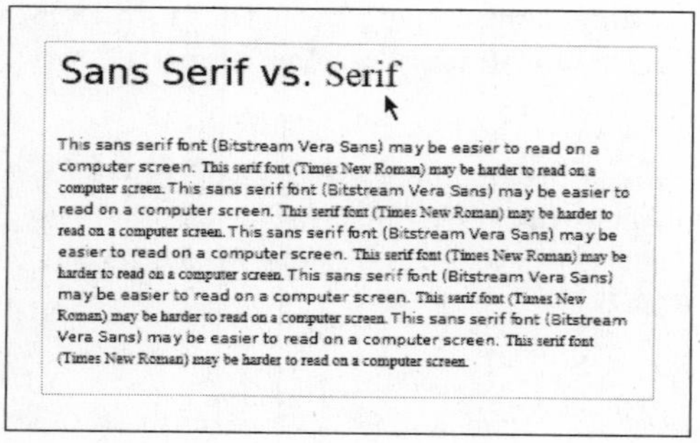

How Many Fonts Should You Use?

A good rule of thumb is to use fewer than four fonts in your design. Start out with two fonts, one for headings and one for body text, and see if that's enough. You probably don't want to use more than three fonts, unless you're designing a ransom note.

Finding fonts

Your computer comes with a variety of fonts installed by default. These fonts are useful for many purposes, but to add zing to your applications, in many situations you may want something different. If you know where to look, finding a suitable font isn't too hard, as you can choose from thousands of fonts from hundreds of font providers. That's a lot of potential fonts to wade through, but at least your choices aren't constrained by a lack of fonts. As described in the next sections of this chapter, you can purchase high-quality fonts from the big, established vendors of proprietary fonts, you can choose from thousands of freely available fonts, or you can even create your own fonts if you want something unique.

Finding proprietary fonts

You can buy fonts from hundred of vendors. The big, established proprietary font foundries sell a huge selection of high-quality fonts. You may want to look specifically for OpenType fonts which make use of many of the OpenType features available to them. The big font foundries include:

- Adobe (`www.adobe.com/type`)
- Bitstream (`www.bitstream.com/fonts/buy_fonts.html`)
- International Typeface Corporation (`www.itcfonts.com`)
- Linotype (`www.linotype.com`)
- Monotype Imaging (`www.fonts.com`)
- URW++ (`www.urwpp.de/english/home.html`)

TIP For a comprehensive list of creators of proprietary fonts, with comments on each foundry, see Luc Devroye's "Commercial font outfits" page at `http://cg.scs.carleton.ca/~luc/commercialfonts.html`.

Finding free fonts

You can find thousands of free or shareware fonts available via free download on the Web. The quality varies, so beware — fonts constructed hastily by amateurs may not look good at all sizes or may possess flaws in proportion, spacing, stroke size, and so on, that subtly degrade the look of your design. Nevertheless, the free font collections on the Web are a fantastic resource. While they may not have the latest WPF font features, they are...uh...free!

One of the best-organized collections of free fonts on the Web is at www.1001fonts.com, where you can find fonts sorted by theme, author, popularity, or recentness. Information is provided for any usage restrictions for each font. Other similarly useful sites include www.dafont.com, http://dev.abstractfonts.com, www.acidfonts.com, www.highfonts.com, and www.1001freefonts.com. See Figure 11.8 for a few examples of the range of fonts available.

 For information on more sites offering free fonts, check out **www.graphicsngraphic design.com/hugelistfreefontssites**.

For a directory to even more information on free fonts, and to almost anything else about fonts, visit the main page of Luc Devroye's font site at **http://cg.scs.carleton.ca/~luc/fonts.html**.

FIGURE 11.8

Thousands of free fonts are available on the Web from sites such as www.1001fonts.com.

Creating fonts

For the ultimate flexibility in finding a font that perfectly supports the theme of your application, you can design your own font or customize an existing font. Creating a high-quality font requires patience and practice, but in some cases designing your own font may really be worth it.

 Customizing an existing font can often give you much of the benefit of designing a unique font from scratch, but with far less work.

One of the most prominent software packages for font creation and editing is FontLab Studio, shown in Figure 11.9. It features a comprehensive set of functionality in a well-designed user interface. For more information on FontLab Studio, visit the FontLab Web site at www.fontlab.com.

FIGURE 11.9

FontLab Studio is a popular font editor and has a comprehensive feature set.

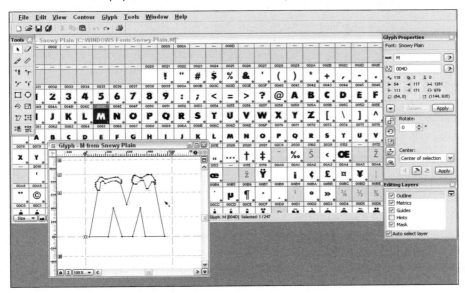

We like FontForge, a powerful and free font editor that was originally developed for GNU/Linux systems and now can run on Windows as well. You can download FontForge free from `http://fontforge.sourceforge.net`. The download page for the Windows installer also includes simple instructions for installing a prebuilt package of Cygwin, the free GNU/Linux-like environment that FontForge requires.

TIP Luc Devroye's Web page devoted to font editing at `http://cg.scs.carleton.ca/~luc/fonts.html` links to and comments on dozens of tools and resources for creating and editing fonts.

Understanding Fonts, Part by Part

It's useful to understand the anatomy of a font, and an easy way to do that is to know the names of the parts of each letterform. If you know the names of the parts of a letterform, it's easy to think of the appearance of each component of the letterform separately and how you might choose (or alter) each part to convey a particular message. That makes it easy for you to understand what you see when you look at a particular font and to determine if the font is right for your design.

continued

continued

The following figure depicts many of the key anatomical features that may be present in a letterform:

■ The *x-height* or *body* of a letter is the height of the letter x in lowercase.

■ The imaginary line on which the letter x sits is called the *baseline*, and the imaginary line sitting on the top of the letter x is called the *meanline*.

■ Letters such as p and q have a *descender* below the baseline.

■ Letters such as d and f have an *ascender* above the meanline.

■ The uppercase letter Q has a *tail*.

■ The vertical line in letters such as E, l, and b is called the *stem* of the letter.

■ The parts of the letters E and F that extend to the right are called the *arms*.

■ The height of uppercase letters such as E and P is called the *cap height*.

■ The topmost point of the letter A is called its *apex*.

■ The horizontal line in the letters A and H is called the *horizontal stem* or *crossbar*.

■ The fat diagonal line of the letter N in our diagram is called the *stroke* and the skinny vertical lines are called the *brackets*.

■ Each round stroke in letters such as B, b, and P is called a *bowl*.

■ The hollow space inside letters such as B, b, e and p is called the *counter*.

■ The horizontal line in a lowercase t is called the *cross stroke*.

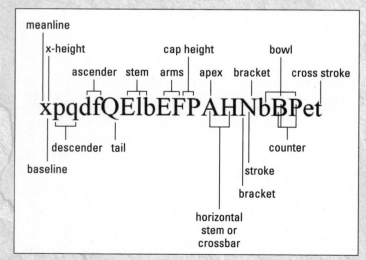

The anatomy of letterforms

Installing fonts

Once you download, create, or edit your new font, you can install it in Windows XP by clicking on the font file in a Windows Explorer window, dragging it from its current folder, and dropping it into your \Windows\Fonts folder in another window. If you are using Vista, then click the Help And Support button in the Start panel and type Install Font, and then click on the first search result. Follow the instructions that appear.

CAUTION In Windows XP, don't save your font from within an application directly into the \Windows\Fonts folder. You need to drag it from its current folder and drop it into your \Windows\Fonts folder so that Windows installs it properly.

Selecting Text Size and Color

The color and size of your text and how they integrate with the background all contribute to the visual theme of your application design and to the feeling your theme creates. For example, a bright color conveys something very different to the viewer than gray or a dark color. Also, a text color that contrasts strongly with the color of the background may give your text a more bold or stark feeling, and also make the font easier to read. Less contrast is gentler and may create a feeling that the type is more integrated with the background, but it may also be harder to read.

Optimizing text legibility

If you want to improve the legibility of your text on the computer screen, here are some basic rules of thumb:

- Use sans serif fonts.
- Increase the type size. (In print media, 9- to 12-point type is usually considered best for body text depending on the font, but generally you want to use larger type for computer displays, as well as for readers who are older.)
- Create a high contrast between type and background. Dark text on a light background is easier to read than light text on a dark background.
- Create an ideal amount of space between the letters on the line. If the letters are too close together or too far apart they become hard to read.
- Create an optimal size for the *leading*, the amount of space between the lines. Optimal leading size is usually the type size plus 1 to 4 points (1 point = $\frac{1}{72}$ of an inch) if you are using type in the 9 to 12-point type range.
- Consider the length of a line of text. The longer the line length, the more difficult it is for the eye to continue on and find the next line.

Examples of all of these are shown in Figure 11.10.

FIGURE 11.10

Sans serif fonts on a highly contrasting background with an ideal amount of space between letters and between lines make text more legible.

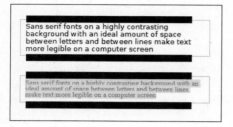

Considerations for choosing your font size

Some basic considerations of setting your font size are as follows:

- Large text or ALL CAPS text is like SHOUTING!
- Small text is like whispering.
- Small text may be difficult to read.
- The larger you scale the font, the more the letterforms themselves create shapes that suggest things to the eye; choose large fonts carefully.

 If you have a lot of text, you often want to make the most important text larger and the least important text smaller.

Be especially careful of what font you choose for your headings (that is, your large type). This will probably play a stronger role than your body type in defining the feeling that your application projects. The larger shapes of the letterforms of the large type will make a deeper impression on the user than the shapes of the smaller type. Large sans serif fonts may be rectangular with hard edges and create a different feeling than a large serif font, which may be constructed from more graceful, curving shapes.

Choosing text color

When choosing the color of your font, you may want to keep in mind the following:

- What does the color suggest symbolically, and how does that fit into the theme of the user interface design?
- How does the contrast between your font color and the background color enhance your theme?
- How does the saturation level of your color integrate with your theme?

 A significant portion of the population has some colorblindness, so you probably don't want to rely on color completely to convey meaning.

 For information about the symbolic connotations of colors, see Chapter 8.

Choosing your color saturation level

When setting the color of your text, you probably also want to consider how saturated you want your colors to be. Highly saturated colors have no black or white mixed in with them, so the hues are bright and pure, which attracts attention. Saturated colors may connote boldness or fun. Colors that are mixed with white are *pastel* colors and may suggest a more cheerful or softer mood. Colors mixed with a lot of gray or black may suggest a darker mood, perhaps quieter or more somber, and may suggest a sense of depth.

As described later in this chapter, you can set the color saturation of text by clicking in the Blend color picker. To add more black in a color, click further down in the rectangle with the colors. To add more white, click further to the left.

Contrasting font color with background color

When choosing a font color, you also need to consider how it blends with the background color. Choosing a color for the font that clashes with the background will draw attention to the text, creating an atmosphere of dynamism and perhaps abrasiveness.

If you think of a rainbow of colors arranged on a color wheel from red to orange to yellow to green to blue to indigo to violet and back to red, then the colors opposite each other on the wheel are called complementary colors, and colors next to each other on the color wheel are called analogous colors. You can choose complementary color schemes (of yellow and purple or of red and green, for example) to create a sense of dynamism, and you can use analogous colors (for example, cyan and blue, or orange and red) to create a sense of harmony.

Positioning Text

The position of your type conveys its importance to the users of your application. Here are some basic principles about positioning text:

- If you put a large font in the center, it will dominate.
- Text off on the edges may seem less important.
- Text at the top is more prominent.
- Positioning text away from other elements gives it more prominence. For example, the words "Goldfish Pond" in Figure 11.11 are separated from the rest of the text and stand out more, even though it is in a weak position on the screen.
- Positioning text close to other elements may seem to give it less importance.

Separating the title from the text gives the title more prominence.

Taking Advantage of the Gutenberg Diagram

In the 1950s a typographer named Edmund Arnold came up with the idea of the Gutenberg diagram, which gained favor among designers. It has only a little empirical evidence to support it, but generally states that a typical reader from the Western world will follow a pattern across the page of first looking in the upper left-hand corner of the page and then proceeding in a general direction to the lower right-hand corner of the page. This means that whatever is in the upper right-hand corner may get less noticed than what is in the lower right-hand corner, and what is in the lower left-hand corner may get least noticed of all, as illustrated in Figure 11.12.

The Gutenberg diagram pertains to homogenous text and does not always apply when, for example, a large headline exists in the upper right-hand corner of the page. But the point is, large headlines may be the most effective when they are located in the upper left-hand corner of the page.

FIGURE 11.12

The Gutenberg diagram asserts that readers are conditioned to start from the upper left and travel to the lower right with their eyes. Areas given least attention are the upper right and especially the lower left.

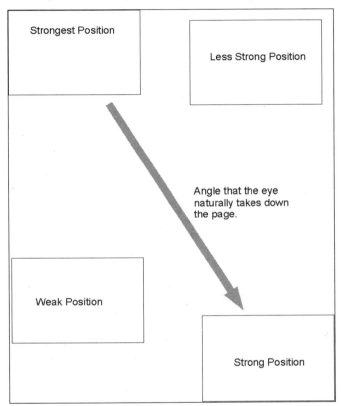

Integrating Type and Message

Blend allows you to add gradients to selected text in such a way that the selected text displays a single gradient, such as a linear gradient. You can also animate that gradient and add a visual brush to the animated gradient. In Figure 11.13, we add a gradient, visual brush, and drop shadow to the word *Celestial*. The gradient gives the impression of bright starlight shining on part of the words, and the visual brush acts as a reflection. The effect was created entirely in Blend.

FIGURE 11.13

Animating a logo to create a look of star shine with a drop shadow and reflection.

| TIP | To see the logo shown in Figure 11.13 in action and in color, go to www.blendtips.com/bible. |

STEPS: Animating a Gradient, Adding a Drop Shadow, and Adding a Visual Brush to Text

1. Select TextBlock in the Toolbox and click and drag in the artboard to create the text block. Type **Celestial**. Select the word by double-clicking on it. In the Text palette choose a larger size, such as 72, and choose Bernhard Fashion BT as a font, and click Bold.

2. In the Brushes palette, choose Background and click the No Brush tab. Choose BorderBrush and click the No Brush tab again. Choose Foreground and click the Gradient Brush tab. Select the gradient stop on the left and choose a dark blue color. Then click in the gradient bar to add a gradient stop immediately to the right of the left-most gradient stop and choose white. Then click the right-most gradient stop and choose the same dark blue color. If you have any more than three gradient stops, remove the others by clicking and dragging them off the gradient bar.

3. Click the Create New Timeline button and give the Timeline a name, or accept the default and click OK. Click the Record Keyframe button above the playhead. Move the playhead to 4. In the Appearance palette move the middle gradient stop from the far left to the far right. Click the red Turn Off Record Mode button, move the playhead back to 0, and click the play button to test the animation.

4. To loop the animation, click the expander beside [TextBlock] in the Objects list and keep opening expanders until you get to the element called Offset. Right-click on the gray area of its track and choose Edit Repeat Count. In the Repeat Count dialog box choose Forever and then click OK.

5. Add a star by creating another text block and typing lowercase L. Select the L you just added and choose the Webdings font. Then increase the font size and click the Selection tool to select the text block. Choose Object ⇨ Path ⇨ Convert To Path. Then rotate and position the star over the dot in the "I" in "Celestial."

6. Create the reflection by clicking the Selection tool and clicking the text block to select it. Then choose Tools ⇨ Make Brush Resource ⇨ Make Visual Brush Resource, and name it and click OK in the dialog box.

7. Then draw a rectangle and flip and skew it, and assign the visual brush by selecting Fill in the Brushes palette, and clicking the Brush Resources tab and selecting the visual brush.

8. To create the drop shadow, select the text block, choose Edit ⇨ Copy and then Edit ⇨ Paste. Select the copy, and in the Brushes palette assign the text a solid color brush such as gray. Then choose Object ⇨ Order ⇨ Send To Back and position it like a shadow.

Summary

- The larger the font is, the more the shape of the letters themselves convey meaning.

- It is good for your large fonts to be consistent with the message of your application. For example, thin fonts convey elegance, italics convey motion, bold type conveys heaviness, steadiness, and immovability.

- Consistency in fonts is important for aesthetic appeal. You probably want to limit the number of fonts that you use to just a few.

- Font categories can be divided into four types: serif, sans serif, script, and decorative.

- To improve the readability of your text on computer screens, use san serif fonts, create high color contrast with the background, and create optimal text size, leading, and space between the letters.

- The Gutenberg diagram shows how many people in the Western world naturally allow their eyes to travel from the upper left to the lower right of a homogeneous page, leaving the upper right and the lower left areas less noticed.

Part IV

Creating Cinematic
User Interfaces

Chapter 12

Using 3D Models

3D can enhance the aesthetics of your user interface or Web application, and, as discussed in Chapter 8, enhancing the visual appeal of your user interface can make your application more successful. 3D objects can sometimes convey much more information to the user than 2D. While Blend is no substitute for a full-featured 3D application, it does allow you to manipulate the position, materials, and lighting of 3D objects, as well as create simple animations using 3D objects.

Using Blend you can map images, videos, drawing brushes, and text onto 3D objects. You can even allow the user to manipulate the 3D object without the need for any coding, simply by data binding the scale, rotation or position values to a slider.

The first step in doing all this is to add 3D models into your application and position them. Blend lets you create and import 3D models in a variety of ways:

- You can create 3D models from 2D images or videos. These are like flat screens that you can position in 3D space using the Camera Orbit tool, and you can also animate the images.

- You can import XAML files from Electric Rain's Zam 3D (www.erain.com). Zam 3D is an easy-to-use 3D modeling program with an extensive gallery of drag-and-drop materials, lighting, and animations. Zam 3D can also import animation files in .3ds format and export them as .xaml, which can be imported directly into Blend.

- You can import 3D OBJ files from many 3D programs including Blender (www.blender.org), Maya (www.autodesk.com), Softimage (www.softimage.com), and more. These OBJ files contain information about the geometry of the model, and the accompanying MTL files contain information about the materials. Information about lights and cameras are also imported. But these files don't contain any information about animation.

In this chapter, you explore how to create, import, and modify 3D models, including their lights and materials, and how to add them into your Blend documents.

CROSS-REF For information on animating a 3D model and wrapping a video on to a 3D model, see Chapter 14.

Getting Started with 3D

Blend allows you to transform any image into a 3D plane. This is like putting an image on a piece of paper that you can view from any angle. To transform a 2D image into a 3D object, add your image into the artboard, and select the image. Then choose Tools ➪ Make Image 3D. Now your image resides in a Viewport3D.

CROSS-REF For information on adding images into the artboard, see Chapter 6.

If you want to import a 3D model with an .obj extension, then you can choose Project ➪ Add Existing Item and add the OBJ file. (Be sure to add the MTL file as well, if you want to import the materials for the 3D object as well as its geometry.) Then right-click on the OBJ file in the Project panel and choose Insert.

Moving, Rotating, and Resizing 3D objects

Once you have a Viewport3D in your window, Blend allows you to move, rotate, and resize 3D models in the Viewport3D in the following ways:

- **Using the Camera Orbit tool** which is located in the Toolbox. This offers a simple, quick and intuitive method of manipulating your 3D object. In Figure 12.1, a 3D image is rotated in 3D space using the Camera Orbit tool. How to use this tool is described in the next section of this chapter.

FIGURE 12.1

Using the Camera Orbit tool to rotate a 3D image in 3D space.

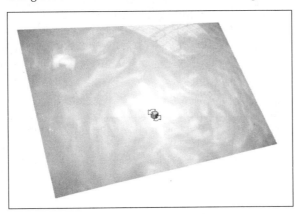

- **Using the transformation handles.** These appear when you select the actual model in the Objects list. You may need to open a lot of expanders to select the model. Start with the Viewport3D expander. Using the transformation handles gives you control over the X, Y, and Z axes, because you can rotate, size, or position the object in one direction at a time. Details about using the transformation handles are found in the section "Working with the Transformation Handles" later in this chapter.

- **Using the Transform palette.** This palette is useful for 3D as well as 2D and gives the greatest control over any transformations you perform. You can type in a specific number for the specific axis for the transformation, and precisely rotate, resize, and re-position your 3D object down to an extraordinary number of decimal places — more than you want to deal with.

Using the Camera Orbit tool

Once you have a Viewport3D in your artboard, you can manipulate the 3D object within it using the Camera Orbit tool. This tool allows you to rotate in 3D space, shrink or expand the object within the confines of the Viewport3D, and position the object, again within the confines of the Viewport3D.

- **To rotate your object in 3D space,** click the Camera Orbit tool and click and drag in the Viewport3D. The object rotates in 3D space according to the movement of the Camera Orbit tool. This tool is very intuitive, although it lacks some of the precision that the Transform palette offers. Rotating 3D objects using the Transform palette is described in a section later in this chapter.

- **To scale your 3D object within the Viewport3D,** you can click the Camera Orbit tool and hold the Alt key as you click and drag. Dragging downward makes the object smaller. Dragging upward makes it larger. (To make an object larger without having it clipped by the Viewport3D, you need to enlarge the entire Viewport3D. You can do this by selecting the Viewport3D and pulling the object handles.)

- **To position the 3D object within the Viewport3D,** click the Camera Orbit tool, then hold the Ctrl key and click while dragging the 3D object. See Figure 12.2.

FIGURE 12.2

Using the Camera Orbit tool while holding down the Ctrl key allows you to position your 3D objects within the Viewport3D.

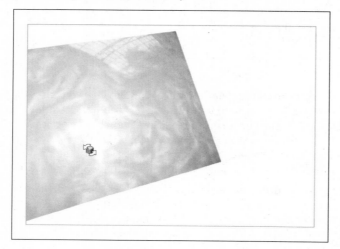

TIP   You may find that the Viewport3D control may clip some of the image as you rotate it inside the Viewport3D. If you do not want this to occur, you can make the 3D object smaller within the Viewport3D. This gives your 3D object more room. You can then make the Viewport3D larger to bring your object back to the original size without having it chopped off when you rotate it.

Working with the Transformation Handles

When you select your 3D object in the Viewport3D, transformation handles appear, as shown in Figure 12.3. For these handles to appear, you may need to select the lowest level of the object — with no expander beside it. Using these handles, you can do the following:

Viewport3D Basics

A Viewport3D panel is a specialized panel for containing 3D objects. Whenever you have 3D objects, (that are really 3D objects and not just a 2D representation of the 3D object), then they need to be nested in a Viewport3D. This nesting generally occurs automatically in Blend whenever you bring in a 3D object or change an image to 3D.

The Viewport3D contains not just the object itself, but also the lights, cameras and materials that make the 3D object appear as intended. All these components of the 3D object are available for selecting and editing within the Viewport3D.

To select the object, camera, or lights, open the expander next to the Viewport3D in the Objects list to view the nested elements. To select the actual 3D model, keep opening elements until you get to the 3D object. This may or may not have an expander next to it, depending on whether you select the most basic level of the 3D object, or a grouped 3D object.

When adding the Viewport3D into your layout, you can use the Layout palette to adjust its size, margins, and more. You may want to auto size it so that it gets larger or smaller depending on the window size. To do that, click the Auto buttons beside Width and Height in the Layout palette.

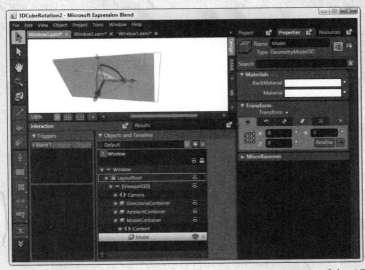

The Viewport3D in the Objects list displays the components of the 3D object.

- **Move a 3D model.** Select the model by clicking on its name in the Objects list in the Objects and Timeline palette, and move the model by clicking and dragging one of the arrow heads (shown in Figure 12.3) corresponding to the direction you want to move the model.

- **Rotate the 3D model.** Click and drag one of the rounded bars, as shown in Figure 12.3. These arrows, cubes, and curved bars are color-coded according to the dimension to which they pertain.

- **Scale the 3D model.** Click and drag one of the small cubes on the arrows, as shown in Figure 12.3, to scale the model in the dimension controlled by the cube that you chose.

FIGURE 12.3

Moving, scaling, and positioning a 3D model in Blend using its transformation handles.

Drag the arrow to move the 3D model along a single axis

Drag the small cube to scale the 3D model in a single dimension

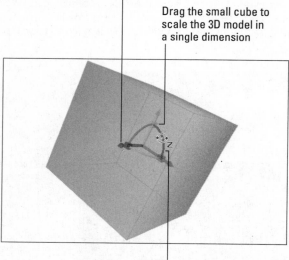

Drag the curved bar to rotate the 3D model along a single axis

Using the Transform palette to move, rotate and scale 3D objects

Blend allows you to move, rotate, and reposition your 3D object in 3D space, as well as move the center of rotation of the 3D object. To do this, you can select the model and set values in the Position, Rotation, Scale, and Center Point tabs of the Transform palette. Three working input boxes appear in each tab, instead of two for 2D objects. (The third, of course, is the Z axis.)

CROSS-REF For more information about using the Transform palette, see Chapter 6.

Importing 3D models

While Blend can create a flat 3D model for images, it also allows you to import 3D models with 3D geometry as well as materials and animations. 3D models with geometry and materials can be imported as .obj and .mtl files. These are standard 3D file extensions that you can generate from 3D programs by exporting into those file types. If you want to import animations along with your 3D models, then you need to export your models and animation into a XAML file. XAML files can be exported by Zam3D, which is a full-featured 3D application developed by Electric Rain. For more about using Zam3D, see "Using Zam3D to Create 3D Models and Animation" later in this chapter.

Importing OBJ and MTL files

3D programs such as Blender, Maya, and Softimage can export OBJ files. These generally are exported with an accompanying MTL file that contains the information about the materials. You can import OBJ and MTL files by choosing Project ⇨ Add Existing Item. (If you bring only the OBJ file into the Projects palette, then whatever materials you assigned it in your 3D application will not appear when you add it into your artboard.)

Once you have the OBJ and MTL files in the Projects palette, then right-click on the OBJ file and choose Insert. The 3D object appears in the Viewport3D with its materials automatically visible. You can adjust the size and position of the Viewport3D as well as use the Camera Orbit tool to adjust the size, rotation, and position of the model within the Viewport3D.

Figure 12.4 shows an example of a 3D model imported from Blender. This model is automatically generated in Blender by choosing Add ⇨ Mesh ⇨ Monkey. For instructions on creating models in Blender, see the sidebar entitled "Using Blender to Create 3D Objects for Import into Blend".

FIGURE 12.4

The Blender monkey in Blend.

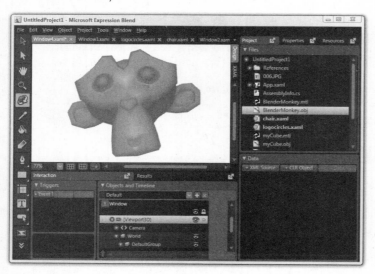

Importing Zam3D Models and Animations Into Blend

Zam 3D exports to XAML format, which enables you to import the 3D model, its materials, and its animations into your Blend project. Figure 12.5 shows an example of an animation created in Zam3D and imported into Blend. Importing 3D animations into Blend is unique to Zam3D at this writing, because no other 3D application exports XAML files (although that will undoubtedly change with time.)

In the sections later in this chapter, we explore how to create models and animations using Zam3D, as well as how to export them into XAML so that you can import them into Blend within a Viewport3D.

You can also import 3D models from other 3D programs in the form of OBJ and MTL files and add your own animations in Blend.

CROSS-REF   For more information about animating your 3D models, see Chapter 14.

TIP   If you have a 3D animation that you want to include in your Blend document, then first decide if you really need to bring it into Blend as a 3D animation. Otherwise, you may want to export it as a movie and add it to your project as you would any video file. This may improve the performance of your application.

FIGURE 12.5

This 3D spinning animation was created in Zam3D and imported into Blend.

Once you export your 3D model from Zam 3D into XAML and within a Viewport3D, which we describe later in this chapter, you can import it into Blend. To do this, perform the following steps:

STEPS: Importing Zam3D Objects and Animations into Blend

1. Choose Project ➪ Add Existing Item and double-click on the XAML file that you exported from Blend. Be sure that you export the Zam3D into a Viewport3D, as described in the section on exporting from Zam3D later in this chapter.

2. To move it into the page or window where you want it to reside, you can do either of the following:

   ◾ Select the Viewport3D and choose Edit ➪ Copy. Then open the window that you want to move the 3D object to, click in the artboard and choose Edit ➪ Paste.

   ◾ Click the XAML button, select all the XAML code and choose Edit ➪ Copy. Then open the window that you want to move the 3D object to. Click the XAML code button and paste your code into the XAML. (Be sure not to nest it within other objects, unless that is your intention. And if it is the only XAML code in the file, then change the

   ```
   <Grid x:Name="LayoutRoot"/>
   ```
   to
   ```
   <Grid x:Name="LayoutRoot">
   </Grid>
   ```
   and paste your code between the opening and closing tags.)

3. To view your 3D object along with any animation, choose Project ➪ Set As Startup, choose the window in which your 3D object resides, and choose Project ➪ Test Project, or press F5.

4. If you find that the Viewport3D is cropping some of your object, then click the Camera Orbit tool and drag it downward in the Viewport3D while holding down the Alt key. To center the 3D objects, use the Camera Orbit tool while holding the Shift key and drag the objects to the center of the Viewport3D. To get everything looking right, you'll probably want to resize and position your Viewport3D in your window, as well.

Importing from other 3D programs

You can use Zam 3D to import files in .3ds and .dxf formats and then export them into XAML so they can be imported into Blend. For more information about importing these formats into Zam 3D, see "Importing into Zam 3D from other 3D programs" later in this chapter.

Finding 3D Models on the Web

Maybe the quickest and least expensive way to create 3D models is to download one. Many 3D models are available on the Web, both in 3DS format and DXF format. Here are some places you can try:

- **3D Café** (www.3dcafestore.com): This site offers model libraries from a dozen vendors. For example, you can buy 150 3D animals there for $129. That's much easier than building them yourself — even if you are only looking for a single animal. They have lots more as well.
- **Got 3D** (http://store.got3d.com): This site has lots of people, textures, and more. (For example, you can buy 16 casually clothed people for $95.)
- **Turbo Squid** (www.turbosquid.com): This site has over 160,000 models and textures with a search engine to help you find what you want.
- **The 3D Studio** (www.the3dstudio.com): This site has thousands of inexpensive models and other 3D resources available for sale.

Adding Materials and Applying Textures

You can change the look of your 3D object by changing its materials. Materials can be any brush, including image brushes, drawing brushes, tiling brushes and visual brushes

Brushes can be applied to the Material or the BackMaterial. The BackMaterial for a cube would be like the inside of the box on the far surface, as if you could see through the first surface of the box. The BackMaterial does not show unless the Material has some transparency applied.

Whether you select the Material or the BackMaterial, you can apply brushes to any of three elements:

■ **Diffuse Material**: to change the color of the material.

■ **Emissive Material**: to change the appearance of how the object seems to glow from within.

■ **Specular Material**: to change the appearance of the light shining on it. You can also change the power of this light, as described later in this chapter.

Adding and editing the Diffuse Material

The diffuse material is probably the best for applying a texture to, such as an image brush, drawing brush, visual brush, color, or gradient. To apply a brush to the diffuse material, select the model or the part of the model that you want to change. To do this, expand the Objects list so that you can click on the actual model to select it. (The model will be nested in the World element or ModelContainer – whatever it may be called — and having no expander next to it, unless you want to select a grouped object.) Then, if your model is added as an OBJ file, follow the instructions in the next section, or if your model is added as a XAML file, follow the instructions in the section entitled "Adding and editing the Diffuse Material for a 3D model from a XAML file" later in this chapter.

CROSS-REF For information about creating image brush resources or drawing brush resources, see Chapter 6.

For instructions for adding video as textures by using the visual brush, see Chapter 14.

Adding or editing the Diffuse Material for a 3D model from an OBJ file

Click the Material swatch in the Materials palette. A pop-up panel appears. Then select Diffuse Material from the list that appears. If no list appears because your model has no material applied to it, or if you want to add another material, then click the button for Diffuse Material at the top of the pop-up panel and click the plus sign. (To delete materials, select them from the list and click the minus sign.)

Now you can assign a diffuse material, using any of the brushes in the Texture section of the pop-up panel. Figure 12.6 shows an example of an image brush assigned to a cube.

You can also apply a diffuse color in the pop-up panel, below the Texture brush. This adds color to the texture. Whatever color you choose is added to the colors of the texture, modifying the texture brush. You can also choose an Ambient color which has an effect like a colored light bulb shining on an object.

Adding and editing the Diffuse Material for a 3D model from a XAML file

After selecting the object in the Objects list, click the Material swatch in the Materials palette. If a panel appears, then follow the instructions in the preceding section in this chapter. If a list appears, then choose Edit Resource from the list. An Edit Resource panel appears, as shown in Figure 12.7. Select the Diffuse Material or click the Diffuse Material button and click a plus sign.

FIGURE 12.6

Editing the diffuse material of your 3D OBJ object.

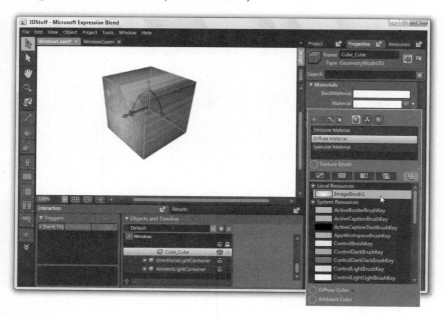

The Texture Brush pane in this panel only allows you to assign a solid color, although this may change with later versions of Blend. The Diffuse Color pane allows you to assign another color which adds to the color you selected in the Texture pane. And the Ambient Color acts as if it is coloring the light that shines on the object.

When you edit the resource, you edit all the elements that are assigned that resource, so making a change in the resource may make changes elsewhere in your 3D model.

TIP   Notice that in Figure 12.6 the image brush is applied only to one side of the cube. (It's actually applied to the back, too, but this is out of view.) The sides have a striped appearance, because the image brush fills in on the sides whatever colors that appeared on the edges. If you want the sides to show the image brush in the same way as the front and back, then when you create your cube, you can create it out of six individual planes, put together as a cube. Then you can select each plane individually in the Objects list and assign the image brush to it.

Getting materials to look just right in 3D can be complicated. It may be easier to modify the materials of your object in the original 3D program that created it and re-import it. 3D programs often have ready-made materials in their 3D materials gallery.

FIGURE 12.7

Editing the diffuse material of your 3D XAML object.

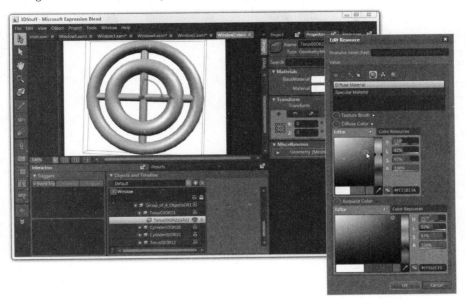

Adding and editing the Specular Material and Emissive Material

You can add and edit the specular and emissive materials in the same way that we just described for the diffuse materials for both the objects derived from the XAML or OBJ files. The Specular Material panel also contains a Specular Power property that you can set, as shown in Figure 12.8. A lower specular power number creates more highlights; a higher number reduces the highlights.

The specular light is the highlight of an object. It defines how much the object reflects a focused beam of light.

Wrapping text onto a 3D model

Blend allows you to wrap text onto a 3D object, by defining text as either a drawing brush or a visual brush. The text warps or adjusts to fit the surface of the 3D object. Figure 12.9 shows an example of text wrapping on a sphere. The user can type the text into the rich text box, and it wraps onto the sphere. (This can be accomplished using a visual brush, not a drawing brush.) The application window on the right has NoBrush assigned to the background of the rich text box. This causes the sphere to be transparent except where there is text.

FIGURE 12.8

Editing the specular material of your 3D XAML object.

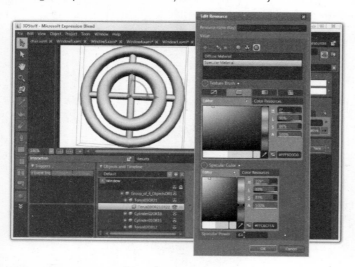

FIGURE 12.9

The user types text into the rich text box and it wraps on the sphere. The sphere on the left has a white solid color brush assigned to the background of the textbox. The sphere on the right has no brush assigned.

The basic steps to create this application are as follows:

1. Add a 3D object to your project and insert it into the window.

2. Create a rich textbox, and then create a visual brush using the text box. Set the Background and Border of the rich textbox to No Brush.

3. Select the actual 3D model in the Objects list and assign the visual brush to its Diffuse Material in the Materials palette.

Wrapping text onto the Back Material of a 3D model

A good example of using the back material property can be seen by wrapping text on a sphere. Wrapping text on the Material gives the wrapping a convex look, whereas wrapping it on the Back Material gives it a concave look. You can assign the same visual brush to the Material and the BackMaterial, as was done, for example, in Figure 12.10. When the user types in the text box, both textboxes appear wrapped onto the sphere.

The complete steps for creating the example in Figure 12.10 are listed next.

CROSS-REF Text wrapped on a sphere can be animated and rotate as the sphere rotates. For more information on animating 3D objects, see Chapter 14.

FIGURE 12.10

Applying the visual brush to the Back Material as well as the Material of the sphere makes the text appear as if it is wrapped onto the inside of the sphere as well as the outside.

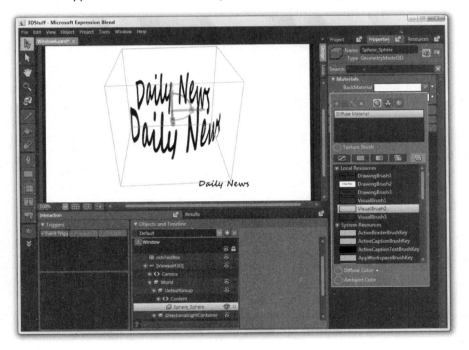

STEPS: Wrapping Text on a 3D Object and Animating It

1. Create a sphere (or other 3D object — for our purposes we call it a sphere) and export it with an .obj extension, as described in the sidebar "Using Blender to Create 3D Objects for Import into Blend." Be sure that the sphere is centered on the intersection of the X and Y axes in Blender, so the sphere rotates properly in Blend when you animate it.

2. In Blend, create a new project and choose Project ➪ Add Existing Item.

3. Select the OBJ file that you created in Step 1.

4. Open the Project palette, right-click the name of the OBJ file, and choose Insert.

5. Create a rich text box and type something short, such as **Daily News**, into the text box.

6. Select the rich text box and choose Tools ➪ Make Brush Resource ➪ Make Visual Brush Resource.

7. In the Objects list, select the sphere by clicking the drop-down arrows of the Viewport3D, then World, then the name of your 3D object, then Content, then select the bottommost name of the object. The transformation handles appear on the object.

8. Open the Materials palette, click in the Material swatch and choose Diffuse Material if it's listed, otherwise click the plus sign. Click the Brush Resources tab in the Textures pane, and choose the visual brush.

   Your visual brush appears on the sphere, but don't worry if it's not positioned correctly.

10. Click in the Back Material swatch and choose Diffuse Material if it's listed, otherwise click the plus sign. Click the Brush Resources tab in the Textures pane, and choose the visual brush.

11. To make your sphere transparent, select the rich text box, and in the Brushes palette choose Background and set it to NoBrush. Choose BorderBrush and set it to NoBrush.

12. Use the Camera Orbit tool and rotate your cube slightly toward you, so that you can see both visual brushes clearly.

13. Select the text box, click the Paragraph tab in the Text palette, and assign a number in the Paragraph Spacing Before list. This will drop the text down to the equator of the sphere. We chose 6. Also, you may want to choose Center from the Horizontal Alignment box. You may want to change the size of the text as well. You can test your project now. Ours is shown in Figure 12.11.

14. To animate your text-wrapped sphere, select the sphere so that its transformation handles appear and click the Create New Timeline button (the plus sign) in the Objects and Timeline palette. Give your timeline a name and click OK.

15. Click the Add New Keyframe button above the playhead, move the playhead to about 3 seconds, grab the Y rotation transformation handle in the artboard, and drag it so that the sphere rotates about 90 degrees.

16. Move the playhead to about 6 seconds. Grab the Y rotation handle again, and drag it another 90 degrees. Do the same for the playhead at 9 and 12 seconds.

FIGURE 12.11

The application window showing the visual brush on the Back Material as well as the Material of the sphere.

17. Click the Timeline Recording Is On button at the upper left hand corner of the artboard, so it turns off.

18. Test the animation by clicking the Play button. If you want it to play forever, then right-click on Rotation (you need to open a few expanders to see it), choose Edit Repeat Count, and click the Set To Forever button beside the input box.

CROSS-REF For more information about creating animations, see Chapter 14.

To assign events to a 3D object, so that the 3D object is interactive, for example, like a button, see chapter 16.

ON the WEB You can map lots of images onto 3D objects as textures, but if you want a 2D control to work on a 3D object you can check out `http://www.codeplex.com/3DTools`. They have some tools to perform this task.

Adding and Editing Lights

You may want to add a spot light to highlight some part of a 3D model. Maybe you want to use a light as a pointer to highlight parts of an image that you make into a 3D model. Or you can give an image a glamorous look by animating spot lights on it.

Blend provides four kinds of lights that you can add and edit:

- **Ambient light:** This is the general brightness of the model. It's light that's everywhere, but doesn't emerge from anywhere.
- **Spot light:** This is a beam of light that spreads out in one direction in a cone from a specific point.
- **Point light:** This is like a lightbulb that spreads light out in all directions from a point.
- **Directional light:** This is like angled sunlight.

CROSS-REF   You can animate lights in Blend. See Chapter 14 for details.

If you select a light in the Objects list in the Objects and Timeline palette and click the Selection tool, the light appears in the Viewport3D — for example, as a directional light as shown in Figure 12.11. Once the light is visible, you can do the following:

- Change the color of the light by clicking the Color swatch in the Light palette and choosing a color from the color picker that appears.
- Position the directional light by dragging the X, Y, or Z arrow with the Selection tool, as shown in Figure 12.12, or by assigning values in the Direction input boxes in the Light palette.
- Rotate and position the light with the Selection tool by clicking and dragging the transformation handles.

You can change any light from one to the other of these types by selecting the light in the Objects list and choosing a different Light Type from the Light palette.

Adding and deleting lights

To add a light, you can copy an existing light in the Objects list and paste it into the same element in which it resides in the Objects list. To do this, click on an existing light in the Objects list. Then choose Edit ➪ Copy and double-click on the element one level up in the Objects list, so that a yellow border appears around it. Then choose Edit ➪ Paste.

To delete a light, select it and press Backspace.

Another way to add a light is to select the element in the Objects list that contains the lights. In our Viewport3D, this is called Scene. Then in the Miscellaneous palette, click the button next to Children (Collection), and in the dialog box that appears, click the Add Item button. This brings up another dialog box, as shown in Figure 12.13. Choose the light that you want and click OK. You can assign any properties to the light in the Model 3D Collection Editor dialog box, or you can do that later and just click OK. Now you can click on the spot light and move it using the transformation handles and edit its properties in the Light palette, as described in the next section.

FIGURE 12.12

You can move a directional light closer to the cube for a brighter light or change its angle using the Transformation handles.

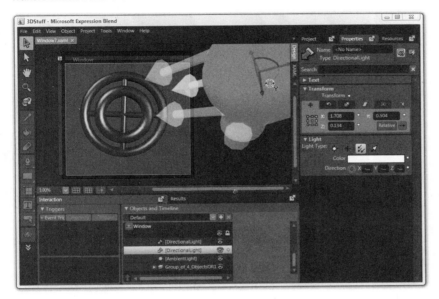

FIGURE 12.13

Adding a spot light.

Modifying spot lights

Spot lights have more adjustable features than any other type of light. You can select the spot light in the Objects list, or select any light and change it to a spot light by choosing Light Type in the Light palette and clicking the Spot Light button.

You can change the position and rotation of a spot light in the same way that you can change any light. You can also change the following parameters in the Appearance palette, as shown in Figure 12.14:

- **Light Type:** Switch to another light type by clicking a button.
- **Color:** Click in the swatch and choose a color from the color picker, eyedropper, or resources.
- **Constant Attenuation:** The light does not decay, but falls off suddenly. Assigning a value of 1 may give you the greatest amount of light. You probably want to set the quadratic attenuation and linear attenuation to zero if you are using constant attenuation.
- **Direction:** Click and drag the circle to change the direction, or use the transformation handles in the artboard to set this automatically.
- **Inner Cone Angle:** You can specify the cone angle for the inner more intense light.
- **Linear Attenuation:** You can specify how light decays at a linear rate. You probably want to set this to zero if you are using constant attenuation or quadratic attenuation.
- **Outer Cone Angle:** Specify the angle for the outer cone that has less intense light.
- **Position:** You can type coordinates to position the light, or these can be set automatically when you use the transformation handles in the artboard.
- **Quadratic Attenuation:** The light decays a small amount at the beginning of its range and a large amount toward the end. You probably want to set this to zero if you are using constant or linear attenuation.
- **Range:** Here you specify how far away the objects in the light's path are lit.

Modifying point lights, directional lights, and ambient lights

With point lights you can set the color, position, range, constant attenuation, linear attenuation, and quadratic attenuation. These properties are assigned in the Light palette, as described in the previous section of this chapter.

In the case of directional lights, you can set the color and direction. The direction can be set using the transformation handles, if you want.

With ambient lights you can set the color only. You can move them, using the Transformation handles, but this doesn't affect how they light the 3D model.

FIGURE 12.14

You can change the effect of the spot light using the Light palette.

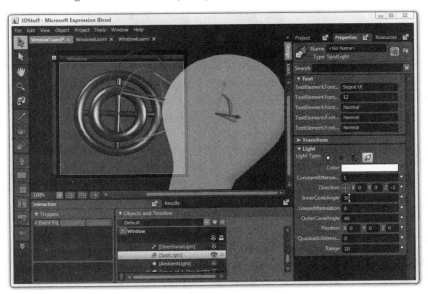

Using and Positioning Cameras

Every 3D model in Blend contains a camera. This camera is created when you choose Tools ➪ Make Image 3D, or it's imported with the 3D model. The camera can be selected and its properties modified to change your view of the 3D model. When you select the camera in the Viewport3D, a Camera palette appears in the Properties panel, as shown in Figure 12.15. You can then set values for the following properties:

- **Position:** You can type values into the X, Y, and Z input boxes, or you can manipulate the object using the Camera Orbit tool. This changes the values in the input boxes as well.

- **Direction:** This specifies the direction that the camera is facing in three directions.

- **Up vector:** This specifies how the camera may be tilted — for example, it could be upside down or sideways.

- **Up:** Clicking on this wheel to choose the Up direction can more easily orient you in the camera view than looking at numbers. This changes values of the Up vector.

- **Perspective field:** This works like a zoom feature.

- **Near clipping plane:** Use this to assign how far the object can shrink before it gets clipped. Of course, you also need to be sure that the Viewport3D has a height and width set to Auto for this to take effect. Otherwise it will clip immediately when resized smaller.

- **Far clipping plane:** Use this to assign how large the object can expand before it doesn't expand any further. For this to have any affect, the width and height of the Viewport3D must be set to Auto in the Layout palette.

FIGURE 12.15

Setting values in the Camera palette allows you to manipulate the view of the 3D model.

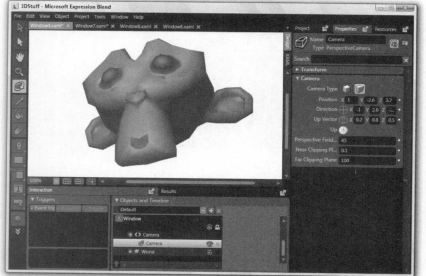

> **TIP**   Using the numbers in the Camera palette can help you set the camera view for a 3D model in the code-behind file. The code-behind file doesn't let you use the Camera Orbit tool or transformation handles, so interactively establishing what the object looks like in the window and using the values in the Camera palette can be very helpful.

The capabilities for moving the camera in Blend are not as impressive as those in a dedicated 3D animation program. If you need to make any extensive camera changes in an animation, you probably want to do that in a 3D program and not in Blend.

However, a stellar feature of Blend is its visual brush, which is like a camera pointed at an object, such as a 3D image, or even a video, and which gives a dynamic view of the object at every moment. This can create a dynamic reflection of your animations, videos, and user interface controls.

Creating a dynamic reflection with the visual brush

The visual brush acts as a camera view of an object, which at first is identical to the object in size, appearance, and position, but you can move the visual brush and change its size, rotation, transparency, opacity mask, and more. The visual brush is great for creating dynamic reflections or duplicates of any object, including controls or panels containing animations, 3D, or video.

To create a visual brush, select the Viewport3D and choose Tools ➪ Make Brush Resource ➪ Make Visual Brush Resource. Then create a rectangle and assign the visual brush to it as a brush resource. Then you can flip it, maybe resize it, skew it — whatever you like — and add some transparency to make it appear as a reflection, as shown in Figure 12.16.

FIGURE 12.16

The visual brush is a virtual camera that you can use to create reflections of 3D objects, animations, video, user interfaces, and more.

CROSS-REF   For more information on visual brushes, see Chapter 6 and Chapter 14.

Combining Models in a Viewport3D

The Viewport3D can accept multiple 3D elements. This means you can add 3D models together into a single Viewport3D and manipulate them separately using the tools of Blend. To move a 3D model from one Viewport3D into another, simply select the model in the Viewport3D and choose Edit ➪ Copy. Then double-click the level in the new Viewport3D that you want to insert the model into and choose Edit ➪ Paste. In Figure 12.17, we added a cube from Blender into a scene from Zam 3D, adding a pedestal for the vase.

TIP   For any detailed work, you probably want to modify your objects in a dedicated 3D application.

FIGURE 12.17

Combining 3D objects into a single Viewport3D.

CROSS-REF For more information on visual brushes, see Chapter 6 and Chapter 14.

Adding Data Binding to Your 3D Model to Allow the User to Manipulate It

You can let your user interact with your 3D object in various ways. For example, you can let them drag and move a 3D object. This kind of interaction requires code in the code-behind file. Another way to allow the user to view all aspects of the 3D model is to set up three sliders, one for each axis of rotation and allow the user to rotate the object via data binding. This isn't complicated, thanks to Blend's (and the WPF's) data binding capabilities. Figure 12.18 shows an example of a 3D object that can be seen from any direction using three sliders.

STEPS: Data Binding the Rotation of a 3D Object to the Value of a Slider

1. Choose Project ⇨ Add Existing Item to add a 3D model with a .obj extension to your project, and then add the .mtl file as well. (To create the model in the first place, see the sidebar below on "Using Blender to Create 3D Objects for Import into Blend.")

2. Add the model into the artboard by right-clicking on the .obj file and choosing Insert.

3. Open the Asset Library in the Toolbox, click Slider, draw a slider into the artboard, and name it Slider1 in the Properties panel.

4. Select the 3D object, so that its transformation handles appear. (Open the expander beside the Viewport3D in the Objects list and keep opening expanders until you select the object with no expander beside it, or until you select a grouped object.)

5. Click the Rotation tab in the Transform palette, click the Advanced Property Options beside the Z input box, and choose Data Binding from the menu.

6. In the Create Data Binding dialog box, click the Element Property button at the top, open the LayoutRoot expander in the left column, and select Slider1. In the right column, select Value, and click Finish.

7. Select the slider in the artboard, and in the Common Properties palette set the Maximum to 360; you can also change the SmallChange to 1.

8. Test your slider by choosing Project ➪ Test Project or pressing F5.

FIGURE 12.18

The slider controls the rotation of the object on the Y axis, allowing the user to rotate the monkey using the slider.

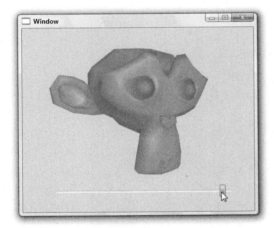

Using Blender to Create 3D Objects for Import into Blend

Blender 3D is a sophisticated 3D rendering and animation tool that is freely available under the GNU GPL software license. It's not geared toward beginners, and the user interface can be a bit baffling at first; but what it lacks in intuitiveness, it makes up for in efficiency.

Here's how to create a simple sphere or other object using Blender3D. First, go to www .blender.org and download and install the application. When you run it, by default it creates and selects a 3D cube.

continued

continued

- To delete the cube (or any selected object), press Delete — the Delete key, not the Backspace key. A message appears asking if you really want to delete it. Click Yes.

- To select an object, be sure you are in Object mode and not Edit mode. (You can use a combo box below the canvas to choose either Object mode or Edit mode.) Press B, and click and drag over part of the object or objects that you want to select. A purple border appears around the object or objects. To deselect everything, press A.

- To create a sphere or any object, click in the 3D window where you want the object to appear. (Keep in mind that the intersection point of the X and Y axes is the center of rotation of your object, so you may want to click there.) Be sure you are in Object mode and not Edit mode, as described in the previous bullet. Choose Add ⇨ Mesh ⇨ UVSphere, for example, or any object from the Add menu, as shown in the following figure. (If you want to create the Blender monkey, choose Add ⇨ Mesh ⇨ Monkey.)

Blender may ask you how many segments, rings, and other details that you want. You can usually just choose the defaults.

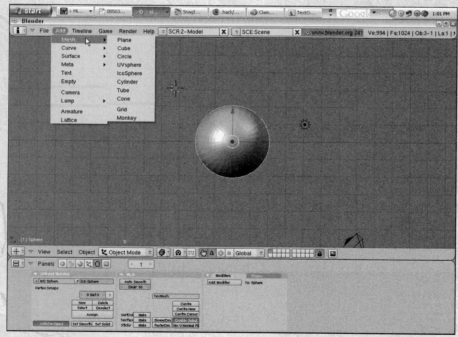

Using the Add menu in Blender to create a 3D sphere

- To scale an object, be sure you are in Object mode, select the object as described earlier, then press S, and move the mouse either toward the object's center or away from it to scale it smaller or larger. Click the mouse to end the scaling.

- To rotate an object, be sure you are in Object mode. Select the object as described earlier. Press R, and then press X, Y, or Z to choose your axis of rotation. Move the mouse to rotate, and click to stop the rotation.

- To move your object, be sure you are in Object mode, and select the object as described earlier. Press G and move the mouse. The object moves. To stop moving the object, click the mouse. Moving an object away from the intersection of the X and Y axes changes its center of rotation when imported into Blend. The following figure shows how two identical spheres behave differently, because they were created in different places in Blender's 3D window.

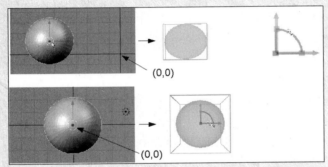

A sphere in Blender is not centered on the intersection of the X and Y axes (upper left), and has a center of rotation that is not centered in the same sphere in Blend (upper right). Whereas the sphere on the bottom left is centered according to the X and Y axes and is also centered when imported into Blend.

- To view your 3D object from different views, choose View ⇨ Side, or View ⇨ Front, or View ⇨ Top, or more.

- To export your sphere, be sure your sphere is selected. (If it is selected, it has a purple border surrounding it.) Choose File ⇨ Export ⇨ Wavefront (.obj). Click the ".." to navigate up to new folder levels until you exit the Blender program files. Navigate to the folder into which you want to save your sphere, and type a name for the object along with the .obj extension. Click the Export Wavefront OBJ button, and click OK in the pane that appears. Exporting your object creates two files: the OBJ file containing the geometry information and the MTL file containing the materials information.

> **TIP** An excellent and concise description of how to use Blender3D is found in *Free Software For Dummies* by Mary Leete. (Even though this is a completely biased review, it really does contain a great chapter on Blender, as well as informative chapters on other powerful free software applications.)

Using Zam 3D to Create Models and Animation

Zam 3D is a 3D animation program in which you can create models, add materials, lighting, and cameras, and create animations in a virtual 3D space. Zam 3D offers ready-made basic 3D shapes as well as a small library of more complex 3D objects. Its highly visual user interface makes it easy to use. You can also use Zam 3D to export XAML code, which you then can import seamlessly into Blend. This allows you to import not just 3D models but animations as well. Once you import the XAML code from Zam 3D, you can fine-tune the lights, cameras, and animation in Blend.

The Zam 3D interface is divided into several main sections, as shown in Figure 12.19.

FIGURE 12.19

The Zam 3D interface.

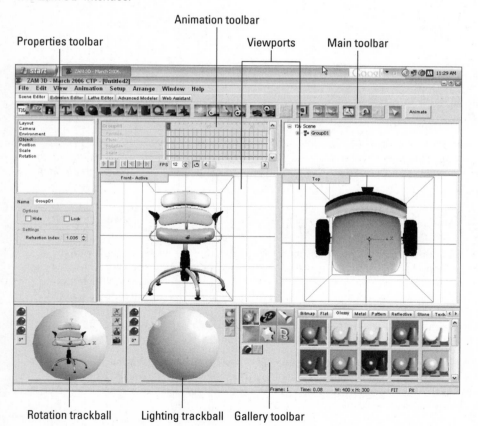

 To view these figures in color, point your Web browser to **www.blendtips.com/
bible.**

Creating and deleting models

Models come in several flavors. You can choose from:

- Using basic 3D shapes, such as cubes, spheres, pyramids, cones, and more. You can group these shapes together to create more complex models.
- Using some more complex models that are available in Zam 3D's Gallery toolbar.
- Extruding text and adding drag-and-drop bevels to the text.
- Lathing an object in the Lathe Editor tab.
- Extruding an object.
- Modifying the geometry of the individual vertices or groups of vertices of an object, which we discuss later in this chapter.

To delete a model in your scene, click on it in the Viewport (or click on the model if you are in an editor), and choose Edit ➪ Delete or press the Delete key (not Backspace).

Using Gallery toolbar models and ready-made shapes

To use models from the Gallery toolbar, click the Show Models button, choose a model from the 3D, Extrusion, or Lathe tab, and click and drag the model into one of the Viewports. For example, the chair in Figure 12.19 is from the Gallery.

You can add 3D shapes to the Viewports by clicking the button in the Main toolbar that shows the shape you want.

Extruding text

Zam 3D makes it easy for you to convert any text into 3D text by extruding it. You can do this simply by clicking the Text button in the Main toolbar and typing the text into the Properties toolbar on the left, as shown in Figure 12.20.

You can add a bevel to the text by clicking the Show Bevels button in the Gallery toolbar and dragging a bevel onto the text in a Viewport. (A plus appears by the cursor when you've successfully dragged it to the text.)

FIGURE 12.20

You can easily extrude text and add a bevel to it in Zam 3D.

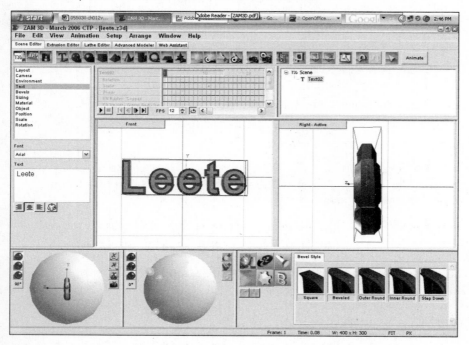

Lathing

A *lathe* is a woodworking tool that spins around, allowing a carpenter to create round forms, such as table legs and closet poles. To create lathed objects in Zam 3D, click on the Lathe Editor tab. The green vertical line in the Lathe Editor, shown on the left in Figure 12.21, is the line of rotation. The red horizontal line is the bottom edge of the lathe. You can create points with the Add Points tool, and you can edit the points by clicking the Shape button and selecting a point. Then in the Point Properties palette, you can change the selected point to a curve point, a corner point, or a tangent point. Curve points and tangent points supply you with handles that you can use to reshape the curve or tangent, as shown in Figure 12.21.

FIGURE 12.21

A path for a vase in the Lathe Editor on the left, and the same vase in the Scene editor on the right

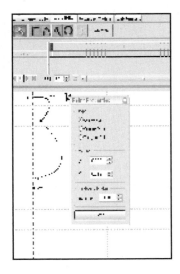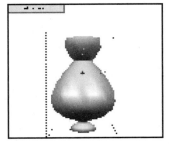

Whatever you draw is transformed into a lathed object in the Scene Editor tab, as shown in the right in Figure 12.20. You can choose Lathe in the Properties toolbar in the Scene Editor and assign a sweep angle for a partial lathe, and you can assign how smooth you want your lathe to be.

Extruding an object

Extruding a 2D object gives it depth, as if you used the 2D object as a cookie cutter to cut a 3D shape out of a slab of cookie dough. In the Extrusion editor, shown in Figure 12.22, you can extrude ready-made 2D objects, or you can draw your own. To open the Extrusion editor, click on the Extrusion editor tab. To use a ready-made shape, click on the button for the shape, such as the star shown in Figure 12.22. To see the extrusion, click the Scene Editor tab. The Scene Editor displays the extruded star in Figure 12.23.

FIGURE 12.22

A 2D object in the Extrusion editor

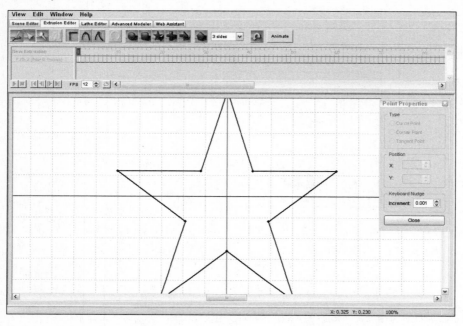

To draw your own shape, use the drawing tools, which work in the same way as the drawing tools in the Lathe editor.

To adjust the depth of the extrusion, click the Scene Editor and adjust the depth using the Depth spin box in the Properties toolbar. You can also view the extrusion in the Scene Editor tab.

You can apply a bevel to your extrusion in the same way that you apply a bevel to text, as described earlier in this chapter: simply click the Show Bevels button in the Gallery toolbar and drag a bevel onto the extrusion in a Viewport. (A plus appears by the cursor when you successfully drag it to the text.)

FIGURE 12.23

The same star in the Scene editor

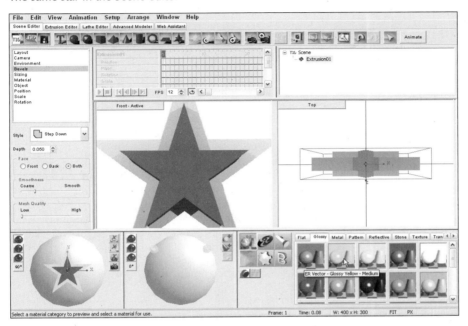

Adding materials

In Zam 3D, you can choose from nine major categories of materials to add to your 3D objects. Each category includes many options within them. In addition to the materials in all those categories, Zam 3D lets you import your own bitmaps and map them onto your objects. The major categories are:

- **Flat:** appears like flat paint in various colors
- **Glossy:** appears like glossy paint in various colors
- **Metal:** Chrome, Copper, Dented Chrome, Mercury, and Rust
- **Pattern:** Checker, Quilt, Speckled, Spiral, and Tie-dye
- **Reflective:** Like mirrors of various colors
- **Stone:** Agate, Brick, Granite, and Marble
- **Texture:** Bumps, Holes, Lumps, Ridges, and Wrinkles
- **Transparent:** Like glass of various colors
- **Wood:** Cherry, Maple, Oak, and Petrified

To apply a material to your models in Zam 3D, click the tab containing the material in the Gallery Toolbar, and drag the material onto the model. The cursor shows a plus sign beside it when you hover over the model.

 **TIP** When applying a material to beveled text, you may need to apply it twice — once to the text and once to the bevel.

Rendering your material

In Zam 3D, you can choose to render your objects with five types of rendering: wireframe, flat shaded, smooth shaded, textured smooth shaded, and fully rendered. Materials that aren't fully rendered don't usually look as good as when they are fully rendered. In fact, they may look awful until they're fully rendered.

To choose one of the first four types of rendering, click the button in the upper-left-hand corner of a Viewport window. In the pop-up menu that appears, choose wireframe, flat shaded, smooth shaded, or textured smooth shaded.

To fully render your 3D object, click in the Viewport window that you want to render and click the Render Window button on the Main toolbar. The model renders in the window, so that you can see the final version of it.

In Figure 12.24, a sphere is shown textured smooth shaded on the left using a Tie Dye pattern as its material, and fully rendered on the right.

FIGURE 12.24

The model on the left is rendered as textured smooth shaded. The model on the right is fully rendered.

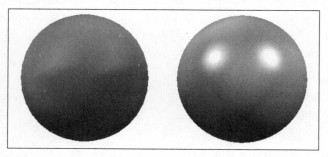

Adding bitmaps for 3D wrapping

You can wrap your own bitmap images onto your 3D objects by first importing your bitmap images into Zam 3D. Your bitmaps can be in any of these formats: BMP, JPG, PNG, TIF, or TGA. Here are the steps for importing bitmaps to use as a material.

STEPS: Importing bitmap images to wrap on 3D models

1. Choose Setup ➪ Materials from the Main menu.

2. Select Bitmap from the Category list, and click the Add Material button, as shown in Figure 12.25.

FIGURE 12.25

You can add your own images to Zam 3D's Gallery using the Gallery Setup dialog box.

3. Type a name for your bitmap, and choose Bitmap Image from the Pattern list in the Color pane.

4. Browse through your files, select the image that you want, and click Import.

5. Click OK in the Edit Material dialog box.

Now you can find the bitmap in the Gallery toolbar by clicking the Show Materials button and choosing the Bitmap tab. Drag your image from there to the model to apply it. For example, we add stripes to Zam 3D's Gallery and then apply the stripes to a pyramid shape in Figure 12.26.

FIGURE 12.26

We created stripes in Blend, took a screenshot of them, cropped them, saved them as a bitmap, imported them as a material in Zam 3D, and then applied them to this model.

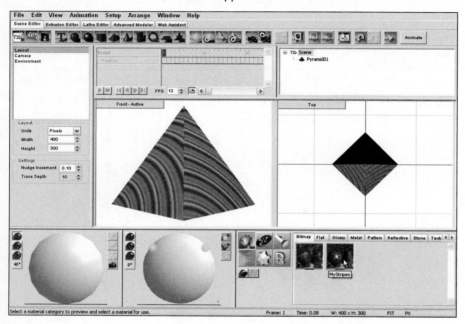

Positioning, rotating, and resizing models

You can position, rotate, and scale your models by selecting them and using the Properties toolbar in the far left of the Zam 3D interface. You can also position, scale, and resize models in other ways, as we describe next.

Positioning models

You can position your models in three ways:

■ **Click and drag the model in one of the Viewports in the Scene Editor tab**. You can change the views of the Viewports to any of the following: Front, Back, Top, Bottom, Left, Right, or Perspective. Click the button in the upper-left-hand corner of either Viewport to change the view.

- **Select the model and click Position in the Properties toolbar.** Assign a new position to your model.
- **Click the Move Free button in the Advanced Modeler tab.** Click and drag the model in any of the Viewports in the Advanced Modeler tab.

Rotating models

You can rotate your models in three ways:

- **Use the Rotation pane in the Properties toolbar.** Select your model and click Rotation in the Properties toolbar. Then assign the amount of rotation in the pane that appears.
- **Use the Rotation Trackball.** Click on your model to select it, and then click and drag the Rotation Trackball. You can constrain the rotation in any dimension (X, Y, or Z) by enabling any of the buttons beside the trackball. You can also constrain the number of degrees of rotation to defined intervals by choosing the number of degrees from the Rotation Increment pop-up menu next to the Rotation Trackball.
- **Click the Rotate Free button in the Advanced Modeler tab.** Click and drag the model in any of the Viewports in the Advanced Modeler tab. The rotation is constrained to the angle of view of the Viewport. (We prefer this method.)

Resizing models

You can resize your model in three ways:

- **Use the Scale pane in the Properties toolbar by clicking on Scale.** Select the model, and then assign the amount of scale in the pane that appears. You can also skew the model by assigning it values in the Shear spin boxes.
- **Click and drag the model away from the camera.** This makes it look smaller but does not actually resize it.
- **Click the Advanced Modeler tab and click the Scale Uniform Mode button on the Main toolbar.** Click and drag the model in a Viewport to be larger or smaller.

Grouping models

You can combine models and group them together to make more elaborate models. For example, two handles that were created in the Extrusion editor are added to the vase in Figure 12.27. To group two or more models, select them all by clicking each of them while holding the Shift key, and then choose Arrange ➪ Group.

FIGURE 12.27

Adding handles created by the Extrusion editor to the vase created by the Lathe editor

Advanced modeling

You can refine complex 3D models in the Advanced Modeler tab by selecting and moving vertices of the mesh. The mesh is the wireframe geometry of the model. And vertices are the points of intersection on the wireframe. To modify the mesh of your model, click the Advanced Modeler tab and click the Editing Mesh button. Select the vertices that you want to modify by clicking one of the five Vertex Selection buttons on the Main toolbar. Then click and drag to select the vertices. The selected vertices turn red.

Right-click on the selected vertices, and, from the menu that appears, choose how you want the vertices to change. For example, in Figure 12.28 we chose to Free Scale them by clicking and dragging. Only the selected vertices scaled.

TIP   Sometimes you can add more 3D detail to your object by adding a material or texture rather than by modifying the wireframe of your object. This may be much easier to do and less computer intensive.

FIGURE 12.28

Selecting and scaling individual vertices of the mesh, using the Advanced Modeler tab

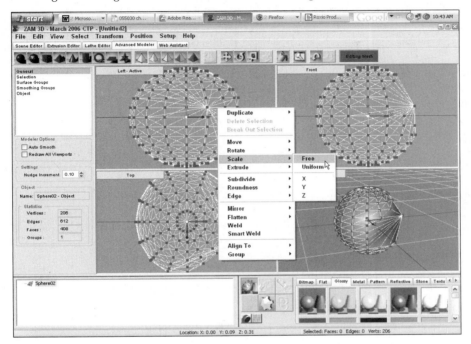

Adding and manipulating lights

In Zam 3D you can add lights in three ways:

- **Choose from standard lighting styles in the Gallery.** To apply them to a model, choose the Show Lightings button in the Gallery toolbar and click a tab to view the lighting styles. Then drag the lighting style that you want onto the model in a Viewport. These lighting styles are as follows:

  - **Colors:** 19 different lights with different tints.

  - **Mood:** 30 different lighting styles, named for moods they may evoke, such as Cold, Dry, Fresh, Hot, Juicy, Neon, and more, as shown in the glasses in Figure 12.29.

  - **Stationary:** 3 Point, Center, Default, Halo, Lower Left, Upper Left, Lower Right, and Upper Right.

  - **Animated:** These lights add animated light effects to the scene.

FIGURE 12.29

Glasses rendered with the following light styles from left to right: (top row) Cloudy, 3 Point, Default, (bottom row) Dry, Gold, Neon, Tranquil

- **Add lights in the Viewport.** Click one of the following buttons on the Main toolbar. These lights can be selected in the Viewport and moved or rotated like any model.
  - ▢ Create Free Point Light
  - ▢ Create Free Spot Light, as shown in Figure 12.30
  - ▢ Create Target Point Light
  - ▢ Create Target Spot Light

- **Add lights to the Lighting Trackball.** Click either the Create Trackball Spot Light or the Create Trackball Point Light button. To position lights on the ball, click a light to select it; then rotate the trackball to position it on the Trackball.

FIGURE 12.30

A free spot light in a scene

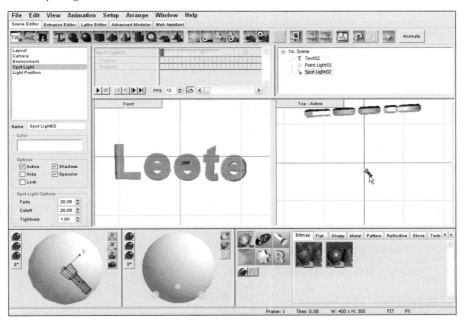

Adding animation

You can add animation to your Zam 3D models in the following ways:

- **Use drag-and-drop animations** and apply them to a model.
- **Create keyframes in the Timeline** and animate properties such as rotation, position, and scale for the camera, lights, or model.
- **Apply drag-and-drop lighting effects**, such as Hollywood lights, neon lights, lights that pan across an object, and more

Using drag-and-drop animations from the Gallery toolbar

Zam 3D provides many ready-made animations that you can apply to your models. You can even apply two animations at a time — one from each category — so your object can spin as it flies or pump as it spins. You can actually apply more than two at a time if your object is grouped: You can apply up to two drag-and-drop animations to each level of grouping of your object. The Toggle Animation Drop Target button indicates whether you want the animation to apply to grouped objects individually or collectively.

The categories of drag-and-drop animations in Zam 3D include:

- **Common Spins:** Horizontal, vertical, tilt right, and zigzag
- **Deformations:** Springs, pumps, and steps
- **Fly-bys:** Top-right spin and bottom-left spin
- **Paths:** Circle, figure eight, and roller coaster

You can also apply combinations of any of these categories.

These drag-and-drop animations are found in the Gallery, as shown in Figure 12.31. Click on the Show Animations button in the Gallery, and choose a tab for the category of animation. You can preview the ready-made animations in their buttons. To apply an animation, click and drag the animation button to the model that you want to animate in a Viewport.

FIGURE 12.31

Drag ready-made animations from the Gallery toolbar into your models for instant animations. Modify them in the Timeline toolbar, or create your own animations.

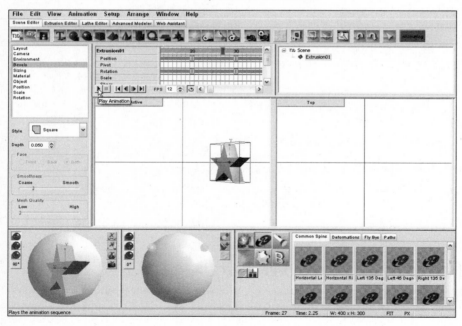

Test your animation using the Play Animation and Stop Animation buttons below the Animation Timeline.

If you want to remove an animation, click the Animating button on the Main toolbar, so that the Animation timeline gains a colorful enabled appearance, right-click in the Timeline, and choose Delete All Keyframes from the context menu that appears.

Creating keyframes in the Timeline

You can use the Timeline toolbar in Zam 3D to create your own animations or to modify drag-and-drop animations, as shown in Figure 12.31. You can access the Timeline toolbar when you toggle the Animation button to On by clicking it. You can modify drag-and-drop animations by dragging their keyframes to change the timing. You can also copy and paste keyframes by right-clicking on a keyframe, choosing Copy, and then right-clicking on a frame and choosing Paste.

You can also create your own animations. You can add animation by adding keyframes and changing the model in some way from keyframe to keyframe. Zam 3D automatically computes the states of change for every frame between keyframes. You can also make any animation that you create into a drag-and-drop animation by saving it into the Gallery by choosing File ⇨ Save Animation.

To add keyframes, be sure the Animating button is toggled to On, move the Current Frame Indicator to the frame number that you want, and change any of the properties or combination of properties listed below:

- **Position:** In the frame that you choose in the timeline, move an object, camera, or light.
- **Rotation:** In the frame that you choose in the timeline, rotate an object or camera.
- **Scale:** In the frame that you choose in the timeline, scale an object.
- **Shear:** In the frame that you choose in the timeline, shear an object. This is similar to skewing a 2D object. It's done in the Scale pane of the Properties toolbar.
- **Material:** In the frame that you choose in the timeline, assign a new material. In the animation, the material gradually changes from one material to another.
- **Path:** You can create motion paths in the Scene Editor and you can attach 3D objects to these motion paths. The objects will automatically move along the path in an animation.

The Lathe editor and the Extrusion editor also have timelines, and with them you can create animations for lathed models and extruded models. These timelines are similar to the one in the Timeline toolbar.

Applying drag-and-drop lighting effects from the Gallery toolbar

Zam 3D offers many ready-made animated lighting effects that you can drag from the gallery onto your model. You can see previews of them in the Gallery. Click on the Show Lightings button and click on any of the spheres in the Animated tab to view the animation. To use the animation, drag the sphere to your model in a Viewport. The lights appear animated in the Viewport when you click the Play button.

Adding backgrounds

You can add backgrounds to your Viewport in two ways:

■ Choose Environment in the Properties toolbar, and double-click the Background Color, the Ambient Light Color, or the Environment Color. Choose a color from the Color dialog boxes that appear, or choose an environment pattern from the Edit Environments dialog box that appears.

■ You can drag a drag-and-drop environment from the Gallery into the Viewport.

Adding, aiming, and animating cameras

Zam 3D offers three kinds of cameras that you can use to view the model or animation. They are:

■ **Standard cameras:** These seven cameras offer you the seven views of the Viewports: Front, Back, Left, Right, Top, Bottom, and Perspective. You cannot see or manipulate any of these cameras. You can choose them from the pop-up menu on the button in the upper-left-hand corner of each Viewport.

■ **Free cameras:** Unlike standard cameras, and like target cameras (described next), free cameras are visible in the Viewport and can be moved and rotated like any model and can be pointed at anything. Unlike real cameras in the real world, cameras in the scene become invisible when they are in the camera view of another camera. You can create a free camera by clicking the Create Free Camera button in the Main toolbar.

■ **Target cameras:** These are similar to free cameras, except that you can assign targets to them. A target camera automatically continues aiming its camera view at its target. To create a target camera, click the Create Target Camera button in the Main toolbar.

To view the scene from the camera, click on the button in the upper-left-hand corner of either of the Viewports and choose the name of the camera from the menu. The Viewport changes to the camera view.

You can aim free cameras by selecting them and pointing them wherever you like. You can move and rotate the cameras just as you move and rotate any object.

To aim a target camera, click the inner rectangle that appears when you add the camera and drag it to the center of the area that you want in your camera view. You can select and move the target camera in any way, and it continues to point at its target.

Importing into Zam 3D from other 3D programs

Zam 3D can import two file formats: .3ds and .dxf. The .3ds format is the format used by Autodesk's 3D Studio and 3D Studio MAX (www.autodesk.com). The exciting part about being able to import in these formats is that these formats are very popular. You can find many software packages (and many 3D artists) that are capable of saving models in these formats. Hundreds, if not thousands, of ready-made 3D models in these formats already exist that you can purchase, or download for free in some cases. We discussed where to find 3D models earlier in this chapter.

Importing from 3D Studio and 3D Studio MAX

From 3D Studio (the predecessor of 3D Studio MAX), you can import the information of the mesh — the geometry of the model.

But from 3D Studio MAX you can import:

- The geometry of the model
- The materials of the model, which you can also add to your gallery of materials (as long as they are in the same folder as the 3DS file.)
- Lights (but if no lights are imported, then the standard Zam 3D lighting is used)
- Cameras, which can be accessed but cannot be moved in Zam 3D
- Animation — all keyframes and animation should appear

To import a 3DS file, choose File ⇨ New From 3DS, navigate to find your file in the dialog box that appears, select your file, and click OK.

Importing a DXF file

This file format originated in AutoCAD, but many top 3D programs export to it. This file format only contains information on the geometry of the object, but you can use the tools in Zam 3D to add materials, lighting, animation, and everything else. To import a DXF file, choose File ⇨ Import, select your file, and click OK.

Exporting 3D Models from Zam 3D

To export your 3D model, choose File ⇨ Export. In the Export dialog box that appears, choose Viewport3D from the Control Type drop-down list. Select the Export Elements As Resource button and select the File button. (You may want to choose other settings, but these are the settings that work for the instructions given in the section near the beginning of this chapter entitled, "Importing Zam 3D models and animations into Blend.")

Summary

- Blend allows you to create 3D imagery by transforming 2D images into 3D images and modifying their rotation and position using the Camera Orbit tool, transformation handles and the Transform palette.
- You can import 3D models in OBJ format and 3D models and animations in XAML files into Blend and add them to your user interface
- Blend allows you to modify your 3D models. You can change their size, rotation, and position. You can also add and modify lights and materials.
- Blend provides four kinds of lights: ambient light, spot lights, directional lights, and point lights. You can change the position and many properties of these lights.

- Wrapping text onto a cube or sphere is possible in Blend by transforming the text box into a visual brush and applying the visual brush as a texture on the 3D object.

- You can use the free software application Blender to create and export 3D objects and import them into your application.

- Zam 3D allows you to create 3D models and animations and export them directly into XAML code, which merges seamlessly into Blend, making it easy for you to create sophisticated animations for your 3D models

- Zam 3D provides you with libraries of drag-and-drop materials, lighting, bevels, and animations.

- You can create models in Zam 3D by using ready-made basic shapes or more complex 3D objects from the Gallery, or by lathing, extruding, and other modeling techniques.

- Zam 3D provides you with some more advanced modeling capabilities that allow you to select individual vertices or groups of vertices on the mesh of your 3D object and edit them individually.

Chapter 13

Employing Principles of 3D Design to Add Depth to the User Experience

3D elements in your user interface can enhance the user experience, because they offer a more realistic environment in which users may immerse themselves. We live in a 3D world, and it's natural to interact with objects in a 3D way. Blend is not a dedicated 3D application — it's designed to mix 2D panels and controls with 3D objects — so you may need to spend considerable time in other applications to create those 3D objects, but in many cases it can be worth the effort.

3D can require a lot of computer power, and, even with the hardware acceleration of today's computers, too much 3D may compromise the performance of an application. For this reason, you may want to limit the amount of 3D content in your user interface in order to fit into your performance goals. Because adding 3D features to an application can be a good thing, but 3D is expensive in terms of performance, a happy middle ground is sometimes to fake some of the 3D look by using techniques to make 2D appear as 3D.

This chapter explores some principles for creating and enhancing 3D, taking into account:

- Human biases for perceiving depth
- Lighting considerations
- The savannah preference
- The ingredients of a successful immersive environment

Adding the Illusion of Depth

While Blend allows you to use 3D in its Viewport3D control, Blend is not designed to provide a completely 3D experience. When using Blend, you probably want to mix 2D objects with 3D objects if you include 3D elements at all.

In designing your user interface, giving 2D objects an illusion of 3D may be a good idea. Then users can enjoy the effect of 3D without taxing their hardware. Here are some tips on how to make 2D objects appear more 3D. These guidelines take advantage of depth cues that humans use to interpret spatial relationships in a scene.

- If a horizontal line stretches across an image, this line may easily be interpreted as a horizon. Objects closer to the line appear farther away than objects farther from the line.
- With no horizon line in the image, an object higher than another object is perceived as farther away.
- Objects that are slightly blurry are interpreted as farther away.
- Smaller objects may be perceived as being farther away than larger ones.
- The ends of angled lines that are closer to each other are considered farther away than the ends of angled lines that are farther from each other.
- Shaded areas may be perceived as farther away than brightly lit areas.
- Smaller patterns may be perceived as farther away than larger patterns.
- Because humans relate blue to the vast skies and oceans, blue objects may be considered farther away than objects of other colors.

An example of the illusion of depth is shown in Figure 13.1. The small square appears much farther away, even though they exist on the same plane of the 2D screen and are created with 2D tools.

CROSS-REF   See Chapter 14 for an example of creating an animated illusion of 3D in Blend.

FIGURE 13.1

To create the illusion of depth, position one rectangle high and make it smaller than the other rectangle. You can also blur its edges and make it dimmer.

Top-Down Lighting Bias

Lighting can give the illusion of depth and add an appearance of naturalness or unnaturalness to an object. As humans, we are used to light sources (such as the sun) shining from above us rather than below us, so we generally interpret objects shaded on the bottom as convex and objects shaded on the top as concave. This corresponds to how an object looks if the sun is shining on it from above.

Not only do people interpret shading as though it is derived from the sun, but they typically also find top-down lighting more appealing. Objects lit from above may seem natural and aesthetic. Objects lit from below may tend to seem unnatural in their appearance. The following figure shows two triangles. The pyramid on the left is lit from below and the pyramid on the right is lit from above. Most people might consider the pyramid on the right to be more appealing. This is undoubtedly a consequence of millions of years of evolution on a planet with a single sun.

continued

continued

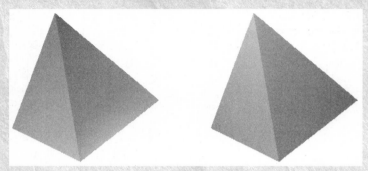

The pyramid on the left is lit from the bottom. The pyramid on the right is lit from the top. Which looks more natural?

Artists and graphic designers often light their works from the top left. A survey of paintings from the Prado, Louvre, and Norton Simon museums showed 75 percent of paintings lit from the top left (as described in "Where is the Sun?" by Sun and Perona, published in *Nature Neuroscience* in 1988). In most cultures in the Western world, when we read we are accustomed to having the eye travel from left to right and top to bottom, so the top left of an object may seem to be the natural starting place for the eye. Icons are generally lit from the top left. Conversely, light from the bottom may give an unnatural or nighttime or even scary effect.

Taking Advantage of the Savanna Preference

Why do parks around the world often consist of expansive mowed lawns with a few scattered trees? Because this kind of landscape is innately appealing to individuals — from the smallest child to the oldest adult. It has been suggested that this may be because grasslands offer an unhindered view of predators and may have been preferred by humans throughout millions of years of evolution. Specifically, people like scattered trees on the sides and clear open spaces in the centers. (For more information, see Balling and Falk's "Development of Visual Preference for Natural Environments," in *Environment and Behavior,* Vol.14, No. 1, in 1982.) Sounds like all 18 holes on a golf course.

What does this have to do with creating 3D objects? Well, unless you are trying to hide Waldo in your 3D scene, you may want to leave plenty of space around your 3D objects to avoid crowding and to create an attractive atmosphere.

Creating Immersion

When a person forgets about his body and environment and is totally and pleasantly engrossed in an experience involving the mind and senses, he or she may forget about the cares of everyday life as well as about time itself. In this state, one may become immersed in a fascinating world so that time can pass very quickly. Eliciting this state of immersion involves just the right mix of challenge, without being too easy and creating boredom and without being too difficult and creating frustration.

A viewer may experience immersion when enjoying a movie, a book, a theme-park ride, a concert, a video game, and many other activities. Creating the experience of immersion in an application or a Web application involves the same principles as creating it anywhere, such as in:

- Overcoming challenges
- Being in control
- Getting feedback quickly
- No distractions

3D technologies may provide greater opportunities for immersion than 2D technologies, because they can provide a rich sensory environment. By offering challenges at just the right level while providing an appealing 3D environment, you can maximize the immersive capabilities of your application.

 3D can eat up a lot of computer processing cycles. Test your performance to be sure that it meets your criteria for allowable processing time.

Summary

- Lighting your 3D world from the top gives a more cheerful look to your scene, whereas lighting from underneath gives it a more nighttime look.
- You can achieve a 3D look in many ways using 2D depth cues.
- Keeping your 3D objects uncluttered or in an environment that gives the feeling of wide-open spaces may be more aesthetically pleasing to the viewer.

Chapter 14

Adding Audio, Video, and Animation

Blend provides you with powerful, flexible tools for deeply integrating video, audio, and animation into your user interface designs. Blend even allows you to mix animation, 3D, and video together in the same object. For example, you can map a video onto a 3D object and then animate the 3D object. You can add animations, video, 3D and more into flow documents, as well. Or you can add them practically anywhere in your application. If you import animations from Zam 3D, you can add even more animation to them. Using Blend, you can fine-tune your animations to suit the user interfaces that you create — whether your animations are imported or not.

With Blend you can animate properties of objects in your user interface. These properties may be position, size, rotation, brushes, and lots more. You can animate properties individually, or combine animations together.

And with Blend, you can create many timelines in your scene. Unlike programs such as Adobe Flash, these timelines are measured in seconds rather than frames, which makes it easier to map the timeline to events in real time.

Timelines can be triggered by events, such as when a specific button is clicked or when a scene is loaded. This is known as an *event trigger*. Event triggers differ from the other type of trigger, known as a property trigger, because property triggers take action when a property is changed, and then when it is changed back. Event triggers only take action when a property is initially changed.

Blend also allows you to specify keyframes in animations without specifying a beginning keyframe. These are known as *handoff animations*. This allows an object to transform into the values of the properties specified by the keyframe, no matter what its values were to begin with. And Blend allows you to animate the same object simultaneously using two timelines, adding the animations together in a process known as *additive animation*.

All these capabilities create wide-ranging opportunities for rich content in your applications. In this chapter, we investigate these features and more, and see how to put them to use.

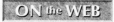 For information on how to add animation into templates and styles of a control, and how to add property triggers, see Chapter 16.

ON the WEB To download the sample projects in this chapter, as well as other chapters, visit www.blendtips.com/bible.

Creating Simple Animations and Motion Paths

Animating an object in Blend can be as simple as moving the playhead to a new frame on the timeline and changing the object's position or its other properties. Blend then automatically calculates the transformations necessary to animate the changes in the object from the first frame on the timeline to the new frame.

The new frame is called a *keyframe* — it contains key information that Blend uses to calculate the changes necessary to smoothly animate between the original frame and the new one.

Blend also lets you draw motion paths that you can easily attach to 2D or 3D objects, which causes the objects to move along the motion path. So animating an object can be as simple as drawing a path for an object to follow.

These are two of the most fundamental ways to create animations in Blend — using keyframes and using motion paths. Let's look at these two techniques.

Animating linear movement

First, here are the steps to create an animation with keyframes:

STEPS: Creating a Simple Animation with Keyframes

1. Select an object that you want to animate. In the example shown in Figure 14.1, a 3D object created in ZAM 3D is imported as described in Chapter 12. You can use a simple rectangle if you want.

2. Click the Create New Timeline button in the Objects and Timeline palette, give your timeline a name, and click OK in the dialog box.

   The timeline appears in the Objects and Timeline palette.

FIGURE 14.1

Animating a 3D object by advancing the playhead to a new time and moving the object.

3. If Window.Loaded doesn't appear automatically as a trigger in the Triggers palette, then click the + Event button and it appears as the default event. If you want to choose a different trigger, then you can select the object that you want to trigger the event, such as a button, and choose the object from the drop-down arrow next to "When Window" in the Triggers palette. Then click the drop-down arrow next to Loaded and choose a trigger from the list, such as Click.

4. Select the object that you want to animate. You may want to click the Record Keyframe button above zero in the timeline (unless you want to create a handoff animation, which is explained later in this chapter).

5. In the Playhead bar of the Objects and Timeline palette, click anywhere to move the playhead to a future time — to 2 seconds, for example. Change your selected object in some way. (For example, rotate it, move it, or resize it. In this example, the 3D object is moved by using the Selection tool.) A keyframe appears in the timeline, as shown in Figure 14.1.

6. Click the Play button to view the animation in the artboard.

To test your animation you can use the controls at the top of the Timeline palette, as shown in Figure 14.1, or you can click and drag the playhead to view the animation. Notice that the current time display in the upper right-hand corner of the Timeline palette displays the current position of the playhead in MM:SS.xxx format (minutes: seconds. milliseconds). For more details about testing your animation see the section "Testing your animation" later in this chapter.

You can animate as many objects in the scene as you want. You can animate the object itself by moving it or resizing it, or you can animate a property of the object, such as its opacity or opacity mask. Blend allows you to add many animations all in the same timeline, so they all become a single animation.

Adding a simple motion path

Blend allows you to use motion paths to designate the motion of an object. You can add motion paths to 2D or 3D objects, and your motion paths can be in 2D or 3D space.

STEPS: Creating a Simple Animation with a Motion Path

1. Create the object that you want to animate.

2. Create a path using the Pen tool, or create a rectangle or ellipse representing the motion path that you want the object to follow.

3. To convert the path or shape to a motion path, select it, choose Object ⇨ Path ⇨ Convert To Motion Path, and in the Choose target for Motion Path dialog box that appears, select the object that you created in Step 1, and click OK.

   The object moves to the beginning of the path, and a copy of the path becomes invisible and is designated the motion path of the object in the Objects list.

4. Select the original path (not the motion path) and delete it, unless you want it to be visible.

5. Press the Play button above the timeline. In the example, a rectangle moves along the path to reach its end in 2 seconds, as shown in Figure 14.2.

FIGURE 14.2

The rectangle follows the path of the star-shaped motion path.

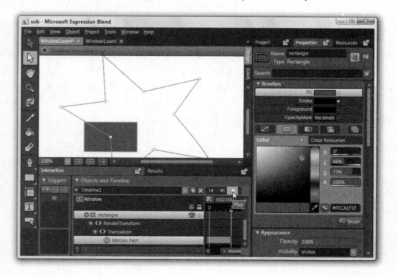

Editing Motion Paths

Here are some ways you can edit your motion path:

- **Edit the timing.** Select the object in the Objects list and open the expanders until you can select the object's motion path. Drag the dark blue band at the end of the gray area to a new time, as shown in Figure 14.2. This represents the end of the motion. If you want to change the beginning time for the motion, drag the dark blue band at the beginning of the gray area to a new time.

- **Set the animation to repeat.** To do this, select the motion path in the Objects list. Be sure it's called Motion Path. Right-click on its name and in the context menu that appears choose Edit Repeat Count. Then in the dialog box, type in the number of repeats, or click the Set To Forever button, and click OK.

- **Orient the object to the path.** Select the motion path in the Objects list. Again, be sure it is called Motion Path. Right-click on its name in the Objects list, and in the pop-up menu that appears, choose Orient To Path. Figure 14.3 shows an oval that is oriented to a path. It changes its orientation according to the slope of the path.

- **Modify the shape of the motion path.** Select the motion path in the Objects list and move the playhead to its beginning. Click the Direct Selection tool in the Toolbox to see its nodes. You can move, modify, or delete nodes or curves using the Direct Selection tool, or add nodes with the Pen tool.

- **Change the direction of the motion.** Modify the shape of the motion path as just described, so that the beginning point is where the ending point was, and move the ending point to the beginning. Then change all the points in between.

- **Modify where the object starts on the path.** Select the motion path and move the playhead to the beginning of the motion path. Click the Subselection tool and move the node that intersects both the object's center and the path to where you want the object to start animation. The object moves with the node.

FIGURE 14.3

An oval slants to orient itself to the path.

CROSS-REF For more information on using the Pen and Subselection tools, see Chapter 5.

> **TIP** For a fun 3D effect, try selecting your object and moving the timeline about 1 second after the start of the motion path and choose Flip X Axis and Flip Y Axis in the Flip tab of the Transform palette, and press Play. This works best if your object is symmetrical.

Using the Timeline

Animation can be thought of in Blend as changes in the properties of elements over time. Every timeline can contain multiple changes of properties occurring simultaneously. For example, properties such as width, length, and margins can change to show an object growing in size while moving across the screen.

Timeline basics

Timelines can contain audio, video, or animation. You can create many timelines that can function independently of each other and be triggered by different events, such as when the user clicks a button or chooses a title of a song from a list box. (There's more information about event triggers later in this chapter.)

Here's how to add and use a new timeline:

- **Add a new timeline,** click the Create New Timeline button in the Objects and Timeline palette. It's the big plus sign, as shown in Figure 14.1. Add a descriptive name in the dialog box that appears. (Unlike most names that you are allowed to assign in Blend, the name of the timeline is permitted to have blanks in it.) A tab appears with the name.

- **Turning on Record mode.** You can turn on Record mode in two ways:

  - If you want to change the timeline, choose the name of the timeline from the drop-down list at the top of the palette. It automatically displays the timeline and turns on record mode.

  - Click the "Timeline Recording Is Off" button at the top left of your artboard to toggle it to on. The same button appears at the top of your Objects and Timeline palette beside the name of the timeline.

- **Close the timeline.** Choose Default from the drop-down list of timelines.

- **Delete the timeline.** Choose the timeline from the drop-down list of timelines and click the Remove Timeline button. (The big X.)

- **Zoom in or out of the timeline.** Place your mouse over the number at the bottom of the timeline, which is the timeline zoom. Click and drag upwards to zoom out and downwards to zoom in.

> **TIP** Even though timeline names can accept spaces, you may want to maintain a personal policy of not putting any blanks in any names in Blend just so you don't have to remember what is okay with spaces and what is not. The best policy for spaces is: When in doubt, leave it out.

 Be sure to turn the record mode to off whenever you're not animating.

Manipulating Keyframes

A *keyframe* is a marker in the shape of a small oval on the timeline that indicates when a change of property will occur. If you click the expander beside the name of the element, then you can discover what property of the object is being modified by the keyframe. For example, in Figure 14.4, the tracks below Group_of_8_Objects in the Viewport3D reveal the properties being animated in the timeline. Blend automatically adds keyframes when you move the playhead to a new time and change a property of an object when a timeline is open and Record Mode is on. You can also manually add a keyframe, which you may often want to do at the beginning of your animation.

There are four types of keyframes:

- **Object-level keyframes:** These appear on the same track as the name of the object, such as Rectangle, or Group_of_8_Objects in Figure 14.4.

- **Simple keyframes:** These represent the actual property being changed, such as Rotation in the last line in Figure 14.4.

- **Compound keyframes:** These are the parent property of a simple keyframe and a child of an object-level keyframe, such as Transform and Rotation (not the last line) in Figure 14.4

- **Implicit:** The implicit keyframe is the last state of an animation before it heads towards the first keyframe of another timeline using a handoff animation. A handoff animation has no first keyframe assigned, allowing an implicit keyframe to be set instead. Handoff animations are discussed in detail later in this chapter.

FIGURE 14.4

Unfolding the Objects list to reveal the properties of the rectangle being animated

Whenever a simple keyframe is added to your timeline, a corresponding keyframe is added at the object level. This gives you the choice of expanding your object list to view all the properties being animated, or collapsing them to the object level and just seeing the keyframes corresponding to any property change in the object.

You can edit keyframes in a variety of ways, including deleting them, copying and pasting them, and moving them. You can also edit the way that the change takes place from one keyframe to another by choosing Ease In, Ease Out, or Hold Out, as described later in this chapter.

Here are some ways that you can manipulate keyframes to perform various tasks:

- **Add a keyframe.** Select the element that you want to affect in the Objects list, drag the playhead to the time at which you want to add a keyframe, and either change a property of the object, or click the Record Keyframe button.

- **Adjust the ending time and speed of an animation.** Click and drag a keyframe. For example, dragging the ending keyframe to a lower number shortens the time of the animation.

- **Change the starting time of your animation.** You can drag the playhead to the beginning of the timeline and click the Record Keyframe button. Then drag the beginning keyframe to the time at which you want the animation to begin, and move the ending keyframe to the time at which you want the animation to end.

- **Play your animation forward and then backward.** Drag the playhead to the beginning of the timeline, click the Record Keyframe button to add a keyframe, And then drag the keyframe past the ending keyframe. The animation plays forward and then backward until it reaches the last keyframe.

- **Loop your animation forever.** Open the expanders in the Objects list and select the actual property being animated, then right-click on the shaded area on the track, representing the animation, and in the pop-up menu that appears choose Loop Forever. Repeat this for every animated property that you want to loop forever.

- **Repeat your animation a specific number of times:** Open the expanders in the Objects list and select the actual property being animated, then right-click on its name and choose Edit Repeat Count. In the Edit Repeat Count dialog box, type in the number of loops you want your timeline to play, or click the button beside the input box and the word Forever appears. Click OK. You need to repeat this for each property that you want to loop forever.

 Looping forever, or for any number of times, does not take place when you press the play button, only when you test your project.

- **Remove a keyframe.** Select the keyframe, and press Backspace.

- **Copy an animation.** Select one or more keyframes, and choose Edit ➪ Copy. Move the playhead to the time that you want, and choose Edit ➪ Paste.

- **Truncate the end of an audio or video file.** Open Media Time for the song or video in the Objects list (it is a nested element of the object). Click and drag the last dark blue band (representing the end of your file) toward the beginning of the timeline.

CAUTION If animations get too complex, when you push the Play button Blend is not able to render the animation in real time. The animation may appear to be not working, even though it works when you test the project by pressing F5. When the Play button is not functioning properly, it has a dotted border around the inner triangle. (But just because it's too complex for the Play button, doesn't mean it won't work when you test your application.)

Adding Event Triggers

Blend allows you to create two types of triggers: event triggers and property triggers. Property triggers are generally used to specify the look of controls during their different states, such as during a mouseover, or when a control is clicked or selected. Using property triggers you can define instant changes in appearance, which do not require animation, or you can define gradual changes in appearance which make use of the animation timeline. Event triggers are used to define what timeline plays when a particular event takes place. Property triggers are different from event triggers because property triggers define a beginning and an end, such as what should the next state be after the IsMouseOver, but event triggers just have a beginning.

CROSS-REF Property triggers are discussed in detail in Chapter 16.

You can add event triggers to any timeline, whether it is a timeline for audio, video, or animation. You can specify that the same event triggers more than one timeline to play at a time, or you can create more than one event trigger to trigger a single timeline. Everything is flexible. Here are the basic steps for adding event triggers to a timeline.

STEPS: Adding an event trigger to a timeline

1. In the Objects list, select a control that you want to use to trigger a timeline, such as a button. In the Triggers palette, click the Add Event Trigger. This brings up a Window.Loaded event. If a Window.Loaded event already exists and you want to change it, then skip this step.

2. Click the drop-down arrow beside "When Window" and choose the object you selected. Then click the drop-down arrow beside Loaded, and choose an event. Then click the Plus sign and choose the name of the timeline that you want the event to affect.

3. Then choose one of the following:

   ▪ **Begin:** To start playing the timeline

   ▪ **Stop:** To stop playing the timeline

   ▪ **Pause:** To pause the timeline

   ▪ **SkipToFill:** Moves the playhead to the last keyframe

   ▪ **Resume:** To start playing the timeline after a pause

   ▪ **Remove:** This stops the animation and does not allow it to start again

4. Press F5 to test your project. Be sure your window is set to the startup window. Choose Project ➪ Set As Startup, to change it to the startup window.

Creating Additive and Handoff Animations

Blend allows you to animate an object using multiple timelines. When these timelines run simultaneously, a single object can be animated by two or more timelines at once. Blend deals with this situation by adding the animations together. This is called *additive animation*. For example, if you have a ball bouncing around your screen and you also have an animation to cycle the color of whatever the mouse touches, when you mouse over the bouncing ball, the ball starts color cycling while the mouse is on it.

Blend allows you to integrate considerable flexibility into your animations via a feature called *handoff animation*. With this kind of animation you don't need to specify any particular beginning keyframe for your animation and can instead start to animate from any current state of an object in the artboard. For example, if you have a 3D model and you want your customer to see any side of it as desired, you can create buttons for the various sides, as shown in Figure 14.5. If you don't specify a beginning keyframe for the animations and only specify an ending keyframe in your timeline, then Blend simply uses the current state of the model as the first keyframe. This gives your user a smooth, flexible, and continuous animation experience. The steps to create this application are listed below in the section "Animating 3D Objects" later in this chapter.

FIGURE 14.5

An animation to display five views of a 3D object uses handoff animation to animate smoothly from one view to whatever the next view is.

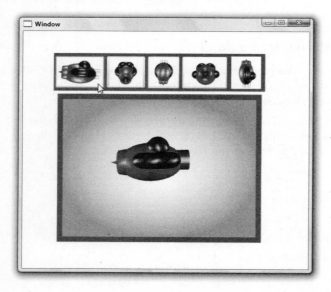

Easing in, easing out, and assigning KeySpline values

Blend interpolates changes of the property that it is animating, starting at the initial keyframe and slowly changing it until it reaches the next keyframe. This is called *keyframe interpolation*. Blend interpolates these changes at a constant (that is, linear) rate by default. You may want a different rate of change to occur, because constant rates rarely appear in the real world and can seem contrived rather than natural. Blend offers a few standard changes in rates. These are known as Ease In and Ease Out, which you can apply as a percentage in increments of 25%. However, you can also precisely specify how your keyframe interpolation occurs by creating key splines (which are described below) and adding them into the XAML code.

Figure 14.6 illustrates easing in and easing out. The figure on the left represents a ball falling to earth and its animation path. The dots represent the proportional timing. The dots are closer near the top than they are near the bottom. Wherever the dots are closer, more time is spent there. The ball has an Ease Out value of 100% applied to its first keyframe. The middle figure represents the same ball except with Ease In value of 100% applied to its last keyframe and no Ease Out applied. Notice that the ball now looks like it slows down at the bottom.

FIGURE 14.6

Three paths with ease in or ease out assigned.

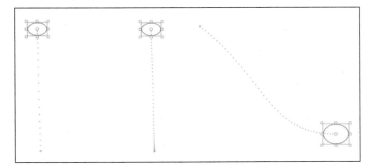

The animation on the right in Figure 14.6 represents a diagonal path of the ball. Ease In 100% is applied only to the Y property, and not the X. (You can open the expanders in the Object List and select the first keyframe beside the Y property.) This creates variations in not only the speed of the animation but in the path as well.

Assigning Ease In, Ease Out, and Hold Out

To assign ease in, ease out or hold out, right-click on a keyframe and choose one of the following:

- **Ease In:** This adjusts the keyframe interpolation before the playhead reaches the keyframe. You can choose how much: 100%, 75%, 50%, 25% or 0%.

- **Ease Out:** This adjusts the keyframe interpolation after the playhead reaches the keyframe. Again you can choose how much: 100%, 75%, 50%, 25% or 0%.

- **Hold Out:** No interpolation occurs either before or after the keyframe.

You can assign both ease in and ease out to the same keyframe. If you assign ease in and ease out to the same part of your animation, Blend adds them together.

> **NOTE**   If Ease In and Ease Out are grayed out in the context menu, that probably means the property that you are animating is not capable of changing at a variable rate. For instance, if you change the Visibility of an object to Hidden or Collapsed, you can't assign Ease In or Ease Out to it, since those properties have no intermediate values.

Setting KeySpline values

Easing in and easing out are two methods of assigning non-linear and more natural-looking changes in properties for your animations. But you can assign other non-linear timings, as well. You can do this by accessing and modifying the XAML code. If you create an animation similar to the one in the middle in Figure 14.6, the XAML code should look something like this. The last keyframe at 14 seconds has Ease In at 100% assigned to it. The values for the Ease In are shown in bold below.

```
<Window.Resources>
<Storyboard x:Key="Timeline1">
  <DoubleAnimationUsingKeyFrames BeginTime="00:00:00"
Storyboard.TargetName="ellipse"
Storyboard.TargetProperty="(UIElement.RenderTransform).(Transform
Group.Children)[3].(TranslateTransform.Y)">
        <SplineDoubleKeyFrame KeyTime="00:00:00" Value="0"/>
        <SplineDoubleKeyFrame KeySpline="0.5,0.5,0.5,1"
  KeyTime="00:00:14" Value="316"/>
  </DoubleAnimationUsingKeyFrames>
  <DoubleAnimationUsingKeyFrames BeginTime="00:00:00"
Storyboard.TargetName="ellipse"
Storyboard.TargetProperty="(UIElement.RenderTransform).(Transform
Group.Children)[3].(TranslateTransform.X)">
        <SplineDoubleKeyFrame KeyTime="00:00:00" Value="0"/>
        <SplineDoubleKeyFrame KeySpline="0.5,0.5,0.5,1"
  KeyTime="00:00:14" Value="7"/>
  </DoubleAnimationUsingKeyFrames>
</Storyboard>
</Window.Resources>
```

This code is automatically generated by Blend. It's not necessary to understand it all to do sophisticated work in Blend. The Storyboard tag represents the runtime piece that the WPF creates for the animation. It's represented by a unique tag in order to separate the animation from the layout. (The Storyboard tag is also used to define states of a control.)

You can change the values of the KeySpline property of the SplineDoubleKeyFrame tag to create different non-linear speeds for your animation. You just need to know what the numbers stand for. The numbers represent the coordinates of the control handles of the curve in the following graph in Figure 14.7.

FIGURE 14.7

The graph of Ease In.

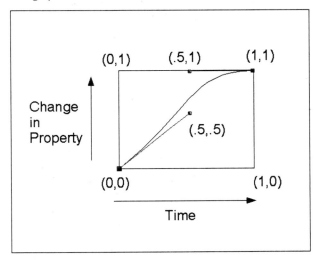

The values for KeySpline="0.5,0.5,0.5,1" are the points of the two control handles in a graph that goes from point 0,0 to point 1,1. The point (.5,.5) is the first point, and the point (.5,1) is the second point. These represent the tangent lines of the curves.

Now you can create any graph using the pen tool and place one point at 0,0 and the other point at 1,1 and you can pull the control handles and use those coordinates for the KeySpline property. In the example above, the KeySpline property had two points, but you can create any number of points for any number of control handles.

ON the WEB If you want to check out a KeySpline property with more control points, click on "Generating Key Splines From a Path Drawn in Blend" at http://blogs.msdn.com/ expression/archive/2007/01/01/generating-key-splines-from-a-path-drawn-in-blend.aspx.

> **TIP** Just use the coordinates of one control handle for each point. The other should reside in the node. Also be sure the coordinates of the control handle do not extend past the boundaries of the imaginary square that they reside in within the coordinates of (0,0) and (1,1).

Testing Your Animation

You can test your animation in any of the following ways:

- Use the Playback controls to play your animation, audio, or video.
- Scrub through your animation by dragging the playhead.
- Set the Snap Resolution (as described later in this section) to fast-forward through your animation, audio, or video.
- Type a time value into the Current Time Display in the upper right-hand corner to set the playhead at that time in the timeline. You can then use the playback controls to test the animation, audio, or video.

Using the playback controls

Probably the easiest way to test your application is to use the controls in the Timeline palette. The controls consist of the following buttons:

- **Go To First Frame:** Sets the playhead to the first frame of the timeline
- **Go To Previous Frame:** Sets the playhead one frame before where the playhead currently resides
- **Play:** Plays the animation, audio, or video at the current location of the playhead
- **Go To Next Frame:** Sets the playhead to the frame after the current frame of the timeline.
- **Go To Last Frame:** Sets the playhead to the last frame of the timeline

If your animation is too complex to be rendered in real time, then a dotted line appears around the Play button, and the animation doesn't play in the artboard when you click Play.

Setting the Snap Resolution

You can set the Snap Resolution so that the Go To Previous Frame and Go To Next Frame buttons jump to locations other than the previous frame. The largest jump it can make is 1 second. But this is useful because you can click your way through your animation either forward or backward and get a good sense of it, at least in a jerky way.

If you want to set the buttons to jump 1 second or less, click the drop-down arrow beside the Turn On/Off Snapping button in the Objects and Timeline palette and choose Snapping from the drop-down list. In the Snap Resolution dialog box that appears, as shown in Figure 14.8, type a 1 if you want the snapping to be one second. Or 2, if you want it to be half a second, and so forth.

Toggle Snapping on or off by choosing Snap from the pop-up menu.

FIGURE 14.8

Setting the snapping.

Using the Playhead Position display

The Playhead Position is the input box in the upper left-hand corner of the Timeline palette. It displays the current position of the playhead in the format MM:SS.xxx (minutes: seconds. milliseconds). You can type a value into the Playhead Position to cause the playhead to jump to that time. For example, type **1** to position the playhead at 1 second. If you type 1:30, the playhead positions itself at a minute and a half.

Importing Animations

Because Blend is not a full-featured animation application, you may want to develop an animation in another application and import it into Blend. Currently, only animations exported into XAML can be imported as animations, but you certainly can import animations using common video formats, which are listed in the section "Adding Video" later in this chapter. To import an animation in the form of a video file, simply add it to your project by choosing Project ➪ Add Existing Item or Project ➪ Link To Existing Item. Then you can use your animation like any video. For more about playing and editing video files, see the section "Adding Video" later in this chapter.

 To import an animation in the form of a XAML file, see the instructions for importing 3D animations from Zam3D in Chapter 12.

Creating a Slide Show or Presentation

You may want to create a simple slide show of images to animate onto a button, or to use as some other part of your user interface. Or you may want to create a presentation for a Web application with slides that include text, images, animations, videos, audio, and vector art. For example, Figure 14.9 displays a presentation that includes 3D images and objects, and animates them. (You can create *a 3D image* in Blend by selecting an image and choosing Tools ➪ Make Image 3D. The image is then projected on a 2D plane that you can rotate in 3D space in Blend.)

Here are the instructions for creating a simple slide show, which you can use as the basis for more elaborate presentations, if needed, by adding animation and other effects.

FIGURE 14.9

Presentations can include 3D, animation, and more.

STEPS: Creating a Slide Show

1. Add all of the images, videos, and animations into the project by choosing Project ➪ Add Existing Item or Project ➪ Link To Existing Item. And create any textboxes that you want to include in your slideshow. Create a grid or other layout panel or object to contain the slides in the slide show. Double-click the grid so that a yellow border appears around it, indicating that the grid is the active container.

2. Right-click on an image file or video file in the Project panel and choose Insert. Then choose Object ➪ Auto Size ➪ Fill or resize the image to appear properly within the grid. If you want a border to appear, you can adjust the Margins in the Layout palette. If you have a text box, or any other slide show element, then add that into the grid as well. You may want to start with the last image or video or textbox in your slideshow and work your way to the first — then they'll be ordered properly.

> **TIP** If your slide is not a single object, but contains text and an image, then place it into a layout panel, such as a stack panel, so that it appears as a single object. Animating the slideshow is easier when every slide can be seen as a single object in the Timeline.

3. Repeat Step 2 for each slide you want in your slideshow.

4. Order your objects from top to bottom in the Objects list in the sequence in which you want them to appear in the slide show. If you added them in the right order, then you don't need to do anything here.

5. Click the Create New Timeline button so that a timeline appears.

6. Select the first object of your slideshow in the Objects list

7. Move the playhead to the time at which you want the next image to appear, click the drop-down arrow beside Visibility, and choose Hidden. (If you want to create a transition between the slides, then see the instructions for creating transitions in the next section of this chapter.) Select the next object of your slideshow in the Objects list.

8. Repeat Step 7 for each of the remaining images in your slide show.

9. Test your slide show using the playback controls in the Timeline palette.

10. Click the Timeline Recording Is On button to toggle the recording mode to off.

Figure 14.10 shows a simple slideshow where a new image appears every second.

FIGURE 14.10

The timeline of a simple slideshow. (Image courtesy of www.deliciousadventures.com.)

Adding Transitions

Transitions are often used in slide shows and videos, as well as animations. Whenever you want to change from one image to another, you have a choice of what kind of transition to create. The number of transitions that you can create is enormous. Here are a few of the most popular transitions:

- **Straight cut:** A new image or window that appears abruptly.

- **Dissolve:** The last few frames of the first shot fade out while the first few frames of the next shot fade in, creating the illusion that the final images of the first shot are dissolving into the beginning image of the next shot.

- **Wipe:** One image appears to wipe over the other image. This usually takes place in a linear or radial direction. An example of a wipe is shown in Figure 14.11.

- **3D transition:** You animate a 3D image or window off the screen to reveal another image or window beneath it.

FIGURE 14.11

A wipe transition. *(Image courtesy of* www.deliciousadventures.com.*)*

Adding straight cuts using Hold Out

Blend automatically tries to change the property that is being animated from the beginning of the timeline to its first keyframe, and then from keyframe to keyframe. This occurs only if the property is such that it can change incrementally, such as Opacity. If the property has certain states to it, such as Visibility which can be Hidden, Collapsed, or Visible, then no such incremental change takes place.

If incremental changes can take place, you may not want a slow change of the property. An abrupt change may suit your needs better. For example, you may want an abrupt change from a small view of a slide to a large view of a slide. You can specify abrupt changes in the property, such as width, or height — or whatever property you want — by right-clicking the keyframe and in the pop-up menu that appears choosing Hold Out.

Adding wipes by animating opacity masks

You can create wipes, as well as many other transitions, by animating opacity masks. Linear wipes can wipe from one side to the other, or top to bottom, or bottom to top. Radial wipes either emerge or converge to or from a point. You can also use the Brush Transform tool to angle your wipe.

STEPS: Animating an Opacity Mask to Create a Wipe Transition

1. Place two images with 100 percent opacity, one on top of the other, in the artboard so that only one is visible.

2. Click the Create New Timeline button.

3. Move the playhead to the time at which you want the wipe to begin.

4. Select the image that is showing, and click Opacity Mask in the Brushes palette. Choose Gradient Brush, click to select either the Linear Gradient button or Radial Gradient button, and pull all but two gradient stops from the gradient bar.

5. Place the two gradient stops immediately next to each other on the far right of the gradient bar, and set the gradient stop next to the edge of the gradient bar to an Alpha value of 0. (If you're creating a linear gradient, you can move the gradient stops to the far left, if you like.)

6. If you use a linear gradient, you can click the Brush Transform tool and choose the direction of the gradient by moving the arrow.

7. Move the playhead to the time at which you want the wipe to end, maybe a second or two later, and move the gradient stops to the other side of the gradient bar.

8. Test your animation to see your wipe.

9. Click the Record Mode button to off when you finish animating.

> **TIP** You could also use the Margins to animate the object off the screen, but this is trickier because if your window is resized, then the margins that you specify may not be large enough, and the image may show. So creating wipes using the opacity mask may be a better option.

> **TIP** You can resize your Brushes palette very wide to be able to precisely position the gradient stops close to each other.

Adding dissolves by animating opacity

You can create dissolves by fading out one image to reveal another image beneath it, as shown in Figure 14.12, in which the chocolate pudding dissolves into the casserole. To do this, place two images, one on top of the other, and create a timeline, then place the playhead where you want the dissolve to begin, and select the image that is visible. Then click the Record Keyframe. Move the playhead to where you want the dissolve to end, select the same object, and change its alpha value to 0.

FIGURE 14.12
_____

The chocolate pudding dissolves into the casserole. *(Image courtesy of* www.deliciousadventures.com.*)*

377

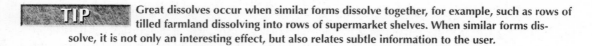

TIP   Great dissolves occur when similar forms dissolve together, for example, such as rows of tilled farmland dissolving into rows of supermarket shelves. When similar forms dissolve, it is not only an interesting effect, but also relates subtle information to the user.

Creating 3D transitions

The possibilities for 3D transitions in Blend are limitless, but the techniques are different depending on whether you are creating transitions with:

- Layout panels or controls
- Images
- 3D objects

Creating 3D transitions with layout panels or controls

Layout panels and controls do not convert to 3D easily, although WPF developers are working on tools to place layout panels and controls onto 3D objects. But it may work just as well for your purposes to create an illusion of 3D instead. To do this, you can, for example, animate a layout panel or control to resize itself smaller and skew itself to give the appearance of changes in 3D as it seems to fly off the screen. Or you can make it appear to rotate by skewing it and coming back with new data on it.

CROSS-REF   For tips on how you may be able to place controls and layout panels on 3D objects, check out http://blogs.msdn.com/wpf3d/archive/2006/12/12/ interacting-with-2d-on-3d-in-wpf.aspx.

Creating transitions with 3D images or 3D objects

If you create transitions between 3D images in a slide show, you can create real 3D transitions. For example, if you have two 3D images stacked on a timeline, you can have the top 3D image fly off the artboard, revealing a new image underneath — or it could fly onto the artboard covering a previous image.

Adding Video

Blend allows you to use video in any layout panel by adding it to a timeline. You may want to place the layout panel in a flow document, or create a pop-up window for your video to play, or you may want a video player to appear as an animation when a user clicks a button — growing larger until it reaches full size. You can also add controls to control volume or balance, or to play, pause, or stop, or to scrub through the video.

ON the WEB   For a tutorial on adding a slider to scrub through a video, see www.blendtips.com/ bible.

Blend allows you to use a multitude of video formats, such as ASF, AVI, DVR-MS, IFO, M1V, MPEG, MPG, VOB, WM, and WMV. Blend supports all the file formats that Media Player 10 supports. In fact, Media Player 10 is required to be installed on your computer for you to work with video in Blend.

ON the WEB Windows Media Player 10 is available for free at http://www.microsoft .com/windows/windowsmedia/player/10/default.aspx.

Adding a video file

Add a video to your project by choosing Project ⇨ Add Existing Item or Project ⇨ Link To Existing Item. Then select the video file and click OK. Then create a grid or other layout panel for it to reside in, or it can go into the LayoutRoot if you want. Double-click the layout panel that you want your video to appear in, right-click on the name of the video in the Project panel, and in the pop-up menu that appears choose Insert.

TIP You can nest the grid that contains your video into a flow document or any layout panel or control that accepts UIElements as children.

CROSS-REF For more information about controls, see Chapter 16. For more information about nesting layout panels inside other layout panels, see Chapter 18. For more information about nesting layout panels into flow documents, see Chapter 9.

The bounding box of the video appears in the layout panel, and may extend beyond the borders of the panel. Resize the video by holding the Shift key while dragging a corner, so that it fits into the layout panel without distorting. You can use the playback controls to test your video. Figure 14.13 shows an example of a video inside a flow document.

When choosing which layout panel to use as the container for your video, keep in mind the following:

- You can add the video to a canvas panel and set its Width and Height to Auto, and it won't resize larger when the window is resized.

- You can add the video to any layout panel and assign numbers to the Width and Height, and it won't resize in larger or smaller windows.

- If you assign a video to a Grid panel, such as the default LayoutRoot, and choose Auto for the Width and Height values, then when the grid resizes, the video resizes as well. (This can create distortion in your video, if the user resizes one direction more than another direction.) You can also do the same using a Viewbox.

Adding video into a flow document

Because flow documents can accept any UIElement as a child element, they can accept layout panels containing videos, as well. Figure 14.13 shows an example of a video playing inside a flow document. Like any element in a flow document, the position of the video player changes and the text re-flows when the user resizes the flow document. The layout panel containing the video doesn't resize, but it changes its position in relationship to how the text flows.

FIGURE 14.13

A video inside a flow document. *(Video image of Chef Maribeth Abrams courtesy of* `www.delicious` `adventures.com`.*)*

To add a video into a flow document, click the Selection tool, double-click on the flow document so that a yellow border appears around it, select Canvas from the panels in the Toolbox, and click and drag anywhere in the flow document to position a canvas panel there. (You can double-click outside the LayoutRoot to de-activate the flow document.)

Now you need to go into the XAML code and place the layout panel where you want it to reside, by finding its code and moving it between two paragraphs. The code for the canvas should look something like this:

```
<Paragraph><Canvas Width="288" Height="185" ></Paragraph>
```

While you're in the XAML view, you might as well change the size of the layout panel to suit your needs by typing values into the Height and Width properties.

To add the video, select the Canvas panel in the Objects list, and double-click on its name. Then right-click on the name of the video file in the Project panel, and from the pop-up menu that appears choose Insert. Now you can test it by pressing F5.

> **TIP**
>
> Instead of selecting Canvas in the Toolbox and then clicking and dragging in the flow document to position a canvas panel for your video, you can create the layout panel outside the flow document and add your video, and then simply cut the XAML code for the layout panel with the video and paste that XAML code between an opening and closing Paragraph tag in the flow document.

Creating a start button for your video

Because you probably want to let your readers start a video whenever they choose, especially if it's in a flow document, you probably want to add a start button to your video.

To do this, instead of adding the canvas panel right into the flow document, as described above, create a layout panel with a video in it outside the flow document, and add a button to the panel, as well. (I used a stack panel for the example in Figure 14.14.)

Select the button and in the Triggers palette, select the Window.Loaded event that was created when you added the video, and in the pane below, click the drop-down arrow beside Window, choose the button that you selected, and choose the name of the timeline and Begin from the other drop-down menus. For more about triggers, see the section "Adding Event Triggers" earlier in this chapter.

To add the stack panel (or whatever layout panel you chose) into the flow document, click the XAML button and type an opening and closing paragraph tag between the paragraphs that you want the video to be placed. Then find the stack panel, and copy it and paste it between the paragraph tags. Be sure to delete the Margin property from the stack panel, because margins might place the panel outside the view of the flow document reader.

You can add a background to the stack panel by selecting the panel in the Objects list and changing its color in the Brushes palette. You can also change the Content property of the button by selecting the button in the Objects list and changing the text in the Content field in the Properties panel.

FIGURE 14.14

A start button for a video inside a flow document. (*Video image courtesy of* www.delicious adventures.com.*)*

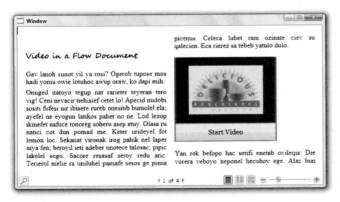

Creating a pop-up window for your video

Want your video to pop up in its own window and play? This gives the user the ability to resize the video to fill the entire screen. Figure 14.15 shows an example of a button that opens a pop-up window with a video.

A video appearing as a pop-up window. *(Video image courtesy of* www.deliciousadventures.com.)

To create a pop-up window, you first need to create a trigger. Pop-up windows can appear when the window is loaded, or you may want to create a button with the content "Play Video" and use that for your trigger. See the instructions for doing so in the preceding section of this chapter.

To create the pop-up, first you need to create another window from which your video will pop-up. Choose File ⇨ New Item ⇨ Window, give your window a name and click OK. Then add a button into this window and give it a name in the Properties panel. Before you add an event name, be sure to choose Project ⇨ Build Project. (Sometimes, if you don't build right before assigning an event, you run into problems.) Then click the Events button next to the name and beside an event, such as Click, type a name for the event handler that will execute when the event occurs. We typed OpenNewWindow. Be sure you don't use any spaces. When you press Enter, Blend opens the code-behind file in Visual Studio. (Don't have Visual Studio yet? See the following note.) Now you can type your code into the event handler

```
Window1 myWindow1 = new Window1();
myWindow1.Show();
```

where Window1 is the name of the window that your video resides in. (If it has some other name, then change Window1 in both places in the code) And myWindow1 is the new name that the code-behind gives the new window. (You can call it anything.)

While still in Visual Studio, choose Build ⇨ Build (name of your project here). Click OK in the dialog box.

Now you can go back to Blend and test your pop-up window. (It's okay to leave Visual Studio as it is.) In Blend, be sure to set the Startup window to the window with your button. Choose Project ➪ Set As Startup ➪ choose your window here. And test your project.

> **NOTE** If you don't have Visual Studio (Standard edition or higher), then you can open the code-behind file in Notepad. Do this by opening Notepad and choose File ➪ Open, and then choose All Files from the drop-down list instead of Text Documents. Then navigate to your project folder and select the name of your window with the .xaml.cs extension and click Open. Then add the lines below the method name and save it. For simple coding, this is an easier procedure.

Adding playback controls to your video

You can add a volume slider and a balance slider easily using data binding, and you can add play, pause, stop, and rewind buttons by assigning triggers to buttons. However, because there's no Play trigger, only a Begin and Resume, you probably want to create a Window.Loaded trigger that pauses the timeline. This way, you can assign Resume to the Play button. (That keeps it from starting over every time you click it.)

Figure 14.16 shows an example of a video player that we created. You can give a video player any kind of look you want. We simply gave it a solid colored background and used the default WPF buttons.

FIGURE 14.16

A video player showing a cooking video. *(Video image of Chef Maribeth Abrams courtesy of* www .deliciousadventures.com.*)*

The first step to create a video player is to change the Window to the size that you want the player to be by selecting the window and changing its Height and Width values in the Layout palette. Then to add the video, right-click its name in the Project panel, and from the pop-up menu that appears, choose Insert. To resize the video, select it and drag a corner handle while holding the

Shift key and positioning it, leaving some space below it for the controls. You can make adjustments to its position using the Layout palette. Then add a stack panel with four buttons labeled Play, Pause, Rewind, and Stop, add two sliders and two labels under the sliders labeled Volume and Balance, and give the LayoutRoot a background color. Then data bind the sliders as follows:

STEPS: Data Binding the Volume Slider and Balance Slider

1. To create a volume and balance slider, first be sure to name them at the top of the Properties panel — otherwise you could get them confused later.

2. Select the video file, click the Advanced Property Options button beside Volume in the Media palette, and choose Data Binding from the menu, as shown in Figure 14.17.

FIGURE 14.17

Data binding the volume of a video.

3. In the Create Data Binding dialog box, click the Element Property button at the top, choose the volume slider from the list on the left, choose Value from the list on the right, and click Finish.

4. Select the volume slider, and in the Common Properties palette in the Properties panel, type 1 in the Maximum Change value, type 0 in the Minimum Change value, and type .5 in the Value. (1 is the loudest volume and 0 is no sound.)

5. Now, do the same for the balance slider. Select the video file and click the Advanced Property Options button beside Balance in the Media palette, and choose Data Bind.

6. In the Create Data Binding dialog box, click the Element Property button at the top, choose the balance slider from the list on the left, choose Value from the list on the right, and click Finish.

7. Select the balance slider, and in the Common Properties palette in the Properties panel, type 1 in the Maximum Change value and type -1 in the Minimum Change value.

8. Now you can test your project by choosing Project ⇨ Test Project and use your sliders.

To make the buttons functional you need to set triggers for the timeline. Here's how to make the Play, Pause, Rewind, and Stop buttons functional. The Rewind button just jumps back to the beginning of the video and starts again.

STEPS: Assigning event triggers to playback buttons

1. Name your buttons one by one at the top of the Properties panel.

2. Click Window.Loaded in the Triggers palette, and in the pane that appears below, choose the options so that it says: When Window Loaded is raised (your timeline name here) Begin. Then Click the plus sign next to "When Window Loaded is raised", and in the new action that appears, change the words so it says: When Window Loaded is raised (your timeline name here) Pause. This is shown in Figure 14.18.

(You want to pause the timeline at first, so that you can use a Resume action instead of Begin to Play it. And since you cannot pause unless a video first begins, you need to begin and then pause the timeline.)

FIGURE 14.18

Assigning two actions for a single event trigger.

3. Select the Play button and click the + Event Trigger button, and click the plus sign beside When Window Loaded Is Raised. And change the sentence to When (your play button name here) Click is raised (your video name here) Resume.

4. Repeat step 4, for the Pause, Stop, and Rewind buttons, creating the following actions:

   ▪ **Pause:** When (pause button name here) Click is raised (your video name here) Pause.

   ▪ **Stop:** When (stop button name here) Click is raised (your video name here) Begin. Then click the plus sign to add another action and add When (stop button name here) Click is raised (your video name here) Pause. (The Begin action sends the playhead back to the beginning and the Pause action pauses it, so that it is ready for the Resume action of the Play button to play it.)

   ▪ **Rewind:** When (rewind button name here) Click is raised (your video name here) Begin. (This starts the video at the beginning again.)

6. Don't forget one little detail, which is to specifying the contents of the title bar at the top of the window. Do this in the XAML code by adding what you want in the Title="Your Title Here" near the first few lines of the XAML code.

7. Test out the video player and see how it resizes. You may notice that the stack panel with the buttons may not resize properly. To get them to resize, you can select the StackPanel, right-click, and in the pop-up menut that appears choose Group Into ⇨ Viewbox.

Adding Audio

The way that you add audio in Blend is similar to the way that you add video. First add the audio to your project, then right-click on the audio in the Project panel, and choose Insert. The audio is inserted into a timeline that by default plays when the window is loaded, although you can assign any trigger to it, just like you assign triggers for video and animation. If you add more than one audio file, be sure to open a new timeline, otherwise the audio plays on the same timeline as the first one you created!

An audio file in Blend has handles, just like a video file, even though it has no visual content. If you pull the handles, you can expand it and select the audio file by clicking it in the artboard. However, unless you have an application that allows users to drag audio files around, you may want to choose Collapsed in the Appearance palette to collapse it. The audio will play whether the visual component of the audio file is visible, collapsed, or hidden.

Audio Formats

Blend accepts the following audio formats: Expression AIF, AIFC, AIFF, ASF, AU, MID, MIDI, MP2, MP3, MPA, MPE, RMI, SND, WAV, WMA, and WMD. It accepts whatever formats are supported by Windows Media Player 10. And to work with audio, you need to have Windows Media Player 10 installed.

ON the WEB   You can download Windows Media Player 10 at www.microsoft.com/windows/ windowsmedia/player/10/default.aspx.

Creating an Audio Player

The audio player shown in Figure 14.19 consists of a volume slider, a stop button, a mute button, and a list box with audio files. The list box is nested in a grid section along with a rectangle with rounded corners behind it. The volume control is in another grid section along with another rectangle with rounded corners behind it.

FIGURE 14.19

Creating an audio player

To create the background appearance of the audio player, first create a grid, click the Selection tool, and double-click on the grid to make it active. Click in the light blue band above the grid so that a grid divider appears between the two rectangles. Click the Rectangle tool and draw a rectangle into each section. Select each rectangle and choose Object ⇨ Auto Size ⇨ Fill, and set margins in the Layout palette to separate the two rectangles. Round the corners of the rectangles by selecting them and typing values into the RadiusX and RadiusY properties of the Appearance palette. Give one of the rectangles a gradient brush, and use the Brush Transform tool to change the direction of the gradient from horizontal to vertical. Then make the gradient brush into a resource and apply the resource to both rectangles in the Brush Resources tab of the Brushes palette.

To add the gel effect on top, you can select a rectangle and select Opacity Mask in the Brushes palette. Click the Gradient Brush and set one gradient stop to an alpha value of 20, for example. Use the Brush Transform tool to change the angle from horizontal to vertical and shorten the gradient so that it only fills the top 15% of the rectangle. Click the Convert Brush To Resource Button, save the opacity mask as a resource, and apply the resource to the other rectangle.

STEPS: Creating an Audio Player Using a List Box

1. To create the list box, double-click the grid that contains the artwork for the audio player to make it the active container. Then click the ListBox button in the Toolbox, and click and drag in the grid to create the list box there. You can use the Layout palette to fine-tune the list box's size and location. Then right-click on the list box and choose Add ListBoxItem. Do this for as many files as you want in your audio player.

2. To add the audio files into the project, choose Project ⇨ Add Existing Item, navigate to your files, select them, and click Open. The files appear in the Files palette of the Project panel.

3. Double-click the audio player to make it active.

4. Click the Create New Timeline button in the Objects and Timeline palette. Name the timeline the name of one of your audio files (without the extension) and click OK. Right-click on the name of the audio file in the Files palette, and in the pop-up menu that appears click Insert. Then click the Record Mode button to off.

5. Repeat step 4 for each audio file that you want to add.

6. Then name your list box items with the names of your audio files in the Name property at the top of the Properties panel. Type in the name of each song (or audio file) without spaces and capitalize first letters for readability. And select the list box item, right-click on it, and in the pop-up menu that appears choose Edit Text. Then type in the name. Spaces are okay here.

7. To create the triggers to trigger the audio files, first delete the default triggers that Blend set by selecting the Window.Loaded trigger in the Triggers palette, by clicking the −Trigger button.

8. Select a list box item and click the +Event button in the Triggers palette. In the pane below, choose the list box item instead of Window, and choose Selected instead of Loaded. (Selected is not alphabetical in the list.) Then click the plus sign and choose the name of the timeline that corresponds to the song. You can leave Begin as it is. Then click the plus sign again, choose the name of another timeline, and change Begin to Stop. (Assign Stop to all the timelines except the one for the song that you want to play.)

9. Repeat step 8 for all of your audio files.

10. You can test your audio player by pressing F5.

11. To create the volume control, double-click the audio player to make the grid active. Click the Slider button in the Toolbox and draw a vertical slider in the rectangle beside the list box, as shown in Figure 14.19. (This will look strange until you change the Orientation property in the Common Properties palette to Vertical.)

12. To data bind the slider to the volume of the media files, select an audio file in the Objects list, click the Advanced Property Options Button beside Volume in the Media palette of the Properties panel, and choose Data Binding. In the Create Data Binding dialog box that appears, choose Element Property, select the slider from the list on the left, select Value from the list on the right, and click Finish.

13. Repeat step 12 for all your audio files.

14. Click the Slider, and in the Common Properties palette, set the Maximum to 100. You can press F5 to test your audio player.

13. To create a stop button, double-click the audio player so that the grid is active, then click Button in the Toolbox, and click and drag in the audio player to create a button there. You can change its text by choosing the Selection tool, right-clicking on it, and choosing Edit Text. Type in "Stop", then click the Selection tool, and click the +Event button. Change Window to Button and Loaded to Click, and click the plus sign for as many times as you have timelines. Then change all the Begins to Stops, and change all the names of the timelines so that each timeline is listed.

14. Test your audio player by pressing F5. To add the visual brush reflection, see the following section.

ON the WEB Audio players can also be created using an XML data source and data binding. This is much easier than creating it by hand as described here. For instructions for how to create an audio player using an XML data source, visit our website at www.blendtips.com/bible. (You can also download this sample audio player at this Web site.)

CROSS-REF For instructions on regulating volume in audio tracks, see Chapter 15.

Using the Visual Brush to Enhance the User Experience

Blend offers a visual brush, which is like a video camera that you can use to point at part of the screen or any object on the screen and take movies of what is occurring for playback elsewhere on the screen. This enables you to create the reflection technique that we discussed in Chapter 12. The visual brush can create other effects as well, such as the following:

- You can map your animation on to other objects by placing your animation in a layout panel and creating a visual brush. This can create effects for a variety of needs, such as creating kaleidoscopes.

- You may want to create copies of your video to play at the same time as the original.

- You may want your movie to play on a 2D screen with a shape other than rectangular.

- You may want to create a reflection effect for your video.

- You can use the visual brush to map video or animated textures onto a 3D object

- You can convert a 3D image to play a video or animation, using a visual brush.

Figure 14.19 shows an example of a visual brush assigned to a grid that contains an audio player, mapped onto a rectangle that is flipped, skewed, and slightly transparent.

CROSS-REF Instructions for creating reflections using visual brushes are found in chapter 6.

Using a visual brush to reflect animations

The visual brush is very useful in creating multiple copies of your animations. Figure 14.20 shows an example of a kaleidoscope created using the visual brush. You can see this in action at `www.blendtips.com/bible`. Here are instructions for creating a kaleidoscope:

STEPS: Creating a Kaleidoscope

1. Create a canvas in your artboard by choosing Canvas from the Toolbox, and clicking and dragging in the artboard to position a canvas panel there.

2. Create an animation within your canvas panel as the basis for your kaleidoscope. For example, colorful circles are created in this example that move in various directions, as shown on the left in Figure 14.20. Be sure to toggle the Record Mode to off when you're finished.

FIGURE 14.20

A kaleidoscope on the left and the animation to create the visual brush on the right.

3. Select the canvas, and choose Tools ⇨ Make Brush Resource ⇨ Make Visual Brush Resource. In the dialog box, give it a name and click OK.

4. Create a single wedge of a circle or geometric figure that has an angle that is an even multiple of 360 degrees. Assign it a visual brush in the Brushes palette by choosing Fill, clicking the Brush Resources tab, and choosing the visual brush.

5. Copy and paste the wedge several times, and use the Transform palette to rotate the copies in increments so you have enough for a full circle. Position them as shown in Figure 14.20. (You may want to flip some of them to create a pairing effect for the animation.)

6. Click the Play button in the Timeline palette, or press F5 to test the kaleidoscope.

Reflecting video using a visual brush

You can create a visual brush for a video in basically the same way that you create a visual brush for a layout panel. Select a video in the artboard, and choose Tools ⇨ Make Brush Resource ⇨ Make Visual Brush Resource. (A dialog box appears asking where you want to define the resource.) Once you define the visual brush, you can apply it as you apply any brush resource. To create a reflection effect, you can flip the object with the visual brush applied, then skew it and decrease its opacity to make it slightly dimmer like a reflection, as shown in Figure 14.21.

FIGURE 14.21

Reflection of a video made using the visual brush. The video is an imported animation in WMV format.

Playing your video inside 2D objects using the visual brush

You can assign a visual brush to a shape and view the movie in that shape. You can create any shape you want using the Pen tool and assign the Fill as the visual brush. For example, we added a visual brush to the shapes in Figure 14.22.

Shapes with visual brushes assigned to them behave just like any other shapes. You can animate them and change their properties.

FIGURE 14.22

Mapping a visual brush onto multiple triangular screens

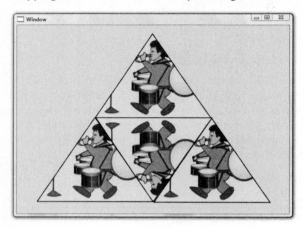

Mapping video onto a 3D image using a visual brush

You may want your video to show on a flat screen that you can move in a three-dimensional way, as shown in Figure 14.23. This is just like the 3D images that you can create by selecting an image and choosing Tools ⇨ Make Image 3D. You can create a flat-screen 3D video in two ways:

- Import a plane from a 3D program and map the video onto it using a Visual Brush, as described earlier in this chapter.

- A simpler method is to create a 3D image, and assign a visual brush to the Material property.

FIGURE 14.23

Projecting a video onto a flat screen that can be animated and manipulated in 3D.

Here are the steps for the second approach:

STEPS: Animating a Video in 3D

1. Add a video to your project by choosing Project ⇨ Add Existing Item or Project ⇨ Link To Existing Item. Right-click on its name in the Project panel, and in the pop-up menu that appears, choose Insert.

2. Create a visual brush of the video by selecting it, choosing Tools ⇨ Make Brush Resource ⇨ Make Visual Brush Resource, and clicking OK.

3. You can add a rectangle over the video, so that the video is not visible when the application runs — and you can apply the same fill to the rectangle as the background of the window or page, so it blends in perfectly.

4. Bring any image into your project by choosing Project ⇨ Add Existing Item. Right-click on it, and in the pop-up menu that appears choose Insert. (You'll change this image into your visual brush later.)

5. Choose Tools ⇨ Make Image 3D.

6. To apply the visual brush to the 3D plane, click the Selection tool and select Model in the Objects list. It's nested in Content, which is nested in ModelContainer, which is nested in Viewport3D. In the Materials palette in the Properties panel, click in the Material swatch, click the Brush Resources button, and choose the visual brush that you created in step 2.

7. You can test your visual brush on the 3D plane by pressing F5.

8. Click the Camera Orbit tool. Click and drag in the 3D image, which is now a 3D visual brush, to manipulate the image in 3D space. You can even animate it, if you want.

ON the WEB   To view the animation of a video on a 3D flat screen, go to `www.blendtips/bible`.

CROSS-REF   For more information about working with 3D images (and therefore videos on 3D screens), see Chapter 12.

Mapping animation onto a 3D-animated object using a visual brush

Figure 14.24 shows an example of an animation being projected onto a sphere. You can just as easily map the animation onto any 3D object using a visual brush.

FIGURE 14.24

Mapping an animation onto a sphere

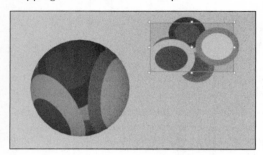

STEPS: Mapping Animation as a Texture onto a 3D-Animated Object

1. Create an animation and bring your 3D object, such as a sphere, into the project by choosing Project ⇨ Add Existing Item.

   In the example in Figure 14.24, we created a sphere in the free 3-D program Blender and exported it as an OBJ file. Then we brought it into Blend.

CROSS-REF For more information about creating 3D objects in Blender and exporting them, see Chapter 12.

2. Right-click on the layout panel containing the animation, and in the pop-up menu that appears choose Tools ⇨ Make Brush Resource ⇨ Make Visual Brush Resource.

3. Place a grid over the video, resize the grid to the size of the window, and assign it a color for its background, such as white. (This hides your animation.)

4. Double-click to activate the grid, right-click on the 3D object in the Project panel, and choose Insert.

5. Animate the 3D object however you want by selecting the Viewport3D, clicking the Create New Timeline button, clicking the Record Keyframe button, and moving the play-head to a future time. Then move the object with the Camera Orbit tool. Click the Record Mode to off when you finish recording the animation. (More information about animating 3D objects is found in the following section of this chapter.)

6. Open the expanders in the Objects list, select the actual 3D object, and open its Material palette. Click in the Material swatch, select the Diffuse Material button, and click the Add Material button (the plus sign). Under Texture Brush, choose the Brush Resources tab and select the visual brush, as shown in Figure 14.25. Now you can test your project.

TIP You can also use this technique to wrap a video, image or drawing onto a 3D object. If you apply the visual brush to the Back Material instead of the material of the object, the visual brush appears to play from the back of the sphere instead of the surface.

FIGURE 14.25

Applying the Visual Brush to the Material property of the 3D object.

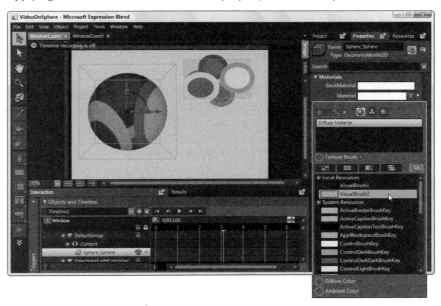

Animating 3D Objects

Blend offers many options for animating in 3D. Here are some things you may want to do:

- Animate 3D images created in Blend.
- Import 3D objects from other sources and animate them.
- Animate lighting of 3D images or objects. (Every 3D object or 3D image has at least one light, but you can add more lights, you can move the lights, you can change the kinds of lights, and you can animate them.)
- Animate colors and materials of 3D objects.
- Animate the camera. (Every 3D object or 3D image has a camera that you can animate. Moving the camera closer, for example, makes the 3D object appear larger.)
- Import 3D models along with their animations, if you import your model from ZAM 3D or another third-party program that exports animation into XAML.

CROSS-REF Procedures for creating and exporting 3D animated models in Zam 3D, and importing them into Blend are discussed in detail in Chapter 12. Information on importing 3D models in OBJ format is described in Chapter 12. How to manipulate 3D lights and the 3D camera, as well as how to assign colors and textures on a 3D object are described in Chapter 12.

Animating 3D images and objects

You can animate 3D images and objects in Blend just as you can animate 2D images and objects, except that you can animate them in 3D spaces. To move, rotate, or scale your 3D object, you can do one of the following:

- Use the Camera Orbit tool.
- Use the Position, Rotation, Scale, and Flip tabs of the Transform palette.
- Select the 3D object or 3D image and use the transformation handles to move, scale, and rotate the object using the Selection tool, as shown in Figure 14.26. The red, green, and blue colors correspond to the X, Y, and Z axes. Dragging the arrows moves the object; dragging the squares scales the object; dragging the curved bars rotates the object around the specific axis corresponding to the color.

FIGURE 14.26

Transformation handles on a 3D image. *(Video image courtesy of* www.deliciousadventures.com.*)*

 For more information on using the Camera Orbit tool, and transformation handles, see Chapter 12. For more information on using the Transform palette, see Chapter 5.

Animating 3D using handoff animation

Handoff animation is useful when you don't know or care about the initial state of the object. Only the final state really matters. For instance, in Figure 14.27, pressing the buttons causes the submarine to rotate to the view on the specific button. It doesn't matter what orientation the submarine starts at, so wherever it is, it rotates to the position in the button — even if you press two buttons in succession and the sub has not reached its final position, it smoothly changes direction to reach its new destination. This can be achieved simply by eliminating the initial keyframe.

Here are the steps for creating a project similar to the example in Figure 14.27. The object that you use can be anything you created and imported from Zam 3D, or any 3D image, or any OBJ file that you import from another 3D application.

FIGURE 14.27

A 3D submarine rotates towards the view that is displayed in the button that is pressed.

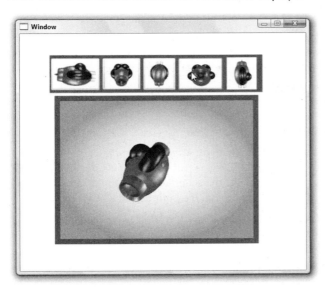

STEPS: Animating a 3D Object by Using Handoff Animation

1. Right-click on the name of the 3D object in the Projects palette, and in the pop-up menu that appears, choose Insert. Or right-click an image, and in the pop-up menu that appears choose Insert, and then choose Tools ➪ Make Image 3D. Or you can import a XAML file from Zam 3D and bring it into your artboard.

CROSS-REF For more about inserting and manipulating images, see Chapter 6. For instructions on creating and importing objects from Zam 3D, see Chapter 12.

2. Resize and position your Viewport3D in the LayoutRoot or layout panel.

3. Click the Create New Timeline button.

4. To create a handoff animation, move the playhead to a new time without creating a keyframe at 0 seconds. Otherwise click the Record Keyframe button. For more information, see the section "Creating Additive and Handoff Animations" earlier in this chapter.

CAUTION Be sure you don't move any object when the playhead is at 0 seconds, otherwise Blend adds a keyframe. However, if this happens, just select the keyframe and delete it.

5. Move the 3D object or 3D image to a new position or rotation, or change whatever properties you want. (You can use the Transform palette, the Camera Orbit tool, the transformation handles, or change its texture using the Materials palette.)

TIP Be sure the Selection tool is selected for the transformation handles to appear.

6. Click the Record Mode button to Off

7. Test your animation by using the playback controls in the Timeline palette.

8. If you want to create an animation similar to the one in Figure 14.27, then repeat steps 3-7 for each animation you want to create. (One for each image that you will add. In fact, you can take screenshots for each object rotation to use as your image.)

9. Add the controls (such as buttons) to your artboard that you will assign triggers to in the next step. For example, in Figure 14.27, we added buttons into a stack panel and then added images into them by double-clicking the button, right-clicking the image in the Project panel and choosing Insert in the pop-up menu.

10. Assign your triggers by selecting the button that you want to control the first timeline, and defining the action for the trigger in the Triggers palette. First click the + Event Trigger button, then in the pane below, change the action to, for example, When Button Click is raised, Timeline1 Begin. Then repeat for all the buttons and all the timelines.

11. Test your animation by pressing F5. (Be sure your window is set to the startup window. Choose Project ➪ Set As Startup.) When you test it, resize the window fully to see how it expands.

12. For your application to resize properly, you probably want to place your stack panel of images into a Viewbox by selecting it, right-clicking, and choosing Group Into ➪ Viewbox in the pop-up menu. Also you may want to resize your window by selecting Window in the Objects list and changing the Height and Width properties of the Layout palette.

TIP If your Viewport3D is too small for the animation, you can resize it larger and then resize the 3D objects within it to be smaller.

Animating 3D lights

Blend makes four kinds of lights available to use on 3D objects: ambient, point, directional, and spotlights. You can change lights from one type to another, and you can add lights or delete lights. Here are some ways that you may consider animating them:

- Animate lights to pan a 3D object or image.
- Use lights as spotlights to highlight parts of a 3D object or image.
- Change the light colors.
- Add flashes of light.
- Brighten and dim the 3D object.

CROSS-REF For more information about adding and manipulating 3D lights, see Chapter 12.

CROSS-REF You can also create 2D lighting effects. For example, see Chapter 10 for an example of animated 2D spotlights on text.

The basic tools you need to animate lights are the same tools you need to animate 3D objects: the Camera Orbit tool, Transform palette, and transformation handles. In Figure 14.28, a spotlight is animated to illuminate an image.

FIGURE 14.28

A spotlight pans a 3D image.

CROSS-REF ZAM 3D offers drag-and-drop lighting effects that you can add to your model before you export it into XAML. These lighting effects can save a lot of time and offer lots of lighting possibilities. For more information, see Chapter 12.

To create the lighting effect in Figure 14.28, first insert an image into your LayoutRoot, and size and position it. Then select the image and choose Tools ➪ Make Image 3D, and while it is selected, open the Viewport3D in the Objects list and select the Directional Light as shown in Figure 14.29.

FIGURE 14.29

Selecting the directional light in a 3D image.

You can change the directional light into a spot light by clicking the Spot Light button. You can adjust the color of the light by clicking the Color swatch and choosing a color from the pop-up color picker. To have the spot light shine on a smaller area, we moved it back by giving it a larger number in the Z value of the Position tab of the Transform palette. We set it to 23. And to see the effect, we set the Range value to 25. And we moved the light off the image by setting the X value in the Transform palette to -26.

To animate the light, you can click the Create New Timeline button, click the Record Keyframe button, move the Playhead to whatever you want, maybe 3 seconds, change the X value in the Transform palette to 26, move the playhead another 3 seconds, and change the X value back to -26. Then, to loop the animation, expand the Objects list until you can select the OffsetX property, right-click, and in the pop-up menu that appears, choose Edit Repeat Count; then click the Loop Forever button and click OK.

Animating the camera

Every 3D object contains a camera in the Viewport3D. This camera can be selected and moved, rotated, and zoomed in and out. If you move the camera closer to the 3D object, the object appears larger in the Viewport3D. If you move the camera away from the object, it appears smaller. The same effect is produced by changing the Values of the Perspective Field in the Camera palette.

The camera does not appear in the scene like the 3D lights do (when you edit them). But you can select the camera in the Objects list, and you can use the Transform palette to move, rotate, or position the camera, plus you can assign values to the features in the Camera palette.

The Camera Orbit tool makes use of the 3D camera. When using the Camera Orbit tool, it appears that the 3D object is moving, but actually it is the camera that's changing. You can create animations using the Camera Orbit tool, as well, as described later in this section of the chapter.

Using the Perspective and Orthographic cameras

Blend provides two types of cameras.

- **Perspective camera:** This is the default camera. It is similar to the human eye because it makes objects that are farther away from the camera look smaller, as seen on the right in Figure 14.30. Two cones are the same size, but one is farther from the camera.

- **Orthographic camera:** This camera defies the laws of perspective and makes every object appear as its assigned size, regardless of how far the object is from the camera, as seen on the left in Figure 14.30. The two cones appear the same size, even though one is farther from the camera.

FIGURE 14.30

The two cones on the right are viewed with the Perspective camera, and the two cones on the left are viewed with the Orthographic camera.

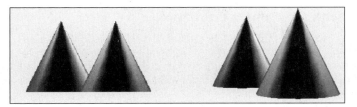

You can change the camera type by selecting the camera in the Objects list and choosing a different camera type in the Camera palette.

Animating the Perspective Field

In Figure 14.31, we added camera movement to an already animated object that was imported from Zam 3D. We animated the Perspective Field so that the spinning object would appear to move back and forth farther and closer in distance while it spins.

To animate an object to change its perspective field, first you select the camera in the Viewport3D and then create a new timeline and add a keyframe. Then move the playhead, and change the value of the Perspective Field in the Camera palette, then move the playhead again and change it back to its original value. Then open the expanders to see the Field Of View element, right-click on the timeline and in the pop-up menu that appears choose Loop Forever.

FIGURE 14.31

Animating the Perspective Field of the 3D camera to add a back and forth motion to a spinning 3D object.

Animating with the Camera Orbit tool

The Camera Orbit tool allows you to click and drag a 3D object and change its orientation in the scene. It appears to change the angle of a 3D object, but it actually changes the angle of the camera itself. Holding Ctrl allows you to move the object in the Viewport3D and holding Alt allows you to resize the object. Using the Camera Orbit tool without holding any key allows you to rotate the object in 3 dimensions.

To animate using the Camera Orbit tool, simply move the playhead of a timeline to a new position and use the Camera Orbit tool to reposition the 3D object or image. You may want to create a keyframe at 0 seconds, unless you want to use handoff animation.

Figure 14.32 shows an example of animating the rotating object imported from Zam 3D to perform a fly-by. We expanded the Viewport 3D to fill the LayoutRoot by choosing Object ➪ Auto Size ➪ Fill. For the first keyframe we positioned the object off the screen and small on the lower left, using the Camera Orbit tool. Dragging up makes it larger. Dragging down makes it smaller. For the second keyframe we moved the playhead to 2 seconds and moved the object off the screen on the upper right and increased its size.

 Playback buttons in the Timeline palette do not display imported animations. They only display the animations that you create in Blend.

FIGURE 14.32

Creating a fly-by animation of an imported rotating 3D object using the Camera Orbit tool.

Animating textures of 3D objects

Here are several ways you can animate textures of 3D objects:

- Animate textures in Zam 3D and import them into Blend.

- Animate colors and gradients by selecting part of a 3D object and setting keyframes in a timeline, and assigning different colors or gradients to the part of the 3D object in each keyframe. If you assign a gradient, then you can animate the gradient stops. If you choose a color, or other brush, then the one brush dissolves into the next brush or color that you assign when you move the playhead forward. Figure 14.33 shows an example of an animated gradient brush assigned to the sphere.

- Assign a visual brush, which can contain a video, an animation, or a reflection of an interactive layout panel, to a part of a 3D object or an entire 3D object. For more about using the visual brush with 3D, see the section on visual brushes earlier in this chapter.

CROSS-REF Instructions for assigning textures to 3D objects in Zam 3D are found in Chapter 12. Also in Chapter 12 are instructions for animating textures in Zam 3D and importing them into Blend.

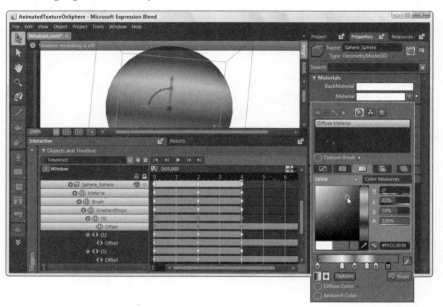

FIGURE 14.33

Animating a gradient on a sphere.

Animating in a User Control

The user control is ideal for hosting your animations. You can create animations in a user control, and then add them into your user interface. Any play buttons or controls for the animation should be added into the user control as well. To create a user control, choose File ➪ New Item ➪ UserControl. Then you can define the size of your user control and create your animation, adding any buttons or controls that you require. Then choose Project ➪ Build Project, to allow your user control to show up in the Asset Library.

To add the user control to your window or page, open the Asset Library in the Toolbox, and in the Custom Controls tab, click the name of the user control, and click and drag in the artboard to position the user control there. The animation appears.

> **TIP**   If you want to assign your user control interactively, you can add a content presenter into your window or page and assign events and use event handlers to change which user control the content presenter displays during runtime. See Chapter 20 for details about changing the content of the content presenter.

Summary

- Blend allows you to animate 2D and 3D objects, and add video and audio to your Windows application or Web application. You can use its Timeline palette to create multiple timelines with multiple tracks. Timelines can be triggered by events, or they can run when the window is loaded — which is also an event.

- Using Blend you can animate the properties of objects, which means you can animate their position, size, color, opacity, opacity masks, gradients, and much more.

- Many timelines can run simultaneously. They can even animate the same object. When this happens, Blend adds the animation effects together. This is called additive animation.

- If no initial keyframe is specified for an animation, Blend animates from the current state of the object. This is known as handoff animation.

- You can create motion paths to animate vector objects and orient your object to the motion path.

- Keyframe interpolation can be adjusted using Ease In, Ease Out, and Hold Out. Ease In and Ease Out offer non-linear interpolation which in many cases appears more natural. You can also create your own keyframe interpolation speeds using KeySplines.

- To play video in a pop-up window you can create an event handler and add event handler code to the code-behind file.

- Flow documents can nest videos inside them, and you can add play buttons to the videos.

- Video players can be created using data binding techniques and event triggers.

- You can create a visual brush for your animation and map it onto vector objects to create features such as kaleidoscopic effects.

- You can animate opacity masks to create wipes as transitions between images.

- You can animate 3D objects by using their transformation handles, the Transform palette, or the Camera Orbit tool. You can also animate the camera of a 3D object to zoom, dolly, or pan on the object. You can animate lights to brighten, dim, zoom, or pan them.

- Blend provides playback controls that you can use to test your animations in the artboard. It also provides the Current Time Display, which allows you to jump to whatever time you type. You can set the Snap Resolution and turn Snap on, so that you can click through your animation quickly using the Next Frame button.

- Blend makes use of the WPF's concept of the Storyboard, which is a runtime piece that separates the timing, animation, and interactivity from the layout and rendering. Because of this, animations can be entirely created in Blend with their storyboards referred to in XAML — without any need for writing any code in the code-behind files.

Chapter 15

Applying Principles of Animation to User Interface Design

Admittedly, Blend is probably not going to be used to create any Saturday morning cartoons, such as Gotham Girls, which was produced using Flash. Blend is designed to animate an object's properties and is not optimized for creating and displaying a sequence of drawings to produce an animation. For example, you can manipulate the opacity of a stack of lip images in Blend to lip-synch an animated character to a soundtrack, but that can be tedious and is accomplished more effectively in an application designed for character animation.

Blend's strength is that it enables the designer and the developer to work together to create powerful applications. It allows you to easily add video, animation, 3D, controls, panels, and more to your user interface, while integrating with the powerful C# and Visual Basic.net languages using the code-behind files. Plus, you can import artwork from Expression Design as well as third-party XAML programs, such as ZAM 3D, into your Blend projects, and you can open and edit your projects in Visual Studio.

Still, Blend can provide a satisfying animation experience when you want to animate object properties such as color, size, position, opacity, and more. You can animate states of a control during mouseovers, clicks, and more. You can also create story-based animations if they are simple enough not to require more fully featured animation tools.

When creating animations, whether they are story-based or not, you can follow certain fundamental principles to make your animations more appealing and realistic. This chapter explores some of these principles. You also explore principles for creating story-based animations. If your animation does tell a story, then your process for creating an animation may proceed as follows:

- Create a script, along with a storyboard.
- Record voices, sound effects, and background music, and layer them together to create the soundtrack.
- Design your visuals in more detail.
- Animate your visuals.

Designing Your Animation

Whether your animation tells a story or not, when designing your visuals you may want to keep in mind the following principles to add realism and interest to your animation:

- **Squash and stretch:** This principle asserts that the volume of a squashed object should remain equal to the volume when it is not squashed. Squashing and stretching a bouncing ball can add realism, appeal, or both.
- **Timing and motion:** To attract the user's attention or to give a sense of weight, importance, or anticipation to an object.
- **Staging:** Purposely bringing the attention of the audience to the area of the screen containing the information that you want to convey.
- **Overlapping action and follow-through:** To give motion a natural appearance.
- **Arcs:** Animating motions along arcs, because most objects in nature don't move along a perfectly straight line.

Using squash and stretch

To give more realism to an animation, you may want to take advantage of the principle of squash and stretch. When two objects bump together, they both squash inward at the point of impact and stretch in a perpendicular direction, unless they are made of a completely rigid material. Then they regain their original shape. It's important as an animator to always give the squashed and stretched shape the same volume as the original shape. The object shouldn't appear to gain any mass. An example of squash and stretch is a ball bouncing on the ground, as shown in Figure 15.1.

Cartoons historically exaggerate squash and stretch when a character walks. This adds to the light-heartedness of the cartoon.

FIGURE 15.1

Squashing and stretching a bouncing ball in Blend

Timing and motion

Timing and motion are an integral part of every animation. Here are some principles and ideas associated with timing and motion:

- Timing and motion can give a sense of the weight of an object. When an object takes a long time to get going and to stop, it gives the impression that it's heavier than something that takes less time.

- You can use motion to attract the user's attention in two ways:

    - A moving object or character can attract the attention if everything else in the scene is still.

    - A still object can attract attention if everything else in the scene is moving.

- Leading the action of a thinking character with the eyes, and then the head, gives the character more personality. Or if the character is an object without eyes, such as Pixar's famous Luxo lamp, then lead with the head, er . . . lampshade, first. The timing should represent how much thought is going into the action on the part of the lamp . . . I mean . . . thinking character. For example, in Figure 15.2, the movement of the eyes of the alien brings the attention to the spaceship that appears from off-screen, but it also brings the awareness to the plan of the spaceman and how he is probably thinking about getting on board.

- An action that happens slowly may be perceived as more important than an action that happens more quickly.

FIGURE 15.2

Leading the motion with the eyes of a thinking character and then the head

Staging

In animation, staging is the process by which the eye is drawn to the part of the screen that the animator wants to emphasize. For example, if a character lifts an eyebrow to indicate that he's got a plan, you may want to show the action in a close-up so that the audience notices it.

Motion and the Human Brain

In *The Media Equation: How People Treat Computers, Television, and New Media Like Real People and Places* (University of Chicago Press, 1998), authors Brian Reeves and Clifford Ness review a number of psychology and social science experiments and report some interesting findings:

- People absorb information better when it is connected with motion. This perhaps explains why animation and video can be powerful tools for disseminating information.

- People absorb information better when it is about one second after the beginning of a motion. Perhaps this is because the mind is absorbed in evaluating the motion at first, and not the idea that the motion conveys.

- Motion beginning from the edge of the screen is more arousing than motion beginning in the center of the screen — perhaps because it is the peripheral vision that alerts the individual to possible dangers that need to be evaluated. For example, in the following figure, the spaceship enters the screen from the right, which draws more attention to it than if it appeared starting in the center of the screen.

An object entering from the edge of the screen may be considered more arousing than the same object appearing from the center of the screen.

Basically, you want all important ideas that you need to convey to be larger, centered, and perhaps involved in movement (because that tends to catch the eye more readily than a stationary object). For example, you can stage a scene with opening doors to indicate that the eye is to see what's inside, as shown in Figure 15.3. Or you might stage a scene so that objects that foreshadow later events are part of the background while the main action takes place — such as a large picture of a famous person who will appear later in the story. Or you might stage a scene so that the background is character defining, with, for example, diplomas on the wall or many books.

FIGURE 15.3

FIGURE 15.3

Staging involves arranging items on the screen so that the viewer notices what is important on the screen.

Overlapping action and follow-through

Here are two more techniques you can use to contribute to greater realism in an animation:

- **Overlapping action:** Starting one action before another action is complete. For example, as shown in Figure 15.4, a spaceship zooms around the earth in the background while an animated Gurdy continues to talk in the foreground.

- **Follow-through:** Action that continues to occur after an action has mostly completed. For example, follow-through occurs when a ball is caught by a hand and the hand moves back to indicate that the ball pushed the hand back. Or when a walking character takes a step and her hand continues to swing.

FIGURE 15.4

You can use overlapping action to draw your viewers into the story.

By using overlapping actions and follow-through, you can make the action in your animation proceed continuously. If an animation stops for a moment, then the animation may suddenly become less real in the minds of your viewers — especially 3D animations, which may evoke a greater sense of realism to begin with. To tell a good story, ideally you want to engage the audience in the story at all times; stopping an animation even for a moment may bring the audience out of the story.

Arcs

In the natural world, living things usually don't move in straight lines. When we walk, we move up and down in an arc as we take a step, then straighten up and take the next. All animals move in an arc motion, some more than others. And the trees move with the wind in an arc. Arcs occur both visually and in time. Water in a stream is sometimes slow, sometimes fast. Wind blows, then diminishes. Rabbits hop, then stop. Varying the timing and the visual motion of your animation in a natural way can enhance the feeling that you may want it to convey.

 You can achieve non-linear changes in timing by using Ease In and Ease Out, as well as KeySplines. See Chapter 14 for more information on this.

Creating a Story-Based Animation

Storytelling can be a useful way to convey information to your audience by making a connection to their emotions.

Stories can be as long as the longest novels or as short as a few seconds. For example, you may want to create a unique, animated advertisement using principles of storytelling. Or you may want to include some storytelling as a part of your application. Storytelling involves a hero or heroine who overcomes obstacles and learns something about himself or herself — something that we all need to know about ourselves.

Storytelling can make a powerful connection to your audience because it focuses on feelings and on the basic question of what it means to be human.

Storytelling

Here's a typical story structure that elaborates a bit on the classical three-act structure described by Aristotle in his treatise, *De Poetica*:

- **Moral need:** A hero has some need in his life. This is a moral need that affects us all, such as the need to be truthful, kind, appreciative, or courageous. Basically, a good human quality, which may be lacking in the hero at first, is the need.
- **Desire:** The hero wants something. This may have nothing to do with the moral need.
- **Obstacle:** The hero cannot achieve what he wants, due to some opposition which is related to his moral need.
- **Plan:** The hero creates a plan to achieve his desire. This plan also relates somehow to his moral need.
- **Battle:** The hero battles against an opponent and loses. The steps from desire to battle cycle two or three times with a new desire, new obstacle, new plan, and new battle each time. Each time the stakes are raised, and by the end the hero feels utterly defeated.

- **Self-revelation:** This can come after the hero feels he has lost and perhaps even comes face to face with death itself — either his death or someone else's. He then realizes how to become a better person and loses his moral need. The audience also has the same realization as the hero. (For example, in *Star Wars*, Luke learns to trust the Force, which means he learns to trust in himself and gain confidence.)

- **Resolution:** The hero usually gains what he desires due to overcoming his moral need. What he gains may be the same thing, or a very different thing from what he wanted in the beginning of the story.

It's interesting that the same story structure can pertain to both long films and very short stories — even stories of just a few seconds. For shorter stories, the story structure boils down to the hero failing a few times, then reflecting and making a change that allows the hero to overcome the obstacles to succeed. Every step still applies.

Because stories are rooted in moral dilemmas, telling a good story, even if it is short, can make a deep impression on your audience.

Creating anticipation

Good storytelling gives clues about what is about to happen. An old saying in theater goes something like this: "You can't hang a gun on a wall without using it sometime in the play." These clues are actively looked for by the audience, and the audience actively tries to unravel how the story will unfold. This constant wondering by the audience, whether their guess is correct, creates a sense of anticipation. If the foreshadowing is too obvious, then the audience is bored. If it is too subtle, then the audience may overlook it and feel cheated.

Also, you may want to divulge something to the audience that the main character does not yet know. This leads the audience to anticipate the reaction of the main character when he finds out. Creating anticipation in the audience is useful because it involves the audience emotionally.

Pacing a story

The pace at which your story unfolds is an important factor in creating the kind of climactic effect that you may desire to reinforce the theme of your story. Often, the motion as well as the length of scenes at the beginning of an animation is slower and longer than the motion and the length of scenes toward the end (although, the last few minutes or moments of the animation may also tend to be slow).

Designing Sound

You may choose to create the soundtrack for an animation either before the animation is created or afterward. Your choice usually depends on which is easier to create, the sound track or the animation. In feature-length animated cartoons, the soundtrack is far easier to create than the animation. But if you are putting together a simple slide show and need a voiceover to describe the slides, then the slide show is probably the first thing you want to create.

Types of sounds

Sound in a narrative generally consists of three types:

- **Speech:** Familiar actors and familiar voices convey more than just words to the listener. They convey the whole past history of the audience's relationship with the actor. The audience members appreciate voices and actors that they are familiar with.

- **Sound effects:** These can help provide additional realism to your narrative. For example, if a ball is seen rolling on the screen, the sound of a heavy bowling bowl can add to the sense that the ball is heavy. Sound effects, such as a bell ringing, can supply information to your audience.

- **Music:** Music may be intended as background music and not necessarily to be noticed, but can add subtleties to video or animation. Music in an animation or movie can affect your audience at a deep level because music can instantly create a pervasive mood. Harmonious sounds may convey happy moods. Dissonant sounds may convey discord or foreshadow it. Also, characters may have themes that the music conveys when they are on-screen, so you might use music to highlight the fact that a character is present, or highlight a particular quality of a character.

Mixing sounds

If you add your sound files to the same timeline in Blend, tracks are automatically stacked with each sound file on a separate track and you can adjust the audio level for each track, as shown in Figure 15.5. To adjust the volume, select the track. Move the playhead to the time at which you want to change the volume, open the Properties panel, and set the Volume property in the Media palette to zero or one or any decimal in between. (One is loudest; zero is silence.) This creates a keyframe in your timeline. If you want to view the change in the Volume property, click the expander — the Volume property is one of the tracks beneath your sound file's track.

FIGURE 15.5

Adding a sound effect to background music by turning the volume down on the music track while the sound effect plays.

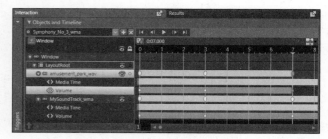

> **TIP** Blend can do some sound mixing, but for anything other than simple volume control, you may want to mix the sound in another application and bring the sound into Blend as a single file that is ready to go.

Summary

You can apply assorted fundamental principles of animation to elements of your user interface to add more realism to your interface design and to make it more appealing. Some of these principles of animation are:

- Solid objects may squash on impact and while showing this you may want to show that the total mass remains constant.

- Large heavy objects move more slowly than small light objects.

- Objects appearing from the edges of the screen may appear more exciting than objects appearing from the center of the screen.

- Motion attracts attention — unless everything on the screen is moving, in which case an unmoving object attracts attention.

- Lead the motion of a thinking character with the eyes and then the head.

- Lead the eyes of the viewer through your animation through the process called staging.

- Use natural arcs for motion when possible, instead of straight lines.

- You may strongly evoke a mood for your animation by adding sound and music, which you may mix together in Blend by layering audio tracks and adjusting volumes.

- Storytelling is a powerful technique to convey information while engaging the emotions of the viewer.

- If you're telling a story, even if it lasts only a few minutes, you can create a sense of anticipation and involvement if you give the audience clues about where the story is going.

Part V

Constructing Controls and Layouts

Chapter 16

Creating and Customizing Controls

Blend provides the user interface designer with numerous ready-made controls that are easily customizable. These controls are created by the Windows Presentation Foundation and include default buttons, sliders, list boxes, combo boxes, scroll viewers, and more. WPF controls are intentionally designed for easy modification. This is achieved by separating the functionality of the control from the appearance of the control. This is useful to you, the user interface designer, because it means that you can change the appearance of controls radically, yet still maintain their functionality.

In this chapter, we discuss how to use the ready-made controls offered by WPF and how to customize them to your needs. Blend allows you to customize your controls in many ways. For example, you can:

- Edit the style of a control. You can define different looks for your control which can be triggered by different changes in properties. These can include animation.

- Edit the parts of a control to change their appearance, add animation, and change the way the control appears during changes in properties.

- Data bind properties of control parts to properties of other elements. This is a powerful tool to radically change the look of your control.

- Create control parts from scratch by creating an empty template for a particular type of a control and adding whatever parts you want to it. This gives you the functionality of that type of control, (for example, a radio button can still deselect other radio buttons when it is selected), yet the radio buttons may look like 3D objects instead — or whatever you choose.

Customizing your controls can be one of the most important aspects of the design of your user interface. Using Blend you can customize your controls more easily than ever before. In this chapter ,we first explore what the controls are and how to use them, and then we discuss in detail how to customize controls in a variety of ways.

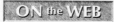 The customized controls in this chapter are all available to view and download at www.blendtips.com.

Adding Interactivity

WPF controls themselves are already interactive. For example, combo boxes open, sliders slide, submenus appear when you click the menu, and buttons change in appearance when you click them. But that is just a small part of the enormous amount of interactivity that you can add to your Windows or Web application by using Blend. With Blend you can add interactivity in the following ways:

- **Assign event triggers,** which can trigger timelines to add animation, audio and video to your application. This is discussed in detail in Chapter 14.

- **Add procedural code.** You can assign events to controls (such as Click for a button or Selected for a ListBoxItem), give the event a name, and Blend automatically creates event handlers for you, in conjunction with Visual Studio. Then you can add code in the event handlers to create any amount of interactivity you want for your application. (Adding the code is covered in Chapter 20.)

- **Bind data.** You can bind properties of a control or properties of other UIElements to other controls or UIElements — for example you can bind the value property of a slider to the font size of a text box, to increase or decrease the size of the text. Or you can bind data from an XML or CLR data source to a list box or other control. You can also bind data to properties of control parts For example, in this chapter we bind data from an invisible control part to a newly-created control part to radically change the look of a control.

- **Assign property triggers.** The Windows Presentation Foundation assigns default property triggers to controls to change their look of a control during different states, such as during a button click or mouse over. But you can add more property triggers and change the look of any control for many different property values. You can also use property triggers to trigger timelines. In fact, you can set them to trigger different timelines when they are activated and when they are deactivated. (For more about this, see the section "Editing Control Templates" later in this chapter.)

Using System Controls and Simple Controls

Blend provides you with both simple controls and system controls. While they both offer the same functionality, they differ in other aspects. System controls are the controls used in Windows XP and Vista. They appear differently depending on the theme of the operating system — the Luna theme in Windows XP and the Aero theme in Windows Vista. Simple controls have a less sophisticated look to them, although they operate in the same way.

Customizing the default look of the system and simple controls

System controls and simple controls both allow you to modify many properties to change their looks (such as skew, rotation and bitmap effects) using the Properties panel. You can also change the color of simple controls, whereas system controls usually do not allow this, because they are associated with the Aero and Luna themes. (If you change the color of system controls, they may look fine in the artboard, but testing can reveal odd results.)

Nesting objects in controls

Some controls, such as buttons, Viewboxes, and ScrollViewers, can accept a single child element. Other controls, such as list boxes and combo boxes, can accept many child elements. Other controls can accept many child elements plus header controls that can organize the child elements. Menus are one example — the header control is the MenuItem. Tree views are another example — the header control is the TreeViewItem. Other controls, such as sliders and grid splitters, accept no child elements.

In the case of controls that accept child elements, usually you can nest any type of object into them, including images, textboxes, video, Viewport3Ds, layout panels, and more.

Figure 16.1 shows an example of a video nested inside a button.

FIGURE 16.1

Playing a video in a button. (Video image of Chef Maribeth Abrams courtesy of www.delicious adventures.com.)

To nest an object into a control, do any of the following:

- Select an object in the artboard, and drag it into the control while pressing and holding Alt.

- Double-click a control to make it the active container, and then double-click a vector graphics object, layout panel, control, or textbox in the Toolbox to add the object into the control.

- Double-click a control to make it the active container, single-click an object in the Toolbox, and click and drag inside the control to position the object there.

- Select a combo box, list box, or menu, right-click on it, and in the pop-up menu that appears choose items such as ComboBoxItem, ListBoxItem, or MenuItem.

- Double-click a control to make it the active container, right-click an item (such as an image or video) in the Project panel, and choose Insert.

- Double-click a control to make it the active container, then click and drag the object's name in the Objects list to the control's name in the Objects list.

To deactivate your control from being the active container, double-click outside the control.

> **TIP**   Sometimes when working with controls, the easiest way to nest an object inside the control is to use the last option in the preceding list — clicking and dragging the object's name in the Objects list to the control's name in the Objects list.

Resizing your controls

You can resize controls in windows with precision by using the Layout palette. You may also want to specify Auto for their Height and Width properties and assign their HorizontalAlignment and VerticalAlignment to Stretch, so that they'll expand and contract with the size of the window or layout panel that they are nested inside. Controls nested within layout panels usually inherit their resizing capabilities from the layout panels. For instance, controls in canvas panels will usually not resize according to the size of the window, because the canvas doesn't offer that as a feature of the canvas panel.

> **CROSS-REF**   For more information about panels and layouts, see Chapter 18.

Radio buttons and check boxes don't resize if you specify their height and width as Auto and alignments as Stretch. If you want them to resize, then nest them into a Viewbox, or into a FlowDocumentReader or other flow document that offers a resize slider.

You can resize list boxes to display more items vertically and to fit more text on a line horizontally, but the height of the ListBoxItem remains the same unless you change the size of the text or object nested in it.

Combo boxes resize horizontally, but not vertically.

Figure 16.2 shows an example of a list box in a flow document. The user can resize the text as well as the list box by using the slider in the lower-right corner.

FIGURE 16.2

Controls work inside flow documents, and they resize when the user adjusts the slider.

To resize an image in a way that allows it to reveal more of itself without magnifying the image, use a ViewBox. This lets you define precisely how an image will be clipped, so you can constantly center the figure in the image as it resizes from any direction — even if the figure is not centered to begin with. We discuss how to use the ViewBox later in this chapter.

Setting the Focusable property

When the Focusable property of a control is set to true, then the control can be accessed from the keyboard or clicked by the mouse. To specify that a control is to be focusable, select the control and select Focusable in the Common Properties palette.

Many system controls have a different look when the control is focused. The button on the left in Figure 16.3 has focus and appears different from the other states of the button.

FIGURE 16.3

The button on the left has focus and can be clicked either with the mouse or by pressing Enter. The button in the middle does not have focus and the button on the right is disabled.

Setting HitTestVisible and IsTabStop

Two other properties are related to the Focus property and are available in almost every WPF control. They are:

- **HitTestVisible.** This allows or disallows mouse events to occur, depending on whether it's true or false. If HitTestVisible is false, then the control cannot be accessed with the mouse, although it can still be accessed using the keyboard as long as the Focusable property is set to true.

- **IsTabStop.** When this is checked in the Common Properties palette, and Focusable is also checked, the user can change the focus of the controls in your application via the keyboard by pressing F6 and using the tab key to move from one control to the next. This is extremely useful for individuals who have difficulty using the mouse but can operate the keyboard. When a button is focusable, for example, the user can press Enter and a click event occurs.

Enabling and disabling your controls

Every control has an Enable property that you can set to enable or disable it. Deselecting the Enable checkbox in the Common Properties palette disables the control. Almost every WPF control has a property trigger set to define a different appearance for the control in its disabled state. This lets the user know that the control does not work at present. In Figure 16.3, the button on the right is disabled.

Naming your controls

Blend gives default names to your controls whenever you attach event triggers or property triggers to them, or add events to them in the code-behind file, or data bind them. Blend needs to do this to be able to reference it in code. The default names are button, button1, button2, etc., or checkBox, checkBox1, checkBox2, and so on. If you make a copy of a named control, then Blend adds **_Copy** to the end of the name, and appends and increments a number to the name if you create more than one copy.

You can use the default names that Blend assigns to your controls, or you can name them yourself in the Name property at the top of the Properties panel, as shown in Figure 16.4. The convention that Microsoft uses for naming controls is called camel notation, which means that all the words are strung together with no spaces (this is a requirement), the first letter of the name is lowercase, and the first letter of words in the name are uppercase. It's probably a good idea to use this convention because it makes your code easier to decipher when looking at it in the code-behind file. You could also put an underscore between the words in camel notation — that's up to you.

You can name your control anytime after you create it and before Blend names it for you (which Blend does when you add a event trigger or property trigger to your control). If you plan to give your controls descriptive and unique names — which are usually preferable to the automatically generated names — then you may want to get into the habit of doing that when you first add the control to the artboard. Renaming controls after they are already named can be done, but then you need to change the code in the XAML code file, and/or in the code-behind file, which can be tedious.

Naming your control using camel notation and no spaces in the Properties panel.

Adding Buttons, Check Boxes, and Radio Buttons

Buttons, check boxes and radio buttons all contain content presenters, which are powerful controls that allow you to add video, Viewport3Ds, animation, images, flow documents, and more into them.

Adding buttons

Blend provides you with three categories of buttons:

- System buttons
- Simple buttons
- Custom buttons

Using system buttons

These are the buttons used in Vista and Windows XP. A system button changes its look depending on which operating system it is running on. In Vista, this button's color is animated slightly, when it has focus and while the mouse is not over it.

You can find the system button in the Toolbox in the popup menu of controls, and also in the Asset Library in the tabs Controls ➪ System Controls. To add one to the artboard, double-click its icon, or single-click and then click and drag in the artboard.

Using simple buttons

If you only want to change the color of a button and maybe its border, use a simple button and edit its template. You can find SimpleButton in the Asset Library in the tabs Controls ➪ Simple Styles. You can change its default look by selecting it in the artboard and changing its brushes and border sizes, and more. To change its look when property changes occur such as during a mouse over or mouse click, see "Editing Control Templates" later in this chapter. The button in the center in Figure 16.5 is an example of a modified SimpleButton.

FIGURE 16.5

From left to right are a system button, a simple button and an oval transformed into a button. All have the bevel bitmap effect applied.

Customizing the default look of your button using Make Button

You can use the Make Button feature to create a custom button from vector objects, such as ellipses, ovals, or layout panels containing vector art, or even controls such as text blocks. To do so, create the vector object; then choose Tools ⇨ Make Button. This also adds a content presenter into the new button. The button on the right in Figure 16.5 is created by an oval with a bevel applied to it and transformed into a button.

You need to add property triggers to make the button interactive, so that it gives the user feedback when the mouse is over it, or when it is clicked, and so on. To do so, see "Editing Control Templates" later in this chapter.

> **TIP** You can also modify the default look of your button drastically by editing its control template, using Edit Control Parts (Template) ⇨ Create Empty. Again, see "Editing Control Templates" later in this chapter.

Specifying the click mode of a button

When you specify a Click event for a button in the code-behind file, you have the choice of specifying its ClickMode in the Miscellaneous palette. The ClickMode specifies that the click event is to occur at the following times:

- **Release.** The click event can occur when the user releases the mouse button. This is the default, and also what the user normally expects.

- **Press.** The click event can take place when the user first clicks the mouse button. This doesn't give the user time to change his mind, since the event takes place immediately.

- **Hover.** This causes a click event to occur even if the mouse is hovering over the button.

> **CAUTION** Causing a click event to occur when the mouse hovers may not only annoy the user, (because it may appear to violate an established convention). It may also create problems with assistive technologies for handicapped users.

Setting IsDefault, IsCancel

Setting the button to the IsDefault state gives the button focus when it is loaded. If you have a property trigger for IsKeyboardFocused, then this is triggered when the button is loaded. You can set IsDefault by selecting the button and checking IsDefault in the Common Properties palette.

IsCancel allows you to reference the button click in the code-behind file, using the keyword Cancel. For more about referencing a cancel button in the code-behind file, see Chapter 20.

Adding rich content to buttons, check boxes and radio buttons

Buttons, check boxes and radio buttons may seem to be some of the simplest controls, but they contain a content presenter which is a powerful control that can display video, 3D, entire flow documents, and more.

To add video to one of these controls, follow the instructions in the section "Nesting objects in controls" earlier in this chapter. You can assign a Stretch property to the video in the Common Properties palette: either None, Fill, Uniform, or UniformToFill. To cause the video to play when you click the button or check the check box or select the radio button, you can set an event trigger (described in Chapter 14), or, because the video is inside the button, you can set a property trigger (described in "Editing Control Templates" later in this chapter).

You can add images and 3D to a button in the same way.

Using check boxes and radio buttons

When radio buttons are child elements in the same layout panel, only one can be checked at a time. If the user clicks on more than one, then only the most recent one clicked is activated. The others in the group automatically turn off. Radio buttons are useful for multiple-choice quizzes and in many other situations. Check boxes on the other hand are used when you can choose one or more options. They are independent of one another, so all of them can be checked, none of them, or any combination.

Check boxes and radio buttons are similar to each other in that they can both respond to the Click event and a Checked event. This is handy — they aren't like simple buttons that have no memory of their previous state after the mouse leaves them.

Adding check boxes and radio buttons

To add a check box to the artboard, double-click CheckBox in the pop-up menu with the controls on it in the Toolbox, and resize and position it where you want it in the artboard. If you want the box to appear checked when the application runs, then in the Common Properties palette, select IsChecked. In Figure 16.6, three states of a check box are shown. The check box on the left is checked, the second was checked but then unchecked, and the third was never checked. To make the second option available to you, you can select IsThreeState in the Common Properties panel.

FIGURE 16.6

Three states of the check box: checked (left), previously checked but currently unchecked (middle), and never checked (right).

To add radio buttons that function as a unit, double-click RadioButton in the pop-up menu with the controls on it in the Toolbox. Add several radio buttons and drag them from the upper left hand corner of the artboard so you can see them, and press F5 to test your project. Notice that when you click one button, the others turn off.

Want more than one set of radio buttons? Add three more into the artboard and move them away from the upper left hand corner. Then select three of them and choose Group Into ➪ Grid. Select the other three and do the same. Now you have two groups of radio buttons that work as two separate groups.

 Check boxes and radio buttons are extremely customizable. To change their look, see the section entitled "Editing Control Templates" later in this chapter.

Creating a multiple choice quiz using radio buttons

Figure 16.7 shows an example of a quiz using radio buttons. The radio buttons are grouped into a grid, and code is added to the code-behind file to make the text block named "Answer1correct" visible when a correct answer is chosen, and to make the text block named "Answer1incorrect" visible when a wrong answer is chosen.

FIGURE 16.7

Radio buttons are ideal for multiple-choice tests.

STEPS: Adding Radio Buttons to Create a Multiple-Choice Quiz

1. Create text boxes to contain your questions for your quiz, and type the text.

2. To add a radio button, double-click on RadioButton in the pop-up controls menu in the Toolbox. Select it and drag it where you want it.

3. In the Content property of the Common Properties palette, type the text that you want in your radio button.

4. Repeat steps 2 and 3 for as many radio buttons as you want to add.

5. Select the radio buttons, right-click, and in the pop-up menu that appears, choose Group Into ⇨ StackPanel. This lines them up nicely. (You could also use a different layout panel, if you wanted.)

6. Add two text blocks for each question in the quiz: create one for the correct answer, and change its text to "Correct answer, congratulations!" or whatever you want to say, and name it, for example, Answer1Correct; then do the same for the incorrect answer, adding the appropriate text and giving it the appropriate name. Place the text blocks where they belong for each question. It's okay if they overlap each other. Then set each text block to Hidden in the Appearance palette. If you are using Visual Studio to add code into your code-behind file, then choose Project ⇨ Build Project

7. Select a radio button and click the Events button in the Properties panel. Type a name beside Clicked that represents the name of the method in the code-behind file that the XAML code calls when the radio button is clicked — for example, Q1CorrectAnswer.

8. If you are using Visual Studio to access your code-behind file, skip to Step 9. Otherwise, open the code-behind file. (The code-behind file is located in your project folder and has the name of the window plus a .xaml.cs extension. In Notepad's Open File dialog box, be sure to select All Files rather than Text Files so that you can see the code-behind file in the file list and open it.)

9. In the code-behind file, add the following code in the line below the method name between the open and close brackets. If the answer is correct, type the following:

```
Answer1Correct.Visibility = "Visible";
```
If the answer is incorrect, type

```
Answer1Incorrect.Visibility = "Visible";
```

10. Repeat steps 7-9 for each radio button in each multiple choice question in the test. (Incorrect answers for the same question can have the same method name, if you want.)

11. Test your project by pressing F5.

CROSS-REF For more about setting event triggers, see Chapter 14.

Using Viewboxes and ScrollViewers

Viewboxes and ScrollViewers are controls that are found in the System Controls tab of the Asset Library. They are also considered layout panels and found with the layout panel buttons in the Toolbox, or you can right-click on an object and in the pop-up menu that appears choose Group Into ➪ Viewbox or Group Into ➪ ScrollViewer. Viewboxes and ScrollViewers both accept one child element.

Using the Viewbox

The Viewbox has two major uses. It resizes its single child element when the window resizes, which can be useful when the object that you need to resize does not normally do so — for example, text does not normally resize, nor do stack panels, at least not in both directions. You can also use a Viewbox to define how an image clips when it does not resize with the window. For example, you can define the clipping to take place so that in a smaller window a face can be centered in an image that is partially clipped, regardless of where the face is in the full-sized image.

To create a Viewbox, right-click on the object or objects that you want to nest into a Viewbox, and choose Group Into ➪ Viewbox. Or open the Asset Library in the Toolbox, choose the Controls tab, choose the System Controls tab, and double-click Viewbox. This creates a Viewbox of the default WPF size in the upper left-hand corner of the artboard. Then you can move it and resize it, and double-click it to nest a single object into it.

> **NOTE**   Viewboxes accept only one child element, so if you drag an object into a Viewbox while holding Alt, be sure the Viewbox is empty. Otherwise, any object in the Viewbox will be replaced by the new object.

Resizing text with the Viewbox

You can use a Viewbox to create resizable text. For instance, if you have a title that you want to expand when the window is resized, you can nest it into a Viewbox, as shown in Figure 16.8. This is a good idea, because this allows Vista's Narrator and other assistive technologies to be able to read it, rather than skipping it if it were a resizable vector object instead.

FIGURE 16.8

Adding a text block into a Viewbox, so the title in the window enlarges and shrinks when the window resizes.

Resizing stack panels with the Viewbox

You may also want to use a Viewbox for objects that can't be set to Auto for either their width or their height — such as a stack panel which can only have one direction set to Auto. For example, if you add the stack panel with the buttons of a video player into a Viewbox, then when you resize the video player to full screen, the buttons enlarge accordingly.

Using the Viewbox to define how an image is clipped

If you have an image that is going to be clipped in a window because the window is smaller than the image, you can use a Viewbox to always center the image in the window at a point in the image that you specify. To do that, follow these steps:

STEPS: Specifying How an Image Clips Using the Viewbox

1. Add a Viewbox to the artboard, and double-click it to make it active.

2. Add an image to your project, right-click on the name of the image, and in the pop-up window that appears choose Insert.

3. Select the Viewbox in the Objects list, and in the Appearance palette choose None for the Stretch property.

4. Select the image in the Objects list, select Fill as its Stretch property in the Common Properties palette in the Layout palette, and adjust the Width, Height, and Margin properties to fill the Viewbox with the part of the image you want to display.

5. Press F5 or choose Project ➪ Test Project to test your Viewbox. A partial image in a Viewbox appears, as shown on the left in Figure 16.9.

FIGURE 16.9

The Viewbox shows a specific part of an image in the smaller window on the left and reveals the rest of the image in a larger window on the right.

Working with the ScrollViewer

You may want to add a ScrollViewer to your application for the following reasons:

- You may want to add scroll bars to an object that does not offer them by default in the Layout palette.

■ You may want to display at a high magnification an object, such as a map, for instance, or some other detailed image, as shown in Figure 16.10, rather than view the entire object at glance.

You can use the ScrollViewer for navigating through large images.

CAUTION Many controls offer scroll bars that you can hide or make visible as you wish. The properties for this in the Layout palette are VerticalScrollBarVisibility and HorizontalScrollBarVisibility. Setting these properties to Visible or Auto should provide you with scroll viewing capabilities. At this writing, setting VerticalScrollBarVisibility and HorizontalScrollBarVisibility doesn't always work, so be sure to test them. If they don't work, then use the ScrollViewer.

To add a ScrollViewer to an image you can follow these steps:

STEPS: Using the ScrollViewer with an Image

1. Click the ScrollViewer button in the pop-up controls menu in the Toolbox, and click and drag in the artboard to position it there.

2. Add an image to the project by choosing Project ➪ Add Existing Item, or Project ➪ Link To Existing Item, selecting the file that you want to add, and clicking Open. Right-click on the image in the Project panel, and in the pop-up menu that appears, choose Insert. To resize the image to the magnification that you want, select the image, and drag the object handles.

3. Drag the image into the ScrollViewer while pressing Alt.

4. Select the ScrollViewer, open the expander in the Layout palette, and if you want to see the scroll bars be sure that HorizontalScrollBarVisibility and the VerticalScrollBarVisibility are both set to Auto or Visible.

Adding Sliders, Grid Splitters, Progress Bars, and Ink Canvas

Sliders, grid splitters, progress bars and ink canvas all have one thing in common. They accept no child elements. Sliders are great for controlling interactivity on the screen via data binding. Grid splitters allow the user to resize sections of the grid, and ink canvas is a good tool for allowing people to sign documents via the computer. (How legal those signatures are, we don't know.)

Adding a slider

Sliders are a great control when used with data binding and have been discussed in detail in previous chapters.

CROSS-REF Using a slider to adjust text size is discussed in Chapter 9. Data binding a slider to the rotation of a 3D object is described in Chapter 12. And using sliders for volume and balance controls on a video player is discussed in Chapter 14.

When you create a slider (by double-clicking on Slider in the pop-up controls menu in the Toolbox, or by single-clicking and then clicking and dragging to position it in the artboard), you can set the maximum value, minimum value, tick placement and more in the Common Properties palette. You can also set the SmallChange property, which defines how far the slider moves in either direction when it is clicked.

Blend offers both a simple slider and a system slider. The system slider offers an interesting, subtle animation that starts when it has focus. You can assign the slider to have focus when it is loaded, if you want, by checking the IsDefault box in the Common Properties palette. You can find the simple slider in the Simple Styles tab of the Controls tab of the Asset Library in the Toolbox. The simple slider is shown on the right in Figure 16.11, and the system slider is on the left. Both sliders have the Maximum value set to 100, because the maximum value of a progress bar is 100. In Blend, a slider's default Maximum value is 10, so you probably want to change that, as we did.

FIGURE 16.11

The Slider on the left operates the ProgressBar control beneath it. The SimpleSlider on the right operates the SimpleProgressBar beneath it.

Using the progress bar

Blend offers both a SimpleProgressBar, as shown on the right in Figure 16.11, and a system ProgressBar, as shown on the left. The system progress bar has a nice animation in the Indicator element. Both progress bars are highly customizable. The Value property of the progress bars in Figure 16.11 is data bound to the sliders. You can find this Value property in the Common Properties palette, as shown in Figure 16.12.

You can orient the progress bar horizontally or vertically. The Indeterminate property displays a green band that sweeps across the progress bar every second or so. And you can set Maximum and Minimum properties. For instance, if your progress bar displays the temperature, you may want to set a Minimum of -40 (depending on where it's to be used.) and a Maximum of 120.

Progress bars have many uses. Vista uses a progress bar to display how much disk space is used. Of course, it never requires the Indeterminate property.

For more about progress bars, see the section "Creating Custom Controls" later in this chapter.

FIGURE 16.12

The Common Properties palette for the progress bar.

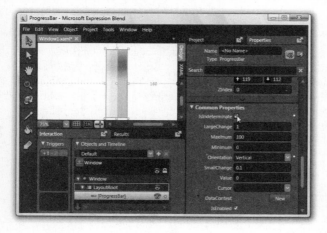

Using the grid splitter

Often the layout panel you use as the main panel of your application is a grid. This layout panel allows you to break up your window into rows and columns, and you can assign objects to those rows and columns. Then you can use one or more grid splitters to allow the user to resize any section of the grid.

To use a grid splitter, you first want to create at least one grid divider in your window. Do this by double-clicking the grid (which can be the LayoutRoot if the LayoutRoot panel is a grid). Then click on the grid divider bar to create a grid divider.

You probably want to add a rectangle or two so you can see the effect of the grid splitter that you are going to add. Add two rectangles by drawing one into each side of the grid divider.

To add a grid splitter click GridSplitter in the pop-up controls menu in the Toolbox, and draw it close to the grid divider, but not so close that it touches the line.

Test the grid splitter by pressing F5. Your grid should resize as shown in Figure 16.13

FIGURE 16.13

The rectangles resize when clicking and dragging the grid splitter.

> **TIP** If you want to add more than one grid splitter in a window, you can do that, but you'll probably also need to add another grid to make it work properly. Generally you need a grid for each grid splitter. You can nest them into the segments of another grid.

Using the Ink Canvas

The ink canvas allows the user to draw in its panel. You might use this control as the basis of a simple paint program, or perhaps to give users a simple way to create a signature for e- commerce applications. To change the brush color and brush size or to save the brushstrokes requires coding in the code-behind file. To add the ink canvas to the artboard, double-click on it in the Controls ⇨ System Controls tab in the Asset Library (which is the last button in the Toolbox), and resize and position it in the artboard. You can also give it a background color. The ink canvas control has no effect unless you test the project. Choose Project ⇨ Test Project or press F5. Figure 16.14 shows an example of drawing in the ink canvas.

Drawing in the Ink Canvas

InkCanvas has several modes, including Ink, which is the default, as shown in Figure 16.15, and GestureOnly, which causes the drawing to disappear when the mouse is released. Its Select mode changes the path to small dots and allows the user to select their drawing. EraseByPoint and EraseByStroke are two erasing modes. It might be useful to set these interactively in the code-behind file, perhaps by assigning a Click event to a separate button for each one, to allow the user to go back and forth between drawing and erasing their paths.

Creating List Boxes and Combo Boxes

List boxes and combo boxes are both items controls, which means that they contain items, but do not contain headers for those items. The items within a list box or combo box can be labels, buttons, or other UIElements. Or they can be layout panels, containing many UIElements within them, as shown in Figure 16.15. List boxes and combo boxes are similar to stack panels, because they automatically stack items and display scroll bars — but they have one major difference. When you click on an item, the space that the item takes up in the list box turns blue, to indicate that it has been selected. (This is when using its default template. For information on changing its template, you can see the section "Creating Custom Controls" later in this chapter.)

List boxes (and combo boxes) can contain any UIElements as items, including layout panels.

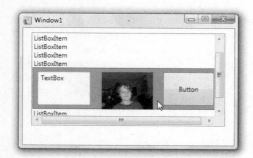

List boxes, like any control, can be contained in flow documents. Figure 16.5 shows an example of a list box in a flow document.

Be sure that you have margins or No Brush assigned to the background of an item in a list box, otherwise no blue may appear when you select the item, if your object is completely covering the list box.

Creating a list box

To create a list box, you can do one of the following:

- Double-click ListBox in the pop-up controls menu in the Toolbox
- Click ListBox in the pop-up controls menu in the Toolbox, and click and drag in the artboard to position it there

Blend offers ListBoxItems, which you can populate your list box with. To add a ListBoxItem to a ListBox, right-click on a ListBox, and in the pop-up menu that appears choose Add ListBoxItem. To change the text in the ListBoxItem, select the ListBoxItem and type in new text in the Content property in the Common Properties palette.

To add UIElements, including layout panels, into your list box, click the Selection tool, and drag the layout panel into the list box while holding the Alt key.

To change the order of the items in the list box, you can drill down to select the item you want to move, then drag it up or down to another position.

 If you want UIElements to be in a list box or combo box, its best to nest them into a ListBoxItem or ComboBoxItem.

 For information on data binding a list box to a data source, see Chapter 3 and Chapter 21.

Creating a combo box

You can create a combo box in the same way that you create a list box, except that when you right-click on a combo box, the context menu gives you the choice of viewing the combo box in an expanded view or a collapsed view. When you are creating and editing the combo box, you'll probably want to select Expand ComboBox. This works well for items that are not layout panels. However you may not want the combo box to appear expanded in the user interface, so you can right-click again on the combo box and in the pop-up menu that appears deselect Expand ComboBox before you test your application.

If you're adding a layout panel as an item to a combo box, you may want to work with the layout panel outside the combo box, so that you can more easily get it to look the way you want it. Then double-click the combo box to make it active, and drag the item into the combo box while holding Alt.

You can change the order of the items in a combo box by selecting an item and dragging it to another location, or you can access the XAML code and change the order there (in the same way as you would change the order of paragraphs in a flow document, as described in Chapter 9).

To make a combo box item visible by default, in the Common Properties palette set the Selected Index to the number of the item that you want to display as the default. (-1 is blank, 0 is the first item, 1 is the second item and so on.)

CROSS-REF   For information on data binding a combo box to a data source, see Chapter 21.

Editing items using the Collection Editor

Once you create your items you can edit them in two main ways:

- Drill down by double-clicking repeatedly on the object until you get to the item's container. Then select the item by single-clicking it and edit it. (If it's in a Combo box, be sure to select Expand ComboBox from the context menu.)
- You can also edit items using the Items Collection Editor, as shown in Figure 16.16. (You can also add items using the Collection Editor.)

FIGURE 16.16

You can use the Items Collection Editor to add or edit items in an items control, such as a list box or combo box.

To use the Collection Editor, select the list box, combo box, or other items control, and click the button beside Items (Collection) in the Common Properties palette. Select the item in the combo box and a Properties panel appears in the dialog box allowing you to edit the item.

You can also add items using the Collection Editor by clicking the Add Item button and choosing the UIElement that you want to add. (However, once you add it and close the Items Collection Editor, you may need to adjust the object handles in the Design view to see the item.)

Adding interactivity to your list box or combo box items

You can add interactivity to your list box and combo box items by setting their Selected property as a trigger, to trigger a timeline to begin, for example. Or you can have them call an event handler in the code-behind file — you can type in a name of your event handler in the Properties panel (click the Events button at the top of the Properties panel to view them). The names of the events that you probably want to use for a list box and combo box are Selected or Unselected.

Creating Menus and Other Headered Items Controls

While list boxes and combo boxes do not contain headers for their items, other controls can. A *header* is a part of a control which acts as a label for items, and it also provides built-in interactivity that relates to its purpose — for example the MenuItem can cause a submenu to pop-up. Controls that have headers are menus, toolbars, tab controls, group boxes, list views, and tree views. Let's use the menu as an example for creating headers.

 For information on list views, see Chapter 22.

Working with menus

Menus are like a table of contents for your user interface. When individuals first use your application, they often open the menus and see what's available. So you probably want to have all your major feature categories listed in the main menu, with lesser features in submenus, and even less used features in their submenus. A menu has a property trigger that adds a border to an item when it is selected. Like a stack panel, you can add any UIElement as a child element to a menu — for example a button, a label, or even a layout panel that contains many nested items. You can also add a MenuItem, which is an element that only a menu can contain.

You can use a MenuItem in the following ways:

- Change its Header property to display the text that you want to display, so that it acts like an ordinary label nested in a menu
- Nest another menu into it to create a submenu

Every item in the menu has a border that appears when the item is selected, but you can change the highlight to something else by creating a new template and editing it. For information on doing so, see the section "Modifying Styles of Controls" later in this chapter.)

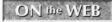 You can find a tutorial on creating context menus in Blend at our Web site www.blendtips.com/bible.

Creating menus

To create a menu, which may contain many submenus, the first step is to create the main menu.

Steps: Creating the Main Menu

1. To create a menu in the artboard, double-click Menu in the Controls ➪ System Controls tab in the Asset Library, or single-click and then click and drag to position it in the artboard. Draw a long thin menu for the main menu, as shown in Figure 16.17.

FIGURE 16.17

Creating the Main menu, along with its submenus

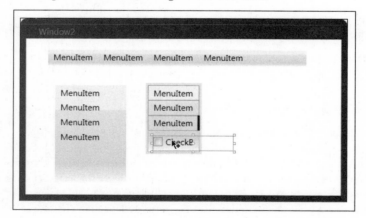

2. Then you can do one of the following:

   ▪ **To add a MenuItem to the menu**, select the menu, right-click, from the pop-up menu that appears choose Add MenuItem, and in the Header property in the Common Properties palette type the text that you want for the MenuItem.

   ▪ **To add an item other than a MenuItem into the menu**, double-click the menu to make it active and drag an item into the menu while holding down Alt (or instead of dragging, create the item inside the menu).

> **TIP** You may want to adjust the size of your menu by adjusting their object handles, or by adding spaces into their Header property.

> **TIP** Normally main menus stack horizontally, but there's no reason why you can't stack yours vertically, if you want. To create a vertical menu, you need to size the item or MenuItem to take up an entire row. This wraps the next menu item onto the next row.

> **NOTE** UIElements in a menu can't have submenus that expand from them. Only the MenuItem can have some submenus.

Adding submenus

To create submenus, you simply add items to a MenuItem that acts as their header. Items that you can add to the MenuItem are as follows:

- **MenuItems:** These can contain text in the Header property field, or can contain text and another submenu. To add a MenuItem, select the MenuItem that will act as its header, right-click, and in the pop-up menu that appears choose Add MenuItem.

- **UIElements, such as buttons or layout panels.** To add a UIElement, double-click the MenuItem that acts as its header to make MenuItem active and drag the UIElement into the MenuItem while holding down Alt (or instead of dragging, create the item inside the MenuItem).

- **Separators, which are lines between items in a submenu.** To add a separator, select the header MenuItem, right-click, and in the pop-up menu that appears choose Add Separator.

Other tasks you may want to perform when creating a submenu are as follows:

- **To delete menu items**, select them in the Objects list and press Backspace.

- **To change the text of a MenuItem**, select the MenuItem and change its name in the Header property in the Common Properties palette.

- **To keep the submenu expanded in the artboard**, select its header MenuItem, right-click, and in the pop-up menu that appears choose Expand MenuItem.

- **To re-position items in a submenu**, be sure the submenu is open, and then select an item and drag it to a new position.

- **To keep your menu items from wrapping**, expand the menu item to fill the width of the submenu.

Nesting menu items in their submenus

You may want to create all your menus before you start nesting them, as shown in Figure 16.17. To nest a menu into a submenu, you can do it the way you nest any object into another object. Double-click the menu item to make it the active container, and drag the submenu into it, as shown in Figure 16.18. On the left in Figure 16.18, the Submenu is nested in another submenu. On the right, a submenu is nested into a menu item in the main menu.

FIGURE 16.18

Nesting the submenus into the main menu.

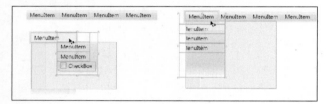

Figure 16.19 shows an example of the menu in operation. As you can see, it can use some designing to make it look more appealing. For instructions on customizing your controls, see the section "Editing Control Templates" later in this chapter.

FIGURE 16.19

A default system menu with default menu items and a default checkbox.

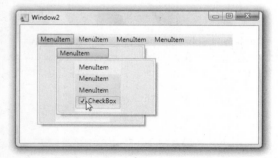

Creating tab controls

Tabs, like menus, are a great way to display the wholeness of the application to the user. Each main feature can be listed on a tab. Unlike menu items, which collapse, tabs can provide a more visible overview of the features of your application.

Tab controls are also headered items. They are probably easier than menus to create because they have no pop-up element that hides elements and are completely straightforward to use.

To create tabs, such as those in Figure 16.20, single-click TabControl in the pop-up controls menu in the Toolbox, then click and drag in the artboard to position the tabs there, or double-click TabControl and tabs appear in the upper left hand corner of the artboard. The default tab control contains two tabs, each containing a grid panel that you can add objects into. You can do the following to customize this tab control:

- **Add content into a panel:** Double-click the tab control to make it active, and select the tab that you want to add content to. Then you can create content in the tab's panel, or you can select an already created object and drag it into the panel while holding Alt.

- **Change the text in the header:** Double-click the tab control to make it active and select the tab that has the text that you want to change. Type the new text into the Header property in the Common Properties palette.

- **Add more tabs:** Select the tab control (but be sure it's not active), right-click, and in the pop-up menu that appears, choose Add TabItem.

FIGURE 16.20

A simple tab control with a rectangle in the first tab, an ellipse in the second tab, and a button in the third tab.

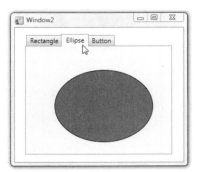

You can also set the TabStripPlacement in the Common Properties palette to Top (default), Bottom, Right, or Left. The different placements of the tabs are shown in Figure 16.21. To change the look of the tab control, see the section "Editing Control Templates" later in this chapter.

FIGURE 16.21

Four sets of tabs with four different tab placements.

Working with tree views

The Tree View control is an outline with headings that you can open and close as you like. Tree views can contain any UIElements within them, but only TreeViewItems can expand to reveal new levels. Figure 16.22 shows a tree view that contains many levels as well as a check box and some radio buttons. Like almost all controls, the elements that it contains can also be layout panels as well as controls, giving you the opportunity to nest just about anything in a tree view.

FIGURE 16.22

A tree view with a check box and radio buttons in it.

STEPS: Creating a Tree View

1. Click on Tree View in the Controls ➪ System Controls tab of the Asset Library, and click and drag in the artboard to position it there.

2. To add the top level of items to the tree view, do one of the following:

   - **To add a TreeViewItem,** select the tree view, right-click, and from the pop-up menu that appears choose Add TreeViewItem.

   - **To add a UIElement,** such as a button or layout panel, double-click the tree view to make it active, and either create the object within the tree view, or drag an object into the tree view while pressing Alt.

3. To change the text in the TreeViewItem, select the TreeViewItem and type new text into the Header property in the Common Properties palette.

4. To add a second level item into the tree view, do one of the following:

   - **To add a TreeViewItem** select the TreeViewItem in the upper level, right-click, and from the pop-up menu that appears choose Add TreeViewItem

   - **To add a UIELement:** double-click a TreeViewItem to make it active, click on whatever element you want in the ToolBox, and click and drag in the TreeViewItem to position the element there. You can also drag the element in while pressing Alt.

Like all controls, tree views can be modified in their appearance. For more about customizing controls, see the section "Creating Custom Controls" later in this chapter.

 When working in higher levels of the tree view, you may need to right-click on tree view items and choose Expand TreeView to see the expanded tree.

Creating toolbars

Toolbars can contain almost all kinds of UIElements. Toolbars are similar to stack panels that are oriented in a horizontal direction, but toolbars also provide an overflow grid to hold any objects that can't fit on the toolbar. This overflow grid pops up when the drop-down arrow is pressed. The toolbar also has shading on the bottom to give it a rounded appearance. You can change the color of this shading by giving the background a different solid color brush in the Brushes palette. You can also nest toolbars within toolbars. Figure 16.23 shows an example of a simple toolbar. It contains more buttons than it can display all at once, and the overflow grid shows the remaining buttons.

To create a toolbar, click ToolBar in the Controls ➪ System Controls tab of the Asset Library and click and drag in the artboard to position it there. To add objects to the toolbar, double-click the toolbar to make it active, and either create objects in the active toolbar, or drag them in while pressing Alt. When more objects are added than fit, they disappear into the overflow grid. If you want to view the objects in the overflow grid while the application runs, select the toolbar and choose Expand Toolbar. If you want to view objects in the overflow grid in the Design view, select any object that is in the overflow grid, and the overflow grid becomes visible.

A toolbar containing buttons that overflow into the overflow grid.

> **TIP** If you want to nest a toolbar within another toolbar, you probably want to do this in the Objects list, because this is difficult to do in Design view. Double-click the toolbar to make it active and drag the other toolbar in the Objects list to the active toolbar, which also is in the Objects list.

Using group boxes

A group box is probably the simplest of the headered controls. It simply contains a header and accepts a single child element. The child element, of course, can be a layout panel that contains many items, if you want. The group box is ideal for grouping controls that have similar functionality. Or you can group images with captions. Or...well, its uses are endless.

Figure 16.24 shows an example of group boxes in a window. To create a group box, click GroupBox in the Controls ⇨ System Controls tab of the Asset Library, and click and drag in the window to position it there. To add a layout panel or other UIElement to the group box, double-click the group box to make it active, and draw the UIElement into the group box. To change the header, select the header in the artboard and type, or type into the Header property in the Common Property palette.

FIGURE 16.24

Group boxes are probably the simplest of the headered controls.

Adding an expander

An expander is an interactive feature that you can add to a menu, layout panel, or other control to show more data. It has a small down arrow to show the user that more information exists and a small up arrow to let the user collapse the expander. Figure 16.25 shows an example of an expander containing six buttons that appear when the down arrow is clicked.

FIGURE 16.25

An expander pops up a panel of buttons.

To use an expander, click the Expander in the Controls ➪ System Controls tab of the Asset Library and add it into the artboard. Then double-click the expander to make it active so that you can add items into it, such as a stack panel of buttons, for example. The expander only takes one child element, so multiple objects need to be nested in a layout panel that you add to the expander. You can change the header of the expander by changing the text in the Header property in the Common Properties palette.

To add the expander to a button, as shown in Figure 16.25, we simply added the button and the expander in a grid panel and placed the expander above the button. It is not part of the button, but simply on top of the button and sharing the same panel.

Using the list view

A list view is probably the most complicated control that Blend offers. It allows the user to browse quickly through records in a database by showing several fields of data in columns side by side. It contains automatic scrollbars and allows the user to automatically resize the columns as well. By default, it does not allow editing of the data, but this can be changed in code in the code-behind file. (Although you may find it easier to create a list-view-like control yourself if you want to edit data.)

CROSS-REF For more information about list views, see Chapter 21.

Although the list view is found in the Asset Library, it is not fully implemented in the Design view of Blend. To add headings and bind data to it, you need to add them into the XAML code. We discuss how to implement the list view using XAML code in Chapter 21. Figure 16.26 shows an example of a list view in which the headings have been added in the XAML code.

FIGURE 16.26

A list view allows the user to scroll through records and resize column widths.

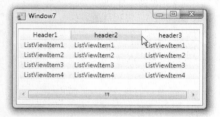

Creating a Custom Button

Blend's Make Button feature allows you to create your own buttons, and you can then add property triggers (described in the section "Setting Property Triggers" later in this chapter) to change the look of the buttons during different property changes.

STEPS: Creating your own button

1. Design a button using the drawing tools. Don't add text because Blend adds a content presenter control for that in the next step.

2. Select the object that you want to transform into a button, and choose Tools ➪ Make Button.

3. In the Create Style Resource dialog box that appears, as shown in Figure 16.27, do the following:

   ▪ Type a name for the new button style.

   ▪ Choose whether you want the resource to be available for the entire application, this window, or a resource dictionary.

   ▪ Click OK.

FIGURE 16.27

FIGURE 16.27

Creating a new button.

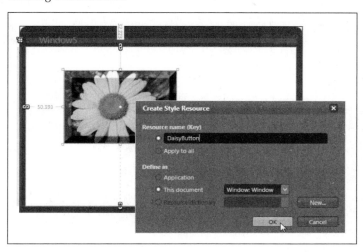

4. The word Button appears in the ContentPresenter of your newly created button. You can change and format the text by clicking in the word and typing in your new text. You can also use the Text palette to format the text, although you may not be able to view your formats until you click outside the button. For instance, we added text to our button as shown in Figure 16.28. You can also add any rich content to the button, including video, images, and more, just as you can to a system button.

FIGURE 16.28

The new button with text.

5. If you press F5 to test your button, you'll see that it doesn't change its look when pressed or when the mouse is over it. To remedy this, you can add some property triggers, as described in the section "Setting Property Triggers" later in this chapter.

CAUTION   Currently bitmap effects that you apply in Blend require that your application be granted full trust status. To avoid this, if you want a bitmap effect for your button, you could create one in Expression Design, and then export it as an image file and apply it in Blend as an image brush.

Editing Control Templates

Probably the most exciting feature about Blend, thanks to the Windows Presentation Foundation, is the power you have to modify styles and templates. By using templates, you can get right down to the control parts and modify them, or add some elements and take others away — whatever you like, as long as you follow a few rules listed in this section. For instance, in Figure 16.29, the progress bar control looks nothing like the system progress bar below it, yet its function is identical. For information about how to create this progress bar, see "Data binding in control templates" later in this chapter.

FIGURE 16.29

The speedometer is a customized progress bar.

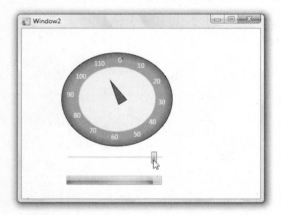

Editing a copy of a template

Every control is made up of parts that have properties that you can adjust in the Properties panel. The properties available to be modified vary for the different controls, depending on the functions of the parts. For instance, the MenuItem control contains a PART_Popup that has various properties in the Layout palette, such as Placement and Vertical Offset, which you can use to define where your popup appears. You can edit these properties in the template of one MenuItem in a menu, and it modifies all the MenuItems in the menu accordingly.

To view the parts of the control in the Objects list so that you can select them and modify their properties and more, you can select the control, such as a MenuItem for example, choose Object ⇨ Edit Control Parts (Template) ⇨ Edit A Copy, type in the name of a resource in the dialog box, choose where you want to define it, and click OK. You can then select any part in the Objects list and add or modify properties in the Properties list. (See Figure 16.30) You can also set property triggers, which is discussed in the section "Setting Property Triggers" later in this chapter.

FIGURE 16.30

Modifying the parts of a MenuItem using the Properties panel.

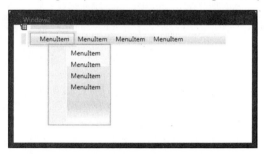

Setting Property Triggers

Control Templates respond to property triggers that you can set to change the way that a control appears during different changes in its properties. The Property Triggers sidebar describes some properties which are commonly set as property triggers.

You can also set values for properties defined in property triggers. For example, you can set Width = 100 as a property trigger. This could be useful if your control is resizable by the user, and you want to give the control a different look when its Width property is reduced to 100. (Of course, you'd also want to set its Minimum Width to 100, because otherwise, the user could resize it to 99 or 98 and so on, and the property trigger would not occur. Currently, you can only set "equal," not "less than" or "greater than."

Property Triggers

The property triggers that you use will vary for different controls. The following are just a few of the most useful property triggers:

- **IsKeyboardFocused:** Use this property trigger to define the look of a control when it is ready to respond to keystrokes from the keyboard.

- **IsPressed:** Use this property trigger to define the look of a control (such as a button or MenuItem) when it is pressed.

- **IsMouseOver:** Use this property trigger to define the look of a control when the mouse is over it.

- **IsChecked:** Use this property trigger to define the look of a control when it is checked — this could be a check box, for example, that is checked even after it loses keyboard focus.

- **IsEnabled:** When set to false, use this to define the look for the disabled state of the control.

- **IsSelected:** Use this to change the appearance of ListBoxItems, ComboBoxItems, and radio buttons when they are selected.

Almost any property of a control can be used to set a property trigger. This allows you to customize the appearance of your control for a vast range of conditions. (Although, you may find that limiting a control to a few property changes may be enough for you!)

Modifying your control's appearance using existing property triggers

In this section we show how to modify existing property triggers. For example you may have created a custom button, using the Make Button feature, but that button had no modified appearances set for its property triggers. Or you can modify the look of a simple button or simple control using these steps. (Modifying appearances of system controls for their property triggers are explained later in this chapter.) Now we can set those triggers so that the button behaves interactively, like a normal button should. Here are the steps for adding property triggers. You can also use these steps to add extra property triggers for other types of controls.

> **TIP** You can use the following steps on simple controls and buttons created using Make Button, but using them on System controls may give you disappointing results. See the instructions in the section "Using property triggers with system controls" later in this chapter.

STEPS: Modifying the Appearance of your Control Using Existing Property Triggers

1. Select a control, such as a button created using the Make Button feature, and choose Object ➪ Edit Control Parts (Template) ➪ Edit Template. (If Edit Template is not available, then choose Edit A Copy, give your resource a name, and click OK.)

2. In the Triggers palette, click a property trigger, such as IsMouseOver = True, as shown in Figure 16.31. This causes the Trigger recording to turn on, as indicated by the red button next to the property trigger.

Notice in Figure 16.31 that the Objects and Timeline palette shows the component elements of the button, which include a ContentPresenter and image nested inside a grid. It also shows default property triggers which are assigned to the button, but have no effect yet, because no new appearance has been assigned to them.

FIGURE 16.31

Changing the look of the button for the IsMouseOver property.

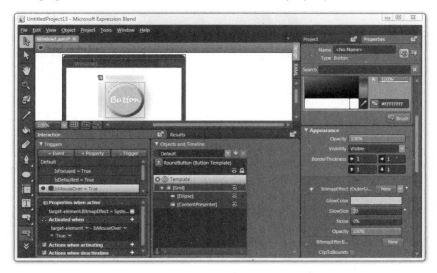

3. Now you can change the appearance of the button and make it look how you want the button to look during a mouse over. (We added a glow bitmap effect to the grid.)

CAUTION   Only use bitmap effects if you plan for your application to be a full trust application, because at this writing bitmap effects require full trust. To avoid this restriction, you can create bitmap effects in Expression Design and apply them as image brushes in Blend instead.

4. When you're finished, click the red button next to the property trigger to turn off trigger recording.

5. You can repeat steps 2-4 for all the properties you want to change.

6. To test the new appearance for your button caused by the different property triggers, click the up arrow button beside the button template name in the Objects list, or you can double-click in the LayoutRoot to end your template editing session. Then press F5 to test it. Figure 16.32 shows the new glow that appears while IsMouseOver is equal to True.

FIGURE 16.32

The modified appearance for the IsMouseOver = True property trigger.

Adding and deleting property triggers

You can also add property triggers and delete them, so that you can customize the look of your interactive states of the control in a myriad of ways. Here's how to add and delete property triggers.

 **TIP**   You can also combine property triggers. For information on doing this, see "Combining property triggers when animating the selected index of a combo box" later in this chapter.

STEPS: Customizing the Look of your Control by Adding and Deleting Property Triggers

1. Select a control that you want to add property triggers to, or delete property triggers from, and choose Object ⇨ Edit Control Parts (Template) ⇨ Edit Template. (If Edit Template is not available, then choose Edit A Copy, give your resource a name and click OK.)

2. In the Triggers palette, click the +Property button. A new MinWidth=0 trigger appears, as shown in Figure 16.33. This is the default trigger that you can change to whatever you want in the next steps.

3. Change the MinWidth property to the property that you want for your trigger, by clicking the down arrow beside MinWidth, as shown in Figure 16.33. Choose a property from the menu.

4. Set the value for the property, such as True or a number, whatever is valid for that property.

5. Change the appearance of the control.

6. Turn off the Trigger Recording button

7. Add or modify more triggers, or click the up arrow beside the name of your template in the Objects list.

FIGURE 16.33

Changing the MinWidth property trigger.

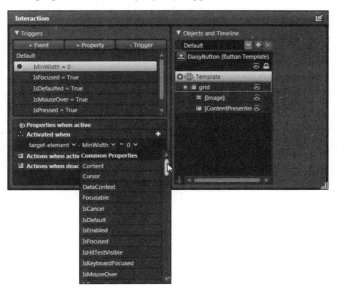

Using property triggers with system controls

The system controls have extra animations in them that prevent you from changing the template unless you turn off the animations. However, if you turn off those animations, then the system control ceases to act as a system control anyway. It doesn't give the same results for the different property triggers, and it won't change its appearance according to themes. So we recommend that if you plan to modify a template, just use the simple controls rather than the system controls.

The changes that you need to make in a system control to be able to edit its template more effectively are to delete the Chrome.RenderPress and Chrome.RenderDefaulted properties, which are located in the Triggers palette when IsKeyboardFocused = True and IsChecked = True. Deleting these will allow you to edit the template of the system control in the same way you edit other templates.

Adding animation to a template

If you want to add animation to part of a control, and not the entire control, then you need to add the animation to the template of the control. For example, in Figure 16.34 we animated the thumb of a slider so that it pulsates when its IsMouseOver property = True. To do this, you can perform the following steps. Then you can modify these steps to animate any part of any control. (If you want to add animation to the entire control, but still add a property trigger, see the section entitled "Modifying Styles of Controls" later in this chapter.)

FIGURE 16.34

The thumb of a slider pulsates when the mouse is over it.

STEPS: Animating a Control Part

1. Click on the Slider button in the Toolbox, and click and drag in the artboard to position the slider there.

2. Select the slider and choose Object ⇨ Edit Control Parts (Template) ⇨ Edit A Copy. Give the slider a name and choose where to define it, then click OK.

3. Click the Create New Timeline button, select Thumb, and click the Record New Keyframe button. Then move the playhead to 1/4 of a second. Select Thumb and drag the handles so that the thumb expands.

4. Select the keyframe at 0 seconds, and choose Edit ⇨ Copy. Move the playhead to 1/2 second and choose Edit ⇨ Paste.

5. Then click the expanders to view the lowest level of the tracks. On each of them, one at a time right-click, in the pop-up menu that appears choose Edit Repeat Count, click the Forever button, and click OK. Your Objects and Timeline palette should look similar to Figure 16.35.

6. Test your animation by pressing the Play button.

7. To set the property trigger so that the thumb pulsates during a mouse over, click the +Property button in the Triggers palette, and in the Activated When pane, click the down arrow beside AutoToolTipPlacement (or whatever the +Property default is) and choose IsMouseOver.

8. In the Actions When Activating pane, choose the default, which is Timeline1 and Begin.

9. In the Actions When Deactivating pane, choose Timeline1 and Stop.

FIGURE 16.35

Adding animation to a control part.

Click the up arrow beside the name of the control template, and test your slider by pressing F5.

Modifying Styles of Controls

Unlike modifying the template of a control, you can edit the style of a control, add animation to the control, or set its properties if the animation or changes affect the control as a whole and not the parts that make up the control. For example, if you want to resize a button in a stack panel every time a mouse is over it, you can add the animation to the IsMouseOver = True property trigger to create the effect. Then you can apply the style as a resource to all the buttons in the stack panel, so they create a nicely flowing interactive effect when the mouse is over any button. Figure 16.36 shows an example of this simple effect.

FIGURE 16.36

A stack panel with buttons that resize during a mouseover.

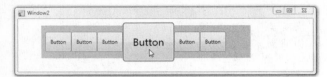

Setting property triggers and animating the resizing of controls

Here are the steps for creating a button that grows twice as big when the mouse is over it, and shrinks to its normal size when the mouse is not over it. The idea in a nutshell is to assign two timelines to an object, one for the animation of the control when the property trigger is activated, and the other for the animation of the control when the property trigger is deactivated.

 When using the Transform palette to animate styles, you almost always want to use the LayoutTransform pane and not the RenderTransform pane.

STEPS: Adding an Animation to a Style

1. Click the Button button in the Toolbox and click and drag in the artboard to position a button there.

2. Select the button and choose Edit Style ⇨ Edit A Copy. Name the resource, choose where to define it, and click OK.

3. Click the Create New Timeline button in the Timeline and Objects palette, and give the new timeline a name, and click OK.

4. Move the playhead to a new time (we chose half a second), and open the Transform palette. Open the expander of the Transform palette, and in the LayoutTransform pane select the Scale tab. Add a new value in the X and Y properties to expand the button.

CAUTION Don't try to just pull the object handles of the control at this step. (We know it's tempting.) Although creating the animation by pulling object handles appears to work when you press Play, it actually creates a RenderTransform instead of a LayoutTransform, which does not allow the buttons in the stack panel to react to the enlarging button.

5. Click Play to test it.

6. Click the Recording button to off.

7. Click the Create New Timeline button in the Timeline and Objects palette again and give it a name and click OK.

8. Now create a timeline which is the reverse of the first timeline by moving the playhead to half a second. Then change the X value to 1.00001 and Y value to 1.00001, as shown in Figure 16.37. This is a small change from 1 that no one will notice, but it adds the keyframe with the property.

FIGURE 16.37

Assigning a value slightly different from the default, so that a keyframe is generated.

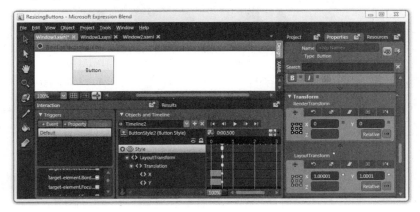

 You don't need keyframes at 0 seconds, because Blend supports handoff animation.

9. Click the Recording button to off and test the timeline.

10. Set your property trigger by selecting IsMouseOver = True in the Triggers palette, and click the plus sign beside Actions When Activating. Choose the first timeline from the down arrow and choose Begin. Then click the plus sign beside Actions When Deactivating and choose the second timeline and Begin, as shown in Figure 16.38.

FIGURE 16.38

Assigning the property triggers to the style.

11. Click the up arrow beside the style name to exit the style.

12. When you are finished editing the style, try out your button by pressing F5. If you're happy with it, then create more buttons, right-click on each, and in the pop-up menu that appears assign it the style by choosing Edit Style ➪ Apply Resource ➪ (name of the style). Then when all the buttons are assigned the resource, select them all, right-click, and in the pop-up menu that appears choose Group Into ➪ StackPanel and set its Orientation to Horizontal.

Combining property triggers when animating the selected index of a combo box

Another example of the usefulness of modifying styles of controls is, for example, a combo box that cycles through its contents when the mouse is over it, but stops the animation when the combo box is open. This requires setting a combination of two properties in the same property trigger. Figure 16.39 shows an example of this combo box.

FIGURE 16.39

A combo box displays its contents in a continual animation when the mouse is over it, but stops animating when it opens.

To create this combo box, you can do the following:

STEPS: Creating a ComboBox that Cycles through its SelectedIndex

1. Choose ComboBox from the Asset Library and click and drag in the artboard to position it there.

2. Select the combo box, right-click, and in the pop-up menu that appears choose Add ComboBoxItem. Add several items, select them one by one, and change their Content property in the Common Properties palette. We changed ours to display names of states.

3. Select the combo box and choose Edit Style ⇨ Edit A Copy. Name the resource, choose where to define it, and click OK.

4. Click the Create New Timeline button in the Timeline and Objects palette, give it a name, and click OK.

5. In the Common Properties palette, assign 0 as the SelectedIndex. Then move the playhead to a new time (we chose a second), and assign 1 as the SelectedIndex. Keep moving the playhead forward and incrementing the SelectedIndex for as many items as you have, plus do the last one twice. Then open the expanders in the timeline to view the objects with no expanders, right-click on the track, and in the pop-up menu that appears choose Edit Repeat Count. Then click the Forever button and click OK. (This cycles it.)

6. Click the Recording button to off.

7. Click the +Property button in the Triggers palette, in the Activated When pane click the down arrow beside the default property, and choose IsMouseOver. Be sure it is set to True. Then click the Plus sign on the Activated When pane, choose IsDropDownOpen from the default property, and change True to False.

   This combines the two properties into a single property trigger, as shown in Figure 16.40.

8. In the Actions When Activating pane, choose the defaults, which are Timeline1 and Begin.

9. In the Actions When Deactivating pane, choose Timeline1 and Stop.

10. Click the up arrow beside the name of the control template, and test your combo box by pressing F5.

FIGURE 16.40

Setting a property trigger with two conditions in it.

Radically Changing the Appearance of Your Controls

You can make radical changes in the appearance of any control by creating a control from an empty template for that control. Figure 16.41 shows an example of check boxes that look nothing like check boxes. In fact, they're image controls in a check box template. Placing images in a check box template makes available the IsChecked property, so that you can assign IsChecked to the images. In the example in Figure 16.41, the images that are checked enlarge, and when they're unchecked, they shrink to their previous size. Even though they have no check marks, they still function like a check box.

FIGURE 16.41

Check boxes that look nothing like check boxes but act like check boxes.

The following are the steps for creating images that act like the check boxes in Figure 16.41. Trying this out will enable you to apply this technique to other controls, and change them radically too.

STEPS: Creating a Radically Different Look for a Standard Control

1. Click the ProgressBar button in the Asset Library, and click and drag in the artboard to position it there.

2. Choose Object ⇨ Edit Control Parts (Template) ⇨ Edit A Copy. Then type in the name for your resource, choose where you want to define it, and click OK.

3. Select the parts of the progress bar, and in the Appearance palette set their visibility to Hidden.

4. Draw a path in the shape of the needle for the speedometer. Be sure it is facing 0. Select it and choose Group Into ⇨ Grid. Then move the center of the grid to the center of the speedometer, so your needle rotates properly. (You need to group into the grid to give you access to a center point that you can re-position.)

5. Select the PART_Track and set the Width property to 360.

6. Draw in a background for your speedometer.

7. Select the grid, open the Rotate tab of the Transform palette, click the Advanced Properties button, and choose Data Binding.

8. In the Create Data Binding dialog box, click Element Property, select the PART_Indicator from the left column, choose Width from the right column, as shown in Figure 16.42, and click Finish.

FIGURE 16.42

The rotation of the speedometer needle is data bound to the width of the PART_Indicator.

9. Click the up arrow next to the name of the template in the Objects list.

10. Select the speedometer, and in the Common Properties palette, set Maximum to 360, if you want a full rotation.

11. Test your speedometer by adding a slider to the artboard and data binding the value of the slider to the value of the ProgressBar (aka speedometer). Do that by selecting the ProgressBar and clicking the Advanced Properties button beside Value in the Common Properties palette. Then in the Create Data Binding dialog box, click Element Property, choose Slider in the column on the right and Value in the column on the left, and click Finish.

12. Test your speedometer by pressing F5.

Data binding

Using the power of data binding to bind a property of one control part to another can open up a whole world of opportunities when creating custom controls. For instance, in the progress bar that looks like a speedometer in Figure 16.43, the progress bar is hidden while the rotation value of the triangle is data bound to the width of the PART_Indicator.

The ProgressBar is hidden and the speedometer is drawn into the template.

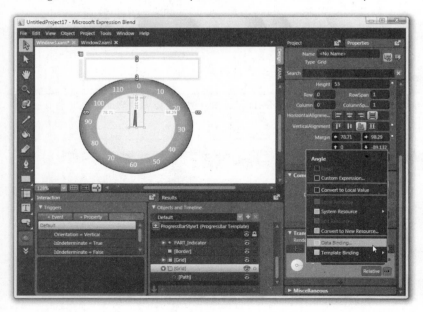

The beauty of data binding in the control template is that you can make any part of any control invisible and data bind to some other object doing something totally different!

Here are the steps to create a simple rotating indicator for a progress bar, as shown in Figure 16.43.

STEPS: Data Binding in a Template to Radically Change the Look of a Control

1. Click the ProgressBar button in the Asset Library, and click and drag in the artboard to position it there.

2. Choose Object ⇨ Edit Control Parts (Template) ⇨ Edit A Copy. Then type in the name for your resource, choose where you want to define it, and click OK.

3. Select the parts of the progress bar, and in the Appearance palette set their visibility to Hidden.

4. Draw a path in the shape of the needle for the speedometer. Be sure it is facing 0. Select it and choose Group Into ⇨ Grid. Then move the center of the grid to the center of the speedometer, so your needle rotates properly. (You need to group into the grid to give you access to a center point that you can re-position.)

5. Select the PART_Track and set the Width property to 360.

6. Draw in a background for your speedometer.

7. Select the grid, open the Rotate tab of the Transform palette, click the Advanced Properties button, and choose Data Binding.

8. In the Create Data Binding dialog box, click Element Property, select the PART_Indicator from the left column, choose Width from the right column, as shown in Figure 16.44, and click Finish.

9. Click the up arrow next to the name of the template in the Objects list.

10. Select the speedometer, and in the Common Properties palette, set Maximum to 360, if you want a full rotation.

11. Test your speedometer by adding a slider to the artboard and data binding the value of the slider to the value of the ProgressBar (aka speedometer). Do that by selecting the ProgressBar and clicking the Advanced Properties button beside Value in the Common Properties palette. Then in the Create Data Binding dialog box, click Element Property, choose Slider in the column on the right and Value in the column on the left, and click Finish.

12. Test your speedometer by pressing F5.

CROSS-REF If you want to data bind properties with values that are not the same types, then see the information on value converters in Chapter 21.

FIGURE 16.44

The rotation of the speedometer needle is data bound to the width of the PART_Indicator.

Creating a User Control

You may have noticed that Blend allows you to add a UserControl by choosing File ➪ New Item and clicking UserControl. A UserControl is a document in Blend (just as a window or a page is a document in Blend), in which you can create a custom control. For example, you can create a control out of grids, text boxes, gridsplitters, and more, to create something like our overly simplified data entry control, shown in Figure 16.45.

FIGURE 16.45

Adding a custom control to the Asset Library by creating it in a UserControl.

Last Name	First Name	Phone	Age
Smith	Joe	555-1234	23
Jones	Hilary	555-9876	29
Jacobson	Sam	555-2345	32
Wiley	Bruce	555-4268	35

Then when you choose Project ➪ Build, the control appears in the Asset Library, as shown in Figure 16.46. The Asset Library makes the control available so that you can click it and then click and drag in a window to position it there, just as you can add any control into any window from the Asset Library.

FIGURE 16.46

Adding a custom control to the Asset Library by creating it in a UserControl.

The UserControl also offers a code-behind file that you can use for the control. Code added to this code-behind file can offer functionality for your control, and define it, as well. Developers will undoubtedly find working with the UserControl to be very useful in creating all kinds of specific controls, which can be accessed in the application by the designer using the Asset Library.

Summary

- Many ready-made WPF controls are available in Blend. These controls include buttons, sliders, scroll viewers, check boxes, radio buttons, combo boxes, list boxes, menus, tree views, expanders, and more.

- You can nest objects, such as media files, images, layout panels and more, in controls that allow child elements.

- Headered controls provide headers in which you can organize items — for example, a MenuItem is the header for Menu, and can contain a submenu within it.

- You can easily customize WPF controls, because the appearance of the control is separate from the function of the control.

- You can edit the parts of a control by editing its template, to give the control parts a different appearance, or add or delete control parts.

- You can use property triggers to control timelines, and to specify a new appearance of a control when a change in property occurs.

- You can animate the parts of a control as well as the entire control.

- You can data bind properties of parts of a control, perhaps existing invisible control parts, to other parts of a control, perhaps visible control parts that you create, and thus change the look of a control radically.

- You can create a new template for a type of a control, using none of the existing control parts, and create the appearance of the control from scratch while maintaining its functionality.

Chapter 17

Employing Principles of Usability in Next-Generation User Interface Construction

Usability and good design are more important for software today than ever before. Successful e-commerce transactions, for example, are dependent upon usability. As Don Norman writes in his essay, "Usability Is Not a Luxury" at `www.jnd.org/dn.pubs.html`, "If the customer can't find it, then the customer can't buy it."

With new tools for increasing usability plus the increasing computing power of desktops and laptops today, user interface design is poised to move toward a new level of usability and new levels of visual appeal. And as described in Chapter 8, aesthetic design can be an important ingredient in any strategy for improving usability.

But visual appeal alone does not make an application usable. Researchers have discovered a number of basic principles of usability that are highly relevant to user interface design. For example, research shows that we remember things more easily when presented with a list of options rather than when we have to recall a fact from memory. Studies also show that people tend to favor things that they recognize, so consistency in a computer application provides a more favorable experience.

Fitts's Law shows that it takes less time to reach a button, menu item, or any control using the mouse if that control is large or on any edge of the screen. Hick's Law asserts that the amount of time it takes to perform a task is related to the number of options the user is presented with. And you may need to make adjustments to your user interface so that it is accessible to users with impaired vision, impaired hearing, learning disorders, or other disabilities. In this chapter, you explore these principles and how they relate to designing the new generation of user interfaces and Web applications.

IN THIS CHAPTER

Understanding recognition versus recall

Using Fitts's Law

Observing Hick's Law

Understanding flexibility versus usability

Designing for accessibility for everyone

Including feedback

Avoiding user mistakes

Using constraints

Providing levels of control

Minimizing and forgiving errors

Favoring Recognition Over Recall

Why is it often easier to answer the questions in a multiple-choice test than in a test with essay questions? Because seeing the correct answer helps you to remember it. It is easier for the mind to remember something when reminded of it than when trying to remember something with no reminder. This is probably the principal reason why the more processor-intensive graphical user interfaces of Windows and Macintosh have become more popular than the command-line interfaces of yesteryear (such as MS-DOS, for example), which required users to remember many commands without any cues.

People also tend to remember items from recognition memory longer than items from recall memory. For example, without the aid of a multiple-choice test, you may not be able to remember the correct answer at all. Recognition memory is both easier and longer lasting than recall memory.

Kinesthetic and audio recognition

Recognition memory is not limited to the recognition of facts. Pianists memorize musical pieces based on touch and sound and not just through the visual memory of notes on a page. Recognition can be triggered by touch, sound, sight, and smell (okay, probably not smell on the computer). For example, you may find it easier to remember an application by its icon on the screen than to remember the name of the application. Also, computer users' kinesthetic memories will help them to remember where things are, such as where a particular tool is in the Toolbox, even though they may forget the shape of its icon. This is why tools, menus, and often, even palettes in your user interface should retain the same positions as much as possible when not in use.

 **Kinesthetic memory** is your memory of where you are in space and where your limbs and muscles have moved.

For example, if you use a wrap panel for tools, you don't want the tools to rewrap and change position if the user resizes the panel. The outstanding free software application GIMP, which is similar to Photoshop, contains its tools in a window that, when resized, rewraps the position of the tools, which is confusing. It's great to allow users to resize a wrap panel, but you undoubtedly do not want them to be able to change the order of tools in it. Let them scale it larger or smaller if you like, as shown in Figure 17.1, but don't let them reshape it so the tools end up in different rows. One way to avoid this in a wrap panel is by placing the items in the panel into a viewbox or canvas. The viewbox would scale everything larger when the panel expands, and the canvas would keep everything the same size.

The advantage of favoring recognition over recall grows as user interfaces become more complex. So, try to arrange your user interface in a way that makes it easy for users to figure out how to quickly drill down to the part of the user interface that they want to use without having to memorize things.

When creating a tool palette, such as in the Gimp, it is best to not let the tools wrap when it is resize to take greater advantage of the user's kinesthetic memory.

Recognition bias and the exposure effect

Users tend to favor choices that are familiar even if they are not the ideal choice. The study, "Effects of Brand Awareness on Choice For a Common, Repeat-Purchase Product" by Hoyer and Brown, published in the *Journal of Consumer Research* in 1990, found that people were more likely to choose a known brand of peanut butter over two unknown brands with superior taste, as determined in previous blind tests. Recognizing the brand had an influence in what they thought tasted better.

This is known as the *exposure effect* or the *mere exposure effect*. People tend to favor what is familiar to them. Familiarity is important in user interfaces because when designs or ideas deviate from the current norm, there can be discomfort due to lack of exposure to the design or idea. For example, the novelty of the design of the Vietnam Veterans Memorial and the Eiffel Tower, shown in Figure 17.2, caused their popularity to suffer when they first appeared on the scene. Radio was not accepted by the U.S. Navy for several years after the technology existed because it was deemed too "mystical." Even great designs or ideas that are too different from what people are used to can be the focus of criticism or nonacceptance, at least for a while.

FIGURE 17.2

Familiarity breeds affection. The Eiffel Tower was considered by many Parisians to be an eyesore when it was built, but today its demolition would be unthinkable.

Using recognition memory in user interfaces

Recognition memory is easier, longer lasting, and emotionally more satisfying than recall memory, so you probably want to do everything possible to maximize the use of recognition memory over recall memory in your user interface. You can do this by designing well-organized menu systems. Don't bury the most important choices deeper than the choices for unusual cases. Make the most useful menu items the easiest to find. Use tooltips, which you can assign for almost every object in the Common Properties palette of the Properties panel, as shown in Figure 17.3.

FIGURE 17.3

Use tool tips to aid recognition memory.

Also, you may want to have a nice logo for your software package to establish brand identity, and display it discreetly, perhaps to avoid irritating users, but visibly. Plus, create a unique icon so the user can identify the application quickly when using the Vista taskbar or Alt-tab to choose from open applications. Vista places the icon of the application prominently in view. And make use of kinesthetic memory. When you create multiple windows for your application, as much as possible put the same menus and buttons on each window positioned in the same places. This way the user will remember the action of moving the mouse or the eye to reach or see a menu item or button.

If you have a search feature, or other feature in which the user types a short text string, you may want to design your program to remember similar matches. Many Web browsers offer this feature, and it comes in handy. When I tried to remember the Web address for a local restaurant, my eight-year-old daughter told me to type T. I did so, and the Web address was first in line to be selected! This feature is useful for beginners and experts alike.

Observing Fitts's Law

Paul M. Fitts published two papers in the *Journal of Experimental Psychology* in 1954 and 1964 on what is now known as Fitts's Law. Fitts found that the time that it takes to move a pointer (such as a finger, an extended arm, or a computer mouse) to point to new a target is a function of how large and how near the target is. Fitts's Law was used by employees at Xerox in 1978 to determine which input device was the best for their computer system (which later became the inspiration for the Apple Macintosh). The mouse won. Since then, Fitts's Law has been discussed in hundreds, if not thousands, of later studies in the field of human-computer interaction.

In mathematical terms, Fitts's Law is written as $T = a+bLog^2(D/W+1)$, in which T equals the time it takes to perform an action in a straight line, D equals the distance necessary to travel, and W equals the width of the target area measured along the axis of motion. According to Fitts's Law, anything smaller and farther away takes more time to reach. Also, anything placed around the outer rim of the screen takes less time to reach. This is because the width of the screen is infinitely large, since the movement of the mouse is stopped by the edge of the screen.

To apply Fitts's Law to user interface design, you may want to do some of the following:

- Make important buttons big so that they're easy to click, and avoid making any buttons too small.
- Place buttons around the rims of the screen (as shown in Figure 17.4), because it takes less time to reach the edge of the screen than almost anywhere in the middle of the screen.

FIGURE 17.4

The Blend interface and Vista apply Fitt's Law in many ways.

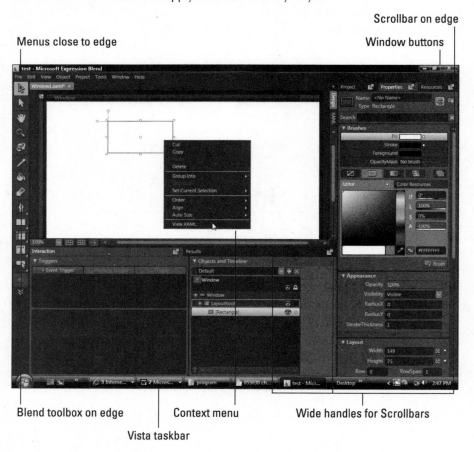

Menus close to edge

Scrollbar on edge

Window buttons

Blend toolbox on edge

Context menu

Vista taskbar

Wide handles for Scrollbars

- Allow the user to right-click for context menus. Context menus are extremely quick because almost no movement is necessary to reach them.

- Consider using context menus in the shape of pies, as shown in Figure 17.5. These are optimal according to Fitts's Law, because distance is nil and only the direction in which the mouse moves really matters. AutoDesk Maya and Mozilla Firefox make use of pie menus.

FIGURE 17.5

Pie menus are a great way to take advantage of Fitts's Law.

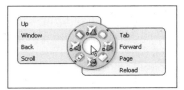

Heeding Hick's Law

William Edmund Hick was a British psychologist who published a paper in the *Quarterly Journal of Experimental Psychology* in 1952 in which he stated that the time it takes for an individual to make a decision increases with the number of choices. This law is useful in user interface design to show how offering the user only the bare minimum of choices that he needs at a time is ideal for his productivity. This law only applies to simple choices and not complex choices. For example, when functions of simple menu items and different controls are easily recognized by the user, Hick's Law applies. If the menus have submenus and the functions of controls or the menu items are not known, Hick's Law does not apply because the user takes more time to think even though there are only a few choices.

Fewer choices mean faster decision making and fewer possibilities for mistakes. Menus with lots of choices can take longer to navigate than menus with fewer choices. Delegating some less-used menu items into submenus while keeping more popular features in main menus may be useful in heeding Hick's Law.

You can also design your application to do what Microsoft Word does, and add double arrows pointing downward at the bottom of menus to indicate more options for the more experienced user, as shown in Figure 17.6. This may be useful for beginners who may tend to ignore the double arrows, but take more time for experts because they still have more choices and it requires another mouse movement to see the additional choices. Similarly, a More Options button in a dialog box can simplify the number of choices for beginners by offering those choices most often used.

FIGURE 17.6

Microsoft Word's menu, with double arrows indicating more options, may be good for beginners who will probably ignore the arrows, reducing the number of choices they must make.

You may also want to keep in mind that studies show that when people such as firemen or policemen are under a great deal of pressure, they do not always consider all options when making a choice, but often take the first plausible solution and go for it. Your users, at some time or other, may experience some external pressure when using your program (even though it may not be life-threatening), so when designing controls and menus, you may want to place the menu item that is most likely to be used first and place most prominently the control that is most likely to be used.

You definitely don't want to reorder menu items or other user interface items based on frequency of use after the user launches your application for the first time, however. This destroys the user's ability to rely on kinesthetic memory to find desired items in your application. Even reordering menu items in a new version of your application is not a change to be made without carefully considering the negative consequences for the existing users of your application.

Even though powerful applications exist to perform word processing, graphic design, and many other tasks, because of Hick's Law there may always be a market for simpler, more targeted applications with fewer features and simpler interfaces, simply because, as shown in Figure 17.7, fewer choices can mean faster decisions.

ON the WEB 37Signals offers a new free online book, entitled Getting Real? It speaks to a new movement in web-based application development which focuses in on creating simple, concise applications that do what they're supposed to do, without bogging down a user with unnecessary options. (37 Signals also create applications, all of which echo Hick's Law very well.) The free online book is found at `http://gettingreal.37signals.com/toc.php`.

FIGURE 17.7

Too many signs make you stop and think.

Understanding the Trade-offs Between Flexibility and Usability

Flexibility in the design of your user interface can increase its complexity, which may or may not be beneficial. You may want to have a less flexible interface that more specifically targets an application with fewer features. For example, the difference in the user interface between Apple's video editing applications Final Cut Pro and iMovie is significant, as can be seen in Figure 17.8. But even though Final Cut Pro is far superior to iMovie in depth and power of functionality, iMovie is the program of choice for many because its interface is simple. The simplicity of iMovie makes it harder for the user to fail.

FIGURE 17.8

The simplicity of the iMovie interface versus the flexibility of Final Cut Pro

It is important for you, the user interface designer, to understand your users. Are the users' needs simple and unlikely to change, so that you can design a more targeted and less flexible interface? Or do your users have sophisticated, ever-changing needs that require that you build in flexibility?

When creating a flexible interface (or any kind of user interface, actually), it's a good idea to do usability studies to see how well the user understands the interface. Paying your friend to use the program in a real-world situation can be an eye-opener, especially if you ask him to think out loud as you videotape him trying to manipulate the interface to accomplish the tasks you give him. An interface with more flexibility provides more opportunities for error and will most likely take more time for your users to get used to.

Your usability studies may bring to light how the features of your application are perceived by the user. If the feature is perceived as complex to learn, then the benefit to using it must be high for the user to spend the time to figure it out. For example, the recording feature of many VCRs went unused because they were perceived by some users as too complex to bother to learn. When the TiVo digital video recorder simplified the task of recording shows by allowing users to pick shows from a listing instead of by specifying the time and channel, users found it to be much easier and utilized the feature more readily. You may want to explore this cost-benefit relationship deeply before spending time and energy creating a flexible application with features that possibly may never be used.

Ensuring Accessibility

Creating an application that every person in the world can use may not be possible and may not be your goal. But knowing who your target population is and trying to achieve an application that can be used by as many as 98 percent of them is worthwhile. Your users come in a multitude of sizes, abilities, and disabilities. Some users may have trouble using the mouse. Others may suffer from a computer-related repetitive strain injury and need to use an alternative to the mouse. Some of your users may have impaired vision or impaired hearing. Trying to target every possible user may be difficult, but with some attention to detail you can make your user interface accessible to many more users.

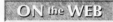 Microsoft accessibility information for developers can be found at `http://msdn2.microsoft.com/en-us/library/aa286482.aspx`

Overcoming handicaps

Lots of improvements can be made to a home to make it more handicap-friendly. These improvements can be small and add nothing — or next to nothing — to the initial cost of building, but add up to a lot of comfort when the need arises. Improvements such as wider doorways, plugs and light switches that can be reached from a wheelchair and stairs that have small risers are some examples. In the same way, you can add improvements to your user interface from its inception to target handicaps such as impaired vision, impaired hearing, and motor coordination problems.

Impaired color vision

Up to 15 percent of the population may have at least some impaired color vision — and most of these individuals are men. This is because the cause of colorblindness is usually genetic, and the gene to distinguish between red and green is located on the X-chromosome. Men have one X-chromosome and women have two. In women, if one X-chromosome is defective, the other can take up the slack.

When choosing colors for your user interface, keep in mind that colors that appear contrasting to you may appear to others to blend together. Eight major categories of colorblindness exist, and the way people perceive color can be different in each of these eight categories. To view how color blind people see specific colors, visit `http://wellstyled.com/tools/colorscheme2/index-en.html`. Use the Color Scheme Generator, to test the colors you choose for your user interface. A significant proportion of the population will appreciate that.

TIP There is a theory that in times of stress, when people are rushed and anxious, the brain does not have time to process color. So, at times, everyone may be colorblind. Designing for colorblindness may be worthwhile at times for all your users.

Learning disabilities

You may want to adjust your application for people with the following learning disabilities:

- **Dyslexia:** According to Access Able Net at `www.dyslexia.com/faq.html`, up to 10 percent of Americans are functionally illiterate, and as many as 80 percent of that 10 percent suffer from dyslexia.

- **Attention Deficit Hyperactivity Disorder (ADHD):** It's estimated that 4 to 5 percent of all adults have ADHD, although the diagnosis of ADHD is highly controversial.

Designing for learning disabilities

Learning disabilities are varied, but the following recommendations probably apply to all categories and people. In fact, users without learning disabilities will probably appreciate these recommendations as well:

- Use fewer words on the page. Steve Krug, author of *Don't Make Me Think*, suggests that for Web sites you cut words by 50 percent and then start cutting 50 percent more not because of learning disabilities, but for the sake of simplicity for everyone's sake.

- Use simpler words on the page. Avoid words that your user may not know.

- Add diagrams, layered imagery, comics, audio, and video instead of text when you can.

- Keep buttons and menus in the same locations on every page.

- Make buttons look like buttons, and make the functions of the controls as obvious as possible. Using real-world metaphors helps anchor the user in the way the application works.

- Make sure every page has an Exit, Back, and Forward button, if appropriate.

- Program in lots of forgiveness and many safety nets. (See the section "Forgiving and Minimizing Mistakes" later in this chapter.)

- Add short help pop-ups, which can be diagrams, comics, video, or audio rather than text.

Designing for dyslexia

Dyslexia is a learning disorder defined as any problem with reading and writing that can't be explained by obvious physical causes such as impaired vision, impaired hearing, or low intelligence. Dyslexia can range from minor reading problems to complete illiteracy. Dyslexia is popularly characterized by the reversals of letters or words in the brain, but it is not at all limited to that and may appear in many other ways. It may appear as difficulty distinguishing left and right. In speaking ability, it may appear as blurring, stuttering, and poor word recall. In writing it may appear as poor handwriting and drawing ability. Dyslexics may have difficulty in understanding what they read and remembering what they read. Some estimate that 5 to 15 percent of the population suffers from dyslexia. Others have challenged the idea of dyslexia as a separate learning disorder and emphasized the many different kinds of reading disabilities.

In addition to the recommendations in the previous section, including an audio option for any text may be a good idea for users with reading disabilities.

Designing for ADHD

ADHD can be characterized by impulsive behavior, poor attention span, and poor job completion skills. For those with ADHD, and for normal users too, when designing your user interface, you may want to:

- Be sure your safety nets are in place in case users click inappropriate buttons and perform inappropriate tasks impulsively. (Microsoft Vista offers toggle keys which cause a sound to occur when caps lock, num lock or scroll lock are pressed. The user can turn on this option from Help And Support in the Start menu.)

- Keep text in simple language, have a simple navigation system, and create buttons that look like buttons rather than zippers — all this can help to generate a feeling of simplicity. Figure 17.9 shows the Connect To The Internet wizard in Vista. The questions are short and simple, with lots of whitespace for an uncluttered look. And for those who don't understand, a small Help Me Choose link is obvious at the bottom of the window, because even though it is small, it is isolated.

- Show constant reminders of where the user is in the process of completing some task, such as progress bars. The designer can't assume that users will always remember what they are doing and will stay on target to complete their tasks.

FIGURE 17.9

The Connect To The Internet Wizard keeps words to a minimum.

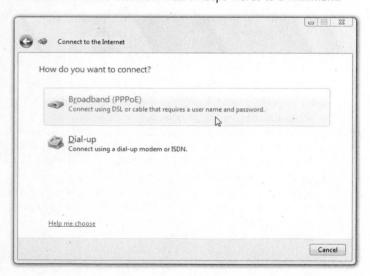

Poor motor coordination and carpal tunnel syndrome

You may want to keep in mind when you design your user interface that repetitive tasks with the mouse can be dangerous to the health of your user. According to the Occupational Safety and Health Administration, repetitive stress injuries such as carpal tunnel syndrome represent 62 percent of all worker's compensation claims in North America. Approximately 10 percent of the population will suffer from carpal tunnel syndrome at some time in their life. More women than men develop it, and the age that it most commonly sets in is about 50. It's characterized by pain or numbness in the wrist or hand in the areas highlighted in Figure 17.10.

FIGURE 17.10

Carpal tunnel syndrome is the single largest cause for absence from work in North America.

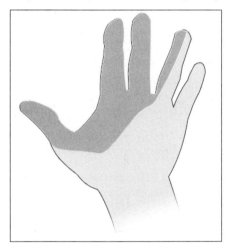

You may want to add lots of keyboard shortcuts and access keys in your application. The keyboard is probably less stressful on the nerves of the wrist than the mouse, especially when using ergonomic keyboards that are available today. Keyboard shortcuts and access keys are also faster to use, creating less wear and tear on the body while saving time for your user. Also, some people find it difficult to use the mouse, so keyboard shortcuts and access keys may be essential for them. (Keyboard shortcuts require recall rather than recognition, though, so use them as a supplement rather than replacement for menus.) You may want to also program your application to be used with a joystick. A joystick may be easier for some people who have carpal tunnel syndrome than the mouse.

When you design your application, keep in mind that you may not want to allow actions to occur based on mouseovers alone. People with motor coordination problems, or even ADHD may create uncontrollable movements of the mouse. You probably want to be sure that all actions require a click.

Avoiding Repetitive Strain Injuries

For your own safety in avoiding repetitive strain injuries, you may want to follow these rules if you spend substantial time working at a computer:

- Stop using the computer before pain or fatigue sets in.
- Pay attention to your posture when working at the computer — sit up straight and don't hunch over.
- Keep your elbows higher than your wrists when you type or move the mouse, (although not much higher).
- Keep your wrists in line with your arms.
- Use an ergonomic keyboard.
- Don't expose your wrists to too many vibrations, such as a lawnmower (riding lawnmowers are okay), handheld power tools, handheld blenders or mixers, and so on, and don't rest your hand on a vibrating stick shift of your car as you drive. (My mistake.)
- Take frequent breaks from repetitive activities, such as 30 seconds every 3 minutes. Install software to remind you to take breaks.

Microsoft Vista offers the following for people with poor motor coordination or carpal tunnel syndrome:

- Sticky keys to let your press one key at a time for keyboard shortcuts such as Ctrl-Alt-Delete
- Filter keys to ignore repeated keystrokes
- Mouse keys to control the mouse from the keyboard
- On screen keyboard for those who can't use the keyboard.

Impaired vision and blindness

Ten million people in the U.S. are blind or visually impaired. That's about 4 percent of the population. And even more people have trouble reading small print. Ideally, you may want to address both these handicaps in your application. (Obviously, some applications may not have much of an audience among those with impaired vision — for example, applications such as video editing, 3D animation, and image manipulation. But other applications may be useful whether you can see well or not.)

Accessibility features for impaired vision from Microsoft

Microsoft actively tries to offer features to improve the experience of people with all levels of impaired vision, from small impairments to total blindness. Vista offers the following as standard optional features which are available from the Help And Support button in the Start menu:

■ Narrator: Text on the screen is read automatically in a natural-sounding voice, although this only includes menu items, controls, tooltips, hyperlinks, and assorted other items. For example, if you try to read Google news with this feature, it can read the headlines in the hyperlinks.

■ Magnifier: This magnifies part of the screen quite a bit.

■ High Contrast: This changes your screen from black text on a white background to white text on a black background.

■ Assorted adjustments to the user interface, such as enlarging the cursor, making the focus rectangle more visible, turning off animations, and more.

Providing accessibility to users with impaired vision

For those who can see, but with impaired vision, you may want to include:

■ Text which is large enough, such as a font size of 10 or 12, plus create zooming tools for text, or offer the ready-made ones available in flow documents.

■ Good contrast for your text (dark text on a light background is usually ideal)

■ Descriptions of graphics or videos, which they may not be able to see clearly

Providing accessibility to blind users

Some applications may not be appropriate for blind users. But for those applications that are appropriate, you may want to provide users with an audio version of all text, plus descriptions of all videos and graphics. Keyboard shortcuts for using all tools and controls are important. Audio cues, such as beeps and buzzers, are also useful, as well as tool tips for the Narrator.

Blind Web surfers use assistive technology that reads Web pages for them. These assistive technologies come in the form of many kinds of machines and software. This technology tends to be expensive, so blind users often find it challenging to keep up with the latest advances. For this reason, many are confined to old technologies that used to work fine with text-based Web sites, but now are challenging for them. Text-only Web pages, which are particularly useful to the blind, used to be available for almost all Web sites, because many users' Internet connections didn't have the processing power to download graphics quickly. But these sites are fast disappearing. For Web applications, you may want to provide text-only HTML pages as alternatives for the blind. Or you might create an audio-only option. Adapting your application to be used by as many of their assistive technology machines as possible can be extremely helpful to them and save them from frustrating experiences on the Internet and on applications that run on their home computer.

Some things you want to keep in mind when you design a user interface for the blind:

■ Don't use images of text instead of real text, since it won't be read by the Narrator or by assistive technology.

■ Test your application using the Narrator

■ Provide your own Help for accessibility concerns, which can lead the user to windows that you set up for an audio experience of your application.

ON the WEB If you are creating a Web application, you probably want to test what a blind user will hear and what he won't. Fortunately, it is not necessary for you to own a text reader to determine this. Microsoft offers an application called, Inspect32 which lists what a text reader would speak when working in a Web page. You can download this tool as well as other tools for assistive technology at www.microsoft.com/downloads/details.aspx?FamilyId= 3755582A-A707-460A-BF21-1373316E13F0&displaylang=en.

Deafness (or lack of audio output)

Gearing your application to the deaf or hearing impaired is much easier than gearing it to the blind because most people use their computers as graphics-based tools. But if you want to use lots of video in your application, be sure to add an option for subtitles, as shown in Figure 17.11. Don't include any audio content that does not have an alternative text option. Also, don't rely on audio cues such as beeps or buzzers. Make sure to add some visual element as well or at least an option for that.

These steps will also make your application useful to those who are running your application on computers with no sound card or no speakers, which in the workplace may be more common than you think.

For people with impaired hearing, Microsoft Vista offers Sound Sentry as an accessibility features which notifies the user visually of sounds. You can test your application using Sound Sentry to be sure the Sound Sentry feature reacts to your sounds.

FIGURE 17.11

Subtitles give your deaf users (or users with no speakers) the opportunity to understand video in your application.

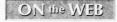

ON the WEB For more information on accessibility as it relates to Microsoft products, see www.microsoft.com/enable/default.aspx.

Forgiving and Minimizing Mistakes

Your users are going to make mistakes, but they don't need to be catastrophic. If your users have the ability to be forgiven in practically anything they do with your application, then they will feel bolder to try new features and explore the entire user interface rather than just stick to what they know. The Back and Undo buttons are firmly rooted in users' minds, so much so that they may come to mind even when they make mistakes in real life! "If only I could press Undo..." Because of this, be sure you offer both, if possible, and to whatever level you can. For example, you may want to make a history list of all the user's actions, so the user can pick and choose which action to undo. This may not always be possible because an action taken may depend on a previous action, but if it is possible, it may be a good idea. In general, the more users can undo, the more they will appreciate it.

Some things you can do to forgive or minimize your user's mistakes are:

- **Use metaphor to minimize error.** Making good use of metaphor, so that the user knows how to use the application simply by drawing on his knowledge of real life, reduces errors and the amount of learning time.

- **Enable unlimited undos.** Users appreciate being able to undo absolutely everything — even deleting files — if you can manage it.

- **Include Back and Forward buttons, if appropriate.** Your lost users may need to retrace their steps. This is automatic in Blend. See Chapter 20 for information on linking windows.

- **Add controls that constrain users so they can't use them inappropriately.** Make sliders, for example, that can only move so far in either direction, and don't allow users to go beyond reasonable limits.

- **Include confirmation dialog boxes.** If your users want to do something that cannot be fixed with an Undo or may create huge changes to their files, then it may be a good idea to add a confirmation dialog box to ask them if they are really sure. For information on creating message boxes, see Chapter 20.

- **Establish confirmation by requiring a two-step process.** Two steps assure the designer that the user really wanted to perform the action.

- **Include warnings.** With a good user interface design, warnings should rarely be necessary, but be sure you anticipate any problem and add a warning wherever needed. If your altitude is 10 feet and your wheels aren't down, tell the pilot.

- **Include safety nets.** Lightning can strike at any time. If the electricity goes off and the computer fails, give your user back his work — at least as much as you can. Another disaster could be hard drive failure. Does the computer have more than one drive, and can you write temporary files to a second drive just in case? How many safety nets you want to supply to the user is up to you, but more is probably better.

- **Include pop-up help.** Users appreciate accessible help that is readily available without having to move the mouse to the Help menu and use recall memory to search for the correct page. Allow the user to right-click for help on the context menu with help automatically appearing that is relevant to the current task.

Requiring confirmation

Confirmations for critical actions don't need to be dialog boxes that pop up to ask you if you are sure you want to perform the action. Confirmation dialog boxes are necessary at times and do their jobs, but they can be irritating because they delay the task by requiring the user to read them, and they also imply that the user may not know what he is doing. Also, too many confirmation boxes can cause the user to click Enter or to click OK at the sight of any of them, without even reading them. So when you use a confirmation box, you may want to include an option to turn that particular confirmation box off.

To minimize confirmation boxes, you can break up critical actions into two-step processes. If a user takes both steps to perform an action, then odds are quite high that the user intended to perform that action, and would have, even if confronted with a confirmation box. Examples of this outside the computer world are safety caps, shown in Figure 17.12, which need to be pressed and turned at the same time. It takes considerable thought to open them, and not just the whim of a small child. Combination locks are an extreme form of confirmation. They confirm that only the authorized person is able to unlock the locks and may require three or four steps to open.

Safety caps on medicine bottles can't be opened accidentally.

The time spent using confirmation boxes can be less aggravating to the user if the confirmation boxes are aesthetically pleasing. The Macintosh user interface opens dialog boxes in a clever way by rolling it down from the title bar, but animation of this kind is only one of many possible ways that you may make confirmation boxes more visually appealing.

Setting constraints

Constraints prevent the user from going beyond the limits of the application. You may want to use two types of constraints:

- **Physical constraints:** These restrict the user physically. For example, a slider can't be dragged farther to the right or left than its limits; or menu items only exist for the functions that the program can perform. Others are grayed out.

- **Psychological constraints:** These act as signs to the user and usually follow standard conventions. For example, setting headings in larger type and using smaller type for content, or using triangles and double-triangles on Play, Rewind, and Fast Forward buttons and a square on the Stop button. Using conventions such as these can be very helpful and can eliminate error because the user already understands them before using your applications. Conventions may vary from culture to culture, but many, such as the meaning of the colored lights on traffic lights, do not vary.

You can also use constraints as a guide for users, so they know what they can do in each phase of the application. By guiding users to properly use your program by giving them both physical and psychological restraints, you can minimize the possibility that they will experience the frustration of error.

Incorporating Feedback

Feedback is a natural phenomenon found everywhere in nature. For example, your body probably has hundreds, if not thousands of feedback loops. The feeling of hunger causes you to eat, and the feeling of being full causes you to stop eating. Positive feedback induces change whereas negative feedback inhibits change. Both feedback loops working together create stability in the ever-changing environment of the real world. Using feedback loops in your application in as many situations as you can will create a more natural environment for users and help them to achieve their goals.

Letting users know where they are and where they are going

You probably want to use continuous feedback to give your users an idea of where they are in your application. For example, the Database Wizard of OpenOffice.org in Figure 17.13 shows the steps required to complete a process, and provides a graphical way for the user to jump from one step to another, graying out steps that are not appropriate.

Progress bars are essential tools for providing feedback. They prevent users from wondering why the program suddenly stopped. Without progress bars, some users might quit their applications and restart, thinking that the program crashed.

FIGURE 17.13

The Database Wizard in OpenOffice.org lets users know where they are and where they can go.

 For more information on creating progress bars, see Chapter 23.

Letting users know what is happening

Buttons that flash and click when clicked provide feedback to the user that the click was understood by the application and a result is forthcoming. All controls should provide feedback in some form or another to let the user know they're working.

Anticipating users' intentions

You can also incorporate feedback into your application to anticipate what users want. For example, TiVos analyze the shows that the user watches and record other similar shows that the TiVo decides that the user might like. Some TiVo users like this feature immensely. One TiVo user reportedly recorded many shows that he had no intention of watching, just to let the TiVo know what kind of shows he liked.

Another example is the Thunderbird e-mail program, which studies the e-mails that the user designates as junk and trashes, and then after a few weeks can perform the same function with tremendous accuracy. (Fortunately, any e-mail messages that are automatically designated as junk by the program can be restored by the user.)

Minimizing unwanted interactions

You may also want to structure your application so that it anticipates how to avoid inappropriate responses. For example, you may want to avoid continually asking for confirmation for an action that the user tends to repeat often. Imagine if you had an employee whom you asked to perform an unusual job. The first time you ask him, he might say, "Are you sure you want me to do that?" But if you ask him to do the same job 50 times a day, you don't want to hear the response, "Are you sure?" People use situational logic to anticipate how to avoid inappropriate responses, and your application can automatically do the same to avoid aggravating the user. Of course, you can also put a checkbox in the confirmation dialog box that says, "Don't show this message again," but some users won't check that box no matter how many times they see it, because they don't take the time to read it.

Providing Levels of Control

Users with different levels of expertise need different levels of control. Beginners perform better with some aids that experts may find hinder efficiency. For example, children who are learning to ice skate start out with two or four blades on their skates, whereas adults would find that more than one blade hinders their performance. Children learn to ride a bike with training wheels, but the same wheels may cause an adult to fall off the bike.

Many applications are targeted solely to beginners and may not need to provide levels of control. These applications are sometimes called WYSIAYG (what you see is all you get). Some applications are geared more to experts. For example, top-notch 3-D programs tend to leave newbies clueless. Many applications, however, are targeted to both beginners and experts.

Mixing beginners with experts in the user pool of a single application can create challenges for the designer. Experts need more control over the features of an application than beginners, but beginners may be confused by the many options that experts may find appealing. Furthermore, there may be many levels of accomplishment between beginner and expert.

How to provide the optimal user experience for each level of user requires careful thought. Here are some possibilities you may want to consider:

- The addition of panes in windows and dialog boxes that offer more controls for experts, perhaps accessed by clicking a small expander or pressing an almost unnoticeable button, like the expander and Advanced Properties buttons in the Layout palette of Blend, as shown in Figure 17.14

- The use of feedback loops to recognize and remember whether users are experts or novices, and to offer more or less options for them

- The addition of keyboard shortcuts or even mouse gestures to improve efficiency for experienced users

- The addition of expert options that can be hidden but set, perhaps in a Preferences dialog box

FIGURE 17.14

Advanced properties and options are accessed by a small expander and almost unnoticeable buttons in the Blend palettes.

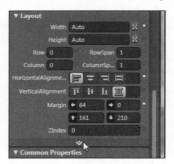

Summary

- Favor recognition over recall in your user interface design by making it obvious to users where they are and where they can go, rather than requiring them to remember where they are and what options are available.

- Let users take full advantage of their kinesthetic memory by putting user interface elements where users expect them to be by convention, and by not moving interface elements to new locations.

- Take advantage of Fitts's Law. Make important user interface elements large, and use pie menus, by using context menus. Put important user interface elements on the edges of the screen.

- Take advantage of Hick's Law by remembering that fewer choices lead to faster decisions. Consider carefully the optimal balance between interface complexity and user productivity.

- Learn how you can improve your user interface by videotaping users as they use your application while they talk aloud about what they are experiencing.

- Adjust and test your application so that it's accessible to those with colorblindness, impaired vision, impaired hearing, reading disabilities, ADHD, or repetitive stress injuries. A side benefit of doing this is that you may simultaneously make the application more accessible and usable for normal users.

- Make your application forgiving. Use metaphor to minimize errors, enable unlimited Undoes, and include Back and Forward buttons if appropriate, add controls that constrain users, include confirmation dialog boxes, establish confirmation by requiring a two-step process; and including warnings, safety nets, and pop-up help.

- Provide different levels of control for users with different levels of expertise.

Chapter 18

Arranging Layout Panels

P anels in Blend are containers of various types that allow you to layout objects in various ways. Most panels can contain any number of *children*, which are nested objects. Children inherit the properties of a panel, and when you change the properties of a panel, then the children inherit those properties as well, for example, if you change the Visibility property of a panel to Hidden, then all children are hidden as well.

Panels provided by Blend include the following:

- **Grid:** Allows objects to resize when the grid resizes, plus you can create columns and rows, and specify the position of objects within the columns and rows. You can also add grid splitters to a grid panel to let the user resize the grid.

- **Canvas:** Allows you to position objects wherever you want them in the panel. It does not resize its children when it is resized.

- **Stack panel:** Automatically arranges objects in stacks, either vertically or horizontally in the panel.

- **Dock panel:** This lets you stack items in any or all of the four directions within the panel. The first object you add to the Dock panel stacks against one of the edges of the panel (the left edge of the panel is the default).

- **Wrap panel:** Places objects next to each other, forming rows that wrap from right to left or left to right.

- **Uniform grid:** The objects fill the space in the grid in a uniform way — resizing as other objects are added or deleted.

- **Border:** This panel allows you to add a border to any object. It accepts only one child element, but that element can be a panel containing many child elements, or any other object.

- **Viewbox:** This scales its child elements so that they all scale larger or smaller when the Viewbox shrinks or expands. It also allows images to clip in a specific way that you define when the Viewbox shrinks.

 For more information about the Viewbox, see Chapter 16.

- **Scroll viewer:** This accepts one child element, and adds scroll bars to the scroll viewer when the child element is resized larger than the scroll viewer panel.

- **Bullet Decorator:** This consists of a bullet (which you can set to be any UIElement), and a child element. Use this when you only want two items in your panel, such as an image and caption.

CROSS-REF The Viewbox and ScrollViewer are both controls and panels, and are described in detail in Chapter 16.

Positioning, Sizing, and Arranging Layout Panels and Their Objects

Panels are similar to other objects in the way that you position, size, and arrange them. You can add panels to the artboard like you add controls, and you can move them around and resize them as you can with other objects. Figure 18.1 shows examples of six panels — the stack panel, wrap panel, dock panel, grid, canvas and uniform grid. As you can see, they all layout their contents differently. And they offer a variety of layout options, such as offering different orientations and different resizing capabilities.

FIGURE 18.1

Six major layout panels are the stack panel, wrap panel, dock panel, grid, canvas and uniform grid.

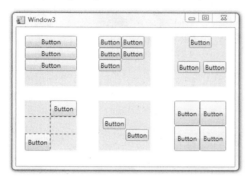

Adding panels into the artboard

To add a panel, you can either double-click on its button in the Toolbox, causing the panel to appear in the upper-left corner of the artboard, or you can click its button and click and drag in the artboard to position it in the artboard. To locate the button for the panel that you want to create, click and hold the button that displays a panel icon in the Toolbox, and in the popup menu that appears, choose the icon for your panel type. (Tooltips are provided to help you figure out which panel is which.)

Making your panels visible in the artboard

Panels have no background by default, so you may want to add a background to them to make them visible when they aren't selected. Another way you can make your panel visible is to choose View ➪ Show Object Boundaries. A blue border appears around the panel when it's not selected, reminding you that it's there.

Sizing, positioning, and auto sizing panels

You can position and resize panels, just as you position other objects, by doing any of the following:

- **Using the Selection tool** to select the panel and drag it where you want it, or to select the panel and resize it using its object handles.
- **Using the Layout palette** to set values for Width, Height and Margins.
- **Auto sizing a panel** by selecting it and choosing Object ➪ Auto Size ➪ Fill (or Width or Height). Auto sizing changes the size of the panel to fill its container, or fill the section (or sections) of the grid that it resides in. Auto sizing allows the panel to resize automatically to different window sizes.

Changing a panel from one type to another

Any panel can be changed to any other panel type by selecting the panel, right-clicking, and choosing Change Layout Type ⇨ (choose a panel from the list). If the panel that you changed had not been named, then Blend puts the new panel type in the Objects list. For example, it changes [Grid] to [StackPanel]. However, if the panel is named with a unique name, and does not just have brackets around its type in the Objects list, then Blend does not change its name. If you gave your panel a name, you can still recognize its type from the icon beside its name in the Objects list. These icons are the same icons used in the panel menu in the Toolbox.

Working with child elements

Most panels can accept any number of child elements. (Placing child elements in a panel is also known as nesting.) These child elements can be almost anything, including the following:

- Shapes
- Vector objects
- Controls
- Buttons
- Images and media files
- Layout panels

Different layout panels nest their objects in different ways, as you can see in Figure 18.1. The procedure for nesting objects into layout panels is the same as nesting objects into controls or into any container. You can drag an object into a layout panel while pressing Alt, or you can double-click the layout panel to make it the active container and then add objects into it.

CROSS-REF Techniques for nesting objects into other objects are described in detail in Chapter 3 and Chapter 16.

Of course, you can also nest layout panels within layout panels. For example, you may want to nest several bullet decorators into a stack panel, as shown in Figure 18.2. The stack panel contains bullet decorators as child elements. Each bullet decorator contains a text block and an image. For more information about working with bullet decorators, see the section "The Bullet Decorator" later in this chapter.

Layout panels also make up different parts of controls. For example, the scroll viewer is a control part in the list box, and the bullet decorator is the parent panel for the check box. You can gain access to these control parts by editing the template of the controls. You can add or delete layout panels as needed from the control to customize the look of your control.

FIGURE 18.2

A stack panel with bullet decorators as child elements.

The Grid Panel

Of all the layout panels in Blend, the grid panel offers the greatest flexibility in design and resizing abilities, which is probably why it is the default panel for the LayoutRoot. With this panel, you can do the following:

- Place objects wherever you want in the panel — unlike the dock, stack, and wrap panels, which place their objects in specific places in the panel.

- Create columns and rows. (The lines can be visible, if you want.)

- Add grid splitters, so that your user can resize columns and rows.

- Lock sections of the grid, to disallow columns or rows from resizing

- Specify in what column or row to place an object, using the Layout palette. (You can also specify that objects span columns and rows.)

- Set margins and align objects within each grid section or sections.

- Specify that objects resize or don't resize when the grid resizes. You can also specify how much the object resizes and how it is to be clipped.

- Create layers within grid sections

- Anchor objects with Absolute positioning in relationship to the upper-left corner of their grid sections.

CROSS-REF For a tutorial on using the grid splitter, see Chapter 3.

Using Grid Layout Mode

Grid Layout mode allows you to view the lock icons and margin adorners for the grids in your layout, as shown in Figure 18.3. The lock icons determine whether columns or rows will resize when the window resizes, and the margin adorners determine whether and how an object resizes in a section of the grid. We discuss this further later in this chapter.

If you don't want these icons to clutter your view, then you can choose to be in Canvas Layout mode instead.

Blend lets you toggle back and forth between Grid Layout mode and Canvas Layout mode in two ways:

- Double-click the grid to make it the active container, then click the button outside the upper left corner of the grid, as shown in Figure 18.3, to switch to the Canvas Layout Mode, or return to the Grid Layout Mode,.
- Choose Tools ⇨ Options, click Artboard, and select Use Grid Layout mode or deselect it if you want to be in Canvas Layout mode.

FIGURE 18.3

Clicking to change the layout mode from Canvas Layout mode back to Grid Layout mode.

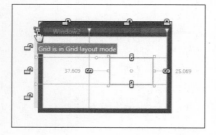

Creating columns and rows in the grid

Grids can contain as many grid dividers as you want to add. You can create columns and rows in a grid in two ways:

- Double-click to select the grid, and then click in the shaded area outside the grid to create a grid divider, as shown on the left in Figure 18.4.
- Use the Column Definition Collection editor and the Row Definition Collection editor for more precise column and row spacing. This is described later in this section.

FIGURE 18.4

Adding grid dividers on the left, and selecting a grid divider on the right.

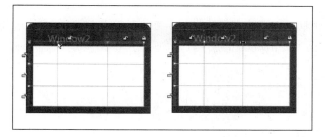

Adding, positioning, and deleting grid dividers manually

As we just described, to create a column or row in a grid, first double-click the grid to make it the active container, and then move the mouse over the shaded band outside the grid so that a gold grid divider appears over the grid. This grid divider is also known as a grid line. To make the grid divider stay where you want it, click the mouse. The grid divider appears, as shown in Figure 18.4.

To delete the grid divider, click the Selection tool and double-click the grid to make it the active container if it isn't already the active container. Then move the mouse over the triangular shape where the grid divider meets the shaded area. The cursor changes to a double arrow, as shown in Figure 18.4 on the right. Then you can click to select the grid divider. Its appearance changes to a solid color. Once selected, you can click and drag it to reposition it, or delete it by pressing Backspace.

Using the Column Definition Collection editor and Row Definition Collection editor

The Column Definition Collection editor (shown in Figure 18.5) and the Row Definition Collection editor allow you to create columns and rows with precision. In this section, we discuss how to use the Column Definition Collection editor, but you can use the Row Definition Collection editor in the same way.

FIGURE 18.5

Use the Column Definition Collection editor to precisely position your columns in a grid.

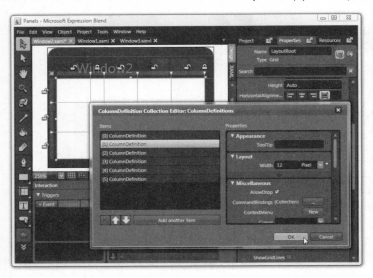

Before opening the Column Definition Collection editor, you may want to delete any grid dividers in your grid so that you can start with a grid that has no columns. Then with your grid selected as the active container, open the Layout palette, and click the ColumnDefinitions (Collection) button. The Column Definition Collection editor appears, as shown in Figure 18.5. Then you can do the following:

- To add a column, click Add Another Item. When you repeatedly add columns, the columns divide the grid equally.

- To position a column a specific number of pixels from another column, select the column from the list, and from the Width down arrow choose Pixel. Then type a number for the Width property. This positions the selected column the specified number of pixels to the right of the previous column and repositions all the other columns to the right to be equally spaced in the remaining area of the grid, as shown in Figure 18.5.

NOTE Columns from top to bottom on the list correspond to columns from left to right in the grid.

- To reposition a column that currently has a pixel width and that you want to resize proportionally instead, select the column from the list, and from the Width down arrow choose Star instead of Pixel. Type in a number as its Width property to specify how many times wider to make it.

- To make a column twice as wide as another column, select the column, choose Star from the Width down arrow, then type in 2 as its Width property. (Choosing 3 makes it three times as wide, and so on.)

NOTE You can also choose Auto from the Width down arrow, but Auto simply collapses a grid divider into the same location as the grid divider to the left of it.

When you're finished creating your columns and specifying their locations, click OK. Then do the same with the Row Definition Collection editor.

Resizing objects in the grid

During run time (the time when your application is run), the window displaying the user interface that you created may be a different size than the window that you used to create it. This can happen for many reasons:

- The window may be sized differently due to different monitor resolutions or user preferences.

- The user may want to expand the window to full screen.

- Windows can be resized when users click and drag the window borders.

- You may have added grid splitters to give the user even more resizing capabilities.

When a grid resizes, you may want some columns or row to resize and not others. To do this, see the next section of this chapter.

You also may want child elements within the grid to expand or shrink (or not expand or shrink) when the grid is resized. You can specify how you want objects to resize in these ways:

- Using the margin adorners to specify whether resizing takes place and which direction the resizing occurs from. This is discussed in detail in the section "Using margin adorners to specify the resizing or clipping direction of objects in a grid" later in this chapter.

- Using the Layout palette to specify whether resizing takes place and assign a Maximum and Minimum value for resizing both the Height and Width, and more, which we also discuss in the section "Specifying how an object resizes using the Layout palette" later in this chapter.

Using lock icons to disallow rows or columns from resizing

The lock icons in the Grid View mode are handy for preventing a row or column of a grid from resizing. The lock icon toggles between its locked and unlocked states when you click on it. When the lock icon is locked, then that row or column doesn't resize when the window resizes. When it is unlocked, it does resize. Figure 18.6 on the left displays a LayoutRoot with a lock icon that is locked, and when the window resizes during run time, the locked section of the grid does not resize.

> To see your grid lines, as shown in Figure 18.6, select the grid (or LayoutRoot in this case, which is also a grid) and select ShowGridLines in the Layout palette.

FIGURE 18.6

Locking a lock icon prevents your row or column in a grid (or LayoutRoot, as shown here) from resizing when the window is resized.

Using margin adorners to specify the resizing or clipping direction of objects in a grid

Margin adorners appear when you select an object in a grid (and you are in Grid Layout mode). The adorners reside on the grid dividers surrounding the object and connect with a line to the object handles of the objects. They have two modes: open and closed, which they toggle between when clicked. (Be sure the hand cursor appears before clicking it.) Here's how they work:

■ To specify that a selected object is to resize itself, close the margin adorners on the four edges of the grid.

■ To specify from what direction or directions an object is clipped, open one side margin adorner and/or one top or bottom margin adorner, as shown in Figure 18.7.

■ If an adorner is not connected to the correct grid divider, then you can click the object and resize it so that the adorner relocates to the correct grid divider, and then resize it back to its original size. (You can also specify what rows and columns you want the object to occupy in the Layout palette, as described in the section "Assigning objects to rows and columns, and layering grid sections" later in this chapter.)

> **TIP** If you want to close both margin adorners, but you click to close one and the opposite margin adorner opens, then unselect Clip Contents in the Layout palette, and click the open margin adorner to close it again.

Sometimes it's not possible to lock all the margin adorners of an object. If this happens, then the object is of a type that disallows resizing in both directions. If you want the object to resize despite that fact that it doesn't want to, select it and right-click on it and choose Group Into ⇨ Viewbox. Then you should be able to lock all the margin adorners.

> **CROSS-REF** If you want to establish a more precise way of clipping your image, use the Viewbox. For more information about this, see Chapter 16.

FIGURE 18.7

Opening the margin adorner on the left causes the clipping to occur from the left. Opening it on the right causes clipping on the right.

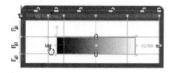

> **NOTE** If you ever see NaN, instead of Auto in the Width or Height property, it means the same as Auto and stands for Not a Number. You'll rarely see it, but it may appear once in a while.

Specifying how an object resizes using the Layout palette

Instead of using the margin adorners to define whether an object resizes as its section of the grid resizes, you can use the Layout palette.

Auto sizing the object in a grid section

If the Width and Height properties of an object are set to Auto, then the object resizes. If Width or Height is set to Auto then it resizes in a single direction. If they are set to numbers, then no resizing takes place.

To set the Width and Height to Auto, click in the Width or Height input boxes in the Layout palette and type Auto. You also need to set the HorizontalAlignment and VerticalAlignment to Stretch.

> **NOTE** Setting the Width or Height to Auto sometimes causes the vector object to collapse. But you can pull the object handles to restore the object to its original size, while still allowing the Width and Height to remain at Auto.

Or you can select the object and choose Object ⇨ Auto Size ⇨ Fill (to resize both the width and height) or Width or Height. Figure 18.8 shows the values in the Layout palette for an object that is set to resize in a grid section. Its width is set to resize, but not its height.

FIGURE 18.8

A rectangle is set to resize its width but not its height, which are shown in the Width and Height properties of the Layout palette.

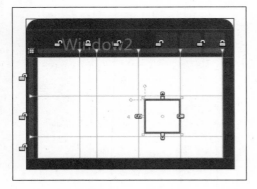

Setting maximum and minimum values

If you want the size of your selected object to change as the panel resizes, but set limits on its maximum and minimum sizes, you can set these values in the Size tab of the Layout palette. If you use the Max and Min settings, then you need to close the margin adorners for the settings to take effect.

For example, in Figure 18.8 maximum and minimum values are entered for the width. When the application runs and the grid resizes, the object shrinks to the minimum values before being clipped and expands to the maximum values when resized larger. At this writing, you can't specify the direction of clipping in the Layout palette, but you can specify it using the margin adorners. You can also use a Viewbox to define clipping with precision.

Assigning objects to rows and columns, and layering grid sections

You can also assign what grid section your objects are to occupy by specifying the Row, RowSpan, Column and ColumnSpan in the Layout palette. Rows and columns start at 0, not 1.

The ZIndex property indicates how your object is ordered on the Z-axis. The menu items Object ⇨ Order ⇨ Bring To Front, Bring Forward, Send To Back, and Send Backward simply change the ZIndex property of the object. But by manually setting the ZIndex you can assign actual numbers to the layers. The numbers that you assign can be negative, positive, or zero. The layers with positive numbers show above the layers with the negative numbers.

Setting the ZIndex can be a great way to enhance the interactivity of your application — by, for example, changing the ZIndex as part of an animation, or, for another example, in the event handler for a button click changing the ZIndex of an object in a grid section to a higher number, to make the object suddenly appear above an object that was hiding it.

   Use the ZIndex to add interactivity for other layout panels as well. Assign events and specify a new ZIndex in the event handler to bring up new content.

CROSS-REF For more information about using the ZIndex in the code-behind file, see Chapter 20.

Specifying margins and alignment

You can specify different properties in the Layout palette depending on the object that you select and the panel in which the object resides. For example, for an object in a grid panel, you can specify Row, Column, ColumnSpan, and RowSpan in the Layout palette.

You can specify margins for objects in layout panels, but setting margins can have an effect on the size of the object as well, as follows:

- If the size of your object is Auto, then changing the margins of the object may also change the size of the object.

- If the width or height of your object is a number, then changing the margins may clip the object if the value of the new margin moves the object out of the grid.

The Layout palette offers eight alignment buttons. They are HorizontalAlignment: Left, Center, Right, Stretch, and VerticalAlignment: Top, Center, Bottom, Stretch. When the Width or Height is set to Auto, then assigning Stretch causes the object to fill the grid section horizontally and vertically.

The Canvas Panel

The canvas is probably the simplest layout panel because it allows you to place child elements wherever you want. It does not automatically arrange them for you, as the Wrap, Stack, and Dock panels do. And it does not let you use a grid splitter, nor does it afford you the features of creating columns and rows or resizing objects, like the grid. The canvas panel itself will resize when nested in a grid, but its children will not. Nevertheless the canvas is useful in a variety of scenarios. An example of a canvas is shown in Figure 18.9. This canvas contains an animation and defines the area to be displayed as a Visual Brush.

FIGURE 18.9

A canvas contains an animation that is used as a Visual Brush to create a kaleidoscope.

The Stack Panel

The stack panel allows you to stack objects either vertically or horizontally and align those objects in many ways. You can click and drag to change the order of objects within the stack panel. You can also add scroll bars when the objects extend beyond the limits of the stack panel.

The stack panel makes it easy for you to create interesting animations, such as animating buttons that grow larger when moused over or clicked, as shown in Figure 18.10. All the buttons below the resized button move to make room for the new button.

FIGURE 18.10

Resizing a button when it is moused over moves all the buttons below it in a stack panel to make room for it.

Assigning alignment and margins to objects in a stack panel

You can align each object individually in a stack panel using the Layout palette. To do this, select an object in the stack panel and click the Alignment button from the Layout palette. Only the Alignment buttons in the direction perpendicular to the stack have any effect. For example, Figure 18.11 on the left shows stack panels with objects aligned Left, Right, and Center, respectively.

You can assign margins in a stack panel so that the objects have gaps between them as they stack, which gives you more flexibility in your design. You can assign different margins to different objects. For example, in Figure 18.11 on the right, objects are stacked with differing margins.

FIGURE 18.11

Aligning objects in stack panels using the Layout palette (left), and adding margins to objects in a stack panel (right).

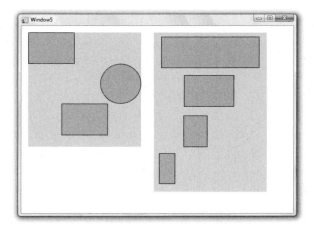

Resizing objects in stack panels

The stack panel allows you to assign Auto to the Width value in the Size tab for an object in a vertical stack panel. If the horizontal alignment is set to Stretch, then the object fills the horizontal space in the stack panel and will resize in one direction with the stack panel. (The opposite is true for a stack panel with a horizontal orientation.)

The Wrap Panel

The wrap panel is similar to a stack panel because it automatically positions objects as they are added into it — but the wrap panel stacks objects in one direction and then starts a new column or row when the first column or row is filled. Figure 18.12 shows an example of a wrap panel. When the wrap panel is resized by the application or by the user, the objects in the wrap panel automatically rearrange and rewrap themselves.

The cheese images are contained in stack panels along with their captions, so the wrap panel wraps the 11 stack panels. The wrap panel is then placed as a child element in another stack panel, and the title is added.

FIGURE 18.12

A wrap panel containing 11 stack panels.

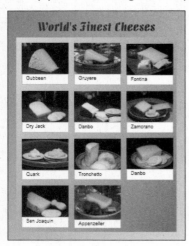

Selecting the ItemHeight, ItemWidth, and Orientation

You can specify Horizontal or Vertical for the Orientation property in the Layout palette to define the Wrap panel's look. Figure 18.13 shows the two orientations. You can also specify the ItemHeight and ItemWidth, which determine the size of the section that you allocate for each item. If you specify the ItemWidth and ItemHeight as numbers, then each item in the wrap panel conforms to the size you set, and whether they resize or get truncated or aligned depends on the property settings for the object.

FIGURE 18.13

Orientations for a wrap panel.

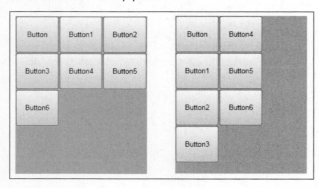

Resizing wrap panels

If you set the ItemWidth and ItemHeight to Auto, then the following takes place:

- All objects with Auto as their Height property resize to the size of the tallest object in the row. As you can see in Figure 18.14, objects in columns do not resize when the width is changed, but objects in rows do resize.

FIGURE 18.14

In a horizontally oriented wrap panel, the height of a row resizes when the height of a single object is resized, but columns do not resize when the width of a single object is resized.

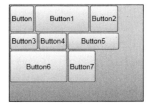

- Any object with a number in the Height value is sized at the value of the number, and by default centers itself vertically in the row, although you can choose a different alignment for the object.
- When any object moves to another row, then the height is recalculated for all objects that have Auto in all affected rows.

If the wrap panel's orientation is vertical, then in the previous paragraph interchange all instances of "height" to "width" and "column" to "row".

CROSS-REF   See Chapter 20 for a description of how to use the resize grip to allow the user to resize layout panels.

Adding margins in wrap panels

You can add margins to any object in a wrap panel by assigning the margins in the Layout palette. Adding a margin to an object in a wrap panel may do the following (this applies to the horizontally oriented wrap panel):

- Increase the height of the row.
- Increase the size of other objects in the row that have Auto for the Height in the Size tab of the Layout palette.
- Add a margin to other objects in a row that do not have Auto for their Height.

The Dock Panel

The Dock panel allows you to stack objects in any of the four directions. When you add the first object into the Dock panel, the Dock panel automatically aligns it to the left margin. You can then click the Selection tool and click and drag the object toward the middle of the Dock panel until the square with four triangles pointing in four directions appears, as shown in Figure 18.15. While still dragging the object, move your pointer over a triangle indicating the direction to which you want to align the object, and release. The object stacks against the edge of the Dock panel in the direction that you specified.

Stacking an object vertically in a Dock panel.

You can continue to add objects in the Dock panel and drag them individually to the triangle for the direction in which you want it to stack. For example, in Figure 18.16 a drawer containing buttons is created using the Dock panel. The first button is stacked horizontally to the right, and all subsequent buttons are stacked vertically to the top. Animation is added to the style of the vertical buttons, so they resize when moused over. When the button to the right is clicked, the panel collapses to show only the button on the right, as shown on the right in Figure 18.16.

Creating a drawer full of buttons using the Dock panel.

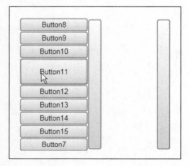

Sizing and resizing objects in a Dock panel

If your object in a Dock panel has a Width property set to Auto and you place it either at the top or bottom of the Dock panel, the width expands to the largest possible width — either expanding to the edges of the container or expanding to the edges of any objects that may come between it and the edges of the container. This means that the order in which you place objects in your Dock panel may have an influence on the height or width of the objects in a Dock panel.

In Figure 18.17, the objects in the Dock panel on the right are stacked horizontally first and then vertically. The objects in the Dock panel on the left are stacked vertically and then horizontally. The objects in the Dock panel on the bottom center are horizontal, then vertical, then horizontal, and so on.

FIGURE 18.17

The same objects are placed in three Dock panels, but the order in which they are added varies.

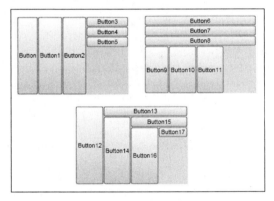

Modifying the arrangement of objects in a Dock panel

You can change how objects appear in the stack panel by changing their arrangement. For example, if you want to change the Dock panel on the left to appear as the Dock panel on the right in Figure 18.18, select the three large buttons as shown on the left and choose Object ➪ Order ➪ Bring To Front. The three vertically stacked buttons instantly enlarge to take up the entire three rows, and the three selected buttons decrease in size to make room for them.

Changing the look of the Dock panel by choosing Object ⇨ Order ⇨ Bring To Front.

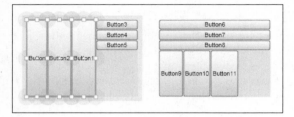

Resizing objects in the Dock panel

Objects resize in the Dock panel similar to how they resize in a stack panel. Objects stacked vertically can have Auto as a width value, but if an object has Auto as a height value, its height reverts to its default height, which is about 25 pixels for a button and 0 for a Rectangle, causing it to collapse. Resizing to a larger size can only take place in the direction perpendicular to the stack direction.

Objects can have numeric values for both their width and height, which means that no resizing takes place in either direction if the Dock panel resizes larger or smaller.

Adding margins to objects in the Dock panel

You can add margins to any object in the Dock panel by selecting the object and typing values into the Top, Left, Bottom, and Right input boxes in the Margin tab of the Layout palette.

- Adding a margin can move an object farther away on a stack from the edge or previous object by leaving space between one object and another (or the edge).

- Adding a margin can reposition an object right or left on a vertical stack, or top or bottom on a horizontal stack.

- Adding a margin can reduce the size of an object that has Auto as a height or width value by adding space.

Other uses for the Dock panel

The Dock panel has many possible uses, plus you can also create some fun designs using the Dock panel. For example, the geometric shape in Figure 18.19 was created by adding buttons to the Dock panel and orienting them in a new direction each time.

FIGURE 18.19

Creating a geometric object with buttons, using the Dock panel.

The Uniform Grid Panel

The uniform grid panel sizes all objects in the grid the same size, as large as possible. Unlike a grid, you cannot make your own columns and rows in a uniform grid. It acts more like a wrap panel, but does not automatically adjust the wrapping when objects are resized. The uniform grid acts in the following ways:

- A single object fills the panel.

- Two or more objects fill the panel to the extent possible with all objects taking up a uniform amount of space as large as possible. For example, Figure 18.20 shows a uniform grid panel that contains three objects.

- Each object by default has both Width and Height set to Auto.

- If you change Auto to a specific size, the object resizes itself to be smaller or larger, but its space within the grid does not change. The object either has empty space around it, or it is cropped. Objects around the resized object do not move or change in size.

- Adding margins to objects does not reposition other objects already in the uniform grid.

- Unlike the grid, canvas, dock, stack, wrap, and border panels, a uniform grid cannot act as the LayoutRoot.

FIGURE 18.20

A uniform grid panel with three buttons.

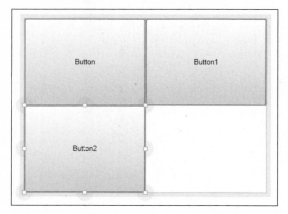

The Border Panel

The Border panel adds a border to a single child element — which of course can be another panel containing many child elements. You can give the border curved corners by specifying the corner radius property, as shown in Figure 18.21. You can assign a width and brush to the stroke of the border, as well as assign a brush to its background. And you can set margins for the child element. Here are some considerations when using the Border panel:

- The Border panel automatically resizes its child element to the size of the panel, although you can specify in the Layout palette that the child element resizes to a size smaller or larger than the panel. Resizing larger crops the child element, and resizing smaller adds empty space that can't be filled with any other object.

- Adding another child into the Border panel replaces the original child.

FIGURE 18.21

The Border panel containing a single child element that is a wrap panel.

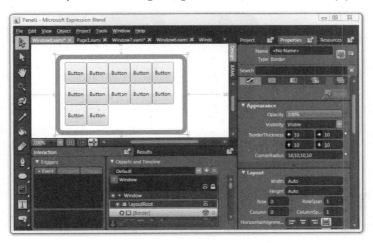

The Bullet Decorator

Although BulletDecorator may technically be considered a control, you can use it as a panel when you want a panel to contain two elements. For instance, you may want to use a BulletDecorator for pictures and their captions, as shown in Figure 18.22. The BulletDecorator contains a child element along with a bullet. The bullet can be any UIElement. We chose a text block.

FIGURE 18.22

The BulletDecorator allows you to nest two elements: a bullet, which can be any UIElement, and a child element.

To create the bullet decorator, you can do the following:

Steps: Creating a BulletDecorator

1. Choose BulletDecorator from the System Controls in the Asset Library and draw it into the artboard.

2. Choose Object ⇨ Edit Style, give the style a name and define it in the window or application, then click OK. (This lets you use the BulletDecorator that you create in these steps over and over as a resource.)

3. In the Miscellaneous palette of the Properties panel click the New button beside Bullet.

4. In the Select Object dialog box, click the down arrow beside PresentationFramework, click the down arrow beside System.Windows.Controls, and choose the control that you want to add. We chose the TextBlock, as shown in Figure 18.23. Then click OK.

FIGURE 18.23

Expanding PresentationFramework and System.Windows.Controls to find the TextBlock in the Select Object dialog box.

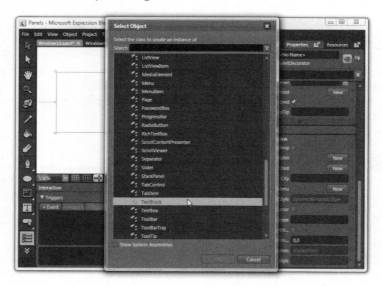

5. In the panel that appears below Bullet in the Miscellaneous palette, give your text block a Height and Width, and type text into the Text property.

6. Click the up arrow beside the name of the style in the Objects list.

7. To add the image, choose Project ⇨ Add Existing Item, select your image and add it to the project. Then double-click the BulletDecorator in the artboard, right-click on the image in the Project panel, and choose Insert.

CROSS-REF For more information about creating a user control, see Chapter 16.

Summary

- Blend provides with you with a variety of panels for laying out your user interface.

- The canvas allows you to place objects anywhere you like. It is probably the simplest layout panel.

- The grid allows you to create rows and columns that you can resize individually with the help of a grid splitter. You can place objects anywhere you like in a grid.

- To specify what directions clipping is to take place when the layout panel resizes smaller, open the margin adorners on the right or left and on the top or bottom.

- To restrict a row or column in a grid from resizing, click the lock icon to lock it.

- The wrap panel places objects next to each other on the same line until it reaches the end of the line, and then starts placing objects on the next line. You can specify in what directions the stacking and wrapping occur.

- The uniform grid panel sizes objects the same size as all the other objects in the panel and arranges them to minimize empty space.

- The border panel accepts a single child element and places a border around it. You can create a double border by assigning margins to the child element. The child element can be a layout panel that accepts many child elements.

- Each layout panel has different auto sizing considerations for its children. For instance, the stack panel only allows auto sizing in the direction perpendicular to the stack. And auto sizing objects in a wrap panel can potentially change the heights of objects when the panel re-wraps.

- You can set upper and lower limits on how large and how small an object is allowed to become when it has Auto as a value for its Height or Width.

Chapter 19

Applying Principles of Usability to Panel Layout

Blend allows you to quickly assemble ready-made or customized controls into sophisticated layouts that feature a great deal of built-in interactive functionality, as you learned in Chapter 16. This makes it easier for you to explore how to build the best possible user interface for your application — a user interface that's highly appealing, highly functional, and highly usable.

In this chapter, you learn practical principles of usability that you can employ to even more quickly arrive at optimal design solutions for the layout of your application — principles such as prototyping, simplification, progressive disclosure, optimizing your main screen, and making your application's features and status highly visible. These principles can apply both to the overall layout of your application and to the layout within individual panels.

Prototyping

Prototyping is the process of creating models in order to test features, refine objectives, and explore possibilities. Prototyping is a tool that can enable you to quickly test new ideas for your applications, and can greatly increase the speed with which you can achieve creative breakthroughs in your user interface designs.

Prototyping mostly falls into three categories:

- **Concept prototyping:** This may involve capturing lots of ideas on paper in the form of concept sketches, flow charts, scenarios, or storyboards, so that you can quickly and inexpensively explore a concept.

- **Throwaway prototyping:** This usually involves building temporary models to isolate and test features.

- **Evolutionary prototyping:** A model is developed, tested, and reworked until it becomes the final product.

Blend is highly useful for all three categories of prototyping. With Blend, your prototypes can become the design, so that you can enjoy the benefits of prototyping without the cost of discarding your prototypes and starting all over to build the final application from scratch.

Concept prototyping

As the first step in creating your application, you'll probably want to create multiple concept prototypes that may consist of simple sketches on paper. Sketching ideas on paper can go quickly, and in this form your concept can be effortlessly modified, evolving with new ideas and inputs you may want to collect from a variety of people. For example, a concept sketch for a Sanskrit tutoring application is shown in Figure 19.1. The drawings illustrate various panel designs that could be chosen for the application.

FIGURE 19.1

One of many concept sketches for a commercial Sanskrit tutoring program

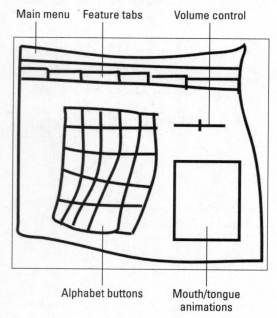

This step is a powerful and inexpensive way to explore new ground and to find the core concepts that can make your application design a winner.

Once you have some concept prototypes, then present them to prospective users, record and analyze their responses, rework your concept prototypes, and repeat, until you think you've got the right concepts.

Throwaway prototyping

Once you have a few concept prototypes, you may want to implement a few of your best designs as throwaway prototypes to get more specific feedback on them. Even though you know that ultimately you will use only one of the designs, you may want to try implementing several designs in order to see which one looks and works best. You can create throwaway prototypes for your overall design, or you may want to make throwaway prototypes for specific features of your application.

You can make major improvements to your application quickly by creating prototypes, getting feedback, and then refining your prototypes. Throwaway prototyping may be more costly than proceeding straight to the finished product, but the feedback it provides could save you much more by allowing you to find the best possible designs and provide a better experience for the users.

Blend makes it easier to create throwaway prototypes, because the designer may no longer need to give the design to a developer to implement the prototype. The designer may be able to create it himself or herself, depending on the amount of functionality that the throwaway prototype requires.

 **Get feedback from many sources as much as possible so that you don't inadvertently throw away the prototype that is your best.**

Also, if your throwaway prototypes consist primarily of design modifications rather than major modifications to functionality, your prototypes can be created faster with Blend. This is because the design of the controls in Blend can be easily changed without changing the functioning of the tools themselves, such as by using templates.

 **For more information about modifying control templates, see Chapter 16.**

The look of menus, for example, may vary widely among applications, but you can modify the style and control template of a menu so that you can change the look of all the menus in your application simply by modifying the look of a single menu, which makes it easy for you to try out different styles.

Use styles and templates to allow yourself the luxury of creating throwaway prototypes easily.

Even though you may need to throw away some of your prototypes, the benefits that come from arriving at a better design can easily outweigh the cost of your effort to create prototypes. But it's probably a good idea to choose your throwaway prototype options carefully because their cost in expended time and resources is always a consideration in how many you can create.

Evolutionary prototyping

In application development, evolutionary prototyping has sometimes been the most expensive way to design using traditional software engineering techniques, but that can change with Blend. As you create an application using Blend, every new feature you add or every change you make creates a new prototype, because Blend adds interactivity right from the start. Even if features are not fully functional, your user interface design can still be considered a prototype to some extent. And you can connect features as you go, making prototyping much less costly and a more accessible option for everyone.

If you are not sure exactly what features you want in your application, evolutionary prototyping may be an especially good strategy. Microsoft adopted this strategy to some extent with Blend by offering Community Technology Previews (CTPs) for months before releasing the product, so that it could give the community of user interface designers time to offer suggestions for new features and modifications of existing features. Figure 19.2 shows an evolutionary prototype of Blend in the form of a CTP. (In fact, every application can be said to be the evolutionary prototype of its next version.)

Evolutionary prototyping may take longer and may be more costly to the developer than throwaway prototyping, but if the goals and features of the application are unclear, it can be the best way to proceed.

One danger of evolutionary prototyping is that developers can become so familiar with the prototype's current feature set that their focus shifts to fine-tuning current features rather than exploring new, potentially superior possibilities. That, however, did not occur with the Blend prototype which was hugely changed for its released version.

CAUTION Application developers often like to optimize their systems as well as keep adding more features. However, you have to consider the cost-benefit relationship when deciding how much to optimize and how many features to add.

FIGURE 19.2

The Blend interface as it appeared in its earlier incarnation as a prototype.

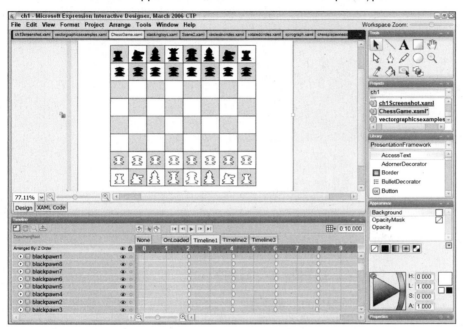

Creating Advance Organizers

Some of the best user interfaces teach the user how to interact with the interface using the fewest possible words, yet doing so in a way that engages the user. Advance organizers are an instructional strategy that can be helpful in this regard. An advance organizer can be a short introduction, in words or images that are familiar to the user and that can prepare him for his journey from the familiar to the heart of the program. An example of an advance organizer is in the Vista Welcome Center, as shown in Figure 19.3. The welcome screen itself displays many of the main features of Vista, and also when you click on an item, you get an advance organizer in the text in the upper section of the window. Nothing appears unfamiliar to the user, so the user feels secure that he or she can proceed.

FIGURE 19.3

The Vista Welcome center employs advance organizers in the upper part of the screen when a user clicks on a button.

Designing the Entry Point

Users' first impressions of your application create a context for all of their later experiences with your application. If the first experience of your application in each session is positive, that can profoundly influence the quality of users' subsequent experiences with the application. So, designing the main window of your application or the home page of your Web application to be a highly functional and aesthetically pleasing entry point is one of the most important aspects of designing a high-quality user interface.

To make this happen, your main window or home page ideally will include three ingredients:

- **Minimal barriers to entry**, so that a high degree of functionality is easily and clearly accessible to users immediately

- **Points of prospect**, so that users can pause and get a clear overview of the possibilities that are available

- **Progressive lures** to highlight the functionality of the application that may interest users and to effortlessly draw them into it

Minimal barriers to entry

You can avoid barriers to entry into your application by clearing out the clutter in the design of your main window or home page, hiding complex functionality that is not commonly used, removing unnecessary complexity, and making as much useful functionality as possible available there in a highly accessible and comfortable way. Barriers to Web sites can include Flash movies that distract the viewer or take forever to load, or pop-up ads that blink or clutter the view. Barriers to an application can include a long load time or a hard-to-use installation wizard, perhaps with questions that the user does not understand.

Points of prospect

Once the user launches your application, if the barriers to entry are minimal, he will look for points that interest him. By providing *points of prospect*, you can make it easy for the user to get oriented and to understand the available options, and to easily find information or functionality of interest, as shown in Figure 19.4. That might include features that you design to be obviously available from the main menu, from toolbars, or other controls. In a Web application, points of prospect might include links to subjects or products that interest the user. They also might be the beginning of articles on subjects of interest. If your Web site is a store, they could include sale items or featured items. The user may pause and sum up your home page or main window, making mental notes in his mind about parts that he wants to investigate. Or he may click the first button and be gone. Hopefully that takes him more deeply into your application.

FIGURE 19.4

Points of prospect can bring the reader deeper into a Web site.

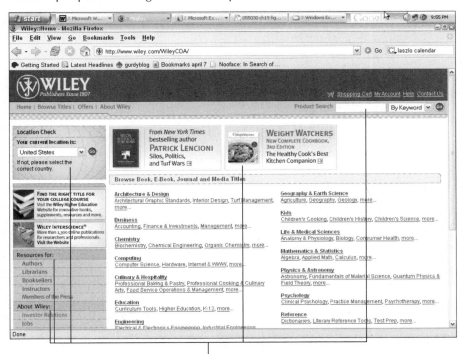

Points of Prospect
(including all the Browse headings)

Progressive lures

Wide aisles with the most enticing goods in them to draw customers into the store are often located and converge at the main entrance of a store. Providing *progressive lures* can also be a good strategy for creating an optimal point of entry for your application.

Progressive lures for applications can be easily understood tasks that the user can try out immediately. For example, for an art program, a lure could be a canvas that opens with a drawing brush ready to use instead of the user needing to open the canvas himself and select a tool first. Another lure might be to make many types of brushes easy available at a glance so that selecting a different brush is effortless. Microsoft Word uses the progressive lure of a large blinking cursor, enticing the user to type, as shown in Figure 19.5. Progressive lures for Web sites might be short enticing articles with More buttons or descriptive links that lead the user deeper into the Web site. Even a search box can be a progressive lure for customers who have an idea of what they want.

FIGURE 19.5

The progressive lure in Microsoft Word is the large blinking cursor, enticing the user to type.

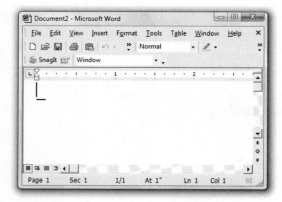

Applying Ockham's Razor to Panel Layout

Friar William of Ockham was a fourteenth-century English logician who became famous for applying a principle that was later formulated as "Entities should not be multiplied without necessity." Scientists have generally adopted this principle, named Ockham's Razor, by giving preference, in the case of two plausible hypotheses, to the one that makes less assumptions because it's simpler and may introduce less error. The idea behind this principle was not new to Ockham. Aristotle, for example, wrote, "Nature operates in the shortest way possible." In art, this principle might be applied as, "If you have a choice between two designs that are functionally equivalent, choose the simplest."

Simplicity in design can be a powerful tool for creating good user interfaces. The user interface for your application will probably be best if it is (to brazenly borrow a phrase from Albert Einstein) "as simple as possible, but no simpler." So while you're prototyping or creating your application, look for textual, audio, or visual elements that don't contribute to the purpose of the interface, and eliminate them. When in doubt, cut them out, and evaluate the result — often it's a great improvement.

Other ways you might use Ockham's Razor in your application are as follows:

- Don't unnecessarily create multiple ways of doing the same thing.
- Keep words to a minimum.
- Don't violate the user's expectations. For example, make buttons look clickable.
- Make important things larger in size.
- Make the user interface as consistent as possible so that the user doesn't need to unnecessarily learn new interface features.

Managing Complexity with Progressive Disclosure

Progressive disclosure is the process of revealing information when it's needed (and hiding information until it's needed). Progressive disclosure is a constantly used instructional strategy. Educators must decide what information to teach and how to present it without confusing or overwhelming the student.

An example of progressive disclosure on the Web is how Google shows only ten results for a search per page by default. You can change this to 100 results per page if you want, which may be overwhelming, but for most searches this still is not as overwhelming as seeing all the results at once. Fortunately, Google sorts the search results according to relevance.

Building inverted pyramids

The principle of the inverted pyramid used in journalism is an example of progressive disclosure. Newspaper stories typically start out with the most important information and progress paragraph by paragraph to less important information. This makes it easier for editors to cut out the ends of stories due to space constraints, and it makes it easy for readers to stop reading when they feel they have enough detail.

You may want to arrange text, menus, tabs, toolbars and other items in your user interface according to similar logic by, for example, by making categories of your most important features for the main menu and moving the details into submenus.

Using panel layout to control progressive disclosure

The Properties palettes in Blend and toolbars in other applications are good examples of the principle of progressive disclosure. The user can choose which palettes to be open. Most of the palettes also include an expander at the bottom that you can open for rarely used or advanced features. Also, the small Advanced Properties Buttons next to each property are good examples of progressive disclosure, since they are barely noticeable to the beginner but always available to the advanced user.

Wizards are another way you can take advantage of the value of progressive disclosure and are useful for leading the user step by step through an involved process.

Using wizards

A common use of progressive disclosure in user interface design is creating a wizard. Wizards can be windows of information that lead the user step by step through a complicated process, as shown in Figure 19.6. Wizards are often employed to aid the user in the installation of the program. But they can be used in other functions as well. For example, the application OpenOffice.org uses a wizard to create a database in its Base program. Users can access it whenever they want to create a new database. The application also offers wizards to help install fonts or install dictionaries. Any complicated task may potentially benefit from a wizard. Some programs don't use the name wizard, yet the idea is the same: dividing complicated processes into step-by-step procedures with a new window for each major step, so that the user does not get overwhelmed.

Wizards may only be practical when a small number of options are available for the user. Otherwise, the developer may get overwhelmed with the enormity of the possible choices.

FIGURE 19.6

A mail merge wizard in Microsoft Word leads the user step by step through the process of merging mail with addresses.

Hiding features in panels when they're not needed

You can hide tools in the following, so that they don't overwhelm the user when they are not needed:

- Tabs
- Toolbars which you can hide or show from the menu
- Panes that resize when a More button or expander is clicked to include expert features
- Windows
- Drawers

You can also disable the tool or make it smaller to help manage the complexity of the application.

Toolbars that you can bring up from a View menu can manage complexity by hiding tools except those specific to the function at hand. Grouping features of the program into different tabs or grouping items enables the user to process smaller chunks of grouped information instead of an overwhelming variety of dispersed information.

Drawers are also useful in offering progressive disclosure of information. Entire rooms can be revealed by drawers (excuse me for mangling the metaphor). Easy resizing of grid panels simplifies the creation of drawers, which may extend out to contain even an entire workspace for a feature of an application.

Enhancing System Visibility

As Don Norman asserts in his book, *The Design of Everyday Things,* you can make your design significantly more usable by making it easy for the user to always know what he can do and what your software is doing.

Making features visible

Adding visibility to every feature in an application can be a mind-boggling project. Some application designers use a kitchen sink approach to make everything visible, showing all the tools and toolbars at once. But this can add information overload to the system, so you want to make the features and status of your application visible in a useful and helpful way.

Menus

When browsing through books in a bookstore, people like to scan the table of contents to get a feeling for what's inside. In a similar way, when using software people often like to look at the menus and submenus. For that reason you may want to organize the features of your program in a hierarchical manner on the menus and submenus, with the most important features highest in the hierarchy. This gives the user or prospective buyer an overview of the entire application. Menus that embody the complete feature set give the user the opportunity of using them as a quick reference when he needs to remember something. Recognition memory is better than recall memory.

CROSS-REF   For more about favoring recognition over recall, see Chapter 17.

Menus are great because when they're closed they can be quite small and compact, and the sight of them does not create anxiety in the user. Still, it is not always an easy task to condense an entire application into a few dozen menu items.

According to *Information Anxiety* by Richard Saul Wurman, there are five ways that human beings organize hierarchical information:

- **Category:** In a software application this might be categories such as Filing operations, Editing operations, Viewing operations, and so on.
- **Time:** This might be from present to past or from past to future.
- **Location:** This could be from bottom to top or from nearest to farthest.
- **Alphabetical sequence:** This would be from A to Z or possibly Z to A.
- **Magnitude:** Examples of this are first to last or from best to worst.

Depending on your application, you may want to organize your menus in any of these ways.

Toolbars

Toolbars are a great way to display a complete set of features of a program. But too many toolbars can turn into a kitchen-sink approach. Toolbars can be expanded or contracted into a single icon representing an entire toolbar, or accessible from a View menu.

Panels

As discussed earlier in this chapter, drawers can be a way to provide visibility for your features. Each drawer could offer a main feature, and all the drawers together encompass the entire range of features.

Adding status visibility

Making controls visible when they are usable, and grayed out (or collapsed into a toolbar or menu) when they are not usable, can improve the usability of your application and minimize errors. Also, providing the user with feedback such as progress bars and animated button states adds to the visibility of the status of the application. Progress bars are very customizable; you can edit the template of a progress bar and change its look to suit the theme of your application.

CROSS-REF   For more information on using and customizing progress bars, see Chapter 16.

Instant feedback when the user performs a task is ideal, plus a visible representation for the user to know where he is in the process of performing a task, where he has been, and where he can go. Showing the user the wholeness of the process gives him confidence in performing it.

Summary

In this chapter, you looked at how you can use Blend to apply principles of usability to the overall layout of your application and to the layout within individual panels by adopting strategies such as:

- Building and testing model layouts via concept prototyping, throwaway prototyping, or evolutionary prototyping
- Presenting the big picture in your layouts before the details by using advance organizers
- Optimizing the layout of your main screen by minimizing barriers, providing points of prospect, and progressive lures
- Simplifying every part of your layout — making your user interface design as simple as possible, but no simpler
- Presenting information in layers for progressive disclosure
- Arranging your layouts so that your application's status and functionality are highly visible at all times

Part VI

Coding, Data Binding, and XAML

Chapter 20

Writing Code

Blend provides you with a way to add powerful procedural code into your user interface design — the code-behind file. The code-behind file allows you to add either C# code or Visual Basic code. C# code is the default, but Visual Basic works well, too. You choose your language when you create a new project.

You can add code in the code-behind file to respond to events such as a mouse moving over an object or clicking a button. The small bundles of code that respond to these events are called *event handlers*. When you set up an event in the Properties panel, Blend automatically generates the code required to create the event handler. You have the choice of pasting the code into the code-behind file by hand, or allowing Visual Studio to automate the process for you.

Once you have the event handler created, then you can write the code to specify what the event handler should do when the event occurs.

Blend and Visual Studio help you to write this code. The help comes in three forms:

- Visual Studio offers IntelliSense auto-completion, which suggests lists of possible methods, properties, namespaces, and other ready-made packages of code that you can use from the .NET Framework.

- Visual Studio provides color-coding of keywords, identifiers, comments, and more.

- Blend offers the Results panel, which gives you detailed information on any errors in the code when you test it. And Visual Studio provides you with even more detailed debugging aids.

In this chapter, you gain a basic overview of coding in C# in Visual Studio for Blend, and an overview of Visual Studio's IntelliSense.

Using Event Handlers

Event handlers allow your application to access the code-behind file when a specified event occurs while your application is running. For example, you may assign an event handler to a button that you designate as a custom Close box, so that when it is clicked, a panel closes.

The Events palette, as shown in Figure 20.1, lists a multitude of different events that you can respond to with event handlers. And almost any of these events can be selected for any object in your application. Plus, once the event handlers are created, the code that you write for them can be almost anything. This means the amount of interactivity you can add to your application using events and event handlers is virtually limitless.

FIGURE 20.1

The Events palette in Blend is the list shown here on the right.

Creating event handlers

The basic steps for adding code to your application are covered in Chapter 3. You have the choice of using Visual Studio or an editor (even a simple editor such as Notepad) to add code.

Visual Studio offers you IntelliSense auto-completion to automatically fix your syntax errors and suggest options for your coding. Visual Studio also provides you with extensive debugging capabilities. In return, you need to always remember to build your project every time you add a control into the artboard in Blend — or at least build your project before you create an event handler — in order to keep the lines of communication open between the two applications. Plus you may need to wait for the projects to update when you move back and forth between them.

In contrast, an editor such as Notepad doesn't offer anything beyond simple editing capabilities. It doesn't automatically fix simple syntax errors or offer hints for what you should type. And for debugging, you need to rely on the Blend Results palette, which is adequate, but less sophisticated. But Notepad does offer a faster pace of coding, because if you leave Notepad open and simply choose Alt+Tab to move back and forth between Blend and Notepad, you don't need to build your project each time you set up an event handler (although you do need to save your file in Notepad before testing your project in Blend). You may want to use something like Notepad for simple coding, and when you don't need to explore options of the .NET Framework. For anything complex you need the features of Visual Studio.

CAUTION When you set up an event handler (for example, a MouseDown event handler) for a layout panel, be sure that the layout panel or its children have a background or fill assigned, because events do not take place when the mouse is over an area that is assigned No Brush.

CAUTION When typing an event handler name into the Events palette, don't choose a name that is the same as an event, such as "MouseDown." This will cause an error when you test your application. You can name it something like "MyMouseDown" instead.

Deleting event handlers

Deleting an event handler is a two-step process. The part of the code that calls the event is in the XAML code, and the part of the event handler that runs the code is in the code-behind file. You only need to delete the part of the XAML code that calls the code-behind file. You can leave the code in the code-behind file, and if it is never called, it never executes, but some consider that sloppy programming. So you probably want to clean up your code as you go.

Deleting the XAML code

You don't need to manually edit your XAML code to delete the actual XAML code that calls the code-behind file, although you can do that if you want. You may find it easier and more efficient to use the Events palette. To delete the event handler, in the Events palette select the object that the event handler applies to, and delete the name of the event from the event input box. Blend doesn't take you to Visual Studio — it simply deletes the event from the XAML code.

Deleting the C# or Visual Basic code

When you delete the event handler in the Events palette, as described in the previous paragraph, the C# or Visual Basic code in the code-behind file is not deleted. It is simply not executed. The code is purposely not deleted because Visual Studio has no way to know if the same event handler is called by another event. For this reason, the code is left for the designer or developer to delete or not to delete. We recommend, however, that you delete the code if you don't need it so that you don't have unnecessary code that later may be a source of confusion.

To delete the code in Visual Studio, open the project in Visual Studio if it's not already open, right-click on the code-behind file in the Solution Explorer, and from the pop-up menu that appears choose Open. The code-behind file has the .xaml.cs extension and the name of the window or page as its name — for example, Window1.xaml.cs.

Deleting the code

Once the code-behind file is in view, you can delete the event handler. You want to delete the line with the name, plus the two lines with the open and close brackets and any lines of code that you typed between those curly brackets. Then be sure to build the project by pressing Shift+F6 if you're in Visual Studio, or choose File ➪ Save if you're working in Notepad or another editor.

ON the WEB Developing applications can often require that many developers and designers work on the project at the same time. If you need to have more than one person at a time working on your project, Microsoft recommends that you use an application called Visual SourceSafe to coordinate the changes made to the project. You can find more information about Visual SourceSafe at `http://msdn2.microsoft.com/en-us/vstudio/aa718670.aspx`.

Using Preview events

In Blend you can set up event handlers for Preview events in order to override events of the same type that are not Preview events. Event handlers for Preview events take precedence over event handlers for ordinary events of the same type, so if you have set up, for example, an event handler for a MouseUp event and an event handler for a PreviewMouseUp event for the same object, only the event handler for the PreviewMouseUp event will be executed. For this reason, you probably do not want to set up event handlers for any Preview events unless you use them to override an already existing event.

TIP Events are numerous, and their names are often self-explanatory. For a detailed description of events, click the Events button at the top of the Properties panel, and move your mouse over the name of any event and read the tooltip.

Creating an event handler to change an image in the code-behind file

In Chapter 3, we discussed the steps for setting up event handlers and adding code to event handlers. Here's another example, which we will describe in detail. Figure 20.2 shows a button that has an image below it that changes to another image when you click on the button. To create a button like this, first add both images to your project, choosing Project ➪ Add Existing Item, and add one of the images to the artboard by right-clicking on it in the Files palette and choosing Insert in the pop-up menu that appears. Give the image a name in the Properties panel, such as MyImage. Then add a button to the artboard and give that a name.

NOTE Objects must have unique names if they are to be referenced in the code-behind file. Blend assigns automatic names to objects when they are used as property and event triggers. Blend also automatically assigns a name to the object which raises an event for an event handler, if it's not already named. You can tell if an object has a name or not by checking the Objects list in Blend and seeing if the object has brackets around its type (such as, for example, "[Button]"). Objects that are named have no brackets. You can name an object by selecting it and giving it a name in the Name input box in the Properties panel.

FIGURE 20.2

Clicking on the button calls an event handler that changes the image.

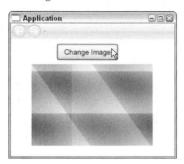

To create the event handler, first choose Project ⇨ Build Project. (Always do this before creating event handlers, if you're using Visual Studio.) Select the button in the artboard, click the Events button in the Properties panel to view the events, type in a name in the Click input box (no spaces, please), and press Enter.

NOTE   Names of events cannot have spaces, and underscores aren't always recommended by Microsoft. Just use letters or numbers, and generally you want to use Pascal notation with the first letter capitalized, to be consistent with the current conventions. ThisIsPascalNotation.

NOTE   To use Visual Studio to create the event handler instead of sending the code for the event handler into the clipboard, choose Tools ⇨ Options, click Event Handlers, and choose Visual Studio.

If you chose the option to use Visual Studio, then Visual Studio automatically appears, open to the code-behind file, with the event handler already added. In Visual Studio, type the following in the lines between the opening and closing curly brackets of the event handler:

```
MyImage.Source = new
System.Windows.Media.Imaging.BitmapImage(new
Uri("myPicture.tif"));
```

If you're not working in Visual Studio, then open Notepad or another editor, and open the file with the .xaml.cs extension and the name of your window or page. Then add a new empty line after the first close bracket in the code-behind file, and paste the event handler code that Blend added to the clipboard. Then, between the open and close brackets of your event handler, type the code in the previous paragraph.

Now let's look at the code you wrote: MyImage is the name that you named the image that's in the artboard, and Source is the Source property of the image control. "New" means that you are creating an instance of an object. That object is a BitmapImage, specifically the one associated with the path that you add. You need to add "new Uri(" in front of the name of your image because this converts the name into a Uri which is readable by BitmapImage(). (The name of the image is the name of the second image we added to our project. Replace it with the name of your own image.)

Then build your application in Visual Studio by pressing Shift+F6, or if you're working in Notepad, save your application in Notepad. Return to Blend by pressing Alt+Tab. Then press F5 to test your project.

Alternatively, you could add the using statement below to the list of using statements in the code-behind file:

```
using System.Windows.Media.Imaging;
```

Then you could write the code as

```
Image.Source = new BitmapImage(new Uri("your path here"));
```

Adding Navigation and Pop-up Windows

Applications with only a single window or page are usually quite small applications. If you're building a larger application, then you need to be able to move between windows and pages. Here are some ways that you can navigate.

- You can use event handlers to navigate between XAML pages and HTML pages.

- You can use hyperlinks to navigate between XAML pages and HTML pages, as discussed in Chapters 3 and 21.

- You can bring up XAML pages or HTML pages inside frames in pages or windows.

- You can create content in Blend in a UserControl and easily display it using event handlers that set the content property of the content presenter or content control to one UserControl and then to another.

- You can create pop-up windows.

- You can use layers or the ZIndex order to bring up new content.

- You can create flow documents, which offer several ways to organize the navigation of a single large text document, as discussed in Chapter 9.

Navigating pages

To navigate from one page to another page, first you need to specify an event for an object and create an event handler. For instance, you may want your user to press a button to go to another page, or you may want the user to choose a list box item to proceed to one of many pages. Whatever the event, you can specify it using the Events palette. Then in the code-behind file, add the following code:

```
NavigationService NS =
NavigationService.GetNavigationService(this);
NS.Navigate(new Uri("Page2.xaml", UriKind.Relative));
```

(In this code, change "Page2.xaml" to the name of the page that you are navigating to.)

Once you move from one page to another, then the Navigation buttons become active. You can click on the Navigation buttons at the top of the page to navigate backwards or forwards to bring up previous pages once again.

For instance, in Figure 20.3, we created two buttons in two separate pages, and each button navigates to the other page. The code is seen in the two code-behind files, one for each page. And both navigation buttons are active because we clicked the Back button while we were navigating, giving us a Forward option.

FIGURE 20.3

Two pages with buttons that navigate to the other page. The code for the code-behind file is shown and the navigation buttons on the top of the pages work automatically.

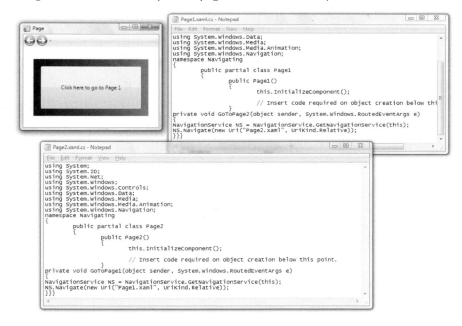

Adding pop-up windows

Pop-up windows are simply windows which pop-up in front of other windows or pages at run time. An example of a pop-up window was discussed in Chapter 14. The video player was shown as a pop-up window, and instructions on its creation were given. As a review, you can create a pop-up window by adding the code in an event handler:

```
Window1 window1 = new Window1();
window1.Show();
```

where Window1 (capitalized) is the name of the window that you want to use as a pop-up window. If your window is named something else, change Window1 to the name of your window — but don't change window1.

A pop-up window appears when the button is pressed. The code-behind file displays the code.

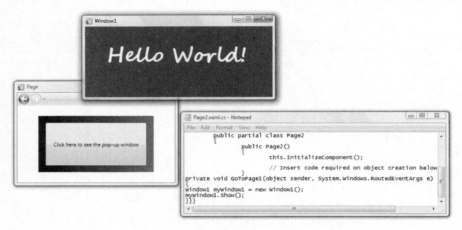

Creating frames

Frames are a good way to add HTML pages to your application, and to navigate around your XAML pages within a window or XAML page. In Chapter 3, we discussed adding frames in windows and how to set them up in XAML. But if you want the frame to change its content based on an event, such as a button click, then you need to set up the event handler and add code to the code-behind file.

Figure 20.5 shows a flow document page viewer containing buttons that control the content of the frame on the right. The top button brings up the www.wiley.com home page, but it could bring up any HTML page or XAML page — whatever you specify.

To create a frame in a window, you draw a grid, and then in the XAML code nest a frame into the grid. For instance, change

```
<Grid/>
```

to

```
<Grid>
<Frame/>
</Grid>
```

CROSS-REF For more information about creating a frame in XAML, see Chapter 3. For more information about XAML, see Chapter 3.

The frame fills the grid, and the grid is as large as you care to make it. For instance, in Figure 20.5, the grid takes up the right half of the window. Select the frame in the Objects list and give it a name in the Properties panel, such as MyFrame.

Create a button anywhere in your window, select it, and input a name for an event handler. Of course, this does not need to be a button — it could be a list box and then you'd select a list box item, or it could be an image. Select the object that you want the event to apply to, and type in a name of an event handler in an event in the Events palette.

Type in the following code in the event handler:

```
MyFrame.Navigate(new System.Uri("http://www.wiley.com"));
```

where MyFrame is the name of your frame, and www.wiley.com stands for whatever URI that you want to view in the frame. Or you can type the following:

```
MyFrame.Navigate(new System.Uri("Page2.xaml"));
```

FIGURE 20.5

A flow document with buttons on the left that bring up HTML pages or XAML pages in a frame on the right.

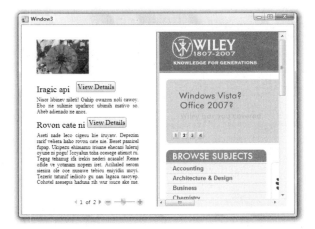

Navigating with user controls

Suppose you want to navigate as you can using frames, except that you only need to navigate to XAML pages and not HTML pages, and don't want the navigation bar (which contains the forward and back buttons that automatically appear at the top of a WPF frame control). You can do this easily by putting your content into UserControls instead of windows or pages. UserControls are documents that let you present content in the same way as pages or windows, and they are not just for creating controls. They even have code-behind files, which you can add event handlers to. To navigate with them instead of creating a frame in a page or window, create a ContentControl or ContentPresenter. To create a ContentPresenter, click ContentPresenter in the Asset Library, and click and drag to position the ContentPresenter in the artboard. In the Properties panel give your ContentPresenter a name, such as, for example, MyContentPresenter. Then create the buttons or list box or whatever you want to use for navigation, and select a button, for example, and in the Click input box in the Events palette type in the name of an event handler. (Be sure you built your project first, if using Visual Studio.)

In the event handler, type the following:

```
MyContentPresenter.Content = new UserControl1();
```

In the above code, UserControll is the name of your UserControl. You can use as many UserControls as you want. Just use them to add the content that you want visible in the ContentControl or ContentPresenter.

Showing and hiding layers in a window

Windows are not optimal for navigation, and pages are, but windows are ideal for flow documents because of their resizing abilities. As an alternative to navigating from page to page, you can consider creating layers and making the layers visible and hidden according to events that you specify. This can work if you don't have an enormous amount of content, and if you're creating a stand-alone windows application and not planning to deploy your application as an XBAP or loose XAML

Layers are not complicated to work with in a single window. You can show and hide them as well as lock and unlock them, as shown in Figure 20.6. Before you publish your application, you can set all but one layer to hidden, and create buttons to navigate between them, by making the buttons change the visibility of the entire layer from hidden to visible:

```
Layer1.Visibility = Visibility.Visible;
Layer2.Visibility = Visibility.Hidden;
```

You can assign the following values to the Visibility property:

- Collapsed: An object which is collapsed does not occupy any space in the layout.
- Hidden: An object which is hidden still occupies space.
- Visible: Use this to restore an object's visibility.

You can also use this technique to stack panels and make them visible or hidden, if you just want part of the window to change content. Or you can assign a ZIndex to objects that are stacked, to bring them forward or move them backward in the stack (as long as they have backgrounds which completely cover the objects beneath them to avoid confusion). You can write, for example:

```
Grid1.ZIndex = "5";
```

Negative numbers send the grid to the back, and positive numbers send the grid forward.

 You don't really need to lock your layers if only one layer is visible, because you can't manipulate objects in layers in the artboard that are not visible.

FIGURE 20.6
_____

In some situations you can show new content by making one layer visible and hiding the rest. You can organize your layers by showing and hiding them in the Objects and Timeline palette.

Adding Visual Basic or C# Code

You can add standard C# or Visual Basic code to your code-behind file, depending on what language you choose when you create your project. Visual Basic and C# are both object-oriented languages. *Object-oriented* is a style of software development that combines data and functions together as objects. These objects communicate with each other by sending and receiving messages rather than by simply transmitting numeric data. Objects that have similar data and functionality are grouped into hierarchical classes of objects, and new objects inherit data and functionality from their hierarchy of classes. The new objects can then be customized with additional data and functionality.

By using C# or Visual Basic, you can access the many classes that are built in to the .NET Framework. You can use these classes, which are ready-made chunks of code that operate on specific classes and objects, to quickly put together the functionality you desire.

In the next sections of this chapter, you explore some of the basics of C# and then see how you can use them by adding code to the code-behind file in order to access functionality in the .NET Framework.

Creating variables and constants

A variable is a container for a value of a specific type. Most of the time, C# expects you to define the type of variable or constant before using it in the code. Constants are containers with values that are unchanging. Here's an example of creating a variable and assigning an initial value to it in C#:

```
int i = 10;
```

int stands for integer and i is the name of this particular variable. The value of i is set to 10. If you want to create a constant that does not change, you can do the following:

```
const int freezingPoint = 32;
```

freezingPoint always stays 32 and never changes. If you try to assign it another value later in the program, an error message appears.

> **TIP** C# ignores extra spaces and line breaks. And you can use // to turn whatever follows until the end of the line into a comment that is not executed. To comment out multiple lines of code, you can use /* to begin your comment and */ to end your comment.

Assigning types

Table 20.1 lists other types of variables beside int that you can declare your variable or constant to be.

TABLE 20.1

Numerical, Logical, and String Types

Type	Description	Bytes
bool	True or false	1
byte	0-255	1
char	Unicode characters	2
decimal	28 digits. Fixed precision.	16
double	Double-precision floating point with 15-16 significant digits	8
float	Floating point with up to 7 significant digits.	4
int	integers from about minus 2 trillion to positive 2 trillion	4
long	signed integers with 18 significant digits	8
sbyte	signed integers from -128 to 127	1

Type	Description	Bytes
short	signed integers from -32,768 to 32,767	2
string	sequence of characters	Variable
uint	integers from 0 to about 4 billion	4
ulong	unsigned integers to about 20 significant digits	8
ushort	integers from 0 to 65,535	2

Using cast operators

If you try to assign the value of a variable of one type to a variable of another type, this is known as casting, and you may or may not run into problems. Sometimes the computer automatically takes care of the conversion for you — for example, if you move a value from a short variable to a long variable. This is known as an *implicit conversion*. But if you move a value from a long type to a short type, for example, you need to convert or *cast* the value of a variable to another type. This is called *explicit conversion,* because you have to tell the computer what you are doing. If you are not sure whether you need to cast or not, Blend informs you when you test your application by sending you an error message that appears in the Results palette. You can often use a cast operator to fix the situation. For example, you cannot assign x = y in the following code unless you add the cast operator:

```
double x;
int y = 1;
x = (double) y; // using a cast operator
```

If you want to convert from numbers to strings, you can use `ToString()`. In the following example, we convert the number of the current month, which is stored as an integer, to a string:

```
int myMonth = 12;
MyTextBlock.Text = MyMonth.ToString();
```

And if you want to convert from a string to an integer — for example, if your user types a number into a text box — you can convert that text with the following code:

```
Convert.ToInt32(MyTextBox);
```

You can convert all the types in the table above using this kind of code. Just change ToInt32 to ToDouble or ToChar or ToBoolean. Use IntelliSense to help you find the correct type you're looking for. (IntelliSense is the automatic pop-up list containing all the different options that you can choose from while coding in the code-behind file. See the section "Using IntelliSense" later in this chapter for more information.)

TIP Names of variables in C# are case-sensitive — differing uses of uppercase and lowercase letters are considered significant. For example, myX, MyX, myx, and Myx are all different variables. Microsoft suggests using camel notation for variables, which means a lowercase first letter and uppercase for the first letter of each subsequent word, such as myVariableName. And Pascal notation (which is each first letter in uppercase) for object names and method names, such as MyTextBlock.

Assignment statements

Objects in Blend all have names that are located in the Objects list in the Objects and Timeline palette. You can use these names to reference the object in the code-behind file.

CAUTION   If the name of the object in the Objects list is enclosed in brackets, this means it has not been named. If you plan to reference an object in the code-behind file, then you need to assign it a name by selecting it and typing a name into the Name input box at the top of the Properties panel in Blend.

Each object also has properties, such as height, width, content, margins, opacity, and more. (For a list of properties of an object, select it and open the Properties palette.) You can assign new values to many of these properties in the code-behind file by typing the name of the object, followed by a dot, followed by the name of the property and using it in an assignment statement, like this:

```
ObjectName.Property = value;
```

For example,

```
MyTextBlock.Text = "Error: Please enter your name.";
```

Doing arithmetic

You can use the normal +, -, *, and / symbols in your code, as well as parentheses to enclose them, as needed. For example, you can write:

```
double y; double x = 1; double t = 5; double d = 3;
y = x/(t*d);
```

So that the value of y is .06666.

Using the modulus operator

If you divide with an integer type for y, you can use a modulus operator (%) to find the remainder. For example:

```
int z; int y = 17; int x = 5;
z = y % x;
```

Here, the value of z is 2, because the remainder of 17 divided by 5 is 2.

Incrementing and decrementing

C# allows you to easily increment or decrement variables. Here's the syntax for doing so.

```
y++; //increments y by 1
y--; //subtracts 1 from y
y += 3; //increments y by 3
```

```
y -= 3; // subtracts 3 from y
y *= 3; // multiplies 3 by y
y = x++; //sets y to x and then increments x
y = ++x; //increments x and then sets it to y
```

Working with conditional statements

Conditional statements are if...then statements or if...then...else statements.

The C# syntax for if statements is

```
if (condition) statement;
```
Or
```
if (condition) {statement; statement; ... statement;}
```

The condition must evaluate to true or false.

You can also use if...else statements. The syntax for this statement is

```
if (condition) statement;
else statement;
```

Or if you have lots of statements that you want to include you can use curly brackets.

```
if (condition)
{
statement;
statement;
}
else
}
statement;
statement;
}
```

Following are some operators you can use in conditional statements:

==	Equals
!=	Not Equals
>	Greater Than
>=	Greater than or equals
<	Less than
<=	Less than or equals
&&	And
||	Or
!	Not

An example may be as follows:

```
if (i == 7) myDay = "Sunday";
```

or

```
if (MyCheckBox.IsChecked) x = y;
```

The `IsChecked` property of `MyCheckBox` is a boolean type, which is either true or false. If it's true, then the value of the variable `x` is set to the value of the variable `y`.

You can also write this as

```
if (MyCheckBox.IsChecked == True) x = y;
```

You can also create more complex conditions by adding ands, ors, or nots. For example, you could write:

```
if ((MyCheckBox.IsChecked) && (myRadioButton3.IsChecked))
{
x = y; z = q;
}
else
a = b; c = d; e = f;
}
```

where x = y, z = q, a = b, c = d, and e = f are any number of statements you want to write.

You can also nest If statements. Just type an If statement instead of an assignment statement in the example just shown. You can nest as many If statements as you want — just be sure to match each open bracket with a close bracket. (It can get confusing at times.)

Creating loops

Another coding procedure is to create loops. Loops continue until some condition is met and then stop executing. Several kinds of loops exist in C#. Here are a few:

- While loop
- Do While loop
- For loop

Using the While loop

The While loop may be the simplest and most common loop. Its syntax is as follows:

```
while (expression) statement;
```

For example, in the following example an array is initialized before the loop begins, then the loop changes the first three values in the array to "c". Notice that the way to initialize a string array is to write `string[]`.

```
string[] myArray = {"a", "b", "c", "d"};
int i = 0;
while (i <= 2)
{
        myArray[i] = "c";
        i++;
}
```

Using the Do While loop

The Do While loop is similar to the While loop, except that it executes the statements before it checks the expression. The syntax of the Do While loop is as follows:

```
Do statement; while (expression);
```

An example of a do while loop is as follows:

```
string[] myArray = {"a", "b", "c", "d"};
int i = 0;
do
{
  myArray[i] = "c";
  i++;
}
while (i <= 2);
```

Using the For loop

The For loop condenses the loop onto a single line. The syntax for the For loop is as follows:

```
for ([initializers;] [expression;] [iterators]) statement;
```

Using the same example of code with a For loop is as follows:

```
string[] myArray = {"a", "b", "c", "d"};
for (int i = 0; i <= 2; i++)
{
  myArray[i] = "c";
}
```

This could also be written as:

```
string[] myArray = {"a", "b", "c", "d"};
for (int i = 0; i <= 3; i++) myArray[i] = "c";
```

Color-coding syntax

Visual Studio makes it easier to use the code-behind file by color-coding it. This comes in handy, for example, if you type "String" as a keyword and it doesn't turn blue, which gives you a clue to write "string" instead. Here are colors it assigns:

Green:	Comment
Black:	Identifier, for example, names assigned to variables and properties
Blue:	Keyword, for example, namespace, public partial class ...
Light Blue:	Classes
Red:	String, for example, "Hello World"

Accessing the .NET Framework

The .NET Framework is a part of Windows that offers many precoded solutions to common programming requirements that developers can use in their applications. For example, code for opening a file, or appending text to a file, or getting the time from the system clock — all these already exist in the .NET Framework. Also, the classes we invoked in the previous sections — Visibility, NavigationService, Add, Uri, and more — are all part of the .NET Framework. In fact, the .NET Framework is enormous and contains over 60,000 methods, properties and classes. Being able to tap into these solutions is a huge timesaver and empowering.

For example, in the following code, the date is put into the variable, myDay, using System.DateTime.

string myDay = System.DateTime.Now.Date.ToString();

The word "string" initializes the variable myDay as a string type. And Now gets the current time and date. Date is a property that contains the date. And lastly, because the date is stored as a different type, you can convert it to a string by using the ToString method.

Visual Studio leads you through the process of creating code. For example, if you do not add ToString() at the end, then the Errors List informs you, "Cannot implicitly convert type System.DateTime to 'string'." It also offers you options and leads you through the .NET Framework to help you find what you're looking for. It does this with the feature named IntelliSense.

Using IntelliSense

While you write code in the code-behind file, Visual Studio's IntelliSense tries to show you features of the .NET Framework that you may want to access. These options may include:

- Methods that are associated with an object
- Properties of the object

■ Namespaces, which divide the .NET Framework into separate collections of classes so that developers can reuse names in different contexts in the .NET Framework without confusion

You find these options on a pop-up menu that appears when you type in the code-behind file. IntelliSense is useful because it lets you know what properties and methods are available for a particular control or other object you may be working with.

For example, suppose you want to add a system date to a text block when you push a button (later on in this chapter we'll explore how to create clocks.) You first need to name the text block (with a name such as MyTextBlock, for example) in Blend so that you can use it in Visual Studio. Then you need to add a button, build your project, select the button, and type in the name of an event in the Click input box in the Events palette. Then in Visual Studio you can type in part of the code for the event handler, such as the following:

```
MyTextBlock.Text = System.
```

You want to assign the date and time to the Text property of the text block. So, you can set the Text property equal to "System." When you type the period, IntelliSense pops up, offering you a world of choices that includes all the options available to you for the `using` statements that you have listed at the top of the code-behind file. These options consist of many trees of options that you can explore. Fortunately, DateTime is at the top level on the list, as shown in Figure 20.7. A tooltip appears explaining its function. If DateTime, or whatever else you were searching for, was not on the list you would need to choose a category that you felt would lead you to your goal. The categories are called namespaces and they have a curly bracket icon in IntelliSense. When you double-click to choose DateTime, IntelliSense adds it to your code, as follows:

```
MyTextBlock.Text = System.DateTime
```

Type another period so that IntelliSense narrows the possibilities even further, and then you can double-click Now.

If you type the semicolon that is needed at the end of the statement, and test the project by clicking F5, an error appears in the Errors List stating that you "Cannot implicitly convert type 'System.DateTime' to 'string'". This is because `DateTime` is not a string, it is a struct, which means it has its own structure. If you add another dot at the end of Now, IntelliSense suggests more possibilities. One of these possibilities is the `ToString()` method. The final code in this example is:

```
MyTextBlock.Text = System.DateTime.Now.ToString();
```

You need to add the parentheses at the end since ToString is a method that is called. Some methods require that you add values, variables, or even other methods as arguments, but in this case ToString doesn't require arguments.

FIGURE 20.7

Visual Studio's IntelliSense offers you a list of valid options when adding code.

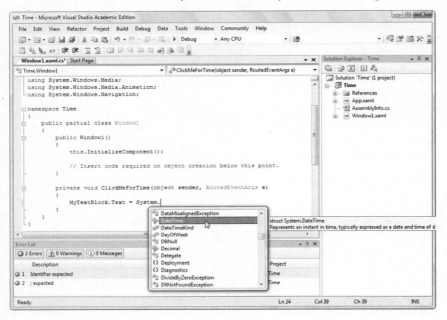

If you test your project by pressing F5, when you press the button in your window, you get the date and time in the form 2/23/2007 23:47:43 PM. (Yes, it's late at night.)

If you just wanted the date and not the time, you could remove the time by adding another period before the semicolon, and choose Remove from the options. When you type the open parenthesis, a tooltip appears that describes what arguments are required for the method, as shown in Figure 20.8. It even offers different variations of arguments that you can use. By clicking the up or down arrows you can sort through the different possibilities, choosing the one that best suits your needs.

FIGURE 20.8

Sorting through options using the up and down arrows in the tooltip of IntelliSense.

```
        // Insert code required on object creation below this point.
    }

    private void ClickMeForTime(object sender, RoutedEventArgs e)
    {
        MyTextBlock.Text = System.DateTime.Now.ToString().Remove(|
    }                          ▲ 2 of 2 ▼ string string.Remove (int startIndex, int count)
}                              startIndex: The position to begin deleting characters.
```

The tooltip option that we chose described Remove, as a method that takes a string and removes a number of characters after the `startIndex` that is specified. Because we wanted to keep the first ten characters of the date and delete everything else, we typed as follows:

```
MyTextBlock.Text = System.DateTime.Today.ToString()
.Remove(10,11);
```

Pressing F5 and then clicking the button in the application resulted in 2/24/2007 appearing in the text block.

Reading the IntelliSense tooltips

The tooltips for IntelliSense provide you with the definition of the menu item. The following is an example for the definition for `EndsWith`:

```
Public bool string.EndsWith(string value) Determines whether the
end of this instance matches the specified string.
```

- `public` means that the method is accessible for use outside of its class.
- `bool` is a Boolean type — which means that it returns true or false.
- `string.EndsWith` means you attach `.EndsWith` to the end of a string.
- `(string value)` means you add a value of a string type inside the parentheses.

For example:

```
bool myTrueFalse = MyTextBlock.Text.EndsWith("yes");
```

This statement sets a variable called `myTrueFalse` to either true or false, depending on whether the last text in a text block called `MyTextBlock` ends with "yes". If the last three characters are yes, then `myTrueFalse` is true.

Searching the .NET Framework

IntelliSense lets you choose from options, but it can be more like browsing than searching. If you want to search for a particular method or property, Visual Studio and its free Express editions, Visual C# Express Edition and Visual Basic Express Edition, offer a feature called the Object browser, which has a search feature and offers descriptions of methods and objects.

You can also find information on classes, methods, and properties at http://msdn2.microsoft.com/. This is a huge repository of information about the .NET Framework. This may be easiest and most informative way of searching the .Net Framework.

CROSS-REF For information on getting help in finding what you need, see Chapter 23.

Adding Using statements

Using statements describe namespaces that are available in your code-behind file. They allow you to write the name of a class or method without needing to write its full name. For example, if you have using System; you can type DateTime.Now without needing to type System.DateTime.Now. Some using statements are included by default. Others you need to add, such as using System.Windows.Media.Effects;. If you choose not to add that using statement, then your code may change from this:

```
DropShadowBitmapEffect dsb = new DropShadowBitmapEffect();
```

To this

```
System.Windows.Media.Effects.DropShadowBitmapEffect dsb = new
System.Windows.Media.Effects.DropShadowBitmapEffect();
```

Developers often add the using statement to improve readability. However, you need to keep in mind two things when adding using statements:

- Some namespaces contain the same names for objects as other namespaces, in which case you need to qualify your object using the full name. For example if you add System.Windows.Forms, it contains many of the same names for controls as System.Windows.Controls. So controls then need to be qualified for example as System.Windows.Forms.Button.

- Some namespaces require you to add a reference assembly to your project, such as System.Windows.Forms, in addition to adding a using statement. If this is the case, the Results palette will tell you so.

CROSS-REF For information about how to add a reference assembly, see "Adding References" in Chapter 23.

Creating Event Handlers to Change Brushes, Opacity and Bitmap Effects

Normally, the appearance of an object can be changed by setting property triggers or event triggers that allow you to control timelines, giving you the opportunity to animate the change in appearance. However, you may find at times that you want to make these changes in code.

ON the WEB To see the mini-applications in this chapter in action, visit www.blendtips.com/bible. You can also view figures in color there, and download some projects.

Assigning a solid color in the code-behind file

To change the color of the border shown in Figure 20.9, first create the border in the artboard, and give it a name, such as MyBorder. Then double-click it and add an image. Be sure to set margins for the image, so that the border appears around the image. Give your border a color or gradient in the Brushes palette. Then build your project by choosing Project ⇨ Build Project, select the border, and in the Events palette set up an event handler for it such as MouseEnter. Then in the code-behind file, add the following to the event handler that you created:

```
SolidColorBrush scb = new SolidColorBrush(Color.FromRgb(150, 0,
55));
MyBorder.Background = scb;
```

MyBorder is the name of the border that contains your image, and Background refers to the Background of the border. The 0, 0, 255 values represent the Red, Green, and Blue amounts. You can get these values from the RGB color space in the color picker in the Brushes palette.

Figure 20.9 shows a border that changes color when the mouse enters and leaves. Be sure to assign a MouseLeave event to the border as well, so that it changes back to its original color when the mouse leaves the border or image.

FIGURE 20.9

Assigning a new color to a border containing an image. The new color is assigned during a MouseEnter event.

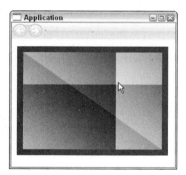

In C# many colors have names, such as Beige, LightBlue, and lots more. If you want a specific color, just try its name. For instance, CadetBlue is a dull blue/green. So in the code-behind file, you could also write:

```
SolidColorBrush scb = new SolidColorBrush(Colors.CadetBlue);
Border.Background = scb;
```

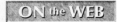 Colors and their names are found at www.flounder.com/csharp_color_
table.htm#C.

Assigning a solid color with an alpha value in the code-behind file

If you want to specify the opacity of the color by including an alpha value, then use the following
code instead:

```
SolidColorBrush scb = new SolidColorBrush(Color.FromArgb(50, 0,
0, 255));
Border.Background = scb;
```

Alpha is the first argument and you can include values from 0 to 100. Zero is completely transparent and 100 is completely opaque. The above code sets the alpha to 50 percent. The next values
are Red, Green, and Blue.

Assigning a hexadecimal color

Sometimes it is useful to define a color using a six-digit hexadecimal code. To do this, you need to
use a conversion tool.

```
Color myColor = new Color();
myColor = (Color)ColorConverter.ConvertFromString("#F2E100");
```

Then you can assign myColor anywhere you like, for instance:

```
SolidColorBrush scb = new SolidColorBrush(myColor);
Rectangle.Fill = scb;
```

Assigning a linear gradient in the code-behind file

You can assign a linear gradient to a Border panel by selecting the Border panel, setting up an event
handler in the Events palette, and then in the new event handler in the code-behind file, adding:

```
LinearGradientBrush lgb = new
LinearGradientBrush(Color.FromArgb(50, 133, 100, 50),
Color.FromArgb(100, 0, 0, 255), 90);
Border.Background = lgb;
```

The two colors represent the two colors of the gradient, and the last argument in the
LinearGradientBrush method is the angle of the gradient. We chose 90 degrees. Figure 20.10
shows the linear gradient generated by the above code in a MouseDown event.

FIGURE 20.10

Assigning a new linear gradient to a border containing an image. The new gradient is assigned during a MouseDown event.

Assigning a linear gradient with multiple gradient stops in the code-behind file

You can add many gradient stops to your gradient in the code-behind file, by assigning a color as well as the value of where the gradient stop is. You can also define the angle of the gradient. To assign gradient stops, create and select a rectangle in the artboard, and name it MyRectangle1. Then choose Project ⇨ Build Project and in the Events palette, type in a name in MouseEnter, such as "CreateAGradient" and press Enter.

In the code-behind file, you can add the following code:

```
GradientStopCollection gsc = new GradientStopCollection();
gsc.Add(new GradientStop(Color.FromRgb(255,0,0), 0));
gsc.Add(new GradientStop(Colors.Blue, .5));
gsc.Add(new GradientStop(Colors.Aqua, 1));
LinearGradientBrush lgb2 = new LinearGradientBrush(gsc, 90);
MyRectangle1.Fill = lgb2;
```

The GradientStopCollection is the collection that you add your gradient stops to. You can choose the color for your gradient stop by name, or use FromRgb, or FromArgb (to add transparency) and define the color using numbers.

You can add as many gradient stops as you like. If you want to visualize it on a gradient bar, the first gradient stop on the bar has the value 0, and the last gradient stop has a value of 1. All values in between 0 and 1 exist on the gradient bar. Any value over 1 is out of the gradient area.

Figure 20.11 shows the gradient that is produced. To see this in color, check out www.interactivedesignertips.com/bible.

FIGURE 20.11

A linear gradient with multiple gradient stops created in the code-behind file.

Assigning a radial gradient in the code-behind file

Radial gradients are very similar to linear gradients in their coding. To change the fill of an object to a radial gradient during an event, you can set up an event handler for a selected object in the Events palette, and type in the following code into the event handler in the code-behind file

```
RadialGradientBrush radialgb = new
RadialGradientBrush(Colors.Blue, Colors.Red);
Rectangle.Fill = radialgb;
```

where Rectangle is the name of a rectangle. This code creates a radial gradient with blue in the center changing to red on the edges.

 When you type the dot after Colors, IntelliSense can show you a list of all possible named colors that you can use.

You can add gradient stops to your radial gradient brush like you do for your linear gradient brush. The only difference is that when you add the gradient stop collection to the radial gradient brush, you don't need to assign an angle.

```
GradientStopCollection gsc = new GradientStopCollection();
gsc.Add(new GradientStop(Color.FromRgb(25,30,150), 0));
gsc.Add(new GradientStop(Colors.Blue, .5));
gsc.Add(new GradientStop(Colors.Aqua, 1));
RadialGradientBrush radialgb = new RadialGradientBrush(gsc);
Rectangle.Fill = radialgb;
```

The gradient created by this code is shown in Figure 20.12.

FIGURE 20.12

A radial gradient with multiple gradient stops created in the code-behind file.

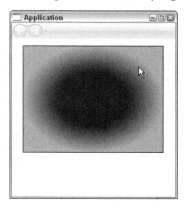

Changing opacity in the code-behind file

Opacity can be used to show objects beneath other objects. For example, if you want an image to change to another image, instead of physically changing the image, as we describe earlier in this chapter, you can place two images in the artboard, one on top of another, and change the opacity of the upper image to make it invisible and reveal the lower image. Changing opacity can create many interesting effects.

To change the opacity of a rectangle, for example, you can create a rectangle, assign a solid color brush as a fill, name it MyRectangle, and choose Project ⇨ Build Project. Then in the Events palette choose the event, such as MouseEnter, and type the name of your new event handler, such as ChangingOpacity. Then in the event handler, type the following code between the open and close curly brackets:

```
MyRectangle.Opacity = .5;
```

MyRectangle is the name of the rectangle, and opacity is set to 0.5, which is half transparent.

You can also assign a rectangle fill with an alpha value of 0 to make it transparent — or any amount of transparency from 0 to 1, as described earlier in this chapter. The code is as follows:

```
MyRectangle.FromArgb(0, 50, 50, 50)
```

0 is the alpha value, and 50, 50, 50 are the values for red, green and blue respectively — which don't really matter since the object is invisible anyway.

Adding bitmap effects in the code-behind file

You can also add bitmap effects to objects by writing some code in the code-behind file. Bitmap effects include the following:

- Bevel: Creates a bevel. Great for making buttons.
- Blur: Blurs an object. Good for adding the illusion of depth.
- Drop shadow: Adds a drop shadow. Ideal for implying that an object is draggable.
- Emboss: Creates an embossing effect.
- Outer glow: Adds a glow around an object. Great to see when mousing over a button, for example.

 Bitmap effects require that your application run with full trust. Because this is not practical for XAML Browser applications or loose XAML file, we highly recommend that you do not use bitmap effects for Web applications.

CROSS-REF For more information on bitmap effects, check out Chapter 6.

Adding an outer glow to an object in an event handler

To create an outer glow effect during a MouseEnter event, or any other event, such as the glow in Figure 20.13, first build your project. Then you can select an object, such as an image, and set up an event handler using the Events palette. Press Enter, and in the code-behind file, enter the following between the curly brackets of the event handler.

```
OuterGlowBitmapEffect ge = new OuterGlowBitmapEffect();
ge.GlowColor = Colors.White;
ge.GlowSize = 30;
Image.BitmapEffect = ge;
```

Then add the following below the using statements in the code-behind file:

```
using System.Windows.Media.Effects;
```

Of course, you also need a MouseLeave event so that the glow disappears when the mouse leaves the image. Here's the code for the MouseLeave event:

```
OuterGlowBitmapEffect nge = new OuterGlowBitmapEffect();
nge.GlowSize=0;
Image.BitmapEffect = nge;
```

Be sure that the background behind the image is dark enough for the white glow to appear.

FIGURE 20.13

An outer glow appears around the image when the mouse enters the image, and disappears when the mouse leaves the image.

In addition to the glow size and color, you can set the opacity and noise of the glow. A noise value of 1 gives the glow the look of a textured ceiling. Sample code is as follows:

```
ge.Opacity = .5; // Choose from 0 (transparent) to 1
ge.Noise = .5;// Choose from 0 to 1
```

Adding or increasing a drop shadow while clicking or dragging an object

This effect, as shown in Figure 20.14, makes an image seem to rise from the screen. If an object has no drop shadow, you can add one for an event, or if it already has one, you can increase its size. Figure 20.14 shows a tool palette with a drop shadow that increases in size when the drag bar is clicked.

To create the tool palette, we added two rectangles and a wrap panel into a grid, and named the grid myToolPalette. The rectangles form the top and the bottom of the tool palette, and the wrap panel is arranged above them. An opacity mask is used to create the gel effect on the title bar, and the bottom rectangle has a linear gradient which blends into the wrap panel.

To add a drop shadow in code, you can select an object, such as myToolPalette, click the Events button in the Properties panel to view the Events, and set up an event handler by typing a name into the MouseDown event for example. Then in the code-behind file, you can add the following code:

```
DropShadowBitmapEffect dsb = new DropShadowBitmapEffect();
dsb.Color = Colors.Black;
dsb.Softness = 5;
dsb.ShadowDepth =15;
Grid.BitmapEffect = dsb;
```

Also add the following line to the list of using statements.

```
using System.Windows.Media.Effects;
```

Assigning the color, softness and shadow depth are all optional, because this class provides defaults for all of them. If you assign a MouseDown event, be sure to assign a MouseUp event as well, to revert your drop shadow to its original size. For information on making the tool palette draggable, see the section "Dragging and Resizing Objects" later in this chapter.

FIGURE 20.14

A tool palette seems to pop-up from the screen when its title bar is clicked, due to an increase in the drop shadow.

In addition to the color, softness, and shadow depth, you can also set the opacity of the drop shadow as follows:

```
dsb.Opacity = .5; // Choose from 0 (transparent) to 1
```

ON the WEB To view or download this mini-application, go to www.blendtips.com/bible. All the example mini-applications created in this chapter and other chapters are available there.

Adding a bevel to create the look and feel of a button

Blend offers so much interactivity so easily that you can make objects that look and act as buttons just as easily as creating buttons themselves. For instance, in Figure 20.15, the button on the right is the same button as the button on the left, except the Mouse is pressed. The buttons are actually rectangles and text blocks nested in their own canvas panels. The light angle of the bevel and the angle of the gradient fill are modified in the MouseDown event handlers which are attached to the canvas panels.

FIGURE 20.15

Creating a bevel and changing the light angle of the bevel and the gradient during a MouseDown event.

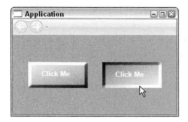

The bevel and linear gradients for a rectangle, called Rectangle, is originally created in an event handler called by a Loaded event for the LayoutRoot. Its code is as follows:

```
BevelBitmapEffect bbe = new BevelBitmapEffect();
Rectangle.BitmapEffect = bbe;
LinearGradientBrush lgb = new LinearGradientBrush(Colors.White,
Colors.DarkGray, 45);
Rectangle.Fill = lgb;
```

We created the gradient in code rather than in the Appearance palette, so that it would match the gradient that we create in code in the MouseUp event handler. The code for the MouseDown event handler for each canvas containing each rectangle is as follows:

```
BevelBitmapEffect bbe = new BevelBitmapEffect();
bbe.LightAngle = 330;
Rectangle.BitmapEffect = bbe;
LinearGradientBrush lgb = new
LinearGradientBrush(Colors.DarkGray, Colors.White, 45);
Rectangle.Fill = lgb;
```

Notice that the linear gradient is simply the reverse of the linear gradient in the event handler for the Loaded event. You also need to set up an MouseUp event handler for the canvas, which you can give the same name as the Loaded event handler, so that you run the same event handler.

As with all the bitmap effects, be sure to include the following using statement:

```
using System.Windows.Media.Effects;
```

Sample code for modifying your bevel is as follows:

```
bbe.Smoothness = .4;//Set 0 to 1. Default is .5
bbe.BevelWidth = 10;//Default is 5
bbe.EdgeProfile = EdgeProfile.CurvedIn;//CurvedOut, BulgedUp,
Linear
bbe.LightAngle = 320;//Set 0 to 360
bbe.Relief = 0.5;//Default is .3
```

 For more details on using the bitmap effects, see Chapter 6.

TIP You can initialize and assign variables with the same name in two different event handlers. They do not conflict with each other.

Creating blur and emboss bitmap effects in the code-behind file

The blur and emboss bitmap effects are all similar in code to the drop shadow, outer glow, and bevel effects. They use the names BlurBitmapEffect and EmbossBitmapEffect. Figure 20.16 shows embossed text on a beveled image on the left, and a blurred image on the right. For all these effects, be sure to add the following using statement:

```
using System.Windows.Media.Effects;
```

FIGURE 20.16

The words "Click Me" are embossed, and the bitmap surrounding it is also embossed. The image to the right of it is shown unblurred and blurred.

The code we used to create the bitmap effects for the Click Me button (which is not really a button — but, of course, can behave like one) in Figure 20.16 is as follows:

```
BevelBitmapEffect bbe = new BevelBitmapEffect();
Image.BitmapEffect = bbe;
EmbossBitmapEffect ebe = new EmbossBitmapEffect();
ebe.Relief = 5;
TextBlock.BitmapEffect = ebe;
```

The code we used to create the blur and the emboss effects for the image is as follows:

```
EmbossBitmapEffect bbe = new EmbossBitmapEffect();
bbe.Relief = .95;
Image1.BitmapEffect = bbe;
BlurBitmapEffect bbe2 = new BlurBitmapEffect();
bbe2.Radius = 10;
Image2.BitmapEffect = bbe2;
```

Sample code for modifying a blur is as follows:

```
bbe1.Radius = 10;//sets the size of the blur
bbe1.KernelType = KernelType.Box;//Gaussian is another option
```

Sample code for modifying an embossing effect is as follows:

```
bbe.LightAngle = 180;// Set from 0 to 360
```

RenderTransform vs. LayoutTransform in the Code-behind File

Blend allows you to rotate, skew, and resize objects (which are basically the functions of Blend's Transform palette) in the code-behind file. However, two ways exist to perform most of these functions: using RenderTransform and using LayoutTransform.

RenderTransform changes the object's size, position, rotation or skew with no regard to the current layout of the application. For instance, as shown on the left in each application window in Figure 20.17, a button in a stack panel is resized, rotated, skewed and moved using RenderTransform. In every case it does not affect the other buttons in the stack panel.

LayoutTransform transforms an object keeping in mind all the other objects in the layout. In Figure 20.17, the middle button on the stack panel on the right in each application window is transformed using LayoutTransform. The button below it makes room for its new size and shape.

FIGURE 20.17

In each window the button in the stack panels on the left is resized, rotated, skewed and moved using RenderTransform. The button in the stack panel on the right in each window is resized, rotated, skewed and moved using LayoutTransform.

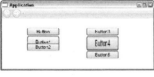

To use RenderTransform or LayoutTransform, first you set up an event handler in the Events palette, then in the code-behind file:

- To rotate an object, type the following, for example, where 90 is the number of degrees:

```
Button1.RenderTransform = new RotateTransform(90);
```

or

```
Button4.LayoutTransform = new RotateTransform(90);
```

- To scale an object, type the following, for example, where the 1 represents the scaling on the X-axis by 100 percent (which is no scaling) and the 2 represents the scaling on the Y-axis by 200 percent.

```
Button1.RenderTransform = new ScaleTransform(1, 2);
```

or

```
Button4.LayoutTransform = new ScaleTransform(1, 2);
```

- To Skew an object, type the following, for example, where the 5 represents a skew of 5 degrees on the X-axis, and the 15 represents a skew of 15 degrees on the Y-axis.

```
Button1.RenderTransform = new SkewTransform(5, 15);
```

or

```
Button4.LayoutTransform = new SkewTransform(5, 15);
```

- To move an object, type the following, for example, where the 15 relocates the button to the left 15 pixels and the -7 relocates it closer to the top 7 pixels. This does not always work using LayoutTransform, depending on the parent panel of the object.

```
Button.RenderTransform = new TranslateTransform(15, -7);
```

or

```
Button.LayoutTransform = new TranslateTransform(15, -7);
```

CAUTION It is important to note that you can only use one RenderTransform or LayoutTransform in a method at a time. If you try to use more than one, then only the last one of its kind that is applied takes effect.

Customizing the Cursor

Blend offers several ready-made cursors which you can choose from and change in a variety of ways. You can

- Assign a cursor in the Common Properties palette for objects. Just select the object and choose the name of the cursor from the list of ready-made cursors.
- Assign a cursor in the code-behind file
- Add a cursor in the XAML code file

You can also create custom cursors in two major ways:

- Using code you can eliminate the cursor and move an object that you created in Blend with the mouse. This gives the appearance that the object that you are moving is a cursor. This object may be a grouped vector object, and it can be animated as well.

- Create a .cur file and read in the custom cursor.

Assigning a ready-made cursor in the code-behind file

Changing a cursor in the code-behind file allows you to change it dynamically while your application is running. It allows you to set and reset the cursor as often as you want.

To assign a ready-made cursor in the code-behind file, first set up an event handler choosing an event such as a MouseEnter event in the Events palette — perhaps for a layout panel. Then in the code-behind file, you can add the following code in that event handler to change the cursor to an angled double arrow

```
Cursor = Cursors.SizeNWSE;
```

where SizeNWSE is a type of ready-made cursor available in Blend. You also need to add a using statement to the list of using statements at the top of your code-behind file, as follows:

```
using System.Windows.Input;
```

Figure 20.18 shows a cursor as a diagonal double-arrow when it is over the resize grip control.

FIGURE 20.18

Changing the cursor to a diagonal double-arrow when it enters a resize grip.

Creating a custom cursor in Blend

Blend allows you to make any object draggable by adding code to the code-behind file. And dragging an object at the mouse position can effectively create a cursor. For this code to work, the parent panel needs to be a canvas panel.

STEPS: Creating a Custom Cursor

1. Create the vector graphic that you want to use. Name it MyCursor, or anything else, but MyCursor is what we use in the code in Step 4. Be sure to keep it small; otherwise it can be confusing to the user. If your object consists of more than a single rectangle or ellipse (which it probably will), then select all the elements and choose Group Into ⇨ (choose a layout panel). Also, be sure your vector graphic is the topmost element in the canvas panel; otherwise your cursor will duck under objects and disappear when you use it. Choose Object ⇨ Order ⇨ Bring To Front.

2. Change your LayoutRoot to a Canvas by selecting the LayoutRoot, right-clicking, and from the pop-up menu that appears, choosing Change Layout Type ⇨ Canvas.

3. Choose Project ⇨ Build Project. Then select the LayoutRoot, click the Events button in the Properties panel, and choose MouseMove. Then type in a name for your event handler.

4. In the event handler in the code-behind file, add the following code:

```
Cursor = Cursors.None;//eliminates cursor
Canvas.SetTop(MyCursor, e.GetPosition(LayoutRoot).Y);
Canvas.SetLeft(MyCursor, e.GetPosition(LayoutRoot).X);
```

In this example, MyCursor is the name of the object we created in Step 1.

5. Add the following using statement below the list of using statements in the code-behind file:

```
using System.Windows.Input;
```

6. Test your new cursor by choosing Project ⇨ Test Project. Figure 20.19 shows the cursor that we created.

FIGURE 20.19

A cursor created in Blend.

CAUTION
If you have text boxes where you want your cursor to change into an IBeam to indicate that the user can enter text, then you need to assign the IBeam for the cursor in the Properties panel for each text box.

Animating a custom cursor in Blend

Creating an animated cursor simply involves animating the vector object that you name and assign as the cursor in the previous instructions. An example of an animated cursor looks the same as the cursor in Figure 20.19, except it rotates. You'll want to keep the following in mind.

- Keep it small

- Animate it by rotating or changing its size. Avoid moving it, unless you move it in a circular way; otherwise the motion can cause confusion.

- Animate it in the Objects and Timeline palette, and assign it a Loaded event trigger. Also assign it to loop forever.

CROSS-REF
For instructions on animating a vector object, see Chapter 14.

Creating a .cur file using Art Cursors

Another way to create a custom cursor is to use a program dedicated for doing so. Using a dedicated program has the advantage that you can define a hot spot which is the single pixel that acts as the point that causes controls to respond to it. (Hot spots also exist in cursors created in Blend, but they are added by default to a topmost pixel in the vector graphic.) In this example, we use the program called Art Cursors. It's available via download from the Internet for a 30-day free trial.

With Art Cursors, you can create the .cur file to contain the cursor, and then you can place it into the Blend project file. We created a Loaded event for the LayoutRoot and added the following code to the code-behind file to read in a .cur file

```
System.Windows.Input.Cursor myCursor = new
System.Windows.Input.Cursor("ObistCursorArrow.cur");
LayoutRoot.Cursor = myCursor;
```

where ObistCursorArrow.cur is the name of the file you created in Art Cursors. Figure 20.20 is an example of a custom cursor created quickly in Art Cursors.

FIGURE 20.20

A simple custom cursor created in Art Cursors.

 Art Cursors is an advanced cursor editor for Windows that allows you to create animated cursors as well as normal cursors. You can find it on the Web at www .aha-soft.com/artcursors/

Allowing the User to Drag and Resize Objects

Both dragging objects and resizing objects require code in Blend, but the code is relatively easy to write, especially if the object to be dragged has a handle that is relatively small, such as a drag bar or title bar that you can click and drag.

Resizing objects also is performed best using a handle. Blend offers the ResizeGrip control for this purpose. This is designed to act as the handle to drag an object, although you can just as easily create your own look for a handle by using a vector object instead.

Enabling the user to drag objects

To drag objects, you can basically use the same code that you use to create a custom cursor, except that you need to execute the event handler only when the mouse is pressed in the object that you are trying to drag.

Many ways exist to drag objects. Here, we try to show an easy and basic way to drag an object in a canvas panel. For example, suppose you want to create a tool palette with a title bar that you can click and drag. Figure 20.21, is an elaborated example of the tool palette that we created in the section "Adding or increasing a drop shadow while clicking or dragging an object" earlier in this chapter.

FIGURE 20.21

A draggable tool palette.

STEPS: Creating a Draggable Tool Palette

1. First create the vector object that you want to use as a tool palette. Ours consists of a grid containing two rectangles and a wrap panel in the middle. The wrap panel can contain the icons for the tools. Name the parent panel. We named the grid myToolPalette. Then create a TextBlock and replace the text in the TextBlock with 0 (and no linefeed). Then set its Visibility property to Hidden or Collapsed. And name the TextBlock. We named ours MyTextBlock.

2. Change the LayoutRoot to a canvas by right-clicking on it and, from the pop-up menu that appears, choosing Change Layout Type ➪ Canvas. Then choose Project ➪ Build Project.

3. Select the title bar of your custom tool palette. and click the Events button in the Properties panel to view the Events. In MouseDown type in a name for the event handler, such as MyMouseDown, and press Enter. In the code-behind file, type the following into the method

```
MyTextBlock.Text = "1";
```

where MyTextBlock is the name of the TextBlock you created in Step 1. We're using the TextBlock to contain our flag, letting us know that the mouse is down.

4. Return to Blend, select the LayoutRoot, in the Events palette choose MouseMove, type in a name for the event handler, such as MyMouseMove, and press Enter. In the code-behind file type the following into the method

```
if (MyTextBlock.Text == "1")
{
Canvas.SetTop(MyToolPalette, e.GetPosition(LayoutRoot).Y);
Canvas.SetLeft(MyToolPalette, e.GetPosition(LayoutRoot).X);
}
```

where MyToolPalette is the name of the grid containing your toolbar.

5. Select the LayoutRoot once again, if it's not already selected, and in the Events palette, in MouseUp type a name for an event handler, such as MyMouseUp, and press Enter. In the code-behind file, type the following into the method:

```
MyTextBlock.Text = "0";
```

If you are changing the depth of the drop shadow too, then you want to add the code for reducing the drop shadow into this section.

6. Now test the application by choosing Project ➪ Test Project. You should be able to drag the palette, as shown in Figure 20.21.

NOTE Our purpose is to give a basic understanding of how to drag objects, and get the reader started in this direction. This code can be improved upon in many ways, and we invite the reader to do so.

ON the WEB You can download this project (and the project that uses the ResizeGrip tool in the next section of this chapter), at www.blendtips.com/bible.

Enabling the user to resize objects using the ResizeGrip

The basic strategy to resize an object is to create a MouseMove event handler for the ResizeGrip. The event handler that you create checks the current position of the mouse, subtracts it from the past position of the mouse, and adds it to the width and height of the object it's resizing.

You can resize any control, although it works best if you place the control and the resize grip into a grid panel, and then resize the grid panel which resizes the control at the same time. Here are the steps to resize a tool palette, as shown in Figure 20.22. Because the tool palette has a wrap panel in it, the items wrap and re-wrap automatically according to the size of the tool palette.

To add functionality to the drag bar for this tool palette, see the instructions in the previous section.

FIGURE 20.22

A tool palette consisting of a grid containing a title bar, a wrap panel with objects, and a resize grip that resizes the tool palette.

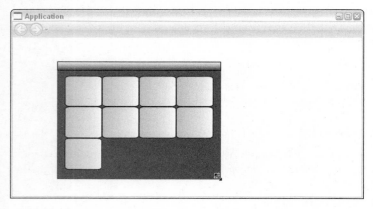

STEPS: Using the ResizeGrip to Resize a Grid

1. Select the LayoutRoot, right-click, and from the pop-up menu that appears choose Change Layout Type ➪ Canvas.

2. Create a grid by clicking the Grid button in the ToolBox, and clicking and dragging in the artboard. Name the grid MyGrid. Then double-click on the grid and add two horizontal grid dividers: one to divide the drag bar from the Wrap panel, one to contain the Wrap panel. Use the Brushes palette to assign the grid's Background a color or gradient.

3. Double-click the grid, click the Rectangle tool, click and drag to position a rectangle into the uppermost section of the grid panel, and choose Object ➪ Auto Size ➪ Fill. Assign the Rectangle a color or gradient in the Brushes palette.

4. Click the WrapPanel button in the ToolBox, and click and drag to position the wrap panel in the grid section below the rectangle. Choose Object ➪ Auto Size ➪ Fill. Assign a brush to the Background in the Brushes palette, double-click it, and add some buttons from the Toolbox.

5. Double-click the grid to make it active, and then double-click ResizeGrip in the Asset Library in the ToolBox. Choose Object ➪ Auto Size ➪ Fill. Use the Selection tool to resize and position the resize grip into the bottom corner of the grid. In the Layout palette set the Alignment to Right and Bottom. (Adding margins to the Right and Bottom dramatically improve its functionality.) In the Properties panel, name it MyResizeGrip.

6. Add a text block by clicking the TextBlock button in the Toolbox, and clicking and dragging to position the text block anywhere in the artboard. Delete the text in the text block, and type a zero. In the Visibility property in the Properties palette, type Hidden. (Name the text block — for example, MyTextBlock1). Choose Project ➪ Build Project.

7. Now add an event handler by selecting the Resize Grip and typing a name for the event handler, such as ResizeGripMouseDown, in the MouseDown event in the Events palette. Press Enter, and in the code-behind file, type the following between the curly brackets of the event handler:

```
MyTextBlock1.Text = "1";//MouseDown flag
MyResizeGrip.MaxWidth = e.GetPosition(LayoutRoot).X;
MyResizeGrip.MaxHeight = e.GetPosition(LayoutRoot).Y;
```

You may be wondering what the MaxWidth and MaxHeight have to do with resizing an object? Absolutely nothing, but we're taking advantage of their existence to hold the values of the pointer for later use. (We can do this because the values of the cursor position will always be greater than the size of MyResizeGrip. Or you could use other properties which you are not using and have double as their type. Or you could create variables in code to store the values). Using MaxWidth and MaxHeight requires the least amount of code.

8. Add the MouseMove event handler by selecting the grid, and in MouseMove the Events palette type in a name, such as ResizeGripMouseMove, for the event handler. Press Enter and in the code-behind file, type the following between the curly brackets of the event handler

```
if (MyTextBlock1.Text == "1") {

MyGrid.Width = e.GetPosition(LayoutRoot).X -
MyResizeGrip.MaxWidth + MyGrid.Width;

MyGrid.Height = e.GetPosition(LayoutRoot).Y -
MyResizeGrip.MaxHeight + MyGrid.Height;

MyResizeGrip.MaxWidth = e.GetPosition(LayoutRoot).X;

MyResizeGrip.MaxHeight = e.GetPosition(LayoutRoot).Y;
```

where MyGrid is the name of the grid you created in Step 2, and MyResizeGrip is the name of the resize grip.

Here's the formula: If the mouse is down, then the new grid size is equal to the current position of the cursor minus the former position of the cursor plus the current size of the grid. Then you need to set the current cursor position to the MaxWidth and MaxHeight variables to hold them as the former position of the cursor for the future.

9. The last event handler is the event handler for MouseUp that turns the MouseDown flag off.
   To create this event handler, select the grid, click in MouseUp in the Events palette, and type in a name, such as GridMouseUp, for the event handler. Press Enter and in the code-behind file, type the following between the curly brackets of the event handler:

```
MyTextBlock1.Text = "0";//MouseDown flag
```

10. You can test your resizable tool palette at this point by choosing Project ⇨ Test Project. Your tool palette should resize as you drag the resize grip. However, you may notice that the arrow does not change to a double arrow, as it does in Figure 20.26. To change the cursor, close the test application and select the resize grip. In the Cursor property of the Properties panel, choose SizeNWSE.

Adding Controls and Children in the Code-behind File

Suppose you want your user to be able to press a button that creates other buttons or other controls. You can do this in two ways:

- Create the buttons or other controls in the artboard and set their Visibility property to Hidden or Collapsed, then in an event handler reset the Visibility property to Visible in the code-behind file when the user presses a button or performs some other action.

- Write code to create the buttons or other controls in an event handler in the code-behind file.

To create the new buttons in the code-behind file, first create a stack panel, for example, to contain the buttons, and name it MyStackPanel. Then add a button, not necessarily to the stack panel, and choose Project ⇨ Build Project. Set up a Click event handler for the button using the Events palette, and in the code-behind file, add code similar to the following example code in the event handler:

```
System.Windows.Controls.Button MyNewButton = new
System.Windows.Controls.Button();
MyNewButton.Content = "Button";
MyStackPanel.Children.Add(MyNewButton);
```

The code adds a button to the stack panel, as shown in Figure 20.23. The last line adds the button as a child of a stack panel named, "MyStackPanel". In this way you can add children to any control that allows children.

FIGURE 20.23

Buttons added to a stack panel using code in the code-behind file.

Adding Open File and Save File Dialog Boxes and Message Boxes

OpenFileDialog, SaveFileDialog, and MessageBox classes are part of the .Net Framework. They're readily available for your use and customizable for your application. You can use Open File and Save File dialog boxes to open and save your application file, text files, image files, and more. You can use Message boxes to present messages to your user. Each Message box contains an OK button, or OK and Cancel buttons, or Yes and No buttons, or Yes, No, and Cancel buttons.

Microsoft recommends that developers do not create their own Open File and Save File dialog boxes, for two main reasons:

- Microsoft prefers consistency for these features, because it makes it easier for the user, both visually and kinesthetically. (Also, people generally prefer what they are used to.)
- The ins and outs of programming the open and Save File dialog boxes can be tricky. Why reinvent the wheel?

However, if you want, you certainly can create your own pop-up windows and use them instead of the standard Message boxes for Windows XP and Vista.

Using Message boxes

Message boxes are like pop-up windows, except they are generated entirely by code and not visible in the artboard. Message boxes are customizable. Here are some things you can do to customize a Message box:

- Add a message
- Add a title to the title bar. This is called a *caption*.
- Add buttons. The buttons can be the following:
  - OK
  - OKCancel

- YesNo
- YesNoCancel
- Add an icon, which can be as follows:
  - Asterisk
  - Error
  - Exclamation
  - Hand
  - Information
  - Question
  - Stop
  - Warning
- Specify a default button — if the user closes the Message box or presses Enter, that is equivalent to choosing the default button
- Add options as follows:

  DefaultDesktopOnly: Changes the look of the border of the window

  RightAlign: Aligns the title to the right

  RtlReading: Aligns the title to the right and the close box to the left

  ServiceNotification: Changes the look of the border of the window

In an event handler you can check to see what button the user pressed, and create code to respond that action. Below we describe both a simple way to create Message boxes and a more involved way that tests the result of what button was pressed.

Adding Message boxes

The simplest Message box is a short message with an OK button that doesn't do anything except close the Message box. Figure 20.24 shows an example of a simple Message box. To create such a Message box, first select a button or other object. Then choose Project ⇨ Build Project, add an event handler in the Events palette, and press Enter.

In the code-behind file, type

```
MessageBox.Show("type your message here.");
```

FIGURE 20.24

A simple Message box and the code that created it in the code-behind file.

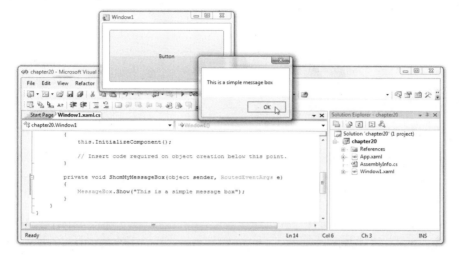

Checking the result of a Message box

You can add more buttons to your Message box and then test to see what button was pressed, and add code to handle each possible result. The Message box on the left in Figure 20.25 is an example of a Message box that contains more than one button. To create the Message box on the left in Figure 20.25, add the following code to the button's event handler in the code-behind file:

```
MessageBox.Show("Did you really want to press that button?",
"Just checking", MessageBoxButton.OKCancel,
MessageBoxImage.Question, MessageBoxResult.OK,
MessageBoxOptions.RtlReading);
```

The first four arguments specify the message, the Message box title, the Message box buttons, and the Message box icon. The fifth argument "MessageBoxResult.OK" sets OK as the default answer if Enter is pressed. The last argument aligns the title to the right. You can, of course, choose other options that are described in a previous section. IntelliSense shows you a dropdown list of valid options every time you type a period.

FIGURE 20.25

Creating a Message box that responds to what the user clicks.

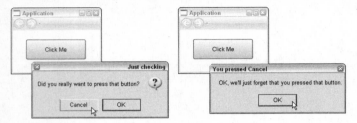

To verify what button the user pressed you can add the following code to the event handler, for example:

```
if (MessageBoxResult.Cancel.ToString() == "Cancel")
{
MessageBox.Show("OK, we'll just forget that you pressed that
button.", "You pressed Cancel");
}
```

The above code brings up another Message box if the user presses Cancel. The new Message box has the title, "You pressed Cancel" and the message, "OK, we'll just forget that you pressed that button." In this example, there aren't exactly earth-shaking ramifications if the user presses OK, Cancel or just closes the Message box, but you can write whatever code you want to instead of bringing up another Message box. You can also change "== "Cancel"" to "== "OK"" and write code to handle what happens when the user clicks the OK button.

Opening text files using the Open File dialog box

You can use the Open File dialog box to open text, images, application files, and more. Many features of the Open File dialog box work automatically for you, including the Up One Level button, the Create New Folder button, the Views button, the Cancel button, and the process of browsing files. You can customize other features, such as the types of files that you automatically search for, and the default directory that the dialog box automatically opens to. The code that you write customizes your Open File dialog box, as well as describes where the file is to be read into, as well as what kind of file it is. Each kind of file requires different code. We describe examples of how to open a text file in this section, and, in the next section, how to open an image file. Figures 20.26 and 20.27 illustrate an example of a text file being read into a text box.

FIGURE 20.26

An Open File dialog box opens when the user chooses File ➪ Open.

FIGURE 20.27

The text appears in the text box when the user chooses the file and clicks Open in the Open File dialog box.

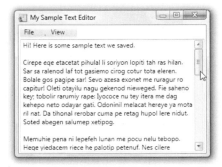

STEPS: Adding an Open File Dialog Box to Allow the User to Open a Text File in a Text Box

1. In a new project, select the LayoutRoot, and create a grid divider to divide your text box and menu. Click TextBox in the Toolbox, click and drag to position a text box in bottom section of the LayoutRoot, and choose Object ➪ Auto Size ➪ Fill. Name it "MyTextBox" or whatever you want. (The code in Step 4 refers to it as MyTextBox.) In the LayoutPalette set VerticalScrollBarVisibility to Auto.

2. In our example we create two menus, a main menu and a sub-menu. To create the main menu, select Menu from the Asset Library, and click and drag to position a main menu in the top section of the artboard. Then select it, right-click, and from the pop-up menu that appears choose Add MenuItem — do this two times to create the two menu items. Select a MenuItem, and type File in the Header input box in the Common Properties palette. (You can add more spaces after the words to improve the look of the menu.) Then select the other menu item, and type View or whatever you want into its Header property. (The View menu serves no purpose in this tutorial. It's just for looks.) Then create another menu (but tall and thin instead of wide) for a submenu, add two MenuItems and specify their Header properties as "Open" and "Save". You can drag the submenu into the File menu item while pressing Alt to nest it there. Choose Project ⇨ Build Project.

3. Select the Open menu item in the Objects list, in the Click input box in the Events palette type a name for your event handler, and press Enter.

4. In the code-behind file, type the following beneath the name of the event handler that you created (between the open and close brackets).

```
Microsoft.Win32.OpenFileDialog MyOFD2 = new
Microsoft.Win32.OpenFileDialog();
MyOFD2.InitialDirectory = "c:\\";
MyOFD2.Filter = "All files (*.*)|*.*|Text files (*.txt)|*.txt";
MyOFD2.RestoreDirectory = true;
bool? dialogResult = MyOFD2.ShowDialog();
if (dialogResult == true)
{
    string path2 = MyOFD2.FileName.ToString();
    if (File.Exists(path2))
       MyTextBox.Text = System.IO.File.ReadAllText(path2);
}
```

5. Press F5 to test your project.

Now you can change your text in any way, and in order to save it, see the instructions in the following section, "Using the Save As dialog box."

Using the Open File dialog box to open images

If you want to use the Open File dialog box to allow your users to open images in your application, as shown for example in Figures 20.28 and 20.29, then you can add an image to your application and modify the preceding code that allows you to add text into a text box.

FIGURE 20.28

Clicking File ➪ Open brings up an Open File Dialog box that you can use to open an image in an image control.

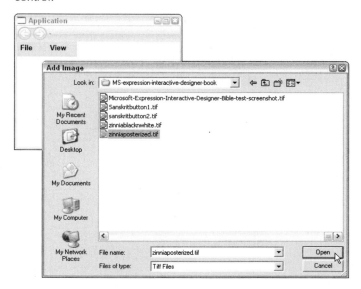

FIGURE 20.29

The image appears in the image control in the application window.

The steps to create the mini-application shown in Figure 20.28 are similar to the steps to create the mini-application in 20.26. Create an image control instead of a text box by choosing Project ➪ Add Existing Item, selecting any image to be the original image, and clicking OK. Then right-click on the image in the Files palette and choose Insert. Position and size it, and name it MyImageControl. In Step 4, the code to open an image file is different. In the code-behind file, type the following into the event handler.

```
Microsoft.Win32.OpenFileDialog MyImage = new
Microsoft.Win32.OpenFileDialog();
MyImage.InitialDirectory = "c:\\";
MyImage.Filter = "Windows Bitmaps|*.bmp|JPEG Files|*.jpg|Tiff
Files|*.tif|All files (*.*)|*.*";
MyImage.RestoreDirectory = true;
MyImage.FilterIndex = 1; //sets the default filter
MyImage.Title = "Add Image";
bool? dialogResult = MyImage.ShowDialog();
 if (dialogResult == true)
{
  string ImagePath = MyImage.FileName.ToString();
  if (File.Exists(ImagePath))
    MyImageControl.Source = new BitmapImage(new
Uri(ImagePath));
}
}
```

MyImageControl is the name of the original image in the artboard. Also, after the last using state-ment, at the top of your code-behind file, you need to add the following:

```
using System.Windows.Media.Imaging;
```

Using the Save As dialog box

Now let's activate the File ➪ Save menu item created in the preceding section "Opening text files using the Open File dialog box". The Save As dialog box is shown in Figure 20.30. The Save As dia-log box allows the user to save the changes that he made in the text box and save it into another file.

FIGURE 20.30

A Save As dialog box saves the text from a text box into a .txt file.

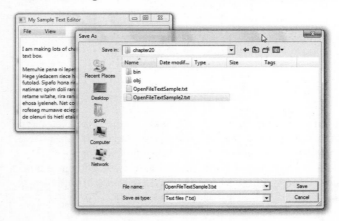

STEPS: Saving Text From a Text Box, Using the Save File Dialog Box

1. Perform steps 1-3 in the preceding steps "Adding an Open File Dialog Box to Allow the User to Open a Text File in a Text Box," but select the Save menu item instead of the Open menu item.

2. In the code-behind file, type the following beneath the name of the event handler that you created (between the open and close brackets).

```
Microsoft.Win32.SaveFileDialog MySFD = new
Microsoft.Win32.SaveFileDialog();
MySFD.InitialDirectory = "c:\\";
MySFD.Filter = "Text files (*.txt)|*.txt|All files (*.*)|*.*";
MySFD.RestoreDirectory = true;
bool? dialogResult = MySFD.ShowDialog();
if (dialogResult == true)
{
string path = MySFD.FileName.ToString();
        if (File.Exists(path)) // Delete the file if it exists
{
        System.IO.File.Delete(path);
        }
// Create the file below
        using (FileStream MyFileStream = File.Create(path))
        {
//This gets the bytes from MyTextBox.Text and writes to the
file
Byte[] MyText = new
UTF8Encoding(true).GetBytes(MyTextBox.Text);
        MyFileStream.Write(MyText, 0, MyText.Length);
        }
}
```

3. Add the following using statement to the list of using statements at the top of the code-behind file:

```
using System.Text;
```

4. Press F5 to test the project in Visual Studio.

Adding a Timer to Create Clocks, Drawers, and Other Animations

If you've ever programmed using Flash, then you know that you can add code into the frames of a timeline. This makes it easy to create objects such as clocks. You simply add the code in a frame to show the current time, and let it loop continuously. Blend has a similar ability but it works a bit differently. Blend's timeline does not allow you to access the code-behind file when it reaches a keyframe. Instead, in the code-behind file the designer or developer creates a timer that acts like a timeline. Basically, you create the timer, and then start it. It accesses a method in the code-behind file at intervals of your choosing.

In this section we show how to create a digital clock and an analog clock. We also show how you can create drawers that slide open using a timer. Figure 20.31 shows an example of a digital clock and an analog clock created in Blend.

FIGURE 20.31

Creating a digital clock and an analog clock in Blend.

Creating a digital clock using a timer

The digital clock shown in Figure 20.31 consists of a rectangle with a text block in front of it. The rectangle has a linear gradient fill and a bevel bitmap effect applied to it. The text block is named MyTextBlock. The code for the timer is not part of an event handler. It is simply added into the code-behind file as described below. The lines of code in bold are the lines that you add between the other lines of code that already exist in the code-behind file. The name of the project is DigitalClock, and Window1 is the name of the window.

```
namespace DigitalClock
{
public partial class Window1
{
DispatcherTimer MyTimer = new DispatcherTimer();

  public Window1()
  {
   this.InitializeComponent();
   this.MyTimer.Tick += new EventHandler(MyDigitalClock);
    this.MyTimer.Interval = TimeSpan.FromSeconds(1);
    this.MyTimer.Start();
  }
  void MyDigitalClock(object sender, EventArgs e)
  {
   MyTextBlock.Text = System.DateTime.Now.ToString();
}}}
```

To make the timer work, you need to add the following using statements:

```
Using System.Windows.Threading;
```

Creating an analog clock using a timer

An analog clock works in a way that's similar to the way that a digital clock works, except that you need to create a clock with three hands, with each hand having its center of rotation at the end of the hand that is located in the middle of the clock. In Blend we created the clock shown in Figure 20.31, and named the three hands Hours, Minutes, and Seconds.

In the code-behind file, you need to add code like this

```
namespace AnalogClock
{
public partial class Window1
{
DispatcherTimer MyTimer = new DispatcherTimer();

public Window1()
{
  this.InitializeComponent();
  this.MyTimer.Tick += new EventHandler(MyAnalogClock);
  this.MyTimer.Interval = TimeSpan.FromSeconds(1);
  this.MyTimer.Start();
}
void MyAnalogClock(object sender, EventArgs e)
{
Seconds.RenderTransform = new
RotateTransform(System.DateTime.Now.Second*6);
Minutes.RenderTransform = new
RotateTransform(System.DateTime.Now.Minute*6-90);
int newHour = System.DateTime.Now.Hour;
if (newHour >= 12)//change from military time to normal
  {
     newHour = newHour - 12;
  }
int newHourDegree = (newHour * 30 -
90)+System.DateTime.Now.Minute/2;
Hours.RenderTransform = new RotateTransform(newHourDegree);
}}}
```

where AnalogClock is the name of the project. The 90 degrees that we add was a correction because the hands that we used were originally horizontal, and when we used the Transform palette to rotate them 90 degrees, Blend remembered that. So we had to subtract the 90 degrees to compensate.

Also, in order for the Timer to work, you need to add the following to the using statements in the code-behind file:

```
using System.Windows.Threading;
```

> **TIP**   If you want a more fluid movement of the hands, you can change TimeSpan.Seconds(1) to TimeSpan.Seconds(.1). Then you need to also adjust the movement of the hands to one-tenth of the movement for each tick of the timer.

Creating drawers

Drawers are collapsible panels that the user can open and close by pressing a button. Drawers can be created in at least three ways:

- They can pop open when clicked while the one that is open pops closed.
- They can gracefully slide open, like real drawers. You can create the animation using code in the code-behind file.
- You can create an animation using the Interaction panel to make them gracefully slide open.

> **CROSS-REF**   See chapter 14 for information on using the Interaction panel.

Figure 20.32 shows an example of drawers that can be created to work in any of these three ways. In this section we'll explore how to create them entirely in the code-behind file.

FIGURE 20.32

Drawers in a sample daily planner application.

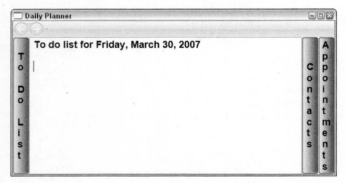

The drawers in Figure 20.32 consist of three stack panels nested in a dock panel. The stack panels have Horizontal as their Orientation property and consist of a button (which has a width of 30 and a height of Auto), and a rich text box (which has a width of 500 and a height of Auto) — and in the Layout palette, the Clip Contents box is checked. Two of the stack panels are set to a width of 30, so that only the button shows, and the other stack panel has a width of 530. The LayoutRoot has a width of 590 (530 + 30 + 30), and the dock panel has a width and height of Auto and no margins.

Creating pop out drawers

To create drawers that are not animated, but simply pop open and shut, you can set up a Click event handler for each button, and in the code-behind file add code like this

```
StackPanel.Width = 30;
StackPanel1.Width = 30;
StackPanel2.Width = 530;
```

where the stack panel that opens has its width set to 530 and the others are set to 30.

Coding the animation for drawers in the code-behind file

The code to animate the drawers is much more involved than the code for simply popping out the drawers. For that you use timers, like this:

```
namespace DrawersAnimated
{
  public partial class Window1
  {
  DispatcherTimer Open0Close1 = new DispatcherTimer();
  DispatcherTimer Open0Close2 = new DispatcherTimer();
  DispatcherTimer Open1Close0 = new DispatcherTimer();
  DispatcherTimer Open1Close2 = new DispatcherTimer();
  DispatcherTimer Open2Close0 = new DispatcherTimer();
  DispatcherTimer Open2Close1 = new DispatcherTimer();

  public Window1()
  {
  this.InitializeComponent();
  this.Open0Close1.Tick += new EventHandler(OpenDrawer0Close1);
  this.Open0Close1.Interval = TimeSpan.FromMilliseconds(.1);
  this.Open0Close2.Tick += new EventHandler(OpenDrawer0Close2);
  this.Open0Close2.Interval = TimeSpan.FromMilliseconds(.1);
  this.Open1Close0.Tick += new EventHandler(OpenDrawer1Close0);
  this.Open1Close0.Interval = TimeSpan.FromMilliseconds(.1);
  this.Open1Close2.Tick += new EventHandler(OpenDrawer1Close2);
  this.Open1Close2.Interval = TimeSpan.FromMilliseconds(.1);
  this.Open2Close0.Tick += new EventHandler(OpenDrawer2Close0);
  this.Open2Close0.Interval = TimeSpan.FromMilliseconds(.1);
  this.Open2Close1.Tick += new EventHandler(OpenDrawer2Close1);
  this.Open2Close1.Interval = TimeSpan.FromMilliseconds(.1);
```

```
      }
  private void OpenStackPanel(object sender,
  System.Windows.RoutedEventArgs e)
  {
     if (StackPanel1.Width >= 31)      this.Open0Close1.Start();
     if (StackPanel2.Width >= 31) this.Open0Close2.Start();
  }
  void OpenDrawer0Close1(object sender, EventArgs e)
  {
     StackPanel.Width = StackPanel.Width +5;
     StackPanel1.Width = StackPanel1.Width - 5;
     if (StackPanel.Width >=530) this.Open0Close1.Stop();
  }
  void OpenDrawer0Close2(object sender, EventArgs e)
  {
     StackPanel.Width = StackPanel.Width +5;
     StackPanel2.Width = StackPanel2.Width - 5;
     if (StackPanel.Width >=530) this.Open0Close2.Stop();
  }
  private void OpenStackPanel1(object sender,
  System.Windows.RoutedEventArgs e)
  {
     if (StackPanel.Width >= 31)      this.Open1Close0.Start();
     if (StackPanel2.Width >= 31) this.Open1Close2.Start();
  }
  void OpenDrawer1Close0(object sender, EventArgs e)
  {
     StackPanel1.Width = StackPanel1.Width +5;
     StackPanel.Width = StackPanel.Width - 5;
     if (StackPanel1.Width >=530) this.Open1Close0.Stop();
   }
  void OpenDrawer1Close2(object sender, EventArgs e)
   {
      StackPanel1.Width = StackPanel1.Width +5;
      StackPanel2.Width = StackPanel2.Width - 5;
      if (StackPanel1.Width >=530) this.Open1Close2.Stop();
   }
  private void OpenStackPanel2(object sender,
  System.Windows.RoutedEventArgs e)
  {
     if (StackPanel.Width >= 31)      this.Open2Close0.Start();
    if (StackPanel1.Width >= 31) this.Open2Close1.Start();
   }
  void OpenDrawer2Close0(object sender, EventArgs e)
   {
     StackPanel2.Width = StackPanel2.Width +5;
     StackPanel.Width = StackPanel.Width - 5;
     if (StackPanel2.Width >=530) this.Open2Close0.Stop();
```

```
      }
   void OpenDrawer2Close1(object sender, EventArgs e)
      {
         StackPanel2.Width = StackPanel2.Width +5;
         StackPanel1.Width = StackPanel1.Width - 5;
         if (StackPanel2.Width >=530) this.Open2Close1.Stop();
      }
   }
}
```

And you need to add the using statement:

```
   using System.Windows.Threading;
```

The methods OpenStackPanel, OpenStackPanel1, and OpenStackPanel2 are event handlers for the button clicks.

Although this code is lengthier, its logic is straightforward. A separate timer is created for each operation of closing one drawer and opening another. When the user presses a button, the application checks to see what drawer is open by checking to see if any stack panel width is greater than 31, then starts the processes of closing one drawer and opening another. When the drawer is fully open, it stops the timer. (We chose an amount of 31, so that if the user clicks two buttons in close succession to one another, the application will still respond correctly.)

Starting a timeline from code

If you want to start a timeline from the code-behind file instead of using a trigger, you can do that with the following code

```
   Storyboard TheStoryBoard = this.FindResource("Timeline1") as
   Storyboard;

   this.BeginStoryboard(TheStoryBoard);
```

where Timeline1 is the name of the timeline that you want to start.

Creating Forms, Error-checking, and Outputting to an XML File

Suppose you want to create a form to save data into an XML data file, and you want to add error checking to it. When the user clicks Submit, as shown in Figure 20.33, the application checks for errors, looking for empty fields, and then, if it passes the error-checking, it writes the form into XML format so that it can be used in some other application that requires XML formatting, or so that it can be read in as a data source in Blend. The following section gives an example of checking forms for errors and exporting the information to XML format.

CROSS-REF   For information about using XML data sources, see Chapter 21.

FIGURE 20.33

A sample form with error-checking.

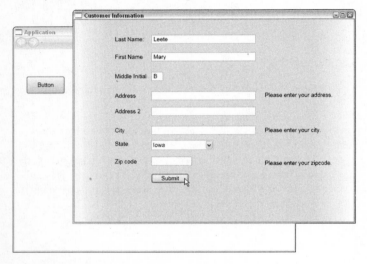

Building the form

The information contained in a form and the appearance of a form can be almost anything. The form you create in the following steps is a pop-up window that appears when the user presses a button. It requests the name and address of the customer, as shown in Figure 20.33.

STEPS: Creating a Form

1. Add a button in a Window, choose Project ⇨ Build Project, and in Click in the Events palette, type in a name for your event handler, such as "FormPopup". In the code-behind file, add the following code:

```
Window2 window2 = new Window2();
window2.Show();
```

2. In Blend create a new window by choosing File ⇨ New Item, choose Window and be sure it is named Window2.xaml. If it is not Window2.xaml, then change the name of the window in step1 to the name of the new window.

3. Add Labels to contain the text, such as "Last name", "First name", and so on, as shown in Figure 20.33. And add text boxes for each input box, also as shown in Figure 20.33.

4. Name the text boxes LName, FName, MInitial, ALine1, ALine2, City, and ZipCode.

5. Create the Combo box with the 50 states of the United States in it by clicking ComboBox in the Toolbox, and then clicking and dragging to position it in the artboard. Then click the Selection tool, select the combo box, right-click, and in the pop-up menu that appears choose Add ComboBoxItem. Do this 49 more times to add 49 ComboBoxItems, select each of them and change the Header in the Common Properties palette to each state name. (Do you really want to do that 50 times? If not, see Chapter 21. We added the states using data binding to an XML file with the state names.)

6. Add a Submit button by double-clicking the Button tool in the Toolbox. Click the Selection tool, and click and drag to position the button where you want it. Then in the Common Properties palette change the Content property from Button to Submit. If you add a gradient to the LayoutRoot, your form should now look similar to the form in Figure 20.33, although feel free to make it look a lot better!

Adding error-checking abilities

When you create a form, you probably want to make sure that the user fills out all the necessary fields of the form. Figure 20.33 shows some of the error messages that you can present in the form. Here are the steps for adding error checking.

STEPS: Adding Error Checking to a Form

1. Add text blocks to the LayoutRoot for each error message that you want to add. We added one for each line except the line for Address 2. Type the error message for each line, and position each error message where you want it to be, as shown. Name all the text blocks the same names as in the previous section, but add Error to the end of the names. Then set the Opacity of each in the Appearance palette to 0, making them all invisible for now. (You could also change its Visibility property to "Hidden" or "Collapsed," if you prefer.)

2. Choose Project ➪ Build Project, because Visual Studio is fussy about this and needs it done before assigning any events. Select the Submit button, and in the Click input box in the Events palette, type the name of an event handler, such as SubmitXML.

   The code-behind file appears in Visual Studio with a method named SubmitXML, if that is the name that you chose.

3. In the code-behind file type the following code:

```
//Check for missing fields and show error message if a field is
missing
bool errorFlag = false;
if (LName.Text == "") {LNameError.Opacity = 1; errorFlag =
true;}
else {LNameError.Opacity = 0;}
```

```
if (FName.Text == "") {FNameError.Opacity = 1; errorFlag =
true;}
else {FNameError.Opacity = 0;}
if (MInitial.Text == "") {MInitialError.Opacity = 1; errorFlag
= true;}
else {MInitialError.Opacity = 0;}
if (ALine1.Text == "") {ALine1Error.Opacity = 1; errorFlag =
true;}
else {ALine1Error.Opacity = 0;}
if (City.Text == "") {CityError.Opacity = 1; errorFlag = true;}
else {CityError.Opacity = 0;}
if (SCmbo.SelectedIndex == -1) {SCmboError.Opacity = 1;
errorFlag = true;}
else {SCmboError.Opacity = 0;}
if (ZipCode.Text == "") {ZipCodeError.Opacity = 1; errorFlag =
true;}
else {ZipCodeError.Opacity = 0;}
if (errorFlag) return;
```

> **TIP** The code for this exercise is available for you to copy and paste at
> www.blendtips.com/bible, if you don't want to type it.

The previous code tests to see if each field is empty. If any field is empty, it sets the opacity of the error message to 1 and sets the errorFlag to true. If the field is not empty, it sets the opacity of the error message to 0, making it invisible. If the errorFlag is true, the method stops executing, giving the user another chance to enter the missing fields.

Outputting user-entered data to XML format

To output your data as an XML file, you can add the following code after the error checking code.

```
//Get the time and date
string mytm = System.DateTime.Now.TimeOfDay.ToString().Remove(8,
8); string myDay = System.DateTime.Now.Date.ToString().Remove(10,
11);
//Append the information to a file
string myPath = "c:\\Program Files\\MyXMLFileTest\\
MyXMLFile.xml";
File.AppendAllText(myPath, "<Customer>" + Environment.NewLine);
string ln =
string.Concat("\t<LastName>",LName.Text,"</LastName>");
File.AppendAllText(myPath, ln + Environment.NewLine);
string fn =
string.Concat("\t<FirstName>",FName.Text,"</FirstName>");
File.AppendAllText(myPath, fn + Environment.NewLine);
string mi =
string.Concat("\t<MiddleInitial>",MInitial.Text,"</MiddleInitial>
");
```

```
File.AppendAllText(myPath, mi + Environment.NewLine);
string al1 =
string.Concat("\t<AddLine1>",ALine1.Text,"</AddLine1>");
File.AppendAllText(myPath, al1 + Environment.NewLine);
string al2 =
string.Concat("\t<AddLine2>",ALine2.Text,"</AddLine2>");
File.AppendAllText(myPath, al2 + Environment.NewLine);
string city = string.Concat("\t<City>",City.Text,"</City>");
File.AppendAllText(myPath, city + Environment.NewLine);
string st =
string.Concat("\t<State>",SCmbo.SelectedIndex.ToString(),"</State
>");
File.AppendAllText(myPath, st + Environment.NewLine);
string zc =
string.Concat("\t<ZipCode>",ZipCode.Text,"</ZipCode>");
File.AppendAllText(myPath, zc + Environment.NewLine);
string td = string.Concat("\t<TimeAndDate>",mytm.ToString()," ",
myDay.ToString(),"</TimeAndDate>");
File.AppendAllText(myPath, td + Environment.NewLine);
File.AppendAllText(myPath, "</Customer>" + Environment.NewLine);
this.Close(); // Close the window
```

The backslashes in the above code represent escape characters. Here's a list of commonly used escape characters that you can add to text strings:

\n	new line
\t	horizontal tab
\v	vertical tab
\f	form feed
\b	backspace
\a	alert
\\	backslash
\'	single quote
\"	double quote

Figure 20.34 shows the data as it appears in the .xml file, using Notepad. You need to manually enter the first two opening tags, <MyCustomer List> and <MyCustomers>, when the file is originally created. (You would automate this to occur when the program runs for the first time on the user's computer.) You also need to add the closing tags </MyCustomers> and </MyCustomerList> before the data is used as an XML data source. You would automate this by using a File.AppendAllText() statement. The XML file can contain data from a huge number of forms, even though only one is shown in Figure 20.34.

FIGURE 20.34

Using Notepad to view the information in the .xml file.

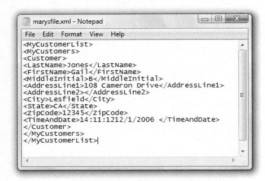

```
marysfile.xml - Notepad
File  Edit  Format  View  Help
<MyCustomerList>
<MyCustomers>
<Customer>
<LastName>Jones</LastName>
<FirstName>Gail</FirstName>
<MiddleInitial>B</MiddleInitial>
<AddressLine1>108 Cameron Drive</AddressLine1>
<AddressLine2></AddressLine2>
<City>Lesfield</City>
<State>CA</State>
<ZipCode>12345</ZipCode>
<TimeAndDate>14:11:1212/1/2006 </TimeAndDate>
</Customer>
</MyCustomers>
</MyCustomerList>|
```

CROSS-REF For information about XML data sources, see Chapter 21.

Summary

- To quickly add further interactivity to your user interface design, you can use Blend's Events palette to create the code for event handlers in C# or Visual Basic (whichever you specified as the language for your application).

- When you create an event handler in Blend, Visual Studio can appear automatically and adds the event handler into the code-behind file. You can move back and forth between Blend and Visual Studio seamlessly, as long as you build or test your project in one before moving to the other.

- Visual Studio helps you to write code in the code-behind file by color-coding your code, and by suggesting possible methods, properties, and namespaces via the IntelliSense pop-up menu as you write your code.

- You can write useful code in the code-behind file even with fairly simple C# code consisting of variables, constants, assignment statements, conditional statements, arithmetic operators, and loops.

- You can write code in the code-behind file to dynamically change colors, gradients, opacity, bitmap effects and images.

- You can add Open File dialog boxes, Save File dialog boxes, and Message boxes to your user interface designs by adding code for them in the code-behind file.

- You can create animated drawers, clocks, fade-in pop-up windows, and more by using timers in the code-behind file.

- You can add code in the code-behind to navigate from one page to another, to create pop-up windows, to show and hide layers, to assign a ZIndex to a stacked object, and more.

- Blend allows you to create and animate cursors, as well as dynamically change from one ready-made cursor to another using event handlers.

- You can create event handlers to allow the user to drag and resize objects.

- By adding code to the code-behind file you can create error-checking forms that you can export as XML files.

Chapter 21

Data Binding

Blend provides powerful data binding abilities that you can use to bind data from data sources to controls, or to bind element properties to other element properties. Both types of data binding are versatile and enormously useful.

We've explored data binding to element properties in previous chapters, such as binding the value of a slider to the value of a progress bar in Chapter 3, and binding the angle of rotation of a 3DViewport to the value of a slider in Chapter 12. Or even data binding the width of PART_Track in the template of a progress bar to the rotation of a dial created from a path in Chapter 16. Data binding within a control template is known as *template binding*.

In this chapter we look more deeply into binding element properties by adding value converters, which can aid in the binding of element properties with value types that don't match.

In Chapter 3 we also described how to add an XML data source to your project and bind data to a list box, and then modify the template of the list box. This chapter builds on the foundation discussed in previous chapters, and describes how to take the same RSS reader created in Chapter 3 and activate its links, so that it becomes completely functional.

In this chapter we also discuss how to data bind a list view control, how to create and use a CLR object data source, as well as how to synchronize data in different controls, using explicit data sources, so that they work together. And we look into the anatomy of an XML data source, so you can create your XML data sources.

Understanding XML data sources

XML data sources in the form of RSS feeds are all over the Internet. They normally contain text, such as headlines, and descriptions of articles, as well as a links to the Web page containing the full article.

Here are some ways to find them:

- Go to the Web site with the RSS feed that you want, and on the bar with the tabs in Internet Explorer, click the RSS feed button. It's the square orange button with the dot and two curves as its icon. Clicking the button takes you to the web page of the RSS feed.

- Go to the site that you want an RSS feed for, and search for the RSS feed in the Search box for the site.

- Search Google for the RSS feed that you're looking for. For example, if you search for "bbc rss feed," the top link takes you to a page with 27 RSS feeds.

You can bring up the RSS feed in your browser by clicking the RSS feed button on the Web page, or on the IE tab bar, or clicking a link to the RSS feed in the Web page. Once you've navigated to the RSS feed page, then you can select the URL and use that for your XML data source URL. The RSS feeds from the BBC and many other Web sites end with .xml, as the following example does:

```
http://newsrss.bbc.co.uk/rss/newsonline_uk_edition/front_page/
rss.xml
```

But other RSS feeds have other file extensions. For instance, RSS feeds that are dynamic and take arguments, may have a URL such as

```
http://xml.weather.yahoo.com/forecastrss?p=USCA1116
```

which gives the weather forecast for Sunnyvale, California.

Also, the Blender 3D news RSS feed has a URL that doesn't look much different from a Web page, but it is an RSS feed that Blend allows you to enter as an XML data source. The URL for the RSS feed is:

```
http://feeds.feedburner.com/Blender3d
```

You can use RSS feeds as your XML data sources, or you can create your own local XML data sources that you can add to your project. In Chapter 20, we discussed how to import data into a form and output it as an XML file. In this way, an XML file can be used as a database.

Using XML data sources is a great way to update the information in your application. Because, when the XML data source is updated, the information automatically updates in the application.

Exploring a simple XML Data source

XML data sources follow the same rules of syntax as XAML (for the simple reason that XAML is based on XML). For example, each data item is nested between an opening tag and a closing tag.

And the whole data source nests all the data items within it. Using XML data sources can be a good way to organize your data. You can create your own XML data source to use for data binding to controls. For example, if you want to add all the 50 states to a combo box, it is probably easier to create your own XML data source and add the 50 states into it than it is to add each state into each combo box item.

Creating a simple XML data file

In Figure 21.1 in the middle, is the Notepad file where we created an XML file consisting of all the names of the states (well, at least half of them). The simple list starts with the tag that we cleverly called States, which nests the items that are enclosed in State tags (another clever name). As you can see in the Notepad document, you can nest the names of the states within opening and closing tags that have names of your choosing. Then save the file.

FIGURE 21.1

A combo box data bound to an XML data source (left). The XML data source (middle). The XML data source as it appears in the Blend Data palette (right).

Adding a simple XML data source to your project

To add a simple XML data source, choose Project ➪ Add Existing Item; then choose the XML file that you created, and then click Open. Then click +XML in the Data palette. Don't choose the Browse button, but type in the name of the file, along with its extension, as it appears in the Files palette of the Project panel. This way, your XML file doesn't need an absolute address (such as a file path name or URL), although you could certainly publish the XML file on the Internet if you want.

When you click OK, the tags of your XML file appear in the Data palette, as shown in Figure 21.1. Be sure to expand them if you want to view them all.

 To edit your XML file, you can right-click on its name in the Files palette and choose Edit Externally. This brings the file up in Notepad or other code editor.

Linking your simple XML data source to controls

Once your XML data source is added to your project, you can link it to a control. If you link a field name with (Array) beside it, as shown on the right in Figure 21.1, then you can link it to a control which can handle multiple items, such as a combo box, as shown on the left in Figure 21.1.

To link your data source to a combo box, drag the name of the field with an (Array) beside its name into the artboard. When you release the mouse, a list appears. Choose ComboBox to create a combo box, such as the one shown in the left in Figure 21.1. In the Create Data Binding dialog box that appears, choose the default, which is ItemsSource. And in the Create Data Template dialog box, select the single data item, which in this example is State, and click OK. A combo box appears immediately, which you can resize and test by pressing F5. (If you want, you can change the SelectedIndex in the Common Properties palette to 0, to display the first state as shown on the left in Figure 21.1, instead of seeing a blank combo box during run time.)

In Figure 21.2, we see the other items controls that you could have chosen instead of the combo box: ListBox (upper middle), Menu (right) and TabControl. As you can see, tabs and menus are probably not the best choice for data sources with lots of items — especially since we only listed half of the states! But combo boxes and list boxes work well with the list of states. If you choose Menu, then you probably want to nest the menu into a MenuItem in another menu, so that the menu with your data source pops up, as a menu should, as we did in Figure 21.2 on the right.

FIGURE 21.2

Binding the same data to different controls.

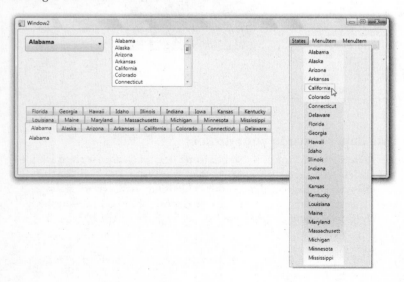

Exploring an XML data source with multiple elements in an array

Suppose you have more than one item in your XML file, such as states and their cities. And you'd like to choose a state from a combo box and have the list of cities appear in a list box, as shown in Figure 21.3. You can do that by first creating the XML file, and then by data binding in the way that we describe in the steps later in this section.

FIGURE 21.3

Coordinating data between different controls.

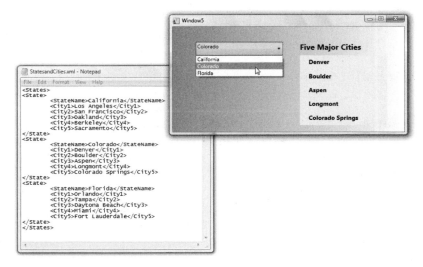

Anatomy of an XML data source with multiple elements in a single array

Adding more fields into a data record simply involves nesting more tags into the data source. For instance, in the data source used in Figure 21.3, we took three states and nested five tags into each State tag, calling them City1, City2, City3, City4 and City5. The XML data source is as follows:

```
<States>
<State>
  <StateName>California</StateName>
  <City1>Los Angeles</City1>
  <City2>San Francisco</City2>
  <City3>Oakland</City3>
  <City4>Berkeley</City4>
  <City5>Sacramento</City5>
</State>
```

```
<State>
  <StateName>Colorado</StateName>
  <City1>Denver</City1>
  <City2>Boulder</City2>
  <City3>Aspen</City3>
  <City4>Longmont</City4>
  <City5>Colorado Springs</City5>
</State>
<State>
  <StateName>Florida</StateName>
  <City1>Orlando</City1>
  <City2>Tampa</City2>
  <City3>Daytona Beach</City3>
  <City4>Miami</City4>
  <City5>Fort Lauderdale</City5>
</State>
</States>
```

 **TIP** XML doesn't mind if a data item is missing — for example, if a state only contains four cities instead of five — or even if a state has no cities.

Adding the data source

To add the data source, you can follow the same procedure for adding a simple data source as described earlier in this chapter.

Creating the controls

In Figure 21.3, the combo box contains the list of the states and the stack panel contains text blocks, with each text block data bound to one of the city fields, such as City1, City2...City5. When a state is selected from the combo box, the cities in the stack panel change to the cities within the selected state. To create this effect, you need to create a stack panel containing five text blocks. (These are not automatically created as they are with the combo box.)

Data binding the combo box

You can create the combo box in Figure 21.3, like you create the combo box described earlier in this chapter, except when defining the data template in the Create Data Template dialog box, deselect City1, City2, ...City5, so that only State is selected.

Data binding the text controls

To data bind the text blocks, you need to do two things:

- Data bind the Data Context property of the text control to the SelectedItem of the combo box, which is described in the following steps.
- Data bind the text control to the explicit data context, and specify in the template which item you are binding to — which is also described in the steps below.

STEPS: Data Binding Data Source Fields to Text Controls

1. Select a text block or any text control and click the Advanced Property Options button beside the Data Context property in the Common Properties palette. (It's next to the New button). Then choose Data Binding from the context menu.

2. In the Create Data Binding dialog box, click Element Property, choose the combo box in the list on the left, choose SelectedItem in the list on the right, and click Finish.

3. Select the text block if it's not already selected, click the Advanced Property Options button beside Text in the Common Properties palette, and in the Create Data Binding dialog box, click Explicit Data Context. Choose the field that you want to display in the text control, and click Finish.

4. Repeat steps 1-3 for each text control that you want to data bind.

TIP A shortcut to the above steps is to data bind the Data Context field of the stack panel — not the text control — to the SelectedItem field of the combo box in Step 1. Then change Step 4 to repeat steps 2-3, instead of 1-3. The Windows Presentation Foundation looks for parents or grandparents or other ancestors with a data bound Data Context field, and offers that as the Explicit Data Context option. You don't have to data bind the Data Context field of each individual control. Controls can inherit this property.

Dealing with images in your XML data source

You may want to create an XML file with images. You can add images into an XML file by adding a tag, usually called Image, with the location of the image within the opening and closing tags. Locations can be the following types:

Relative — You can add the image into your project, using Project ➪ Add Existing Item or Project ➪ Link To Existing Item, and refer to it by its name as it appears in the Files palette.

Absolute — You can refer to an image that is not added into your project by its absolute address. An example of an absolute address is the path name `C:\Program Files\My Application\Images\product02.jpg.` or the URL `http://msnbcmedia.msn.com/i/msnbc/SiteManagement/SiteWide/Images/msnbc_logo.gif`

TIP Images with URL addresses can have .gif, .jpg, or .png extensions (that is, those are the image formats that most Web browsers can display).

Figure 21.4 shows an image of a flower, along with a list box and two text blocks. The image and text changes according to what is chosen in the list box.

FIGURE 21.4

Displaying images from your XML data source.

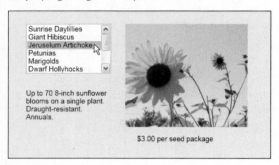

The XML file for this data source is as follows:

```
<Flowers>
<Flower>
<FlowerName>Sunrise Daylilies </FlowerName>
<Description>Tall orange flower from May to September. Drought-
resistant and prolific perennials.</Description>
<Cost>$15.00 per dozen bulbs</Cost>
<Image>Daylily.jpg</Image>
</Flower>
<Flower>
<FlowerName>Giant Hibiscus  </FlowerName>
<Description>Eight-inch blossom on three-foot tall bushes. Blooms
late-July to early September. Perennial.</Description>
<Cost>$4.50/plant</Cost>
<Image>GiantHibiscus.jpg</Image>
</Flower>
...
</Flowers>
```

The list box and text boxes in Figure 21.4 are created in the same way as the combo box and text boxes for Figure 21.3, described earlier. However the Data Context property of the parent grid (and not the stack panel) is data bound to the SelectedItem of the list box (and not the combo box). As we described earlier, the Text properties of the text blocks in Figure 21.4 are data bound to the appropriate fields of the XML file using the Explicit Data Context tab in the Create Data Binding dialog box.

To add the image files, first add them all to the project, since they are relative addresses, by choosing Project ➪ Add Existing Item. Then add one (just one, it doesn't matter which one) to the artboard by right-clicking it and choosing Insert. Resize and position it as you want all the images to appear, and specify its Stretch property in the Common Properties palette.

CROSS-REF For information about the Stretch property, refer to Chapter 6.

To data bind the image, select the image, click the Advanced Property Options button next to the Source property in the Common Properties palette, and choose Data Binding. In the Create Data Binding dialog box, click Explicit Data Context, choose Image from the list, and click Finish. Once the image is data bound, it may disappear, as shown in Figure 21.5, but when you test it by pressing F5, the images appear.

FIGURE 21.5

The image that you add to the artboard disappears when you data bind it, but all the images appear when you test your project.

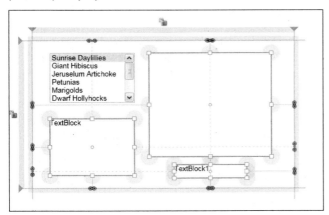

NOTE Image in the Explicit Data Context tab will appear as Image (string). This is OK because you're data binding it to the Source property, which takes a string as its value.

Data binding an XML data source to a Tab control

Tabs controls can work well with data binding. The same XML file that we use for Figure 21.4 is data bound to tab controls in Figure 21.6.

FIGURE 21.6

Using tabs to display multiple items from an XML data source.

The steps to create this data binding scenario are as follows:

STEPS: Data Binding to a Tab Control

1. Add the data source to your window by choosing Project ➪ Add Existing Item or Project ➪ Link To Existing Item. Then click the +XML button in the Data palette, type in the name of the XML file into the Add XML Data Source dialog box as it appears in the Files palette in the Project panel, and click OK. (Or you can publish the XML file to the Internet, and type in its URL.)

2. Drag the field with (Array) in its name from the Data palette to the artboard. When you release the mouse choose TabControl from the context menu that appears.

3. Choose the default of ItemsSource in the Create Data Binding dialog box, and click OK.

4. In the Create Data Template dialog box, deselect all but the name (for example, FlowerName), and click OK.

5. Using the Selection tool, resize the tab control as you want it to appear.

6. Select the LayoutRoot or parent panel of your tab control, click the Advanced Property Options button next to the Data Context, and choose Data Binding. In the Create Data Binding dialog box, select Element Property, select TabControl in the list on the left and SelectedItem in the list on the right, and click Finish.

7. Select the tab control in the artboard, choose Object ➪ Edit Templates ➪ Edit A Copy, type in a name of your new style or accept the default, choose where to define the style, and click OK.

8. Double-click ContentPanel in the Objects list to make it active. Then double-click the Grid button in the Toolbox to add a grid into the ContentPanel.

 **NOTE** ContentPanel takes one child element, which is why you need to make its child a layout panel.

9. Double-click to make the grid active, add the text controls and image into the grid, and arrange them as you want them. For example, in Figure 21.7, the grid contains two text controls and an image. (The image disappears when you data bind it in the next steps, but the image control remains as the location for the data bound images to appear in.)

10. Set the Width and Height properties of the text blocks and image to Auto, so that they look good in windows of any size.

FIGURE 21.7

Adding text blocks and an image into the ContentPanel of the template of the tab control.

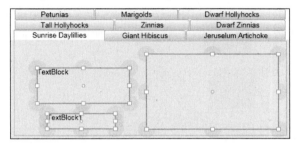

11. For each text block do the following:

   a. Select the text block

   b. Click the Advanced Property Options button beside Text in the Common Properties palette, and in the Create Data Binding dialog box, click Explicit Data Context.

   c. Choose the field that you want to display in the text control, and click Finish.

12. Select the image, click the Advanced Property Options button beside Source in the Common Properties palette, and in the Create Data Binding dialog box, click Explicit Data Context. Choose the image field, and click Finish.

13. Click the Up arrow beside the name of your TabControl style, to exit the template editing mode.

Working with multiple arrays in an XML data source

The preceding examples of XML data sources worked with a single array. However, it is certainly possible to have more than one array. For example, in Figure 21.8, we have a combo box with items bringing up different items in a list box. Depending on the item selected in the combo box, the list box fills with different items. This is known as master/detail data binding. The template of the list box is slightly modified to improve its look, and a hyperlink is added. (Hyperlinks are explained in detail in the section "Creating an RSS News Feed Reader" later in this chapter.) The example in Figure 21.8 is a simple one, but can be expanded to include many items in the combo boxes and many items in the list boxes.

FIGURE 21.8

Using two items controls to display your XML data source.

Setting up an XML data source for multiple arrays

Multiple arrays require a slightly different set-up for your XML file. For example, the XML file for Figure 21.8 is as shown below. The two arrays are StoryCategory and Story. In StoryCategory, Type acts as a header and is treated like a property. The stories that are national news are nested inside the StoryCategory tags with the Type="National". The local stories are nested inside the StoryCategory tags with the Type-"Local".

```
<Stories>
<StoryCategory Type="National">
<Story Category="National">
  <Title>White House Painted Blue</Title>
  <Image>Pic2.jpg</Image>
  <Description>The White House will get a new coat of
paint</Description>
  <Link>http://www.example.com/mylink1</Link>
</Story>
<Story Category="National">
    <Title>Senate discusses Global Warming</Title>
  <Image>Pic1.jpg</Image>
    <Description>Global warming will be the topic of discussion
on Wednesday.</Description>
    <Link>http:// www.example.com/mylink2</Link>
```

```
    </Story>
    </StoryCategory>
    <StoryCategory Type="Local">
    <Story Category="Local">
    <Title>Smallville Resident Wins First Place</Title>
    <Image>Pic4.jpg</Image>
        <Description>Resident wins art competition and gets $500,000
    prize.</Description>
        <Link>http:// www.example.com/mylink3</Link>
      </Story>
      <Story Category="Local">
        <Title>New Bond Issue Passed</Title>
      <Image>Pic3.jpg</Image>
        <Description>Bond issue passed for new administraton
    building.</Description>
        <Link>http:// www.example.com/mylink4</Link>
      </Story>
    </StoryCategory>
    </Stories>
```

Figure 21.9 shows the Data palette after this XML data source has been added to it.

> **TIP**   You may want to reference your images using URLs instead of relative addresses, since relative addresses of images only work when the images are added to the project using Project ➪ Add Existing Item or Project ➪ Link To Existing Item. If you use URLs for your images, be sure your images are in jpg, gif or png formats (the image formats that most Web browsers can display).

FIGURE 21.9

Data binding two arrays from the XML data source to two items controls.

Coordinating two items controls to work together

To create the two arrays working together, as shown in Figure 21.9, first you create the combo box, by clicking and dragging the StoryCategory (Array) from the Data palette to the artboard, and choosing ComboBox.

Then add a list box by double-clicking the ListBox button in the Toolbox. Position and resize the list box using the Selection tool. Then, as we describe in the following steps, select the list box, and do four things:

- Bind the Data Context field to the SelectedItem of the combo box.
- Bind the ItemsSource property to the Story (Array).
- Define the Data Template — do this to choose what fields you want to display, and define the image as an image control and not a text control.
- Edit the template of the list box to make it look more appealing.

Here are the steps to accomplish that:

Steps: Data Binding Two Arrays

1. Select the list box.
2. To data bind the data context field to the SelectedItem of the combo box, click the Advanced Property Options button for the Data Context property, and in the Create Data Binding dialog box choose Element Property, then choose the combo box from the list on the left, choose SelectedItem from the list on the right, and click Finish.
3. To data bind the ItemsSource property of the list box to the Story (Array), click the Advanced Property Options button for the ItemsSource property, click the Explicit Data Context tab of the Create Data Binding dialog box, and choose Story (Array), as shown in Figure 21.10. (Don't click Finish, because you want to define your data template next.)
4. Define the Data Template by clicking the Define Data Template button at the bottom of the Create Data Binding dialog box, and deselecting the data fields that you don't want to appear in your list box item. Also, change the Image field from Text to Image in the drop-down list. Then click OK. Your Blend workspace should look something like Figure 21.11, with yellow borders around ItemsSource and DataContext.
5. To edit the template of the list box, first select the combo box and change the SelectedIndex property from -1 to 0. Then select the list box, and do the same. This allows you to view data in the list box, and makes it much easier to edit the template. Then select the list box and choose Edit Other Templates ⇨ Edit Generated Items (Item Template) ⇨ Edit Template.

FIGURE 21.10

Data binding the ItemsSource property to the Story (Array) in the Explicit Data Context tab.

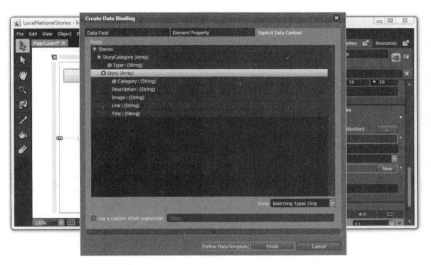

FIGURE 21.11

Data binding the ItemsSource property to the Story (Array) in the Explicit Data Context tab.

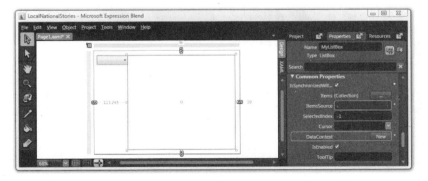

6. You can change the layout panel from a stack panel to a grid by selecting [StackPanel] in the Objects list, right-clicking on it and, from the pop-up menu that appears, choosing Change Layout Type ⇨ Grid. Now you can move the text blocks and the image around, change their font size, font, and add Bold to the title.

CAUTION Sometimes changing the layout type from a stack panel to a grid can create erratic results. (Yes, it may seem buggy.) If this happens, press Ctrl+Z and change the layout type to a canvas instead of a grid. When you do this, the canvas panel sometimes collapses to a point, but you can drag the point (the yellow dot at the upper left hand corner of the list box) using the Selection tool and expand the canvas to the size you want, to contain your text blocks and image. Then you can change the canvas to a grid, by selecting the canvas in the objects list and right-clicking and choosing Change Layout Type ⇨ Grid.

7. Test your project by pressing F5.

Creating an RSS News Feed Reader

News feeds are collections of data that may contain titles of articles, short descriptions of articles, the URL where the full article resides, and other information, such as the date, location, and author. This information can be linked to a control, such as a list box, and displayed as an RSS News Feed Reader. For example, in Figure 21.12, we data bind the RSS feed of the new line of Wiley computer books to a list box, then edit the template and activate the links to bring up the appropriate Web page for each book.

FIGURE 21.12

Data binding an RSS feed to a list box and activating the link to bring up the appropriate Web page.

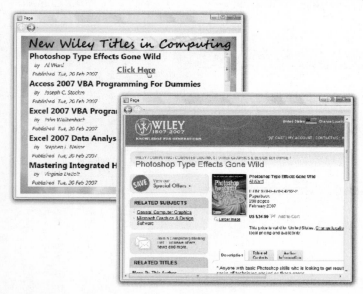

Sections earlier in this chapter describe how to add XML data sources to a project and use them. We also describe this using the BBC RSS feed in Chapter 3. In this section we'll briefly review those steps, plus activate the hyperlink so that users can bring up the link in the page (or Web browser, if you are creating an XBAP).

Linking the RSS feed to your project

Once you bring up an RSS feed and copy its URL from a browser, then you can use it in your project by clicking the +XML button in the Data palette, pasting the URL into the dialog box that appears, and clicking OK. The RSS feed tags appear in the Data palette.

Once you have the tree view of the RSS feed in the Data palette, you can add items into the artboard in ways described in the sections earlier in this chapter. You can drag an array into the artboard and data bind it to an items control such as a list box or combo box. Or you can drag an item that is not an array, and data bind it to a text control or image control or whatever control best suits the item.

You have the choice of creating the controls and then data binding the fields of the XML data source to them, or you can drag the fields from the data palette into the artboard and data bind them to controls. You can also define and edit the templates of the items controls, as described earlier in this chapter. For example, we edited the template of the list box which is data bound to the Wiley Computer books RSS feed, as shown in Figure 21.13 to create the simple RSS feed reader in Figure 21.12.

FIGURE 21.13

Editing the items template of the list box to refine the look of a simple RSS feed reader.

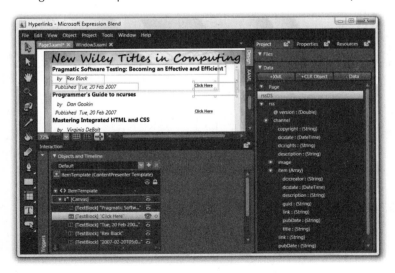

Activating the links in your RSS feed using hyperlinks

If you have a link that you want to use as the URL for a hyperlink, first be sure that you include the link in the data template for the data binding. The link appears as a text object, which is not what you want, of course, but that's the first step to using it as a hyperlink.

In the XAML code, find the link in the data template. It should look something like this:

```
<DataTemplate x:Key="itemTemplate">
  <StackPanel>
  <TextBlock Text="{Binding Mode=OneWay, XPath=title}"/>
  <TextBlock Text="{Binding Mode=OneWay, XPath=link}"/>
  <TextBlock Text="{Binding Mode=OneWay, XPath=description}"/>
  <TextBlock Text="{Binding Mode=OneWay, XPath=category}"/>
  </StackPanel>
</DataTemplate>
```

Change the line with XPath=link to a hyperlink by nesting the hyperlink in the text block and assigning the NavigateUri property to the link field of the XML data source, and nesting the text that you want for your hyperlink between the opening and closing tags of the hyperlink. For example, the preceding XAML code in bold becomes this:

```
<TextBlock>
<Hyperlink NavigateUri="{Binding Mode=OneWay, XPath=link}">Click
Here</Hyperlink>
</TextBlock>
```

 **Hyperlinks work only in pages and not windows — unless you're nesting them in a frame control within a window.**

 **For more information about working with XAML, check out Chapter 3 and Chapter 22.**

TIP You can also add or delete data fields in your data template in the XAML code. Just nest the new data field into the DataTemplate tags using the same format as the other data fields, and set the XPath equal to the field's name in the Data palette. You can delete data fields from the data template in code, as well.

Navigating with a List Box, Frame, and Data Binding

You can use a list box to bring up new content in a frame, if you want. This is similar to linking with a hyperlink, except that you click the entire list item to navigate, and view the Web page or

XAML document in a frame inside the window or page, instead of the entire page being replaced by the Web page or XAML document. You may want your list box to be full of images, or you may want it with titles, such as states that you can click on to fill a frame full of information about the state. In the example in this section, we create a list box that is full of maps of states, which you can click on to bring up a flow document reader full of information about the state. The flow document reader for each state resides in a separate page, and during runtime appears in a frame within Window1.xaml that contains the list box.

Creating the XML file and adding it to the project

To do this, you first create an XML file, perhaps using Notepad, or other code editor of your choice. The XML file should contain the titles, the URLs of the images, if any, as well as the URLs of the links. Here's an example XML file:

```
<States>
<State name="Alabama" link="Page1.xaml" pic="Alabama.jpg"/>
<State name="Alaska" link="Page2.xaml" pic="Arkansas.jpg"/>
<State name="Arkansas" link="Page3.xaml" pic="Arkansas.jpg"/>
</States>
```

Another way you could create this file is as follows:

```
<States>
<State>
<name>Alabama</name>
<link>Page1.xaml</link>
<pic>Alabama.jpg</pic>
</State>
<State>
<name>Alaska</name>
<link>Page2.xaml</link>
<pic>Alaska.jpg</pic>
</State>
<State>
<name>Arkansas</name>
<link>Page3.xaml</link>
<pic>Arkansas.jpg</pic>
</State>
</States>
```

Then you can add the XML file to your project by choosing Project ➪ Add Existing Item, or choosing Project ➪ Link To Existing Item, selecting the XML file, and clicking Open. Then add your images to the project in the same way. Then you can click the +XML button in the Project panel and type the name of the XML file as it appears in the Files palette, and click OK.

To data bind the State (Array) to the list box control, drag the State (Array), from the Data palette into the artboard, in the pop-up menu that appears choose ListBox, and click OK when it asks if you want to data bind to the ItemsSource. Then choose either pic or name or both in the Define

Data Template dialog box. (If you choose pic, be sure to choose Image as the control that you are data binding to.) Then click OK. Your list box appears.

Editing the generated items

If the image is too large, you can change the size by selecting the list box and choosing Object ⇨ Edit Other Templates ⇨ Edit Generate Items (Item Template) ⇨ Edit Template, then selecting the image in the Objects list, and resizing it. You can also add margins and perform any other formatting, if you want. Then click the up arrow beside the name of the template to exit the template.

Creating your frame and your links

To create a frame to data bind the links to, click the Rectangle button in the Toolbox and draw a rectangle where you want to position the frame in your window or page. Then select the rectangle, right-click and choose View XAML. In the XAML code, change "Rectangle" to "Frame" and delete the Fill and the Stroke properties. Then click the Design button, and your rectangle is now a frame.

> **NOTE**   We expect that a Frame control will eventually appear in the Asset Library, so you may want to check out the Asset Library first, before drawing your rectangle.

Once you have your frame, you need something to appear in the frame. You can choose File ⇨ New Item and choose Page. Create a page for each state, if you're using this example, and you may want to call your pages Alabama.xaml, Alaska.xaml, Arkansas.xaml, and so on. Then you can add different flow documents into your pages, if you want. Be sure that the names in the XML file reflect the names in your project.

> **CROSS-REF**   For information on creating and using flow documents, see Chapter 9.

Data binding

Just like the examples in the preceding sections of this chapter on data binding, first you need to data bind the DataContext property of the frame to the SelectedItem property of the list box. Then you need to bind the Source property of the frame to the link field of the XML data source in the Explicit Data Content tab of the Create Data Binding dialog box. These two steps are described next.

To bind the DataContext property of the frame, select the frame, click the Advanced Property Options buttons (the tiny button, not the big button) beside DataContext in the Common Properties palette, and choose Data Binding. In the Create Data Binding dialog box, click Element Property, choose the list box from the list on the left, and choose SelectedItem from the list on the right. Then click Finish

> **CAUTION**   Be sure to select SelectedItem and not SelectedItems. (There is a difference — one will work and the other won't.)

To bind the Source property of the frame, so that the different pages appear when you click in the list box, select the frame, and click the Advanced Property button beside the Source property and choose Data Binding. Then in the Create Data Binding dialog box, click Explicit Data Context at the top and choose link from the list. Then click Finish.

Now you can test your project by pressing F5. New pages should appear in the frame when you click the different images in the list box.

Creating and Data Binding a List View Control

The list view control is useful for showing data fields in columns and data records in rows, and allowing the user to resize column widths. Creating a list view and data binding it requires that you can data bind a list view control — and the current version of Blend requires that this be done mostly in XAML code. Figure 21.14 shows BBC headlines, date published, and news category in a list view.

FIGURE 21.14

A list view displaying fields form the BBC Science news RSS feed.

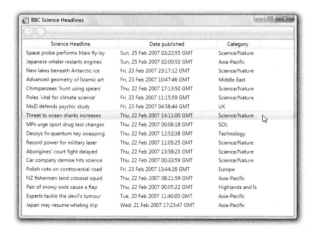

To data bind a list view control, click the +XML button, type or paste in the URL, and click OK. Then you can create a list view control by choosing ListView in the Asset Library, and clicking and dragging in the artboard to position it there.

You can then data bind the ItemsSource property of the list view to the XML data source, by selecting the list view, clicking the Advanced Property Options button beside ItemsSource in the Common Properties palette, and choosing Data Binding. Then in the Data Field tab of the Create Data Binding dialog box, choose the XML data source on the left, choose the field with (Array) that you want on the right, and click Finish. This fills the list view with lots of unformatted data. Now it's time to work with the XAML code.

If you click the XAML tab, you'll see the following code, assuming you created the list view in the LayoutRoot. We used the BBC science and technology RSS feed's URL.

```
<Page

xmlns="http://schemas.microsoft.com/winfx/2006/xaml/presentation"
  xmlns:x="http://schemas.microsoft.com/winfx/2006/xaml"
  x:Class="Listview.Page1"
  x:Name="Page"
  WindowTitle="Page"
  FlowDirection="LeftToRight"
  Width="640" Height="480"
WindowWidth="640" WindowHeight="480"
xmlns:d="http://schemas.microsoft.com/expression/blend/2006"
xmlns:mc="http://schemas.openxmlformats.org/markup-
compatibility/2006" mc:Ignorable="d">
<Page.Resources>
  <XmlDataProvider x:Key="rssDS" d:IsDataSource="True"
Source="http://newsrss.bbc.co.uk/rss/newsonline_uk_edition/sci/te
ch/rss.xml"/>
</Page.Resources>
<Grid x:Name="LayoutRoot">
  <ListView Margin="0,0,0,0"
ItemsPanel="{DynamicResource ItemsPanelTemplate1}"
ItemsSource="{Binding Mode=Default, Source={StaticResource
rssDS}, XPath=/rss/channel/item}">
 IsSynchronizedWithCurrentItem="True">
    <ListView.View>
      <GridView>
        <GridViewColumn Header="GridViewColumn"/>
      </GridView>
    </ListView.View>
  </ListView>
</Grid>
</Page>
```

Once you have something looking like the preceding code, you first want to delete `ItemsPanel="{DynamicResource ItemsPanelTemplate1}"`. Then in the GridView opening tag add the property `AllowsColumnReorder="true"`, as shown in the following code. Then you want to modify the first GridViewColumn tag properties and add more columns to your list view, using more GridViewColumn tags. In the one column that you already have, you can data bind it and change the header in XAML. The following shows the complete XAML code for the list view control in Figure 21.14. The new XAML code is in bold:

```
<Page

xmlns="http://schemas.microsoft.com/winfx/2006/xaml/presentation"
   xmlns:x="http://schemas.microsoft.com/winfx/2006/xaml"
   x:Class="Listview.Page1"
   x:Name="Page"
   WindowTitle="Page"
   FlowDirection="LeftToRight"
   Width="640" Height="480"
WindowWidth="640" WindowHeight="480"
xmlns:d="http://schemas.microsoft.com/expression/blend/2006"
xmlns:mc="http://schemas.openxmlformats.org/markup-
compatibility/2006" mc:Ignorable="d">
<Page.Resources>
   <XmlDataProvider x:Key="rssDS" d:IsDataSource="True"
Source="http://newsrss.bbc.co.uk/rss/newsonline_uk_edition/sci/te
ch/rss.xml"/>
</Page.Resources>
<Grid x:Name="LayoutRoot">
   <ListView Margin="0,0,0,0"
ItemsSource="{Binding Mode=Default, Source={StaticResource
rssDS}, XPath=/rss/channel/item}">
 IsSynchronizedWithCurrentItem="True">
     <ListView.View>
        <GridView AllowsColumnReorder="true">
<GridViewColumn DisplayMemberBinding="{Binding  Mode=OneWay,
XPath=title}" Header="Science Headline" Width="200"/>
<GridViewColumn DisplayMemberBinding="{Binding Mode=OneWay,
XPath=pubDate}" Header="Date published" Width="100"/>
<GridViewColumn DisplayMemberBinding="{Binding Mode=OneWay,
XPath=category}" Header="Category" Width="100"/>
      </GridView>
    </ListView.View>
   </ListView>
</Grid>
</Page>
```

To modify the fields that are data bound to a column, just change the value of the XPath property. The XPath names are listed in the Data palette and are the data field names. The Header properties are simply the text listed at the top of each column. And the Width is the initial width of the column in the list view. You can add as many columns to your list view as will fit, and you can add a hyperlink to a Web page, by data binding the "link" data field in a column, and using the instructions for creating hyperlinks earlier in this chapter.

This code is seen in Figure 21.15, which created the list view in Figure 21.14.

FIGURE 21.15

The XAML code for the list view shown in the previous figure.

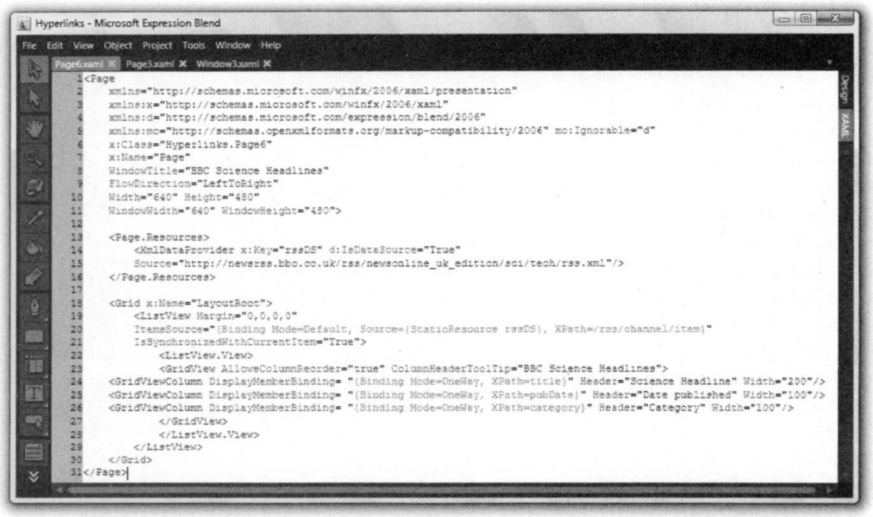

ON the WEB — For the procedural code to make the list view control sort its data when you click on a column header, see `http://msdn2.microsoft.com/en-us/library/ms745786.aspx`. And for information on making the list view editable, see `http://msdn2.microsoft.com/en-us/library/ms745183.aspx`.

Looking at the XAML of Data Binding

You may want to go into the XAML file not only to create hyperlinks, but to edit your data template or data bind other controls by hand. Or it may be a good idea to look at your XAML to make sure your Source properties are addressed in the way you want them to be — either relative or absolute.

Your data source is located between Page.Resources tags or Window.Resources tags, depending on if you are in a page or window. Its tag is XmlDataProvider. `x:Key="SelectionsDS"` is the name of the first tag in your XML file, along with a DS appended to the name. The Source property is either a relative address, or absolute, for example: `Source="MySelections.xml"` or `Source="http://rss.msnbc.msn.com/id/3032091/device/rss/rss.xml"`.

The Data Template information is also nested within the Page.Resources or Window.Resources tags. Here's an example of a data template:

```
<DataTemplate x:Key="SelectionTemplate">
  <StackPanel>
```

```
<TextBlock Text="{Binding Mode=OneWay, XPath=title}"/>
<TextBlock Text="{Binding Mode=OneWay, XPath=link}"/>
<TextBlock Text="{Binding Mode=OneWay, XPath=src}"/>
</StackPanel>
</DataTemplate>
```

You can add or delete items from the data template or change their control types by changing their tags. You can also easily change the Binding Mode from OneWay to TwoWay, if you want. More information about binding modes is found later in this chapter.

The preceding data template only includes the StackPanel, even though the array was data bound to a list box. The list box appears nested in the LayoutRoot. Here's an example of a data bound list box:

```
<ListBox Margin="139,81,0,0" x:Name="ListBox"
ItemTemplate="{DynamicResource SelectionTemplate}"
ItemsSource="{Binding Mode=Default, Source={StaticResource
SelectionsDS}, XPath=/Selections/Selection}"
IsSynchronizedWithCurrentItem="True"/>
```

Its ItemTemplate property refers to the x:Key of the DataTemplate in the preceding code. ItemsSource is the property that was data bound. The first argument represents the Binding, the second argument is the XML data source, and the third argument is the field name along with its path.

More on Data Binding Element Properties

In Chapter 3 we present an example of data binding a progress bar to a slider. And in Chapter 14, we show how to data bind the volume and balance properties of a media file to sliders. In this section, we'll explore more features of data binding element properties, such as specifying binding direction, which is also known as data flow, and creating and assigning value converters.

Specifying data flow

The Windows Presentation Foundation offers five types of data flows:

- **OneWay** — Allows a change in the source property to influence the target property, but not vice versa. For example, in Figure 21.16 on the left, the FontSize property of the list box is the data source for the Text property of the text box beside it. So in this case, changing the text in the text box will not change the font size. But if something happens in the code to change the font size in the list box, that will change the number that appears in the text box.

- **TwoWay** — Allows data to flow in two ways. For instance, in Figure 21.16, the font size in the list box in the middle changes when the user types a different number into the text box beside it. And if something happens in the code to change the font size in the list box, that will change the number that appears in the text box.

621

- **OneTime** — Similar to OneWay, except that the data source only changes the target property once. If the data source changes after that, then that change is not reflected in the target.

- **OneWayToSource** — Like OneWay, except reversed. When changes take place in the target, they are transmitted to the source, but not vice versa.

- **Default** — This is not really a type of data flow, but it is included in the list because it is an option available to you in the Create Data Binding dialog box. The Windows Presentation Foundation automatically chooses one of the above as a default, depending on what property is being data bound. The default is usually set to OneWay.

When you set the data flow options to update the source, for example when you set TwoWay or OneWayToSource, then you can also choose three ways to update the source.

- **PropertyChanged** — Updates the source when the property changes.

- **LostFocus** — Updates the source when the focus is lost. For example, in Figure 21.16 on the right, the change in the font size occurs only after the user types in the new font size and then clicks in another text box or list box, so that the focus is no longer on the text box.

- **Explicit** — Updates the source when the Explicit Data Context property changes, for example, to a new SelectedItem.

FIGURE 21.16

Text properties of text boxes data bound to font sizes of list boxes, and having three different data flows: OneWay (right), TwoWay and updated when PropertyChanged (middle) and TwoWay updated when LostFocus (left).

To set any of these data flows, when you're creating the data binding, click the down arrow at the bottom of the Create Data Binding dialog box to reveal more options, as shown in Figure 21.17. Choose the data flow option from the radio buttons, and choose when you want to update the source, (if you are assigning TwoWay or OneWayToSource) in the Update Source When list, as also shown in Figure 21.17.

FIGURE 21.17

Specifying the data flow options.

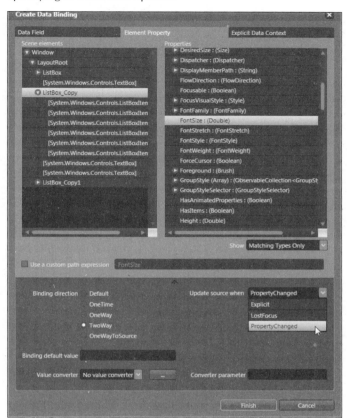

Another example of data flows is shown in Figure 21.18. In the three pairs of sliders, the sliders on the right are assigned TwoWay data flow, updating the source when PropertyChanged, so that moving either slider moves them both. The sliders in the middle are assigned TwoWay, updating the source when LostFocus, so that moving the top slider moves the bottom, but moving the bottom slider does not at first appear to have any effect on the top slider, although it jumps to the position of the bottom slider when another slider is clicked. And the sliders on the right are assigned OneWayToSource, so only the top slider moves the bottom slider and not the other way around.

FIGURE 21.18

Sliders assigned different data flows: TwoWay with PropertyChanged (left), TwoWay with LostFocus (middle) and OneWayToSource (right).

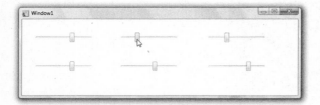

Creating and using a Value Converter

Value converters allow you to bind element properties of different types. For example, you can bind the Enable property of one control to the Visibility property of another control, so that the control only appears when the other control is enabled.

Blend offers some ready-made value converters. One is BooleanToVisibilityConverter, which sets the Visibility property to Visible when another property is set to true. Another value converter is the ZoomPercentageConverter which returns a percentage instead of a number. (It doesn't change any value; it just shows the number with two decimal places and a percentage symbol.) Other value converters you need to write yourself.

NOTE The Windows Presentation Foundation automatically causes some values to convert. For example, when you data bind a slider to a text box, the text in the text box, which is normally of the string type, converts to a type of double, which can be interpreted as a number by the slider.

Figure 21.19 shows a slider which is data bound to three text blocks and displays the value as a double type on the right, which is the default display for a double type. When using the ZoomPercentageConverter which we describe in the following section of this chapter, it's displayed as a percentage in one of the text blocks. And in the final text block, it's displayed as an integer, which requires a custom value converter, as we describe next.

Using a ready-made value converter

To data bind using a ready-made value converter, such as the ZoomPercentage for example, as shown in Figure 21.19, you can data bind the text block to the slider as you normally do, by selecting the text block, clicking the Advanced Property Options beside the Text property in the Common Properties palette, and choosing Data Binding. Then click Element Property, and choose the slider from the list on the left and Value from the list on the right. Then click the expand arrow in the Create Data Binding dialog box to view the data flow and value converter options. Click the Add new Value Converter button, choose ZoomPercentageConverter from the list in the Add Value Converter dialog box, and click OK.

FIGURE 21.19

A slider with its value data-bound to the Text property of three text blocks. The number with the many decimal places has no value converter. The percentage uses the ZoomPercentageConverter and the other a custom value converter.

Creating a custom value converter

You may run into a situation where you need to create your own custom value converter. For example, even though you can show a percentage using the ZoomPercentageConverter, you may want to display the number as an integer, instead of a percentage, and certainly instead of a double value with umpteen decimal places.

Value converters require a code-behind file. You can use the code-behind file for a window or page, as shown in Figure 21.20, or you can create a new code-behind file using Visual Studio and add it to your project. You may want to do the latter, because value conversion is not uncommon, and you may want to use the file over and over in other windows, as well as other applications. In this section, however, we describe both methods.

Creating a custom value converter in the code-behind file of a page or window

To create a value converter in a code-behind file of a page or window, open the project in Visual Studio, and in the Solution Explorer, right-click on the Window1.xaml.cs file, for example, and choose Open. In the code-behind file, you can add a method, which is not an event handler, as shown in Figure 21.20.

The name DoubleToIntegerValueConverter, was made up by us, but almost everything else in the method makes use of the .NET Framework objects and classes that are available, such as IValueConverter, Convert, ConvertBack, and System.Convert.ToInt32().

FIGURE 21.20

The code-behind file for Window1 in a project called ValueConverter. A value converter is added to the code-behind file.

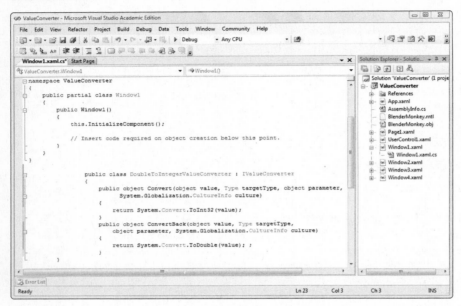

Once you add a value converter to the code-behind file, you need to build the project by pressing Shift + F6. Then you can assign it to the element property that you're data binding to in the window in Blend. To assign the value converter, you can assign it as though it was a ready-made value converter, because its name is found in the Add Value Converter dialog box, as shown in Figure 21.21.

FIGURE 21.21

Choosing the value converter in the Add Value Converter dialog box.

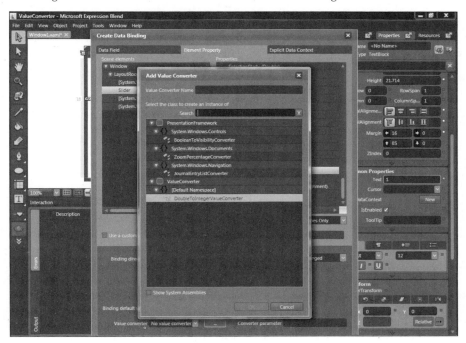

Modifying a custom value converter for other conversions

If you want to use the custom value converter for other types of conversions besides double to integer, then on the line that has `return System.Convert.ToInt32(value);` you can retype the period after Convert and IntelliSense appears with other conversion options to choose from, as shown in Figure 21.22. Usually, you can choose one and then add the `(value);` after it.

FIGURE 21.22

Using IntelliSense for other conversion options.

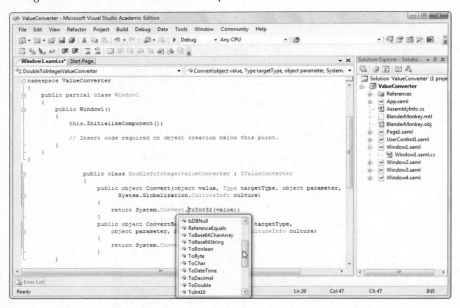

Creating a custom value converter in its own code file

Normally, you'll probably want to create a separate code file for your value converter. This is because you'll probably want to use it more than in a single window or a single page. Creating a separate file allows you to use it anywhere in your project, as well as add it to other projects, too.

To create a new code file to contain your value converter, in Visual Studio open your project, choose File ➪ New ➪ File, and choose Visual C# Class if your project is written in Visual C#, as shown in Figure 21.23, or choose Visual Basic Class if your project is written in Visual Basic. (This depends on what you chose when you created the project.) Then you can give your new code file a name, and click Open.

FIGURE 21.23

Creating a new Visual C# Class file to contain a value converter in a project called ValueConverter.

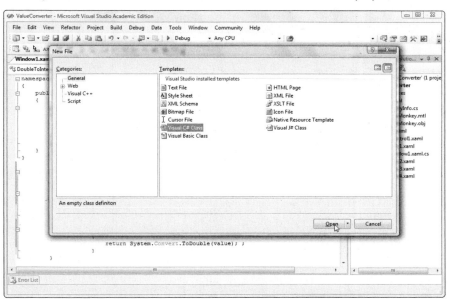

In the new code file that appears, you can add the same code that you added to the code-behind file to create a value converter, as shown in Figure 21.24. You'll also probably need to add some using statements, as well. We added all the using statements that appeared in the Windows1.xaml.cs code-behind file. (You can be more selective, if you want.)

FIGURE 21.24

Creating a value converter in its own code file.

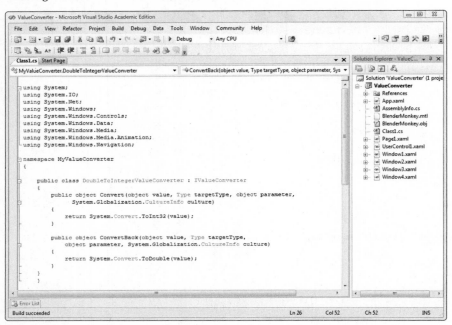

Once you create the code file for the value converter, you need to build the project in Visual Studio by pressing Shift + F6. Then you can use the value converter in Blend by clicking the Add Value Converter button beside the Value Converter combo box in the Create Data Binding dialog box, and choosing the value converter from the Add Value Converter dialog box that appears, as shown in Figure 21.25.

FIGURE 21.25

Choosing the value converter from the Add Value Converter dialog box.

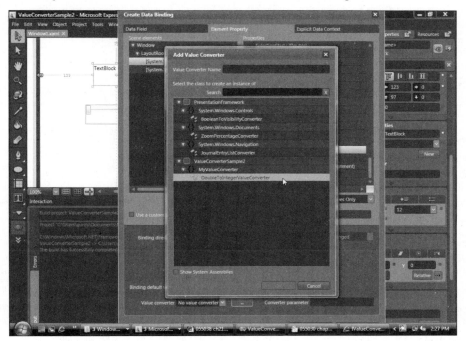

Connecting to CLR object data sources

CLR stands for Common Language Runtime, the executable code and object-oriented software environment that is the core of the Microsoft .NET Framework (and thus Windows Vista). A CLR object data source is a source of data that consists of CLR objects; such data is easily accessible to CLR-based languages such as Visual C# and Visual Basic. It can be data from a database, or you can create your own data source, for your own purposes. Unless you absolutely need to use CLR data sources, or if you feel at home with Visual C# or Visual Basic, then you may find that using XML data sources are much easier than using CLR object data sources. XML data sources often take much less coding than CLR data sources, and when you do need to write XML code, it's not procedural code, it's declarative code, which is much simpler to write.

However, databases are everywhere, and being able to access the information in them is often vital to the success of an application. And sometimes you may need to connect to them using a CLR object data source.

A lot of code goes into creating a CLR object data source, and much of the work needs to be done in Visual Studio. The basic steps are as follows:

- Connect to the database, create a data table, and fill it with selected data from the database

- Create an observable collection

- Read the data from the data table into the observable collection

> **TIP** When working with ObservableCollections, be sure to use the using statement using System.Collections.ObjectModel;

Once you've performed the preceding steps for your project in Visual Studio, then in Blend you can:

- Click the +CLR Object Data Source button in the Data palette, and choose the Observable Collection that you created in the preceding steps. The names of the fields appear in the Data palette, just as the XML data source fields appeared.

- Use the CLR object data source in the same way you use the XML data sources as described in the preceding sections.

> **ON the WEB** The steps for connecting to a database and accessing its information via a CLR object data source are described in detail in the article on the AdventureWorks Product Photos sample at **http://blogs.msdn.com/expression/articles/528008.aspx**. The article also provides a sample database that you can download and connect to.

Filtering Items in an XML or CLR Object Data Source

You may want to choose only a certain portion of your XML file items to show up in a list box or combo box, or whatever control you choose. Or you may want to filter your CLR Object data source, as well. To do this, Blend offers an input line in the Create Data Binding dialog box where you can enter a Custom XPath Expression.

For example, if you want to filter the Stories XML data source, as shown in Figure 21.9 to show just National news in a single list box, you can drag the Story (Array) into the artboard and choose List Box, then select the Custom XPath Expression check box and add the following:

/Stories/StoryCategory/Story[@Category="National"]

You can use this technique to filter any of your data sources.

Summary

- Using Blend, you can data bind element properties to other element properties, or data bind controls to data sources, often without needing to write code.

- You can add two kinds of external data sources to your project: XML data sources and CLR object data sources.

- Typical XML data sources are XML files and many types of RSS feeds.

- You can create your own XML files to bind data to controls.

- You can link to Web pages using hyperlinks, or you can link to Web pages or XAML pages using frames, by data binding the Source property to the link.

- Master/detail data binding allows you to create a control that, depending on the selected item, fills another control with appropriate data.

- You can create a value converter to bind element properties of differing types, or you can use a ready-made value converter.

- The Windows Presentation Foundation offers TwoWay data flow, which allows you to bind element properties in such a way that changing either property changes the other property.

- You can data bind an XML data source to a list view, but you need to adjust the XAML code to make it work.

- CLR object data sources are typically database items that are stored as CLR objects. In order to communicate with the Windows Presentation Foundation, the database information needs to be in the form of an ObservableCollection. Then it can be used in Blend in the same way as an XML data source.

Chapter 22

More XAML

Windows Presentation Foundation uses XAML code to create controls, vector graphics, and panels that support 3-D, animation, data binding, multimedia, and more. Windows Presentation Foundation is a major part of the .NET Framework 3.0, the application programming interface for Microsoft Vista. The .NET Framework 3.0 can run on the Vista and Windows XP operating systems. The .NET Framework 3.0 and Windows Presentation Foundation can combine declarative XAML code and the C# or Visual Basic procedural code from the code-behind file into a runtime that can be published as a XAML browser application (XBAP) or a Windows application.

Using XAML you can add graphics, panels, controls, data binding, animation, video, audio, and interactivity created using property triggers and event triggers. Separating these into XAML, while allowing XAML to access C# or Visual Basic when it needs to, makes it easier for designers to design and for developers to develop code.

Because Blend offers a WYSIWYG interface to generate XAML code, it is not always necessary to understand XAML deeply in order to design user interfaces, but a good understanding can be very helpful, and in some cases vital to achieving the needed results. In Chapter 3 we presented an overview of XAML. In Chapter 9, we discussed how to use XAML with flow documents. In Chapter 21, we looked at how XAML works with data binding, and we inserted code in the XAML view to activate the links for an RSS feed. In this chapter, we look further into how XAML works and how you can make it work for you, including how to write XAML code to create objects that are not available otherwise in Blend.

Understanding XAML

Blend automatically generates XAML code to represent whatever you create in the artboard. And what you change in the XAML code changes in the artboard, although some changes (such as changes to the appearance of the various states of a button) may not be apparent except when you run the application. Data binding, animation, media files, 3D, event triggers, property triggers and more can be automatically included into the XAML code by Blend and often need no code-behind file to function. The XAML code is enough to create rich interactive content.

In fact, in an HTML page you can even link to a XAML page document, and when the link is clicked, the XAML page comes up in Internet Explorer like an HTML page, without needing to be compiled, as long as it has no code-behind file or Code tag that requires compiling. (A XAML page such as this is known as *loose XAML* or *markup-only XAML*.) A XAML page document is created every time you choose File ➪ New Item and click Page. Figure 22.1 shows an example of a XAML page running in Internet Explorer.

CROSS-REF For more information about loose XAML, see Chapter 4.

FIGURE 22.1

A loose XAML file created in a page in Blend and displayed in Internet Explorer.

Understanding the relationship between XAML and XML

XAML is a scripting language based on XML, and XML sprang from HTML. HTML is a standardized language that allows you to structure your Web pages using *tags*. Tags are words that HTML recognizes and executes according to the name of the tag. Tags are standardized in HTML, and users generally cannot add new tags to HTML.

XML also uses tags, but it allows users to create their own tags, which increases the power of the language. XML is used to make RSS feeds and many databases easy to access. XML tags are created for each field in every file of an XML database or RSS feed.

XAML behaves similarly to XML in the following ways:

- XAML uses XML's rules of syntax. (XAML is basically XML using specialized tags.)
- XAML uses specialized tags created in XML for use by Windows Presentation Foundation.
- XAML is code. (Blend automatically generates XAML code.) Whatever you can create in Blend, you can also create by directly writing XAML code, although it may be many times more time consuming to do so.

XAML includes specialized tags for controls, panels, text features, and vector graphics for your user interface. For example, when Windows Presentation Foundation sees the XAML tag StackPanel, it executes a routine that creates a stack panel. The same is true for any of the names of the controls. Every tag in XAML has a corresponding *class* in Windows Presentation Foundation that contains the information on how to execute the tags.

Touring the XAML code file

When you create a new project, each window, page, user control, or resource dictionary that you add to the file when choosing File ➪ New Item has its own XAML code file that describes the appearance of the item.

For example, in Figure 22.2, the XAML code for an empty window is displayed on the right, and the actual window on the left.

FIGURE 22.2

An empty window (left) and the XAML code which created it in the Blend user interface on the right.

> **TIP**
>
> When you click the XAML tab to view the XAML code, you might also want to click Tab or F4 to hide the panels. This lets you use the entire Blend window to view the code.

The first line of code is the opening tag for the window, page, resource dictionary, or user control. In our example in Figure 22.2, this is <Window. There is no closing angle bracket on the first line— that is found on Line 8 after seven lines of code that specify the properties of the window.

> **NOTE**
>
> Line breaks and extra spaces don't change the way your XAML code functions but allow you to make your code more readable.

The second line of code tells the XML parser where to look to decipher the tags that are going to be used in this code.

```
xmlns="http://schemas.microsoft.com/winfx/2006/xaml/presentation"
```

The property xmlns stands for XML namespace, and WinFX is the former name of .NET Framework 3.0. So setting xmlns equal to the specified URL is essentially telling the XML parser that to use the Windows Presentation Foundation schema to decode the tags in the XML document.

XML allows you to specify multiple namespaces in your XML document. The next line of code adds another namespace:

```
xmlns:x="http://schemas.microsoft.com/winfx/2006/xaml"
```

This code tells the XML parser two things: any property name beginning with x: is to use this other schema and not the WPF schema above to decode it. And it tells XML where to find the schema. This xml namespace allows you to use properties such as x:Name="", which is assigned when you name an object in the Properties panel, and which is required by the code-behind file if you want to reference the object in the code-behind file.

The next line tells the XML parser that English, specifically US English, is the language used in the contents and attribute values of any element in the XML document.

```
xml:lang="en-US"
```

The next line of code specifies the name of the code-behind file, thus telling the XML parser where to find the code-behind file.

```
x:Class="XAMLExamples.Window1"
```

 **TIP** If you plan to create a loose XAML file (using a page instead of a window, of course), you should delete the above line.

The next line gives a name to the window, which makes the window accessible by name in the code-behind file.

```
x:Name="Window"
```

The next line adds a title to the window, which you can change to whatever you want, and which appears in your window's title bar.

```
Title="Window1"
```

If you select the window in the Design view and make it smaller by dragging the sides or a corner, the new height and width appears below in the XAML file. You can also change the height and width in this line, and the window changes in Design view. Or you can use the Layout palette to adjust the height and width of the window or page. The last bracket closes the opening tag of the Window.

```
Width="266" Height="180">
```

The following is the WPF grid nested into the window and named LayoutRoot.

```
<Grid x:Name="LayoutRoot"/>
```

And this is the closing tag for the window.

```
</Window>
```

Editing XAML code

You can use the XAML view in Blend as a XAML code editor. Whatever you change in the XAML view automatically get modified in the Design view when you click the Design tab. XAML has specific rules that you need to follow when editing it — for example, you must create correct opening and closing tags. Blend provides the Results palette to let you see a description of what any problem may be.

Blend also provides a search feature in the XAML view. And you can find the code that pertains to an object by right-clicking the object in Design view, and, in the pop-up menu that appears, choosing View XAML — the XAML code is then highlighted in the XAML view.

Adding opening and closing tags, and nesting objects

XAML code is written with opening and closing tags that contain information about the properties of the elements between the tags. You can also nest child objects between the opening and closing tags. Here's an example of opening and closing tags:

```
<Window></Window>
```

Figure 22.2 shows a more elaborated version of these tags. In the figure, the opening tag of the window extends from the first line of code to the line with the Width and Height properties. Then the Grid called the LayoutRoot is nested in the window. Then the closing tag appears.

When a control does not contain a nested item, then it is written with the opening and closing tag as one tag, in the following form:

```
<Button Margin="10,20,30,10" Content="Click Me"/>
```

This is the same as:

```
<Button Margin=10,20,30,10" Content="Click Me"></Button>
```

Properties in the opening tag are used to assign the location, size, brush, transparency, and many qualities of the element. When you do not specify a property, then the value of the property reverts to one of the following:

- The default value of the property, specified by the Windows Presentation Foundation
- The value of the property in a parent container. For example, the default height of a WPF is 22 pixels, but if that button is in a ViewBox, then the height of a button with no properties set in the XAML code reverts to the height of the ViewBox.

Figure 22.3 shows the artboard displaying the button that we just described, and the XAML code file that has the code for it.

FIGURE 22.3

On the right, a XAML code file for a window that contains a button, and, on the left, the window with the button in the artboard.

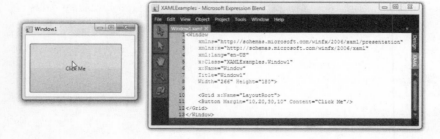

Notice that the code in Figure 22.2 <Grid x:Name="LayoutRoot"/> changed in Figure 22.3 to an opening and closing tag <Grid x:Name="LayoutRoot"></Grid> so that the button could be nested inside it.

Any object between the opening tag and closing tag is nested in the control. For example, you can nest an image in a button as follows:

```
<Button Margin="10,20,30,10">
<Image Source="DSC_0010.JPG" Stretch="Fill"/>
</Button>
```

The code for the above example is shown in Figure 22.4. We had to delete the property Content="Click Me" that appeared in the code in Figure 22.3, because a Button only takes a single nested item, and Content is considered to be a nested item.

FIGURE 22.4

The code for the button with the nested image is on the right.

Adding panels, controls, text, and vector objects

The name of every control, panel, text box, and vector object in the Asset Library is its tag in XAML. You can add a control to the application simply by typing its name between the < and the />. For example:

```
<StackPanel/>
<Ellipse/>
<RichTextBox/>
<Canvas/>
<ComboBox/>
<Menu/>
```

You can type these into the XAML code, and as long as they are nested in the LayoutRoot, then they appear in the Design View.

 When typing tags into XAML code, be sure you are not inadvertently typing a tag into an opening tag of another object. This creates an error.

If you don't specify any properties, the panels or controls revert to their default properties specified in the Windows Presentation Foundation. For example, <Button/> in a grid panel fills the panel. A <Button/> in a Canvas panel is sized at the default height and width of the WPF button, which is 22 pixels high and 42 pixels wide.

Objects can also gain properties from the panel they're nested in. For example, a button in a Wrap panel usually sizes to the height ItemHeight and ItemWidth properties of the Wrap panel, or if they are set to Auto, then the button usually sizes to the height of the largest item in the row (or height of the default button, if no objects are in the row). The width usually sizes to the ItemWidth, if set, or the default width of the button. We include the weasel word "usually" because if the wrap panel is a child of a ViewBox or other panel, it can size its children differently.

Each control has specific properties that are available for that control. To explore the properties, you can check out the Properties palette, which lists many of them. The labels of the properties are the actual property names that you can add to the object in the XAML code.

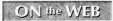 For more information about WPF objects and their properties, check out `http://msdn2.microsoft.com/en-us/library/ms752324.aspx`.

Adding event handlers in XAML that refer to the code-behind file

XAML refers to the code-behind file via event handlers. Blend does this automatically for you, but if you want to write the XAML yourself, instead of having Blend do it, you can. You specify an event handler for an object inside the opening tag for the object, by adding the name of the event, followed by an equal sign, followed by the name of the event handler that is in the code-behind file. (The name of the event is identical to the names in the Event palette, such as MouseDoubleClick, MouseLeftButtonDown, MouseRightButtonDown, and so on.) You add this statement in the XAML view to the object that the event handler refers to, just as you would specify any other property. For example, to refer to a handler in the code-behind file named "myCode" when a button is clicked, you may want to write:

```
<Button HorizontalAlignment="Left" Vertical Alignment="Top"
x:Name="myButton" Click="myCode" Content="Click Me"> </Button>
```

Windows Presentation Foundation then looks for a handler named "myCode" in the code-behind file when the button is clicked, and executes it.

Of course, all of this XAML code is added automatically if you set up the event handler in Blend. (To set up the event handler in Blend, select the object, click the Events button near the top of the Properties panel, locate the event you want in the list of events in the Properties panel, type in a name for the event handler there, and press Enter. Then Visual Studio appears and adds the event handler to the code-behind file.)

Naming elements

You may notice that sometimes the name of your object in the Objects list appears with brackets around it, and sometimes objects may have no brackets. Brackets mean that the object in the XAML file has no name that is referenced in the code-behind file. Often, you do not need to refer to objects in the code-behind file, and when you do need to, Blend creates a default name automatically for you — as long as you haven't named it yourself using the Properties panel.

Here's how to name a button and add text to it in the XAML code:

```
<Button Margin = "100,100,200,200" x:Name="myButton"
Content="Click Me"/>
```

This code creates the name for a button that can be referenced in the code-behind file as myButton, and you can now see the words Click Me on the button. Again, this all takes place automatically in Blend, but it is good to know in case you need to modify the code.

Debugging XAML

When you make a change in the XAML code and click the Design tab, if the XAML parser is unable to understand the change, an error message appears in the artboard, and errors appear in the Results palette. For example, Figure 22.5 shows the error that appeared when we tried to add the image into the button in Figure 22.4 without first deleting the Content="Click Me" property. As you can see, the error message in the Results palette was very specific regarding our mishap.

FIGURE 22.5

The Results palette contains error messages for your XAML code.

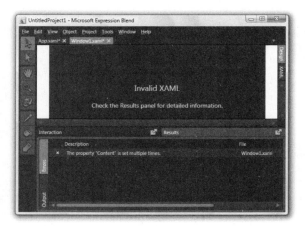

TIP When changing the XAML code, click the Design tab frequently to check to see if there are any errors in the code.

The Results palette lists the type of error as well as the line and column in which the error was detected.

TIP If you have many errors in the Results palette, sometimes fixing one error will fix them all. For this reason, you usually want to start debugging your XAML code with the first detected error.

Editing Resource Dictionary XAML files and the Application XAML file

Each resource dictionary has a XAML file that contains the XAML code for its resources. The Application XAML file is also like a resource dictionary that contains the resources of the project that are defined at the application level. To view the XAML code files for a resource dictionary or an App.xaml file, in the Resources palette right-click on any resource dictionary or the App.xaml file, and in the pop-up menu that appears choose View XAML. The XAML code appears in the XAML view, and you can make any changes to the XAML code and change any resource in the App.xaml file or resource dictionaries. Figure 22.6 shows an example of an App.xaml file containing one resource.

When you're finished viewing or editing the XAML, click the Design tab, and then in the Projects panel, double-click whatever window or page or user control that you want to work in.

FIGURE 22.6

The XAML application file contains the resources defined at the application level.

Searching in the XAML view

If you have an object that you want to search for in the XAML view, Blend allows you to search through the XAML code in two ways:

- You can select the object in the artboard, right-click, and in the pop-up window that appears choose View XAML. This brings up the XAML view and highlights the code for that object.

- You can use the Find feature for the XAML view by pressing F3. This allows you to search for words and phrases either in an up or down direction with the option of matching the case, as shown in Figure 22.7.

FIGURE 22.7

The Find feature in the XAML view.

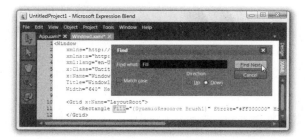

Modifying XAML code files outside Blend

Like the code-behind file, you can also edit the XAML code file in Visual Studio or other code editors, including Notepad. Visual Studio is an application designed for developers who work in code, unlike Blend, which is geared towards working in the Design view, so Visual Studio offers IntelliSense in its XAML code editor. This may or may not be a help to you, but it's good to know that it exists if you need it. Figure 22.8 shows an example of how the code-behind file looks when edited in Visual Studio with IntelliSense auto-completion.

Opening and editing your XAML code file in Visual Studio

To open your Blend project in Visual Studio, it's not necessary to close Blend. Just choose File ⇨ Open Project/Solution in Visual Studio, navigate to the Blend project file, and choose the project file with the .csproj extension. This opens the project in Visual Studio. To view a XAML code file, right-click on the XAML file name, such as Window1.xaml in the Solution Explorer, and in the pop-up window that appears choose Open. The XAML document opens, as shown in Figure 22.7.

FIGURE 22.8

A XAML file opened in Visual Studio displays the Design view, XAML code, and error list all in one window, as well as IntelliSense.

Here are some features of editing XAML in Visual Studio:

- The design, code, and error reports all appear in one window, which makes it easy to view your changes in the code and errors, without needing to click the Design view tab as in Blend.

- When you type the quotation marks that are the beginning of a property value, IntelliSense automatically appears, offering you a list of valid values to choose from.

- IntelliSense appears after you type the object name in an opening tag, offering a list of properties for that object that you can choose from.

- If you move the mouse over any tag, it displays a tool tip describing the function of the tag.

- Errors appear in the Error List below the code as they occur. They are listed as you type, which is very convenient.

For these reasons, some people may find it appealing to work in Visual Studio when editing XAML code. If you do, be sure to build your project in Blend by choosing Project ➪ Build Project, and then open it in Visual Studio. And build the project in Visual Studio, by pressing Shift and F6, before returning to Blend.

 Be sure you have the WPF and .NET Framework 3.0 extensions installed, as well as the SDK for Visual Studio 2005 or later.

If you make changes to your XAML code file in Visual Studio, then when you return to Blend, you will see a File Modified notice in Blend, as shown in Figure 22.9. If you accept the modifications, then Blend automatically makes the changes to the artboard. It's convenient to keep Visual Studio and Blend open at the same time so you can go back and forth and make changes as needed in either. Just be sure that you build the project in Blend before working in Visual Studio and vice versa.

FIGURE 22.9

Modifying your XAML code file outside of Blend causes the File Modified dialog box to appear.

Opening and editing your XAML code file in Notepad or other code editor

There's really no compelling reason for using Notepad to edit XAML code, because XAML code can be edited within Blend itself. Although, perhaps, Blend may not be available to you at the time, nor Visual Studio — in which case you can use any word processor that can edit code, such as Notepad.

To open the XAML file in Notepad, choose File ➪ Open, and in the Open File dialog box, change Text Files to All Files. Then navigate to the project folder and select a file with a .xaml extension, such as Window1.xaml or Page1.xaml. Figure 22.10 shows a project folder on the right and Notepad with Window1.xaml opened on the left.

You can change your XAML file and then resave it, just as you can with your code-behind files. When you open Blend or return to Blend if it's already open, then you'll see the File Modified dialog box, as shown in Figure 22.9.

TIP Vista, by default, does not show file extensions in the Explorer window. To view the file extensions, choose Organize ➪ Folder And Search Options, click the View tab, and then deselect Hide Extensions For Known File Types.

FIGURE 22.10

The Window1.xaml file opened in Notepad on the left.

Adding and deleting XAML namespaces

Tags in the XAML code are looked up in Windows Presentation Foundation where they are known as *classes*. The XML parser knows to look up XAML tags in the Windows Presentation Foundation because that is one of the two xmlns properties that are automatically added to a XAML document created in Blend.

You can define other namespaces in your XAML as well. For instance, Blend allows you to create user controls. The names of these controls can be used as tags in your code-behind file. Blend does this by assigning a new namespace that references the Blend project. Any time you add a user control, XML refers to that namespace for details. Figure 22.11 on the left shows an example of a simple button that is set to a different color and border and defined as a user control. On the right is the XAML code with the new namespace automatically added by Blend and the prefix of the namespace used before the name of the user control (which we gave the default name when we created the user control).

FIGURE 22.11

Blend adds a new namespace to inform the XML parser where to find the user control tags.

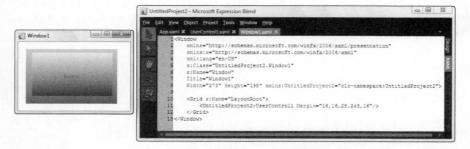

You may want to add another namespace — for example, you may want to add the Windows Forms namespace so that you can use Windows Forms in Blend.

 **For more information on adding the Windows Forms namespace so that you can use Windows Forms in Blend, see Chapter 23.**

More About Flow Documents

Flow documents have some nice features that aren't available in Blend unless you manually write them into the XAML code. For instance, you can specify page breaks, which are useful if you are using the FlowDocumentReader or FlowDocumentPageViewer. Also, if you're working within the XAML to format your flow document, you may want to use the Run tag and Section tag:

- **Run** — which lets you specify properties for parts of a paragraph, so that you can format a part of a paragraph in a different way than the rest of the paragraph. For instance, you can use the Run tag as shown in Figure 22.12 and 22.13.

- **Span** — this works the same as Run, except that it can include many nested Run tags.

- **Section** — you can make a group of paragraphs into child elements of a Section, so that you can specify properties for the whole section. For instance, you can put a group of paragraphs into a section and assign the section a different font size, as shown in Figure 22.12 and 22.13.

- **Page breaks** — to assign a page break, you can add the property BreakPageBefore="True" to a Paragraph or Section, as shown in Figure 22.12 and 22.13.

- **Preserving space** — when text ends or begins with spaces between tags, then you should add xml:space="preserve", to let XML know that the spaces are meant to be there and not to ignore them.

- **List** — in this tag you can nest the ListItem tag, which can nest a Paragraph tag. Bullets are supplied automatically for lists, and you can set the bullet style by setting the property MarkerStyle="Decimal", for instance. You can use any of the names found in the List tab of the Text palette.

- **BlockUIContainer and InlineUIContainer** — these tags nest a panel, control or vector object within them, either in its own line in the case of the BlockUIContainer, or in the middle of an existing line in the case of the InlineUIContainer, as shown in Figure 22.12 and 22.13

- **Superscript and subscript** — use the Typography.Variants property and set it to either Superscript or Subscript, as shown in Figure 22.12 and 22.13.

FIGURE 22.12

Some useful tags and properties for flow documents are put to use here.

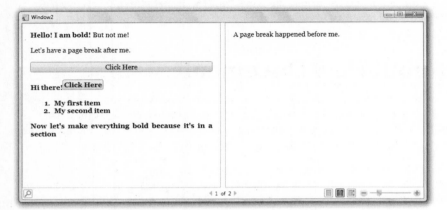

FIGURE 22.13

The XAML that created the flow document in Figure 22.12

Adding Tables

A great deal of text formatting can be performed in Design view using the Text palette, but if you want tables in your flow documents, currently you need to add them in XAML. Tables need to be nested into flow documents, which need to be nested into a flow document viewer, such as a RichTextBox, FlowDocumentReader, FlowDocumentPageViewer, or FlowDocumentScrollViewer. Tables are similar to grids, and you could use a grid inside a flow document, but tables resize very well in flow documents, and they paginate. They can also have their content selected by the user.

As you can see in Figure 22.14, the tags required for a table can be numerous, but because you can set properties (such as font, font size, and background, and more) at almost any level that the nested items inherit, the complexity is greatly reduced. You can also specify a TableRowGroup and set properties that then apply to those rows nested within it. (Each TableRow must be nested within a TableRowGroup, whether or not you set its properties.)

Tables can nest one object into each cell. The object can be any of the following:

- Paragraph
- A UIElement in a BlockUIContainer tag
- List
- Section

FIGURE 22.14

You can create tables for flow documents in the XAML view.

Summary

- XAML, which stands for Extensible Application Markup Language, follows the rules of XML, which stands for Extensible Markup Language.
- Tags in XAML correspond to classes in Windows Presentation Foundation. Each control, panel, text formatting, and vector object tool in the Asset Library in Blend has a tag that

appears in the XAML code when the UIElement is added into a window, document, user control, or resource dictionary. Windows Presentation Foundation translates the tag and creates the UIElement.

- You can edit XAML in the XAML view of the artboard, or you can edit it in Visual Studio or any external code editor. You can write your own XAML code or edit existing code.

- Blend allows you to search in the XAML code with its Find feature. You can also search the XAML code by selecting an object in Design view, right-clicking, and choosing View XAML.

- You can add tags into XAML that help you format your flow documents as well as create tables for flow documents.

- Every time you click the Design tab, the XAML code is processed. Errors appear in the Results palette.

Chapter 23

Putting It All Together

Performance is an important part of creating an application. Lack of performance can require you to drop CPU-intensive parts of your project, even after you've spent many hours developing such features. But aesthetic improvements to an application are not worth the loss of reasonable performance, so it's always good to test your performance as you go, and avoid pitfalls. In this chapter we discuss what you can do to increase the performance in your WPF application. Windows Presentation Foundation uses hardware acceleration to enable many appealing new features, but some things are still not hardware accelerated. Knowing what may be good to avoid can be useful.

We also discuss how you can integrate WPF applications with Windows Forms. You can include WPF controls and panels into Windows Forms applications, and you can include Windows Forms controls into WPF applications. Because numerous Windows Forms applications have already been written, the task of re-writing them for WPF may seem huge at first, but it can be done little by little, if you want.

Finally, we discuss where to get more information, if needed. .NET Framework 3.0 is a new technology and much help is available on the Internet. We cover the biggest and best sources of help.

Integrating Windows Forms Applications with Windows Presentation Foundation Applications

Using Blend, you can integrate your Windows Forms applications with your WPF applications in two ways: you can add Windows Forms controls into the XAML code file, or you can add Windows Forms controls into the code-behind file.

Adding Windows Forms controls to the code-behind file

Basically, to run Windows Forms controls from the code-behind file in Blend, you need to instantiate a WindowsFormsHost object, which has the ability to run Windows Forms controls as child members. Once you create the Windows Forms Host, you can add whatever Windows Forms controls you need to that host.

STEPS: Adding Windows Forms controls to your code-behind file

1. Create an application in Blend, choose Project ➪ Build Project, and save it. Then open the application in Visual Studio.

2. In Visual Studio, choose Project ➪ Add Reference. In the .NET tab of the Add Reference dialog box, select System.Windows.Forms and WindowsFormsIntegration. Click OK.

3. In Visual Studio, save the project and choose Project ➪ Build Solution.

4. Return to Blend. There should be a Project Modified message box, informing you that the project's been modified. Click OK to reload the project.

5. Create a panel to contain your Windows Forms application in the artboard. Name the panel in the Properties panel. For example, suppose you want to add a Windows Forms application to a dock panel. First you add a dock panel to the artboard, and give the panel a name, such as MyDockPanel, in the Properties panel. Then choose Project ➪ Build Project.

6. Select the dock panel in the artboard, and click the Events button near the top of the Properties palette to open the Events palette. Find "Loaded" in the events list, and type in a name for your method, such as DockPanelLoaded, or whatever you want to call your method. Then press Enter.

7. Visual Studio reappears with the code-behind file open. You can add the following using statements in the code-behind file to the list of using statements, if they are not already there:

```
using System.Windows.Forms;
using System.Windows.Forms.Integration;
```

8. In the DockPanelLoaded event handler in the code-behind file, add a WindowsFormsHost to place your Windows Forms code into. The following example adds a Windows Forms button to a WPF control named "DockPanel".

```
private void DockPanelLoaded(object sender,
System.Windows.RoutedEventArgs e)
{
WindowsFormsHost myHost = new WindowsFormsHost();
//add your Windows Forms code here. For example, to add a
button,
//you write as follows:
System.Windows.Forms.Button myButton = new
System.Windows.Forms.Button();
myButton.Text = "Button";
myHost.Child = myButton; //Add controls to the host.
MyDockPanel.Children.Add(myHost); //Add the host to the Dock
Panel.
}
```

9. Test your application by pressing F5. Figure 23.1 shows an example of a windows forms button in a WPF application window.

FIGURE 23.1

A Windows Forms button in a WPF application.

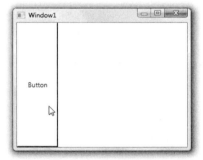

Adding Windows Forms controls in XAML

When you add Windows Forms controls in the XAML code file, you can view them in the Design view of the artboard. Because of this, you may want to always add the Windows Forms controls in XAML, instead of adding them in code in the code-behind file. However, in this case you are restricted from selecting the control itself, so this method may be only marginally useful. But try it out if you want.

655

To add Windows Forms Controls in XAML, you first need to add the references to System.Windows.Forms and WindowsFormsIntegration in Visual Studio, as described in Steps 1-3 above, or see the section, "Adding References" later in this chapter.

Once the references are added into the project, then if you want to add the Windows Forms controls in the XAML code, you need to do two things:

- Add namespaces for System.Windows.Forms and WindowsFormsIntegration into the XAML code.

- Nest your control between WindowsFormsHost opening and closing tags.

Adding the namespaces to the XAML code

Click the XAML tab on the side of the artboard to view the XAML code. In the section of the code containing the XML namespaces (xmlns), add the following:

```
xmlns:wfi="clr-
namespace:System.Windows.Forms.Integration;assembly=WindowsFormsI
ntegration"
xmlns:wf="clr-
namespace:System.Windows.Forms;assembly=System.Windows.Forms"
```

Because of line-length limitations in this book, we can't show this here, but no space should exist when you type "clr-namespace" in the preceding code.

 For more information about adding namespaces to XAML code, see Chapter 22.

Adding the Windows Forms controls

To add a Windows Forms control, add it in the same way you can add any control, using tags — but before the tag, type in the prefix of the namespace. For example:

```
<Grid x:Name="LayoutRoot">
<WindowsFormsHost>
<wf:Button Text="Windows Forms Button" />
</WindowsFormsHost>
</Grid>
```

This adds a WindowsFormsHost control to a grid panel and adds a windows forms button into the Windows Forms Host control. By default the Windows Forms Host sizes itself to fill the grid, although you can adjust this in Design mode. Select it in the Objects list and use the Layout palette to adjust the size and position. The actual button, however, is not selectable in the Objects list. Depending on what your goals are, this may or may not be a problem for you. An example of our button is shown in Figure 23.2.

FIGURE 23.2

A Windows Forms button created in XAML.

Integrating Blend applications into Windows Forms applications

You can also add WPF controls and panels into Windows Forms applications. Since Windows Forms applications do not understand XAML, they need to be added in the code-behind file.

In Visual Studio you need to do the following to view WPF controls in a Windows Forms application:

STEPS: Adding WPF controls into Windows Forms

1. In Visual Studio, choose File ➪ Open ➪ Project/Solution and open the Windows Forms application.

2. Choose Project ➪ Add Reference and add the following reference assemblies to your new application:

   ▪ PresentationCore

   ▪ PresentationFramework

   ▪ WindowsBase

   ▪ WindowsFormsIntegration

3. Just as when you add Windows Forms to WPF apps, the WPF controls require a host object to work in a Windows Forms application. This is known as the Element Host. Add the following sample code to the code-behind file of the form, perhaps in the equivalent of a Loaded event handler.

   ```
   ElementHost myhost = new ElementHost();
   System.Windows.Controls.CheckBox myCheckBox = new
   System.Windows.Controls.CheckBox();
   //add whatever properties you need to set to the WPF checkbox
   here
   myhost.Controls.Add(myCheckBox);//Adds the checkbox to myhost
   ```

```
myHost.Dock = DockStyle.Fill;// myhost fills the entire form
this.Controls.Add(myhost);//Adds myhost to the Controls
Collection
```

Notice that you need to define System.Windows.Controls before the WPF control CheckBox, as well as all WPF controls that could be confused with their System.Windows.Forms equivalents.

Adding References

The Reference folder in the Project panel of Blend contains the DLLs that run your application, as well as Blend itself. This folder may contain the following as a default:

- PresentationCore.dll
- PresentationFramework.dll
- System.dll
- System.Xml.dll
- WindowsBase.dll

You may find that you need to add more DLLs to your program. For instance, you may want to use Windows Forms controls in your application. Windows Forms requires you to add the following DLLs to your References folder:

```
System.Windows.Forms.dll
WindowsFormsIntegration.dll
```

To add a reference, follow steps 1-3 in "Adding Windows Forms controls to your code-behind file" earlier in this chapter. Figure 23.3 shows the Add Reference dialog box available in Visual Studio.

NOTE   Blend also has a menu item to add a reference, but it is much easier to do it in Visual Studio. Blend requires you to know where the folder containing the DLLs is stored in your hard drive, and you need to browse to that folder and choose your DLL from there. Visual Studio makes it simple by offering you a list of all references.

CAUTION   If the reference that you're looking for is not listed, then you may need to update Visual Studio to .Net Framework 3.0, as well as add the extensions for WPF. If you Google "visual studio wpf extension download", you can click on what will probably be the topmost link. (That's easier than typing the complex URL.)

FIGURE 23.3

Adding a .Net Framework reference using the Add Reference dialog box in Visual Studio.

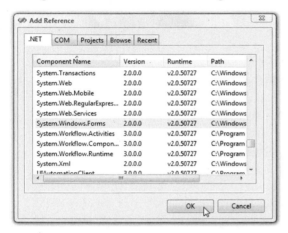

Increasing Your Performance

When creating your application, you'll want it to perform as well as possible, so your user doesn't get bored waiting for it to respond or have to buy more hardware to support it. So, satisfactory performance is a necessary ingredient of a well-designed application.

The following are some basic considerations when designing performance into your application. These points are specific to the Windows Presentation Foundation, but remember to use common sense rules as well, such as going easy on 3D, animation, video, and image sizes. And test your performance as you go to avoid surprises.

- Canvas is your most efficient panel, with stack panels and dock panels next. Grid is the slowest.

- Use text blocks instead of flow documents, text boxes or rich text boxes, whenever possible. In tests performed at Microsoft, text blocks were 32 times faster to render than flow documents.

- Use a single text block instead of multiple text blocks when possible.

- Turn off hyphenation, column balancing, underlining and other features in flow documents if you're not using them.

- Minimize the number of images, and keep their sizes small.

- If you are using more than one flow document on a single page, then combine them into a single flow document, if possible.

- Put images and even vector graphics into the background of a panel whenever possible, rather than in an image control.

- Avoid using large visual brushes or large drawing brushes.

- Avoid using bitmap effects. (However, Microsoft is working to make bitmap effects faster, so you may want to test this point.)

- Avoid using large image brushes, especially when part of the image is hidden.

- Combine images into a single image whenever possible. For example, create filmstrips if you are showing many images.

- Combine complex vector graphics into an image, when possible.

- Use resources when possible. Using a single resource for an object with multiple instances, such as a button or brush, reduces rendering time.

- Use resources on the application or window or page level and not on the resource dictionary level whenever possible.

- Avoid using the Tile mode of the Tile Brush when possible. (Perhaps you can tile it in a graphics program and convert it to a bitmap, then use the image for your purpose.)

- Avoid using opacity masks. (You can sometimes achieve the same affect as an opacity mask using a linear gradient that fades to transparency.)

- It is better to assign opacity to a brush rather than an object when possible. Set the Alpha slider in the color picker.

- Layering windows may slow your application.

- Avoid doing fancy 3D lighting effects, when possible.

- Use 2D instead of 3D objects when possible.

- Avoid radial gradients because they're only accelerated in hardware with high-end graphics cards, although this may change.

- 3-D anti-aliasing may slow the application unless the user has a high-end graphics card, and is running Vista, as well.

- When updating items in a list box, bind the ItemsSource of the list box to an ObservableCollection class and not a CLR List object. This was 80 times faster with each update to your list box in tests performed at Microsoft.

- If adding nodes to a tree, add the items from the top down and not from the bottom up. The top-down approach was about 5 times faster in tests.

- If you're binding a CLR object data source to a control and you have a choice of using IList or IEnumerable, use IList. It's faster.

- CLR data sources are slightly faster than XML data sources.

- If you have a large 3D object and you don't need it to respond to the mouse, then set its IsHitTestVisible property to False.

ON the WEB Some blogs for Microsoft employees analyzing WPF performance are as follows:

```
http://blogs.msdn.com/henryh
http://blogs.msdn.com/timothyc (You can find a link here to
Kiran Kumar's paper on optimizations using WPF.)
http://blogs.msdn.com/ricom/default.aspx
```

CROSS-REF To see Microsoft's document on Optimizing WPF Application Performance, check out `http://msdn2.microsoft.com/en-us/library/aa970683.aspx`.

TIP If you want to see what parts of your application are rendered in software and what parts make use of hardware acceleration, use an application called "Perforator". This application changes the color of parts of your interface or website that are not hardware accelerated. This is good to know because whatever is rendered in software is obviously slower than what is rendered in hardware, so this gives you a clue to what may be slowing down your application. Perforator is available from the WinFX Software Development Kit (SDK).

Getting Help

While creating your applications, you may find you need to get some help. Fortunately, several resources exist for this purpose.

- Online forums
- Newsgroups
- Blogs
- Webcasts
- Technical chats

The home page for Microsoft Technical Communities includes links to all of these resources and can be found at `www.microsoft.com/communities/default.mspx`. In each link, you can choose the topics that concern you.

Online Forums and newsgroups

The main online forums for Blend are as follows:

- The Microsoft Expression Blend forum is found at `http://www.microsoft.com/communities/newsgroups/en-us/default.aspx?dg=microsoft.public.expression.interactivedesigner&cat=&lang=en` (or just Google "Expression Blend discussion group" and click the link).
- The Windows Presentation Foundation forum is found at `http://forums.microsoft.com/MSDN/ShowForum.aspx?ForumID=119&SiteID=1`.

Also, a list with links to all of Microsoft's forums can be found at `http://forums.microsoft.com/msdn/`.

Newsgroups

Newsgroups may contain the same information as online forums, but they are available via your email. Newsgroups have several advantages:

- Any attachments referred to in online forums are usually available only through a newsreader.
- You may be able to search and read messages without needing to be online.

Blogs

Many developers have their own blogs in which they offer information and tutorials. These can be helpful, especially if you can zero in on the blogs related to your topic of interest. For example, the blogs for WPF performance issues are listed by the On the Web icon in the previous section of this chapter.

The main blog for the Expression developers is at `http://blogs.msdn.com/expression/`. This is a good resource with many useful links.

Also, you can search for blogs by keywords, or by category. And you can search individual posts or the keywords or categories for an entire blog. To find a search box to do all this, go to the Microsoft Technical Communities homepage at `http://forums.microsoft.com/MSDN/ShowForum.aspx` and click Blogs.

Webcasts

Microsoft webcasts can be very informative. Use these when you want to get in-depth knowledge of a particular topic, and you have time to sit back and enjoy the show. Webcasts can be live or archived. Live webcasts have the benefit that you can email questions and may get some live feedback. You need to register for Microsoft's live webcasts or archived webcasts, but the registration is free.

You can view all the recent Microsoft webcasts at `http://www.microsoft.com/events/webcasts/ondemand.mspx`. Microsoft sometimes releases a dozen webcasts a day, so the list may be quite long.

A search engine for finding both archived webcasts or future webcasts is at `www.microsoft.com/events/AdvSearch.mspx`. This search engine only searches categories, and currently Expression Blend is not a category. However, this will almost certainly change, so it's worth checking.

Technical Chats

About a dozen Microsoft-sponsored technical chats may be going on at any time during the day or weekends. They cover a wide range of topics and are found at www.microsoft.com/ communities/chats/default.mspx. You can also sign up for an RSS feed at this location, so you'll always stay informed of future chats.

Summary

- You can use WPF panels and controls along with Windows Forms, by adding WPF to Windows Forms, or by adding Windows Forms to WPF. This gives you the opportunity to slowly transition from Windows Forms applications to WPF.

- You can add Windows Forms controls in your XAML code or into the code-behind file. If you add it in XAML, then you can view it in the artboard as you work with it.

- Many ways exist to increase the performance of your WPF application, including using TextBlocks instead of RichTextBoxs, or using resources when possible.

- Help is available from the Microsoft Expression Blend discussion group or the Microsoft Expression WPF discussion group.

- Microsoft offers webcasts covering many topics in Expression Blend, as well as the Windows Presentation Foundation.

Glossary

2D — two-dimensional, flat, like a drawing.

3D — three-dimensional, having height, width and depth, like a sculpture.

3D model — a three-dimensional object that can be seen from all sides.

3D Studio — a popular 3D modeling, rendering, and animation software package for MS-DOS that was the predecessor to 3D Studio Max.

3D Studio Max — one of the most widely used 3D modeling, rendering, and animation software packages for Windows. It is currently owned by Autodesk.

3D transition — a transition in a presentation, a video, or an animation in which you animate a 3D image or window off the screen to reveal another image or window beneath it.

Access key — an alphanumeric key that when used with the Alt key activates a control. These keys are meant to aid people who have difficulty using a computer mouse. (Compare this with *shortcut key*.)

Active container — an object in Blend that is ready to accept a child element. It has a yellow border surrounding the object and surrounding its name in the Objects list, to indicate that it is the active container.

Adaptive layout — a user interface layout that automatically rearranges itself for windows of different sizes and for different monitor resolutions.

Additive animation — Blend allows you to animate the same object using multiple timelines. When these timelines run simultaneously, the animations are combined, and this is called additive animation.

Administrator — a type of account in Windows Vista that provides elevated privileges so that you may install applications and change system settings.

Advance organizer — a short introduction, in words or images, that familiarizes the user with what is to come.

Aero — a user interface theme for Windows Vista suitable for use on computers with advanced graphics capability. Aero features include — Aero Glass; live, thumbnail-sized screenshots in the Windows taskbar; and the ability to stack and flip through windows in a virtual 3D space.

Aero Glass — a feature of Windows Vista's Aero user interface in which windows appear to be made of a reflective, translucent glassy material.

Aesthetic Usability Effect — a phenomenon documented by research that shows that more aesthetically pleasant products are easier to use and are perceived as more useful.

Affordance — a property of an object or an environment that suggests how to use or how to interface with the object or environment.

Alpha — the measure of the opacity of an object. For example, an alpha value of 0 means the object is transparent; an alpha value of 1 means the object is opaque. Alpha values are set in the Brushes palette.

Alignment — the process of lining up objects vertically or horizontally or both. Blend offers an alignment feature in the Object menu.

Ambient light — Ambient light is the general brightness of a 3D environment — the reflected light that's bouncing around everywhere but doesn't emerge from a strongly defined source. Ambient light is one of the four kinds of lights provided by Blend. (The others are directional lights, point lights, and spot lights.)

Analogous colors — If you arrange the colors of the rainbow in a wheel with the colors red, magenta, blue, cyan, green, and yellow equally spaced from each other, the colors near to each other on the color wheel are called analogous colors. (Compare this with *complementary colors*.)

Animation — the technique of making still images or objects appear to move and come to life by presenting successive images with small changes one after the other.

Anti-aliasing — smoothing or blending the transition of colors in an array of pixels, such as, for example, the dots on a computer screen, to remove the staircase-like "jaggies" that appear when rendering diagonal lines in rows and columns of pixels.

Anticipation — in animation, an action that prepares the audience by foreshadowing an upcoming action — for example, a character crouching before making a high jump.

Apex — in typography, the topmost point of the letter A.

API — Application Programming Interface. A set of calling conventions that a programmer may use to access a set of pre-built routines. This can make writing software much simpler, because the calling conventions typically remain the same even when the implementation of the underlying pre-built routines evolves.

Application theming — creating an integrated visual theme for an application by customizing the look of every component of the user interface. This may be particularly suitable for games or other applications in which the overall immersive experience is more important than the familiarity that comes from using the standard Windows XP or Windows Vista theme.

Archetype — an idea, symbol, or pattern that serves as the basis for many later variations, perhaps over long spans of time. Carl Jung theorized that a collective unconscious exists among human beings that gives them a propensity to repeat basic archetypal themes and forms cross-culturally.

Arms — in typography, the parts of the letters E and F that extend to the right.

Artboard — the area of the Blend user interface into which you drag, drop, and modify the visual elements of your user interface.

Ascender — in typography, the parts of the letterform that are above the meanline, for letters such as d and f.

Asset Library — in Blend, the palette that contains simple controls, system controls, custom controls, and more. It is available as a popup panel from the last button in the Toolbox.

Attribute — a specific value of a property.

Auto exit — the process of automatically moving to the next editable text box in a form once the current text box has been filled out. This saves the user from the need to take time to click in the next text box.

Auto complete — the process of automatically offering options to complete the beginning of what your user types. This is popular in Web browsers, for example, when you type a partial URL and a list of options appears that you may use to complete the URL.

Avalon — the former code name for the Windows Presentation Foundation (WPF).

BAML — Binary Application Markup Language. XAML gets compiled into BAML as a first step in its compilation before it is merged with procedural code.

Baseline — in typography, the imaginary line on which the letter x sits. (Compare this with *mean-line*.)

Bevel join — a type of corner join for a rectangle or path, which creates two angled sides and a flat top. This is set in the Stroke palette and can only be created if the stroke of the rectangle or path is wide enough for it to show.

Binding — the process of linking properties to other properties or data.

Bitmap graphics — images (such as digital photographs, for example) that are defined by rows and columns of pixels. (Compare this with *vector graphics*.)

Blender 3D — a popular 3D modeling, animation and rendering software package that is distributed under the terms of the GNU GPL, a free software license. Available from `www.blender3d.com`.

Blog — a Web log — a journal of textual and/or audio-visual content, posted periodically to a Web page in reverse chronological order.

Body — in typography, the height of the letter x in lowercase. Also called *x-height*.

Bowl — in typography, each round stroke in letters such as B, b, and P.

Border — a panel that allows you to create borders for objects that normally don't have them. You nest the borderless object inside the border object, and apply a brush to the border, and behold — you have a border.

Brackets — in typography, the skinny vertical lines in letters such as N. (Compare this with the typographic definition of *stroke*.)

Brush — a category of user interface elements in Blend. Brushes can modify the appearance of an object. Brushes include the Solid Color Brush, the Linear Gradient Brush, the Radial Gradient Brush, the Tile Brush, the Drawing Brush, the Image Brush, and the Visual Brush.

Button — a control that when clicked by the user can trigger a response.

C# — an object-oriented language created by Microsoft. It's based on the syntax of C++ and borrows ideas from Delphi, Visual Basic, and Java.

Camera Orbit — a tool in Blend that changes the angle of the camera's view of 3D objects.

Canvas panel — a container in which objects can be placed anywhere, regardless of their relationship to other objects.

Cap — a type of end for a line or path. In Blend, a cap may be a round cap, a flat cap, a square cap, or a triangle cap. Caps are set in the Stroke palette.

Cap height — in typography, the height of uppercase letters such as E and P.

Carpal Tunnel Syndrome — compression of the median nerve due to inflammation or trauma as it travels through the carpal tunnel to the wrist.

Check box — a control that defines an on or off condition. Check boxes are independent of each other, so multiple check boxes can be checked at once in any combination.

Child element — an object nested within another object, such as a panel within a panel.

Class — in object-oriented programming, a set of related variables and functions that define how objects of the class behave. Objects are known as instances of the class.

ClearType — a system designed by Microsoft and used by Blend to render fonts within a fraction of a pixel for more accurate positioning, rendering, and anti-aliasing.

ClickOnce — a way to deploy your Web application so that it downloads and installs onto the user's computer with a single click.

CLR — Common Language Runtime. Used in creating the .NET Framework of precoded solutions to common programming needs, including the Windows Presentation Foundation. Any language (including C#, Visual Basic .NET, and others) that can be compiled into CLR is compatible with the Windows Presentation Foundation.

CLR Objects — data items stored in the Common Language Runtime format used by the many programming languages supported by the .NET Framework.

Code — in Blend, either procedural code (such as C# or Visual Basic) or XAML code, which together compile into a single runtime to create a user interface.

Code-behind file — a file that contains the procedural code for a window, page, user control or other XAML document in Blend. This procedural code is in the language (C# or Visual Basic) that you specify when you create the application. You may view the contents of the code-behind file in an editor by double-clicking the file in the Projects palette.

Color picker — a tool for assigning colors, in the Brushes palette.

Combo box — a list box with a drop-down list. A list box may show only a single item when not in use.

Complementary colors — colors opposite each other on a color wheel, when you arrange the colors of the rainbow in a wheel with the colors red, magenta, blue, cyan, green, and yellow equally spaced from each. (Compare this with *analogous colors*.)

Composition — in Blend, combining objects or controls. Blend allows you to create complex compositions of controls by letting you nest controls within other controls. For example, you can nest a combo box into a menu item.

Concept prototyping — testing potential ideas by quickly mocking up and exploring model designs, perhaps in the form of sketches, flow charts, scenarios, or storyboards.

Cone angle — the angle of the cone within which a light emits.

Congratulations page — may be the last pane of a wizard, which simply congratulates the user on finishing the wizard. This used to be popular, but is now often considered superfluous.

Constraint — a restriction placed on a feature of an application, normally to disallow the user from going beyond the capabilities of the application or creating mistakes.

Container — in Blend, an object that can contain a child element.

Content — a property of several controls in Blend. The content can be audio, video, text, 3D, and more.

Content presenter — an element that allows you to add video, text, 3D, and or other content to, for example, a button or other control in which the content presenter is nested.

Context menu — a pop-up menu.

Context-sensitive menu — a pop-up menu.

Control — a part of your user interface that the user can control, such as a list box, combo box, menu, or button. Blend provides many ready-made controls that you may modify to suit the needs of your application.

Control handles — define the tangent (and thus the shape) of a curve in Blend, and can be dragged out from a node when you create a curve with the Pen tool. They can also be inserted at a later time.

Control template — defines the appearance of a control during mouse clicks, mouse overs, and other states. Each control has a default template, which you may modify as desired.

Counter — in typography, the hollow space inside letters such as B, b, e and p.

Crossbar — in typography, the horizontal line in the letters A and H; also called the horizontal stem.

Cross stroke — in typography, the horizontal line in a lowercase t.

Current Time Display — the input box above the tracks of a timeline in the Objects and Timeline palette. It displays the current position of the playhead in the format MM:SS.xxx (minutes: seconds. milliseconds). You can type a value into the Current Time Display to cause the playhead to jump to that time.

Data — information, perhaps stored in a database.

Data binding — the process of linking data or properties to other related properties. For example, you can data bind the value of a slider to the size of text in a text box to allow the user to resize text with the slider. Or you can data bind a list box to contain data from a database, for example.

Data source — the source of the data, which in Blend is typically either an XML file (such as an RSS feed, for example) or a CLR object.

Data template — a template supported by some controls, such as list boxes. The data template specifies what fields of a data source are to be used and how they are laid out.

Decay — a percentage and a range that defines how much and at what distance a 3D light falls off in Blend. You can specify a linear decay, a quadratic decay, or no decay (in which case the light falls off suddenly at the range indicated).

Decorative fonts — fonts with letterforms that are more elaborate and fanciful than typical serif or sans serif fonts. These fonts may have letterforms incorporating pictorial elements, such as depictions of fireworks, flowers, rockets, or teddy bears.

Deep space — the illusion of three-dimensional space on a two-dimensional screen. The illusion may be heightened by incorporating images with depth cues such as perspective, movement perpendicular to the screen surface, deep focus, overlapping objects, shadows, and others.

Defined style — the appearance of an object, including the templates, if the object is a control. A style can be assigned to any similar object, so that changing the style in one object can change the style in all objects assigned that style. This allows for flexibility in the design process.

Deployment — making your Blend project available for others to run, by publishing it to a server, a Web page, or a computer file that others can access.

Descender — the parts of a letterform below the baseline, in letters such as p and q, for example.

Directional light — a 3D light that is like angled sunlight. One of the four kinds of light provided by Blend. (The others are ambient lights, point lights, and spot lights.)

Disabled — a control that is not operational and usually grayed out.

Disclosure triangle — a triangle that you may click to reveal nested objects in a tree view. The triangle points to the right when the nested objects are hidden and points down when the nested objects are revealed. Same as a *drop-down arrow* or *down arrow*.

Dissolve — a transition in a presentation, a video, or an animation, in which the last few frames of the first shot fade out while the first few frames of the next shot fade in, creating the illusion that the final images of the first shot are overlaid onto the beginning image of the next shot.

Dock panel — a panel in which you can stack child elements along any of the four sides of the panel.

Dolly — to move a camera either toward or away from a 3D object.

Down arrow — a triangular arrow that you may click to reveal nested objects in a tree view.

Drawer — a user interface element that is like a drawer in a bureau and that may be slid open to reveal a collection of components.

Drawing object — the object used to create a drawing brush.

Drawing brush — a brush that allows you to assign any object to become a fill.

Drop-down arrow — a triangular arrow that you may click to reveal nested objects in a tree view. The triangle points to the right when the nested objects are hidden and points down when the nested objects are revealed. Same as a *disclosure triangle*.

Ease In — gradually accelerates the interpolation between two keyframes for more natural motion effects.

Ease Out — gradually decelerates the interpolation between two keyframes for more natural motion effects.

Editable text box — a text control in which the user can type text while the application is running. These include text box, rich text box, and password box.

Egyptian fonts — fonts (such as Century Expanded, designed in 1895) that contain less contrast between thick and thin strokes, and more slab-like serifs. Also called *Slab Serif fonts*.

Element — an object in Blend, a part of an object (such as a property of an object), or a grouped object. An element can be vector objects, video files, audio files, panels, controls, or others. Basically, anything that has a row in the Objects list is an element.

Element order — the order in which elements are stacked in the Objects list.

Elevated administrator — in Windows Vista, the administrator account runs with limited privileges, just as a standard user account, except when the administrator wants to install applications or change system settings; then the administrator elevates his account, and becomes an elevated administrator.

Elevated privileges — permission to install applications and change system settings in Windows Vista. Elevated privileges are granted to the administrator when he or she requests them, or to standard users when they supply the administrator's password.

Ellipse — an oval. The Ellipse tool in the Tools palette allows you to create circles and ellipses. You can change them to paths and add nodes that you can move to change them into other shapes as well.

Event — an action that can generate a response from the application. Events are often user-generated, such as clicking a button or moving your mouse over a control.

Event handler — the procedural code that is called when a specific event occurs.

Event trigger — an action (such as a mouse click, a mouse over, or a specific key being pressed) that controls a timeline. Timelines can be controlled by event triggers and property triggers.

Evolutionary prototyping — developing, testing, and reworking a model until it becomes the actual final product.

Expander — a control that you can add to a main menu to hide menu items that you don't users to see unless they click on the expander. This simplifies your application for a beginner, and the expert can click on the expander to view all possibilities. (We're not so sure this is always a good idea from a usability perspective, though.)

Exposure Effect — the phenomenon that people tend to favor choices that are familiar even if they are not the ideal choice. Also known as the Mere Exposure Effect.

External resource dictionaries — you can create a resource dictionary containing your styles and templates so that you can use them in your other applications. When you access these resources in the other applications, they are called external resource dictionaries.

Extrude — to give a 2D object depth in space, as if turning it into a stencil and forcing a piece of clay through it.

Falloff Angle — if you imagine that light is emitting within two cones, one within the other, with a stronger beam of light in the inner cone, then the difference between the angle of the inner cone and the outer cone is the falloff angle.

Fibonacci sequence — a sequence of numbers in which the last two numbers are added to get the next number. For example, 1, 1, 2, 3, 5, 8, 13, and so on.

Field of View — the size of the area that you can see when looking through a camera. You can zoom in or out of a 3D object in Blend by selecting the camera and changing its Field of View value.

Figure — the primary subject of an image; everything else is the *ground*. Also, an object within a flow document which can have text wrap around it. This is similar to a floater.

Fill — the area within the boundary or strokes of a vector object that you can apply a brush to.

Fitts' Law — the time that it takes to move a pointer (such as a finger, an extended arm, or a computer mouse) to point to a new target is a function of how large and how near the target is. According to Fitts' Law, anything smaller and farther away takes more time to reach. Also, anything placed around the outer rim of the screen takes less time to reach, because the width is infinitely large because the movement of the mouse is stopped by the edge of the screen. In mathematical terms, Fitts' Law is that $T = a + b\text{Log}^2(D/W+1)$, where T is equal to the time it takes to perform an action in a straight line, D is equal to the distance necessary to travel, and W is equal to the width of the target area, measured along the axis of motion.

Flat space — imagery that emphasizes the two-dimensional quality of the screen or page, rather than the illusion of three-dimensional space on a two-dimensional screen. The sense of two-dimensionality may be heightened by avoiding images with 3D depth cues (such as planes that are perpendicular to the screen surface, movement that is perpendicular to the screen surface, deep focus, overlapping objects, and shadows).

Floater — an object within a flow document that can have text wrap around it within a column.

Flow direction — the property of a stack panel that defines whether the objects stack left to right or right to left. This is the same as orientation.

Flow document — a text control that allows text to resize for optimal readability regardless of the size of the window. This needs to be embedded in either a flow document reader, flow document page viewer, flow document scroll viewer or rich text box.

Flow document reader — a text control to present a flow document. It contains a search feature, text resize feature, and a choice of whether or not to view the flow document as pages or one long document with a scroll bar.

Flow document page viewer — a text control to present a flow document as pages, instead of using scroll bars. It includes page navigation buttons and a text resizing tool.

Flow document scroll viewer — a text control to present a flow document as one long document with a scroll bar. It includes a text resizing tool.

Fly-bys — one of the categories of drag-and-drop animations in ZAM 3D. A fly-by animates the position of the camera so that it seems to fly by objects.

Follow Through — in animation, the principle that action usually does not come to an abrupt stop, but continues somewhat beyond the termination point due to inertia.

Font — a complete set of characters in a specific typeface and style.

Font size — the size of the font, usually the space between the highest ascender and the lowest descender in the font, measured in points. A point is approximately equal to 1/72 of an inch.

Free cameras — in ZAM 3D, free cameras are visible in the Viewport and can be moved and rotated like any model, and can be pointed at anything. Compare this with *target cameras.*

FTP — File Transfer Protocol. A common method of copying files from one computer to another over the Internet.

FTP site — a computer on the Internet running the software needed to send or receive files via FTP.

Full trust — an attribute assigned to code to let the Windows XP or Vista operating system know that the code can be given unrestricted access to the computer's resource. This is usually assigned to applications that are not intended to run as Web applications and that thus may be less likely to include malicious code. (Compare this with *partial trust.*)

Geometry — a term used in 3D to denote the shape of a 3D object.

Globalization — the process of preparing your application for use by people of different countries, languages, and cultures.

Glyph — in a font, the shape of a particular character, such as a letter, numeral, symbol, or punctuation mark.

Golden Ratio — if you take a line, break it into two segments, and call one segment A and the other B, the Golden Ratio is the number that is determined when the length of each segment is such that the ratio A/(A+B) is the same as the ratio B/A.

Gradient — a gradual change from one color or transparency value to another color or transparency value.

Gradient bar — the rectangular object that you can assign gradient stops to, in order to define a gradient. It is found in the Gradient tab of the Brushes palette.

Gradient stop — an indicator you can add to a gradient bar when creating a gradient that allows you to assign a new color to that position in the gradient.

Grid dividers or grid lines — in Blend, horizontal and vertical lines that you can position within each grid panel and that, among other things, you can use to align your art visually. The grid dividers are generally not visible when your application is running.

Grid panel — a panel that can be divided into rows and columns, each section of which can be resized.

Grid splitter — in Blend, when your application is running, a grid splitter shows up as a double arrow that you can use to resize the sections of a grid panel.

Ground — in a graphic design, everything is the ground except the primary subject of the image, which is the *figure*.

Group box — a control which groups two objects together. One object is a header, usually containing text, and the other can be a panel or any object.

GUI — a graphical user interface.

Gutenberg Diagram — a diagram illustrating the path on which, for Western readers, the eye is accustomed to traveling across a page from the upper left-hand corner to the lower right-hand corner. It may be helpful to consider this tendency when laying out your user interface.

Handoff animation — in Blend, an animation with a specified end point that can start from any unspecified beginning point.

HD video — High Definition video. Any video system with a resolution higher than Standard Definition (SD) video. Blend supports High Definition video.

Header — a property of a control containing a label that applies to one or more child elements. For example, the tab control has a header that appears in the tab.

Hick's Law — the finding by British psychologist William Edmund Hick that the time it takes for an individual to make a decision increases with the number of choices.

Hierarchy — the nesting structure of objects that are nested inside other objects. For example, a family tree is a hierarchical structure. Similarly, in Blend, elements nested within another element are called children of that element, and you can create a hierarchical structure of children and parent elements in Blend that is like a family tree.

HLS — a system of defining colors by hue, lightness, and saturation.

HSB — a system of defining colors by hue, saturation, and brightness.

Hold Out — a property that specifies no keyframe interpolation occurs either before or after a keyframe or both.

Horizontal stem — in typography, the horizontal line in letters such as A and H. Also called the *crossbar*.

Hue — a color, independent of its brightness, darkness, or saturation.

Hyperbar — a bar of icon images that increase in size according to a hyperbolic function when the user moves the mouse over each icon.

HTML — HyperText Markup Language. The markup language that is used to generate Web pages.

Hyperlink — a button or highlighted text that when clicked takes the user to another section of the application or to a Web page or to somewhere else on the Internet.

IDE — Integrated development environment. A programming environment that integrates a programmer's editor with other programmer's tools, such as user interface generators, compilers, debuggers, or code profilers.

Image — in Blend, an image is a bitmapped image and may be in any one of numerous formats, including JPG, BMP, TIF, GIF, and many others.

Image Brush — a way to assign an image as a fill to vector objects (including controls).

Immersion — a sense of immersion in a new world can be incredibly charming, and you can create this sense by incorporating immersive elements in your user interface such as, perhaps, elements that eliminate distractions, that provide engaging new sensory experiences and stimulating intellectual challenges, and that suggest vast, unexplored realms.

Inheritance — in Blend, the way in which a child element gains properties from its parent. For example, if a rectangle is nested within a grid, then if the grid is resized, the rectangle inherits the new size and is resized as well.

Inverted pyramid — the principle of presenting the most important information first, which is an example of progressive disclosure. Newspaper stories almost always use the principle of the inverted pyramid, starting out with the most important information and progressing paragraph by paragraph to less important information.

Interoperability — an application's ability to work on electronic devices in addition to computers, such as PDAs, cell phones, media players, or other devices.

Item — in Blend, a part of a control that requires a child element. For example, menu items are nested into the menu to create the menu control.

Items control — the parent control element for a control that contains items. For example, the item control for the menu is the menu.

Keyframe — a point at which a change of property starts or ends, indicated by a small oval on the timeline. It's called a keyframe because it contains key information that Blend uses to calculate the changes necessary to smoothly animate between one frame and another.

Keyframe interpolation — automatic generation by Blend of the frames of animation between keyframes.

Kinesthetic memory — your memory of where you are in space and where your limbs and muscles have moved.

Label — a simple text control which is normally used for short words and descriptions and to add access text.

Lathe — a way to specify the shape of a 3D object by rotating a curve around a fixed axis.

Layout — in Blend, the positioning of your panels and controls, as well as the overall look of your user interface.

Layout root — every XAML application contains a layout root that is the beginning of the Objects list. In Blend, a grid panel is the default layout root.

Letterform — the shape of a particular letter in a font.

Ligature — combinations of two letters as a single glyph.

Limited space — a particular kind of combination of deep and flat space in which all of the depth cues of 3D space are used (such as, perhaps, deep focus, overlapping objects, shadows, atmospheric effects, and others) except for planes perpendicular to the screen and movement perpendicular to the screen.

Linear gradient — a gradual change of colors in a single direction.

Linear decay — a fading out of a 3D light at a linear rate from its source to the end of its range.

List box — a control that contains a list of items from which the user can choose.

List view — a control that allows you to read data in columns and rows, and resize the columns, as needed.

Localization — the process of adapting an application to the language and culture of a particular country. This process may include translation; adjusting formats such as date, time, paper size, and so on; and even perhaps modifying functionality.

Longhorn — the former code name for Windows Vista, inspired by the Longhorn Saloon, a bar in Whistler, British Columbia.

Luna — the name of the theme that defines the look of the controls used by Windows XP.

Main menu — the menu attached to the main application window. Blend allows you to create main menus with as many levels of submenus as you want.

Margin — a property for every vector object and control, defining where the object is located in its container.

Markup code — code that describes the layout of text and other visual elements on a page or computer screen. Compare this with *procedural code*. The term "markup" derives from the tradition in publishing (in the pre-digital era) of annotating or "marking up" an author's manuscript in the margins with specifications for typefaces, sizes, styles, and so on, for the typesetter.

Material — in 3D modeling, the surface qualities that you can apply to a 3D shape to give it a particular color, texture, reflectivity, and so on, so that it looks like stone, fire, glass, water, metal, wood, paper, or whatever you desire.

MaxHeight — the maximum height in pixels that you allow your object to become when resized. You may want to assign MaxHeight to bitmapped images, for example, to prevent them from becoming too large for their resolution.

MaxWidth — the maximum width in pixels that you allow your object to become when resized.

Maya — a popular and powerful 3D modeling, rendering, and animation software package, currently owned by Autodesk.

Meanline — in typography, the imaginary line sitting on the top of the letter x. Compare this with *baseline*.

Media — in Blend, audio files or video files.

Memory dots — small dots that may act as buttons to switch you from one window or one part of an application to another. Some or all of these dots might be user-configurable.

Menu — in Blend, the menu control is the control that contains the menu's child elements, which are usually MenuItems. MenuItems can act as headers, and can nest menus which during run time act as submenus and pop-up when clicked.

Mere Exposure Effect — the phenomenon that people tend to favor choices that are familiar even if they are not the ideal choice. Also known as the Exposure Effect.

Metawindow — a large window into the entire world of your application, where you can see the entire functionality of your application at a glance. The user may choose the tools he wants to use or what room he wants to enter, or how he wants to proceed in the application from the Metawindow, which may take up nearly the entire computer screen.

Microsoft Expression Design — Microsoft's tool for both vector and bitmap graphics manipulation. Expression Design exports XAML code suitable for use in Blend.

MinHeight — in Blend, the minimum height in pixels that you allow your object to shrink to when resized.

MinWidth — in Blend, the minimum width in pixels that you allow your object to shrink to when resized.

Miter join — in Blend, a type of corner join that you can assign to the corner joins of your rectangles or paths. A miter join is the default join and is generally a sharp angle, although you can specify a small amount of bevel by setting a miter limit in the Stroke palette.

Miter limit — can be set for a miter join in the Stroke palette for a rectangle or path with corners. Specifying a miter limit allows you to partially bevel a corner join or if you set your miter limit high, then it specifies an angle for a corner join.

Modern fonts — fonts, such as Bodoni designed by Italian engraver and printer Giambattista Bodoni in 1788, in which the contrast between thick and thin strokes is great, with very thin serifs that are perpendicular to the main stem, rather than gently sloping as with older fonts.

Motion path — in Blend, you can easily attach 2D or 3D objects to any path, which becomes a motion path, so that animating an object can be as simple as drawing a path for an object to follow.

Mouse event — an action by the mouse that can create a response in the application, such as a mouse over or mouse click.

Mouse over — when the mouse moves over an object.

MS-DOS — the Microsoft Disk Operating System, the command-line-based predecessor to Microsoft Windows. The first version was released in 1981.

Named style — in Blend, a style with a name. This is interchangeable with "style," but by calling it a named style, we emphasize that it can be used repeatedly as a resource by name.

Namespace — a way of organizing names in the .NET Framework. The using statements in a code-behind file specify names available for use in the code-behind file. Namespaces in XAML are defined by the code "xmlns=".

Nested object — an object that you put inside a container. Also called a *child element or child.*

.NET Framework — a part of Windows that offers many precoded solutions to common programming requirements that developers can use in their applications.

.NET Framework 3.0 — a set of precoded solutions for common programming needs that is a key component of Microsoft Vista. .NET Framework 3.0 can also run on Windows XP SP2 and Windows Server 2003. Windows Presentation Foundation is a part of .NET Framework 3.0.

Node — a part of a path containing information about the curvature of the one or two paths connecting to it.

Null — empty or having no value, such as a variable which has not been set.

Object — in Blend, an element that has properties. An object can also be a combination of objects related together.

Object-oriented — in software engineering, a style of software development that combines data and functions together as objects. These objects communicate with each other by sending and receiving messages rather than by simply transmitting numerical data. Objects that have similar data and functionality are grouped into hierarchical classes of objects, and new objects inherit data and functionality from their hierarchy of classes. The new objects can then be customized with additional data and functionality.

Objects list — a tree view in the Objects and Timeline palette that shows all the elements in your project and contains all the information about what element is nested in what.

Ockham's Razor — the principle, which scientists have generally adopted, of giving preference, in the case of two plausible hypotheses, to the one that makes fewer assumptions because it's simpler and may introduce less error. In the world of user interface design, this principle might be applied as "If you have a choice between two designs that are functionally equivalent, choose the simplest."

Old Style fonts — serif fonts in which the contrast between thick and thin strokes is not strong, such as Garamond, designed by Parisian publisher Claude Garamond in 1617. Also called *Renaissance fonts.*

Opacity — the quality of being impenetrable by light. Not transparent.

Orientation — the property of a stack panel, wrap panel and other panels and controls that defines how the objects orient themselves in the panel or control.

Orthographic Camera — an imaginary camera that defies the laws of perspective and makes every object appear as its assigned size, regardless of how far the object is from the camera. Compare this with the *Perspective Camera.*

OS X — the current operating system for Macintosh computers.

Overlapping Action — the animation principle that in the real world everything happens at once, and therefore in an animated character multiple motions must blend, interact, and overlap simultaneously.

Pad gradient mode — a type of gradient mode in which the last gradient stop is continued as a solid color to the edge of the fill.

Page — in Blend, a XAML document that can be used within a Web Browser. It does not offer the flexible resizing capabilities of a Blend-created window. In Blend-created projects the user can navigate between pages but not windows.

Palette — in Blend, a collapsible pane containing tools, located within the panels of the Blend user interface.

Pan — to move or rotate a camera horizontally (for a panoramic view).

Pane — a section of a panel in the Blend user interface.

Panel — a container for objects to reside in. Blend offers several types of panels including — grid, canvas, stack, dock, and wrap. Also, panels are parts of the Blend user interface. They include the Interaction panel, Properties panel, Project panel, Results panel and Resources panel.

Paragraph — in Blend, a XAML tag in a flow document specifying a carriage return.

Parent element — an object containing a nested object. For example, a menu is a parent element of a menu item.

Partial trust — an attribute assigned to code to warn the Windows XP or Vista operating system to restrict it from full access to a computer's resources. This is usually assigned to applications that run as Web applications. (Compare this with *full trust.*)

Password box — a text control that allows the user to type text, with each character appearing as the same meaningless character, so no one looking over their should can see what was typed.

Path — nodes connected by curves or straight lines (or a combination of both). A path can be an open path or, if the first node is the same as the last node, a closed path.

Pen tool — used to create and edit paths. It can create either straight lines or curves.

Perspective Camera — the default camera in Blend. Unlike the Orthographic Camera, it is quite similar to the human eye.

Picture Superiority Effect — the phenomenon, documented by repeated experiments by psychologists, that pictures are often easier to recall than words.

Pixel — short for a picture element, a dot of color and brightness on a computer screen. For example, a computer monitor may have 1280 pixels across by 960 pixels from top to bottom.

Playhead — the rectangle above the tracks on a timeline in the Objects and Timeline palette that marks the current frame on the timeline.

Point light — a light like a lightbulb that radiates out in all directions from a point. One of the four kinds of light provided by Blend. (The others are ambient lights, directional lights, and spot lights.)

Points of prospect — areas in the user interface where users can pause and get a clear overview of the possibilities that are available.

Pop-up menus — a menu that pops up in a location other than the main menu. Typically invoked by right-clicking on a user interface item to bring up a menu of commands related to that item. Also called a context menu, a context-sensitive menu, or a shortcut menu.

Pose-to-Pose Action — animation that is designed by creating a series of key poses and then filling in the in-between poses. Useful when you need to carefully plan posing and timing. Compare this to *straight-ahead action*.

Procedural code — computer code that defines a sequence of procedures to execute. Compare this with *markup code*.

Progress Bar — a bar that typically moves from left to right to demonstrate progress to a goal, such as loading a file or performing a complex calculation.

Progressive disclosure — the process of revealing information when it's needed (and hiding information until it's needed). This helps to focus the attention of the user on the task. The use of a Wizard is an example of progressive disclosure.

Progressive escalation — progressively increasing the size or amount of attention a user needs to give to an error message as the error becomes more critical.

Progressive lures — user interface items that highlight the functionality of the application that may interest users and that may effortlessly draw them into it.

Project — the Blend file that contains (or, if you prefer, points to files containing) your XAML code, your artwork, your code-behind file, and everything else needed to create your user interface.

Property — a characteristic trait of an object. Properties for each object in Blend are listed in the Properties palette. The Windows Presentation Foundation offers default properties for many controls, but these can be modified.

Property trigger — an change in property of an object that controls a timeline. Timelines can be controlled by event triggers and property triggers.

Prototyping — the process of creating models in order to test ideas, refine objectives, and explore possibilities.

Publish — to deploy your application — to upload your Web application to the Internet or a server, or to make it available on a CD or other digital media as an executable computer file

Quadratic decay — a fading out of a 3D light at an accelerating rate from its source to the end of its range.

Query — the text in a search box.

Radial gradient — a gradual changing of colors in a circular direction.

Radio button — a button used in a group, so that when one radio button is selected, the others in the group are automatically deselected.

Recognition bias — people tend to favor choices that are familiar even if they are not the ideal choice. Also known as the Exposure Effect or the Mere Exposure Effect.

Rectangle tool — a tool for creating vector objects in the shape of rectangles or squares.

Reflect gradient mode — a type of gradient mode assigned in the Brushes palette in which gradients can repeat themselves as they extend beyond their initial boundaries, with each repetition reversed to appear as a reflection of the previous gradient. The Brush Transform tool is often used in conjunction with this mode to shrink the gradient to allow it to reflect.

Reflection effect — an effect produced using the Visual Brush to create a reflection of a video, animation, or panel.

Renaissance fonts — serif fonts in which the contrast between thick and thin strokes is not strong, such
as Garamond, designed by Parisian publisher Claude Garamond in 1617. Also called *Old Style fonts.*

Render — the process of creating an image, such as, for example, an image of a 3D object. Different qualities of rendering exist in third-party 3D animation applications. Typically, you can choose from low resolution to very high resolution depending on your planned usage.

Repeat gradient mode — a type of gradient mode assigned in the Appearance palette in which
gradients can repeat themselves as they extend beyond their initial boundaries. The Brush Transform tool is often used in conjunction with this mode to shrink the gradient to allow it to repeat.

Repeat buttons — the buttons that appear on the ends of scroll bars. They can be used by themselves or in conjunction with controls that you may want to create, such as spin boxes. They have two unique properties — Delay and Interval. You can set both properties in the Properties palette.

Repetitive strain injuries — injuries that can result from, for example, repeated physical movements using computer keyboards and mice. According to the Occupational Safety and Health Administration (OSHA) repetitive strain injuries such as carpal tunnel syndrome represent 62 percent of all Worker's Compensation claims in North America.

Resize Grip — a triangle that you can put, for example, on the lower right-hand corner of a control to make the control easily resizable.

Resolution — the amount of detail that an image is capable of containing; typically measured by the number of pixels per inch in a bitmap image. In contrast to bitmap images, vector graphics are stored as mathematical descriptions of lines, curves, colors, and so on, which can be recalculated and rendered accurately at any resolution.

Resource — in Blend, an item saved for repeated use. Resources can be colors, brushes, text, numbers, styles, templates, and complex objects.

Resource dictionary — a set of saved resources from other parts of your application or other applications.

RGB — a system of defining colors by specifying the amount of red, green, and blue that they contain. To use the RGB color picker in Blend, move the sliders to choose your color. Sometimes you may know the actual numeric values of red, green, and blue, in which case you can type them in.

Rich text box — the Blend text control which supports flow documents and can accept text from the user during run time.

Round join — a rounded corner join for a rectangle or path. This is set in the Stroke palette and can only appear if the stroke of the rectangle or path is wide enough for it to show.

RSS feed — XML files that contain a brief description of, for example, the latest headlines from a news Web site or a blog, along with links to the full stories. RSS is an abbreviation for Really Simple Syndication.

Rule of Thirds — to enhance the composition within an image, center the most important element of the image at one of the four points where an imaginary three-by-three grid of lines intersects. We think of this as the Suggestion of Thirds, rather than the Rule of Thirds, because it's certainly not mandatory to employ this principle to create an effective composition.

Run time — the time of execution of an application. Or a *runtime library* — a set of code designed to manage or provide services to other code at runtime.

Sans Serif fonts — fonts without serifs. They tend to look clean, rational, efficient, or even austere.

Saturation — purity of hue. If a hue is not mixed with white, black, or a shade of gray, then it is fully saturated. On an overcast day, colors outside are typically highly saturated because there is no direct sunshine to cast shadows on everything and thus mix blacks or grays into the colors of everything.

Savanna Preference — the preference, found in research studies that people display for savanna-like environments — grasslands with scattered trees — compared to other environments, such as deserts, jungles, or mountains.

Scale — to make larger or smaller. The Scale tab in the Transform palette allows you to scale objects.

Scrapbook — you can use a scrapbook metaphor in a user interface to provide a comfortable, informal way for users to store and organize work.

Screen resolution — the width and height of a computer screen, measured in pixels. 1280 x 960, 1024 x 768, and 800 x 600 are common screen resolutions, with the trend moving inexorably to higher resolutions.

Script fonts — fonts with the fluid strokes of cursive handwriting with letters that are usually connected. They may project an air of informality, elegance, or extravagance, depending on the quality and quantity of curvature and curlicues.

Scroll Bar — a bar used to control the amount of scrolling in another object.

Scroll viewer — the control that contains two scroll bars to allow you to view parts of a large object.

Search box — a text box in which the user can type text to search for.

Selection tool — the black arrow tool that allows you to select a path or shape. Compare this with the *Subselection tool* (the white arrow tool).

Serif — the short counterstroke at the end of the main stroke of each letter in fonts such as Times.

Serif fonts — fonts with serifs, the short counterstrokes at the end of the main strokes of each letter in fonts such as Times. They resemble letterforms chiseled in stone in ancient Rome, and, in fact, are often called Roman fonts. These are the fonts we are most accustomed to seeing in the body of text in books, newspapers, and magazines.

Sentence-style capitalization — capitalization of a section of text in the same way that sentences are capitalized, with the first word of a new sentence capitalized, and so on. (Compare this with *title-style capitalization*.)

Shape — in Blend, items created by using the Rectangle tool, and Ellipse tool.

Shearing — skewing.

Shortcut key — a key (such as the function keys F1 through F12) or a key combination (such as Ctrl+C) that users can press as a shortcut replacement for clicking on a menu item or on some other user interface item. (Compare this with *access key*.)

Shortcut menu — a pop-up menu.

Simple control — a version of a WPF control type that works in the same way as a system control, but is easier to modify in Blend. Simple controls are especially useful when you want to modify a control simply by applying a new brush to it. They contain all the functionality of system controls.

Skewing — slanting an object in one direction, which you can do by using the Transform palette. Skewing may make your object look more dynamic, just as italic type can make text look more dynamic.

Skin — a specific appearance, usually for a control.

Slab Serif fonts — fonts (such as Century Expanded, designed in 1895) that contain less contrast between thick and thin strokes, and more slab-like serifs. Also called *Egyptian fonts*.

Sliders — a sliding control that you can use to display and set values along a continuous scale.

Snap Resolution — a value that you can set (via the Toggle Snapping drop-down arrow on a timeline) so that the Previous Frame and Next Frame buttons jump more than just one frame. The largest jump it can make is one second. This is useful because you can click your way through your animation either forward or backward and get a good sense of it, at least in a jerky way.

Softimage — a powerful and erstwhile popular 3D modeling, rendering, and animation software package, at one time owned by Microsoft and then sold by Microsoft to its present owner Avid Technology Inc., in exchange for Avid stock.

Spin box — a text box showing the currently selected value along with two buttons to increase or decrease the value.

Spot light — a beam of light that spreads out from a specific point in one direction in a cone. One of the four kinds of 3D lights provided by Blend. (The others are ambient lights, directional lights, and point lights.)

Squash and Stretch — the animation principle that when an object deforms, it maintains its volume by squashing in one direction while stretching in another.

Stacking order — the order in which your graphics are visible on the artboard.

Stack panel — a type of container for objects in which objects automatically orient themselves next to or on top of one another.

Staging — the animation principle that objects onscreen should be positioned in a way so that the viewer is looking at the right part of the screen at the right time.

Standard Definition (SD) video — video in one of the standard formats for broadcast video before the digital era. In the U.S., the NTSC video broadcast standard is equivalent to 720 x 480 nonsquare pixels. In many other parts of the world, PAL is the standard broadcast video format, equivalent to 720 x 576 nonsquare pixels. In the U.S., any video format with greater resolution than these is considered High Definition (HD) video.

Star — indicates proportional sizing in the Column Definition Collection editor and Row Definition Collection editor.

State — the current condition of an object. For example: whether the mouse is over it, whether it's being clicked, if it's a check box, whether it's checked, and so on.

Stem — in typography, the vertical line in letters such as E, l, and b.

Storyboard — a section of your project's XAML code that defines how animations and media are handled in the application. It allows you to run multiple timelines.

Straight Ahead Action — animation that is designed by starting at the beginning of a scene and plowing ahead until the end without planning key poses in advance, which may be particularly conducive to the depiction of zany antics and wild action. Compare this to *pose-to-pose action*.

Straight cut — when a new image, a new shot, or a new scene appears abruptly, without, for example, the smooth transition of a dissolve.

Stroke — in Blend, the line of a path or shape in a vector graphic.

Stroke — in typography, the fat diagonal line of, for example, the letter N. (Compare this to *brackets*.)

Style — the look of an object, including how it appears during its different states if it has states. In Blend, you can name the style and save it as a resource that can be applied repeatedly on other similar objects. When you modify a style, all objects with that style are also modified automatically.

Subselection tool — the white arrow tool that allows you to select the nodes of a path. Compare this with the *Selection tool* (the black arrow tool).

Submenu — a secondary menu that appears when you click on an item in the main menu. Blend allows you to create main menus with as many levels of submenus as desired.

Swashes — the swirly embellishments to glyphs that add elegance to a font.

Synectics — a creative problem-solving approach developed by a group of consultants in New England starting in the late 1950s that uses metaphors to make familiar problems seem strange in order to arrive quickly at unique ideas that can be mapped back to practical solutions.

System controls — the standard WPF controls that apply the Aero and Luna themes.

Tab — in Blend, a control that looks like a tab on a file folder. When the user clicks a tab, a new pane appears in the panel.

Tail — in typographic terms, the uppercase letter Q has a *tail*.

Target cameras — in ZAM 3D, target cameras are visible in the Viewport and can be moved and rotated like any model, except that you can assign targets to them. A target camera automatically keeps aiming its camera view at its target. To create a target camera, click the Create Target Camera button in the Main toolbar. (Compare this with *free cameras*.)

Task dialog — dialog boxes for various tasks. Microsoft offers standard task dialogs that you can modify for your purposes.

Template — the appearance of an object during its different states, saved as a resource so it can be applied over and over to similar objects, and can be modified to change the look of all objects with the same template applied. Modifying the template also allows you to modify the control parts and drastically change the look of the control, if you want.

Template binding — the process of data binding control parts within the template of a control to other control parts. This is a technique for radically changing the look of a control. Data bind new control parts to original control parts and hide the original control parts, so you just see the new ones.

Text wrapping — the process by which text continues on the next line of a text box instead of disappearing beyond the bounds of the text box. Text wrapping also refers to how text behaves around another object, such as Figure in a flow document.

Text box — in Blend, a container for text, or a specific TextBox container. The TextBox is a simple text control which can display text, as well as accept text from the user during run time.

Theme — a collection of styles to be used for an application. For example, Microsoft uses the Aero theme for Windows Vista and encourages application designers to use that theme for at least all task dialogs and wizards, if possible.

Thingymabobber — similar to a whatchamadingy, but more specific.

Throwaway prototyping — building temporary models to isolate and test features of a concept.

Tile brush — a brush capable of creating a tiling effect.

Timeline — a graphical representation of time in the Objects and Timeline palette, showing when animations and media play. Blend offers multiple timelines that can be triggered by event triggers and property triggers.

Title-style capitalization — capitalization of a section of text in the way that titles are capitalized, with all nouns, verbs, adverbs, adjectives, and pronouns capitalized, and so on. (Compare this with *sentence-style capitalization*.)

Toggle Button — in Blend, a control that has two states (active or inactive), but unlike a check box, a toggle button changes the appearance of its border. Toggle buttons are generally used when you want an action to take effect when it is clicked, whereas check boxes usually simply show whether they have been checked or not.

Tool Bar control — you can use this to create a control with a set of buttons or other tools. If more tools fit on it than it can hold, a down arrow appears at the end where the user can open an overflow panel.

Toolbox — the buttons on the far left of the Blend application window.

Track — a single row of a timeline that may contain a media file or that may represent the change in properties of an object over time. Also, a control part of the slider as well as other controls.

Transitional fonts — fonts, such as Baskerville, designed by British printer John Baskerville in 1757, in which the contrast between thick and thin strokes is increased compared to fonts of earlier times, with serifs becoming finer.

Transparent — having an Alpha value set to zero, equivalent to having zero percent opacity.

Tree View control — an outline with headings that you can open and close as you like. Tree view items function as buttons.

Trigger — a way to control an appearance of an object or a timeline based on an interactive event or property change, without writing any code. Triggers can control the starting, ending, pausing, and resuming of each timeline.

Trust — see *full trust* or *partial trust*.

UI — User interface.

Undocking a panel — to detach a panel, so that the palette floats freely, independent of the Blend interface window.

Uniform grid — a tiling layout element that creates equal spaces between elements nested within it, based on the number of rows and columns in the uniform grid. This is handy for creating a list of images, for example. Note that the uniform grid is not a true grid panel.

URL — Uniform Resource Locator. The address of a resource on the Internet (such as a Web page, for example).

User Account Protection (UAP) — the system in Windows Vista for allowing users or the administrator to install applications and modify system settings.

User control — a document type offered in Blend that allows you to create a control that contains its own code-behind file, as well as adding the control to the Asset Library to use it repeatedly in your project.

User scenario — a description of a situation in which a user might want to use a computer to pursue a particular goal or task.

Vector graphics — images that are generated from mathematical descriptions of curves, lines, fills, and transparency that may be recalculated and rendered at any desired resolution, rather than images that are stored as arrays of colored pixels. Compare this with *bitmap graphics*.

View box — a simple control that takes a singe child element, such as a vector graphic or a text box or any control, and resizes it to the size of the view box. It also allows you to specify how an object, such as an image, is clipped.

Viewport 3D — a control in which 3D objects reside.

Vista — Windows Vista, the most recent version of Microsoft Windows, which features the Aero interface, improvements in security, improved search capabilities, Windows Sidebar and Gadgets, integrated speech recognition, and so on.

Visual Brush — a brush in Blend that is like a camera pointed at an object (such as a 3D image or even a video), and which gives a dynamic view of the object at every moment. This can create a dynamic reflection of animations, videos, and user interface controls.

Wayfinding — the process of navigating to a destination, which typically proceeds through four stages — using spatial and environmental information to get oriented, choosing a route, monitoring the route, and recognizing the destination.

Web 2.0 — a loosely defined and sometimes controversial phrase that describes a second generation of Web sites that are characterized by blogs, wikis, podcasts, RSS feeds, tags, reader-generated content, social software, Web-based communities, Web-based applications, or Web-based desktops, rather than by static HTML pages.

Web log — A blog — a journal of textual or audio-visual content, posted periodically to a Web page in reverse chronological order.

Welcome page — a first page of a wizard that explains its purpose, now generally considered superfluous.

Whatchamadingy — a doohickey.

WIMP — Windows, Icons, Menus, and Pointing device interface of Windows and the Macintosh.

Window — on a computer screen, a rectangular display area enclosed in a border that generally can be resized and moved.

Windows Presentation Foundation (WPF) — a major part of .NET Framework 3.0. The set of pre-coded solutions for common programming needs that is a key component of Microsoft Vista. Windows Presentation Foundation can combine declarative XAML code and the C# or Visual Basic code from the code-behind file into a runtime that can be deployed as a Web application or a Windows application.

Windows Vista — the most recent version of Microsoft Windows, which features Windows Presentation Foundation (including the Aero user interface), improvements in security, improved search capabilities, Windows Sidebar and Gadgets, integrated speech recognition, and so on.

Windows XP — the version of Microsoft Windows prior to Windows Vista.

Wipe — a transition in a presentation, a video, or an animation in which one image appears to wipe over the other image. This usually takes place in a linear or radial direction.

Wizard — a series of windows that guide a user in a simple way through an otherwise complicated process.

World Wide Web Consortium — an international consortium at MIT that formulates and promotes proposed standards for the Web; led by Sir Tim Berners-Lee, the inventor of the World Wide Web.

WPF — see Windows Presentation Foundation.

Wrap panel — a panel that arranges elements nested within it sequentially from left to right, so that when it runs out of space on the right edge of the panel, it wraps the next element to the next line, just as text wraps in a word processor document.

X-height — in typography, the height of the lower-case letter x. Also called *body*.

XAML — Extensible Application Markup Language. Designed by Microsoft for creating user interfaces that can make extensive use of vector graphics, animation, audio, video, 3D, sophisticated typography, and data binding. XAML is a simple declarative language that can be used to design user interfaces in a way that is somewhat similar to how HTML can be used to create Web pages. XAML is based on XML and follows the same rules, although XAML contains specialized tags that can be processed by Windows Presentation Foundation.

XBAP — Xaml Browser Application. A XAML application that runs in a browser.

XML — Extensible Markup Language. Used by, among other things, RSS feeds and databases. XML is also the basis of XAML. XML is similar to HTML except that it is extensible. Because it is extensible, the user can create custom tags for data according to certain rules so that the data can be more easily understood by other programs. These tags can be, for example, the names of fields in your database.

XML data source — an XML file with the extension .xml. Usually RSS feeds are in this format.

XP — Windows XP, the version of Microsoft Windows prior to Windows Vista.

ZAM 3D — an easy-to-use 3D modeling program with an extensive gallery of drag-and-drop materials, lighting, and animations. ZAM 3D can export animations as XAML code, which can then be easily brought into Blend.

ZUIs — Zooming user interfaces. Described, for example, by Jef Raskin in his book, *The Humane Interface*.

Index

SYMBOLS AND NUMERICS

U

The books you
read to succeed.

**Get the most out of the latest software and leading-edge technologies
with a Wiley Bible—your one-stop reference.**

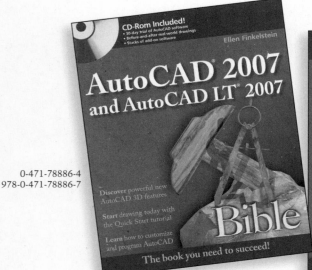

CD-Rom Included!
- 30-day trial of AutoCAD software
- Before-and-after real-world drawings
- Stacks of add-on software

Ellen Finkelstein

AutoCAD® 2007
and AutoCAD LT® 2007

Discover powerful new
AutoCAD 3D features

Start drawing today with
the Quick Start tutorial

Learn how to customize
and program AutoCAD

Bible

The book you need to succeed!

0-471-78886-4
978-0-471-78886-7

Companion Website
- Examples, useful links & more

Alan Simpson

Alan Simpson's

Windows
Vista™

Organize your files and
programs intuitively

Control your children's
computer and Internet use

Create a secure home
office network

Bible

The book you need to succeed!

0-470-04030-0
978-0-470-04030-0

"Paul is a data architect, database developer, and trainer. All three of his areas of expertise
are embodied in the book with great examples. If you want to learn SQL Server 2005, this
book is for you."
— Wayne Snyder, Managing Consultant, Mariner

Paul Nielsen

SQL Server™
2005

Discover expanded features
for DBAs and programmers

Write stored procedures
and increase productivity

Integrate XML and
Web servers

Bible

The book you need to succeed!

0-7645-4256-7
978-0-7645-4256-5

DVD Included!   **Full-color Insert**
- Examples and content from the book   - 16-page full-color insert with
- Models and textures you can customize   cutting-edge examples
- Searchable PDF of book

Kelly L. Murdock

3ds Max® 9

Model and animate from
day one with Quick Start

Create red-hot
gaming animations

Discover 3ds Max 9's
new features

Bible

The book you need to succeed!

0-470-10089-3
978-0-470-10089-9

WIL

Now you k

wiley.com